FRANK WOOD'S
BUSINESS ACCOUNTING
UK GAAP

Visit the *Business Accounting, UK GAAP 2* Companion Website at
www.pearsoned.co.uk/wood to find valuable **student** learning
material including:

- Learning objectives for each chapter
- Multiple choice questions to help test your learning
- Review questions and answers
- Links to relevant sites on the web
- Searchable online glossary
- Flashcards to test your knowledge of key terms and definitions

Frank Wood

1926–2000

FRANK WOOD'S
BUSINESS ACCOUNTING 2
UK GAAP

FRANK WOOD BSc (Econ), FCA

and

ALAN SANGSTER BA, MSc, Cert TESOL, CA

Prentice Hall
FINANCIAL TIMES

An imprint of **Pearson Education**

Harlow, England • London • New York • Boston • San Francisco • Toronto • Sydney • Singapore • Hong Kong
Tokyo • Seoul • Taipei • New Delhi • Cape Town • Madrid • Mexico City • Amsterdam • Munich • Paris • Milan

Pearson Education Limited

Edinburgh Gate
Harlow
Essex CM20 2JE
England

and Associated Companies throughout the world

Visit us on the World Wide Web at:
www.pearsoned.co.uk

First published 2008

© Pearson Education Limited 2008

The rights of Frank Wood and Alan Sangster to be identified as
authors of this work have been asserted by them in accordance with
the Copyright, Designs and Patents Act 1988.

ISBN 978-0-273-71880-2

British Library Cataloguing-in-Publication Data
A catalogue record for this book is available from the British Library

Library of Congress Cataloging-in-Publication Data
Wood, Frank, 1926–2000.
    Frank Wood's business accounting UK GAAP / Frank Wood and Alan Sangster. – 1st ed.
        p. cm.
    Includes bibliographical references and index.
        ISBN 978-0-273-71876-5   ISBN 978-0-273-71880-2 (pbk. : alk. paper)   1. Accounting–Standards–Great Britain.
I. Sangster, Alan. II. Title. III. Title: Business accounting UK GAAP.
        HF5616.G7.W66 2008
        657.0941—dc22

                                                                                                2008018137

10 9 8 7 6 5 4 3 2 1
12 11 10 09 08

Typeset in 9.5/11.5pt Sabon by 35
Printed and bound by Ashford Colour Press, Gosport

The publisher's policy is to use paper manufactured from sustainable forests.

Also available:
Book-keeping and Accounts (ISBN 978-0-273-71805-5)
Frank Wood's A-Level Accounting (ISBN 978-0-273-68532-6)
Frank Wood's Business Accounting UK GAAP Volume 1 (ISBN 978-0-273-71876-5)
Frank Wood's Business Accounting Volume 1 (ISBN 978-0-273-71212-1)
Frank Wood's Business Accounting Volume 2 (ISBN 978-0-273-71213-8)

Contents

Part 10   The emerging business environment of accounting

Supporting resources

Visit **www.pearsoned.co.uk/wood** to find valuable online resources:

Companion Website for students

- Learning objectives for each chapter
- Multiple choice questions to help test your learning
- Review questions and answers
- Links to relevant sites on the web
- Searchable online glossary
- Flashcards to test your knowledge of key terms and definitions

For instructors

- Complete, downloadable Solutions Manual
- PowerPoint slides that can be downloaded and used for presentations

Also: The Companion Website provides the following features:

- Search tool to help locate specific items of content
- E-mail results and profile tools to send results of quizzes to instructors
- Online help and support to assist with website usage and troubleshooting

For more information please contact your local Pearson Education sales representative or visit **www.pearsoned.co.uk/wood**

Guided tour of the book

Part opening

Learning objectives outline what you will need to have learned by the end of the chapter.

A wide range of **exhibits** offer clear examples of accounting practice and methodology.

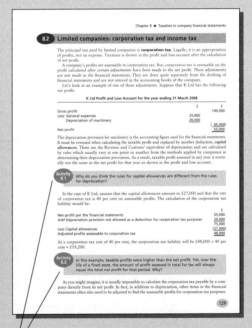

Activities occur frequently throughout the book to test your understanding of new concepts.

A number of **worked examples** are provided
to guide you through more difficult concepts.

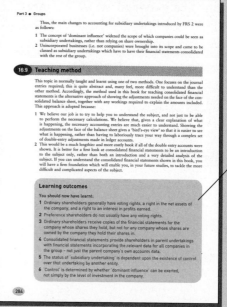

Learning outcomes
revisit and reinforce
the major topics
covered in the
chapter.

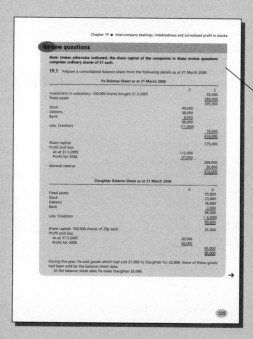

Each chapter ends with a selection of
practice questions to prepare you for
your examinations.

Guided tour of the Companion Website

Business Accounting UK GAAP 2 is supported by a fully interactive Companion Website, available at **www.pearsoned.co.uk/wood**, which contains a range of additional learning material.

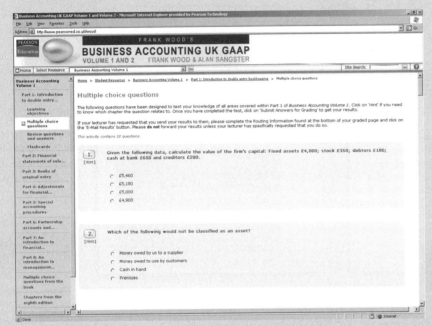

Multiple choice questions test your learning and provide helpful feedback to improve your results.

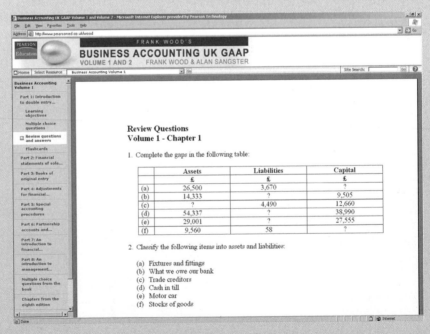

Review questions and answers provide practice at answering examination questions.

Weblinks to useful accounting sites.

Flashcards provide an interactive revision tool for all key terms.

Notes for teachers and lecturers

This textbook has been written so that a very thorough introduction to accounting is covered in two volumes. The split into two volumes is a recognition of the fact that many students new to accounting will find all that they require in Volume 1. This second volume takes students who have completed their first accounting course to a more advanced stage. As is explained below, what was originally one book (*Business Accounting*) and then became two (*Business Accounting 1* and *2*) has now become four: *Business Accounting 1* and *2* (covering International GAAP) and *Business Accounting UK GAAP 1* and *2* (covering UK GAAP).

This book completes the coverage of the financial accounting part of quite a few examinations in accounting which are focused upon UK GAAP. As examination syllabuses are constantly being revised, it would not make sense to be too specific as to which chapters would be needed by students taking each of the various examinations. In particular, it can be said to be very suitable for students who are studying the subject for A-level, Scottish Higher Grade, or General Certificate of Secondary Education examinations, the Open University Certificate in Accounting, and for those studying with the Association of Accounting Technicians, the Institute of Secretaries and Administrators, or any of the six UK and Irish Chartered Accountancy bodies.

The general public have tended to view accounting as a traditional, never-changing subject. This is not true; despite common appearances, accounting is a dynamic subject. The big change, begun in 2005, and continuing for the next few years, is the move in the UK from domestic accounting rules to international rules. Specifically, the rules that have been developed in the UK since 1970, known as Statements of Standard Accounting Practice (SSAPs) and Financial Reporting Standards (FRSs), are effectively being phased out. Coming in their place are International Financial Reporting Standards (IFRSs).

This change is being introduced gradually, with all companies across the European Union, including the UK, that are listed on a stock exchange in the EU, using the international set of standards from 2005. Other companies broadly the small and medium-sized ones, will continue to use the old UK standards for the time being. However, it seems likely that all companies will move to using international standards in the medium term and the UK standards will then presumably wither away. Indeed, the UK's standard setters are currently working on convergence of UK and international rules.

This means that UK accounting is currently in the middle of a major transition. This book is based on the terminology and rules of the UK standards. Some reference is made to international accounting standards, but only so as to tell you where to look if you need to know what they say on a particular topic. If you are studying for examinations based on international accounting standards, you should use the version of this book which is based upon them: *Business Accounting 2*.

The pedagogical devices used in this book include:

1 Each chapter:
  (*a*) starts with *Learning Objectives*;
  (*b*) contains *Activities* designed to broaden and reinforce students' understanding of the concepts being covered and, in some cases, to introduce new concepts in such a way that they do not come as a surprise when introduced formally later in the book;
  (*c*) ends with *Learning Outcomes* that can be mapped back to the Learning Objectives, so reinforcing the major topics and concepts covered in the chapter;
  (*d*) contains answers to all the Activities immediately after the Learning Outcomes.
2 The book has an alphabetical Glossary (in Appendix 3) of all the significant terms introduced. Each entry is referenced back to the chapter in which it appeared.

3 A set of Notes for Students appears at the front of the book. This covers how to use this book, how to tackle the end-of-chapter Review Questions, and how to study for and sit examinations. It should be read by students before they start working through the main text.

4 Additional colours have been introduced to enhance readability and bring out key points in the text.

● Chapter 2, *Hire Purchase Accounts*, has been revised to use a ledger account for the trading account, rather than an extract from the financial statement. This should make it easier to follow the entries being made.

● Chapter 15, *Contract Accounts*, has been renumbered to become Chapter 3, and the numbers of previous chapters 3 to 14 have been increased by one.

● Chapter 11, *Accounting Standards and Related Documents*, has been updated to incorporate UK and international standards in issue in December 2007.

● Chapter 15, *Cash Flow Statements*, now focuses on FRS 1.

● The book has been fully updated in line with the Companies Act 2006.

● The dates used in examples and in Review Questions have been changed to 'real' dates (e.g. 2008) instead of the artificial 'X' dates (e.g. 20X8).

● Over 20 Review Questions have been replaced with new questions.

● All examples and Review Questions reflect the change brought about as a result of FRS 21 whereby dividends declared or unpaid after the balance sheet are no longer to be treated as a liability in the balance sheet.

In addition, in response to further requests from reviewers, Exhibit 6.11, which shows the T-account entries for a sinking fund established in order to redeem debentures, has been further amended to show the entries in a more complete and so more meaningful way.

We hope that you find these changes helpful and appropriate and would welcome comments on these and any other changes you feel ought to be made in future editions. You can contact Alan Sangster by email at **a.j.a.sangster@btinternet.com** or by letter via the publishers.

Three chapters from the *eighth* edition (3, *Container Accounts*; 17, *Value Added Statements*, and 18, *Investment Accounts*) can be found on the *Frank Wood website*.

We would like to thank all those teachers and lecturers who gave us their advice as to the changes they would like to see incorporated in this edition.

We also wish to acknowledge the contribution of Mike Rogers, Basingstoke College of Technology, to Chapter 32 (*Corporate Governance*) and Chapter 33 (*Public Sector Accounting*).

A *Solutions Manual* giving suggested solutions to those questions with the suffix A in the book (e.g. 5.8A) is available from the publishers free of charge to teachers and lecturers adopting this book on their course, or can be downloaded from the lecturers' section of the Companion Website for *Business Accounting UK GAAP 1* and *Business Accounting UK GAAP 2* at **www.pearsoned.co.uk/wood**

Frank Wood and Alan Sangster

Notes for students

This textbook is organised to provide you with what has been found to be the most appropriate sequencing of topics as you build upon the foundations of accounting knowledge that you developed when you studied *Business Accounting 1*. You will find that a number of features of the book, properly used, will enhance your understanding and extend your ability to cope with what will possibly appear, at first, to be a mystifying array of rules and procedures.

While a lot, but by no means all, of what follows was written in *Business Accounting 1*, all of the advice given to you in that book will apply to you throughout your studies of accounting, whatever the level. We therefore offer no apologies for repeating some of it here along with new advice appropriate to the level of *Business Accounting 2*.

In order to make best use of this resource, you should consider the following as being a proven path to success:

- At the start of each chapter, **read the Learning Objectives**. Then, while you work through the material, try to detect when you have achieved each of these objectives.
- At the end of each chapter **check what you have learnt against the Learning Outcomes** that follow the main text.
- If you find that you cannot say 'yes, I have achieved this' to any of the Learning Outcomes, look back through the chapter and reread the topic you have not yet learnt.
- **Learn the meaning of each new term as it appears.** Do not leave learning what terms mean until you are revising for an exam. Accounting is best learnt as a series of building blocks. If you don't remember what terms mean, your knowledge and ability to 'do' accounting will be very seriously undermined, in much the same way as a wall built without mortar is likely to collapse the first time someone leans against it.
- **Attempt each of the Activities in the book at the point** *at which they appear.* This is *very* important. The Activities will reinforce your learning and help set in context some of the material that may otherwise appear very artificial and distant from the world you live in. The answers are at the end of each chapter. **Do not look at the answers before you attempt the questions; you'll just be cheating yourself.** Once you have answered one, check your answer against the one in the book and be sure you understand it before moving on.
- Above all, remember that accounting is a vehicle for providing financial information in a form that assists decision making. Work hard at presenting your work as neatly as possible and remember that pictures (in this case, financial figures) only carry half the message. When you are asked for them, words of explanation and insight are essential in order to make an examiner appreciate what you know and that you actually understand what the figures mean.

There are two subjects we would like you to consider very carefully: making best use of the end-of-chapter Review Questions and your examination technique.

Review questions: the best approach

As we did in *Business Accounting 1*, we have set Review Questions at the end of most chapters for you to gauge how well you understand and can apply what you have learnt. **If you simply read the text without attempting the questions, then we can tell you now that you will not pass your examinations.** You should first of all attempt the question, and then check it fully against the answers at the back of the book.

What you should not do is perform a 'ticking' exercise. By this we mean that you should not simply compare the question with the answer and tick off the bits of the answer which relate to each part of the question. No one ever learnt to do accounting properly that way. It is tempting to save time in so doing but, believe us, you will regret it eventually. We have deliberately had the answers printed using a different page layout to try to stop you indulging in a 'ticking' exercise.

Need for practice

You should also try to find the time to answer as many Review Questions as possible. Our reasons for saying this are as follows:

1 Even though you may think you understand the text, when you come to answer the questions you may often find your understanding incomplete. The true test of understanding is whether or not you can tackle the questions competently.

2 It is often said that practice makes perfect, a sentiment we don't fully agree with. There is enough sense in it, however, in that if you don't do quite a lot of accounting questions you will almost certainly not become good at accounting.

3 You simply have got to get up to a good speed in answering questions: you will always fail accounting examinations if you are a very slow worker. The history of accountancy examinations so far has always been that a ridiculously large amount of work has been expected from a student during a short time. However, examining boards maintain that the examination could be completed in the time by an adequately prepared student. You can take it for granted that *adequately prepared students* are those who not only have the knowledge, but have also been trained to work quickly and at the same time maintain accuracy and neatness.

4 Speed itself is not enough; **you also have to be neat and tidy**, and follow all the proper practices and procedures while working at speed. Fast but really scruffy work can also mean failing the exam. Why is this so? At this level the examiner is very much concerned with your practical ability in the subject. Accounting is a practical subject, and your practical competence is about to be tested. The examiner will therefore expect the answers to be neat and well set out. Untidy work with figures spread over the page in a haphazard way, badly written figures, and columns of figures in which the vertical columns are not set down in straight lines, will incur the examiner's displeasure.

5 Appropriate presentation of information is important. Learn how to present the various financial statements you may need to produce in an examination. Examiners expect to see the items in trading and profit and loss accounts, balance sheets and cash flow statements in the correct order and will probably deduct marks if you don't do so. Practise by writing down examples of these statements without any numbers until you always get the layout correct. One exam trick most students overlook is that the layout of a financial statement is often included in an examination paper as part of one question while another question asks you to produce the same financial statement. The one you need to produce will contain different numbers but the general layout should be very similar.

Need for headings

The next thing is that work should not only be neat and well laid out. **Headings should always be given, and any dates needed should be inserted.** The test you should apply is to imagine that you are a partner in a firm of professional accountants and you are away on holiday for a few weeks. During that time your assistants have completed all sorts of work including reports, drafting final accounts, various forms of other computations and so on. All of this work is deposited on your desk while you are away. When you return you look at each item in the pile awaiting your attention.

Suppose the first item looks like a balance sheet as at 31 December in respect of one of your clients. When you looked at it you could see that it was a balance sheet, but you didn't know for which client, neither did you know which year it was for. Would you be annoyed with your staff? Of course you would. So therefore in an examination why should the examiner accept as a piece of your work a balance sheet answer without either the date or the name of the business or the fact that it is a balance sheet written clearly across the top? If proper headings are not given you may lose a lot of marks. **Don't wait until your examination to start this correct practice.** Always put in the headings properly. Similar attention should be paid to sub-totals which need showing, e.g. for Fixed assets, Current assets.

We will be looking at examination technique in the next section.

The examiner

Really, what you should say to yourself is: 'Suppose I were in charge of an office, doing this type of accounting work, what would I say if one of my assistants put on my desk a sheet of paper with accounting entries on it written in the same manner as my own efforts in attempting this question?' Just look at some of the work you have done in the past. Would you have told your assistant to go back and do the work again because it is untidy? If you say that about your own work, why should the examiner think any differently?

Anyone who works in accounting knows well that untidy work leads to completely unnecessary errors. Therefore the examiner's insistence on clear, tidy, well laid out work is not an outdated approach; they want to ensure that you are not going to mess up the work of an accounting department. Imagine going to the savings bank and the manager says to you: 'We don't know whether you've got £5 in the account or £5,000. You see, the work of our clerks is so untidy that we can never sort out exactly how much is in anybody's account.' We would guess that you would not want to put a lot of money into an account at that bank. How would you feel if someone took you to court for not paying a debt of £100 when in fact you owed them nothing? This sort of thing would happen all the time if we simply allowed people to keep untidy accounts. The examiner is there to ensure that the person to whom they give a certificate will be worthy of it, and will not continually mess up the work of any firm at which they may work in the future.

We can imagine quite a few of you groaning at all this, and if you do not want to pass the examination please give up reading here. If you do want to pass, and your work is untidy, what can you do about it? The answer is simple enough: **start right now to be neat and orderly in your work.**

Quite a lot of students have said to us over the years: 'I may be giving you untidy work now, but when I actually get in the exam room I will then do my work neatly enough.' This is as near impossible as anything can be. You cannot suddenly become able to do accounting work neatly, and certainly not when you are under the stress and strain of an examination. Even the neatest worker may well find in an examination that their work may not be of its usual standard as nervousness will cause them to make mistakes. If this is true, then if you are an untidy worker now, your work in an examination is likely to be even more untidy. Have we convinced you yet? Present your work neatly.

The structure of the questions

We have tried to build up the Review Questions in a structured way, starting with the easiest and then going on to more difficult ones. We would have liked to omit all the difficult questions, on the basis that you may well spend a lot of time doing them without adding very much to your knowledge about accounting. However, if all the questions were straightforward, the shock of meeting more complicated questions for the first time in an examination could lead you to fail it. We have therefore tried to include a mixture of straightforward and complicated questions to give you the maximum benefit.

The answers

At the back of the book, you will find answers to approximately half of the Review Questions. The answers to the other Review Questions (indicated by the letter 'A' after the question number) are only available to you from your teacher or lecturer. Don't worry if you are studying this subject on your own. There are still more than sufficient Review Questions with answers in this book to ensure you know and can confirm that you understand the material.

Examination technique

If you were completely devoid of examination technique you would probably not have advanced to this stage of your accounting studies. A lot of what follows was written in *Business Accounting 1*. Don't avoid reading it just because you read it when you were studying the material in that book.

In your first accounting examination you were competing with people who had probably never sat an accounting examination before. A lot of them will not get past Stage 1. In Stage 2 you are competing against people who have already proved they have a certain degree of competence in the subject. You might have got away with a certain amount of poor examination technique at Stage 1, but that will not be as easy at Stage 2.

Here we want to concentrate on the main deficiencies noted by examiners. These have never changed during the past 50 years. Students really should read examiners' reports – they will learn a lot from them.

Students do not read the questions properly

A large number of students do not answer the questions as set by the examiner, because they have not read the question properly. They answer what they think the examiner wants, not what the examiner is asking for.

Let us take a simple example. Suppose the examiner sets the following question: 'Describe the use of accounting ratios in assessing the performance of businesses.'

A lot of students will immediately start to describe how to calculate various accounting ratios. Marks which will be obtained – nil. The question asked for the *use* of accounting ratios, not *how to calculate* them.

Many other students will have concentrated on the word *use*. They will then write their answer based on comparing this year's accounting ratios in a business with those of last year. They may well even mention trend ratios which will earn them some extra marks. If they keep their discussion to comparing ratios in a business in the year with other years, however, they cannot get top marks, no matter how well they have written their answers.

Why not? Well, they picked up the word *use*, but from then on they stopped reading properly. The question does not in any way limit itself to the ratios of one business only. First of all you can compare the performance of a business with its own performance in the past. Secondly, you may be able to compare one business with another business of a similar kind. In addition, if you miss out mentioning interfirm comparisons you will lose marks.

Therefore, (a) *read* the question carefully, (b) *underline* the *key* words to get to the meaning of the question, (c) *think carefully* about how widespread your answer should be.

On the other hand, there is no point in widening the question more than is needed. It is for the *use* of *accounting* ratios, *not* the use of *all types* of ratios. Besides accounting ratios there are marketing ratios – e.g. size of share of market, how long it takes to supply orders, ratios of defective goods etc. The question does not ask for all of these. If you give them, you will not get any extra marks.

Poor time management

Using time well to gain the highest possible marks is essential. Examiners constantly report that examinees are very poor in this aspect of tackling an examination. How, then, can you avoid the usual pitfalls?

First of all, **read the *rubric* carefully**. These are the instructions at the top of the paper, e.g. 'Attempt four questions only: the three questions in Section A and one from Section B. Begin each answer on a separate page.'

You would be surprised to know that a lot of students would try to answer more than one question from Section B. If you tackle two questions from Section B, you will get marks for only one of your answers. Few examiners will mark both and then give you the marks for your highest marked answer. Many will simply mark the first of the optional questions answered and ignore the next, unnecessary answer.

Secondly, **start each answer on a new page**. You'll only annoy the examiner if you don't. It is your job to make the examiner's work as easy as possible. Examiners are only human, and it would be surprising if their annoyance did not result in its influencing the marking of your paper.

You really must attempt each and every question you are required to answer according to the rubric of the examination. If you have to answer five questions then you must avoid attempting only four questions.

Students often feel that they would be better off by handing in the complete answers to only four questions, instead of five incomplete answers. In accounting examinations this is not true. Why is this so?

1   Examiners use positive marking in accounting examinations. If you have done 80 per cent of an answer worth 20 marks in total, and you have got it absolutely correct, then you get 80% of 20 = 16 marks.
2   The first marks in a question are the easiest to obtain. Thus it is easier to get the first 10 marks out of 20 than it is to get the second lot of marks to get full marks. By ensuring that you get the easiest marks on every question it therefore makes your task easier.

To ensure that you tackle (not necessarily finish) each question you should **mark the number of minutes to be allowed by *yourself* for each question**. Thus a 20-mark question, in a 100-mark examination, should be given 20 per cent of the time, i.e. 20% of 3 hours = 36 minutes. When 36 minutes have passed, *stop answering the question* unless it is the last question to be attempted, and go on to the next question.

If you don't know the answer, or part of an answer, you should guess. You don't lose marks for guessing, and if you guess correctly you get the marks. Intuition will often give the correct answer. Very often if you don't guess on part of a computational question you will be unable to go on to the remainder of the question which you can answer.

Workings

You may wonder why we have put this under a separate heading. We cannot emphasise enough how important it is that you should:

(*a*) submit all your workings, and
(*b*) ensure that the workings are set out so that the examiner can follow them.

A very high percentage of candidates in an examination are near the pass mark, within either a few percentage points above it or below it. If you are one of these candidates – and, as we have said, there are a lot of them – handing in workings which can be understood by the examiner will often ensure you a pass mark. Conversely, no workings, or completely unintelligible workings, may well ensure you fail the examination.

This last point is important. Some students think that putting down a set of random jottings and calling them 'workings' will gain marks. It won't. **Examiners won't waste time searching through random jottings for something relevant.** Treat your workings as if they, themselves, are part of your answer. **Insert titles and headings to indicate what a particular working is about.**

Tackle the easiest questions first

Never start off your examination by tackling a difficult question. You must be able to settle down properly and not let your nerves get out of control. Starting off on the easiest question is the best way to enable you to get off to a good start. Much more about this was written in *Business Accounting 1*.

State your assumptions

It does happen that sometimes a question can contain ambiguities. Examination bodies try to prevent it happening, but it does occur occasionally. Unfortunately, questions do sometimes contain errors.

In both of these cases you must point out the ambiguity/error. You should then make an assumption, based on what you thought the examiner meant, and carry on with your answer. **You must, however, state what your assumption is.** Try to make your assumption as sensible as possible. The examiner will then mark your answer accordingly. If you make a ridiculous assumption, it is unlikely that you will be given any marks for that part of your answer. Don't be sarcastic in your comments or complain about inefficiency – there are other times and places for that.

Answering essay questions

The problem

Unlike computational-type answers, you will not know whether your written answers are up to the mark until you receive your examination result. Likewise, written questions lack the certainty and precision of accounting problems and it is often difficult to fathom out exactly what the examiners require of you. For this reason, sound examination technique is absolutely essential together with precise knowledge of relevant law and regulations.

There are several major aspects to success in written papers. *Plan* your answer, answer the question *as set*, pay attention to good *layout*, and explain in clear and simple terms what you are doing. Remember you can only be marked on what you write down. You have no opportunity to explain some ambiguity or other and if what you write is unclear you will *not* get the benefit of the doubt.

Plan

First read the question and jot down the key *verb*, i.e. your instructions; this may be to discuss, explain, advise, set out, list, draft an audit programme, write a letter, etc.

If the question requires a discussion or an explanation it should be written in proper paragraph form. Each paragraph should be self-contained and explain the point it makes. Sentences should be short and to the point. The ideal length for a paragraph is three sentences with four as a maximum. Over four and you are probably making more than one point and should have gone into two paragraphs.

Plan how many points you are going to make and what the answer is. This is essential as otherwise your answer will 'drift' as you struggle to come to some conclusion. The plan should consist of arrows connecting points to each other so that the answer will flow and be logical. The plan need not be too extensive; it is silly to waste time on a 'mini-answer'. It should consist of the *headings* you are going to use.

Layout

Whenever examiners meet to discuss results, or write down their commentary on students' performance, they all agree on the importance of good layout; yet students generally tend to take no notice. The range of marks between good papers and poor papers tends to be quite small. Anything you can do to put the examiner on your side will pay off in those few extra marks.

The main areas for good layout are:

1 *Tabulate* in numbered points, unless you are writing an essay-type question (as explained above).

2 Leave at least a clear line between each point or paragraph.

3 Use headings whenever possible to indicate what major point or series of points you are about to make. Make it easy for the examiner to read your work and follow what you are doing. A solid mass of material is difficult to read, provides no respite for the eye and shows a lack of discipline. Remember that you are taking a *professional* examination and there is no room for academic licence.

4 Take care with your *language*. Be objective and avoid the use of the words 'I' or 'we' at too frequent intervals. Be direct and concise, say what you mean, do not use pompous terminology, and use technical words with their correct meaning.

Short sentences are far more effective and punchy than long ones. An accounting programme or evaluation of an internal control system could well start with a series of *verbs*. Good ones are: test, examine, inspect, calculate, reconcile, compare, summarise, inquire, investigate. These key words will help you to construct answers to these types of questions much more direct and to the point. If you start with them you are bound to avoid falling into the trap of being long-winded, or of padding out your answer. You only have a limited time and everything you write down must earn you marks.

5 *Think* while you are writing out your answer to make sure you are answering the question *as set*. Keep on reading the instructions and make sure you are following them. Use the question to help you to get the answer and, while this should be tackled at the planning stage, it is always possible that inspiration will strike while you are writing out your answer. In which case jot the point down on your plan, otherwise you might forget it and that can cause frustration. What you say should be relevant, but if you are in doubt about the relevance but sure about the accuracy – include it in your answer. You cannot lose and it may be one of the key points the examiner was looking for.

Key points

Do try to find a couple of key points to each question. These are points which you feel are vital to answer the question. You may well be right, and anyway, jotting them down after you have read the question carefully can help to give your answer much needed direction.

Practice

You will need to practise the above routine. Written answers in fact need more practice than computational ones. Have a go at the question. Write out the answer as you would in the examination. Compare with the suggested answers.

Write out at the foot of your answer what you left out and what you got wrong. Learn from the answers and from the work you do, so that when you see a similar question you will produce a better answer.

Time pressure

You will experience a lot of pressure of time as you progress with written questions. Do not worry; this is a good sign.

In the examination, spread your time sensibly. Start with the questions you like the look of most and, if you have to go slightly over the time you allotted for those, do so. End with the question you think you cannot answer or will be hardest to answer, but do give yourself time to have a reasonable go at it.

If a written question is included in a computational paper do not go over the time on it but *do spend the allocated time*. **Examiners pay great attention to the written parts of computational papers, so do not skimp on this part.**

All this sounds formidable and, of course, it is. It requires skill, application and, above all, confidence. Practice makes perfect and once the skill is acquired then, like riding a bicycle, it will not be forgotten. Take pride in your work and be critical of your own efforts, but do not imagine your answers will have to be perfect to pass the examination. Suggested answers tend to be too long because tutors are afraid to reveal any signs of weakness or ignorance.

Go for the main points and make them well. That is the secret of success.

Summary

Remember:

1 Read the rubric, i.e. the instructions.
2 Plan your time before you start.
3 Tackle the easiest questions first.
4 Finish off answering each question when your time allocation for the question is up.
5 Hand in all your workings.
6 Do remember to be neat, also include all proper headings, dates, sub-totals, etc. A lot of marks can be lost if you don't.
7 Only answer as many questions as you are asked to tackle by the examiner. Extra answers will not normally be marked.
8 Underline the *key* words in each question to ensure that you answer the question set, and not the question you wrongly take it to be.
9 Never write out the text of essay questions.

Best of luck with your examination. We hope you get the rewards you deserve!

Frank Wood and Alan Sangster

Publisher's acknowledgements

We are very grateful to teachers of accounting in many schools, colleges of further education and universities whose generous advice has contributed to the development of this edition. We wish to thank, in particular:

Ann-Marie Ward, Queens University, Belfast
Bhagwan Moorjani, University of Westminster
Georgios Iatridis, Manchester University
Chris McMahon, Liverpool John Moores University
Adil Mahmood, Bradford College
Graeme Reid, Hull University
Rohan Chambers, University of Technology, Jamaica
Mike Rogers, Basingstoke College of Technology
Lindsay Whitlow, Dudley College
Paul Wertheim, Solihull College
David Gilding, Park Lane College, Leeds
Malcolm Rynn, Greencroft School, County Down
Eric Edwards, University of Northumberland
Helen Khoo, Sunway College, Petaling Jaya, Malaysia
Caroline Teh Swee Gaik, Inti College, Nilai, Malaysia
Christopher Foo, St George's School, Malaysia
Dave Knight, Leeds Met
Patrick Devlin, Glasgow Cale
Sally Nower, Colchester
Pushpa Kalu, Silpa
Penny Gardner, Napier
Sarah Knight, Huntingdon

We are grateful to the following for permission to reproduce examination questions:

Association of Accounting Technicians (AAT), Assessment and Qualifications Alliance (NEAB/AQA and AEB/AQA), Association of Chartered Certified Accountants (ACCA), Institute of Chartered Secretaries and Administrators (ICSA), London Qualifications Ltd trading as Edexcel, Chartered Institute of Management Accountants (CIMA), Institute of Chartered Accountants in England & Wales (ICAEW), Welsh Joint Education Committee (WJEC), and Oxford, Cambridge and RSA Examinations; Exhibit 11.1: Adapted from Accounting Standards Board, Accounting Standards Board Statement of Principle 1991. Copyright © Accounting Standards Board Ltd (ASB). Reproduced with the kind permission of the Financial Reporting Council. All rights reserved. For further information please visit **www.frc.org.uk/asb** or call +44 (0)20 7492 2300.

All answers to questions are the authors' own work and have not been supplied by any of the examining bodies.

Part **1**

SPECIAL ACCOUNTS

Introduction

The first two chapters of this part are concerned with two items that are treated in a similar way, irrespective of the form of business involved. The third deals with something, the treatment of which may vary.

Accounting for branches

1.1 Background

This topic was the genesis for accounting as we know it today. Merchants in 13th-century Europe were able to travel along the trade routes established in the Crusades and their knowledge of 'what lay where' had developed well beyond knowing simply what existed within a few days' walk or ride of their homes. The more adventurous merchants started travelling further afield, some to fairs in other towns, districts and even countries. There, they would sell their own products and buy or barter the products of others to take home and sell to their fellow townsfolk.

In time, this grew to the point where a merchant had simply too many opportunities and too much to do. Agencies were formed in other towns and countries and employees taken on to fill the role previously undertaken by the merchant. Merchants stopped travelling so much and stayed home. Some of these merchants were so successful that they became 'merchant princes' with power, wealth and authority to rival the aristocracy. Nowhere was this more so than in what is now the northern part of Italy. From Naples to Milan in the west and from Perugia to Venice in the east, merchants' businesses became increasingly large.

A method had to be found for merchants to record and monitor the activities of their salesmen and their branches. The result is what we know as 'joint venture accounting' (see *Business Accounting UK GAAP 1*) and branch accounting, the topic of this chapter.

1.2 Accounting records and branches

There are two commonly used methods for recording transactions for branches of an organisation:

(*a*) the headquarters keeps all the accounting records, or
(*b*) each branch has its own full accounting system.

It is easier to understand accounting for branches if these two main methods are dealt with separately. The first is shown in Sections 1.3–1.8; the second in Sections 1.9–1.13. Sections 1.12 and 1.13 may also apply to the first method.

1.3 If the headquarters maintains all the accounting records

The ledgers are used for three main purposes:

(*a*) to record transactions showing changes in assets, liabilities and capital;
(*b*) to ascertain the profitability of each branch; and
(*c*) to enable checks to be made that might indicate whether anyone at the branches is stealing goods or cash.

This third purpose is very important for businesses that have many branches. The people who manage or work in these branches may be receiving and paying out large sums of money. In addition they may be handling large amounts of stocks of goods. The branches may be a considerable distance away from the head office, i.e. the headquarters of the business. Being at a distance from control can be tempting to some people for whom distance equates to freedom to do what they wish. Some may think that it includes being able to steal things without being caught.

1.4 Methods for checking stock and cash

If a firm with just a few branches sells only very expensive cars, it would be easy to check on purchases and sales of the cars. The number of cars sold would be relatively small. Checking that cars or money have not been stolen would be easy. However, a business with branches selling many thousands of cheap items could not be checked so easily. To maintain a check on each carton of salt or bag of flour sold would be almost impossible. Even if it could be done, such checks would cost much more than they could possibly save.

One solution to this problem is to record all transactions at the branch in terms of selling prices. For each accounting period, it should be possible to check whether the closing stock is as it should be. For a small branch, you may be given the following figures:

	£
Stock on hand at 1 January – at selling price	5,000
January – Goods sent to the branch by the head office – at selling price	20,000
January – Sales by the branch – obviously at selling price	18,000

The calculation of the closing stock is:

	£
Opening stock (selling price)	5,000
Add Goods sent to the branch (selling price)	20,000
Goods which the branch had available for sale (selling price)	25,000
Less Goods sold (selling price)	18,000
Closing stock should be (selling price)	7,000

1.5 Allowances for deficiencies

In every business there will be:

(a) wastage of goods for some reason – goods may be damaged or broken, or they may be kept too long and become unsaleable;

(b) stealing by customers, especially in a retail business;

(c) thefts by employees.

No one can be certain how much stock is wasted or stolen during a period. Only experience will enable a good estimate of these losses to be made.

1.6 The double column system

At regular intervals, at least once a year but usually more frequently now that accounting for branches is virtually always computerised, headquarters prepares a special type of trading account for each branch. The trading account can be shown in a form similar to a 'T-account' but with two columns on each side.

The right hand column on the left side shows goods sent to the branch or held in inventory at cost price, i.e. the normal basis for any business. The other columns show all trading account items at selling price. This allows dificiencies in trading to be compared with the normal allowance for wastages, etc. of the business.

When such a system is in place, it is easy for head office to tell if the branch is operating as expected; and, of course, easy for the branch itself to assess its own operations against the norms for the business.

Exhibit 1.1

Branch Trading Account for the year ending 31.12.2008					*At selling price*	
		At selling price				
	£	£		£	£	
Stock 1 Jan 2008	1,600	1,200	Sales	7,428	7,428	
Goods from head office	8,000	6,000	Deficiency (difference)	172		
	9,600	7,200				
Less Stock 31 Dec 2008	2,000	1,500				
	7,600	5,700				
Gross profit c/d		1,728				
	7,600	7,428		7,600	7,428	
			Gross profit b/d		1,728	

Exhibit 1.1 is drafted from the following details for a business which sells goods at a uniform mark-up of $33\frac{1}{3}$ per cent on cost price:

	£
Stock 1 Jan 2008 (at cost)	1,200
Goods sent to the branch during the year (at cost)	6,000
Sales (selling price)	7,428
Stock 31 Dec 2008 (at cost)	1,500

Allowances for wastage, etc., 1 per cent of sales.

As the actual deficiency of £172 exceeds the amount expected, i.e. 1 per cent of £7,428 = £74, an investigation will be made.

This method is suitable where all the sales are for cash, there being no sales on credit, or when debtors make their payments to the branch where the sale took place.

Activity 1.1 Why should it make any difference if debtors make payment to a branch other than the one where the sale took place?

1.7 The stock and debtors system

Further adjustments are needed when there are credit sales as well as cash sales. There are two ways of making the entries. These are:

(a) using memoranda columns *only* to keep a check on stock;
(b) integrating stock control into the double entry system. This is often called an 'integrated method'.

Under both these approaches, information is kept relating to stock and debtors.

Using the following data, Exhibit 1.2 presents the records in the Headquarters books when (a), the memoranda method, is used. Exhibit 1.3 shows (b) the records when the integrated method is used.

Data: A branch sells all its goods at a uniform mark-up of 50 per cent on cost price. Credit customers are to pay their accounts directly to the headquarters.

		£
First day of the period:		
Stock (at cost)	(A)	2,000
Debtors	(B)	400
During the period:		
Goods sent to the branch (at cost)	(C)	7,000
Sales – cash	(D)	6,000
Sales – credit	(E)	4,800
Cash remitted by debtors to head office	(F)	4,500
At the close of the last day of the period:		
Stock (at cost)	(G)	1,800
Debtors	(H)	700

Note: The letters A to H beside the figures have been inserted to identify the entries in Exhibits 1.2 and 1.3.

(a) Memoranda columns method

Exhibit 1.2

Branch Stock

		Selling price (memo only) £	£			Selling price (memo only) £	£
Stock b/d	(A)	3,000	2,000	Sales: Cash	(D)	6,000	6,000
Goods sent	(C)	10,500	7,000	Credit	(E)	4,800	4,800
Gross profit to				Stock c/d	(G)	2,700	1,800
profit and loss			3,600				
		13,500	12,600			13,500	12,600
Stock b/d	(G)	2,700	1,800				

Branch Debtors

		£			£
Balances b/d	(B)	400	Cash	(F)	4,500
Branch stock	(E)	4,800	Balance c/d	(H)	700
		5,200			5,200
Balance b/d		700			

Goods Sent to Branches

	£			£
Headquarters trading	7,000	Branch stock	(C)	7,000

Cash Book

		£	
Branch stock – cash sales	(D)	6,000	
Branch debtors	(E)	4,500	

The branch stock account is similar to the branch trading account you saw in Exhibit 1.1. However, in addition a branch debtors account is in use.

The balance of the goods sent to the branches account is shown as being transferred to the headquarters trading account at cost. This figure is deducted from the purchases in the headquarters trading account, so that goods bought for the branch can be disregarded when the gross profit earned by the business is calculated.

(b) The integrated method

The integrated method introduces the idea that gross profit can be calculated by reference to profit margins. It relies upon all selling prices being set strictly on the basis of the profit margins adopted by the business. For example, assume that a travelling salesman sells all his goods at cost price plus 25 per cent. At the start of a week he has £80 of goods at cost, he buys goods costing £800, he sells goods for £900 (selling price) and he has goods at the end of the week which have cost him £160. A trading account based on this data is shown below.

Trading

	£		£
Stock b/d	80	Sales	900
Purchases	800	Stock c/d	160
Gross profit c/d	180		
	1,060		1,060
		Gross profit b/d	180

This could be shown as an extract from the trading and profit or loss account or could be presented as:

	£
Profit made when opening stock is sold	20
Profit made when purchases are sold	200
Profit made when all goods are sold	220
But he still has left unsold goods (cost £160) on which the profit still has to be realised	(40)
Therefore profit realised	180

This could be expressed in account form as:

Salesman's Profit Adjustment

	£		£
Gross profit realised	180	Unrealised profit b/d	20
Unrealised profit c/d	40	Unrealised profit when goods were bought	200
	220		220

The integrated system uses an adjustment account because goods sent to the branch are shown at cost price in a 'goods sent to branch account'. (This is the same as under the memoranda column method.) In the branch stock account, these goods are shown at selling price. Obviously, if one entry is made at cost price and the other at selling price, the accounts would not balance. As the integrated method does not use memoranda columns, to correct this an extra account called a 'branch adjustment account' is opened. As with the Salesman's Profit Adjustment shown above, entries in this account are in respect of the profit content *only* of goods.

The branch stock account acts as a check upon stock deficiencies. The branch adjustment account shows the amount of gross profit realised (i.e. earned) and unrealised during the period.

Exhibit 1.3 shows the ledger accounts needed for the integrated system from the same information given on page 6 that was used to complete Exhibit 1.2. (For simplicity, there is no deficiency of stock in this example.) The letters A to H in Exhibit 1.3 conform to the letters A to H shown against the information on page 6.

Exhibit 1.3

Branch Stock (Selling Price)

		£			£
Balance b/d	(A)	3,000	Sales: Cash	(D)	6,000
Goods sent to branch	(C)	10,500	Credit	(E)	4,800
			Balance c/d	(G)	2,700
		13,500			13,500
Balance b/d	(G)	2,700			

Branch Debtors (Selling Price)

		£			£
Balances b/d	(B)	400	Cash	(F)	4,500
Branch stock	(E)	4,800	Balances c/d	(H)	700
		5,200			5,200
Balances b/d	(H)	700			

Goods Sent to Branch (Cost Price)

	£			£
Headquarters trading	7,000	Branch stock	(C)	7,000

Branch Adjustment (Profit Content)

		£			£
Gross profit to profit and loss		3,600	Unrealised profit b/d	(A)	1,000
			Branch stock – goods sent	(C)	3,500
Unrealised profit c/d	(G)	900			
		4,500			4,500
			Unrealised profit b/d	(G)	900

The opening and closing stocks are shown in the branch stock account at selling price. However, the balance sheet should show the stock at cost price. The previous balance sheet should therefore have shown stock at cost of £2,000. This is achieved by having a compensating £1,000 credit balance brought forward in the branch adjustment account so that the debit balance of £3,000 in the branch stock account, when it comes to being shown in the balance sheet, has the £1,000 credit balance deducted to show a net figure of £2,000. Similarly, at the close of the period the balance sheet will show stock at £1,800 (branch stock debit balance £2,700 *less* branch adjustment credit balance £900).

Compare the entries in the branch adjustment account to the differences between the memoranda and 'real' column figure in the branch account shown in Exhibit 1.2. You should be able to see how both methods show the same information, one (the *memoranda columns method*) using gross amounts as the basis for presentation while the other (the *integrated method*) presents the gross profits as separate amounts.

1.8 The stock and debtors integrated method – further points

Returns

Goods may be returned:

(*a*) from the branch stock to the head office
(*b*) from customers of the branch to the branch
(*c*) from customers of the branch to the headquarters of the business.

Exhibit 1.4

To examine the entries needed, suppose a business sells goods at cost plus 25 per cent profit, and goods sold at the following prices were returned: (*a*) £90, (*b*) £150, (*c*) £30. The entries needed are:

Branch Stock (Selling Price)

		£				£
Returns from debtors	(*b*)	150	Returns to headquarters	(*a*)		90

Branch Adjustment (Profit Loading)

		£	
Returns from branch	(*a*)	18	
Returns from debtors	(*c*)	6	

Goods Sent to Branch (Cost Price)

		£	
Returns from branch	(*a*)	72	
Returns from debtors	(*c*)	24	

Branch Debtors (Selling Price)

			£
Returns to branch	(*b*)		150
Returns to headquarters	(*c*)		30

Entries (*b*), both being in accounts shown at selling price, were two in number, i.e. £150 Dr and £150 Cr; entries (*a*) and (*c*) each needed entries in three accounts, (*a*) being £45 Cr and £18 Dr and £72 Dr, (*c*) being £30 Cr and £24 Dr and £6 Dr.

1.9　If each branch maintains full accounting records

Branches rarely maintain full accounting records. When they do, it is usually in a business with just a few branches, and is normally done only when a branch is large enough to justify employing its own accounting staff.

A branch cannot operate on its own without resources, and it is the business as a whole which provides these in the first instance. It will want to know how much money it has invested in each branch, and from this arises the concept of branch and headquarters current accounts. The relationship between the branch and the headquarters is seen as that of a debtor/creditor. The current account shows the branch as a debtor in the headquarters records, while the headquarters is shown as a creditor in the branch records. (This is similar to what you learnt about joint venture accounting in *Business Accounting Essentials 1*.)

The current accounts are used for transactions concerned with supplying resources to the branch or in taking back resources. For such transactions, full double entry records are needed, both in the branch records and in the headquarters records: i.e. each item is recorded twice in each set of records. Some transactions will, however, concern the branch only, and these will merely need two entries in the branch records and none in the headquarters records. Exhibit 1.5 shows several transactions and the records needed:

Exhibit 1.5

A company with its headquarters in London opened a branch in Manchester. The following transactions took place in the first month:

(A) Opened a bank account at Manchester by transferring £10,000 from the London bank account.
(B) Bought premises in Manchester, paying by cheque drawn on the London bank account, £50,000.
(C) Manchester bought a motor van, paying £6,000 from its own bank account.
(D) Manchester bought fixtures on credit from A B Equipment Ltd, £2,900.
(E) London supplied a machine valued at £2,500 from its own machinery.
(F) Manchester bought goods from suppliers, paying by cheque on its own account, £2,700.
(G) Manchester's cash sales banked immediately in its own bank account, £30,000.
(H) Goods invoiced at cost to Manchester during the month by London (no cash or cheques being paid specifically for these goods by Manchester), £28,000.
(I) A cheque is paid to London by Manchester as a return of funds, £18,000.
(J) Goods returned to London by Manchester – at cost price, £1,000.

The exact dates have been omitted. You will see later that complications arise because of differences in the timing of transaction for the two locations. For example, a cheque sent on one day will arrive on another day. Each transaction has been identified by a capital letter. The relevant letter will be shown against each entry in the accounts.

Headquarters Records (in London)
Manchester Branch Current Account

		£			£
Bank	(A)	10,000	Bank	(I)	18,000
Bank – premises	(B)	50,000	Returns from Branch	(J)	1,000
Machinery	(E)	2,500			
Goods sent to Branch	(H)	28,000			

Bank

		£			£
Manchester Branch	(I)	18,000	Manchester Branch	(A)	10,000
			Manchester premises	(B)	50,000

Machinery

			£
	Manchester Branch	(E)	2,500

Goods Sent to Branch

		£				£
Returns from Branch	(J)	1,000	Manchester Branch	(H)	28,000

Branch Records (in Manchester)
Headquarters Current Account

		£			£
Bank	(I)	18,000	Bank	(A)	10,000
Returns	(J)	1,000	Premises	(B)	50,000
			Machinery	(E)	2,500
			Headquarters current: goods	(H)	28,000

Bank

		£			£
Headquarters current	(A)	10,000	Motor van	(C)	6,000
Cash sales	(G)	30,000	Purchases	(F)	2,700
			Headquarters current	(I)	18,000

Premises

		£	
Headquarters current	(B)	50,000	

Motor Van

		£	
Bank	(C)	6,000	

Fixtures

		£	
A B Equipment Ltd	(D)	2,900	

A B Equipment Ltd

			£
	Fixtures	(D)	2,900

Machinery

		£	
Headquarters current	(E)	2,500	

Purchases

		£	
Bank	(F)	2,700	

→

Sales

			£
	Bank	(G)	30,000

Goods from Headquarters

		£				£
Headquarters current	(H)	28,000	Headquarters current: returns	(J)		1,000

Note: **It can be seen that items C, D, F and G are entered only in the Manchester records. This is because these items are purely internal transactions and are not concerned with resources flowing between London and Manchester.**

1.10 Profit or loss and current accounts

The profit or loss earned by the branch does not belong to the branch. It belongs to the business and must therefore be shown as such. The headquarters represents the central authority of the business and profit of the branch should be credited to the Headquarters Current Account, any loss being debited.

The branch will therefore maintain its own trading account and profit and loss account (T-accounts). After agreement with headquarters the net profit will then be transferred to the credit of the Headquarters Current Account. The headquarters will then debit the Branch Current Account in its own records and credit its own profit and loss account (T-account). Taking the net profit earned in Exhibit 1.5 as £7,000 the two sets of books would be:

Headquarters Records (in London)
Headquarters Profit and Loss

		£
	Net profit earned by the Manchester Branch	7,000

Manchester Branch Current Account

	£		£
Bank	10,000	Bank	18,000
Bank: premises	50,000	Returns from Branch	1,000
Machinery	2,500		
Goods sent to Branch	28,000		
Headquarters profit and loss: net profit	7,000	Balance c/d	78,500
	97,500		97,500
Balance b/d	78,500		

Branch Records (in Manchester)
Manchester Profit and Loss

	£	
Headquarters current: net profit	7,000	

Headquarters Current Account			
	£		£
Returns to Headquarters	1,000	Bank	10,000
Bank	18,000	Premises	50,000
		Machinery	2,500
		Goods from Headquarters	28,000
Balance c/d	78,500	Profit and loss	7,000
	97,500		97,500
		Balance b/d	78,500

The trading and profit and loss account for the business can then be prepared.

1.11 The combined balance sheet

After the company's trading and profit and loss account has been drawn up a balance sheet can be done. The branch sends its trial balance to headquarters which adds the assets and liabilities of the branch to those in the headquarter's trial balance.

In the trial balances, the Headquarters Current Account will be a debit balance while the Branch Current Account will be a credit balance, e.g. the figures of £78,500 in the London books and Manchester books. These therefore cancel each other out and are not shown in the combined balance sheet. This is the correct treatment, as the two balances do not represent assets or liabilities of the business.

Activity 1.2 If the current account balances do not represent assets or liabilities, what do they represent?

1.12 Items in transit

Earlier in this chapter, it was mentioned that the timing of transactions could raise complications. These are similar to those that give rise to the need for bank reconciliations, which you learnt about in *Business Accounting Essentials 1*. Obviously, a cheque sent by post by a Manchester branch would probably arrive in London the next day, while goods sent from London to Manchester, or returned from Manchester to London, could arrive on the same day or anything up to several days later.

Both the headquarters and the branch will have entered the transactions at the dates of remittance or receipt and, as the remittance from one place will occur on one day and the receipt may occur at the other place on another day, items which are in transit at the end of a financial period may not be recorded in both sets of books. That is, the two sets of books will not contain identical figures and the balances on the current accounts will not be equal to one another.

Not surprisingly, they must be adjusted to agree at the correct amount so that they will cancel out when the combined balance sheet is prepared. As the two sets of records contain some figures which are different from each other they must somehow be reconciled so that the balances carried down are the same.

When preparing a bank reconciliation, permanent adjustments are made to the bank account balance recorded in the books. In contrast, when dealing with reconciliations of branch and headquarters current accounts, adjustments are made that are then carried down as balances to the next period. Which set of figures is to be altered? The amendments are all made in the headquarters books. Otherwise, when several branches are involved, things could get very confusing indeed.

Exhibit 1.6 is for a second month of the business shown in Exhibit 1.5. However, while there were no items in transit at the end of the first month, this is not the case at the end of the second month.

Exhibit 1.6

Headquarters records (showing current accounts only)	£
Goods sent to Branch	37,000
Cheques received from Branch	29,500
Returns received from Branch	4,400
Branch records	
Goods received from Headquarters	35,000
Cheques sent to Headquarters	30,300
Returns sent to Headquarters	5,000

The net profit shown by the profit and loss account of the branch is £8,000.

Branch Records (in Manchester)
Headquarters Current Account

	£		£
Bank	30,300	Balance b/d	78,500
Returns to Headquarters	5,000	Goods from Headquarters	35,000
Balance c/d	86,200	Net profit	8,000
	121,500		121,500
		Balance b/d	86,200

Headquarters Records (in London)
Manchester Branch Current Account

		£			£
Balance b/d		78,500	Bank	(B)	29,500
Goods sent to Branch	(A)	37,000	Returns received	(C)	4,400
Net profit		8,000			

At this point, the following items are found to be in transit at the end of the period (these should be confirmed to ensure that they are not merely errors in accounting records):

(A) Goods sent to the branch amounting to £2,000 (£37,000 – £35,000).
(B) Cheques sent by the branch amounting to £800 (£30,300 – £29,500).
(C) Returns from the branch amounting to £600 (£5,000 – £4,400).

● (A) needs amending to £35,000. This is done by crediting the account with £2,000.
● (B) needs amending to £30,300. This is done by crediting the account with £800.
● (C) needs amending to £5,000. This is done by crediting the account with £600.

As these are items in transit, they need to be carried down as balances into the next period. The branch current account will now be completed.

It may seem strange that all the items in transit are shown as debit balances. However, all goods (including returns) and money in transit are assets of the business at the end of a financial period. That they are in transit does not alter the fact that they belong to the business. Assets are always shown as debit balances and there is no reason why it should be different just because they have not reached their destination on a certain date.

Manchester Branch Current Account

	£		£
Balance b/d	78,500	Bank	29,500
Goods sent to branch	37,000	Returns received	4,400
Net profit	8,000	Goods in transit c/d	2,000
		Cheques in transit c/d	800
		Returns in transit c/d	600
		Balance c/d	86,200
	123,500		123,500
Balance b/d	86,200		
Goods in transit b/d	2,000		
Cheques in transit b/d	800		
Returns in transit b/d	600		

All of these four balances are shown in the trial balance. When the combined balance sheet is being prepared the balance of the two current accounts (in this case £86,200) will cancel out as it is a debit balance in one trial balance and a credit balance in the other. The goods in transit £2,000 and the returns in transit £600, both being goods, are added to the stock in the balance sheet. This is because at the end of the second month, stock is made up of the following items:

	£
Stock at London	
Add Stock at Manchester	
Add Stocks in transit (£2,000 + £600)	2,600
Total stock	

Similarly, the balance for cheques or remittances in transit is added to the bank balances at London and Manchester:

	£
Bank balance at London	
Add Bank balance in Manchester	
Add Remittances in transit	800

This is rather like a man who has £14 in one pocket and £3 in another. He takes a £5 note from the pocket containing the larger amount and is transferring it to his other pocket when someone asks him to stay perfectly still and calculate the total cash in his possession. He therefore has:

	£
Pocket 1 (£14 – £5)	9
Pocket 2	3
Cash in transit	5
	17

1.13 Items in transit and the balance sheet

Using the figures already given in Exhibit 1.6, but adding some further information, trial balances for the London headquarters and the Manchester branch are shown in Exhibit 1.7 *after* the trading and profit and loss account on the business has been prepared for the second month and trial balances for both headquarters and the branch have been drawn up.

Exhibit 1.7

Trial Balances as at end of month 2	London Headquarters		Manchester Branch	
	Dr	Cr	Dr	Cr
	£	£	£	£
Premises	100,000		50,000	
Machinery	20,000		2,500	
Fixtures	31,000		2,900	
Motor vans	15,000		6,000	
Closing stock	38,000		7,000	
Debtors	11,000		8,000	
Bank	122,000		21,600	
Headquarters Current Account				86,200
Branch Current Account	86,200			
Goods in transit	2,000			
Cheques in transit	800			
Returns in transit	600			
Creditors		13,000		11,800
Capital account as at start of month 1		378,600		
Net profit for the two months from the trading and profit and loss accounts (Branch £15,000 + Headquarters £20,000)		35,000		
	426,600	426,600	98,000	98,000

The combined balance sheet can now be drawn up.

Balance Sheet as at 29 February 2008		
	£	£
Fixed assets		
Premises		150,000
Machinery		22,500
Fixtures		33,900
Motor vans		21,000
		227,400
Current assets		
Stocks (Note 1)	47,600	
Debtors (Note 2)	19,000	
Bank	144,400	
	211,000	
Less Current liabilities		
Creditors	(24,800)	
Working capital		186,200
Net assets		413,600
Capital		
Balance at 1 January 2008		378,600
Add Net profit:		
London		20,000
Manchester		15,000
		413,600

Notes:

	£			£
(1) Stocks: London	38,000	(2) Bank: London		122,000
Manchester	7,000	Manchester		21,600
In transit (£2,000 + £600)	2,600	In transit		800
	47,600			144,400

1.14　Foreign branch accounts

The treatment of the accounts of foreign branches is subject to only one exception from that of branches in your own country. This is concerned with the fact that when the trial balance is drawn up by the branch, this will be stated in a foreign currency. To amalgamate these figures with your own country's figures will mean that the foreign branch figures will have to be translated into your currency.

There are rules for general guidance as to how this can be done. These are given in SSAP 20: *Foreign currency translation*. These are the ones which will be shown. (Before you read further you should check whether or not this topic is part of your examination requirements.)

The amount of a particular currency which one can obtain for another currency is known as the exchange rate. Taking an imaginary country with a currency called *chips*, there might be a general agreement that the exchange rate should stay about 5 chips to £1. At certain times the exchange rate will exactly equal that figure, but due to all sorts of economic reasons it may well be 5.02 chips to £1 on one day and 4.97 chips to £1 several days later. In addition, some years ago there may have been an act of devaluation by one of the countries involved; the exchange rate could then have been 3 chips to £1. To understand more about exchange rates, devaluation and revaluation of currencies, you may wish to consult a relevant economics textbook.

All items in the trial balance should NOT be converted to your currency on the basis of the exchange rate ruling at the date of the trial balance. The rules in SSAP 20 have been devised in an attempt to bring about conversion into your currency in a way that does not to distort reported trading results.

1.15　SSAP 20 conversion rules

1. (*a*) Fixed assets at the exchange rate ruling when the assets were bought – the **temporal method**. If fixed assets have been bought on different dates, then different rates will have to be used for each separate purchase.
   (*b*) Depreciation on the fixed assets at the same rate as the fixed assets concerned.
2. Current assets and current liabilities – at the rate ruling at the date of the trial balance. This is known as the **closing method**.
3. Opening stock in the trading account – at the rate ruling at the previous balance sheet date.
4. Goods sent by the headquarters to the branch, or returns from the branch – at the actual figures shown in the Goods Sent to Branches Account in the headquarters books.
5. Trading and profit and loss account items, other than depreciation, opening and closing stocks, or goods sent to or returned by the branch – at the average rate for the period covered by the accounts.
6. The Headquarters Current Account – at the same figures as shown in the Branch Current Account in the headquarters books.

1.16　Conversion of trial balance figures

When the conversion of the figures into your currency is completed, the totals of the debit and credit sides of your currency trial balance will not normally be equal to one another. This is due to different exchange rates being taken for conversion purposes. A balancing figure will therefore be needed to bring about the equality of the totals. For this purpose, a **difference on exchange account** will be opened in which a debit entry will be made if the lesser total is on the debit side of the trial balance. When the headquarters redrafts the profit and loss account, any debit balance on the difference on exchange account should be transferred to it as an expense. A credit balance on the difference on exchange account should be transferred to the credit of the profit and loss account as a gain.

In consolidated accounts, special rules are applied to foreign exchange conversion.

Exhibit 1.8

An example of the conversion of a trial balance into UK currency is now shown. The branch is in Flavia, and the unit of currency is the Flavian dollar. The exchange rates needed are:

(a) On 1 January 2003, 10 dollars = £1
(b) On 1 January 2005, 11 dollars = £1
(c) On 1 January 2008, 17 dollars = £1
(d) On 31 December 2008, 15 dollars = £1
(e) If no further information were given the average rate for 2008 would have to be taken as (c) + (d) ÷ 2, i.e. 16 dollars = £1. This is not an advisable procedure in practice; the fact that the average has been calculated from only two readings could mean that the average calculated might be far different from a more accurate one calculated from a larger number of readings.

Trial Balance as at 31 December 2008					
	Dr (F$)	Cr (F$)	Exchange rates	Dr (£)	Cr (£)
Fixed assets:					
Bought 1 Jan 2003	10,000		10 = £1	1,000	
Bought 1 Jan 2005	8,800		11 = £1	800	
Stock 1 Jan 2008	6,800		17 = £1	400	
Expense accounts	8,000		16 = £1	500	
Sales		32,000	16 = £1		2,000
Goods from Headquarters	21,900		£ per account in Headquarters books	1,490	
Headquarters current account		43,000	£ per account in Headquarters books		3,380
Debtors	9,000		15 = £1	600	
Creditors		4,500	15 = £1		300
Bank	15,000		15 = £1	1,000	
	79,500	79,500		5,790	5,680
Difference on exchange account					110
				5,790	5,790

The value of the stock at 31 December 2008 is 12,000 Flavian dollars. When the trading account is drawn up, this is converted at F$15 = £1, i.e. £800.

Note: don't forget that either the term, 'head office' or the word, 'headquarters' may be used by examiners.

Learning outcomes

You should now have learnt:

1 There are two main methods used to record transactions of the branches of an organisation:
  (a) all accounting records are kept by the headquarters;
  (b) each branch has its own full accounting system.

2 When all sales are for cash, a double column trading and profit and loss account can be used in order to monitor any unexpected losses.

3 When some sales are on credit, either memoranda columns can be used in the branch stock account in order to monitor stock or stock control can be integrated into the double entry system.

4 Foreign branch figures need to be translated using the principles set down in SSAP 20: *Foreign currency translation*.

Answers to activities

1.1 When a second branch or headquarters is also involved in receiving payments from debtors of another branch, the focus of control shifts from being purely connected with one branch. More sophisticated methods of recording the transaction data are therefore required.

1.2 They are merely a measure of the resources at the branch. The underlying assets and liabilities they represent are already included in the balance sheet.

Review questions

1.1 L Pacioli Ltd has a branch in Bath at which a full set of books is kept. At the end of the year the following summary is compiled of the transactions between the branch and the headquarters as recorded in the latter's books:

	£
Balance due from branch 1 April	72,600
Cash received from branch	110,000
Goods supplied to branch	74,200
Goods returned by branch	2,600
Expenses paid on behalf of branch	17,800

At 30 September the branch profit and loss account showed a net profit of £63,000 for the six months.

(a) Show the above items as they would appear in the ledger of the head office.
(b) How can any resulting balance from these figures be proved, and what does it indicate?

1.2 Haddock Ltd, whose head office is in Perth, operates a branch in Inverness. All goods are purchased by headquarters and invoiced to and sold by the branch at cost plus 40 per cent.
  Other than a sales ledger kept in Inverness, all transactions are recorded in the books in Perth.
  The following particulars are given of the transactions at the branch during the year ended 30 June 2006.

→

→

	£
Stock on hand, 1 July 2005, at invoice price	40,012
Debtors on 1 July 2005	28,000
Stock on hand, 30 June 2006, at invoice price	26,488
Goods sent from Aberdeen during the year at invoice price	170,100
Credit sales	149,590
Cash sales	21,000
Returns to headquarters at invoice price	7,560
Invoice value of goods stolen	4,200
Bad debts written-off	1,540
Cash from debtors	131,600
Normal loss at invoice price due to wastage	812
Cash discount allowed to debtors	3,156

You are required to write up the branch stock account and branch total debtors account for the year ended 30 June 2006, as they would appear in the headquarters books, showing clearly any abnormal wastage.

1.3 RST Limited is a family-controlled company which operates a chain of retail outlets specialising in motor spares and accessories.

Branch stocks are purchased by a centralised purchasing function in order to obtain the best terms from suppliers.

A 10 per cent handling charge is applied by headquarters to the cost of the purchases, and branches are expected to add 25 per cent to the resulting figure to arrive at normal selling prices, although branch managers are authorised to reduce normal prices in special situations. The effect of such reductions must be notified to headquarters.

On 1 April 2006, a new branch was established at Derham. The following details have been recorded for the year ended 31 March 2007:

	£
Purchase cost to headquarters of stock transferred to Derham	82,400
Derham branch sales: cash	89,940
credit	1,870
Stocks transferred from Derham to other branches, at normal selling prices	3,300
Authorised reductions from normal selling prices during the year	2,250

All records in respect of branch activities are maintained at headquarters, and the branch profit margin is dealt with through a branch stock adjustment account.

Required:
(a) Prepare:
  (i) the branch stock account (maintained at branch selling prices);
  (ii) the branch stock adjustment account.
  The *book stock* should be taken for this part of the question.
(b) List four of the possible reasons for the stock difference revealed when a physical stocktaking at the Derham branch on 31 March 2007 showed stock valued at selling prices amounting to £14,850.
(c) State which of the following is the figure to be included in RST Limited's balance sheet at 31 March 2007, for Derham branch stock:
  (i) £11,138
  (ii) £11,880
  (iii) £10,800
  (iv) None of these.

Justify your choice with appropriate calculations.

(*Chartered Institute of Management Accountants*)

1.4A Paper Products has a head office in London and a branch in Bristol. The following information has been extracted from the head office books of account as at 31 March 2006:

Information relating to the branch

Balances	Opening £000	Closing £000
Branch bank account (positive balance)	3	12
Branch debtors	66	81
Branch stock (at transfer price)	75	90

Transactions during the year	£000	
Bad debts written off	15	
Branch general expenses (paid from bank branch account)	42	
Cash received from credit customers and banked	390	
Cash sales banked	120	
Cash transferred from branch to head office bank account	459	
Credit sales	437	
Discounts allowed to credit customers	9	
Goods returned by credit customers	8	
Goods returned from branch (at transfer price from head office)		30
Goods sent to branch (at transfer price from head office)		600

Information relating to head office

Balances	Opening £000	Closing £000
Stock	180	220

Transactions during the year	£000
Bad debts written off	24
Cash sales	1,500
Credit sales	2,000
Discounts allowed to credit customers	29
General expenses	410
Goods returned by credit customers	40
Purchases	2,780

Additional information:

1 Most of the accounting records relating to the branch are kept by the head office in its own books of account.

2 All purchases are made by the head office, and goods are invoiced to the branch at selling price, that is, at cost price plus 50 per cent.

Required:

(a) Write up the following ledger accounts for the year to 31 March 2006, being careful to bring down any balances as at that date:

    (i) branch stock account;

    (ii) goods sent to branch account;

    (iii) branch stock adjustment account;

    (iv) branch debtors account; and

    (v) branch bank account.

(b) Compile Paper Products' trading, and profit and loss account for the year ending 31 March 2006.^{Authors' note}

(c) Examine briefly the merits and demerits of Paper Products' method of branch bookkeeping including comments on the significance of the 'balancing figure' in the branch stock account.

(Association of Accounting Technicians)

Authors' note: **Part (b) should show a column for headquarters, a column for the branch, and a column for the total.**

→

→ **1.5** Packer and Stringer were in partnership as retail traders sharing profits and losses: Packer three-quarters, Stringer one-quarter. The partners were credited annually with interest at the rate of 6 per cent per annum on their fixed capitals; no interest was charged on their drawings.

Stringer was responsible for the buying department of the business. Packer managed the head office and Paper was employed as the branch manager. Packer and Paper were each entitled to a commission of 10 per cent of the net profits (after charging such commission) of the shop managed by him.

All goods were purchased by head office and goods sent to the branch were invoiced at cost.

The following was the trial balance as on 31 December 2004.

	Head Office Books Dr	Head Office Books Cr	Branch Books Dr	Branch Books Cr
	£	£	£	£
Drawings accounts and fixed capital accounts: Packer	2,500	14,000		
Stringer	1,200	4,000		
Furniture and fittings, at cost	1,500		1,100	
Furniture and fittings, provision for depreciation as at 31 December 2003		500		350
Stock on 31 December 2003	13,000		4,400	
Purchases	37,000			
Goods sent to branches		18,000	17,200	
Sales		39,000		26,000
Provision for doubtful debts		600		200
Branch and head office current accounts	6,800			3,600
Salaries and wages	4,500		3,200	
Paper, on account of commission			240	
Carriage and travelling expenses	2,200		960	
Administrative expenses	2,400			
Trade and general expenses	3,200		1,800	
Sundry debtors	7,000		3,000	
Sundry creditors		5,800		400
Bank balances	600			1,350
	81,900	81,900	31,900	31,900

You are given the following additional information:

(a) Stocks on 31 December 2004 amounted to: head office £14,440, branch £6,570.
(b) Administrative expenses are to be apportioned between head office and the branch in proportion to sales.
(c) Depreciation is to be provided on furniture and fittings at 10 per cent of cost.
(d) The provision for doubtful debts is to be increased by £50 in respect of head office debtors and decreased by £20 in the case of those of the branch.
(e) On 31 December 2004 cash amounting to £2,400, in transit from the branch to head office, had been recorded in the branch books but not in those of head office; and on that date goods invoiced at £800, in transit from head office to the branch, had been recorded in the head office books but not in the branch books.

Any adjustments necessary are to be made in the head office books.

You are required to:
(a) prepare trading and profit and loss accounts and the appropriation account for the year ending 31 December 2004, showing the net profit of the head office and branch respectively;
(b) prepare the balance sheet as on that date; and
(c) show the closing entries in the branch current accounts giving the make-up of the closing balance.

Income tax is to be ignored.

(*Institute of Chartered Accountants*)

1.6A LR, a trader, commenced business on 1 January 2009, with a head office and one branch.

All goods were purchased by the head office and goods sent to the branch were invoiced at a fixed selling price of 25 per cent above cost. All sales, both by the head office and the branch, were made at the fixed selling price.

The following trial balance was extracted from the books at the head office at 31 December 2009.

Trial Balance

	£	£
Capital		52,000
Drawings	1,740	
Purchases	123,380	
Sales		83,550
Goods sent to branch (at selling price)		56,250
Branch current account	24,550	
Fixed assets	33,000	
Debtors and creditors	7,980	11,060
General expenses	8,470	
Balance at bank	3,740	
	202,860	202,860

No entries had been made in the head office books for cash in transit from the branch to head office at 31 December 2009, £1,000.

When the balances shown below were extracted from the branch books at 31 December 2009, no entries had been made in the books of the branch for goods in transit on that date from head office to branch, £920 (selling price).

In addition to the balances which can be deduced from the information given above, the following balances appeared in the branch books on 31 December 2009.

	£
Fixed assets	6,000
General expenses	6,070
Debtors	7,040
Creditors (excluding head office)	1,630
Sales	51,700
Balance at bank	1,520

When stock was taken on 31 December 2009, it was found that there was no shortage at the head office, but at the branch there were shortages amounting to £300, at selling price.

You are required to: prepare trading and profit and loss accounts (*a*) for head office and (*b*) for the branch, as they would have appeared if goods sent to the branch had been invoiced at cost, and a balance sheet of the whole business as on 31 December 2009.

Head office and branch stocks are to be valued at cost.

Ignore depreciation of fixed assets.

(*Institute of Chartered Secretaries and Administrators*)

→

1.7 Nion is a retail stock outlet operating from a head office in London and a branch in Brighton. The following trial balances have been extracted from the books of account as at 31 October 2011.

| | Head Office Books | | Branch Books | |
| | Dr | Cr | Dr | Cr |
	£	£	£	£
Drawings	40,000			
Fixed assets: at cost	350,000		100,000	
accumulated depreciation				
(at 1 November 2010)		140,000		30,000
Stock (at 1 November 2010)	8,000		20,000	
Provision for unrealised profit		4,000		
Purchases	914,000			
Goods sent to branch at invoiced value		380,000	375,000	
Sales		850,000		437,000
Provision for doubtful debts		9,000		2,500
Head office/branch current accounts	175,000			120,000
Distribution expenses	80,500		5,000	
Administrative expenses	200,000		16,500	
Trade debtors	60,000		60,000	
Trade creditors		50,000		
Cash and bank balances	15,500		13,000	
Capital		410,000		
	£1,843,000	£1,843,000	£589,500	£589,500

Additional information:
1 All goods are purchased by the head office. Those goods sent to the branch are invoiced at cost plus 25 per cent.
2 Stocks were valued at 31 October 2011 as being at head office, £12,000; and at the branch, £15,000 at their invoiced price.
3 Depreciation is to be provided for the year on the fixed assets at a rate of 10 per cent on the historic cost.
4 The provision for doubtful debts is to be maintained at a rate of 5 per cent of outstanding trade debtors as at the end of the financial year.
5 As at 31 October 2011, there was £50,000 cash in transit from the branch to the head office; this cash was received in London on 3 November 2011. There was also £5,000 of goods in transit at invoice price from the head office to the branch; the branch received these goods on 10 November 2011.

Required:
Prepare in adjacent columns: (*a*) the head office, and (*b*) the branch trading and profit and loss accounts for the year ending 31 October 2011; and a **combined** balance sheet for Nion as at that date.

Notes:
(*i*) a combined trading and profit and loss account is NOT required; and
(*ii*) separate balance sheets for the head office and the branch are also NOT required.

(Association of Accounting Technicians)

1.8A Star Stores has its head office and main store in Crewe, and a branch store in Leek. All goods are purchased by the head office. Goods are invoiced to the branch at cost price plus a profit loading of 20 per cent. The following trial balances have been extracted from the books of account of both the head office and the branch as at 31 December 2009:

	Head Office Books		Branch Books	
	Dr	Cr	Dr	Cr
	£000	£000	£000	£000
Administrative expenses	380		30	
Distribution costs	157		172	
Capital (at 1 January 2009)		550		
Cash and bank	25		2	
Creditors and accruals		176		20
Current accounts	255			180
Debtors and prepayments	130		76	
Motor vehicles:				
at cost	470		230	
accumulated depreciation at 31 December 2009		280		120
Plant and equipment:				
at cost	250		80	
accumulated depreciation at 31 December 2009		120		30
Proprietor's drawings during the year	64			
Provision for unrealised profit on branch stocks at 1 January 2009		5		
Purchases	880			
Sales		1,200		570
Stocks at cost/invoiced amount at 1 January 2009	80		30	
Transfer of goods to the branch/from the head office		360	300	
	£2,691	£2,691	£920	£920

Additional information:
1 The stocks in hand at 31 December 2009 were estimated to be as follows:

	£000
At head office (at cost)	100
At the branch (at invoiced price)	48

In addition, £60,000 of stocks at invoiced price had been despatched to the branch on 28 December 2009. These goods had not been received by the branch until 5 January 2010 and so they had not been included in the branch books of account.
2 On 31 December 2009, the branch had transferred £15,000 of cash to the head office bank, but this was not received in Crewe until 2 January 2010.

Required:
(a) Prepare in adjacent columns and using the vertical format: (*i*) the head office, and (*ii*) the branch trading accounts and profit and loss accounts for the year ending 31 December 2009 (*note*: a combined profit and loss account is NOT required); and
(b) Prepare in the vertical format, Star Stores' balance sheet as at 31 December 2009 (*note*: separate balance sheets for the head office and the branch are NOT required).

(Association of Accounting Technicians)

→

1.9 EG Company Limited, a manufacturing business, exports some of its products through an overseas branch whose currency is 'florins', which carries out the final assembly operations before selling the goods.

The trial balances of the head office and branch at 30 June 2008 were:

	Head Office		Branch	
	£	£	'Fl.'	'Fl.'
Freehold buildings at cost	14,000		63,000	
Debtors/creditors	8,900	9,500	36,000	1,560
Sales		104,000		432,000
Authorised and issued capital		40,000		
Components sent to branch		35,000		
Head office/branch accounts	60,100			504,260
Branch cost of sales			360,000	
Depreciation provision, machinery		1,500		56,700
Head office cost of sales				
(including goods to branch)	59,000			
Administration costs	15,200		18,000	
Stock at 30 June 2008	28,900		11,520	
Profit and loss account		2,000		
Machinery at cost	6,000		126,000	
Remittances		28,000	272,000	
Balance at bank	4,600		79,200	
Selling and distribution costs	23,300		28,800	
	220,000	220,000	994,520	994,520

The following adjustments are to be made:

1 The cost of sales figures include a depreciation charge of 10 per cent per annum on cost for machinery.
2 A provision of £300 for unrealised profit in branch stock is to be made.
3 On 26 June 2008 the branch remitted 16,000 'Fl.'; these were received by the head office on 4 July and realised £1,990.
4 During May a branch customer in error paid the head office for goods supplied. The amount due was 320 'Fl.' which realised £36. It has been correctly dealt with by head office but not yet entered in the branch books.
5 A provision has to be made for a commission of 5 per cent of the net profit of the branch after charging such commission, which is due to the branch manager.

The rates of exchange were:

At 1 July 2007	10 'Fl.' = £1
At 30 June 2008	8 'Fl.' = £1
Average for the year	9 'Fl.' = £1
On purchase of buildings and machinery	7 'Fl.' = £1

You are required to prepare, for internal use:
(a) detailed operating accounts for the year ended 30 June 2008;*
(b) combined head office and branch balance sheet as at 30 June 2008;
(c) the branch account in the head office books, in both sterling and currency, the opening balance on 1 July 2007 being £25,136 (189,260 'Fl.').
Taxation is to be ignored.

(*Chartered Institute of Management Accountants*)

Authors' note: The question is looking for a trading and profit and loss account for both the branch and head office showing overall net profit.)

1.10 OTL Ltd commenced business on 1 January 2010. The head office is in London and there is a branch in Highland. The currency unit of Highland is the crown.

The following are the trial balances of the head office and the Highland branch as at 31 December 2010:

| | Head Office | | Highland Branch | |
	£	£	Crowns	Crowns
Branch account	65,280			
Balances at bank	10,560		66,000	
Creditors		21,120		92,400
Debtors	18,480		158,400	
Fixed assets (purchased 1 January 2010)	39,600		145,200	
Head office account				316,800
Profit and loss account (net profit for year)		52,800		79,200
Issued share capital		86,400		
Stocks	26,400		118,800	
	160,320	160,320	488,400	488,400

The trial balance of the head office was prepared before any entries had been made in respect of any profits or losses of the branch.

Remittances from head office to branch and from branch to head office were recorded in the books at the actual amounts paid and received.

The rates of exchange were:

On 1 January 2010	5 crowns = £1
Average rate for year 2010	4.4 crowns = £1
On 31 December 2010	4 crowns = £1

Required:

(a) The trial balance of the Highland branch as at 31 December 2010, in sterling.
(b) The closing entries, as at 31 December 2010, in the branch account in the books of the head office.
(c) A summary of the balance sheet of OTL Ltd as at 31 December 2010.
Ignore depreciation of fixed assets.
Ignore taxation.

(*Institute of Chartered Secretaries and Administrators*)

1.11A Home Ltd is incorporated in the UK and rents mobile homes to holidaymakers in this country and in Carea. The company has a head office in London and a branch in Carea where the local currency is 'Mics'. The following balances are extracted from the books of the head office and its 'self-accounting' branch at 31 December 2004.

	Head Office £	Branch Mics
Debit balances		
Fixed assets at cost	450,000	900,000
Debtors and cash	17,600	36,000
Operating costs	103,700	225,000
Branch current account	42,600	
	613,900	1,161,000
Credit balances		
Share capital	200,000	–
Retained profit, 1 January 2004	110,800	–
Sales revenue	186,300	480,000
Creditors	9,700	25,000
Head office current account	–	420,000
Accumulated depreciation	107,100	236,000
	613,900	1,161,000

→

→ The following information is provided regarding exchange rates, some of which is relevant.

The fixed assets of the branch were acquired when there were 8 Mics to the £. Exchange rates ruling during 2004 were:

	Mics to the £
1 January	6
Average	5
31 December	4

There are no cash or goods in transit between head office and branch at the year end.

Required:
The final accounts of Home Ltd for 2004. The accounts should be expressed in £s sterling and, for this purpose, the conversion of Mics should be made in accordance with the temporal method of translation as specified in SSAP 20: *Foreign currency translation.*

(*Institute of Chartered Secretaries and Administrators*)

You can find a range of additional self-test questions, as well as material to help you with your studies, on the website that accompanies this book at **www.pearsoned.co.uk/wood**

Hire purchase accounts

Learning objectives

After you have studied this chapter, you should be able to:

- explain the term 'hire purchase'
- explain what distinguishes hire purchase from outright purchase
- explain what distinguishes hire purchase from a lease
- record the entries relating to hire purchase transactions

Introduction

In this chapter you'll learn about the nature of hire purchase; of the difference to the cost to the buyer of paying the same amount each period as compared with paying a variable amount linked to the outstanding amount owed; and the accounting treatment and entries required when hire purchase transactions occur. You will also be introduced to leases and to the differences between leases and hire purchase agreements.

2.1 Nature of hire purchase

Hire purchase is a way of buying assets that avoids the need to pay in full either at the time of purchase or very soon thereafter. While the term 'hire purchase' is now rarely used in shops, it is the correct term to use to describe purchases when payment is made in instalments.

The essential differences between a hire purchase and a 'normal' purchase are:

1 The asset does not belong to the purchaser when it is received from the supplier. Instead it belongs to the supplier providing the hire purchase.
2 The purchaser will pay for the item by instalments over a period of time. This may be for as long as two or three years, or even longer.
3 The cost to the buyer will be higher than it would have been had the item been paid for at the time of purchase. The extra money paid is interest.
4 The asset does not legally belong to the purchaser until two things happen:
   (a) the final instalment is paid, and
   (b) the purchaser agrees to a legal option to buy the asset.

If the purchasers wanted to, they could stop paying the instalments. They would then have to give the asset back to the seller. They would not be able to get a refund of instalments already paid.

If the purchaser is unable to continue paying the instalments, the seller could normally repossess the asset. The seller would keep all the instalments already paid.

Activity 2.1 Why do you think organisations purchase assets on hire purchase?

2.2 Law of hire purchase

The Hire Purchase Act 1964 governs all hire purchase transactions in the UK.

2.3 Interest payable on hire purchase

Each payment made on a hire purchase contract consists of two things:

1 **Capital.** Paying off some of the amount owing for the cash price of the asset.
2 **Interest.** Paying off some of the interest that has accrued since the start of the agreement.

The total payment (1) + (2) made for each instalment may be the same, or may differ. Normally, however, the same amount in total is paid each time an instalment is due.

Exhibit 2.1 Unequal instalments

1 A high-spec notebook PC is bought from A King at the start of Year 1. Cash price is £2,000.
2 Hire purchase price is £2,300.
3 Payable in two annual instalments at the end of each year. Each instalment to be £1,000 plus interest accrued for that year.
4 Rate of interest is 10 per cent per annum.

			£
Year 1:	Cash price	(A)	2,000
	Add Interest 10% of (A) £2,000		200
			2,200
	Less Instalment paid		(1,200)
	Owing at end of Year 1	(B)	1,000
Year 2:	*Add* Interest 10% of (B) £1,000		100
			1,100
	Less Instalment paid		(1,100)
	Owing at end of Year 2		–

Exhibit 2.2 Equal instalments

The facts are the same as in Exhibit 2.1, except that each instalment is £1,152. (Each figure of interest is rounded down to the nearest £.)

			£
Year 1:	Cash price	(A)	2,000
	Add Interest 10% of (A) £2,000		200
			2,200
	Less Instalment paid		(1,152)
	Owing at end of Year 1	(B)	1,048
Year 2:	*Add* Interest 10% of (B) £1,048		104
			1,152
	Less Instalment paid		(1,152)
	Owing at end of Year 2		–

Note: The interest for Year 1 is the same for both the equal and the unequal instalments in Exhibits 2.1 and 2.2, as the whole of the cash price is owed in both cases for a full year.

Activity 2.2 Why is the amount paid in Year 2 in Exhibit 2.2 different from the amount paid in Year 2 in Exhibit 2.1?

Note: **In this example, no payment was made until 12 months after the transaction occurred. Often, the first instalment is paid at the time of the transaction, if so, it is a repayment of capital. The difference shown between unequal instalments and equal instalments would still be similar to those shown in Exhibit 2.1 because some of the amount due includes interest and interest due depends upon how it is calculated.**

2.4 Accounting for hire purchase

Accounting treats assets bought on hire purchase as though they belong immediately to the purchaser.

This is because businesses normally buy assets on hire purchase with the intention of paying all the instalments, so that the asset finally will belong to them. As they mean to keep the asset and legally own it after the final payment, accounting treats it as though legal ownership occurred on purchase.

This is an illustration of the use of the 'substance over form' concept. Legally the firm does not yet own the asset (form) yet it does own it from an economic perspective (substance).

The total purchase price is split into two parts for the financial statements:

1 **Cash price.** This is the amount to be debited to the fixed asset account.
2 **Interest.** This is an expense of borrowing money and is changed to an expense account, i.e. hire purchase interest account.

As interest accrues over time, each period should be charged only with the interest accrued for that period. This is shown in Exhibit 2.3:

Exhibit 2.3

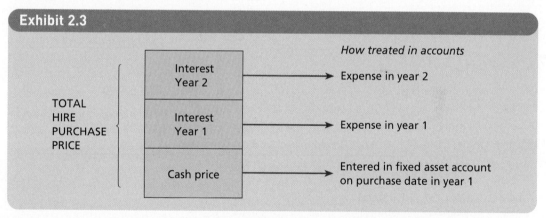

2.5 Illustrations of purchaser's accounts

The double entry needed is:

(A) Cash price:
    Debit fixed asset
      Credit supplier

(B) Hire purchase interest (for each period's interest):
    Debit hire purchase interest
      Credit supplier

(C) Hire purchase instalments:
    Debit supplier
      Credit bank

(D) Charge interest to profit and loss:
    Debit profit and loss
      Credit hire purchase interest

We can now look at the ledger accounts which would have been used to enter the facts as in Exhibit 2.1. (For simplicity, depreciation has been omitted from the example.) Letters entered against the entries refer to the double entries given above.

Notebook PC

		£	
Year 1			
Jan 1 A King	(A)	2,000	

Hire Purchase Interest

		£					£
Year 1			Year 1				
Dec 31 A King	(B)	200	Dec 31 Profit and loss	(D)	200
Year 2			Year 2		
Dec 31 A King	(B)	100	Dec 31 Profit and loss	(D)	100

A King

		£			£
Year 1			Year 1		
Dec 31 Bank	(C)	1,200	Jan 1 Notebook PC (A)	2,000
31 Balance c/d		1,000	Dec 31 HP interest (B)	200
		2,200		2,200
Year 2			Year 2		
Dec 31 Bank	(C)	1,100	Jan 1 Balance b/d	1,000
			Dec 31 HP interest (B)	100
		1,100		1,100

Cash Book

					£
			Year 1		
			Dec 31 A King	(C)	1,200
			Year 2		
			Dec 31 A King	(C)	1,100

Profit and Loss

		£	
Year 1			
Dec 31 HP interest	(D)	200	
Year 2			
Dec 31 HP interest	(D)	100	

2.6 Depreciation and assets bought on hire purchase

Depreciation is based on the cash price. Hire purchase interest is an expense in the profit and loss account and so does not enter depreciation calculations. Only the initial (cash) price of the asset is depreciated.

2.7 Balance sheets and assets bought on hire purchase

In the balance sheet for a sole trader or a partnership, purchases on hire purchase of assets can be shown as follows:

Fixed assets	£	£
Machinery at cost[1]		20,000
Less Owing on hire purchase[2]	6,000	
Depreciation to date	10,000	
		(16,000)
		4,000

Notes

(1) This is the cash price of the machinery.

(2) This is the amount of the original cash price still unpaid.

In Exhibit 2.1 above, if the notebook PC had been depreciated using the straight line method at 25 per cent, the balance sheet entries would have been:

Balance Sheet (end of Year 1)

Fixed assets	£	£
Notebook PC at cost		2,000
Less Owing on hire purchase*	1,000	
Depreciation to date	500	
		(1,500)
		500

*This is the balance of A King's account and does not include interest.

Balance Sheet (end of Year 2)

Fixed assets	£	£
Notebook PC at cost		2,000
Less Depreciation to date		(1,000)
		1,000

Note: At the end of Year 2 there was nothing owing to A King for hire purchase.

However, in company balance sheets this is *not* allowed. The Companies Acts do not permit an amount owing on a hire purchase contract to be deducted from the value of the asset in the balance sheet. (In general, netting off of assets and liabilities is not permitted. The only exception is where the same entity is both a debtor and a creditor of an entity.)

In a company's balance sheet, the entries relating to Exhibit 2.1 would be:

Balance Sheet (end of Year 1)

Fixed assets	£	£
Notebook PC at cost		2,000
Less Depreciation to date		(500)
		1,500
Liabilities		
Creditors (Owing on hire purchase)*		1,000

*This is the balance of A King's account and does not include interest.

Balance Sheet (end of Year 2)

Fixed assets	£
Notebook PC at cost	2,000
Less Depreciation to date	(1,000)
	1,000

2.8 A fully worked example

Exhibit 2.4 illustrates hire purchase more fully. It covers three years of hire purchase and shows the balance sheet figures that would appear if sole traders and partnerships adopted the first approach shown in Section 2.7. We'll also be using this example in Sections 2.9 and 2.10.

Exhibit 2.4

1 A machine is bought by K Thomas for £3,618 on hire purchase from Suppliers Ltd on 1 January 2003.
2 It is paid by 3 instalments of £1,206 on 31 December of 2003, 2004 and 2005.
3 The cash price is £3,000.
4 Rate of interest is 10 per cent per annum on the balance outstanding at the start of the year.
5 Straight line depreciation of 20 per cent per annum is to be provided.

Note: The letters (A) to (F) refer to the description of entries following the account.

Machinery

2003				£		
Jan	1	Suppliers Ltd	(A)	3,000		

Suppliers Ltd

2003				£	2003					£
Dec	31	Bank	(B)	1,206	Jan	1	Machinery	(A)	3,000
	31	Balance c/d	(D)	2,094	Dec	31	HP interest	(C)	300
				3,300					3,300
2004					2004				
Dec	31	Bank	(B)	1,206	Jan	1	Balance b/d	(D)	2,094
	31	Balance c/d	(D)	1,097	Dec	31	HP interest	(C)	209
				2,303					2,303
2005					2005				
Dec	31	Bank	(B)	1,206	Jan	1	Balance b/d	(D)	1,097
					Dec	31	HP interest	(C)	109
				1,206					1,206

Hire Purchase Interest

2003				£	2003				£
Dec	31	Suppliers Ltd	(C)	300	Dec	31	Profit and loss	(E)	300
2004					2004				
Dec	31	Suppliers Ltd	(C)	209	Dec	31	Profit and loss	(E)	209
2005					2005				
Dec	31	Suppliers Ltd	(C)	109	Dec	31	Profit and loss	(E)	109

Provision for Depreciation: Machinery

				2003				£
				Dec	31	Profit and loss	(F)	600
				2004				
				Dec	31	Profit and loss	(F)	600
				2005				
				Dec	31	Profit and loss	(F)	600

Balance Sheets as at 31 December

		£	£	£
2003	Machinery (at cost)		3,000	
	Less Depreciation	600		
	Owing on hire purchase agreement	2,094		
			(2,694)	
				306
2004	Machinery (at cost)		3,000	
	Less Depreciation to date	1,200		
	Owing on hire purchase agreement	1,097		
			(2,297)	
				703
2005	Machinery (at cost)		3,000	
	Less Depreciation to date		(1,800)	
				1,200

Description of entries:

(A) When the asset is acquired the cash price is debited to the asset account and the credit is in the supplier's account.
(B) The instalments paid are credited to the bank account and debited to the supplier's account.
(C) The interest is credited to the supplier's account for each period as it accrues, and it is debited to the expense account, later to be transferred to the profit and loss account for the period (E).
(D) The balance carried down each year is the amount of the cash price still owing.
(F) Depreciation provisions are calculated on the full cash price, as the depreciation of an asset is in no way affected by whether or not it has been fully paid for.

In the case of a company, the balance sheet entries consist of balance (A), the cash price, *less* balance (F), the amount of the cash price apportioned as depreciation. Balance (D), the amount of the cash price still owing at each balance sheet date, is shown separately under creditors.

2.9 The seller's books: apportionment of profits

There are many ways of incorporating sales on hire purchase in the financial statements. The method used should be the one most suitable for the business.

The total profit for the seller of goods on hire purchase breaks down as follows:

	£
Profit on item sold: Cash price *less* cost	xxx
Profit made from interest charged	xxx
	xxx

In Exhibit 2.4, Suppliers Ltd sold a machine to K Thomas. Assume that the machine cost Suppliers Ltd £2,100. The total profit upon the final instalment being paid is found as follows:

		£	£
Profit on sale of machine: Cash price		3,000	
Cost		(2,100)	
			900
Profit earned by charging interest:	2003	300	
	2004	209	
	2005	109	
			618
Total profit over 3 years			1,518

Apportionment of profit on sale

There are two main methods for allocating the profit on sale (£900) between the years of the agreement. (This profit does *not* include the hire purchase interest.)

1 It is considered profit in the period in which it was first sold to the purchaser. In this case, all the £900 would be shown as profit for 2003.
2 The profit is divided among the three years.

The ratio is calculated as follows:

$$\frac{\text{Cash received in period}}{\text{Total cash to be received}} \times \text{Profit}$$

In this case the profits will be shown as:

$$2003 \quad \frac{£1,206}{£1,206 \times 3} \times £900 = {}^1/_3 \times £900 = £300$$

$$2004 \quad \frac{£1,206}{£1,206 \times 3} \times £900 = {}^1/_3 \times £900 = £300$$

$$2005 \quad \frac{£1,206}{£1,206 \times 3} \times £900 = {}^1/_3 \times £900 = £300$$

Total profit on sale for three years   £900

This case shows equal profits because equal instalments were paid each year. Unequal payments would result in unequal profits.

Apportionment of interest to profit and loss

The interest accrued for each period should be taken into profit calculations. As the amount owed reduces, so does the interest:

	£
Year 2003	300
Year 2004	209
Year 2005	109
Total interest for the three years	618

2.10 The seller's books: accounts needed

We can now look at Exhibit 2.5 taking the details from Exhibit 2.4 as it would appear in the seller's books. Items (A) to (C) have already been shown in Exhibit 2.4:

Exhibit 2.5

(A) The machine was sold on 1 January 2003 to K Thomas on hire purchase terms. Cash price was £3,000 plus hire purchase interest.
(B) Hire purchase interest was at a rate of 10 per cent per annum.
(C) There are to be three instalments of £1,206 each, receivable on 31 December of 2003, 2004 and 2005. These were paid by K Thomas on the correct dates.
(D) This was the only hire purchase sale during the three years.
(E) The profit on the cash price is to be shown as profits for 2003, the year in which the sale was made.
(F) The cost of the machine to Suppliers Ltd was £2,100.

Hire Purchase Sales

2003			£	2003				£
Dec	31	Trading	3,000	Jan	1	K Thomas	(A)	3,000

K Thomas

2003				£	2003				£
Jan	1	Sales	(A)	3,000	Dec	31	Bank	(C)	1,206
Dec	31	HP interest	(B)	300			Balance c/d		2,094
				3,300					3,300
2004					2004				
Jan	1	Balance b/d		2,094	Dec	31	Bank	(C)	1,206
Dec	31	HP interest	(B)	209			Balance c/d		1,097
				2,303					2,303
2005					2005				
Jan	1	Balance b/d		1,097	Dec	31	Bank	(C)	1,206
Dec	31	HP interest	(B)	109					
				1,206					1,206

Hire Purchase Interest

2003			£	2003				£
Dec	31	HP trading	300	Dec	31	K Thomas	(B)	300
2004				2004				
Dec	31	HP trading	209	Dec	31	K Thomas	(B)	209
2005				2005				
Dec	31	HP trading	109	Dec	31	K Thomas	(B)	109

Hire Purchase Goods

2003				£	2003			£
Jan	1	Bank	(F)	2,100	Dec	31	HP trading	2,100

Cash Book

2003				£	2003				£
Dec	31	K Thomas	(C)	1,206	Jan	1	HP goods	(F)	2,100
2004									
Dec	31	K Thomas	(C)	1,206					
2005									
Dec	31	K Thomas	(C)	1,206					

Hire Purchase Trading

2003			£	2003			£
Dec	31	HP goods	2,100	Dec	31	HP sales	3,000
		Gross profit	1,200			HP interest	300
			3,300				3,300
2004				2004			
Dec	31	Gross profit	209	Dec	31	HP interest	209
2005				2005			
Dec	31	Gross profit	109	Dec	31	HP interest	109

In Exhibit 2.5 all the profit was taken as being earned in 2003 other than the interest allocated to 2004 and 2005. If we decided to take the profit as being earned when the instalments are received, then the only account which would be altered would be the trading account plus, another account is opened: the hire purchase profit deferred account. All the other accounts would be exactly the same as in Exhibit 2.5.

The amendments needed are shown as Exhibit 2.6:

Exhibit 2.6

Hire Purchase Trading

2003		£	2003		£
Dec 31	HP goods	2,100	Dec 31	HP sales	3,000
	HP profit deferred (G)	600		HP interest	300
	Gross profit	600			
		3,300			3,300
2004			2004		
Dec 31	Gross profit	509	Dec 31	HP profit deferred (H)	300
				HP interest	209
		509			509
2005			2005		
Dec 31	Gross profit	409	Dec 31	HP interest deferred (I)	300
				HP interest	109
		409			409

Hire Purchase Profit Deferred

2003		£	2003		£
Dec 31	Balance c/d	600	Dec 31	HP trading (G)	600
2004			2004		
Dec 31	HP trading	300	Jan 1	Balance b/d	600
	Balance c/d	300			
		600			600
2005			2005		
Dec 31	HP trading (H)	300	Jan 1	Balance b/d	300

The double entry needed was:

(G) In year of sale: Debit hire purchase trading account with profits carried to future years
Credit hire purchase profit deferred
(H) In following years: Debit hire purchase profit deferred with profits earned in each year
Credit hire purchase trading account

Note: **The entries for hire purchase interest have not changed.**

2.11 Repossessions

When customers stop paying their instalments before they should, the goods can be taken away from them. This is called **repossession**. The amounts already paid by the customers will be kept by the seller.

The repossessed items should be entered in the books of the seller, as they are now back in stock, but they will be valued as used goods.

Exhibit 2.7 shows the entries that must be made in the hire purchase trading account:

1 On 1 January 2004 we buy 15 electronic agendas for £300 each.
2 On 1 January 2004 we sell 12 of them for a cash price of £480 plus £120 interest to be paid = £600 total.
3 24 monthly instalments are to be paid of £25 each = £600.
4 Because of the difficulties of apportioning interest, each instalment is taken to include £5 interest, i.e. 24 × £5 = £120 interest.
5 On 1 November 2004, after 10 instalments have been received, a customer who bought 2 of the agendas cannot pay any more instalments. Both of them are returned by him. We do not have to repay the instalments paid by him.
6 The 2 agendas returned are valued at £140 each. Also in stock on 31 December 2004 are 3 of the agendas bought on 1 January 2004 for £300 each and still valued at that amount.
7 Profit is to be calculated based on the number of instalments paid.

Exhibit 2.7

Hire Purchase Trading

2004		£	2004		£
Purchases	(a)	4,500	Sales at cash price	(b)	4,800
Hire purchase profit deferred	(f)	900	Hire purchase interest	(c)	600
			Instalments received on repossessions	(d)	500
Gross profit	(g)	1,680	Stock	(e)	1,180
		7,080			7,080

Notes
Calculations are made as follows:
(a) 15 × £300 each = £4,500.
(b) 10 were sold (and not returned) at cash price of £480 each.
(c) Interest on 10 sold (and not returned) × £5 × 12 months = £600.
(d) 10 instalments paid (including interest) on 2 agendas = 10 × £25 × 2 = £500.

		£
(e) Stock = new items 3 × £300	=	900
repossessed items 2 × £140	=	280
		1,180

		£
(f) Profit per agenda = cash price £480 − cost £300	=	180
To be paid: 12 instalments out of 24 = ½ profit	=	90
Number sold and not returned, 10 × £90	=	900

(g) Gross profit can be checked:

		£		£
Earned to date 10 × £90			=	900
Interest earned to date £5 × 10 × 12 months			=	600
Profit on repossessions:				
Instalments received			500	
Less: Loss of value on repossessions	£			
Cost 2 × £300	600			
Value taken back	(280)	=	(320)	
				180
				1,680

2.12 SSAP 21: Accounting for leases and hire purchase contracts

Leasing and hire purchase contracts are means by which organisations acquire the right to use (lease) or purchase (hire purchase) fixed assets. In the UK there is normally no provision in a lease contract for legal title to the leased asset to pass to the lessee during the term of a lease. In contrast, under a hire purchase contract the hirer may acquire legal title by exercising an option to purchase the asset upon fulfilment of certain conditions (normally the payment of an agreed number of instalments).

Lessors fall into three broad categories: (i) organisations, including banks and finance houses, which provide finance under lease contracts to enable a single customer to acquire the use of an asset for the greater part of its useful life; (ii) businesses which rent out assets for varying periods of time, probably to more than one customer; or, (iii) manufacturers or dealer lessors (such as car salerooms) which use leasing as a means of marketing their products, which may involve leasing a product to one customer or to several customers.

As a lessor and lessee are both parties to the same transaction it is appropriate that the same definitions should be used and the accounting treatment recommended should ideally be complementary. However, because the pattern of cash flows and the taxation consequences will be different, the recorded balances in both sets of financial statements will often be different.

There are two types of leases: **finance leases** and **operating leases**. The distinction between a finance lease and an operating lease will usually be evident from the contract between the lessor and the lessee. A lease is classified as a finance lease if it transfers substantially all the risks and rewards incidental to ownership. If it does not, it is an operating lease.

A *finance lease* usually involves repayment to a lessor by a lessee of the full cost of the asset together with a return on the finance provided by the lessor. As such, a lease of this type is normally non-cancellable or cancellable only under certain conditions, and the lessee enjoys substantially all the risks and rewards associated with the ownership of an asset, other than the legal title. A finance lease is, therefore, very similar to a hire purchase agreement.

An *operating lease* involves the lessee paying a rental for the hire of an asset for a period of time which is normally substantially less than its useful economic life. The lessor retains the risks and rewards of ownership of an asset in an operating lease and normally assumes responsibility for repairs, maintenance and insurance.

SSAP 21 requires that a finance lease should be accounted for by the lessee as if it were the purchase of the proprietory rights in an asset with simultaneous recognition of the obligation to make future payments, in the same way that a hire purchase is normally accounted for.

Under an operating lease, only the rental will be taken into account by the lessee. The asset involved does not appear in the balance sheet of the lessee. The standard recognises that the substance of the transaction rather than its legal form should govern the accounting treatment.

Learning outcomes

You should now have learnt:

1 Hire purchase is a means of buying assets where:
   (a) the asset does not belong to the purchaser until the final instalment is paid *and* the purchaser agrees to a legal option to buy the asset; *but*
   (b) for accounting purposes, the asset is treated immediately as if it belongs to the purchaser.

2 Each payment made on a hire purchase contract is part interest and part payment of the cash price of the asset.

3 How to record the various entries relating to hire purchase.

4 How to treat hire purchase transactions in the hire purchase trading account, the trading and profit and loss account and the balance sheet.

5 The difference between hire purchase and leasing.

6 The difference between a finance lease and an operating lease.

Answers to activities

2.1 An organisation may have a shortage of cash, or may prefer to use its cash for other purposes. It may not wish to keep the asset permanently and may buy it on hire purchase so that after a couple of years it can stop paying the instalments. Sometimes, hire purchase is offered at zero interest so it is actually cheaper to purchase an item on hire purchase (because interest can be earned by the buyer on the amount not yet paid).

2.2 Because £48 less was paid in Exhibit 2.2 at the end of Year 1. Interest was charged at 10% on that £48, resulting in an additional £4 having to be paid in Year 2 as well as the £48 that was not paid in Year 1. Overall, this meant that the Year 2 payment in Exhibit 2.2 was £52 greater than in Exhibit 2.1. However, over the two years, the difference in cost to the buyer was the £4 interest that arose as a result of the first-year payment having been slightly lower in Exhibit 2.2.

Review questions

2.1 An engineering company purchased a machine on hire purchase over a period of three years, paying £2,672 on 1 January 2006, and further annual payments of £5,700 due on 31 December 2006, 2007 and 2008.

The cash price of the machine was £17,100, the vendor company charging interest at 9 per cent per annum on outstanding balances at the start of each year.

Show the appropriate ledger accounts in the purchaser's books for the three years and how the items would appear in the balance sheet at 31 December 2006; depreciation at 25 per cent per annum straight-line is to be charged and interest calculated to the nearest £.

2.2A On 1 January 2005 P Wriggle bought a computer (cash price £1,046) from Dowe Ltd on the following hire purchase terms. Wriggle was to make an immediate payment of £300 and three annual payments of £300 on 31 December in each year. The rate of interest chargeable is 10 per cent per annum on the balance at the start of the year.

→ P Wriggle depreciates this computer by 40 per cent reducing balance each year.

(a) Make the entries relating to this computer in Wriggle's ledger for the years 2005, 2006 and 2007. (All calculations are to be made to the nearest £.)

(b) Show how the item 'computer' would appear in the balance sheet as at 31 December 2005.

2.3 Bulwell Aggregates Ltd wish to expand their transport fleet and have purchased three heavy lorries with a list price of £18,000 each. Robert Bulwell has negotiated hire purchase finance to fund this expansion, and the company has entered into a hire purchase agreement with Granby Garages plc on 1 January 2001. The agreement states that Bulwell Aggregates will pay a deposit of £9,000 on 1 January 2001, and two annual instalments of £24,000 on 31 December 2001, 2002 and a final instalment of £20,391 on 31 December 2003.

Interest is to be calculated at 25 per cent on the balance outstanding on 1 January each year and paid on 31 December each year.

The depreciation policy of Bulwell Aggregates Ltd is to write off the vehicles over a four-year period using the straight line method and assuming a scrap value of £1,333 for each vehicle at the end of its useful life.

The cost of the vehicles to Granby Garages is £14,400 each.

Required:

(a) Account for the above transactions in the books of Bulwell Aggregates Ltd, showing the entries in the profit and loss account and balance sheet for the years 2001, 2002, 2003 and 2004.

(b) Account for the above transactions in the books of Granby Garages plc, showing the entries in the hire purchase trading account for the years 2001, 2002, 2003. This is the only hire purchase transaction undertaken by this company.

Calculations to the nearest £.

(*Association of Accounting Technicians*)

2.4A D Lane purchased two cars for his business under hire purchase agreements:

	DL 1	DL 2
Registration number	DL 1	DL 2
Date of purchase	31 July 2002	30 November 2002
Cash price	£27,000	£36,000
Deposit	£4,680	£7,200
Interest (deemed to accrue evenly over the period of the agreement)	£2,880	£3,600

Both agreements provided for payment to be made in 24 monthly instalments commencing on the last day of the month following purchase.

On 1 September 2003, vehicle DL 1 was involved in a crash and was declared a write-off. In full settlement on 20 September 2003:

(a) the motor insurers paid out £18,750, and

(b) the hire purchase company accepted £10,700 for the termination of the agreement.

The firm prepares its financial statements to 31 December and provides depreciation on a straight line basis at a rate of 25 per cent per annum for motor vehicles, apportioned as from the date of purchase and up to the date of disposal.

All instalments were paid on the due dates.

The remaining balance on the hire purchase company account in respect of vehicle DL 1 is to be written off.

Required:

Record these transactions in the following accounts, carrying down the balances as on 31 December 2002 and 31 December 2003:

(a) Motor vehicles
(b) Depreciation
(c) Hire purchase company
(d) Assets disposal.

2.5 On 31 March 2004, D Biggs, who prepares his financial statements to 31 March, bought a lorry on hire purchase from Truck Fleet Ltd. The cash price of the lorry was £61,620. Under the terms of the hire purchase agreement, Biggs paid a deposit of £20,000 on 31 March 2004, and two instalments of £23,981 on 31 March 2005 and 2006. The hire vendor charged interest at 10 per cent per annum on the balance outstanding on 1 April each year. All payments were made on the due dates.

Biggs maintained the motor lorry account at cost and accumulated the annual provision for depreciation, at 40 per cent on the reducing balance method, in a separate account. A full year's depreciation is charged in the year of purchase, irrespective of the date acquired.

Required:
(a) Prepare the following accounts as they would appear in the ledger of D Biggs for the period of the contract:
   (i) Truck Fleet Ltd
   (ii) Motor lorry on hire purchase
   (iii) Provision for depreciation of motor lorry
   (iv) Hire purchase interest payable.
(b) Show how the above matters would appear in the balance sheet of D Biggs at 31 March 2005.

Truck Fleet Ltd prepares its financial statements to 31 March, on which date it charges D Biggs with the interest due.
Make calculations to the nearest £.

2.6 J Wild started business on 1 April 2002 selling one model of digital cameras on hire purchase. During the year to 31 March 2003 he purchased 2,000 cameras at a uniform price of £90 and sold 1,900 cameras at a total selling price under hire purchase agreements of £150 per camera, payable by an initial deposit of £45 and 10 quarterly instalments of £10.50p.

The following trial balance was extracted from Wild's books as at 31 March 2003.

	£	£
Capital		136,026
Drawings	40,000	
Fixed assets	9,500	
Purchases	180,000	
Cash collected from customers		125,400
Rent, business rates and insurance	5,000	
Wages	27,000	
General expenses	5,100	
Balance at bank	7,246	
Sundry trade creditors		12,600
	274,026	274,026

The personal accounts of customers are memorandum records (i.e. they are not part of the double entry system).

Wild prepares his financial statements on the basis of taking credit for profit (including interest) in proportion to cash collected from customers.

Prepare Wild's hire purchase trading and profit and loss account for the year ended 31 March 2003 and a balance sheet as at that date.^Authors' note

Ignore depreciation of fixed assets.

Authors' note: the financial statement is required, not the T-accounts.

→

→ **2.7** RJ commenced business on 1 January 2008. He sells refrigerators, all of one standard type, on hire purchase terms. The total amount, including interest, payable for each refrigerator, is £300. Customers are required to pay an initial deposit of £60, followed by eight quarterly instalments of £30 each. The cost of each refrigerator to RJ is £200.

The following trial balance was extracted from RJ's books as on 31 December 2008.

Trial Balance

	£	£
Capital		100,000
Fixed assets	10,000	
Drawings	4,000	
Bank overdraft		19,600
Creditors		16,600
Purchases	180,000	
Cash collected from customers		76,500
Bank interest	400	
Wages and salaries	12,800	
General expenses	5,500	
	£212,700	£212,700

850 machines were sold on hire purchase terms during 2008.

The annual accounts are prepared on the basis of taking credit for profit (including interest) in proportion to the cash collected from customers.

You are required to prepare the hire purchase trading account, and the profit and loss account for the year 2008 and balance sheet as on 31 December 2008.

Ignore depreciation of fixed assets.

Show your calculations.

(*Institute of Chartered Secretaries and Administrators*)

2.8A Object Limited is a retail outlet selling word processing equipment both for cash and on hire purchase terms. The following information has been extracted from the books of account as at 31 August 2006:

	Dr £	Cr £
Authorised, issued and fully paid share capital (ordinary shares of £1 each)		75,000
Administration and shop expenses	130,000	
Cash at bank and in hand	6,208	
Cash received from hire purchase customers		315,468
Cash sales		71,000
Depreciation of premises and equipment (at 1 September 2005)		45,000
Hire purchase debtors (at 1 September 2005)	2,268	
Premises and equipment at cost	100,000	
Profit and loss account (at 1 September 2005)		8,000
Provision for unrealised profit (at 1 September 2005)		1,008
Purchases	342,000	
Stock (at 1 September 2005)	15,000	
Trade creditors		80,000
	595,476	595,476

Additional information:
1 The company's policy is to take credit for gross profit (including interest) for hire purchase sales in proportion to the instalments collected. It does this by raising a provision against the profit included in hire purchase debtors not yet due.

2 The cash selling price is fixed at 50 per cent and the hire purchase selling price at 80 per cent respectively above the cost of goods purchased.

3 The hire purchase contract requires an initial deposit of 20 per cent of the hire purchase selling price, the balance to be paid in four equal instalments at quarterly intervals. The first instalment is due three months after the agreement is signed.

4 Hire purchase sales for the year amounted to £540,000 (including interest).

5 In February 2006 the company repossessed some goods which had been sold earlier in the year. These goods had been purchased for £3,000, and the unpaid instalments on them amounted to £3,240. They were then taken back into stock at a value of £2,500. Later on in the year they were sold on cash terms for £3,500.

6 Depreciation is charged on premises and equipment at a rate of 15 per cent per annum on cost.

Required:
Prepare Object Limited's trading, and profit and loss account for the year ending 31 August 2006, and a balance sheet as at that date.
   Your workings should be submitted.

(*Association of Accounting Technicians*)

2.9A On 1 January 2006, F Limited commenced business selling goods on hire purchase. Under the terms of the agreements, an initial deposit of 20 per cent is payable on delivery, followed by four equal quarterly instalments, the first being due three months after the date of sale. During the year sales were made as follows:

	Cost price	HP sales price
	£	£
10 January	150	225
8 March	350	525
12 May	90	135
6 July	200	300
20 September	70	105
15 October	190	285
21 November	160	240

The goods sold in July were returned in September and eventually sold in November for £187 cash. All other instalments are paid on the due dates.

It may be assumed that:

(*a*) gross profit and interest are credited to profit and loss account in the proportion that deposits and instalments received bear to hire purchase price; or
(*b*) the cost is deemed to be paid in full before any credit is taken for gross profit and interest.

You are to prepare for the first year of trading, a hire purchase trading account compiled firstly on assumption (*a*) and secondly on assumption (*b*) and give the relevant balance sheet entries under each assumption.
   Workings should be clearly shown.

(*Chartered Institute of Management Accountants*)

2.10A On 1 January 2007, Carver bought a machine costing £20,000 on hire purchase. He paid a deposit of £6,000 on 1 January 2007 and he also agreed to pay two annual instalments of £5,828 on 31 December in each year, and a final instalment of £5,831 on 31 December 2009.
   The implied rate of interest in the agreement was 12 per cent. This rate of interest is to be applied to the amount outstanding in the hire purchase loan account as at the beginning of the year.
   The machine is to be depreciated on a straight line basis over five years on the assumption that the machine will have no residual value at the end of that time.

→

→ **Required:**
(a) Write up the following accounts for each of the three years to 31 December 2007, 2008 and 2009 respectively:
   (i)   machine account;
   (ii) accumulated depreciation on machine account; and
   (iii) hire purchase loan account; and
(b) Show the balance sheet extracts for the year as at 31 December 2007, 2008 and 2009 respectively for the following items:
   (i)   machine at cost;
   (ii) accumulated depreciation on the machine;
   (iii) long-term liabilities: obligations under hire purchase contract; and
   (iv) current liabilities: obligations under hire purchase contract.

(Association of Accounting Technicians)

2.11 Dundas Limited purchased a machine under a hire purchase agreement on 1 January 2008. The agreement provided for an immediate payment of £2,000, followed by five equal instalments of £3,056, each instalment to be paid on 30 June and 31 December respectively.

The cash price of the machine was £10,000. Dundas estimated that it would have a useful economic life of five years, and its residual value would then be £1,000.

In apportioning interest to respective accounting periods, the company uses the 'sum of digits'[Authors' note] method.

Required:

(a) Write up the following ledger accounts for each of the three years to 31 December 2008, 2009 and 2010 respectively:
   (i) machine hire purchase loan account; and
   (ii) machine hire purchase interest account; and
(b) Show the following balance sheet extracts relating to the machine as at 31 December 2008, 2009 and 2010 respectively:
   (i)   fixed assets: machine at net book value;
   (ii) creditors: amounts payable within one year – obligation under hire purchase contract; and
   (iii) creditors: amounts falling due after more than one year – obligation under hire purchase contract.

Authors' note – Sum of digits
This is very similar to the 'rule of 78', explained in Section 45.12. It is explained in detail in *Business Accounting UK GAAP 1*. In brief, if a machine is expected to last 4 years, you write off the cost by weighting year 1 as 4, year 2 as 3, year 3 as 2 and year 4 as 1. The total of these weights is used as the denominator. Thus, year 1 depreciation would be 4/10 of the amount to be written off; year 2 would be 3/10, year 3 would be 2/10 and year 4 would be 1/10.

(Association of Accounting Technicians)

You can find a range of additional self-test questions, as well as material to help you with your studies, on the website that accompanies this book at **www.pearsoned.co.uk/wood**

Contract accounts

Learning objectives

After you have studied this chapter, you should be able to:

- describe the factors that are involved in accounting for contracts
- describe how accounting records of contracts are maintained
- explain the need to apply prudence when assessing profit or loss on a contract that is still in progress
- describe some of the requirements of SSAP 9 relating to long-term contracts

Introduction

In this chapter you'll learn how to record revenues and expenditures arising on contracts in contract accounts and how to estimate profits and losses on long-term contracts so that appropriate entries may be included in the financial statements for internal use.

3.1 Financial statements and the business cycle

The span of production differs between businesses, and some fit into the normal pattern of annual financial statements more easily than others. A farmer's financial statements are usually admirably suited to the yearly pattern, as the goods they produce are in accordance with the seasons, and therefore repeat themselves annually. With a firm whose production span is a day or two, the annual financial statements are also quite suitable.

On the other hand, there are businesses whose work does not fit neatly with a financial year's calculation of profits. Assume that a firm of contractors has only one contract in progress, the construction of a large oil refinery complex which is expected to take five years to complete. Until it is completed, the actual profit or loss on the contract cannot be accurately stated – too many things could happen that would affect the final profit or loss over the five years of the contract. However, if the company was formed solely for the purpose of undertaking this contract, the shareholders would not want to wait for five years before the profit could be calculated and dividends paid. As a result, an attempt must be made to calculate profits earned to date at the end of each financial year. Some companies will have more than one contract under way at a time, each at a different stage, in which case the profit earned to date on each contract must be calculated.

3.2 Contract accounts

When a company starts a long-term contract, an account is opened for it. It is, in fact, a form of trading account. As an example, if a company has a contract to construct a new college building, it may be called Contract 71, in which case an account for 'Contract 71' would be opened. All expenditure traceable to the contract is charged to the account. This is far easier than apportioning expenses to specific products manufactured in a factory, as any expenditure on the contract site will be expenses of the contract, e.g. wages for the manual workers, rental of telephone lines, hire of machinery, wages for the timekeepers, clerks, etc.

Activity 3.1
As each contract has or will have a unique flow of revenue, it makes sound business sense to know the profit or loss it generates. Hence the use of individual contract accounts. When financial statements are produced that include long-term contracts (those that extend into future accounting periods), which fundamental accounting concept is adhered to by maintaining a separate contract account for each contract?

3.3 Certification of work done

When a building is being constructed, the contractor is paid on the basis of architects' certificates. In the case of an engineering contract, it is on the basis of an engineers' certificate. The architect, or engineer, will visit the site at regular intervals and will issue a certificate stating his or her estimate of the value of the work done, in terms of the total contract price (the sale price of the whole contract). For example, a certificate may be issued for £90,000 which represents the proportion of the total contract amount which he or she believes has been completed.

Normally, the terms governing the contract will contain a clause concerning 'retention money'. This is the amount, usually stated as a percentage, which will be retained, i.e. held back, in case the contract is not completed by a stated date, or in case there are claims made for faulty workmanship, etc. A 10 per cent retention in this case would lead to £81,000 being payable by the organisation for whom the contract was being performed.

3.4 Allocation of overheads

Any administration overhead expenses that are not directly traceable to individual contract sites may be split between the contracts using an appropriate base, such as the overall contract amount or the labour cost to date. Of course, if there were only one contract then all the overhead expenses would quite rightly be chargeable against it. On the other hand, if there are twenty contracts, any apportionment will be arbitrary. No one can perfectly apportion the administration overhead expenses of, for example, the managing director's salary, the cost of advertising to give the business the right 'image', or the costs of running the accounting system for the whole company, and these are only a few of such difficult to apportion expenses.

Similar to the effects of apportioning overheads in departmental accounts, as covered in Chapter 36 of *Business Accounting Essentials 1*, the allocation of overheads to individual contracts may sometimes produce misleading results. It is, therefore, far better for the administrative overhead expenses which are obviously not chargeable to a contract to be omitted from the contract accounts. The surplus left on each contract account would, therefore, represent the 'contribution' of each contract to administrative overhead expenses and, thus, to profit.

Let's look at a worked example.

3.5 A worked example of a contract account

In many cases, contracts will start and finish in the same financial period. In such cases, there is no need to estimate profits and losses at the period end. However, when a contract extends into one or more periods after it started, it is known as a 'long-term contract' and an appropriate estimate of profits or losses must be made so that appropriate entries can be made in the financial statements. In the example which follows, Contract 44 extends into a second accounting period.

This example shows how profit or loss may be calculated for inclusion in financial statements prepared for internal purposes. As you will later learn, when financial statements are prepared for publication, a more complex approach to the calculation of profit or loss must be used.

Exhibit 3.1

Contract 44 is for a school which is being built for the Blankshire County Council. By the end of the construction company's financial year, the following items have been charged to the contract account:

Contract 44

	£
Wages – labour on site	50,000
Wages – foreman and clerks on the site	32,000
Materials	40,000
Subcontractors on the site	9,000
Other site expenses	3,000
Hire of special machinery	2,000
Plant bought for the contract	20,000

The entries concerning expenditure traceable direct to the contract are relatively simple. These are charged to the contract account. These can be seen in the contract account shown below.

Architects' certificates have been received during the year amounting to £147,000. It is assumed that the certificates relate to all work done up to the year end. A retention of 10 per cent is to be made, and the Blankshire County Council has paid £132,300 so far. The £147,000 has been credited to a holding account called an Architects' Certificates Account and debited to the Blankshire County Council Account.

The total of the Architects' Certificates Account now needs to be transferred to the Contract 44 account. It is, after all, the 'sale' price of the work done so far, and the contract account is a type of trading account. The £132,300 received has been debited to the bank and credited to Blankshire County Council Account, which now shows a balance of £14,700 representing the retention money.

The cost of the materials on the site at the end of the period is not included in the value of the architects' certificates and is, therefore, carried forward to the next period at cost. The value of the plant at the end of the year is also carried forward. In this case the value of the cost of the plant not yet used is £14,000. This means that £20,000 has been debited for the plant and £14,000 credited thus, effectively, charging £6,000 for depreciation. Assume that the unused materials cost £8,000.

The Contract 44 account will appear as follows:

Contract 44

	£		£
Wages – labour on site	50,000	Architects' certificates	147,000
Wages – foreman and clerks on the site	32,000	Stock of unused materials c/d	8,000
		Value of plant c/d	14,000
Materials	40,000		
Subcontractors on the site	8,000		
Other site expenses	3,000		
Hire of special machinery	2,000		
Plant bought for the contract	20,000		

> **Activity 3.2** What is the profit to date on Contract 44?

3.6 Profit estimation

In order to estimate the profit or loss on Contract 44, more information is needed beyond the values shown in the contract account. The contract is only part-completed, and costly snags may crop up which would dissipate any potential profit earned, or problems may have developed already, such as subsidence which has remained unnoticed as yet. It is not possible to identify all known factors of this type. To minimise the risk of profits being overstated or losses understated, the concept of prudence is applied and the profit is reduced according to an 'appropriate' modifier.

Before SSAP 9 was revised in 1988, the custom had developed of multiplying the profit shown on the contract account by two-thirds and then multiplying the result by the proportion of work certified for which cash had been received. **While the current, and far more complex SSAP 9 approach must be adopted in practice when preparing financial statements for publication, the previous, simpler approach is an excellent example of the prudence concept and is still used in examinations. You will, therefore, need to learn how to apply it.**

It is relatively straightforward to apply, as shown in the following example:

$$\text{Apparent profit} \times \frac{2}{3} \times \frac{\text{Cash received}}{\text{Work certified}} = \text{Amount available for dividends, etc.}$$

For example: the apparent profit earned to date on Contract 44 is £14,000 (*see* Activity 3.2)

$$£14,000 \times \frac{2}{3} \times \frac{132,300}{147,000} = £8,400.$$

On the basis of the £8,400 profit calculated above, the Contract 44 Account can now be completed.

Contract 44

	£		£
Wages – labour on site	50,000	Architects' certificates	147,000
Wages – foreman and clerks on		Stock of unused materials c/d	8,000
the site	32,000	Value of plant c/d	14,000
Materials	40,000		
Subcontractors on the site	8,000		
Other site expenses	3,000		
Hire of special machinery	2,000		
Plant bought for the contract	20,000		
Profit to the profit and loss account	8,400		
Reserve **(the part of the apparent**			
profit not yet recognised as			
earned) c/d	5,600		
	169,000		169,000
Stock of unused materials b/d	8,000	Reserve b/d	5,600
Value of plant b/d	14,000		

Profit and Loss Account

	£
Profits from contracts:	
Contract 43	–
Contract 44	8,400
Contract 45	–

3.7 Anticipated losses

In the above case, there was an apparent profit earned to date of £14,000 but we only recognise £8,400 in the financial statements. If instead of revealing such a profit, the contract account had shown a loss, *all* the loss would be recognised *now*. Thus, if the loss were £9,000, that would be the amount transferred to the profit and loss account. This is in accordance with the concept of prudence which states that profits may be underestimated but never losses.

As is the case with stock valuation, it is not always the case that an engineer or architect will certify the work done on the last day of the financial year. He or she may call several days before or after the year end. The cost of any work done but not certified at the year end is carried down at cost as a balance to the next period when certification will take place.

So far, we have considered how the various figures to be included in the financial statements prepared for internal use may be calculated. When financial statements are prepared for external use, i.e. for publication, the more complex SSAP 9 approach must be adopted.

You may not need to know the current accounting standard rules relating to long-term contracts. It depends upon which examinations you are studying for. If you do, Section 3.8 provides an introduction to the rules contained in SSAP 9 but you will need to consult the relevant accounting standard or a more advanced textbook on the subject before tackling your examinations.

3.8 Long-term contracts and SSAP 9

When SSAP 9: *Stocks and long-term contracts* was revised in 1988, this custom-based *rule of thumb* was replaced with a far more complex calculation that focuses upon turnover and the work certified valued in relation to the overall contract amount.

According to SSAP 9, long-term contracts should be assessed on a contract-by-contract basis. They should be reflected in the profit and loss account by recording turnover and related costs as contract activity progresses. Turnover should be ascertained in a manner appropriate to the stage of completion of the contract, the business and the industry in which it operates. Where the outcome of a contract can be assessed with reasonable accuracy, profit should be recognised (so far as prudence permits) as the difference between recognised turnover and related costs. Any foreseeable losses identified should be immediately recognised.

The amount of long-term contracts, at costs incurred, net of amounts transferred to cost of sales, after deducting foreseeable losses and payments on account not matched with turnover should be classified as 'long-term contract balances' and disclosed separately within the balance sheet heading of 'stocks'. The balance sheet note should disclose separately the balances of 'net cost less foreseeable losses' and 'applicable payments on account'.

Profit recognition

SSAP 9 provides two definitions relevant to any consideration of long-term contracts: those of 'attributable profit' and 'foreseeable losses'.

Attributable profit is that part of total profit currently estimated to arise over the duration of the contract, after allowing for estimated remedial and maintenance costs and increases in costs (so far as not recoverable under the terms of the contract), that fairly reflects the profit attributable to that part of the work performed at the accounting date. There can be no attributable profit until the outcome of the contract can be assessed with reasonable certainty.

Foreseeable losses are those losses estimated to arise over the duration of the contract, after allowing for estimated remedial and maintenance costs and increases in costs (so far as not recoverable under the terms of the contract), *whether or not* work has commenced, and irrespective of both the proportion of work completed and profits expected on other contracts.

SSAP 9 does not prescribe a point at which profit on long-term contracts should start to be recognised. The requirement that a contract's outcome must be capable of being assessed with reasonable certainty before any profit should be recognised. This leaves it entirely to individual judgement as to when to start recognising profit on a long-term contract. One company may recognise profit after the first six months, while another may wait until a year has passed. As a result, inter-firm comparability is impaired. However, the standard does assist in intra-company comparison from one year to the next as it requires consistent application of the method of ascertaining attributable profit both within the business, and from year to year.

Clearly, future costs must be estimated in arriving at a figure for attributable profit or foreseeable losses. Unfortunately, no two people are likely to independently arrive at exactly the same amount. Thus, the profits and losses recognised are likely to vary considerably from one company to another and inter-company comparability is further impaired.

Turnover valuation

Turnover should be ascertained in a manner suitable to the industry and the specific contracts concerned. The valuation of work carried out may be used to derive a value for turnover and profit is then calculated; or profit should be regarded as earned in relation to the *amount* of work performed to date. These two approaches often produce different results, but the profit recognised needs to reflect the proportion of the work carried out and to take into account any known inequalities of profitability in the various stages of a contract. Consequently, when there is a work certified value, this should be used as the turnover value and the costs incurred in achieving that turnover charged to cost of sales.

Where no work certified figure exists, costs to date as a proportion of total expected costs should be applied to the contract value in order to determine the figure for turnover. Where the work certified value is not available for all work completed, a combination of the two approaches would be appropriate. One further point regarding turnover concerns settlements of claims against the purchaser arising from circumstances not foreseen in the contract: these should only be incorporated when there is sufficient evidence that payment will be received.

Complexity

The standard is extremely complex and it is beyond the scope of this book, where this topic is being introduced rather than developed in detail, to extend coverage to the level of complexity that would be required in order to cover the SSAP 9 rules adequately. As previously mentioned, if you require a sound understanding of the current SSAP 9 rules concerning long-term contracts you should refer to the standard, where the appendix covers the topic in detail, or to a specialised text on the subject.

From the perspective of the review questions that follow at the end of this chapter, apart from question 3.5A, *unless otherwise indicated in the question*, you should apply the two-thirds rule of thumb given above. Doing so will develop an awareness of the complexity of contract accounts without the added complexity of applying the SSAP 9 rules. By adopting this approach, you will be well placed to progress to an understanding of the SSAP 9 rules, knowing well the underlying factors involved in contract accounts. The answer to question 3.5A is based on the SSAP 9 rules, and is provided for the benefit of anyone who chooses to study those rules independently of this book.

Learning outcomes

You should now have learnt:

1 A separate contract account should be opened in respect of every contract.

2 Profits or losses on each uncompleted contract must be estimated at the end of each accounting period.

3 Losses should be written off immediately they are identified.

4 An appropriate amount of any profit should be included in the financial statements.

5 Some of the definitions and requirements of SSAP 9 relating to long-term contracts.

6 The rule of thumb profit/loss ascertainment approach adopted in this chapter is necessarily simplified in order to ensure the topic is well understood; SSAP 9 should be consulted for the definitive approach to adopt when preparing financial statements.

Answers to activities

3.1 While it is ongoing, each contract represents an asset or liability. The separate determination concept – see Section 10.6 in *Business Accounting Essentials 1* – requires that the amount of each individual asset or liability be determined separately from all other assets and liabilities. Maintaining a separate contract account for each contract enables compliance with this fundamental accounting concept.

3.2 The difference between the two sides (Credit side £169,000; Debit side £155,000) is £14,000. At this stage, as the contract is incomplete, the £14,000 simply reflects the excess of potential revenue over expenditure to date on the contract. It does not necessarily mean that the contract will ultimately result in a profit and it certainly does not mean that there is a profit to date on the contract of £14,000 – the stock of materials, for example, would need to be sold for precisely the amount shown and the plant disposed of at the amount it is valued at, neither of which is particularly likely.

Review questions

3.1 The financial statements of J. Foot Ltd are made up to 31 March in each year. Work on Contract 349 started on 1 July 2006 and completed on 31 January 2008. The total contract price was £580,000, but a penalty of £10,000 was suffered for failure to complete by 31 December 2007.

The following is a summary of receipts and payments relating to the contract:

	Year to 31 March	
	2007	2008
Payments		
Materials	64,000	82,000
Wages	73,000	109,000
Direct expenses	7,000	11,000
Purchases of plant on 1 July 2006	42,000	–
Receipts		
Contract price (*less* penalty)	156,000	416,000
Sale, on 31 January 2008, of all plant purchased on 1 July 2006	–	14,000

The amount received from the customer in 2007 represented the contract price of all work certified in that financial year less 20 per cent retention money.

When the financial statements to 31 March 2007 were prepared, it was estimated that the contract would be completed on 31 December 2007, and that the market value of the plant would be £24,000 on that date. It was estimated that further expenditure on the contract would be £198,000.

For the purposes of the financial statements, depreciation of plant is calculated, in the case of uncompleted contracts, by reference to the expected market value of the plant on the date when the contract is expected to be completed, and is allocated between accounting periods by the straight line method.

Credit is taken, in the financial statements, for such a part of the estimated total profit, on each uncompleted contract, as corresponds to the proportion between the contract price of the work certified and the total contract price.

Required:
Prepare a summary of the account for this contract, showing the amounts transferred to the profit and loss account at 31 March 2007 and 31 March 2008.

3.2 Stannard and Sykes Ltd are contractors for the construction of a pier for the Seafront Development Corporation. The value of the contract is £300,000, and payment is by engineer's certificate subject to a retention of 10 per cent of the amount certified; this is to be held by the Seafront Development Corporation for six months after the completion of the contract.

The following information is extracted from the records of Stannard and Sykes Ltd.

	£
Wages on site	41,260
Materials delivered to site by supplier	58,966
Materials delivered to site from store	10,180
Hire of plant	21,030
Expenses charged to contract	3,065
Overheads charged to contract	8,330
Materials on site at 30 November 2008	11,660
Work certified	150,000
Payment received	135,000
Work in progress at cost (not the subject of a certificate to date)	12,613
Wages accrued to 30 November 2008	2,826

Required:
Prepare the Pier Contract Account to 30 November 2008, and suggest a method by which profit could be prudently estimated.

(*Association of Chartered Certified Accountants*)

3.3A Cantilever Ltd was awarded a contract to build an office block in London and work commenced at the site on 1 May 2005.

During the period to 28 February 2006, the expenditure on the contract was as follows:

	£
Materials issued from stores	9,411
Materials purchased	28,070
Direct expenses	6,149
Wages	18,493
Charge made by the company for administration expenses	2,146
Plant and machinery purchased on 1 May 2005, for use at site	12,180

On 28 February 2006, the stock of materials at the site amounted to £2,164 and there were amounts outstanding for wages £366 and direct expenses £49.

Cantilever Ltd has received on account the sum of £64,170 which represents the amount of Certificate No. 1 issued by the architects in respect of work completed to 28 February 2006, after deducting 10 per cent retention money.

The following relevant information is also available:

(a) the plant and machinery has an effective life of five years, with no residual value, and
(b) the company only takes credit for two-thirds of the profit on work certified.

Required:
(a) prepare a contract account for the period to 28 February 2006, and
(b) show your calculation of the profit to be taken to the credit of the company's profit and loss account in respect of the work covered by Certificate No. 1.

(*Institute of Chartered Accountants*)

3.4A You are required to prepare the contract account for the year ended 31 December 2010, and show the calculation of the sum to be credited to the profit and loss account for that year.

On 1 April 2010 MN Ltd commenced work on a contract which was to be completed by 30 June 2011 at an agreed price of £520,000.

MN Ltd's financial year ended on 31 December 2010, and on that day expenditure on the contract totalled £263,000 made up as under:

	£
Plant	30,000
Materials	124,000
Wages	95,000
Sundry expenses	5,000
Head office charges	9,000
	263,000

Cash totalling £195,000 had been received by 31 December 2010 representing 75 per cent of the work certified as completed on that date, but in addition, work costing £30,000 had been completed but not certified.

A sum of £9,000 had been obtained on the sale of materials which had cost £8,000 but which had been found unsuitable. On 31 December 2010 stocks of unused materials on site had cost £10,000 and the plant was valued at £20,000.

→

→ To complete the contract by 30 June 2011 it was estimated that:

(a) the following additional expenditures would be incurred:

	£
Wages	64,000
Materials	74,400
Sundry expenses	9,000

(b) further plant costing £25,000 would be required;
(c) the residual value of all plant used on the contract at 30 June 2011 would be £15,000;
(d) head office charges to the contract would be at the same annual rate plus 10 per cent.

It was estimated that the contract would be completed on time but that a contingency provision of £15,000 should be made. From this estimate and the expenditure already incurred, it was decided to estimate the total profit that would be made on the contract and to take to the credit of the profit and loss account for the year ended 31 December 2010, that proportion of the total profit relating to the work actually certified to that date.

(*Chartered Institute of Management Accountants*)

Note: The next question requires the application of the rules contained in SSAP 9.

3.5A *General information on the Lytax group of companies*:
    Lytax Ltd is a company in the building construction industry.
    It has three regional offices, North Borders, Midlands and South Downs, which are constituted as separate units for accounting purposes.
    On 25 May 2010 Lytax Ltd acquired 90 per cent of the ordinary share capital of Ceprem Ltd, a company which manufactures building materials.
    Lytax Ltd has for 3 years held 15 per cent of the ordinary share capital of Bleco plc. This company carries out specialist research and development activities into building and construction materials, technology and techniques. It then sells the results of these activities to other companies.

Details of long-term contract work undertaken by Lytax Ltd:
At 31 October 2010, Lytax Ltd was engaged in various contracts including five long-term contracts, details of which are given below:

	1 £000	2 £000	3 £000	4 £000	5 £000
Contract price	1,100	950	1,400	1,300	1,200
At 31 October 2010:					
Cumulative costs incurred	664	535	810	640	1,070
Estimated further costs to completion	106	75	680	800	165
Estimated cost of post-completion guarantee/rectification work	30	10	45	20	5
Cumulative costs incurred transferred to cost of sales	580	470	646	525	900
Progress payments					
Cumulative receipts	615	680	615	385	722
Invoiced:					
Awaiting receipt	60	40	25	200	34
Retained by contractee	75	80	60	65	84

It is not expected that any contractees will default on their payments.

Up to 31 October 2009, the following amounts had been included in the turnover and cost of sales figures.

	1	2	3	4	5
	£000	£000	£000	£000	£000
Cumulative turnover	560	340	517	400	610
Cumulative costs incurred transferred to cost of sales	460	245	517	400	610
Foreseeable loss transferred to cost of sales	–	–	–	70	–

It is the accounting policy of Lytax Ltd to arrive at contract turnover by adjusting contract cost of sales (including foreseeable losses) by the amount of contract profit or loss to be regarded as recognised, separately for each contract.

Required:

(a) Calculate the amounts to be included within the turnover and cost of sales figures of the profit and loss account of Lytax Ltd for the year ending 31 October 2010, in respect of the long-term contracts.

(b) Prepare extracts from the balance sheet of Lytax Ltd at 31 October 2010 incorporating the financial effects of the long-term contracts.

Your answer should comply with the requirements of SSAP 9 (Stocks and Long-Term Contracts) and should include any supporting notes required by that standard.

Workings for individual contracts which build up to the total for each item must be shown.

All calculations should be made to the nearest £1,000.

(Association of Chartered Certified Accountants)

You can find a range of additional self-test questions, as well as material to help you with your studies, on the website that accompanies this book at **www.pearsoned.co.uk/wood**

COMPANIES

Part
2

Introduction

This part is concerned with the accounts and financial statements of limited companies. It considers how various accounting transactions should be entered in the books and how the financial statements should be presented, including the requirements of the Companies Acts and of accounting standards.

Limited companies: general background

Learning objectives

After you have studied this chapter, you should be able to:

- explain the legal nature of limited companies
- explain the importance of the concept of limited liability
- describe the statutory framework governing limited companies
- describe some of the major characteristics of limited companies
- explain the difference between the Memorandum of Association and the Articles of Association

Introduction

In this chapter, you'll learn about the legislation that governs how companies are formed and lays out the rules within which companies operate in the UK. You'll learn about the importance of limited liability and of the relationship between companies, their shares and the stock exchange.

4.1 Preliminary study

An introduction was made to the financial statements of limited companies in *Business Accounting Essentials 1*. It was intended to show some of the basic outlines of the financial statements of limited companies to those people who would be finishing their studies of accounting with the completion of *Business Accounting 1*. This volume now carries the study of limited companies accounting to a more advanced stage.

4.2 The Companies Acts

The Acts of Parliament governing limited companies in the UK are the Companies Act 2006 and the Companies Acts 1985, 1989 and 2004. The Companies Act 2006 is mainly concerned with the legal aspects of companies and relevant definitions of terms used, whereas the three previous Companies Acts are concerned with the content of financial statements. The Companies Act 2006 appealed and replaced much of the earlier Acts. In this volume, we cannot deal with many of the complicated issues arising from the Companies Act. These are better left until readers have reached a more advanced stage in their studies.

The Companies Act is the descendant of modern limited liability company legislation which can be traced back to the passing of the Companies Act 1862. This Act was a triumph for the development of the limited liability principle which had been severely restricted since the 'Bubble Act' of 1720, which was introduced to address a multitude of spectacular frauds perpetrated behind the cloak of limited liability. Not until 1862 was prejudice against the principle of limited liability overcome, and the way paved for the general use of the limited liability principle which is now commonplace. Company law consists of the Companies Act 2006, together with a considerable body of case law which has been built up over the years. Apart from companies that have been formed since the first Companies Act came into force in 1862, there are companies dating from earlier times which were incorporated either by Royal Charter, such as the Hudson's Bay Company, or by special Acts of Parliament. While such companies may have been subject to different rules at the time of their formation, they are subject to the same Companies Act as all other companies so far as their financial reporting is concerned.

4.3 Changes in company law

Company law has changed considerably since the mid-1960s. This has been brought about largely because of the obligation to observe the company law directives issued by the Council of European Communities, i.e. the EU. Such changes have not completely eliminated the differences in company law throughout the European Union, but they have considerably reduced such differences and have provided a set of minimum common standards to be observed.

The 1985 and 1989 Companies Acts laid down detailed rules of the format of the financial statements of limited companies. These were based on the formats contained in the 4th Directive of the Council of European Communities.

Banks and insurance companies do not come under the same legislation as that which applies to other companies. A separate part of the 1989 Act deals with banks, while insurance companies are the subject of a special directive.

4.4 Other forms of company

The Companies Acts cover companies with unlimited liability, of which there are very few. They also cover companies limited by guarantee, which may or may not have share capital, though the Companies Act 1985 prohibited the future formation of such companies unless they have no share capital.

The Companies (Audit, Investigations and Community Enterprise) Act 2004 established another form of company: a community interest company. Companies with or without share capital can become community interest companies, including companies limited by guarantee. A community interest company cannot issue share capital but can issue interest bearing preference shares – they can then pay dividends up to a fixed percentage above the base rate of interest.

These types of limited company and chartered companies are relatively unimportant, so any future reference in this book to 'a limited company' or 'a company' will be concerned with limited liability companies.

4.5 Separate legal entity

The outstanding feature of a **limited company** is that, no matter how many individuals have bought shares in it, it is treated in its dealings with the outside world as if it were a person in its own right: it is said to be a separate 'legal entity'. A prime example of its identity as a separate legal entity is that it may sue other business entities, people – even its own shareholders – or, in turn, be sued by them.

Just as the law can create this separate legal person, it can also eliminate it, but only by using the proper legal procedures. The identity of the shareholders in a large company may change daily as shares are bought and sold by different people but this, itself, has no immediate impact upon the existence or nature of the company.

On the other hand, a small private company may have the same shareholders from the day it is incorporated (when it legally came into being), until the date when liquidation is completed (the cessation of the company, often known also as 'winding up' or being 'wound up').

 Activity 4.1 Why would it be advantageous for a company to be able to sue other business entities, rather than for the directors or an employee to do so?

The legal formalities by which a company comes into existence can be found in any textbook on company law. It is not the purpose of this book to discuss company law in any great detail; this is far better left to a later stage of your studies. As companies must, however, comply with the law, the essential company law concerning accounting matters will be dealt with in this book as far as is necessary.

What is important is that the basic principles connected with company financial statements can be seen in operation. So that you are not unduly confused, points which rarely occur, or on which the legal arguments are extremely involved and may not yet have been finally settled, will be left out completely or merely mentioned in passing. This means that some generalisations made in this book will need to be expanded upon when your accounting studies reach a more advanced stage.

4.6 Memorandum and Articles of Association and company registration

Memorandum of association

A memorandum of association is a memorandum stating that the subscribers wish to form a company under the Companies Act and agree to become members of the company and, in the case of a company that is to have a share capital, to take at least one share each.

Articles of association

A company must have articles of association prescribing regulations for the company. Unless it is a company to which default model articles apply (i.e. articles prescribed for a company of that description as in force at the date on which the company is registered), it must register articles of association which must be contained in a single document, and be divided into paragraphs numbered consecutively.

Default application of model articles

On the formation of a limited company, if articles are not registered or, if articles are registered, in so far as they do not exclude or modify the relevant model articles, the relevant model articles (so far as applicable) form part of the company's articles in the same manner and to the same extent as if articles in the form of those articles had been duly registered.

Company registration

The memorandum of association must be delivered to the registrar together with an application for registration of the company, the documents required by this section and a statement of compliance.

The application for registration must state:

(*a*) the company's proposed name,
(*b*) whether the company's registered office is to be situated in England and Wales (or in Wales), in Scotland or in Northern Ireland,
(*c*) whether the liability of the members of the company is to be limited, and if so whether it is to be limited by shares or by guarantee, and
(*d*) whether the company is to be a private or a public company,
(*e*) in the case of a company that is to have a share capital, a statement of capital and initial shareholdings,
(*f*) in the case of a company that is to be limited by guarantee, a statement of guarantee,
(*g*) a statement of the company's proposed officers.

The application must also contain a statement of the intended address of the company's registered office; and a copy of any proposed articles of association (to the extent that these are not supplied by the default application of model articles).

Statement of capital and initial shareholdings

The statement of capital and initial shareholdings required to be delivered in the case of a company that is to have a share capital must state:

(*a*) the total number of shares of the company to be taken on formation by the subscribers to the memorandum of association,
(*b*) the aggregate nominal value of those shares,
(*c*) for each class of shares:
  ● prescribed particulars of the rights attached to the shares,
  ● the total number of shares of that class, and
  ● the aggregate nominal value of shares of that class, and
  ● the amount to be paid up and the amount (if any) to be unpaid on each,
  ● share (whether on account of the nominal value of the share or by way of premium).

It must contain such information as may be prescribed for the purpose of identifying the subscribers to the memorandum of association.

It must state, with respect to each subscriber to the memorandum the number, nominal value (of each share) and class of shares to be taken by him on formation, and the amount to be paid up and the amount (if any) to be unpaid on each share (whether on account of the nominal value of the share or by way of premium).

Where a subscriber to the memorandum is to take shares of more than one class, the information is required for each class.

4.7 Limited liability

The principle of limited liability underlying item (c) in the registration list has been of great importance in industry and commerce. Without it, it is inconceivable that large business units, such as GlaxoSmithKline plc or Marks and Spencer plc, could have existed. The investor in a limited company, i.e. someone who owns shares in the company, is a shareholder. The most he or she can lose is the money paid for the shares although, where they are only partly paid, the shareholder is also liable for the unpaid part. With public companies, whose shares are traded on a stock exchange, shares can be sold easily whenever a shareholder wishes. Selling shares in a private company is normally far more difficult.

Activity 4.2 Why is it unlikely that many large companies could have existed if limited liability did not exist?

4.8 Classes of shares

The main types or classes of shares are **ordinary shares** and **preference shares**. Unless otherwise stated, preference shares are assumed to be of the cumulative variety – see *Business Accounting Essentials 1*.

There are also a variety of other shares. The rights attaching to these shares are purely dependent upon the skill and ingenuity of the person who prepares the company's registration. An entirely new type of share may be created provided it does not contravene the law.

The shares which carry the right to the whole of the profits remaining after dividends have been paid on any preference shares (and any other fixed dividend shares) are often known as 'equity share capital' or as '**equities**'.

4.9 Distributable profits

The calculation of dividends from profits available for distribution was described in *Business Accounting 1*. Clearly, in order to do this, there needs to be some way of knowing what the amount of **distributable profits** is.

A company's realised profits and losses are '*those profits and losses which are treated as realised in the financial statements, in accordance with principles generally accepted with respect to the determination of realised profits and losses for accounting purposes at the time when those accounts are prepared*'. In accounting, the realisation concept recognises profit or loss at the point when a contract is made in the market to buy or sell assets. The definition of realised profits and realised losses also applies for the purpose of calculating a company's distributable profits.

4.10 A company's constitution

A company's constitution comprises the regulations contained in the Articles of Association and any resolutions or agreements passed subsequently by the company. Among those regulations are those governing the rights and duties of the directors. Any such regulations are of the utmost importance when it is realised that the legal owners of the business, the shareholders, have entrusted the running of the company to the directors.

The shareholders' rights are largely limited to attending meetings, such as the annual general meeting, where they have the right to vote. However, some shares do not carry voting rights and the holders of these shares may attend but not vote at such meetings.

The Companies Acts make the keeping of proper sets of accounting records and the preparation of Final Accounts (financial statements) compulsory for every company. In addition, the financial statements for large companies must be audited, this being quite different from the situation in a partnership or a sole trader's business where an audit is not compulsory.

Companies with limited liability, whether they are private or public companies, have to send a copy of their Final Accounts (i.e. their financial statements), drawn up in a prescribed manner, to the Registrar of Companies. Public companies must submit them within six months of their financial year end; private companies within nine months of their financial year end.

Look at Chapters 12–14 for the accounting requirements of the Companies Acts.

4.11 Public companies and the Stock Exchange

Dealings in the shares of most public companies are conducted on one or other of the recognised stock exchanges. The shares of private companies cannot be bought or sold on any stock exchange, as this would contravene the requirements for the company being recognised as a 'private' company.

The only entry made in a company's books when a shareholder sells all, or some, of his shares to someone else, is to record the change of identity of the shareholders. The price at which the shares were sold on the stock exchange is not entered into the company's books.

Although no accounting entries are made, the price of the shares on the Stock Exchange does have repercussions upon the financial policy of the company.

Activity 4.3 Why?

Stock exchanges are the 'second-hand markets' for company shares. Companies do not actually sell (normally called **issue**) their shares in a stock exchange. Companies issue new shares directly to the people who make application to them for the shares at the time when they have shares available for issue. Shares of a public company sold and bought on stock exchanges are passing from one shareholder to another person who will then become a shareholder. So far as the company is concerned, the number of shares in issue is unchanged.

4.12 Stocks and shares

Later in this book you will learn about the procedure whereby the shares of a company may be made into **stock**. Thus 500 ordinary shares of £1 each may be made into £500 stock. The dividends paid on the shares or the stock would be the same, and the voting powers would also be the same. Apart from administrative convenience there is really no difference between shares and stock.

Learning outcomes

You should now have learnt:

1 Limited companies are governed by the Companies Acts and EU directives.

2 Limited companies are each a separate legal entity.

3 Each company is governed by its constitution which, initially, is contained in its Articles of Association.

4 What is meant by 'limited liability'.

5 Investors in limited companies can only lose the amount they paid (plus any amount still unpaid if the shares are only part-paid) when they acquired their investment in the company, i.e. they have 'limited liability'.

Answers to activities

4.1 If a director sued another business entity on behalf of a company, the director would be liable for any legal costs incurred were the case unsuccessful. Perhaps more meaningfully, if companies could not be sued, directors and employees could be exposed to the risk of being sued for actions taken by the company, even when they were not personally involved in what had occurred. In effect, granting companies a legal identity separate from their owners makes it possible to operate limited liability effectively.

4.2 Without limited liability, investors would be very unwilling to buy shares in companies. They would fear that they may lose everything they owned if the company failed. Companies would, therefore, find it very difficult to raise funds other than from banks and other financial institutions. Such funds would carry interest costs that would have to be paid irrespective of how well the companies were doing. In the early years of a new business, it can take quite a long time to become profitable and the reliance upon loan funding would increase the possibility that the company will fail. As a result, in an economic environment where there was no limited liability, the investors in the failed company could lose everything they own. It is unlikely that many would be willing to take this risk. Hence, it is unlikely that many large companies would exist were it not for limited liability.

4.3 If some new shares are to be issued, the price they are to be issued at will be largely dependent on the stock exchange valuation. If another business is to be taken over by the company, part of the purchase price being paid using some of the company's shares, then the stock exchange value will also affect the value placed upon the shares being given. A takeover bid from another business may well be caused because the stock exchange value of the shares has made a takeover seem worthwhile.

You can find a range of additional self-test questions, as well as material to help you with your studies, on the website that accompanies this book at **www.pearsoned.co.uk/wood**

The issue of shares and debentures

Learning objectives

After you have studied this chapter, you should be able to:

- explain the terminology relating to the issue of shares and debentures
- describe the steps in the process of issuing of shares and debentures
- record the accounting entries relating to the issue of shares and debentures
- make the necessary entries in the ledger accounts when shares are forfeited

Introduction

In this chapter, you'll learn about the alternatives available to companies when they wish to issue shares and of the various entries to be made in the ledger accounts. You'll learn about how to record the issue of shares at a price greater than their nominal value and how to record the issue of shares to existing shareholders, rather than to non-shareholders wishing to purchase them. You will also learn about the difference in accounting entries made when debentures (a form of loan capital) rather than shares, are issued.

5.1 The issue of shares

The cost of issuing shares can be very high. As a result, the number of shares issued must be sufficient to ensure the cost of doing so is relatively insignificant compared to the amounts received.

When shares are issued, they may be payable, either (*a*) immediately on application, or (*b*) by instalments. Issues of shares may take place on the following terms connected with the price of the shares:

1 Shares issued at par. This would mean that a share of £1 nominal value would be issued for £1 each.
2 Shares issued at a premium. In this case a share of £1 nominal value would be issued for more than £1 each, say for £3 each.

Note: At one time, shares could be issued at a discount. Thus, shares each of £5 nominal value might have been issued for £3 each. However, this was expressly forbidden in the Companies Act 1980.

Activity 5.1 Why do you think companies may wish to issue shares at a discount and how do you think companies avoid being in this position?

5.2 Share premiums and discounts

This will all seem rather strange at first. How can a share with a nominal value of 10p, which states that value on the face of it, be issued for £3, and who would be foolish enough to buy it? The reasons for this apparently strange state of affairs stem from the Companies Act requirement that the share capital accounts always show shares at their nominal value, irrespective of how much the shares are worth or how much they were issued for. To illustrate this, the progress of two companies, A Ltd and B Ltd, can be looked at. Both started in business on 1 January 2001 and issued 1 million ordinary shares each of 10p nominal value at par. Ignoring any issue expenses, each of the balance sheets on that date would be identical:

Balance Sheet as at 1 January 2001

	£
Bank	100,000
Capital	100,000

Five years later, on 31 December 2005, the balance sheets show that the companies have fared quite differently. It is to be assumed here, for purposes of illustration, that the balance sheet values and any other interpretation of values happen to be identical.

A Ltd needs £100,000 more capital, and this is to be met by issuing more ordinary shares. Suppose that another 1 million ordinary shares of 10p nominal value each are issued at par. Column (*a*) below shows the balance sheet before the issue, and column (*b*) shows the balance sheet after the issue has taken place.

Exhibit 5.1

A Ltd Balance Sheets (Solution 1) as at 31 December 2005

	(a) £	(b) £
Fixed and current assets (other than bank)	225,000	225,000
Bank	25,000	125,000
	250,000	350,000
Financed by:		
Ordinary share capital	100,000	200,000
Profit and loss	150,000	150,000
	250,000	350,000

Share premiums

Now the effect of what has happened can be appreciated. Before the new issue there were 1 million shares. As there were £250,000 of assets and no liabilities, each share was worth 25p. After the issue, there are 2 million shares and £350,000 of assets, so each share is now worth 17.5p. This would be extremely disconcerting to the original shareholders who have seen the value of each of their shares fall by 30 per cent (7.5p).

On the other hand, the new shareholder who has just bought shares for 10p each saw them rise in value immediately by 75 per cent to be worth 17.5p each. Only in one specific case would this be fair, and that is where each original shareholder buys an equivalent number of new shares.

What is required is a price which is equitable as far as the interests of the old shareholders are concerned, and yet will attract sufficient applications to provide the capital required. As in this case the balance sheet value and the real value are the same, the answer is that each old share was worth 25p and therefore each new share should be issued at a price of 25p. If this were done, the balance sheets would become as shown in Exhibit 5.2:

Exhibit 5.2

A Ltd Balance Sheets (Solution 2) as at 31 December 2005

	(a) £	(b) £
Fixed and current assets (other than bank)	225,000	225,000
Bank	25,000	275,000
	250,000	500,000
Financed by:		
Ordinary share capital (at nominal value)	100,000	200,000
Share premium (*see note below*)	–	150,000
Profit and loss	150,000	150,000
	250,000	500,000

Thus in (*a*) above, 1 million shares own between them £250,000 of assets = 25p each, while, in (*b*) 2 million shares are shown as owning £500,000 of assets = 25p each. Both the old and new shareholders are therefore satisfied with the bargain that has been made.

Note: **The share premium shown on the capital side of the balance sheet is needed because the balance sheet would not balance without it.** If shares are stated at nominal value but issued at another price, the actual amount received increases the bank balance, but the share capital is increased by a different figure. The share premium therefore represents the excess of the cash received over the nominal value of the shares issued.

Share discount

The other company, B Ltd, has not fared so well. It has, in fact, lost money. The accumulated losses are reflected in a debit balance on the profit and loss account as shown below in column (*c*). There are £80,000 of assets to represent the shareholders' stake in the firm of 1 million shares, i.e. each share is worth 8p. If more capital was needed, 1 million more shares could be issued. From the action taken in the previous case it will now be obvious that each new share of 10p nominal value would be issued for its real value of 8p each, were it permitted. The balance sheets would appear:

Exhibit 5.3

B Ltd Balance Sheets (correct solution) as at 31 December 2005

	(c)	(d)
Fixed and current assets (other than bank)	55,000	55,000
Bank	25,000	105,000
	80,000	160,000
Ordinary share capital	100,000	200,000
Discounts on shares (*see below*)		(20,000)
Profit and loss – debit balance	(20,000)	(20,000)
	80,000	160,000

Although shares cannot now be issued at a discount, some companies still exist which issued shares at a discount before 1980. In these cases, a separate heading will have to be inserted in the balance sheet for the discount.

Once again, as the share capital is shown at nominal value but the shares are issued at a different figure, the discount on the shares issued must be shown in order that the balance sheet balances. It is, of course, a balancing figure needed because the entries already made for an increase in the ordinary share capital and the increase in the bank balance have been at different figures. The figure for discounts on shares therefore rectifies the double entry 'imbalance'.

A balance sheet is a historical view of the past based on records made according to the company's interpretation and use of accounting concepts and conventions. When shares are being issued it is not the view of the past that is important, but the view of the future. Therefore the actual premiums on shares being issued are a matter not merely of balance sheet values, but of the issuing company's view of the future and its estimate of how the investing public will react to the price at which the shares are being offered.

It is to be noted that there are *no* restrictions on issuing shares at par or at a premium. Let's now look at the double entries that need to be made when shares are issued. First we'll consider the case where the full amount is due in one payment made at the time of issue.

5.3 Shares payable in full on application

The issue of shares in illustrations (1) and (2) which follow are based on the balance sheets that have just been considered. First, let's look at the entries when shares are issued at their par value.

1 Shares issued at par

One million ordinary shares with a nominal value of 10p each are to be issued. Applications, together with the necessary money, are received for exactly 1 million shares. The shares are then allotted to the applicants.

Bank

		£			
Ordinary share applicants	(A)	100,000			

Ordinary Share Applicants

		£			£
Ordinary share capital	(B)	100,000	Bank	(A)	100,000

Ordinary Share Capital

				£
	Ordinary share applicants	(B)	100,000

It may appear that the ordinary share applicants account is unnecessary, and that the only entries needed are a debit in the bank account and a credit in the ordinary share capital account. However, applicants do not always become shareholders; this is shown later. The applicant must make an offer for the shares being issued, accompanied by the necessary money: this is the application. After the applications have been vetted, the allotments of shares are made by the company. This represents the acceptance of the offer by the company and it is at this point that the applicant becomes a shareholder. Therefore (A) represents the offer by the applicant while (B) is the acceptance by the company. **No entry must be made in the share capital account until (B)**

happens, for it is not until that point that the share capital is in existence. The share applicants account is an intermediary account pending allotments being made.

Now let's look at the entries to be made when the shares are issued at more than their par value.

2 Shares issued at a premium

One million ordinary shares with a nominal value of 10p each are to be issued for 25p each (*see* Exhibit 5.2 A Ltd previously). Thus a premium of 15p per share has been charged. Applications and the money are received for exactly 1 million shares.

Bank

	£		
Balance b/d	25,000		
Ordinary share applicants	250,000		

Ordinary Share Applicants

		£			£
Ordinary share capital	(A)	100,000	Bank		250,000
Share premium	(B)	150,000			
		250,000			250,000

Share Premium

			£
	Ordinary share applicants	(B)	150,000

Ordinary Share Capital (A Ltd)

			£
	Balance b/d		100,000
	Ordinary share applicants	(A)	100,000

Note: **(A) is shown as £100,000 because the share capital is shown at nominal value, not total issued value. The £150,000 share premiums (B) must therefore be credited to a share premium account to preserve double entry balancing.**

Let's now look at the entries to be made when the number of shares applied for is not equal to the number of shares on offer.

3 Oversubscription and undersubscription for shares

When a company invites investors to apply for its shares it is obviously rare indeed if applications for shares equal exactly the number of shares to be issued. Where more shares are applied for than are available for issue, then the issue is said to be **oversubscribed**. Where fewer shares are applied for than are available for issue, then the issue has been **undersubscribed**.

With a new company, an amount is set in advance as being the minimum necessary to carry on any further with the running of the company. If the applications are less than the minimum stated, then the application monies are returned to the senders. This does not apply to an established company.

If 1 million shares of 10p each are available for issue, but only 875,000 shares are applied for, then only 875,000 shares will be issued. The accounting entries will be in respect of 875,000 shares, no entries being needed for the 125,000 shares not applied for, as they do not represent a transaction.

The opposite occurs when shares are oversubscribed. In this case, rationing is applied so that the issue is restricted to the shares available for issue. The process of selecting which applicants will get how many shares depends on the policy of the company. Some, for example, prefer to have large shareholders because this leads to lower administrative costs.

You can see why by considering the cost of calling a meeting of two companies each with 200,000 shares. H Ltd has 20 shareholders with an average holding of 10,000 shares. J Ltd has 1,000 shareholders with an average holding of 200 shares. They all have to be notified by post and given various documents including a set of the financial statements. The cost of printing and sending these is less for H Ltd with 20 shareholders than for J Ltd with 1,000 shareholders. This is only one example of the costs involved, but it will also apply with equal force to many items connected with the shares. Conversely, the directors may prefer to have more shareholders with smaller holdings, one reason being that it decreases the amount of voting power in any one individual's hands.

The actual process of rationing the shares is straightforward once a policy is in place. It may consist of scaling down applications, of drawing lots or some other chance selection, but it will eventually bring the number of shares to be issued down to the number of shares available. Excess application monies received will then be refunded by the company.

An issue of shares where 1 million ordinary shares of 10p nominal value each are to be issued at par payable in full but 1.55 million shares are applied for, will be recorded as follows:

Bank

	£		£
Ordinary share applicants	155,000	Ordinary share applicants (refunds)	55,000

Ordinary Share Applicants

	£		£
Bank	55,000	Bank	155,000
Ordinary share capital	100,000		
	155,000		155,000

Ordinary Share Capital

			£
		Ordinary share applicants	100,000

Let's now look at the entries to be made when payment for shares purchased is to be made in instalments.

5.4 Issue of shares payable by instalments

The shares considered so far have all been issued as paid in full on application. Conversely, many issues are made which require payment by instalments. These are probably more common with public companies than with private companies. It should be noted that a public company is now not allowed to allot a share (i.e. pass ownership to the subscriber) unless a sum equal to at least one-quarter of its nominal value plus the whole of any premium has been paid on it. When the premium is large compared to the nominal value, this clearly affects the manner in which the instalments are divided.

The various stages, after the initial invitation has been made to the public to buy shares by means of advertisements (if it is a public company) etc. are as follows:

(A) Applications are received together with the application monies.
(B) The applications are vetted and the shares allotted, letters of allotment being sent out.

(C) The excess application monies from wholly unsuccessful applicants, or, where the application monies received exceed both the application and allotment monies required, from wholly and partly unsuccessful applicants, are returned to them. Usually, if a person has been partly unsuccessful, his excess application monies are held by the company and will reduce the amount needed to be paid by him on allotment.

(D) Allotment monies are received.

(E) The next instalment, known as the first call, is requested.

(F) The monies are received from the first call.

(G) The next instalment, known as the second call, is requested.

(H) The monies are received from the second call.

This carries on until the full number of calls have been made, although there is not usually a large number of calls to be made in an issue.

The reasons for the payments by instalments become obvious if it is realised that a company will not necessarily require the immediate use of all the money to be raised by the issue. Suppose a new company is to be formed: it is to buy land, erect a factory, equip it with machinery and then go into production. This might take two years altogether. Suppose the total sum needed was £1 million, required as follows:

Ordinary Share Capital

	£
Cost of land, payable within 1 month	300,000
Cost of buildings, payable in 1 year's time	200,000
Cost of machinery, payable in 18 months' time	200,000
Working capital required in 2 years' time	300,000
	1,000,000

A decision may be made to match the timing of the payment of the instalments of the share issue to the timing of the requirement for funding. If so, the share issue may be on the following terms:

	Per cent
Application money per share, payable immediately	10
Allotment money per share, payable within 1 month	20
First call, money payable in 12 months' time	20
Second call, money payable in 18 months' time	20
Third call, money payable in 24 months' time	30
	100

The entries made in the share capital account should equal the amount of money requested to that point in time. However, instead of one share applicants account, there are usually several accounts each representing one of the instalments. For this purpose application and allotment are usually joined together in one account, the *application and allotment account*. This cuts out the need for transfers where excess *application monies* are held over and set off against allotment monies needed. That is, instead of refunding excess application monies, they are retained and used to meet subsequent instalments.

When allotment is made, and not until then, an entry of £300,000 (10 per cent + 20 per cent) would be made in the share capital account. On the first call, an entry of £200,000 would be made in the share capital account; likewise £200,000 on the second call and £300,000 on the third call. The share capital account will therefore contain not the monies received, but the amount of money requested. Exhibit 5.4 now shows an example of a share issue with payments by instalments.

Exhibit 5.4

A company is issuing 100,000 7 per cent preference shares of £1 each, payable 10 per cent on application, 20 per cent on allotment, 40 per cent on the first call and 30 per cent on the second call. Applications are received for 155,000 shares. A refund of the money is made in respect of 5,000 shares while, for the remaining 150,000 applied for, an allotment is to be made on the basis of 2 shares for every 3 applied for (assume that this will not involve any fractions of shares). The excess application monies are set off against the allotment monies asked for. The remaining requested instalments are all paid in full. The letters by the side of each entry refer to the various stages outlined earlier.

Bank

		£				£
Application and allotment:			Application and allotment refund (C)			500
Application monies	(A)	15,500				
Allotment monies						
(£100,000 × 20% *less* excess						
application monies £5,000)	(D)	15,000				
First call	(F)	40,000				
Second call	(H)	30,000				

Application and Allotment

		£				£
Bank – refund of application monies	(C)	500	Bank		(A)	15,500
Preference share capital	(B)	30,000	Bank		(D)	15,000
		30,500				30,500

First Call

		£				£
Preference share capital	(E)	40,000	Bank		(F)	40,000

Second Call

		£				£
Preference share capital	(G)	30,000	Bank		(H)	30,000

7 per cent Preference Share Capital

	£				£
Balance c/d	100,000	Application and allotment		(B)	30,000
		First call		(E)	40,000
		Second call		(G)	30,000
	100,000				100,000
		Balance b/d			100,000

If more than one type of share is being issued at the same time, e.g. preference shares and ordinary shares, then separate share capital accounts and separate application and allotment accounts and call accounts should be opened.

Now let's look at the entries to be made when a purchaser of the shares fails to pay the instalments due.

5.5 Forfeited shares

Sometimes, some shareholders fail to pay the calls requested. If drawn up with care, the Articles of Association of the company will provide that the defaulting shareholder forfeits the shares allocated. In this case, the shares will be cancelled. The instalments already paid by the shareholder will be forfeited and retained by the company.

After the forfeiture, the company may or may not choose to reissue the shares (though, in some cases, there may be a provision in the Articles of Association which prevents their reissue). There are regulations governing the prices at which such shares can be reissued. The amount received on reissue plus the amount received from the original shareholder should at least equal (a) the called-up value where the shares are not fully called up, or (b) the nominal value where the full amount has been called up. Any premium previously paid is disregarded in determining the minimum reissue price.

Exhibit 5.5

Take the same information as that contained in Exhibit 5.4, but, instead of all the calls all being paid in full, Allen, the holder of 10,000 shares, fails to pay the first and second calls. He had already paid the application and allotment monies on the required dates. The directors conform to the provisions of the Articles of Association and (A) Allen is forced to suffer the forfeiture of his shares; (B) The amount still outstanding from Allen will be written off; (C) The directors then reissue the shares at 75 per cent of nominal value to J. Dougan; (D) Dougan pays for the shares.

First Call

		£				£
Preference share capital		40,000	Bank			36,000
			Forfeited shares	(B)		4,000
		40,000				40,000

Second Call

		£				£
Preference share capital		30,000	Bank			27,000
			Forfeited shares	(B)		3,000
		30,000				30,000

7 per cent Preference Share Capital

		£				£
Forfeited shares	(A)	10,000	Application and allotment			30,000
Balance c/d		90,000	First call			40,000
			Second call			30,000
		100,000				100,000
Balance c/d		100,000	Balance b/d			90,000
			J. Dougan	(C)		10,000
		100,000				100,000
			Balance b/d			100,000

Forfeited Shares

		£			£
First call	(B)	4,000	Preference share capital	(A)	10,000
Second call	(B)	3,000			
Balance c/d		3,000			
		10,000			10,000
J. Dougan*		2,500	Balance b/d		3,000
Balance c/d		500			
		3,000			3,000
			Balance b/d		500

Bank

		£		
First call (£90,000 × 40%)		36,000		
Second call (£90,000 × 30%)		27,000		
J. Dougan	(D)	7,500		

J. Dougan

	£			£
Preference share capital	10,000	Bank	(D)	7,500
		Forfeited shares (discount on reissue)*		2,500
	10,000			10,000

*The transfer of £2,500 from the forfeited shares account to J. Dougan's account is needed because the reissue was entered in the preference share capital account and Dougan's account at nominal value, i.e. following standard practice by which a share capital account is concerned with nominal values. But Dougan was not required to pay the full nominal price. Therefore the transfer of £2,500 is needed to close his account.

Activity 5.2   Why do you think companies make new share issues?
[Note: these are not the same as the shares issued when a company is first formed.]

The balance of £500 on the forfeited shares account can be seen to be: cash received from original shareholder on application and allotment £3,000 + from Dougan £7,500 = £10,500. This is £500 over the nominal value so the £500 appears as an extra credit balance. This could be transferred to a profit on reissue of forfeited shares account, but it would be pointless for small amounts. More normally it would be transferred to the credit of a share premium account.

Having looked at what is done when payments are not made, let's consider the treatment of payments being received early or received late.

5.6   Calls in advance and in arrear and the balance sheet

At the balance sheet date some shareholders will not have paid all the calls made. These are collectively known as **calls in arrear**. On the other hand, some shareholders may have paid amounts in respect of calls not made by the balance sheet date. These are **calls in advance**.

Calls in arrear, i.e. **called-up share capital not paid**, is shown in the balance sheet in one of the positions shown in the format per the Companies Act 1985 (*see* Chapter 13). There is no specified place in the Companies Act format for calls in advance, so this is inserted in the balance sheet as an extra heading.

So far, we have looked at the issue of shares to anyone, whether or not they are existing shareholders. Now, let's look at what happens when a company wishes to offer shares for sale to existing shareholders.

5.7 Rights issues

The costs of making a new issue of shares can be quite high. One way to reduce the costs of raising new long-term capital in the form of issuing shares is to do so in the form of a **rights issue**. To do this, the company contacts the existing shareholders, and informs them of the number of shares which each one of them is entitled to buy of the new issue. In most cases, shareholders are allowed to renounce their rights to the new shares in favour of someone else to whom they sell the right to purchase the shares.

A rights issue is usually pitched at a price which enables the rights to be sold. If any shareholders do not either buy the shares or transfer their rights, the directors have the power to dispose of the shares not taken up by issuing them in some other way. Alternatively, they may choose not to issue them.

So far in this chapter, we have looked at the issue of shares. Companies may also raise funds by issuing long-term loans. These are called **debentures**.

5.8 Debentures

A **debenture** is a certificate acknowledging a loan to a company. It is usually issued under the company's seal (i.e. is an official document issued by the company, similar to a share certificate) and bears a fixed rate of interest (similar to preference shares). However, unlike shares, which normally depend on profits out of which to appropriate dividends, debenture interest is payable whether or not profits are made.

A debenture may be **redeemable**, i.e. repayable at or by a specified date. Conversely it may be irredeemable, redemption taking place only when the company is eventually liquidated, or in a case such as when the debenture interest is not paid within a given time limit.

People lending money to companies in the form of debentures will obviously be interested in how safe their investment will be. In the case of some debentures, the debenture holders are given the legal right that on certain happenings they will be able to take control of specific assets, or of the whole of the assets. They can then sell the assets and recoup the amount due under their debentures, or deal with the assets in ways specified in the deed under which the debentures were issued. Such debentures are known as being secured against the assets, the term **mortgage debenture** often being used. Other debentures carry no prior right to control the assets under any circumstances. These are known as **simple** or **naked debentures**.

Debenture are also known as 'loan notes'.

Activity 5.3 Why do you think companies issue debentures rather than making a new share issue?

5.9 The issue of debentures

The entries for the issue of debentures are similar to those for shares but, nowadays, they are normally issued at their nominal value. If the term 'debentures' is substituted for 'share capital' in the T-accounts you saw earlier in this chapter, the entries in the ledger accounts would be identical.

5.10 Shares of no par value

You should now realise that a fixed par value for a share can be very confusing. For anyone who has not studied accounting, it may come as a shock to find that a share with a par value of £1 might have been issued for £5. If the share is dealt in on the Stock Exchange, they might find a £1 share selling at £10 or even £20 or, equally well, it may sell for only 10p.

Another problem with the use of a par value is that it can give people entirely the wrong impression of the amount of dividend paid. If a low par value is used, the dividend (which is declared as a percentage of the par value) can look excessive when it really isn't.

Exhibit 5.6

Jones bought a share 40 years ago for £1. At the time, he was satisfied with a return of 5 per cent on his money. With a 5 per cent dividend he could buy a certain amount of goods which will be called *x*. Now, 40 years later, to buy that same amount of goods, he would need, say, 20 times as much money. Where previously £5 would have bought *x*, now he would need £100. To keep the dividend at the same level of purchasing power, he would need a dividend now of 100 per cent, as compared with the 5 per cent dividend of 40 years ago.

In many countries, including the USA and Canada, no par value is attached to shares being issued. A share is issued at whatever price is suitable at the time, and the money received is credited to a share capital account.

Activity 5.4 Why do you think companies are not allowed to issue shares at no par value in the UK?

Learning outcomes

You should now have learnt:

1 Shares may be issued either:
   (a) at par, or nominal value – i.e. a £1 ordinary share would be issued in exchange for payment of £1, or
   (b) at a premium, i.e. if a £1 ordinary share were issued at a premium of 25p, it would cost the buyer £1.25 (and the 25p would be put into the issuing company's *share premium* account).

2 How to make the accounting entries when shares are issued.

3 How to make the accounting entries when shares are forfeited.

4 How to make the accounting entries when debentures are issued.

5 The accounting entries made on the issue of debentures are identical to the accounting entries made on the issue of shares though, obviously, debenture ledger accounts are used rather than share capital ledger accounts.

Answers to activities

5.1 If a company is not performing very well and its share price has fallen below its nominal value, it would find it very difficult to issue shares at par or above. Hence, it may wish to issue shares at a discount. As companies are prohibited from doing so, it is common nowadays for shares to be given very low nominal values and then issued, in the first instance, at a price considerably in excess of their nominal value. This makes the likelihood of companies ever being in a position where they would wish to issue shares at a discount extremely rare. In effect, by adopting very low nominal values, companies make the restriction on their being able to issue shares at a discount irrelevant.

5.2 Nowadays, companies often make new share issues in order to obtain funds or in order to use the new shares to purchase another business entity.

5.3 Issuing shares may not be appropriate because the current share price is low and it is felt that issuing new shares at this time will enable investors to buy into the company too cheaply, with the result that when the share price rises, the new investors will make substantial profits on their investment. A company may prefer to wait until the share price is higher before selling new shares. It may also be the case that the share price is low because investors do not feel that the company is a good investment at present. Selling new shares may be difficult. Debentures do not involve transference of rights of ownership. Buyers of debentures receive interest, rather than a share of profit. If the company feels its profits are going to grow, it may prefer to issue debentures so that existing shareholders receive the maximum long-term benefit of their investment in the company. That is, their share of future profits is not diluted by the issue of new shares.

5.4 When shares are issued at a premium, the excess above the nominal value is put into a reserve (the share premium account). Such a reserve can, in certain circumstances, be distributed or utilised. Doing so has no effect upon the share capital account. If shares are issued with no nominal value, share capital in the balance sheet would represent the total amount received by a company when it issued shares. The share premium account would no longer be readily identifiable. In fact, it would not and could not exist (as no notion of par value would exist). By requiring shares to have a nominal value, additional flexibility is granted to the company in how it uses the funds received when it issues shares.

Review questions

5.1 Shift Ltd has a nominal share capital of £400,000 comprising 400,000 ordinary shares of £1 each. The whole of the capital was issued at par on the following terms:

	Per share
Payable on application	20p
Payable on allotment	25p
First call	30p
Second call	25p

Applications were received for 600,000 shares and it was decided to allot the shares on the basis of two for every three for which applications had been made. The balance of application monies was applied to the allotment, no cash being refunded. The balance of allotment monies was paid by the members.

The calls were made and paid in full by the members, with the exception of one who failed to pay the first and second calls on the 2,000 shares allotted to him. A resolution was passed by the directors to forfeit the shares. The forfeited shares were later issued to N Butt at 90p each.

Show the ledger accounts recording all the above transactions, and the relevant extracts from a balance sheet after all the transactions had been completed.

5.2 Feliz Ltd has an authorised capital of £500,000 comprising 1 million ordinary shares of 50p each. The 1 million shares were issued at par, payments being made as follows:

	Per share
Payable on application	10p
Payable on allotment	25p
First call	35p
Second call	30p

Applications were received for 1.28 million shares. It was decided to refund application monies on 80,000 shares and to allot the shares on the basis of five for every six applied for. The excess application monies sent by the successful applicants is not to be refunded but is to be held and so reduce the amount payable on allotment.

The calls were made and paid in full with the exception of three members holding a combined total of 6,000 shares who paid neither the first nor the second call and another member who did not pay the second call on 2,000 shares. The shares were forfeited and reissued to C Lamb at a price of 85p per share.

You are to draft the ledger accounts to record the transactions.

5.3 The authorised and issued share capital of Cosy Fires Ltd was £75,000 divided into 75,000 ordinary shares of £1 each, fully paid. On 2 January 2007, the authorised capital was increased by a further 85,000 ordinary shares of £1 each to £160,000. On the same date 40,000 ordinary shares of £1 each were offered to the public at £1.25 per share payable as to £0.60 on application (including the premium), £0.35 on allotment and £0.30 on 6 April 2007.

The lists were closed on 10 January 2007, and by that date applications for 65,000 shares had been received. Applications for 5,000 shares received no allotment and the cash paid in respect of such shares was returned. All shares were then allocated to the remaining applicants pro rata to their original applications, the balance of the monies received on applications being applied to the amounts due on allotment.

The balances due on allotment were received on 31 January 2007, with the exception of one allottee of 500 shares and these were declared forfeited on 4 April 2007. These shares were reissued as fully paid on 2 May 2007, at £1.10 per share. The call due on 6 April 2007 was duly paid by the other shareholders.

You are required:
(*a*) To record the above-mentioned transactions in the appropriate ledger accounts; and
(*b*) To show how the balances on such accounts should appear in the company's balance sheet as on 31 May 2007.

(*Association of Chartered Certified Accountants*)

5.4A During the year to 30 September 2007, Kammer plc made a new offer of shares. The details of the offer were as follows:

1 100,000 ordinary shares of £1 each were issued payable in instalments as follows:

	Per share £
On application at 1 November 2006	0.65
On allotment (including the share premium of £0.50 per share) on 1 December 2006	0.55
On first and final call on 1 June 2007	0.30
	£1.50

2 Applications for 200,000 shares were received, and it was decided to deal with them as follows:
  (*a*) to return cheques for 75,000 shares;
  (*b*) to accept in full applications for 25,000 shares; and
  (*c*) to allot the remaining shares on the basis of three shares for every four shares applied for.
3 On the first and final call, one applicant who had been allotted 5,000 shares failed to pay the due amount, and his shares were duly declared forfeited. They were then reissued to Amber Ltd on 1 September 2007 at a price of £0.80 per share fully paid.

Note: Kammer's issued share capital on 1 October 2006 consisted of 500,000 ordinary shares of £1 each.

Required:
Record the above transactions in the following ledger accounts:

(*a*) ordinary share capital;
(*b*) share premium;
(*c*) application and allotment;
(*d*) first and final call;
(*e*) forfeited shares; and
(*f*) Amber Ltd's account.

(*Association of Accounting Technicians*)

5.5 M Limited has an authorised share capital of £1,500,000 divided into 1,500,000 ordinary shares of £1 each. The issued share capital at 31 March 2007 was £500,000 which was fully paid, and had been issued at par. On 1 April 2007, the directors, in accordance with the company's Articles, decided to increase the share capital of the company by offering a further 500,000 ordinary shares of £1 each at a price of £1.60 per share, payable as follows:

On application, including the premium	£0.85 per share
On allotment	£0.25 per share
On first and final call on 3 August 2007	£0.50 per share

On 13 April 2007, applications had been received for 750,000 shares and it was decided to allot the shares to applicants for 625,000 shares, on the basis of four shares for every five shares for which applications had been received. The balance of the money received on application was to be applied to the amounts due on allotment. The shares were allotted on 1 May 2007, the unsuccessful applicants being repaid their cash on this date. The balance of the allotment money was received in full by 15 May 2007.

With the exception of one member who failed to pay the call on the 5,000 shares allotted to him, the remainder of the call was paid in full within two weeks of the call being made.

The directors resolved to forfeit these shares on 1 September 2007, after giving the required notice. The forfeited shares were reissued on 30 September 2007 to another member at £0.90 per share.

You are required to write up the ledger accounts necessary to record these transactions in the books of M Limited.

(*Chartered Institute of Management Accountants*)

5.6A Applications were invited by the directors of Grobigg Ltd for 150,000 of its £1 ordinary shares at £1.15 per share payable as follows:

	Per share
On application on 1 April 2008	£0.75
On allotment on 30 April 2008 (including the premium of £0.15 per share)	£0.20
On first and final call on 31 May 2008	£0.20

Applications were received for 180,000 shares and it was decided to deal with these as follows:

1 To refuse allotment to applicants for 8,000 shares.
2 To give full allotment to applicants for 22,000 shares.
3 To allot the remainder of the available shares pro rata among the other applicants.
4 To utilise the surplus received on applications in part payment of amounts due on allotment.

An applicant, to whom 400 shares had been allotted, failed to pay the amount due on the first and final call and his shares were declared forfeit on 31 July 2008. These shares were reissued on 3 September 2008 as fully paid at £0.90 per share.

Show how the transactions would be recorded in the company's books.

(*Association of Chartered Certified Accountants*)

You can find a range of additional self-test questions, as well as material to help you with your studies, on the website that accompanies this book at **www.pearsoned.co.uk/wood**

Companies purchasing and redeeming their own shares and debentures

Learning objectives

After you have studied this chapter, you should be able to:

● explain, in the context of shares and debentures, the difference between the terms 'purchasing' and 'redeeming'

● describe the alternative ways in which a company may purchase or redeem its own shares and debentures

● explain the difference between the purchase/redemption opportunities available to private companies, and those available to other companies

● record the accounting entries relating to the purchase and the redemption of shares and debentures

Introduction

In this chapter, you'll learn the difference between the terms 'redemption' and 'purchase' of a company's own shares and debentures and the rules relating to companies that do either of these things. You will learn how to record such activities in the ledger accounts and of the effects of such activities upon the balance sheet.

6.1 Purchasing and redeeming own shares

In the context of shares and debentures, to all intents and purposes, the words 'purchasing' and 'redeeming' may appear to be identical and interchangeable. They both involve an outflow of cash incurred by a company in getting back its own shares so that it may then cancel them. However, legally, 'redeeming' means the buying back of shares which were originally issued as 'redeemable shares'. That is, the company stated when they were issued that they would or could be bought back at sometime in the future by the company. The actual terms of the redemption are declared at the time when the shares are issued. In contrast, when shares issued are not stated to be redeemable, if they are subsequently bought back by the company, the company is said to be 'purchasing' its own shares rather than 'redeeming' them.

Since 1981, if authorised by its Articles of Association, a company may:

(*a*) issue redeemable shares of any class (preference, ordinary, etc.). Redeemable shares include those that are to be redeemed on a particular date as well as those that are merely liable to be redeemed at the discretion of the shareholder or of the company. There is an important proviso that a company can only issue redeemable shares if it has in issue shares that are *not* redeemable. Without this restriction a company could issue only redeemable shares, then later redeem all of its shares, and thus finish up without any shareholders;

(*b*) 'purchase' its own shares (i.e. shares that were not issued as being redeemable shares). Again, the company must, *after* the purchase, have other shares in issue at least some of which are not redeemable. This again prevents a company redeeming its whole share capital and thus ceasing to have any shareholders.

Activity 6.1 Why do you think the rules concerning purchase and redemption were changed in 1981?

6.2 Advantages to companies of being able to purchase and redeem their own shares

There are many advantages to a company arising from its being able to buy back its own shares. For public companies, the main advantage is that those with surplus cash resources can return some of this surplus cash to its shareholders by buying back some of their own shares, rather than being pressurised to use such cash in other, less economic ways.

However, the greatest advantages are for private companies and relate to overcoming problems which occur when shareholders cannot sell their shares on the 'open market'. This means that:

1 They can help shareholders who have difficulties in selling their shares to realise their investment when needed.
2 People will be more willing to buy shares from private companies. The fear of not being able to dispose of them previously led to finance being relatively difficult for private companies to obtain from people other than the original main proprietors of the company.
3 In many 'family' companies, cash is needed to pay for taxes on the death of a shareholder.
4 Shareholders with grievances against the company can be bought out, thus contributing to the more efficient management of the company.
5 Family-owned companies are helped in their desire to keep control of the company when a family shareholder with a large number of shares dies or retires.
6 As with public companies, private companies can return unwanted cash resources to their shareholders.
7 For both private companies and public companies whose shares are not listed on a stock exchange, it may help boost share schemes for employees, as the employees would know that they could dispose of the shares fairly easily.

6.3 Accounting entries

The accounting entries for the purchase and the redemption of shares are exactly the same, except that the word 'redeemable' will appear as the first word in the title of the ledger accounts for shares that are redeemable. The figures to be entered will naturally be affected by the **terms** under which shares are redeemed or purchased, but the **location** of the debits and credits to be made will be the same.

You will understand better the rather complicated entries needed if you realise that protection of the creditor was uppermost in the minds of Parliament when, for the first time, it permitted companies to purchase their own shares in the 1981 Companies Act. The general idea is that **capital** should not be returned to the shareholders, except under certain circumstances. If capital is returned to the shareholders, thus reducing the cash and bank balances, then the creditors could lose out badly if there was not then sufficient cash/bank balances to pay their claims. Thus the shareholders, seeing that things were not progressing too well in the company, could get their money out, leaving the creditors with nothing.

There are dividends which can quite legitimately be paid to the shareholders out of distributable profits but, in order to prevent shareholders withdrawing all their capital, included under the general heading of 'capital' are reserves which *cannot* be used for the payment of cash dividends.

There are exceptions to this, namely the reduction of capital by public companies (*see* Chapter 10) and the special powers of a private company to purchase or redeem its own shares out of capital (which you will learn about later in this chapter). However, apart from these special cases, company law regulations are intended to ensure that capital does not decrease when shares are redeemed or purchased. This is what lies behind the accounting entries which we'll now consider.

6.4 Rules for redemption or purchase

In *all* cases, shares can be redeemed or purchased only when they are fully paid.

> **Activity 6.2** Why do you think shares need to be fully paid before they can be redeemed or purchased?

The safeguards for the protection of capital contained in the Companies Acts are summarised in the next five sections.

6.5 Nominal value

In respect of the **nominal value** of shares redeemed or purchased, either (*a*) there must be a new issue of shares to provide the funds for redemption or purchase or (*b*) sufficient distributable profits must be available (i.e. a large enough credit balance on the appropriation account) which could be diverted from being used up as dividends to being treated as used up for the purpose of redeeming or purchasing the shares.

Therefore, when shares are redeemed or purchased other than by using the proceeds of a new share issue, the amount of distributable profits treated as being used up to redeem or purchase the *nominal* value of the shares redeemed or purchased is debited to the appropriation account and credited to a **capital redemption reserve**. (Previously, this was called a 'capital redemption reserve fund'.)

Thus, the old share capital amount is equal to the total of the new share capital *plus* the capital redemption reserve. The capital redemption reserve is a 'non-distributable' reserve. It *cannot* be transferred back to the credit of the appropriation account, and so increase the profits available for distribution as cash dividends. The process of diverting profits from being usable for dividends means that the non-payment of the dividends leaves more cash in the company against which creditors could claim if necessary.

Note: In all the examples that follow, as the entries are the same, no attempt is made to indicate whether or not the shares being redeemed/purchased are redeemable shares. In a real company, the titles of the accounts would indicate which shares were redeemable.

In Exhibit 6.1, journal entries are shown first, followed by the changes in the balance sheet amounts.

Note: In all these examples, the amounts involved are kept small so that you can follow more easily the entries and changes that arise.

Exhibit 6.1

£2,000 preference shares are redeemed/purchased at par. In order to do so, a new issue is to be made of £2,000 ordinary £1 shares at par. The journal entries are:

		Dr £	Cr £
(A1)	Bank	2,000	
(A2)	Ordinary share applicants		2,000
	Cash received from applicants		
(B1)	Ordinary share applicants	2,000	
(B2)	Ordinary share capital		2,000
	Ordinary shares allotted		
(C1)	Preference share capital	2,000	
(C2)	Preference share purchase*		2,000
	Shares to be redeemed/purchased		
(D1)	Preference share purchase*	2,000	
(D2)	Bank		2,000
	Payment made to redeem/purchase shares		

*To make it easier to follow, all these examples refer only to the redemption of preference shares. The process is identical whatever the type of shares being redeemed or purchased, only the names of the accounts to be used are different. When ordinary shares are redeemed, they are transferred to a 'share redemption account'. If they are purchased, a 'share purchase account' is used instead of a 'preference share purchase account'.

	Balances before £		Effect Dr £		Cr £	Balances after £
Net assets (except bank)	7,500					7,500
Bank	2,500	(A1)	2,000	(D2)	2,000	2,500
	10,000					10,000
Ordinary share capital	5,000			(B2)	2,000	7,000
Ordinary share applicants	–	(B1)	2,000	(A2)	2,000	–
Preference share capital	2,000	(C1)	2,000			–
Preference share purchase	–	(D1)	2,000	(C2)	2,000	–
Total 'capitals'*	7,000					7,000
Profit and loss	3,000					3,000
	10,000					10,000

*Total 'capitals' remain the same as the preference share capital has been replaced with additional ordinary capital.

Exhibit 6.2 shows the journal entries and the changes to the balance sheet amounts when reserves are used to redeem or purchase shares.

Exhibit 6.2

£2,000 preference shares are redeemed/purchased at par, with no new issue of shares to provide funds for the purpose. Therefore an amount equal to the nominal value of the shares redeemed *must* be transferred from the profit and loss appropriation account to the credit of a capital redemption reserve.

		Dr £	Cr £
(A1)	Preference share capital	2,000	
(A2)	Preference share purchase		2,000
	Shares to be redeemed/purchased		
(B1)	Preference share purchase	2,000	
(B2)	Bank		2,000
	Cash paid as purchase/redemption		
(C1)	Profit and loss appropriation	2,000	
(C2)	Capital redemption reserve		2,000
	Transfer to reserve on redemption of shares		

	Balances before £		Effect Dr £		Cr £	Balances after £
Net assets (except bank)	7,500					7,500
Bank	2,500			(B2)	2,000	500
	10,000					8,000
Ordinary share capital	5,000					5,000
Preference share capital	2,000	(A1)	2,000			–
Preference share purchase	–	(B1)	2,000	(A2)	2,000	–
Capital redemption reserve	–			(C2)	2,000	2,000
Total 'capitals'*	7,000					7,000
Profit and loss	3,000	(C1)	2,000			1,000
	10,000					8,000

*The total 'capitals' (i.e. share capital + non-distributable reserves) remain the same at £7,000.

Exhibit 6.3 shows the journal entries and the changes to the balance sheet amounts when both the Exhibit 6.1 and Exhibit 6.2 approaches are used.

Exhibit 6.3

£2,000 preference shares are redeemed/purchased at par, being £1,200 from issue of ordinary shares at par and partly by using the profit and loss appropriation account balance.

		Dr £	Cr £
(A1)	Bank	1,200	
(A2)	Ordinary share applicants		1,200
	Cash received from applicants		
(B1)	Ordinary share applicants	1,200	
(B2)	Ordinary share capital		1,200
	Ordinary shares allotted		
(C1)	Profit and loss appropriation	800	
(C2)	Capital redemption reserve		800
	Part of redemption/purchase not covered by new issue		
(D1)	Preference share capital	2,000	
(D2)	Preference share purchase		2,000
	Shares being redeemed/purchased		
(E1)	Preference share purchase	2,000	
(E2)	Bank		2,000
	Payment made for redemption/purchase		

	Balances before £		Effect Dr £		Cr £	Balances after £
Net assets (except bank)	7,500					7,500
Bank	2,500	(A1)	1,200	(E2)	2,000	1,700
	10,000					9,200
Ordinary share capital	5,000			(B2)	1,200	6,200
Ordinary share applicants	–	(B1)	1,200	(A2)	1,200	–
Preference share capital	2,000	(D1)	2,000			–
Preference share purchase	–	(E1)	2,000	(D2)	2,000	–
Capital redemption reserve	–			(C2)	800	800
Total 'capitals'*	7,000					7,000
Profit and loss	3,000	(C1)	800			2,200
	10,000					9,200

*Total 'capitals' remain the same.

6.6 Premiums

Another requirement of the Companies Acts is that when shares are being redeemed/purchased at a premium that were *not* originally issued at a premium, then an amount equal to the premium *must* be transferred from the profit and loss appropriation account to the credit of the share purchase/redemption account. As before, this is required so as to maintain total capitals by diverting profits from being distributable to being part of the non-distributable capital.

Exhibit 6.4

£2,000 preference shares which were originally issued at par are redeemed/purchased at a premium of 20 per cent. There is no new issue of shares for the purpose. The ordinary shares were issued at a premium, thus the reason for the share premium account being in existence. However, as it is *not* the ordinary shares which are being redeemed, the share premium *cannot* be used to source the premium paid on the redemption/purchase.

		Dr £	Cr £
(A1)	Preference share capital	2,000	
(A2)	Preference share purchase		2,000
	Shares being redeemed/purchased		
(B1)	Profit and loss appropriation	400	
(B2)	Preference share purchase		400
	Premium on purchase/redemption of shares *not* previously issued at premium		
(C1)	Profit and loss appropriation	2,000	
(C2)	Capital redemption reserve		2,000
	Transfer because shares redeemed/purchased out of distributable profits		
(D1)	Preference share purchase	2,400	
(D2)	Bank		2,400
	Payment on purchase/redemption		

	Balances before £	Effect Dr £		Effect Cr £		Balances after £
Net assets (except bank)	7,500					7,500
Bank	2,500			(D2)	2,400	100
	10,000					7,600
Ordinary share capital	4,500					4,500
Preference share capital	2,000	(A1)	2,000			–
Preference share purchase	–	(D1)	2,400	(A2)	2,000	
				(B2)	400	–
Capital redemption reserve	–			(C2)	2,000	2,000
Share premium	500					500
Total 'capitals'*	7,000					7,000
Profit and loss	3,000	(C1)	2,000			
		(B1)	400			600
	10,000					7,600

*Once again, the total 'capitals' remain the same.

Under the Companies Acts, when shares are being redeemed or purchased at a premium, *and* they were originally issued at a premium, *and* a new issue of shares is being made for the purpose, then the share premium account *can* have an amount calculated as follows transferred to the credit of the share purchase/redemption account. This is shown as (E) below.

Share Premium Account

		£
Balance before new issue	(A)	xxx
Add Premium on new issue	(B)	xxx
Balance after new issue	(C)	xxx
Amount that *may* be transferred is the lesser of:	(E)	
Premiums that were received when it first issued the shares now being redeemed/purchased	(D)	xxx
or		
Balance after new issue above		xxx
Transfer to share purchase/redemption (the lesser of D and C)	(E)	(xxx)
New balance for balance sheet (could be nil)		xxx

Where the amount being deducted (E) is *less* than the premium paid on the *current* redemption or purchase, then an amount equivalent to the difference must be transferred from the debit of the profit and loss appropriation account to the credit of the share purchase/redemption account. (An example of this is shown below in Exhibit 6.5.) This again diverts the appropriate amount of profits away from being distributable.

Exhibit 6.5

£2,000 preference shares of three companies which were originally issued at a premium of 20 per cent are now purchased/redeemed at a premium of 25 per cent. The changes to the share premium account are shown below for the three companies.

● Company 1 issues 2,400 ordinary £1 shares at par.
● Company 2 issues 2,000 ordinary £1 shares at 20 per cent premium.
● Company 3 issues 1,600 ordinary £1 shares at 50 per cent premium.

Share Premium Account

		Company 1 £	Company 2 £	Company 3 £	
Balance before new issue	(A)	150[Note (a)]	400	400	
Premium on new issue		__	400	800	(B)
Balance after new issue	(C)	150	800	1,200	
Amount transferable to share purchase/ redemption is therefore lower of (C) or original premium on issue (£400)		(150)[Note (b)]	(400)[Note (b)]	(400)[Note (b)]	
New balance for balance sheet		–	400	800	

Note (a): In Company 1 it is assumed that, of the original £400 premium, the sum of £250 had been used to issue bonus shares (see Chapter 10).

Note (b): As these figures are less than the premium of £500 *now* being paid, the differences (Company 1 £350; Companies 2 and 3 £100 each) must be transferred from the profit and loss account to the preference share/purchase redemption account.

→ *Journal entries:*

	Company 1 Dr £	Company 1 Cr £	Company 2 Dr £	Company 2 Cr £	Company 3 Dr £	Company 3 Cr £
(A1) Bank	2,400		2,400		2,400	
(A2) Ordinary share applicants		2,400		2,400		2,400
Cash received from applicants						
(B1) Ordinary share applicants	2,400		2,400		2,400	
(B2) Ordinary share capital		2,400		2,000		1,600
(B3) Share premium		–		400		800
Ordinary shares allotted						
(C1) Preference share capital	2,000		2,000		2,000	
(C2) Preference share purchase		2,000		2,000		2,000
Shares being redeemed/purchased						
(D1) Share premium account	150		400		400	
(D2) Preference share purchase		150		400		400
Amount of share premium account used for redemption/purchase						
(E1) Profit and loss	350		100		100	
(E2) Preference share purchase		350		100		100
Excess of premium payable over amount of share premium account usable for the purpose						
(F1) Preference share purchase	2,500		2,500		2,500	
(F2) Bank		2,500		2,500		2,500
Amount paid on redemption/purchase						

Exhibit 6.6

The following balance sheets for the three companies in Exhibit 6.5 are given *before* the purchase/redemption. The balance sheets are then shown *after* purchase/redemption.

Balance Sheets (*before* redemption/purchase)

	Company 1 £	Company 2 £	Company 3 £
Net assets (except bank)	7,500	7,500	7,500
Bank	2,500	2,500	2,500
	10,000	10,000	10,000
Ordinary share capital	4,850	4,600	4,600
Preference share capital	2,000	2,000	2,000
Share premium	150	400	400
	7,000	7,000	7,000
Profit and loss account	3,000	3,000	3,000
	10,000	10,000	10,000

Balance Sheets (*after* redemption/purchase)			
	Company 1 £	Company 2 £	Company 3 £
Net assets (except bank)	7,500	7,500	7,500
Bank	2,400	2,400	2,400
	9,900	9,900	9,900
Ordinary share capital	7,250	6,600	6,200
Share premium	–	400	800
	7,250	7,000	7,000
Profit and loss account	2,650	2,900	2,900
	9,900	9,900	9,900

6.7 Private companies: redemption or purchase of shares out of capital

The Companies Act 1981 introduced a new power for a *private* company to redeem/purchase its own shares where *either* it has insufficient distributable profits for the purpose *or* it cannot raise the amount required by a new issue. Previously it would have had to apply to the court for **capital reduction** (which you will learn about in Chapter 10). The 1981 legislation made it far easier to achieve the same objectives, in terms of both time and expense.

The full details of the various matters which must be dealt with by private companies who pursue this option are beyond the scope of this textbook. If you wish to go into this topic in greater detail, you will need to consult a book on company law. For our purposes, a very brief outline is as follows:

1 The private company must be authorised to redeem or purchase its own shares out of capital by its Articles of Association.
2 **Permissible capital payment** is the amount by which the price of redemption or purchase exceeds the aggregate of (*a*) the company's distributable profits and (*b*) the proceeds of any new issue. This means that a private company must use its available profits and any share proceeds before making a payment out of capital. (This is dealt with in greater detail in the next section.)
3 Directors must certify that, after the permissible capital payment, the company will be able to carry on as a going concern during the next twelve months, and be able to pay its debts immediately after the payment and also during the next twelve months.
4 The company's auditors make a satisfactory report.

Activity 6.3 Why do you think the rules are less restrictive for private companies?

6.8 Permissible capital payments

1 Where the permissible capital payment is *less* than the nominal value of shares redeemed/ purchased, the amount of the difference *shall* be transferred to the capital redemption reserve from the profit and loss account or other reserve, such as a repairs reserve.
2 Where the permissible capital payment is *greater* than the nominal value of shares redeemed/ purchased, *any* non-distributable reserves (e.g. share premium account, capital redemption reserve, revaluation reserve, etc.) or fully paid share capital can be reduced by the excess.

This can be illustrated by taking two companies, R and S, with similar account balances *before* the purchase/redemption, which are redeeming their shares on different terms.

(*Note*: To ensure maximum clarity, the values used have been kept unrealistically low.)

Exhibit 6.7

Company R	Before £	Dr £			Cr £	After £
Net assets (except bank)	2,500					2,500
Bank	7,500			(B2)	4,000	3,500
	10,000					6,000
Ordinary shares	1,000					1,000
Preference shares	4,000	(A1)	4,000			–
Non-distributable reserves	2,000					2,000
Capital redemption reserve				(C2)	3,000	3,000
Preference share purchase	–	(B1)	4,000	(A2)	4,000	
	7,000					
Profit and loss	3,000	(C1)	3,000			
	10,000					6,000

The preference shares were redeemed at par, £4,000. No new issue was made.
(A1) and (A2) represent transfer of shares redeemed/purchased.
(B1) and (B2) represent payment to shareholders.

Therefore pay	4,000
Less Profit and loss account	(3,000)
Permissible capital payment	1,000
Nominal amount of shares redeemed/purchased	4,000
Less Permissible capital payment	(1,000)
Deficiency to transfer to capital redemption reserve (C1 and C2)	3,000

The steps taken were:	Dr	Cr
(A1) Preference shares	4,000	
(A2) Preference share purchase		4,000
(B1) Preference share purchase	4,000	
(B2) Bank		4,000
(C1) Profit and loss	3,000	
(C2) Capital redemption reserve		3,000

Company S	Before £	Dr £			Cr £	After £
Net assets (except bank)	2,500					2,500
Bank	7,500			(D2)	7,200	300
	10,000					2,800
Ordinary share capital	1,000					1,000
Preference shares	4,000	(A1)	4,000			–
Non-distributable reserves	2,000	(C1)	200			1,800
Capital redemption reserve	–					–
Preference share purchase		(D1)	7,200	(A2)	4,000	
				(B2)	3,000	
				(C2)	200	
	7,000					2,800
Profit and loss	3,000	(B1)	3,000			–
	10,000					2,800

The preference shares were redeemed/purchased at a premium of 80%. No new issue was made.

(A1) and (A2) represent shares redeemed/purchased.
(B1) and (B2) are transfers to redemption/purchase account of part of source of funds.
(D1) and (D2) are payment to shareholders.

Therefore pay		7,200
Less Profit and loss account		(3,000)
Permissible capital payment		4,200
Permissible capital payment		4,200
Less Nominal amount redeemed/purchased		(4,000)
Excess from *any* non-distributable reserves (or capital) (C1 and C2)		200

The steps taken were:	Dr	Cr
(A1) Preference shares	4,000	
(A2) Preference share purchase		4,000
(B1) Profit and loss	3,000	
(B2) Preference share purchase		3,000
(C1) Non-distributable reserves	200	
(C2) Preference share purchase		200
(D1) Preference share purchase	7,200	
(D2) Bank		7,200

6.9 Cancellation of shares purchased/redeemed

All shares purchased/redeemed must be cancelled immediately. They cannot be kept by the company and later traded.

6.10 Redemption of debentures

Unless they are stated to be irredeemable, debentures are redeemed according to the terms of the issue. The necessary funds to finance the redemption may be from:

(*a*) an issue of shares or debentures for the purpose;
(*b*) the resources of the company.

As (a) resembles the redemption of redeemable preference shares, you won't be surprised to learn that no transfer of profits from the profit and loss account to a reserve account is needed. However, when financed as in (b), it is good accounting practice, although not legally necessary, to divert profits from being used as dividends by transferring an amount equal to the nominal value redeemed from the profit and loss account to a reserve account.

Redemption may be done in one of three ways:

(*a*) by annual transfers out of profits;
(*b*) by purchase in the open market when the price is favourable, i.e. when it is less than the price which will have to be paid if the company waits until the last date by which redemption has to be carried out;
(*c*) in a lump sum to be provided by the accumulation of a **sinking fund**.

These three approaches can now be examined in more detail.

1 Redeemed by transfers out of profits

(a) When debentures are redeemed at a premium

In this case, the source of the funds with which the premium is paid should be taken to be (i) the share premium account, or if this does not exist, or the premium paid is in excess of the balance on the share premium account, then any part not covered by a share premium account is deemed to come from (ii) the profit and loss appropriation account. Exhibit 6.8 shows the effect on a balance sheet where there is no share premium account, while Exhibit 6.9 illustrates the case when a share premium account is in existence with a balance large enough to source the premium.

Exhibit 6.8

Starting with the *before* balance sheet, £400 of the debentures are redeemed at a premium of 20 per cent, i.e. £80.

(*Note:* As before, the values involved have been kept unrealistically low for greater clarity.)

Balance Sheets

	Before	+ or –	After
	£	£	£
Other assets	12,900		12,900
Bank	3,400	−480 (A)	2,920
	16,300		15,820
Share capital	10,000		10,000
Debenture redemption reserve	–	+400 (B)	400
Debentures	2,000	−400 (A)	1,600
Profit and loss	4,300	−400 (B)	
		−80 (A)	3,820
	16,300		15,820

Exhibit 6.9

Starting with the *before* balance sheet, £400 of the debentures are redeemed at a premium of 20 per cent, i.e. £80.

Balance Sheets

	Before	+ or –	After
	£	£	£
Other assets	13,500		13,500
Bank	3,400	−480 (A)	2,920
	16,900		16,420
Share capital	10,000		10,000
Share premium	600	−80 (A)	520
Debenture redemption reserve	–	+400 (B)	400
Debentures	2,000	−400 (A)	1,600
Profit and loss	4,300	−400 (B)	3,900
	16,900		16,420

In both Exhibits 6.8 and 6.9 the balance on the debenture redemption reserve account is increased by the nominal value of the debentures redeemed each year. Any element of the redemption sourced by the share premium account is entered as a debit to that account and is not included in the debenture redemption reserve.

When the whole issue of debentures has been redeemed, the balance on the debenture redemption reserve account is transferred to the credit of a general reserve account. It is, after all, an accumulation of undistributed profits.

(b) When debentures are redeemed but originally issued at a discount

The discount on issue was given in order to attract investors to buy the debentures and is, therefore, as much a cost of borrowing as is debenture interest. The discount therefore needs to be written off during the life of the debentures. It might be more rational to write it off to the profit and loss account but accounting custom, as permitted by law, would first of all write it off against any share premium account and, secondly, against the profit and loss appropriation account.

The amounts written off over the life of the debentures are:

(*a*) equal annual amounts over the life of the debentures; or
(*b*) in proportion to the debenture debt outstanding at the start of each year. Exhibit 6.10 shows such a situation.

Exhibit 6.10

£30,000 debentures are issued at a discount of 5 per cent. They are repayable at par over five years at the rate of £6,000 per annum.

Year	Outstanding at start of each year	Proportion written off		Amount
	£			£
1	30,000	$30/90 \times £1,500$	=	500
2	24,000	$24/90 \times £1,500$	=	400
3	18,000	$18/90 \times £1,500$	=	300
4	12,000	$12/90 \times £1,500$	=	200
5	6,000	$6/90 \times £1,500$	=	100
	90,000			1,500

---

2 Redeemed by purchase in the open market

A sum equal to the cash actually paid on redemption is transferred from the profit and loss account to the debenture redemption reserve account. The sum actually paid will have been credited to the bank account and debited to the debentures account.

Any discount (or profit) on purchase will be transferred to a reserve account. Any premium (or loss) on purchase will be deemed to come out of such a reserve account, or if no such account exists or if it is insufficient, then it will be deemed to come out of the share premium account. Failing the existence of these accounts any loss must come out of the profit and loss account. It may seem that purchase would not be a good idea if the debentures had to be redeemed at a premium. However, it would still be opportune if the premium paid was not as high as the premium to be paid if the final date for redemption was awaited.

3 Redemption of debentures sourced from a sinking fund

Where debentures are issued which are redeemable (which most are), consideration should be given to the availability of cash funds at the time.

This method involves the investment of cash outside the business. The aim is to make a regular investment of money which, together with the accumulated interest or dividends, is sufficient to finance the redemption of the debentures at the requisite time.

As each period's interest (or dividend) from the investment is received, it is immediately reinvested to earn more interest. In addition, an equal amount is invested each period.

If, for example, the money is to be invested at 5 per cent per annum, and the debenture is £500 to be redeemed in five years' time, how much should be invested each year? If £100 were invested at the start of each year for five years, the interest earned would mean that more than £500 was set aside by the end of the five-year period. Therefore, an amount less than £100 per annum is needed. The exact amount can be calculated by the use of the compound interest formula. Chapter 45 illustrates how the amount needed can be calculated. As these calculations are left until later in this book, a summarised set of tables is shown below in Exhibit 6.11.

Exhibit 6.11

	Annual sinking fund instalments to provide £1				
Years	3%	3½%	4%	4½%	5%
3	0.323530	0.321933	0.320348	0.318773	0.317208
4	0.239028	0.237251	0.235490	0.233744	0.232012
5	0.188354	0.186481	0.184627	0.182792	0.180975
6	0.154597	0.152668	0.150761	0.148878	0.147017
7	0.130506	0.128544	0.126609	0.124701	0.122819
8	0.112456	0.110476	0.108527	0.106609	0.104721
9	0.098433	0.096446	0.094493	0.092574	0.090690
10	0.087230	0.085241	0.083291	0.081378	0.079504

The table gives the amount required to provide £1 at the end of the relevant number of years at a given rate of interest. To provide £1,000 multiply by 1,000; to provide for £4,986 multiply by 4,986; and so on.

Now, let's look at the double entries required when a **sinking fund** is being used.

6.11 Double entries for a sinking fund

When the annual instalment has been found, the double entry needed each year is:

1 Annual instalment:
   Dr Profit and loss appropriation (*or* profit and loss – *see* note)
      Cr Debenture redemption reserve
2 Investment of 1st instalment:
   Dr Debenture sinking fund investment
      Cr Bank
3 Interest/dividends on sinking fund investment:
   Dr Bank
      Cr Debenture redemption reserve
4 Investment of second and later instalments (these consist of equal annual instalment plus interest/dividend just received):
   Dr Debenture sinking fund investment
      Cr Bank

Note: In all the examples so far we have made transfers from the profit and loss account; these will normally be shown in the note on movements in shareholders' funds. While it is understandable that many books state that the debit of these entries is made to the profit and loss appropriation account, this is only the case for the financial statements prepared for internal use – this has been the custom and practice for many years. However, under UK GAAP, this account may exist but does not have a place in published financial statements. Nevertheless, many companies do have a profit and loss appropriation account in their ledger and many examiners expect use of a T-account of that name to be used for the entries. For this reason, the account is shown in Exhibit 6.12; it could just as easily have been entitled 'profit and loss'!

Exhibit 6.12

Debentures of £10,000 are issued on 1 January 2001. They are redeemable five years later on 31 December 2005 on identical terms (i.e. £10,000). The company therefore decides to set aside an equal annual amount which, at an interest rate of 5 per cent, will provide £10,000 on 31 December 2005. According to the table in Exhibit 6.11, £0.180975 invested annually at 5 per cent will provide £1 in five years' time. Therefore, £0.180975 × 10,000 will be needed annually = £1,809.75

Profit and Loss Appropriation

		£			
2001 Debenture redemption reserve	(B)	1,809.75			
2002 Debenture redemption reserve	(E)	1,809.75			
2003 Debenture redemption reserve	(H)	1,809.75			
2004 Debenture redemption reserve	(K)	1,809.75			
2005 Debenture redemption reserve	(N)	1,809.75	2005 Debenture redemption reserve	(R)	10,000

Debenture Redemption Reserve

2001		£	2001			£
Dec 31 Balance c/d		1,809.75	Dec 31 Profit and loss appropriation	(B)		1,809.75
2002			2002			
Dec 31 Balance c/d		3,709.99	Jan 1 Balance b/d			1,809.75
			Dec 31 Bank interest (5% of £1,809.75)	(D)		90.49
			Dec 31 Profit and loss appropriation	(E)		1,809.75
		3,709.99				3,709.99
2003			2003			
Dec 31 Balance c/d		5,705.23	Jan 1 Balance b/d			3,709.99
			Dec 31 Bank interest (5% of £3,709.99)	(G)		185.49
			Dec 31 Profit and loss appropriation	(H)		1,809.75
		5,705.23				5,705.23
2004			2004			
Dec 31 Balance c/d		7,800.24	Jan 1 Balance b/d			5,705.23
			Dec 31 Bank interest (5% of £5,705.23)	(J)		285.26
			Dec 31 Profit and loss appropriation	(K)		1,809.75
		7,800.24				7,800.24
2005			2005			
Dec 31 Profit and loss appropriation (Reserve no longer required)	(R)	10,000.00	Jan 1 Balance b/d			7,800.24
			Dec 31 Bank interest (5% of £7,800.24)	(M)		390.01
			Dec 31 Profit and loss appropriation	(N)		1,809.75
		10,000.00				10,000.00

Debenture Sinking Fund Investment

2001			£				£
Dec	31	Bank	(C)	1,809.75			
2002							
Dec	31	Bank Note (a)	(F)	1,900.24			
2003							
Dec	31	Bank Note (b)	(I)	1,995.24			
2004							
Dec	31	Bank Note (c)	(L)	2,095.01			
2005					2005		
Dec	31	Bank Note (d)	(O)	2,199.76	Dec 31 Bank	(P)	10,000.00
				10,000.00			10,000.00

Notes:

Cash invested

	(a)	(b)	(c)	(d)
	£	£	£	£
The yearly instalment	1,809.75	1,809.75	1,809.75	1,809.75
Add interest received on sinking fund balance	90.49	185.49	285.26	309.01
	1,900.24	1,995.24	2,095.01	2,199.76

Bank (extracts)

2001				£	2001				£
Jan	1	Debentures (issued)	(A)	10,000.00	Dec	31	Debenture sinking fund investment	(C)	1,809.75
2002					2002				
Dec	31	Debenture redemption reserve (interest on investment)	(E)	90.49	Dec	31	Debenture sinking fund investment	(F)	1,900.24
2003					2003				
Dec	31	Debenture redemption reserve (interest on investment)	(G)	185.49	Dec	31	Debenture sinking fund investment	(I)	1,995.24
2004					2004				
Dec	31	Debenture redemption reserve (interest on investment)	(J)	285.26	Dec	31	Debenture sinking fund investment	(L)	2,095.01
2005					2005				
Dec	31	Debenture redemption reserve (interest on investment)	(M)	390.01	Dec	31	Debenture sinking fund	(O)	2,199.76
	31	Debenture sinking fund	(P)	10,000.00		31	Debenture (redemption)	(Q)	10,000.00
				20,000.00					20,000.00

Debentures

2005				£	2001				£
Dec	31	Bank (redemption)	(Q)	10,000.00	Jan	1	Bank	(A)	10,000.00

The final payment into the sinking fund of £2,199.76 would probably not physically happen unless it was a condition of the investment that a fifth deposit was made before the amount invested could be withdrawn. (There is no point in paying money out of the bank account into the sinking fund and then, on the same day, withdrawing it from the sinking fund and redepositing it in the bank account.) The entries are presented in this way so as to make it clear that the entire £10,000 has been set aside over the five years. If no transfer was shown (of the £2,199.76), the balance on the sinking fund would be £7,800.24 and this amount would be transferred to the bank account. The amount available in the bank account would still be £10,000.

Sometimes debentures bought in the open market are not cancelled but are kept 'alive' and are treated as investments of the sinking fund. The annual appropriation of profits is credited to the sinking fund account, while the amount expended on the purchase of the debentures is debited to the sinking fund investment account. Interest on such debentures is debited to the profit and loss account and credited to the sinking fund account. Thus the interest, so far as the sinking fund account is concerned, is treated in the same fashion as if it was cash actually received by the business from an outside investment. The sum expended on investments will then be equal to the annual appropriation + the interest on investments actually received + the interest on debentures kept in hand.

6.12 Convertible loan stock

Particularly in periods of high inflation, but at other times too, the attraction to lenders to provide funds at reasonable rates of interest is much reduced as they stand to lose significantly on the real value of the funds lent, since the repayment of the loan is normally fixed at its original cash value. One way of attracting lenders is to give them the right to convert their loan into shares. The right can usually be exercised at a given rate of conversion from loan to shares, once a year over a stated length of time. The value of the conversion right will depend on the performance of the shares in the market. If the shares increase in value significantly, the conversion value will increase and attract the lender to opt into shares. If the shares do badly, the lender can retain the loan stock with its higher levels of security.

The accounting entries are the same as those described in Section 6.10 for the redemption of debentures. The value of the shares issued to meet the redemption will be fixed under the terms of the original agreement by reference to their market prices at specified dates.

Learning outcomes

You should now have learnt:

1 The difference between the terms 'redemption' and 'purchase' in the context of shares and debentures.

2 How to make the accounting entries relating to the redemption or purchase by a company of its own shares.

3 The accounting entries made on the redemption by a company of its own shares are the same as when it purchases its own shares, except that the word 'redeemable' will appear as the first word in the title of the accounts for shares that are redeemed.

4 In order to protect creditors, companies *must* still have irredeemable shares in issue after undertaking any purchase or redemption of their own shares.

5 A company cannot redeem or purchase its own shares unless they are fully paid.

6 The rules on reserves to use when purchasing or issuing their own shares at a premium are less strict for private companies.

7 How to make the accounting entries relating to the redemption or purchase by a company of its own debentures.

8 Debentures are redeemed according to the terms of their issue.

Answers to activities

6.1 Apart from moving into line with the rest of Europe, the restriction that remained (of having one member, i.e. shareholder) minimised the risk of abuse of creditors, which was the main reason for having the rule preventing purchase and redemption in the first place.

6.2 If this occurred, it would suggest that the company issued them only to have free use of the funds they realised for a short time. In effect, they were simply a form of interest-free loan. By requiring that shares be fully paid before being redeemed or purchased back by the company, the possibility that companies would engage in this form of sharp practice is minimised.

6.3 Private companies are much smaller than public ones. Their shares are often held by a far smaller group of shareholders, often all known to each other. There is not, therefore, the same need to protect shareholders, but there is often a greater need to assist shareholders wishing to reduce their shareholdings. Private companies also tend to have far smaller and less extensive groups of creditors in need of protection. If you refer back to the advantages listed in Section 6.2, you can see why it is important that private companies have greater flexibility in this respect than public ones.

Review questions

6.1 Exercises (a) to (e) are based on the following balance sheet.

RSV Ltd
Balance Sheet

	£
Net assets (except bank)	20,000
Bank	13,000
	33,000
Preference share capital	5,000
Ordinary share capital	15,000
Share premium	2,000
	22,000
Profit and loss	11,000
	33,000

Note also that each of exercises (a) to (e) is independent of any other. The exercises are not cumulative.

Required:
(a) RSV Ltd redeems £5,000 preference shares at par, a new issue of £5,000 ordinary shares at par being made for the purpose. Show the balance sheet after completion of these transactions. Workings are to be shown as journal entries.
(b) RSV Ltd redeems £5,000 preference shares at par, with no new issue of shares to provide funds. Show the balance sheet after completing the transaction. Workings: show journal entries.
(c) RSV Ltd redeems £5,000 preference shares at par. To help finance this an issue of £1,500 ordinary shares at par is effected. Show the balance sheet after these transactions have been completed; also show the necessary journal entries.
(d) RSV Ltd redeems £5,000 preference shares at a premium of 25 per cent. There is no new issue of shares for the purpose. In this question the share premium account is taken as being from the issue of ordinary shares some years ago. Show the balance sheet after these transactions have been completed, and the supporting journal entries.
(e) RSV Ltd redeems £5,000 preference shares at a premium of 40 per cent. There is an issue of £7,000 ordinary shares at par for the purpose. The preference shares had originally been issued at a premium of 30 per cent. Show the balance sheet after these transactions have been completed, and also the supporting journal entries.

6.2A Exercises (a) to (e) are based on the following balance sheet.

BAR Ltd
Balance Sheet

	£
Net assets (except bank)	31,000
Bank	16,000
	47,000
Preference share capital	8,000
Ordinary share capital	20,000
Share premium	4,000
	32,000
Profit and loss	15,000
	47,000

Note also that exercises (a) to (e) are independent of each other. They are not cumulative.

Required:
(a) BAR Ltd purchases £10,000 of its own ordinary share capital at par. To help finance this £7,000 preference shares are issued at par. Show the necessary journal entries and the balance sheet after the transactions have been completed.
(b) BAR Ltd purchases £12,000 of its own ordinary shares at a premium of 20 per cent. No new issue of shares is made for the purpose. It is assumed that the share premium account is in respect of the issue of preference shares some years before. Show the balance sheet after the transactions have been completed, and also the supporting journal entries.
(c) BAR Ltd purchases all the preference share capital at par. These shares were not originally redeemable preference shares. There is no new issue of shares to provide funds. Show the requisite journal entries, and the closing balance sheet when the transaction has been completed.
(d) BAR Ltd purchases £12,000 of its own ordinary shares at par, a new issue of £12,000 preference shares at par being made for the purpose. Show the journal entries needed and the balance sheet after completing these transactions.
(e) BAR Ltd purchases £6,000 ordinary shares at a premium of 50 per cent. They had originally been issued at a premium of 20 per cent. There is an issue of £10,000 preference shares at par for the purpose. Show the amended balance sheet, together with the journal entries.

6.3 A company's balance sheet appears as follows:

	£
Net assets (except bank)	40,000
Bank	48,000
	88,000
Preference share capital	20,000
Ordinary share capital	50,000
Non-distributable reserves	10,000
	80,000
Profit and loss	8,000
	88,000

Required:
(a) If £10,000 of the ordinary shares were purchased at par, there being no new issue of shares for the purpose, show the journal entries to record the transactions and the amended balance sheet.
(b) If, instead of (a), £10,000 ordinary shares were purchased at a premium of 100 per cent, there being no new issue of shares for the purpose, show the journal entries to record the transactions and the amended balance sheet.

→ **6.4A** Debentures of £30,000 are issued on 1 January 2003. Redemption is to take place, on equal terms, four years later. The company decides to put aside an equal amount to be invested at 5 per cent which will provide £30,000 on maturity. Tables show that £0.232012 invested annually will produce £1 in four years' time.

You are required to show:
(a) debenture redemption reserve account
(b) debenture sinking fund investment account
(c) debentures account
(d) profit and loss account extracts.

6.5 Some years ago M plc had issued £375,000 of 10 per cent debentures 2006/2010 at par. The terms of the issue allow the company the right to repurchase these debentures for cancellation at or below par, with an option to redeem, at a premium of 1 per cent, on 30 September 2006. To exercise this option the company must give three months' notice, which it duly did on 30 June 2006 indicating its intention to redeem all the debentures outstanding at 30 September 2006.

M plc had established a sinking fund designed to accumulate the sum of £378,750 by 30 September 2006 and had appropriated profits annually and invested these, together with the interest from such investments and the profits made on any realisations from time to time. A special No. 2 bank account was established specifically to deal with the receipts and payments relating to the debentures and the sinking fund.

By 30 June 2006 annual contributions amounting to £334,485, together with the interest on the sinking fund investments of £39,480, had all been invested except for £2,475 which remained in the No. 2 bank account at that date.

The only investments sold, prior to 30 June 2006, had cost £144,915 and realised £147,243. This was used to repurchase debentures with a par value of £150,000.

Transactions occurring between 1 July and 30 September 2006 were:

(i) interest received on the sinking fund investments:

7 July	£1,756
13 September	£1,455

(ii) proceeds from the sale of investments:

2 August	£73,215 (book value was £69,322)
25 September	£160,238 (remaining investments)

(iii) redemption of all the debentures, on 30 September, with the exception of £15,000 held by B Limited. The company had received notice of a garnishee order.*
(iv) M plc deposited with the W Bank plc the sum of £15,150 on 30 September 2006.

You are to ignore debenture interest and income tax.

You are required, from the information given above, to prepare the ledger accounts (including the No. 2 bank account) in the books of M plc for the period 30 June to 30 September 2006, showing the transfer of the final balances to the appropriate accounts.

Note – Garnishee order
This order, issued by the court, instructs M plc not to release the money owing to B Limited until directed by the court to do so.

(*Chartered Institute of Management Accountants*)

6.6A The following information relates to White Rabbit Trading plc:

Summarised Balance Sheet as at 31 January 2007

	£000
Fixed assets	2,400
Investments	120
Net current assets	1,880
	4,400

Financed by:	£000
Capital and reserves	
Ordinary shares of 50p each fully paid	2,000
Redeemable shares of £1 each (2007/2011)	500
Share premium	200
Revaluation surplus	400
Profit and loss account	900
	4,000
Long-term liabilities	
8% debentures (2007/2010)	400
	4,400

On 1 February 2007 the company closed the list of applications for 400,000 ordinary shares at a premium of 50p. The shares were to be paid for as follows: 60p on application, 25p on allotment and 15p on the first and final call, which was to be made on 1 May 2007. A total of £1,320,000 was received, the shares were allotted and £1,032,000 was returned to unsuccessful applicants. The call money was received by 31 May from all shareholders, with the exception of two shareholders, one of whom had been allotted 500 shares. The other subscriber for 100 shares still owed £25 for allotment in addition to the call money. Eventually both lots of shares were forfeited and reissued to an existing shareholder for a payment of £500 which was duly received.

At a board meeting on 15 February 2007 the directors decided to make a fresh issue of 500,000 £1 redeemable shares at a premium of 60p, and to redeem all of the existing redeemable shares at a premium of 40p. The shares had originally been issued for £1.20 each. All moneys due on application were duly received by 31 March 2007, and the redemption took place on 6 April 2007.

In January 2005 White Rabbit Trading plc had purchased, for cash, 80,000 25p ordinary shares in March Hares Ltd for £25,000, and this is included in investments on the balance sheet at 31 January 2007. On 1 April 2007 the company purchased 400,000 out of a total issue of 500,000 25p ordinary shares in March Hares Ltd, by exchanging 200,000 of its own ordinary shares.

The 8 per cent debentures were redeemed on 15 May 2007 at a 10 per cent premium, and on the same date £500,000 7 per cent debentures (2010/2013) were issued at a discount of 5 per cent.

Required:
Show the full journal entries to record the above events, including cash/bank transactions, in the books of White Rabbit Trading plc.

(*Association of Chartered Certified Accountants*)

6.7 During the year to 30 September 2009, Popham plc issued 100,000 £1 ordinary shares. The terms of the offer were as follows:

2009		£
31 March	on application	0.30 (including the premium)
30 April	on allotment	0.70
30 June	first and final call	0.20

Applications were received for 200,000 shares. The directors decided to allot the shares on the basis of 1 for every 2 shares applied for and apply the excess application money received against the amount due on allotment.

→   All amounts due on application and allotment were received on the due dates, with the exception of one shareholder who had been allotted 10,000 shares, and who defaulted on the first and final call. These shares were forfeited on 31 July 2009, and reissued on 31 August 2009 at a price of £1.10 per share.

Required:
Write up the above details in the books of account of Popham plc using the following ledger accounts:
(*i*)   application and allotment
(*ii*) first and final call
(*iii*) investment – own shares.

(*Association of Accounting Technicians*)

6.8A Alas plc has an authorised share capital of 150,000 ordinary shares of £10 each. Upon incorporation, 50,000 shares were issued and fully paid. The company has decided to issue another 50,000 shares, the details of which are as follows:

	Per share £
Upon:	
Application	3
Allotment (including a premium of £5)	8
First call	2
Final call	2
	15

Additional information:
1 Applications were received for 85,000 shares out of which 10,000 shares were rejected, the cash being returned immediately to the applicants. The remaining applicants were allotted two shares for every three shares applied for, and the surplus application money was carried forward to the allotment stage.
2 The total amount due on allotment was duly received.
3 All cash due at the first call was received, but the final call resulted in 5,000 shares being forfeited. These shares were subsequently reissued at a price of £13 per share.

Required:
Compile the following ledger accounts:
(*a*) ordinary share capital
(*b*) ordinary share applications
(*c*) ordinary share allotment
(*d*) share premium
(*e*) ordinary share first call
(*f*) ordinary share final call
(*g*) investments – own shares (originally known as the forfeited shares account).

6.9 The following information relates to Grigg plc:

1 On 1 April 2008 the company had £100,000 10 per cent debentures in issue. The interest on these debentures is paid on 30 September and 31 March.
2 The debenture redemption fund balance (relating to the redemption of these debentures) at 1 April 2008 was £20,000. This fund is being built up by annual appropriations of £2,000. The annual appropriation (along with any dividends or interest on the investments) is invested on 31 March.
3 Debenture redemption fund investments can be realised at any time in order to purchase debentures in the open market either at or below par value. Such debentures are then cancelled.
4 On 31 December 2008 £10,000 of investments were sold for £11,400 and the proceeds were used to purchase debentures with a par value of £12,000.
5 Dividends and interest on redemption fund investments during the year to 31 March 2009 amounted to £1,600.
6 The cost of dealing with the above matters and any taxation effects may be ignored.

Required:
Write up the following ledger accounts for the year to 31 March 2009:
(a) 10 per cent debentures
(b) debenture redemption fund
(c) debenture redemption fund investments
(d) debenture redemption
(e) debenture interest.

Note: The debenture redemption fund is sometimes known as a **sinking fund**.

You can find a range of additional self-test questions, as well as material to help you with your studies, on the website that accompanies this book at **www.pearsoned.co.uk/wood**

Limited companies taking over other businesses

Learning objectives

After you have studied this chapter, you should be able to:

- explain how goodwill may arise on the purchase of a business
- explain the difference between goodwill and negative goodwill
- record the accounting entries relating to a limited company taking over another business
- describe the difference in the accounting treatment of takeovers by limited companies of sole traders, partnerships and limited companies
- describe the two methods whereby a limited company may take over another limited company
- deal with pre-incorporation profits and losses
- deal with formation expenses

Introduction

In this chapter, you'll learn about goodwill and negative goodwill and you will learn how to record the purchase of a business in the books of the purchaser using a variety of methods of paying for the purchase. You will also learn about how to deal with pre-incorporation losses and profits and formation expenses.

7.1 Background

From time to time, limited companies take over other businesses. The purchase may be: (i) in cash; (ii) by giving the company's shares to the sellers; (iii) by giving the company's debentures; or (iv) by any combination of the three.

Never be mistaken into thinking that because the assets bought are shown in the selling entity's books at one value, the purchasing company must record the assets taken over in its own books at the same value. The values shown in the purchasing company's books are those values at which the company is buying the assets (known as their 'fair' values), such values being frequently quite different from those shown in the selling firm's books.

For example, the selling entity may have bought premises many years earlier for £100,000 which are now worth £250,000. The company buying the premises will obviously have to pay £250,000 for the premises and it is this value that is recorded in the buying company's books. Alternatively, if its value has fallen, the value at which it is recorded in the buying company's books would be less than that shown in the selling entity's books.

The recording of the transactions is the simple part. The negotiations that take place before agreement is reached, and the various strategies undertaken by the various parties, are a study in themselves. The accounting entries are, in effect, the tip of the iceberg, i.e. that part of the whole affair which is seen by the eventual reader of the financial statements.

Where the total purchase consideration exceeds the total value of the identifiable assets as recorded in the ledger of the purchasing company, the excess is the **goodwill** and is entered as a debit in a goodwill account in the purchasing company's books.

Should the total purchase consideration be less than the values of the identifiable assets recorded in the purchasing company's ledger, the difference is known as **negative goodwill** and is entered as a credit in the goodwill account. (**Note: the goodwill amount is** *always* **shown in the assets section of the balance sheet, even when it has a credit balance.**)

Activity 7.1 Why do you think the amount paid for a business may be different from the total value of its net assets as shown in its financial statements?

Let's now look at how business takeovers are recorded in the accounting records of the purchaser.

7.2 Taking over a sole trader

We'll start with the takeover of the simplest sort of business unit, that of a sole trader. Some of the balance sheets shown will be deliberately simplified so that the principles involved are not hidden behind a mass of complicated calculations.

Exhibit 7.1

Earl Ltd is to buy the business of M Kearney. The purchase consideration is to be £60,000 cash, the company placing the following values on the assets taken over – machinery £30,000; stock £10,000. The goodwill must therefore be £20,000, because the total price of £60,000 exceeds the sum of the values of the machinery £30,000 and stock £10,000 by £20,000. The company's balance sheets before and after the takeover are shown below:

M Kearney
Balance Sheet

	£
Machinery	30,000
Stock	10,000
	40,000
Capital	40,000

Earl Ltd
Balance Sheets

	Before £	+ or – £	After £
Goodwill		+20,000	20,000
Machinery	110,000	+30,000	140,000
Stock	50,000	+10,000	60,000
Bank	90,000	–60,000	30,000
	250,000		250,000
Share capital	200,000		200,000
Profit and loss	50,000		50,000
	250,000		250,000

If shares had been issued to Kearney instead of cash, the new balance sheet of Earl Ltd would be as above except that bank would be £90,000 and share capital would be £260,000, as shown in Exhibit 7.2:

Exhibit 7.2

Earl Ltd
Balance Sheets

	Before £	+ or − £	After £
Goodwill		+20,000	20,000
Machinery	110,000	+30,000	140,000
Stock	50,000	+10,000	60,000
Bank	90,000		90,000
	250,000		310,000
Share capital	200,000	+60,000	260,000
Profit and loss	50,000		50,000
	250,000		310,000

Exhibit 7.3

If the purchase had been made by issuing 50,000 shares of £1 each at a premium of 50 per cent, then the total consideration would have been worth £75,000 which, if the assets of £40,000 are deducted, leaves goodwill of £35,000. The balance sheets would then be:

Earl Ltd
Balance Sheets

	Before £	+ or − £	After £
Goodwill		+35,000	35,000
Machinery	110,000	+30,000	140,000
Stocks	50,000	+10,000	60,000
Bank	90,000		90,000
	250,000		325,000
Share capital	200,000	+50,000	250,000
Share premium		+25,000	25,000
Profit and loss	50,000		50,000
	250,000		325,000

You should now realise just how straightforward the balance sheet changes are. You simply adjust the balance sheet for the assets (and liabilities) acquired and for the items used in order to complete the purchase. Whatever the difference is between the two parts of the balance sheet, must be the goodwill.

In each of Exhibits 7.1 to 7.4 it has been assumed that all transactions were started and completed at the same time. In reality, an intermediary account would first be created but then closed almost immediately when the purchase consideration was handed over.

Taking Exhibit 7.3 as an example, a credit entry will be made in the share capital account and another in the share premium account, plus debit entries in the goodwill, machinery and stock accounts. Think about this. Shares cannot be issued to goodwill, machinery or stocks. They have, in fact, been issued to M Kearney. This means that there should have been an account for M Kearney involved in the double entries, but the balance on it was cancelled when the purchase was completed. The actual accounts used for Exhibit 7.3 in the books of Earl Ltd were:

Share Premium

			£
		M Kearney	25,000

Share Capital

	£		£
Balance c/d	250,000	Balance b/d	200,000
		M Kearney	50,000
	250,000		250,000
		Balance b/d	250,000

Profit and Loss

			£
		Balance b/d	50,000

Goodwill

	£		
M Kearney	35,000		

Machinery

	£		£
Balance b/d	110,000	Balance c/d	140,000
M Kearney	30,000		
	140,000		140,000
Balance b/d	140,000		

Stock

	£		£
Balance b/d	50,000	Balance c/d	60,000
M Kearney	10,000		
	60,000		60,000
Balance b/d	60,000		

(The £10,000 may have been entered in the purchases account. However, Kearney's £10,000 stock obviously increased the actual amount of stock held after the takeover of Kearney's business.)

Bank

	£		
Balance b/d	90,000		

M Kearney

	£		£
Consideration passing:		Assets taken over:	
Share capital	50,000	Goodwill	35,000
Share premium	25,000	Machinery	30,000
		Stock	10,000
	75,000		75,000

Some accountants use a business purchase account instead of a personal account such as that of M Kearney.

Sometimes the company taking over the business of a sole trader pays for the assets and takes over the creditors of the business acquired. Take the case of a sole trader with assets valued at premises £50,000 and stock of £40,000. To gain control of these assets, a company is to pay the sole trader £110,000 in cash. In addition, the company will pay off the creditors £10,000. Goodwill is, therefore, £30,000:

	£	£
Paid by the company to gain control of the sole trader's assets:		
Cash to the sole trader		110,000
Cash to the sole trader's creditors		10,000
		120,000
The company receives assets:		
Premises	50,000	
Stock	40,000	
		(90,000)
Excess paid for goodwill		30,000

Exhibit 7.4

If the purchase had been made by the issue of 10,000 shares of £1 each at a premium of 40 per cent, £30,000 worth of 7 per cent debentures at par and £40,000 in cash, the total purchase consideration would be ordinary shares valued at £14,000, debentures valued at £30,000 and £40,000 in cash, making a total of £84,000. The assets are valued at £40,000, so the goodwill must be £44,000. The balance sheets would be:

Earl Ltd
Balance Sheets

	Before £	+ or – £	After £
Goodwill		+44,000	44,000
Machinery	110,000	+30,000	140,000
Stocks	50,000	+10,000	60,000
Bank	90,000	–40,000	50,000
	250,000		294,000
Less Debentures	–	+30,000	(30,000)
	250,000		264,000
Share capital	200,000	+10,000	210,000
Share premium		+4,000	4,000
Profit and loss	50,000		50,000
	250,000		264,000

7.3 Taking over a partnership

The entries are virtually the same as those made when taking over a sole trader. The main difference is the distribution of the purchase consideration. In the case of a sole trader, the sole trader gets all of it. In a partnership, it has to be divided between the partners.

This means that a partnership realisation account will have to be drawn up to calculate the profit or loss on sale of the partnership business which is attributable to each partner. The profit or loss on sale will then be shared between the partners in their profit/loss-sharing ratios.

The double entry needed *in the partnership books* is:

(A) Transfer assets being disposed of to the realisation account:
    Dr Realisation
       Cr Assets (various)

(B) Transfer liabilities being disposed of to the realisation account:
   > *Dr* Liabilities (various)
   >> *Cr* Realisation

(C) Enter purchase price:
   > *Dr* Limited company (purchaser)
   >> *Cr* Realisation

(D) If profit on sale:
   > *Dr* Realisation
   >> *Cr* Partners' capitals (profit-sharing ratio)

(E) If loss on sale:
   > *Dr* Partners' capitals (profit-sharing ratio)
   >> *Cr* Realisation

(F) Receipt purchase price:
   > *Dr* Cash
   > *Dr* Shares (if any) in limited company
   > *Dr* Debentures (if any) in limited company
   >> *Cr* Limited company (purchaser)

(G) Final settlement with partners:
   > *Dr* Partners' capital and current accounts
   >> *Cr* Cash
   >> *Cr* Shares (if any) in limited company
   >> *Cr* Debentures (if any) in limited company

Exhibit 7.5 shows how this is done.

Exhibit 7.5

Kay and Lee were in partnership, sharing profits and losses in the ratio 2:1 respectively. The following was their balance sheet as at 31 December 2004.

Kay and Lee
Balance Sheet as at 31 December 2004

	£	£
Fixed assets		
Buildings		300,000
Motor vehicles		150,000
		450,000
Current assets		
Stock	80,000	
Debtors	60,000	
Bank	10,000	
	150,000	
Current liabilities		
Creditors	(50,000)	
		100,000
		550,000
Capitals: Kay	320,000	
Lee	160,000	
		480,000
Current accounts: Kay	30,000	
Lee	40,000	
		70,000
		550,000

On 1 January 2005, Cayley Ltd took over the assets, other than bank. The purchase price is £800,000, payable by £600,000 in £1 shares in Cayley Ltd at par, plus £200,000 cash. Kay and Lee will pay off their own creditors. Shares are to be divided between the partners in their profit-sharing ratio.

First, let's look at the closing entries in the accounts of Kay and Lee. The only asset account shown will be the bank account. The individual creditors' accounts are also not shown. The letters in brackets refer to the description of the double entry already given.

Books of Kay and Lee
Realisation

		£			£
Assets taken over:			Cayley Ltd	(C)	800,000
Buildings	(A)	300,000			
Motor vehicles	(A)	150,000			
Stock	(A)	80,000			
Debtors	(A)	60,000			
Profit on realisation:					
Kay $^2/_3$	(D) 140,000				
Lee $^1/_3$	(D) 70,000	210,000			
		800,000			800,000

Cayley Ltd

		£			£
Realisation: sale price	(C)	800,000	Bank	(F)	200,000
			Shares in Cayley Ltd	(F)	600,000
		800,000			800,000

Shares in Cayley Ltd

		£			£
Cayley Ltd	(F)	600,000	Capital accounts: Kay	(G)	400,000
			Lee	(G)	200,000
		600,000			600,000

Capital Accounts

		Kay £	Lee £			Kay £	Lee £
Shares in Cayley	(G)	400,000	200,000	Balances b/d		320,000	160,000
Bank	(G)	60,000	30,000	Realisation (profit)	(D)	140,000	70,000
		460,000	230,000			460,000	230,000

Current Accounts

		Kay £	Lee £			Kay £	Lee £
Bank	(G)	30,000	40,000	Balances b/d		30,000	40,000

Bank

		£		£
Bank b/d		10,000	Creditors	50,000
Cayley Ltd	(F)	200,000	Capital accounts: Kay	60,000
			Lee	30,000
			Current accounts: Kay	30,000
			Lee	40,000
		210,000		210,000

Note: It would have been possible to transfer the balances of the current accounts to the capital accounts before settlement.

Assuming that Cayley values the buildings at £410,000 and the stock at £70,000, its balance sheet at 1 January 2005 would appear as in (B) below. The items shown under (A) were the balances before the takeover.

Balance Sheet(s)

	(A) *Before* £	+ £	– £	(B) *After* £
Goodwill		110,000		110,000
Buildings	500,000	410,000		910,000
Motor vehicles	250,000	150,000		400,000
Stock	280,000	70,000		350,000
Debtors	170,000	60,000		230,000
Bank	300,000		200,000	100,000
	1,500,000	800,000	200,000	2,100,000
Share capital (£1 shares)	1,000,000	600,000		1,600,000
Profit and loss	400,000			400,000
Creditors	100,000			100,000
	1,500,000	600,000		2,100,000

7.4 The takeover of one company by another

There are two methods by which one company may take over another:

1 Buying all the assets of the other company with cash, shares or debentures. The selling company may afterwards be wound up: the liquidators may distribute the purchasing company's shares and debentures among the shareholders of the selling company, or the shares and debentures of the buying company may be sold and the cash distributed instead.
2 Giving its own shares and debentures in exchange for the shares and debentures of the selling company's share and debenture holders.

The two methods are shown in Exhibit 7.6:

Exhibit 7.6

The following are the balance sheets of three companies as at the same date.

Balance Sheets

	R Ltd £	S Ltd £	T Ltd £
Buildings	130,000	–	10,000
Machinery	40,000	20,000	10,000
Stock	30,000	10,000	20,000
Debtors	20,000	10,000	30,000
Bank	10,000	20,000	30,000
	230,000	60,000	100,000
Share capital (£1 shares)	180,000	30,000	50,000
Profit and loss	20,000	10,000	40,000
Current liabilities	30,000	20,000	10,000
	230,000	60,000	100,000

R takes over S by exchanging with the shareholders of S two shares in R at a premium of 10 per cent for every share they hold in S.

R takes over T by buying all the assets of T, the purchase consideration being 120,000 £1 shares in R at a premium of 10 per cent, and R will pay off T's creditors. R values T's assets at buildings £20,000; machinery £6,000; stock £14,000; debtors £25,000; and the bank is £30,000, a total of £95,000.

R's deal with the shareholders of S means that R now has complete control of S Ltd, so that S Ltd becomes what is known as a subsidiary undertaking of R Ltd, and will be shown as an investment in R's balance sheet.

On the other hand, the deal with T has resulted in the ownership of the assets resting with R. These must therefore be added to R's assets in its own balance sheet. As R has given 120,000 £1 shares at a premium of 10 per cent plus taking over the responsibility for creditors of £10,000, the total purchase consideration for the assets taken over is £120,000 + £12,000 (10 per cent of £120,000) + £10,000 = £142,000. Identifiable assets as already stated are valued at £95,000 therefore the goodwill is £142,000 − £95,000 = £47,000.

The distinction between the acquisition of the two businesses can be seen to be a rather fine one. With S, the shares are taken over, the possession of these in turn giving rise to the ownership of the assets. In the books of R this is regarded as an investment. With T, the actual assets and liabilities are taken over so that the assets now directly belong to R. In the books of R this is therefore regarded as the acquisition of additional assets and liabilities and not as an investment (using the meaning of 'investment' which is used in the balance sheets of companies). The balance sheet of R Ltd therefore becomes:

R Ltd
Balance Sheet

	Before £	+ or −	£	After £
Goodwill		+(T)	47,000	47,000
Buildings	130,000	+(T)	20,000	150,000
Machinery	40,000	+(T)	6,000	46,000
Investment in S at cost		+(S)	66,000	66,000
Stock	30,000	+(T)	14,000	44,000
Debtors	20,000	+(T)	25,000	45,000
Bank	10,000	+(T)	30,000	40,000
	230,000			438,000
Less Current liabilities	(30,000)	+(T)	10,000	(40,000)
	200,000			398,000
Share capital	180,000	+(S)	60,000	
		+(T)	120,000	= 360,000
Share premium		+(S)	6,000	
		+(T)	12,000	= 18,000
Profit and loss	20,000			20,000
	200,000			398,000

No entry is necessary in the books of S Ltd, as it is merely the identity of the shareholders that has changed. This would be duly recorded in the register of members, but this is not really an integral part of the double entry accounting system. As you will see later, when group financial statements are prepared the assets and liabilities of S are added to those of R and the goodwill at the time of R's acquisition of S (of £26,000) is also shown on the group balance sheet.

If, however, T Ltd is now liquidated, then a realisation account must be drawn up and the distribution of the shares (or cash if the shares are sold) to the shareholders of T Ltd must be shown. Such accounts would appear as follows:

Books of T Ltd
Realisation

	£		£
Book values of assets disposed of:		R Ltd: Total purchase	
Buildings	10,000	consideration	142,000
Machinery	10,000		
Stock	20,000		
Debtors	30,000		
Bank	30,000		
Profit on realisation transferred			
to sundry shareholders	42,000		
	142,000		142,000

Share Capital

	£		£
Sundry shareholders	50,000	Balance b/d	50,000

Profit and Loss

	£		£
Sundry shareholders	40,000	Balance b/d	40,000

Creditors

	£		£
R Ltd – taken over	10,000	Balance b/d	10,000

R Ltd

	£		£
Realisation:		Creditors	10,000
Total consideration	142,000	Sundry shareholders: 120,000	
		£1 shares received at premium	
		of 10 per cent	132,000
	142,000		142,000

Sundry Shareholders

	£		£
R Ltd: 120,000 £1 shares at premium		Share capital	50,000
of 10 per cent	132,000	Profit and loss	40,000
		Realisation (profit)	42,000
	132,000		132,000

It can be seen that the items possessed by the sundry shareholders have been transferred to an account in their name. These are (*a*) the share capital which obviously belongs to them, (*b*) the credit balance on the profit and loss account built up by withholding cash dividends from the shareholders, and (*c*) the profit on realisation which they, as owners of the business, are entitled to take. As there were 50,000 shares in T Ltd, and 120,000 shares have been given by R Ltd, then each holder of 5 shares in T Ltd will now be given 12 shares in R Ltd to complete the liquidation of the company.

7.5 The exchange of debentures

Sometimes the debentures in the company taking over are to be given in exchange for the debentures of the company being taken over. This may be simply on the basis of a £1 debenture in company A for each £1 debenture in company B. However, when the exchange is in terms of one or both sets of debentures being at a discount or at a premium, it becomes more complex. This form of exchange may occur because:

1 There is a desire to persuade the debenture holders in company B to give up their debentures but they need some form of inducement, such as letting them have A's debentures at a discount, even though they may well be worth their par value.
2 There may be a difference between the interest rates of the two debentures. For instance, a person with a £100 7 per cent debenture would not normally gladly part with it in exchange for a £100 6 per cent debenture in another company. The first debenture gives the investor £7 a year interest, the second one only £6 per year. Thus, the debenture in the second company may be issued at a discount so that holders who switch to it continue to receive £7 a year for each £100 they originally invested. As the amount of interest is only one factor – others include the certainty of the debenture holder regaining his/her money if the business had to close down – the precise terms of the exchange cannot be based merely on arithmetical calculations of interest rates, but it is one of the measures taken when negotiating the exchange of debentures and is the most obvious.

Exhibit 7.7

1 D Ltd is to give the necessary debentures at a discount of 10 per cent required to redeem £9,000 debentures in J Ltd at a premium of 5 per cent. The problem here is to find exactly what amount of debentures must be given by D Ltd.

$$\frac{\text{Total nominal value of debentures}}{\text{to be redeemed (exchanged)}} \times \frac{\text{Redeemable value of each £100 debenture of J Ltd}}{\text{Issue value of each £100 debenture of D Ltd}}$$

= Total nominal value of D Ltd to be issued

$$= £9,000 \times \frac{105}{90}$$

$$= £10,500$$

Thus, to satisfy the agreement, debentures of D Ltd of a total nominal value of £10,500 are issued at a discount of 10 per cent to the debenture holder of J Ltd.

2 H Ltd is to give the necessary debentures at par to redeem £5,000 debentures in M Ltd at a premium of 4 per cent.

$$£5,000 \times \frac{104}{100} = \text{Debentures of £5,200 nominal value are given by H Ltd at par}$$

3 I Ltd is to give the necessary amount of 5 per cent debentures at par to redeem £20,000 debentures of 6 per cent of K Ltd.

£20,000 × 6% = £1,200 interest per year

$$\therefore \frac{£1,200}{0.05} = \text{£24,000 debentures of 5 per cent must be issued by I Ltd in exchange for the £20,000 debentures of 6 per cent in K Ltd.}$$

Now, let's move on to look at something that often happens when a company is first formed – profits or losses have been earned prior to incorporation.

7.6   The treatment of profits (or losses) prior to incorporation

Quite frequently, companies are formed after a business has been in existence for some time and profits or losses have been earned. For example, it could be that two people enter into business and start trading with the intention of running the business as a limited company. However, it takes more than a few days to attend to all the necessary formalities before the company can be incorporated. The actual time taken depends on the speed with which the formation is pushed through and the resolution of any problems which arise.

When a company is incorporated, it may enter into a contract whereby it adopts all the transactions retrospectively to the date that the business had started trading. This means that the company accepts all the benefits and disadvantages which have flowed from the transactions which have occurred. The example used was that of a new business. It could have been an old, established business that was taken over from a date predating incorporation of the company.

Legally, a company cannot earn profits before it comes into existence (i.e. incorporated). Therefore, to decide what action to take, profits must be calculated. Any such profits are of a capital nature and must be transferred to a capital reserve account, normally titled *Pre-incorporation Profit Account* or *Profit Prior to Incorporation Account*. That this should be done is obvious if you realise that, even though the actual date from which the transactions have been adopted falls before the date of incorporation, the price at which the business was taken over was influenced by the values of the net assets of the business at the date when the company was incorporated.

Let's consider an example. Suppose that Doolin and Kershaw start a business on 1 January 2005 with £1,000 capital, and very shortly afterwards Davie and Parker become involved and the four of them form a company in which they will all become directors – Davie and Parker to start active work when the company is incorporated.

The company is incorporated on 1 May 2005 and the original owners of the business, Doolin and Kershaw, are to be given shares in the new company to compensate them for handing over the business. If they know that the original £1,000 assets have grown to net assets of £6,000 then they would not part with the business to the company for £1,000. Ignoring goodwill, they would want £6,000 of shares. Conversely, if the net assets have shrunk to £400, would Davie and Parker be happy to see £1,000 of shares handed over? This means that the price at which the business is taken over is dependent on the expected value at the date of the company incorporation, and that value clearly includes profits or losses earned to that date.

In the case where net assets have increased to £6,000 the £5,000 difference is made up of profits. If these profits could be distributed as dividends, the capital payment of £6,000 in shares is being partly used for dividend purposes. This is inappropriate and is in direct contradiction to the normal accounting practice of keeping capital intact. The £5,000 profits must, therefore, be regarded as not being available for dividends. They are a capital reserve.

Although **pre-incorporation profit** cannot be regarded as free for use as dividends, any **pre-incorporation loss** can be used to restrict the dividends which could be paid out of the profits made after incorporation. This is an example of application of the prudence concept and, if the price paid on takeover was higher than was justified by the net worth of the business at that time, and it was discovered later that a pre-incorporation loss had been made, then the restriction of dividends leads to the capital lost being replaced by assets held back within the business.

It is possible for the profits up to the date of incorporation to be calculated separately from those earned after incorporation. (This is invariably the case in examination questions.) However, the cost of doing so may not be worthwhile incurring when there is no legal requirement to do so.

Therefore, when the financial statements for the full financial year are prepared, they will consist of profits pre- and post-incorporation. The financial statements must, therefore, be split to reveal the two sets of profit (or loss), so that distinction can be made between those profits usable, and those not usable, for dividend purposes. There is no hard-and-fast rule as to how this is done. Known facts must prevail and, where an arbitrary apportionment must be made, it should meet the test of common sense. Exhibit 7.8 shows an attempt to determine the amount of pre- and post-incorporation profits.

Exhibit 7.8

Slack and King are partners. Their business was taken over as from 1 January 2004 by Monk Ltd which is incorporated on 1 April 2004. It was agreed that all profits made from 1 January 2004 should belong to the company, and that Slack and King are entitled to interest on the purchase price from 1 January to the date of payment.

The purchase price was paid on 30 April 2004, including £1,600 interest. A profit and loss account is drawn up for the year ending 31 December 2004. This is shown as column (X). This is then split into pre-incorporation, shown as column (Y), and post-incorporation as column (Z). The methods used to apportion the particular items are shown after the profit and loss account, the letters (A) to (I) against the items being references to notes below the profit and loss account.

These methods of apportionment must *not* be used in all cases for similar expenses; they are only an indication of different methods of apportionment. The facts and the peculiarities of each business must be taken into account, and no method should be adopted simply because it was used before.

Assume for this example that all calendar months are of equal length.

Monk Ltd
Profit and Loss Account for the year ending 31 December 2004

		(X) Full year £	£	(Y) Pre-incorporation £	£	(Z) After £	£
Gross profit	(A)		38,000		8,000		30,000
Less							
Partnership salaries	(B)	1,000		1,000			
Employees' remuneration	(C)	12,000		3,000		9,000	
General expenses	(C)	800		200		600	
Commission on sales	(D)	1,700		200		1,500	
Distribution expenses	(E)	1,900		400		1,500	
Bad debts	(F)	100		20		80	
Bank overdraft interest	(G)	200				200	
Directors' remuneration	(H)	5,000				5,000	
Directors' expenses	(H)	400				400	
Debenture interest	(H)	500				500	
Depreciation	(C)	1,000		250		750	
Interest paid to vendors	(I)	1,600		1,200		400	
			(26,200)		(6,270)		(19,930)
Net profit			11,800				
Transferred to capital reserves					1,730		
Carried down to the appropriation account							10,070

Notes:

(A) For the three months to 31 March sales amounted to £40,000, and for the remaining nine months they were £150,000. Gross profit is at a uniform rate of 20 per cent of selling price throughout the year. Therefore the gross profit is apportioned (Y) 20 per cent of £40,000 = £8,000, and (Z) 20 per cent of £150,000 = £30,000.

(B) The partnership salaries of the vendors, Slack and King, obviously belong to (Y), because that is the period of the partnership.

(C) These expenses, in this particular case, have accrued evenly throughout the year and are therefore split on the time basis of (Y) three-twelfths, (Z) nine-twelfths.

(D) Commission to the salesforce was paid at the rate of $\frac{1}{2}$ per cent on sales up to 31 March, and 1 per cent thereafter. The commission figure is split:

(Y) $\frac{1}{2}$ per cent of £40,000 =   200
(Z) 1 per cent of £150,000 = 1,500
                        1,700

(E) In this particular case (but not always true in every case) the distribution expenses have varied directly with the value of sales. They are therefore split:

(Y) $\frac{\text{Y sales}}{\text{Total sales}} \times \text{Expenses} = \frac{40,000}{190,000} \times £1,900 = \frac{4}{19} \times £1,900 = £400$

(Z) $\frac{\text{Z sales}}{\text{Total sales}} \times \text{Expenses} = \frac{150,000}{190,000} \times £1,900 = \frac{15}{19} \times £1,900 = £1,500$

(F) There were two bad debts:
  (i) in respect of a sale in January, the debtor dying penniless in March, £20;
  (ii) in respect of a sale in June, the debtor being declared bankrupt in December, £80.

(G) The bank account was never overdrawn until June, so that the interest charged must be for period (Z).

(H) Only in companies are such expenses as directors' salaries, directors' expenses and debenture interest to be found. These must naturally be shown in period (Z).

(I) The interest paid to the vendors was due to the fact that the company was receiving all the benefits from 1 January but did not in fact pay any cash for the business until 30 April. This is therefore, in effect, loan interest which should be spread over the period it was borrowed, i.e. three months to (Y) and 1 month to (Z).

7.7 The treatment of formation expenses

These are also known as 'preliminary expenses'. They may be written-off immediately to profit or loss or capitalised and amortised over an appropriate period. Normally, they would be written-off.

Learning outcomes

You should now have learnt:

1 Why goodwill may arise when a business is taken over.
2 The difference between goodwill and negative goodwill.
3 The basic accounting entries are the same whether a limited company takes over a sole trader or a partnership.
4 Limited companies may take over other limited companies either:
  (a) by buying all the assets of the other company, or
  (b) by giving its own shares and debentures in exchange for the shares and debentures of the company being taken over.
5 How to record pre-incorporation losses and profits.
6 Pre-incorporation profits are not available for distribution.
7 The alternative treatments of formation expenses.

Answer to activity

7.1 Apart from the obvious difference that may arise between the net book value of an individual asset and its fair value (i.e. its true worth), such as in the example of the property given in the text, when a business is sold, the purchaser may have to pay extra to cover the value of intangible assets that do not appear in the balance sheet. Examples would include the reputation and customer base of the business being purchased, neither of which can appear in a balance sheet.

It is also possible that less may be paid than the net worth of a business because some assets may be considered as not being worth the amounts shown in the financial statements – it may be considered, for example, that debtors are likely to be overvalued or that individual assets are worth less to the purchaser than the values shown in the financial statements.

Of course, buyers generally try to pay as little as possible for a business. If a seller is very keen to sell, a price may be agreed that is below the net worth as shown in the balance sheet, even though that value is correct. It all depends on how the transaction is negotiated by the purchaser and the seller.

Review questions

7.1 Deal Ltd was incorporated on 1 September 2004 and took over the business of Fish and Chip on 1 June 2004. It was agreed that all profits made from 1 June should belong to the company and that the vendors should be entitled to interest on the purchase price from 1 June to the date of payment. The purchase price was paid on 31 October 2004 including £3,300 interest.

The following is the profit and loss account for the year ending 31 May 2005:

	£	£	£
Gross profit			104,000
Less: Expenses			
Salaries of Fish and Chip		6,800	
Wages and general expenses		32,400	
Rent		3,600	
Distribution expenses		6,800	
Commission on sales		2,600	
Bad debts		1,420	
Interest paid to vendors		6,200	
Directors' remuneration		15,000	
Directors' expenses		2,200	
Depreciation			
Vans	7,600		
Machinery	2,300		
		9,900	
Bank interest		440	(87,360)
Net profit			16,640

You are given the following information:

1 Sales amounted to £72,000 for the three months to 31 August 2004 and £132,000 for the nine months to 31 May 2005. Gross profit is at a uniform rate of 50 per cent of selling price throughout the year, and commission at a rate of 1 per cent is paid on all sales.
2 Salaries of £6,800 were paid to the partners for their assistance in running the business up to 31 August 2004.
3 The bad debts written-off are:
   (a) a debt of £480 taken over from the vendors;
   (b) a debt of £940 in respect of goods sold in November 2004.

4 On 1 June 2004, two vans were bought for £28,000 and machinery for £20,000. On 1 August 2004 another van was bought for £12,000 and on 1 March 2005, another machine was added for £12,000. Depreciation has been written off vans at 20 per cent per annum, and machinery 10 per cent per annum. Depreciation is written off for each month in which an asset is owned.

5 Wages and general expenses and rent all accrued at an even rate throughout the year.

6 The bank granted an overdraft facility in September 2004.

Assuming all calendar months are of equal length:

(a) set out the profit and loss account in columnar form, so as to distinguish between the period prior to the company's incorporation and the period after incorporation;

(b) state how you would deal with the profit prior to incorporation;

(c) state how you would deal with the results prior to incorporation if they had turned out to be a net loss.

7.2 On 30 June 2004 Smith and Sons Ltd acquired all the assets, except the investments, of Firefly Ltd. The following are the summaries of the profit and loss account of Firefly Ltd for the years ending 30 June 2002, 2003 and 2004:

	2002	2003	2004		2002	2003	2004
Motor expenses	9,400	9,900	10,300	Gross profit	164,800	178,200	177,400
Management salaries	32,000	35,000	36,000	Investment income	2,100	2,900	4,200
Depreciation of plant							
and machinery	12,000	9,600	7,680	Rents received	7,800	3,300	–
Overdraft interest	440	1,120	1,360	Profit on sale of			
Wrapping expenses	5,010	5,730	6,120	property	–	23,200	–
Preliminary expenses							
written off	–	4,400	–				
Net profit	115,850	141,850	120,140				
	174,700	207,600	181,600		174,700	207,600	181,600

The purchase price is to be the amount on which an estimated maintainable profit would represent a return of 20 per cent per annum.

The maintainable profit is to be taken as the average of the profits of the three years 2002, 2003 and 2004, after making any necessary adjustments.

You are given the following information:

(a) The cost of the plant and machinery was £60,000. It has been agreed that depreciation should have been written off at the rate of 10 per cent per annum using the straight line method.

(b) A new type of wrapping material means that wrapping expenses will be halved in future.

(c) By switching to a contract supply basis on motor fuel and motor repairs, it is estimated that motor expenses will fall by 25 per cent in future.

(d) Stock treated as valueless at 30 June 2001 was sold for £4,700 in 2003.

(e) The working capital of the new company is sound and it is felt that there will be no need for a bank overdraft in the foreseeable future.

(f) Management salaries have been inadequate and will have to be increased by £35,000 a year in future.

You are required to set out your calculation of the purchase price. All workings must be shown. In fact, your managing director, who is not an accountant, should be able to decipher how the price was calculated.

→

7.3 CJK Ltd was incorporated on 15 December 2009 with an authorised capital of 200,000 ordinary shares of £0.20 each to acquire as at 31 December 2009 the business of CK, a sole trader, and RP Ltd, a company.

From the following information you are required to prepare:

(a) the realisation and capital accounts in the books of CK and RP Ltd showing the winding up of these two concerns;
(b) the journal entries to open the books of CJK Ltd, including cash transactions and the raising of finance;
(c) the balance sheet of CJK Ltd after the transactions have been completed.

The balance sheet of CK as at 31 December 2009 is as follows:

Balance Sheet

	£
Freehold premises	8,000
Plant	4,000
Stock	2,000
Debtors	5,000
Cash	200
	19,200
Capital	16,000
Creditors	3,200
	19,200

The assets (excluding cash) and the liabilities were taken over at the following values: freehold premises £10,000, plant £3,500, stock £2,000, debtors £5,000 less a bad debts provision of £300, goodwill £7,000, creditors £3,200 less a discount provision of £150. The purchase consideration, based on these values, was settled by the issue of shares at par.

The balance sheet of RP Ltd as at 31 December 2009 is as follows:

Balance Sheet

	£
Freehold premises	4,500
Plant	2,000
Stock	1,600
Debtors	3,400
	11,500
Share capital: 10,000 shares at £0.40 each	4,000
Revenue surplus	2,500
Creditors	1,500
Bank overdraft	3,500
	11,500

The assets and liabilities were taken over at book value with the exception of the freehold premises which were revalued at £5,500. The purchase consideration was a cash payment of £1 and three shares in CJK Ltd at par in exchange for every two shares in RP Ltd.

Additional working capital and the funds required to complete the purchase of RP Ltd were provided by the issue for cash of:

(i) 10,000 shares at a premium of £0.30 per share;
(ii) £8,000 7 per cent debenture stock at 98.

The expenses of incorporating CJK Ltd were paid, amounting to £1,200.

(*Chartered Institute of Management Accountants*)

7.4A The balance sheet of Hubble Ltd as at 31 May 2010 is shown below.

Hubble Ltd

	£	£
Fixed assets		
Freehold premises at cost		375,000
Plant and machinery at cost		
Less Depreciation £48,765		101,235
Motor vehicles at cost		
Less Depreciation £1,695		6,775
		483,010
Current assets		
Stock-in-trade	102,550	
Debtors	96,340	
Cash in hand	105	
		198,995
		682,005
Authorised share capital		
650,000 ordinary shares of £1 each		650,000
Issued share capital		
400,000 ordinary shares of £1 each fully paid		400,000
Profit and loss account		180,630
Current liabilities		580,630
Trade creditors	63,200	
Bank overdraft	38,175	
		101,375
		682,005

Hubble Ltd agreed to purchase at this date the freehold premises, plant and machinery and stock of A Bubble at agreed valuations of £100,000; £10,000; and £55,000 respectively. The purchase price was to be fully settled by the issue to Bubble of 120,000 ordinary shares of £1 each in Hubble Ltd, and a cash payment to Bubble of £25,000. Bubble was to collect his debts and to pay his creditors.

Hubble Ltd sold one of its own premises prior to taking over Bubble for £75,000 (cost £55,000) and revalued the remainder at £400,000 (excluding those acquired from Bubble).

You are required to:
(a) show the journal entries, including cash items, in the books of Hubble Ltd to give effect to the above transactions; and
(b) show the balance sheet of Hubble Ltd after completing them.

(*Association of Chartered Certified Accountants*)

7.5A From the following information you are required to prepare a statement apportioning the unappropriated profit between the pre-incorporation and post-incorporation periods, showing the basis of apportionment:

VU Limited was incorporated on 1 July 2009 with an authorised share capital of 60,000 ordinary shares of £1 each, to take over the business of L and Sons as from 1 April 2009.

The purchase consideration was agreed at £50,000 for the net tangible assets taken over, plus a further £6,000 for goodwill.

Payment was satisfied by the issue of £30,000 8 per cent debentures and 26,000 ordinary shares both at par, on 1 August 2009. Interest at 10 per cent per annum on the purchase consideration was paid up to this date.

The company raised a further £20,000 on 1 August 2009 by the issue of ordinary shares at a premium of £0.25 per share.

→

The abridged profit and loss account for the year to 31 March 2010 was as follows:

	£	£
Sales:		
1 April 2009 to 30 June 2009	30,000	
1 July 2009 to 31 March 2010	95,000	
		125,000
Cost of sales for the year	80,000	
Depreciation	2,220	
Directors' fees	500	
Administration salaries and expenses	8,840	
Sales commission	4,375	
Goodwill written off	1,000	
Interest on purchase consideration, gross	1,867	
Distribution costs (60 per cent variable)	6,250	
Preliminary expenses written off	1,650	
Debenture interest, gross	1,600	
Dividend paid on ordinary shares	7,560	
		115,862
Unappropriated profit carried forward		9,138

The company sells one product only, of which the unit selling price has remained constant during the year, but due to improved buying the unit cost of sales was reduced by 10 per cent in the post-incorporation period as compared with the pre-incorporation period.

Taxation is to be ignored.

(*Chartered Institute of Management Accountants [part (a) of question only]*)

7.6A Rowlock Ltd was incorporated on 1 October 2008 to acquire Rowlock's mail order business, with effect from 1 June 2008.

The purchase consideration was agreed at £35,000 to be satisfied by the issue on 1 December 2008 to Rowlock or his nominee of 20,000 ordinary shares of £1 each, fully paid, and £15,000 7 per cent debentures.

The entries relating to the transfer were not made in the books which were carried on without a break until 31 May 2009.

On 31 May 2009 the trial balance extracted from the books is:

	£	£
Sales		52,185
Purchases	38,829	
Wrapping	840	
Postage	441	
Warehouse rent and rates	921	
Packing expenses	1,890	
Office expenses	627	
Stock on 31 May 2008	5,261	
Director's salary	1,000	
Debenture interest (gross)	525	
Fixed assets	25,000	
Current assets (other than stock)	9,745	
Current liabilities		4,162
Formation expenses	218	
Capital account – Wysocka, 31 May 2008		29,450
Drawings account – Wysocka, 31 May 2008	500	
	85,797	85,797

You also ascertain the following:

1 Stock on 31 May 2009 amounted to £4,946.
2 The average monthly sales for June, July and August were one-half of those for the remaining months of the year. The gross profit margin was constant throughout the year.
3 Wrapping, postage and packing expenses varied in direct proportion to sales, whilst office expenses were constant each month.
4 Formation expenses are to be written off.

You are required to prepare the trading and profit and loss account for the year ending 31 May 2009 apportioned between the periods before and after incorporation, and the balance sheet as at that date.

(*Chartered Institute of Management Accountants*)

You can find a range of additional self-test questions, as well as material to help you with your studies, on the website that accompanies this book at **www.pearsoned.co.uk/wood**

Taxation in company financial statements

Learning objectives

After you have studied this chapter, you should be able to:

- explain why profit per the profit and loss account is normally different from assessable profit for corporation tax calculations
- explain how income tax on interest affects companies and individuals
- describe how the 'imputation system' operates
- describe how and why deferred tax is relevant to capital allowances

Introduction

In this chapter, you'll learn that in the UK depreciation is not allowed as an expense for tax purposes and that something called a 'capital allowance' is granted instead. You'll also learn that the result of replacing depreciation with capital allowances when calculating tax is that taxable profit is very rarely the same amount as the figure shown for net profit in the financial statements. You'll learn how to apportion taxable profit across two tax periods, when corporation tax is payable, and the differences between the UK tax system for companies compared with the one that operates for sole traders and partnerships. Finally, you will learn about deferred tax and how it is calculated and applied to avoid financial statements being misleading in the way they present future tax liabilities in the balance sheet.

8.1 Background

This chapter is concerned with the entries made in the financial statements of companies in respect of taxation. It is not concerned with the actual calculation of the taxes as tax legislation is extremely complex and contains too many exceptions to the general rules applicable to companies for us to attempt to cover the entire subject in this book. It should be appreciated, therefore, that although the rules described in this chapter apply to the great majority of UK companies, there are many for which more complex tax rules will apply.

Taxation that affects UK companies can be split between:

1 Value added tax (VAT). This was covered in *Business Accounting 1*.
2 Direct taxes, payable to Revenue and Customs, the government department responsible for the calculation and collection of the taxes. For a company, the relevant taxes are corporation tax and income tax. FRS 16: *Current tax* deals with the treatment of taxation in company financial statements and will be adhered to in this chapter.

8.2 Limited companies: corporation tax and income tax

The principal tax paid by limited companies is **corporation tax**. Legally, it is an appropriation of profits, *not* an expense. Taxation is shown in the profit and loss account after the calculation of net profit.

A company's profits are assessable to corporation tax. But, corporation tax is assessable on the profit calculated *after certain adjustments have been made* to the net profit. These adjustments are not made in the financial statements. They are done quite separately from the drafting of financial statements and are not entered in the accounting books of the company.

Let's look at an example of one of these adjustments. Suppose that K Ltd has the following net profit:

K Ltd Profit and Loss Account for the year ending 31 March 2008

	£	£
Gross profit		100,000
Less: General expenses	25,000	
Depreciation of machinery	20,000	
		(45,000)
Net profit		55,000

The depreciation provision for machinery is the accounting figure used for the financial statements. It must be reversed when calculating the taxable profit and replaced by another deduction, **capital allowances**. These are the Revenue and Customs equivalent of depreciation and are calculated by rules which usually vary at one point or another from the methods applied by companies in determining their depreciation provisions. As a result, taxable profit assessed in any year is normally not the same as the net profit for that year as shown in the profit and loss account.

Activity 8.1

Why do you think the rules for capital allowances are different from the rules for depreciation?

In the case of K Ltd, assume that the capital allowances amount to £27,000 and that the rate of corporation tax is 40 per cent on assessable profits. The calculation of the corporation tax liability would be:

	£
Net profit per the financial statements	55,000
Add Depreciation provision not allowed as a deduction for corporation tax purposes	20,000
	75,000
Less Capital allowances	(27,000)
Adjusted profits assessable to corporation tax	48,000

At a corporation tax rate of 40 per cent, the corporation tax liability will be £48,000 × 40 per cent = £19,200.

Activity 8.2

In this example, taxable profits were higher than the net profit. Yet, over the life of a fixed asset, the amount of profit assessed in total for tax will always equal the total net profit for that period. Why?

As you might imagine, it is usually impossible to calculate the corporation tax payable by a company directly from its net profit. In fact, in addition to depreciation, other items in the financial statements often also need to be adjusted to find the assessable profits for corporation tax purposes.

8.3 The rate of corporation tax

The rate of corporation tax covering the period from 1 April to 31 March of the following year is fixed by the Chancellor of the Exchequer in the Budget, presented to Parliament each year. This rate is applied to the assessable profits of companies earned during this period. A company which has a financial year end other than 31 March spans two tax years, and apportions its taxable profits across the two periods.

Let's look at an example of this in Exhibit 8.1:

Exhibit 8.1

Company T Ltd: adjusted profits for the year ended 31 December 2008 = £160,000.

Rates of corporation tax:
For the tax year ended 31.3.2008, 45 per cent.
For the tax year ended 31.3.2009, 40 per cent.

	£
3 months' profit 1.1.2008 to 31.3.2008	
3/12 months × £160,000 = £40,000 × 45 per cent	18,000
9 months' profit 1.4.2008 to 31.12.2008	
9/12 months × £160,000 = £120,000 × 40 per cent	48,000
Corporation tax payable on adjusted profits for the year ended 31 December 2008	66,000

8.4 Corporation tax – when payable

All companies have a payment date of nine months after the end of their accounting period. For the rest of this chapter, although companies with relatively small profits can pay tax at a lower rate than companies with greater profits, unless mentioned otherwise corporation tax will be assumed to be 40 per cent.

8.5 Income tax

You've just learnt that companies pay corporation tax, not income tax. In the case of a sole trader, income tax is not directly connected with the business, as the individual *not* the business is liable to pay tax on the profits earned. Calculation of the tax due depends on many factors including, for example, whether the sole trader has other taxable income. The income tax paid by a sole trader should be treated as drawings if paid from the business bank account.

Activity 8.3
If a sole trader has the same net profit each year as is earned by a small company, all other things being equal, which business will show the greater accumulated profits if

(a) the sole trader pays income tax out of the business bank account;
(b) the sole trader pays income tax out of a personal bank account and does not draw any extra funds out of the business to cover the payment?

Why are these two answers different?

The income tax charged upon a partnership is also subject to the personal situation of the partners. The actual apportionment of the tax between the partners must be performed by someone who has access to the personal tax computations. It is *not* apportioned in the partners' profit-sharing ratios but on the basis of how much income tax each partner was required to pay. When the apportionment has been made, each partner should have the relevant amount debited to his drawings account. Remember, neither sole traders nor partnerships are liable to corporation tax and income tax does not appear in their financial statements.

In contrast, income tax does appear in the accounts of companies. When a company pays a dividend or pays charges such as debenture interest, it deducts income tax from the amount paid. This figure of income tax is then payable by the company to the Revenue and Customs. In effect, the company is acting as a tax collector on behalf of the Revenue and Customs, similar to the position a company is in regarding VAT.

Let's look at an example. Suppose a company has a thousand different debenture holders. It is far easier for the Revenue and Customs if the company pays only the net amount (i.e. the amount of debenture interest less income tax) due to each debenture holder and then pays the income tax deducted, in one figure, to the Revenue and Customs. This saves the Revenue and Customs having to trace a thousand debenture holders and then collect the money from them. It obviously cuts down on the bad debts that the Revenue and Customs might suffer, and makes it more difficult to evade the payment of income tax, plus it makes it cheaper for the Revenue and Customs to administer the system. This system is similar to the way PAYE on wages or salaries is operated, something you learnt about in *Business Accounting 1*.

For clarity, throughout the rest of this chapter it will be assumed that the basic rate of income tax is 25 per cent. The real rate will obviously differ from time to time. In addition, when someone has a relatively high or low income, the rate of income tax they pay may be higher or lower than 25 per cent. However, even though individual debenture holders may have to pay income tax at higher rates, or indeed pay lower rates or no income tax at all, companies deduct income tax at the basic rate.

Thus, if a company has issued £100,000 of 8 per cent debentures, cheques amounting to a total of £6,000 (8 per cent of £100,000 = £8,000 less 25 per cent income tax, £2,000 = £6,000) will be paid to the debenture holders. A cheque for £2,000 will then be paid to the Revenue and Customs by the company.

Let's consider some possible scenarios relating to this company's debenture holders (Exhibit 8.2).

Exhibit 8.2

If debenture holder AB pays income tax at the rate of 25 per cent, and he received £75 net (i.e. £100 gross less income tax £25), on his debenture of £1,250 then he has already suffered his rightful income tax by deduction at source. He will not get a further bill from the Revenue and Customs for £25 tax. The company has already paid the £25 income tax he owed as part of the total income tax cheque it paid of £2,000.

On the other hand, debenture holder CD is not liable to income tax because his income is low. He also has a debenture of £1,250 and so also receives a cheque for interest of £75. As he is not liable to income tax, but £25 of his money has been included in the total cheque paid by the company to Revenue and Customs of £2,000, he will be able to claim a refund of £25 from Revenue and Customs. Such a claim is made direct to the Inland Revenue, not to the company.

A third debenture holder EF pays tax at a rate of 40 per cent on his income. If he also has a debenture of £1,250, the company will pay a cheque to him of £75. But, he is really liable to pay tax of £40, not £25. As £25 income tax has been taken from him and handed over by the company in the total cheque of £2,000 income tax paid to Revenue and Customs, Revenue and Customs will send an extra demand to him for income tax of £15. Once again, the company has nothing to do with this extra demand.

8.6 Income tax on interest

Of course, a company may well have bought debentures or may own royalties, for example, in another company. This may mean that the company not only pays charges, such as debenture interest, but also receives similar items from other companies. The company will receive such items net after income tax has been deducted. When the company both receives and pays such items, it may set off the tax already suffered by it from such interest etc. received against the tax collected by it from its own charges, and pay the resultant net figure of income tax to Revenue and Customs. Again, this is similar to the treatment of VAT.

The figures of charges to be shown as being paid or received by the company in the company's own profit and loss account are the gross charges, i.e. the same as they would have been if income tax had never been invented. Exhibit 8.3 illustrates this more clearly:

Exhibit 8.3

RST Ltd has 7 per cent debentures amounting to £100,000 and has bought a £40,000 debenture of 10 per cent in a private company, XYZ Ltd. During the year, cheques amounting to £5,250 (£7,000 less 25 per cent) have been paid to debenture holders, and a cheque for £3,000 (£4,000 less 25 per cent) has been received from XYZ Ltd. Instead of paying over the £1,750 income tax deducted on payment of debenture interest, RST Ltd waits until the cheque is received from XYZ Ltd and then pays a cheque for £750 (£1,750 collected less £1,000 already suffered by deduction by XYZ Ltd) to Revenue and Customs in settlement.

Debenture Interest Payable

	£		£
Cash	5,250	Profit and loss	7,000
Income tax	1,750		
	7,000		7,000

Debenture Interest Receivable

	£		£
Profit and loss	4,000	Cash	3,000
		Income tax	1,000
	4,000		4,000

Income Tax

	£		£
Unquoted investment income	1,000	Debenture interest	1,750
Cash	750		
	1,750		1,750

It may well have been the case that although the income tax had been deducted at source from both the payment out of the company and the amount received, no cash has been paid specifically to Revenue and Customs by the company by the balance sheet date. In this case, the balance of £750 owing to Revenue and Customs will be carried down as a credit balance and will be shown under current liabilities in the balance sheet.

8.7 Deferred taxation

It was pointed out earlier in the chapter that *profits according to the financial statements* and *profits on which tax is payable* are often different from each other. The main reasons for this are as follows:

1 The figure of depreciation shown in the profit and loss account may be different from Revenue and Customs figure for 'capital allowances', which is *their* way of calculating allowances for depreciation.
2 Some items of expense charged in the profit and loss account will not be allowed by Revenue and Customs as expenses. Examples are political donations, fines for illegal acts and expenses for entertaining UK customers.

Timing differences

In the case of capital allowances under (1) above, as you learned in Activity 8.2, the amount of 'depreciation' charged for an asset over the years will eventually equal the amount allowed by Revenue and Customs as 'capital allowances'. Where the difference lies is in the periods when these items will be taken into account.

For instance, take an asset which cost £4,800 and will be sold after three years for £2,025. The depreciation rate is $33^{1}/_{3}$ per cent straight line. Revenue and Customs capital allowances are 25 per cent reducing balance.

Years ended 5 April*	2002	2003	2004	Overall
	£	£	£	£
Depreciation	925	925	925	2,775
Capital allowances	1,200	900	675	2,775
Timing differences	+275	−25	−250	nil

*The Revenue and Customs tax year actually ends on 5 April, not 31 March, though 31 March is used for companies.

Activity 8.4   Why do you think the depreciation is £925 per year?

Thus, over the economic life of the asset, the same amount was deducted from profit for depreciation as was allowed as a deduction in the form of capital allowances.

What about retained profits, are they the same too? If profits for each year after depreciation were £1,000:

Years ended 5 April	2002	2003	2004	Overall
	£	£	£	£
Profits after depreciation	1,000	1,000	1,000	3,000
Profits for tax purposes	725	1,025	1,250	3,000
Differences	−275	+25	+250	nil

As you can see, profits have in fact remained the same overall at £1,000. It is the difference in the timing of the deduction of capital allowances compared to that for depreciation which causes there to be different taxable profit figures each year compared to the net profit figures. These are known as 'timing differences'. Taking the point of view that profits of £1,000 per year give a more sensible picture than the £725, £1,025 and £1,250 per the Revenue and Customs calculations, the company's way of depreciating is probably more appropriate for individual companies than Revenue and Customs method which does not vary between companies.

You may well be wondering if it matters what amount is deducted for depreciation. Analysts and potential investors and shareholders themselves place a great reliance on something called 'earnings per share after tax'. Suppose that corporation tax was 40 per cent for each of the three years and that there were 1 million shares. This would give the following figures:

Tax based on net profit, i.e. the company's calculations:

	2002	2003	2004
	£000	£000	£000
Profit per financial statements before taxation	1,000	1,000	1,000
Less Corporation tax (40%)	(400)	(400)	(400)
Profit after tax	600	600	600
Earnings per share = Profit after tax ÷ 1 million =	60p	60p	60p

Tax based on Revenue and Customs calculations:

	2002	2003	2004
	£000	£000	£000
Profit per financial statements before tax	1,000	1,000	1,000
Less Corporation tax:			
40% of £725	(290)		
40% of £1,025		(410)	
40% of £1,250			(500)
Profit after tax	710	590	500
Earnings per share = Profit after tax ÷ 1 million =	71p	59p	50p

In truth, all of the years have been equally profitable – this is shown by the company's calculation of 60p earnings per share each year. On the other hand, if no adjustment is made, the financial statements when based on actual tax paid would show 71p, 59p and 50p. This could confuse shareholders and would-be shareholders.

In order not to distort the picture given by financial statements, the concept of deferred taxation was brought in by accountants. There have been three UK accounting standards on this topic. The latest, FRS 19: *Deferred tax*, was issued in December 2000.

FRS 19 requires that deferred tax is provided on timing differences relating to:

● capital allowances and depreciation;
● accruals for pension costs and other post-retirement benefits;
● the elimination of unrealised intragroup profits;
● unrelieved tax losses;
● annual revaluations of assets where changes in fair value are taken to the profit and loss account;
● other short-term timing differences.

The double entry is as follows:

1 In the years when taxation is lower than it would be on comparable accounting profits, e.g. £40 on £200 net profit instead of £80:

Dr Profit and loss appropriation account
    Cr Deferred taxation account

with the amount of taxation understated.

Capital allowances etc. have reduced taxable profit this year but at some point in the future, the reverse will occur.

2 In the years when taxation is higher than it would be on comparable accounting profits, e.g. £100 on £200 net profit instead of £80:

> Dr Deferred taxation account
> Cr Profit and loss appropriation account

with the amount of taxation overstated.

By making these adjustments, a 'fair' amount of tax has either been set aside or paid each year. As a result, when the timing differences reverse, the retained profits will neither suddenly fall nor suddenly rise.

Let's now look at how the profit and loss account and the T-accounts for corporation tax and for deferred taxation would have been drawn up in the last example. We shall use the wording which applies to published company financial statements. As a result, instead of 'Profit per financial statements before taxation', we shall use 'Profit on ordinary activities before taxation'.

Exhibit 8.4

Profit and Loss Account extracts for the years ended 5 April

	2002 £000	2002 £000	2003 £000	2003 £000	2004 £000	2004 £000
Profit on ordinary activities before taxation		1,000		1,000		1,000
Tax on profit on ordinary activities:						
Corporation tax	290		410		500	
Deferred taxation	110	(400)	(10)	(400)	(100)	(400)
Profit on ordinary activities after taxation		600		600		600

For stakeholders, such as shareholders, stock exchange analysts, and would-be shareholders, the profit after taxation figures on which earnings per share (EPS) would be calculated is £600,000 in each of the three years. The timing difference distortion has thus been eliminated by inclusion of the deferred tax adjustments.

Assuming that corporation tax is payable on 1 January following each accounting year end, the ledger accounts for corporation tax and deferred tax would be as follows:

Corporation Tax

2002		£000	2002		£000
Apr 5	Balance c/d	290	Apr 5	Profit and loss	290
		290			290
2003			2002		
Jan 1	Bank	290	Apr 6	Balance b/d	290
			2003		
Apr 5	Balance c/d	410	Apr 5	Profit and loss	410
		700			700
2004			2003		
Jan 1	Bank	410	Apr 6	Balance b/d	410
			2004		
Apr 5	Balance c/d	500	Apr 5	Profit and loss	500
		910			910
			2004		
			Apr 6	Balance b/d	500

→

→

Deferred Taxation

2002			£000	2002			£000
Apr	5	Balance c/d	110	Apr	5	Profit and loss	110
			110				110
2003				2002			
Apr	5	Profit and loss	10	Apr	6	Balance b/d	110
	5	Balance c/d	100				
			110				110
2004				2003			
Apr	5	Profit and loss	100	Apr	6	Balance b/d	100
			100				100

The balance sheets would appear:

	2002	2003	2004
	£000	£000	£000
Creditors: amounts falling due within one year			
Corporation tax	290	410	500
Provisions for liabilities and charges			
Deferred taxation	110	100	–

Permanent differences

No adjustments are made to the accounting profit for differences between it and the taxable profit that arise because of non-tax-deductible items, such as political donations, and some entertaining expenses.

A fully worked example

Exhibit 8.5 shows the ledger accounts in which tax will be involved for the first year of a new company, Harlow Ltd. Exhibit 8.6 shows the second year of that company. **This should help make your understanding of this topic clearer – to consider just one year very often leaves many unanswered questions.**

Exhibit 8.5

Harlow Ltd has just finished its first year of trading on 31 December 2004. Corporation tax throughout was 35 per cent, and income tax was 25 per cent. You are given the following information:

(A) Net trading profit for the year was £165,000, before adjustment for debenture interest.
(B) Debenture interest (net) of £12,000 was paid on 31 December 2004 and (C) the income tax deducted was paid on the same date.
(D) An ordinary interim dividend of 10 per cent on the 210,000 £1 ordinary shares was paid on 1 July 2004.
(E) A proposed final ordinary dividend of 25 per cent for the year is to be accrued.[Note]
(F) Depreciation of £12,000 has been charged before arriving at net trading profit. Capital allowances of £37,000 have been approved by the Revenue and Customs. Account for timing differences.
(G) Corporation tax on the first year's trading is expected to be £38,500.

You are required to:
(a) show double entry accounts (other than bank) to record the above;
(b) prepare extracts from the profit and loss account and balance sheet.

Note: Dividends proposed do not appear in financial statements, nor are they accrued. This would appear only as a note to the financial statements.

Debenture Interest

2004			£	2004		£
Dec 31	Bank	(B)	12,000	Dec 31 Profit and loss		16,000
Dec 31	Income tax	(C)	4,000			
			16,000			16,000

Income Tax

2004			£	2004		£
Dec 31	Bank	(C)	4,000	Dec 31 Debenture interest (C)		4,000

Ordinary Dividends

2004			£	2004		£
Jul 1	Bank	(D)	21,000	Dec 31 Profit and loss (reserve)Note		21,000

Note: This does not appear in the financial statement. It is an appropriation of profits and appears in the note of movements in shareholders' funds.

Deferred Taxation

2004		£	2004			£
Dec 31	Balance c/d	8,750	Dec 31 Profit and lossNote	(F)		8,750

Note: (F) allowed £37,000 but only charged £12,000 = £25,000 × 35% corporation tax deferred = £8,750.

Corporation Tax

2004		£	2004			£
Dec 31	Balance c/d	38,500	Dec 31 Profit and loss	(G)		38,500

Profit and Loss Account extracts for the year ending 31 December 2004

		£	£
Net trading profit	(A)		165,000
Less Debenture interest	(B)		16,000
Profit on ordinary activities before taxation			149,000
Corporation tax	(G)	38,500	
Deferred taxation	(F)	8,750	
			(47,250)
Profit on ordinary activities after taxation			101,750

Balance Sheet (extracts) as at 31 December 2004

Creditors: amounts falling due within one year	£
Corporation tax	38,500
Deferred tax	8,750

Exhibit 8.6

Harlow Ltd, as per Exhibit 8.5, has now finished its second year of trading. From 2004 there will be two ledger account balances to be brought forward from Exhibit 8.5. These accounts are:

| Deferred taxation | (a) | Cr | £8,750 |
| Corporation tax | (b) | Cr | £38,500 |

You are given the following information:

(c) The proposed ordinary dividend £52,500 was paid on 1 March 2005.
(d) Corporation tax remains at 35 per cent and income tax remains at 25 per cent.
(e) Shares had been bought in STU Ltd and a dividend of £1,500 was received on 31 August 2005.
(f) An interim dividend of 15 per cent on the 210,000 £1 ordinary shares was paid on 1 July 2005.
(g) Debentures had been bought in RRR Ltd and interest (net) of £4,500 was received on 30 December 2005.
(h) Harlow Ltd paid its own debenture interest (net) of £12,000 on 31 December 2005, and (i) the income tax account (net) was paid on the same date.
(j) The corporation tax due for 2004 was paid on 30 September 2005.
(k) A final ordinary dividend for the year of 30 per cent was proposed. This will be paid in March 2006.
(l) Corporation tax for the year ended 31 December 2005 is expected to be £41,300.
(m) Depreciation of £28,000 has been charged in the accounts, while capital allowances amounted to £22,000.
(n) Net trading profit after deducting depreciation but before adjusting for the above was £178,000.

To record these items, we open a tax on profit on ordinary activities account and transfer tax items to it. After all entries have been made, the balance on the account is transferred to the profit and loss account.

Ordinary Dividends

2005			£	2005		£
Mar	1	Bank (c)	52,500			
Jul	1	Bank interim (f)	31,500	Dec 31 Profit and loss		84,000
			84,000			84,000

Investment Income

2005		£	2005		£
Dec 31	Profit and loss	1,500	Aug 31 Bank (e)		1,500
		1,500			1,500

Debenture Interest Payable

2005			£	2005		£
Dec	31	Bank (h)	12,000	Dec 31 Profit and loss		16,000
	31	Income tax	4,000			
			16,000			16,000

Debenture Interest Receivable

2005		£	2005		£
Dec 31	Profit and loss	6,000	Dec 30 Bank (g)		4,500
			30 Income tax		1,500
		6,000			6,000

Income Tax

2005			£	2005			£
Dec	30	Debenture interest receivable	1,500	Dec	31	Debenture interest payable	4,000
	31	Bank (i)	2,500				
			4,000				4,000

Deferred Taxation

2005			£	2005			£
Dec	31	Tax on profit on ordinary activities (6,000 × 35%) (m)	2,100	Jan	1	Balance b/d (C)	8,750
	31	Balance c/d	6,650				
			8,750				8,750

Corporation Tax

2005			£	2005			£
Sep	30	Bank (j)	38,500	Jan	1	Balance b/d (b)	38,500
Dec	31	Accrued c/d	41,300	Dec	31	Tax on profit on ordinary activities (l)	41,300
			79,800				79,800

Tax on Profit on Ordinary Activities

2005			£	2005			£
Dec	31	Corporation tax (n)	41,300	Dec	31	Deferred taxation (m)	2,100
					31	Profit and loss	39,200
			41,300				41,300

Profit and Loss account extracts for the year ending 31 December 2005

	£	£
Net trading profit (O)		178,000
Add Debenture interest received	6,000	
Investment income	1,500	
		7,500
		185,500
Less Debenture interest payable		(16,000)
Profit on ordinary activities before taxation		169,500
Tax on profit on ordinary activities		(39,200)
Profit on ordinary activities after taxation		129,700

Balance Sheet (extracts) as at 31 December 2005

Creditors: amounts falling due within one year	£
Corporation tax	41,300
Deferred tax	6,650

Learning outcomes

You should now have learnt:

1 Depreciation is not allowed as an expense when calculating tax liability.

2 Capital allowances are the equivalent of depreciation that the government allows to be deducted when calculating tax liability.

3 The profit shown in the financial statements is normally different from assessable profit for corporation tax calculations.

4 Deferred tax eliminates the differences that arise as a result of depreciation being replaced by capital allowances when calculating corporation tax payable.

5 FRS 19: *Deferred tax* regulates the calculation of the figure for deferred tax that appears in the balance sheet.

Answers to activities

8.1 To answer this question, you need to consider why each of these rules is in place. Depreciation is governed by FRS 15: *Tangible fixed assets*. It is calculated so as to reflect the reduction in economic value of an asset over an accounting period. In other words, it is intended to give a true and fair view of the true remaining value of an asset, subject to the effect of the basis upon which the base value of the asset has been derived. For example, if historical cost is the base, the remaining amount after depreciation has been deducted represents that proportion of the original value of the asset that remains at the balance sheet date.

Capital allowances are the government's assessment of how much of the historical cost of an asset can legitimately be treated as an expense in a given year. In most cases, the rate and method of calculation selected bear little relation to either the actual expected economic life of an individual asset or to the extent to which use of an asset has reduced its future economic life.

In some cases, capital allowances are intended to encourage successful business by enabling taxable profits to be reduced significantly in one year so that tax is lower than it would otherwise be. For example, capital allowances of 100 per cent may be permitted for any company operating in economically depressed parts of the UK. The motivation for capital allowances is, therefore, very different from the principles underlying depreciation provisions.

8.2 Capital allowances are allowed as a deduction against profit over the life of a fixed asset, as is depreciation. Thus, although in any particular period the amount of capital allowance is usually different from the depreciation charged in the profit and loss account, by the end of the life of a fixed asset, the amount granted in capital allowances will be the same as the total amount of depreciation charged.

8.3 (a) Both businesses will have the same amount of accumulated profits.

(b) The sole trader's business will have a greater amount of accumulated profits. It will, therefore, appear more successful than the company, even though both businesses are making the same annual profits. In fact, because the sole trader will have more assets in the business than the company (due to the fact that less cash has been paid out), it can be argued that it is the company that is the more successful business.

The answers are different because the sole trader has chosen to accept a lower level of net annual income than the owners of the company.

8.4 You will either have found this question simple, straightforward and obvious, or you will have struggled to find the answer. Whichever position you were in, it is important that you remember this question whenever you are thinking about depreciation and/or about deferred tax. The answer is that depreciation is based on the difference between cost and the estimated disposal value of the asset. This asset cost £4,800. It is to be used for three years and its disposal value is estimated at £2,025. The amount to be depreciated over the three years is, therefore, £2,775. At $33\frac{1}{3}$ per cent per annum straight-line, the annual depreciation charge is £925.

Review questions

Note: **Questions 8.5 and 8.6 will be sufficient for those taking examinations with little tax content.**

8.1 Camden Lock Ltd has just finished its first year of trading to 31 December 2006. Corporation tax throughout was 40 per cent and income tax 20 per cent. You are given the following information:

(*i*)   Net trading profit, after adjustment for (*ii*) but before other adjustments, was £390,000.
(*ii*)   Depreciation of £70,000 was charged. Capital allowances were £110,000.
(*iii*)   An interim dividend of 4 per cent on 800,000 £1 ordinary shares was paid on 1 July 2006.
(*iv*)   Debenture interest of £14,000 (net) was paid on 31 December 2006.
(*v*)   Income tax deducted from debenture interest was paid on 31 January 2007.
(*vi*)   A final dividend of 6 per cent was proposed for the year.
(*vii*)   Corporation tax for the year was estimated to be £145,000.

You are required to:
(*a*) draw up the double entry accounts recording the above (except bank);
(*b*) show the relevant extracts from the profit and loss account and the balance sheet.

Note that Question 8.2A is concerned with the second year of trading for Camden Lock Ltd.

8.2A Camden Lock Ltd has just finished its second year of trading to 31 December 2007. Balances from Question 8.1 need to be brought forward into this question. Tax rates are the same as for 2006. The following information is available:

(*i*)   The proposed final dividend for 2006 (*see* Review Question 8.1) was paid on 31 January 2007.
(*ii*)   Shares in Strand Ltd were bought on 1 January 2007. A dividend of £4,200 was received on 30 September 2007.
(*iii*)   Debentures in Strand Ltd were bought on 1 July 2007. Debenture interest of £8,400 (net) was received on 31 December 2007.
(*iv*)   Debenture interest of £14,000 (net) was paid by Camden Lock Ltd on 31 December 2007.
(*v*)   Income tax owing to the Inland Revenue for 2007 was not paid until 2008. The 2006 income tax was paid on 30 January 2007.
(*vi*)   An interim dividend of 5 per cent on 800,000 £1 ordinary shares was paid on 10 July 2007.
(*vii*)   A final dividend of 9 per cent was proposed for the year.
(*viii*)   Depreciation of £90,000 was charged. Capital allowances were £120,000.
(*ix*)   Net trading profit (before taking into account (*ii*), (*iii*), and (*iv*)) was £540,000.
(*x*)   The corporation tax due for 2006 was paid on 1 October 2007. Corporation tax for the year to 31 December 2007 is expected to be £160,000.

You are required to:
(*a*) Draw up the double entry accounts recording the above (except bank).
(*b*) Show the relevant extracts from the profit and loss account for the year and balance sheet at the year end.

Note: **Question 8.3 is in the style of a typical professional accounting body's examination question. It is not easy. Remember to bring forward the balances from the previous year, some of which will often have to be deduced. The letters (A) to (L) against the information will make it easier for you to check your answer against the one at the back of the book.**

To answer question of this type, first prepare all the T-accounts.

8.3 Corporation tax for the tax years 2007, 2008, and 2009 was 40 per cent and income tax for each year was 20 per cent.

(A)   Skim Ltd's draft profit and loss account for the year ended 31 December 2008 shows a net trading profit from operations of £1.2 million. This figure is before taking into account (B) and (C1) and (C2).

→

(B) Debenture interest paid on 5 December 2008 (gross) was £200,000. Ignore accruals.
(C1) Fixed rate interest received is £60,000 (net). Date received 9 November 2008. Ignore accruals.
(C2) A dividend of £2,000 was received from Beef Ltd on 1 October.
(D) Depreciation was £180,000. This compares with £260,000 capital allowances given by the Inland Revenue. There is to be full provision for all timing differences for 2008.
(E) The income tax bill (net) in respect of (B) and (C1) was paid on 19 December 2008.
(F) Preference dividend paid on 6 July 2008 £32,000.
(G) Ordinary interim dividend paid 8 August 2008 £180,000.
(H) Proposed final ordinary dividend for 2008 (paid in 2009) was £300,000.
(I) Proposed final ordinary dividend for 2007 (paid 10 March 2008) was £240,000.
(J) There was a credit balance on deferred taxation account at 31 December 2007 of £170,000.
(K) Tax for 2007 had been provided for at £280,000 but was finally agreed at £272,000 (paid on 6 October 2008).
(L) Corporation tax for 2008 is estimated to be £340,000.

You are required to enter up the following accounts for the year ended 31 December 2008 for Skim Ltd: Deferred tax; Income tax; Interest receivable; Debenture interest; Investment income; Corporation tax; Tax on profit on ordinary activities; Preference dividends; Ordinary dividends; Profit and loss account extract. Also prepare the relevant balance sheet extracts as at 31 December 2008.

8.4A Joytan Ltd has a trading profit, before dealing with any of the undermentioned items, for the year ended 31 December 2004 of £500,000. Prepare the profit and loss account for the year.

(a) The standard rate of income tax is 25 per cent.
(b) Joytan Ltd has bought £100,000 of 8 per cent debentures in another company. Joytan Ltd receives its interest, less income tax, for the year on 6 November 2004.
(c) Joytan has issued £300,000 of 10 per cent debentures, and pays interest, less income tax for the year on 22 December 2004.
(d) No cheque has been paid to the Revenue and Customs for income tax.
(e) Joytan Ltd has a liability for corporation tax, based on the year's profits for 2004, of £210,000.
(f) Joytan Ltd owns 90,000 ordinary shares of £1 each in Plax Ltd, and receives a cheque for the dividend of 15 per cent in October 2004. Plax Ltd is neither a subsidiary company nor a related company of Joytan Ltd.
(g) Joytan Ltd proposed a dividend of 9 per cent on its 500,000 ordinary shares of £1 each, payable out of the profits for 2004.
(h) Transfer £50,000 to general reserve.
(i) Unappropriated profits brought forward from last year amounted to £122,000.

8.5 Moontan Ltd has an operating profit for the year ended 31 December 2002, before dealing with the following items, of £200,000. Complete the profit and loss account.

(a) The standard rate of income tax is 20 per cent.
(b) Moontan Ltd had issued £100,000 of 7 per cent debentures. It paid the interest for the year, less income tax, on 31 December 2002.
(c) Moontan Ltd owns £10,000 of 5 per cent debentures in another company. It received a year's interest, less income tax, on 27 December 2002.
(d) No cheque has been paid to the Revenue and Customs for income tax.
(e) Moontan Ltd has 40,000 ordinary shares of £1 each in Sunshine Ltd. Sunshine Ltd paid a dividend to Moontan Ltd of 8 per cent on 24 November 2002. Sunshine Ltd is a 'related company' of Moontan Ltd.
(f) Moontan Ltd had a liability for corporation tax, based on profits for 2002, of £106,000.
(g) Moontan proposed a dividend of 10 per cent on its 200,000 ordinary shares of £1 each, out of the profits for 2002.
(h) Transfer £10,000 to general reserve.
(i) Unappropriated profits brought forward from last year amounted to £22,480.

8.6 The following information relates to Kemp plc for the year to 31 March 2009:

	£m
1 Dividends	
Proposed final ordinary dividend for the year to 31 March 2008 paid on 31 August 2008	28
Interim ordinary dividend paid on 31 December 2008	12
Proposed final ordinary dividend for the year 31 March 2009 to be paid on 31 July 2009	36
2 Deferred taxation account	
Credit balance at 1 April 2008	3
During the year to 31 March 2009 a transfer of £5 million was made from the profit and loss account to the deferred taxation account.	
3 Tax rates	
Corporation tax 35 per cent	
Income tax 25 per cent	

Required:

Write up the following accounts for the year to 31 March 2009, being careful to insert the appropriate date for each entry and to bring down the balances as at 31 March 2009:

(*i*) ordinary dividends;
(*ii*) deferred taxation.

(*Association of Accounting Technicians*)

8.7A The following figures appeared in W Ltd's balance sheet at 31 March 2002:

Current liability – corporation tax	£600,000
Deferred taxation	£300,000

During the year ended 31 March 2003, W Ltd made a payment of £520,000 to the Collector of Taxes in settlement of the company's corporation tax for the year ended 31 March 2002. Dividend payments totalling £60,000 were made during the year ended 31 March 2002 and a further dividend of £200,000 had been proposed at the year end.

Two dividend payments were made during the year ended 31 March 2003. A payment of £200,000 was made for the final dividend for the year ended 31 March 2002. An interim dividend of £40,000 was paid for the year ended 31 March 2003. These payments were made in May 2002 and September 2002 respectively. The directors have provided a final dividend of £240,000 for the year ended 31 March 2003.

W Ltd received a dividend of £12,000 from a UK quoted company. This was received in August 2002.

W Ltd's tax advisers believe that corporation tax of £740,000 will be charged on the company's profits for the year ended 31 March 2003. This amount is net of the tax relief of £104,000 which should be granted in respect of the exceptional loss which the company incurred during the year. It has been assumed that corporation tax will be charged at a rate of 35 per cent. The basic rate of income tax was 25 per cent.

It has been decided that the provision for deferred tax should be increased by £20,000. No provision is to be made in respect of timing differences of £400,000.

You are required:

(*a*) to prepare the note which will support the figure for the provision for corporation tax in W Ltd's published profit and loss account for the year ended 31 March 2003;
(*b*) to calculate the liability for corporation tax which will appear in W Ltd's published balance sheet at 31 March 2003;
(*c*) to prepare the deferred tax note which will support the figure for the liability which will appear in W Ltd's published balance sheet at 31 March 2003.

(*Chartered Institute of Management Accountants*)

You can find a range of additional self-test questions, as well as material to help you with your studies, on the website that accompanies this book at **www.pearsoned.co.uk/wood**

Chapter 9

Provisions, reserves and liabilities

Learning objectives

After you have studied this chapter, you should be able to:
● explain the difference between a provision and a liability
● explain the difference between revenue reserves and capital reserves
● describe how capital reserves may be used
● describe what normally comprises distributable profits

Introduction

In this chapter, you'll learn about the difference between provisions and liabilities and about the difference between revenue reserves and capital reserves. You will also learn about some of the restrictions on the use of reserves and learn more about what is meant by 'distributable profit'.

9.1 Provisions

A **provision** is an amount written off or retained in order to provide for renewals of, or diminution in value of assets, or retained to provide for any known liability of which the amount cannot be determined with 'substantial' accuracy. This therefore covers such items as **provisions for depreciation** and **provisions for doubtful debts**. A **liability** is an amount owing which can be determined with substantial accuracy.

Sometimes, therefore, the difference between a provision and a liability hinges around what is meant by 'substantial' accuracy. Rent owing at the end of a financial year would normally be known with precision, so would obviously be a liability. Legal charges for a court case which has been heard, but for which the lawyers have not yet submitted their bill, would be a provision.

See Chapter 12 for clarification of the need for the distinction between liabilities and provisions when the requirements of the Companies Acts regarding disclosures in the financial statements are examined.

9.2 Revenue reserves

A **revenue reserve** is an account to which an amount has been voluntarily transferred from the profit and loss account, thus reducing the amount of profits left available for cash dividend purposes and crediting the appropriate **reserve account**. The reserve may be for some particular purpose, such as a **foreign exchange reserve account** created just in case the business should ever meet a situation where it would suffer loss because of foreign currency exchange rate movements; or it could be a **general reserve account** that could be used for any purpose.

> **See Section 9.3 for a further look at general reserves.**

Such transfers are an indication to the shareholders that it would be unwise at the time of the transfer to pay out all the available profits as dividends. The resources represented by this part of the profits should be retained, at least for the time being. Revenue reserves can be called upon in future years to help swell the profits retained in the profit and loss account as being available for dividend purposes. This is effected quite simply by debiting the particular reserve account and crediting the profit and loss appropriation account.

 Activity 9.1 Why do you think special revenue reserves are used, rather than simply leaving everything in the profit and loss account (which is, itself, a revenue reserve)?

9.3 General reserve

A general reserve is one that can be used for any purpose. For example, it may be needed because of the effect of inflation: assume a company needs £4,000 working capital in 2003 and that the volume of trade remains the same for the next three years but that during that time, the general level of prices increases by 25 per cent: the working capital requirement will now be £5,000. If all the profits are distributed, the company will still have only £4,000 working capital which cannot possibly finance the same volume of trade as it did in 2003. Transferring annual amounts of profits to a general reserve instead of paying them out as dividends is one way to help overcome this problem.

 Activity 9.2 In terms of the amount of working capital, what is the difference between doing this and leaving the amount transferred in profit and loss?

On the other hand, it may just be the conservatism convention asserting itself, with a philosophy of 'better be safe than sorry', in this case to restrict dividends because the funds they would withdraw from the business may be needed in future. This is sometimes overdone, with the result that a business has excessive amounts of liquid funds being inefficiently used when, if they were paid out to the shareholders, who are, after all, the owners of the business, the shareholders could put the funds to better use themselves.

This then leaves the question of the balance on the profit and loss account. If it is a credit balance, is it a revenue reserve? Yes. If profits are not distributed by way of dividend, they are revenue reserves until such time as they are converted into share capital or transfered to other reserves.

9.4 Capital reserves

A **capital reserve** is a reserve which is *not* available for cash dividends. Most capital reserves can never be utilised for cash dividend purposes – notice the use of the word 'cash', as it will be seen later that bonus shares may be issued as a 'non-cash' dividend.

Let us look at the ways in which capital reserves are created.

Capital reserves created in accordance with the Companies Acts

The Companies Acts state that the following are capital reserves and can never be utilised for the declaration of dividends payable in cash:

1 Capital redemption reserve – *see* Chapter 6.
2 Share premium account – *see* Chapter 5.
3 Revaluation reserve – where an asset has been revalued, an increase is shown by a debit in the requisite asset account and a credit to a revaluation reserve account. The recording of a reduction in value is shown by a credit in the asset account and a debit in the revaluation reserve account.

Capital reserves created by case law

Distributable profits as defined by the Companies Acts have been described earlier in this book. The definition includes the words 'in accordance with principles generally accepted'. As accounting develops and changes there will obviously be changes made in the 'principles generally accepted'.

Quite a few legal cases have established exactly whether an item represents a distributable profit and, therefore, is available for cash dividend purposes. Where it is not, the item that is not distributable should be transferred to a capital reserve account. These cases will be studied at the more advanced stages of accounting, so will not be dealt with here.

9.5 Using capital reserves

These can be used only in accordance with the Companies Acts. The following description of the actions which can be taken assumes that the Articles of Association (*see* Chapter 4) are the same as Table A for this purpose, and that therefore there are no provisions in the articles to prohibit such actions.

Capital redemption reserve (for creation *see* Chapter 6)

1 To be applied in paying up unissued shares of the company as fully paid shares. These are commonly called bonus shares, and are dealt with in Chapter 10.
2 Can be reduced only in the manner as to reduction of share capital (*see* Chapter 10).
3 Can be reduced, in the case of a private company, where the permissible capital payment is greater than the nominal value of shares redeemed/purchased (*see* Chapter 6).

Share premium account (for creation *see* Chapter 5)

1 The same provision referring to bonus shares as exists with the capital redemption reserve.
2 Writing off expenses and commission paid on the issue of shares or debenture that gave rise to the share premium used for this purpose.
3 Providing any premium payable on redemption or purchases of shares or debentures.

Revaluation reserve

Where the directors are of the opinion that any amount standing to the credit of the revaluation reserve is no longer necessary then the reserve must be reduced accordingly. An instance of this would be where an increase in the value of an asset had been credited to the revaluation account, and there had subsequently been a fall in the value of that asset.

The revaluation reserve may also be reduced where the permissible capital payment exceeds the nominal value of the shares redeemed/purchased.

Profits prior to incorporation (for creation *see* Chapter 7)

These can be used for the issuing of bonus shares, paying up partly paid shares, or alternatively they may be used to write down goodwill or some such similar fixed asset.

Created by case law

These can be used in the issue of bonus shares or in the paying up of partly paid shares.

9.6 Distributable profits

Distributable profits have already been defined. Accounting standards will apply unless they come into conflict with the Companies Acts themselves.

Normally the revenue reserves, including any credit balance on the profit and loss account, would equal distributable profit.

Depreciation on revalued assets

There is a conflict here between FRS 15: *Tangible fixed assets* and the Companies Acts. The Companies Acts require depreciation on revalued assets to be based on the revalued amounts. However, the Companies Acts allow the extra depreciation because of the revaluation to be *added back* when calculating distributable profit.

Distributions in kind

Where a company makes a non-cash distribution, for example by giving an investment, and that item (i.e. in this case the investment) has been revalued, it could generally be said that part of the distribution was unrealised profit locked into investment. However, the Companies Acts allow this because the 'unrealised' profit is 'realised' by the distribution (from the company's viewpoint, anyway).

9.7 Distributions and auditors' reports

The Companies Acts prohibit any particular distribution if the auditor's report is qualified, with one exception. The exception is that if the amount involved is *not* material and the auditor agrees to this fact, then distribution of an item can take place.

If a distribution is unlawfully made, any member knowing it to be so could be made to repay it. If the company could not recover such distributions then legal proceedings could be taken against the directors.

Learning outcomes

You should now have learnt:

1 Provisions involve uncertainty over the precise amount involved, it being impossible to determine the amount with 'substantial' accuracy.

2 Liabilities can be determined with 'substantial' accuracy.

3 There are two main categories of reserves:
   (a) revenue reserves (can be freely distributed)
   (b) capital reserves (subject to restrictions on their distribution).

4 There is often no need to transfer amounts from profit and loss into a revenue reserve. However, doing so does signal the likelihood of some future event and so could improve the true and fair view of the financial statements.

5 Some of the uses that can be made of capital reserves.

6 What normally comprises distributable profits.

Answers to activities

9.1 There is no simple answer to this question. Reserves of this type were fairly common some years ago, mainly because they signalled that the business was being prudent and preparing to meet some future expense. Some people might suggest that some transfers of this type were made so as to retain cash in the business and thus avoid the interest costs of borrowing funds. (Funds already held by a business are the cheapest form of finance available.) It could be argued that transferring reserves from the profit and loss account to a repairs reserve, for example, stops shareholders complaining that they have not received a high enough dividend, thus enabling the company to use its cash resources for other purposes.

However, nowadays, investors are more sophisticated than in the past and they are unlikely to be confused by such a transfer between reserves. That is, the fact that reserves had been transferred into a repairs reserve would not prevent investors from complaining that they had not received a high enough dividend. Also, nowadays, they would both wish to know why the transfer had taken place *and* expect it to be used for the purpose indicated.

In reality, it matters not a bit whether businesses make reserve transfers of this type. They may feel it is more informative to do so, but there is no need for such transfers to occur.

9.2 There is no difference. The cash has not been paid out so, in both cases, working capital increases accordingly. Transferring the amount from profit and loss to a general reserve simply indicates that some funds are being retained for an undefined purpose.

Review question

9.1 An extract from the draft financial statements of Either Ltd at 30 November 2005 shows the following figures before allowing for any dividend which might be proposed:

	£000
Ordinary shares of £1 each	400
6% preference shares of £1 each	150
Capital redemption reserve	300
Revaluation reserve	125
General reserve	80
Profit and loss account	13
	1,068
Operating profit before taxation for the year	302
Taxation	145
	157

Additional information includes:

(*i*) The revaluation reserve consists of an increase in the value of freehold property following a valuation in 2003. The property concerned was one of three freehold properties owned by the company and was subsequently sold at the revalued amount.

(*ii*) It has been found that a number of stock items have been included at cost price, but were being sold after the balance sheet date at prices well below cost. To allow for this, stock at 30 November 2005 would need to be reduced by £35,000.

(*iii*) Provision for directors' remuneration should be made in the sum of £43,000.

(*iv*) Included on the balance sheet is £250,000 of research and development expenditure carried forward.

(*v*) No dividends have yet been paid on either ordinary or preference shares for the year to 30 November 2005, but the directors wish to pay the maximum permissible dividends for the year.

(*vi*) Since the draft accounts were produced it has been reported that a major customer of Either Ltd has gone into liquidation and is unlikely to be able to pay more than 50p in the £ to its creditors. At 30 November 2005 this customer owed £60,000 and this has since risen to £180,000.

(*vii*) It has been decided that the depreciation rates for plant and machinery are too low but the effect of the new rates has not been taken into account in constructing the draft financial statements. The following information is available:

Plant and machinery	£
Purchases at the commencement of the business on 1 December 2001 at cost	100,000
Later purchases were: 1 June 2003	25,000
29 February 2004	28,000
31 May 2004	45,000
1 December 2004	50,000

In the draft financial statements depreciation has been charged at the rate of 25 per cent using the reducing balance method and charging a full year's depreciation in the year of purchase. It has been decided to change to the straight line method using the same percentage but charging only an appropriate portion of the depreciation in the year of purchase. There have been no sales of plant and machinery during the period.

Required:

(*a*) Calculate the maximum amount which the directors of Either Ltd may propose as a dividend to be paid to the ordinary shareholders whilst observing the requirements of the Companies Acts. Show all workings and state any assumptions made.

(*b*) Outline and discuss any differences which might have been made to your answer to (*a*) if the company were a public limited company.

For the purposes of this question you may take it that corporation tax is levied at the rate of 50 per cent.

(Association of Chartered Certified Accountants)

You can find a range of additional self-test questions, as well as material to help you with your studies, on the website that accompanies this book at **www.pearsoned.co.uk/wood**

The increase and reduction of the share capital of limited companies

Learning objectives

After you have studied this chapter, you should be able to:

● explain the various ways in which a limited company may alter its share capital

● describe the difference between a bonus issue and a rights issue of shares

● explain why a company may introduce a scheme for the reduction of its capital

● describe the effect upon the balance sheet of bonus issues, rights issues and schemes for the reduction of capital

Introduction

Sometimes companies need to alter their issued share capital. In this chapter, you'll learn about the alternatives available. You'll learn about the difference between scrip issues and rights issues and how to record the appropriate ledger account entries when either occurs. You will also learn that the nominal value of share capital can be reduced, and how to do so.

10.1 Alteration of capital

A limited company may, if authorised by its Articles, and if the correct legal formalities are observed, alter its share capital in any of the following ways:

1 Increase its share capital by issuing new shares, e.g. increase authorised share capital from £500,000 to £1 million and then issue more shares.

2 Consolidate and divide all or any of its share capital into shares of a larger nominal value than its existing shares, for instance convert 500,000 ordinary shares of £1 each into 100,000 ordinary shares of £5 each.

3 Subdivide all, or any, of its shares into shares of smaller denominations, e.g. convert 1 million ordinary shares of £1 each into 2 million ordinary shares of £0.50 each, or 4 million ordinary shares of 25p each.

4 Cancel shares which have not been taken up. This is known as 'diminution of capital', and is not to be confused with 'reduction of capital', described later in the chapter. Thus, a company with an authorised share capital of £200,000 and an issued share capital of £175,000 can alter its share capital to authorised share capital of £175,000 and issued share capital of £175,000.

5 Redenominate shares from a fixed nominal value in one currency (e.g. £) to a fixed nominal value in another currency (e.g. €).

**Activity
10.1** Why do you think a company would wish to change its share capital?

10.2 Bonus shares

These are shares issued to existing shareholders free of charge. An alternative name often used is **scrip issue**.

If the articles give the power, and the requisite legal formalities are observed, the following may be applied in the issuing of bonus shares:

1 The balance of the profit and loss account.
2 Any other revenue reserve.
3 Any capital reserve, e.g. share premium.

This thus comprises all of the reserves.

The reason why this should ever be needed can be illustrated by taking the somewhat exaggerated example shown in Exhibit 10.1.

Exhibit 10.1

When Better Price Ltd started in business 50 years ago, it issued 10,000 ordinary shares of £1 each and deposited £10,000 in the bank. The company has constantly retained a proportion of its profits to finance its operations, thus diverting them from being used for cash dividend purposes. This has preserved an appropriate level of working capital.

The firm's balance sheet as at 31 December 2007 is shown as:

Better Price Ltd
Balance Sheet as at 31 December 2007
(before bonus shares are issued)

	£
Fixed assets	150,000
Current assets *less* current liabilities	150,000
	300,000
Share capital	10,000
Reserves (including profit and loss balance)	290,000
	300,000

If an annual profit of £45,000 was being earned (i.e. 15 per cent on capital employed) and £10,000 were paid annually as cash dividends, then the dividend declared each year would be 100 per cent (i.e. a dividend of £10,000 on shares with a nominal value of £10,000).

It is obvious that the dividends and the share capital are out of step with one another. Employees and trade unions could start complaining due to a lack of accounting knowledge (or even misuse of it) because they believe that the company is making unduly excessive profits. Customers may also be deluded into thinking that they are being charged excessive prices. Even though this could be demonstrated not to be true because of the prices charged by competitors, they may still have the feeling that they are somehow being duped.

In fact, an efficient company in this industry may only be achieving 'average' rewards for the risks it has taken if it is making a profit of 15 per cent on capital employed. The figure of 100 per cent for the dividend is due to the very misleading convention in accounting in the UK of calculating dividends in relationship to the nominal amount of the share capital, rather than the capital employed.

If it is felt that £80,000 of the reserves could not be used for dividend purposes, due to the fact that the net assets should remain at a minimum of £90,000, made up of fixed assets £80,000 and working capital of £10,000, then besides the £10,000 share capital which cannot be returned to the shareholders there are also £80,000 of reserves which cannot be rationally returned to them. Instead of this £80,000 being called reserves, it might as well be called capital, as it is needed by the business on a permanent basis.

To remedy this position, as well as some other less obvious needs, the concept of bonus shares was developed. The reserves are made non-returnable to the shareholders by being converted into share capital. Each holder of one ordinary share of £1 each will receive eight bonus shares (in the shape of eight ordinary shares) of £1 each. The balance sheet, if the bonus shares had been issued immediately, would be:

Better Price Ltd
Balance sheet as at 31 December 2007
(after bonus shares are issued)

	£
Fixed assets	150,000
Current assets *less* current liabilities	150,000
	300,000
Share capital (£10,000 + £80,000)	90,000
Reserves (£290,000 − £80,000)	210,000
	300,000

When the annual dividends of £10,000 are declared in the future, they will represent:

$$\frac{£10,000}{£90,000} \times \frac{100}{1} = \text{a dividend of 11.1 per cent}$$

This will cause fewer problems in the minds of employees, trade unions and customers.

Of course the issue of bonus shares may be seen by any of the interested parties to be some form of excessive generosity on the part of the company. To give eight shares of £1 each free for one previously owned may be seen as unfair by employees and their trade unions. In fact, the shareholders have gained nothing. Before the bonus issue there were 10,000 shareholders who owned between them £300,000 of net assets. Therefore, assuming for this purpose that the book 'value' is the same as any other 'value', each share was worth £30. After the bonus issue, each shareholder has nine shares for every one share held before. If a shareholder had owned one share only, he now owns nine shares. He is therefore, the owner of $^9/_{90,000}$ of the company. The 'value' of the net assets is £300,000, and he owns $^9/_{90,000}$ of them, so his shares are worth £30. This is exactly the same 'value' as that applying before the bonus issue was made.

It would be useful, in addition, to refer to other matters for comparison. Anyone who had owned a £1 share 50 years ago, then worth £1, would now have nine £1 shares. A new house of a certain type 50 years ago might have cost £x; it may now cost £9x. Price inflation affects different items in different ways. The cost of a bottle of beer may now be y times greater than it was 50 years ago, a loaf of bread may cost z times more, and so on. But, at least the shareholders now have some tangible increase in the nominal value of their investment. Of course, the company has brought a lot of trouble on itself by waiting so many years to capitalise its reserves. It should have been done in several stages over the years.

This is a very simplified example, but it is a situation many companies have had to face. There is, also, no doubt that a misunderstanding of accounting and financial matters has caused a great deal of unnecessary friction in the past and will probably still do so in the future. Yet another very common misunderstanding is the assumption that the asset balance sheet values equal the amount they could be sold for. Thus, a profit of £100,000 when the book value of the net assets is £200,000 may appear to be excessive, yet if the realisable value of the net assets were used, the net worth of the company may be £2 million, making a profit of £100,000 appear perhaps a little low, rather than appearing excessive.

The accounting entries when bonus shares are issued are to debit the reserve accounts utilised, and to credit a bonus account. The shares are then issued and the entry required to record this is to credit the share capital account and to debit the bonus account. The journal entries in our example would be:

The Journal

	Dr	Cr
	£	£
Reserve account(s) (show each account separately)	80,000	
Bonus account		80,000
Transfer of an amount equal to the bonus payable in fully paid shares		
Bonus account	80,000	
Share capital account		80,000
Allotment and issue of 80,000 shares of £1 each, in satisfaction of the bonus declared		

10.3 Rights issue

You learnt in Chapter 5 that a company can also increase its issued share capital by making a **rights issue**. This is the issue of shares to existing shareholders at a price lower than the ruling market price of the shares. You will remember that the price is lower so as to compensate for the reduction in value of shares held previously.

The price at which the shares of a profitable company are quoted on the Stock Exchange is usually higher than the nominal value of the shares. For instance, the market price of the shares of a company might be quoted at £2.50 while the nominal value per share is only £1.00. If the company has 800,000 shares of £1 each and declares a rights issue of one for every eight held at a price of £1.50 per share, it is obvious that it will be cheaper for the existing shareholders to buy the rights issue at this price instead of buying the same shares in the open market for £2.50 per share. Assume that all the rights issue were taken up, then the number of shares taken up will be 100,000 (i.e. 800,000 ÷ 8), and the amount paid for them will be £150,000. The journal entries will be:

The Journal

	Dr	Cr
	£	£
Cash	150,000	
Share capital		100,000
Share premium		50,000
Being the rights issue of 1 for every 8 shares held at a price of £1.50 nominal value being £1.00		

As the nominal value of each share is £1.00 while £1.50 was paid, the extra 50p constitutes a share premium to the company.

Notice also that the market value of the shares will be reduced or 'diluted' by the rights issue, as was the case for bonus shares. Before the rights issue there were 800,000 shares at a price of £2.50, giving a market capitalisation of £2 million. After the rights issue there are 900,000 shares and the assets have increased by £150,000. The market value may now be £2.39 [(£2 million + £150,000)/900,000], although the precise market price after the rights issue will be influenced by the information given surrounding the sale about the future prospects of the company and may not be exactly the £2.39 calculated above.

10.4 Reduction of capital

Where capital is not represented by assets

Any scheme for the reduction of capital needs to go through legal formalities via the shareholders and other interested parties, and must receive the consent of the court.

Capital reduction means that the share capital – all of it if there is only one class such as ordinary shares, or all or part of it if there is more than one class of shares – has been subjected to a lessening of its nominal value, or of the called-up part of the nominal value. Thus:

(a) a £4 share might be converted into a £3 share;
(b) a £5 share might be converted into a £1 share;
(c) a £3 share, £2 called up, might be converted into a £1 share fully paid up;
(d) a £5 share, £3 called up, might be converted into a £3 share £1 called up;

plus any other variations.

Why should such action be necessary? The reasons are rather like the issue of bonus shares in reverse. However, in this case, the share capital has fallen out of line with the assets, in that the share capital is not fully represented by assets. For example, Robert Ltd may have a balance sheet as follows:

Robert Ltd
Balance Sheet as at 31 December 2007

	£
Net assets	300,000
Ordinary share capital	
100,000 ordinary shares of £5 each, fully paid	500,000
Less Profit and loss (debit balance)	(200,000)
	300,000

The net assets are shown at £300,000, and it is felt that the book value represents a true and fair view of their actual value. The company will almost certainly be precluded from paying dividends until the debit balance on the profit and loss account has been eradicated and replaced with a credit balance. If profits remaining after taxation are now running at the rate of £30,000 per annum, it will be seven years before a dividend can be paid. One reason for buying shares is to provide income (although there may well enter another reason, such as capital appreciation). Consequently, the denial of income to the shareholders for this period of time could seriously affect the company.

A solution would be to cancel, i.e. reduce, the capital which was no longer represented by assets. In this case, £200,000 of the share capital can lay no claim to any assets. The share capital should therefore be reduced by £200,000. This is done by converting the shares into £3 shares fully paid instead of £5 shares. The balance sheet would become:

Robert Ltd
Balance Sheet as at 31 December 2007

	£
Net assets	300,000
	300,000
Ordinary share capital	300,000
	300,000

Now that there is no debit balance on the profit and loss appropriation account, the £30,000 available profit next year can be distributed as dividends.

Of course, the Robert Ltd example has been simplified to make what is being explained easier to understand. Often, both preference and ordinary shareholders are involved. Sometimes, debenture holders as well. Even creditors occasionally sacrifice part of the amount owing to them, the idea being that the increase in working capital so generated will help the firm to achieve prosperity, in which case the creditors hope to once again enjoy the profitable contact that they used to have with the company.

Capital reduction schemes are matters for negotiation between the various interested parties. For instance, preference shareholders may be quite content for the nominal value of their shares to be reduced if the rate of interest they receive is increased accordingly. As with any negoti-ation, the various parties will put forward their points of view and discussions will take place until a compromise solution is arrived at. When the court's sanction has been obtained, the accounting entries are:

1 For amounts written off assets:
     Dr Capital reduction account
        Cr Various asset accounts

2 For reduction in liabilities (e.g. creditors):
     Dr Liability accounts
        Cr Capital reduction account

3 The reduction in the share capital:
     Dr Share capital accounts (each type)
        Cr Capital reduction account

4 If a credit balance now exists on the capital reduction account:
     Dr Capital reduction account (to close)
        Cr Capital reserve

It is unlikely that there would ever be a debit balance on the capital reduction account, as the court would rarely agree to any scheme which would bring this about.

Capital reduction schemes for private companies are used less frequently now than previously, thanks to companies having been granted the right to purchase their own shares.

Where some of the assets are no longer needed

Where some of the assets are no longer needed, probably due to a contraction in its activities, a company may find itself with a surplus of liquid assets. Subject to the legal formalities being observed, in this case the reduction of capital is effected by returning cash to the shareholders, i.e.:

1 Dr Share capital account (with amount returnable)
        Cr Sundry shareholders

2 Dr Sundry shareholders
        Cr Bank (amount actually paid)

The Creditors could object to such a scheme if it affected their interests.

Learning outcomes

You should now have learnt:

1 A limited company may alter its share capital if it is authorised to do so by its Articles of Association.

2 Alterations to share capital can be made by a limited company:
   (a) issuing new shares;
   (b) consolidating all or any of its share capital into shares of a higher nominal value;
   (c) subdividing all or any of its share capital into shares of a lower nominal value;
   (d) cancelling shares that have not been 'taken up' – the difference between the 'authorised share capital' and the 'issued share capital';
   (e) redenominating shares into a different currency.

3 Some reasons why companies change their share capital.

4 Where share capital is overvalued in relation to assets, a capital reduction scheme may be adopted in order to bring the share capital into line with the underlying asset value of the business as reported in the balance sheet.

Answer to activity

10.1 As you will see later in this chapter, there are many possible reasons. It may be that the nominal value of the share capital is significantly understated compared with current earnings. An increase in nominal share capital would help redress this imbalance and make things like earnings per share more intuitively meaningful. Alternatively, it may be that large reserves have been built up and the company wishes to increase the amount of its share capital by converting the reserves into shares. Another possibility is that the share price has risen significantly since the shares were first quoted on the Stock Exchange and it now appears unreasonably high relative to comparable shares. By splitting each share into a number of shares of a lower nominal value, the share price can be brought back to an appropriate level. Don't forget, companies can both increase and reduce the nominal value of their share capital.

Review questions

10.1 The Merton Manufacturing Co Ltd has been in business for many years making fitted furniture and chairs. During 2004 and 2005 substantial losses have been sustained on the manufacture of chairs and the directors have decided to concentrate on the fitted furniture side of the business which is expected to produce a profit of at least £22,500 per annum before interest charges and taxation. A capital reduction scheme has been proposed under which:

(i) a new ordinary share of 50p nominal value will be created;
(ii) the £1 ordinary shares will be written off and the shareholders will be offered one new ordinary share for every six old shares held;
(iii) the £1 6 per cent redeemable preference shares will be cancelled and the holders will be offered for every three existing preference shares and one new ordinary share;
(iv) the existing 11 per cent debenture will be exchanged for a new debenture yielding 8 per cent at a rate of 2 old debentures for 3 new debentures. In addition, existing debenture holders will be offered one new ordinary share for every £4 of the old debenture held;
(v) existing reserves will be written-off;

(*vi*) goodwill is to be written-off;

(*vii*) any remaining balance of write-off which is necessary is to be achieved by writing down plant and equipment; and

(*viii*) existing ordinary shareholders will be invited to subscribe for two fully paid new ordinary shares at par for every three old shares held.

The balance sheet of the Merton Manufacturing Co Ltd immediately prior to the capital reduction is as follows:

	£	£	£
Fixed intangible assets			
Goodwill at cost less amounts written off			50,000
Fixed tangible assets			
Freehold land and buildings at cost			95,000
Plant and equipment at cost		275,000	
Less Depreciation to date		(89,500)	
			185,500
			330,500
Current assets			
Stocks		25,000	
Debtors		50,000	
		75,000	
Current liabilities			
Creditors	63,500		
Bank overdraft	15,850		
		(79,350)	
Excess of current liabilities			(4,350)
			326,150
Long-term loan			
11$\frac{1}{2}$ per cent debenture, secured on the freehold land and buildings			(100,000)
			226,150

	£
Share capital and reserves	
£1 ordinary shares fully paid	90,000
6 per cent £1 redeemable preference shares fully paid	150,000
Share premium account	25,000
Profit and loss account	(38,850)
	226,150

On liquidation, freehold land and buildings are expected to produce £120,000; plant and equipment £40,000; stocks £15,000; and debtors £45,000. Goodwill has no value.

There are no termination costs associated with ceasing the manufacture of chairs.

Required:

(a) Assuming that the necessary approval is obtained and that the new share issue is successful, produce a balance sheet of the company showing the position immediately after the scheme has been put into effect.

(b) Show the effect of the scheme on the expected earnings of the old shareholders.

(c) Indicate the points which a preference shareholder should take into account before voting on the scheme.

Corporation tax may be taken at 33$\frac{1}{3}$ per cent.

(*Association of Chartered Certified Accountants*)

→

→ **10.2** Deflation Ltd, which had experienced trading difficulties, decided to reorganise its finances. On 31 December 2005 a final trial balance extracted from the books showed the following position:

	£	£
Share capital, authorised and issued:		
150,000 6 per cent cumulative preference shares of £1 each		150,000
200,000 ordinary shares of £1 each		200,000
Share premium account		40,000
Profit and loss account	114,375	
Preliminary expenses	7,250	
Goodwill (at cost)	55,000	
Trade creditors		43,500
Debtors	31,200	
Bank overdraft		51,000
Leasehold property (at cost)	80,000	
(provision for depreciation)		30,000
Plant and machinery (at cost)	210,000	
(provision for depreciation)		62,500
Stock in hand	79,175	
	577,000	577,000

Approval of the Court was obtained for the following scheme for reduction of capital:

1 The preference shares to be reduced to £0.75 per share.
2 The ordinary shares to be reduced to £0.125 per share.
3 One £0.125 ordinary share to be issued for each £1 of gross preference dividend arrears; the preference dividend had not been paid for three years.
4 The balance on share premium account to be utilised.
5 Plant and machinery to be written down to £75,000.
6 The profit and loss account balance, and all intangible assets, to be written off.

At the same time as the resolution to reduce capital was passed, another resolution was approved restoring the total authorised capital to £350,000, consisting of 150,000 6 per cent cumulative preference shares of £0.75 each and the balance in ordinary shares of £0.125 each. As soon as the above resolutions had been passed 500,000 ordinary shares were issued at par, for cash, payable in full upon application.

You are required:
(a) to show the journal entries necessary to record the above transactions in the company's books; and
(b) to prepare a balance sheet of the company, after completion of the scheme.

(Institute of Chartered Accountants)

10.3 On 31 March 2002, the following was the balance sheet of Planting Trees Ltd.

Balance Sheet

	£	£	£
Fixed assets			
Goodwill and trade marks as valued		160,000	
Plant and machinery (at cost *less* depreciation)		430,000	
Furniture and fittings (at cost *less* depreciation)		28,000	
			618,000
Current assets			
Stock		230,000	
Sundry debtors		84,000	
Cash		2,000	
Less: Current liabilities		316,000	
Sundry creditors	55,000		
Bank overdraft	71,000	(126,000)	
			190,000
			808,000
Authorised capital			
100,000 5 per cent preference shares of £1 each		100,000	
6 million ordinary shares of 25p each		1,500,000	
		2,600,000	
Issued and fully paid capital			
100,000 5 per cent preference shares of £1 each			100,000
3,600,000 ordinary shares of 25p each			900,000
			1,000,000
Capital reserve		90,000	
Less: Profit and loss		(282,000)	(192,000)
			808,000

The following scheme of capital reduction was sanctioned by the Court and agreed by the shareholders:

(a) Preference shares were to be reduced to 60p each.
(b) Ordinary shares were to be reduced to 15p each.
(c) The capital reserve was to be eliminated.
(d) The reduced shares of both classes were to be consolidated into new ordinary shares of £1 each.
(e) An issue of £400,000 7 per cent debentures at par was to be made to provide fresh working capital.
(f) The sum written off the issued capital of the company and the capital reserve to be used to write off the debit balance of the profit and loss account and to reduce fixed assets by the following amounts:

Goodwill and trade marks	108,000
Plant and machinery	80,000
Furniture and fittings	20,000

(g) The bank overdraft was to be paid off out of the proceeds of the debentures which were duly issued and paid in full.

A further resolution was passed to reduce the authorised capital of the company to 1,750,000 ordinary shares of £1 each.

Required:
Prepare journal entries (cash transactions to be journalised) to give effect to the above scheme and draw up the balance sheet of the company after completion of the scheme.

→

10.4A The balance sheet of Tatters Ltd on 31 December 2008 was as follows:

Balance Sheet

	£	£
Goodwill		50,000
Fixed assets		190,000
		240,000
Current assets		
Stock	21,000	
Work in progress	3,000	
Debtors	25,000	
Bank	18,000	
		67,000
Capital expenses		
Formation expenses		3,000
		310,000
Less: Current liabilities		
Creditors		(30,000)
		280,000
Less: 5 per cent debentures		(60,000)
		220,000
Issued share capital		
200,000 ordinary shares of £1 each		200,000
100,000 4 per cent cumulative preference shares of £1 each		100,000
		300,000
Less: Profit and loss		(80,000)
		220,000

The dividend on the preference shares is £12,000 in arrears. A scheme of reconstruction was accepted by all parties and was completed on 1 January 2009.

A new company was formed, Rags Ltd, with an authorised share capital of £250,000, consisting of 250,000 ordinary shares of £1 each. This company took over all the assets of Tatters Ltd. The purchase consideration was satisfied partly in cash and partly by the issue, at par, of shares and 6 per cent debentures by the new company in accordance with the following arrangements:

1 The creditors of the old company received, in settlement of each £10 due to them, £6 in cash and four fully paid ordinary shares in the new company.
2 The holders of preference shares in the old company received nine fully paid ordinary shares in the new company to every ten preference shares in the old company and four fully paid ordinary shares in the new company for every £5 of arrears of dividend.
3 The ordinary shareholders in the old company received one fully paid share in the new company for every four ordinary shares in the old company.
4 The holders of 5 per cent debentures in the old company received £50 in cash and £50 of 6 per cent debentures issued at par for every £100 debenture held in the old company.
5 The balance of the authorised capital of the new company was issued at par for cash and was fully paid on 1 January 2009.
6 Goodwill was eliminated, the stock was valued at £15,000 and the other current assets were brought into the new company's books at the amounts at which they appeared in the old company's balance sheet. The balance of the purchase consideration represented the agreed value of the fixed assets.

You are required to show:
(a) the closing entries in the realisation account and the sundry shareholders account in the books of Tatters Ltd.
(b) your calculation of:
  (i) the purchase consideration for the assets, and
  (ii) the agreed value of the fixed assets;
(c) the summarised balance sheet of Rags Ltd as on 1 January 2009.

10.5A The ledger balances of Tick Tick Ltd at 31 March 2011 were as follows:

	£
Freehold premises	90,000
Plant	300,000
Stock	82,000
Debtors	96,000
Development expenditure*	110,000
Cash at bank	11,000
Profit and loss (debit balance)	121,000
250,000 8 per cent preference shares of £1 each	250,000
500,000 ordinary shares of £1 each	500,000
Creditors	60,000

A capital reduction scheme has been sanctioned under which the 250,000 preference shares are to be reduced to 80p each, fully paid; and the 500,000 ordinary shares are to be reduced to 20p each, fully paid.

Development expenditure and the debit balance on profit and loss account are to be written off, the balance remaining being used to reduce the book value of the plant.

Required:
Prepare the journal entries recording the reduction scheme and the balance sheet as it would appear immediately after the reduction. Narrations are not required in connection with journal entries.

***Development expenditure is a fixed asset. (*See* Chapter 11.)**

You can find a range of additional self-test questions, as well as material to help you with your studies, on the website that accompanies this book at **www.pearsoned.co.uk/wood**

Accounting standards and related documents

Learning objectives

After you have studied this chapter, you should be able to:

● explain the measures being taken by the Accounting Standards Board to develop a framework for the preparation and presentation of financial statements

● describe the full range of UK accounting standards currently in issue, their aims and objectives, and identify the equivalent international accounting standards

Introduction

In this chapter, you'll learn about the background to the formation of the UK Accounting Standards Board and of the range of UK accounting standards issued since 1971.

11.1 Why do we need accounting standards?

Accounting is used in every kind of business and organisation, from large multinational organisations to your local shop, from sole traders to companies. It can cover an unlimited range of activities as different as breweries, charities, churches, dentists, doctors, lawyers, mines, oil wells, betting shops, banks, cinemas, circuses, funeral undertakers, farms, waste disposal, deep-sea diving, airlines, estate agents and so on.

Let's assume that you have received a copy of the published financial statements of a company. You want to be sure that you can rely on the methods it selected to calculate its revenues, expenditures and balance sheet values. Without this assurance you would not be able to have any faith at all in the figures, and could not sensibly take any decision concerning your relationship with the company.

It is the same for all investors. People invest in organisations of all types and they would all like to have faith and trust in the figures reported in their financial statements. But this diversity of type of business, and also of size, means that, while general principles can be laid down, detailed regulations that it would make sense to apply to one company would be wholly inappropriate for another company. It is, quite simply, impossible to provide 100 per cent assurance of the validity of the financial statements of every conceivable organisation through the creation of a single set of rules and procedures. There has to be some flexibility within the rules laid down.

If it isn't feasible to produce a set of all-encompassing regulations, why bother with rules at all? To understand why there was a move to regulation, we need to look back to what happened in the 1960s.

11.2 The background

In the late 1960s there was a general outcry that the methods used by different businesses were showing vastly different profits on similar data. In the UK, a controversy had arisen following the takeover of AEI Ltd by GEC Ltd. In fighting the takeover bid made by GEC, the AEI directors had produced a forecast, in the tenth month of their financial year, that the profit before tax for the year would be £10 million. After the takeover, the financial statements of AEI for that same year showed a loss of £4.5 million. The difference was attributed to there being £5 million of 'matters substantially of fact' and £9.5 million of 'adjustments which remain matters substantially of judgement'.

The financial pages of the national press started demanding action, calling for the accounting profession to lay down consistent principles for businesses to follow.

In December 1969, the Institute of Chartered Accountants in England and Wales issued a *Statement of Intent on Accounting Standards in the 1970s*. The Institute set up the Accounting Standards Steering Committee in 1970. Over the following six years, it was joined by the five other UK and Irish accountancy bodies and, in 1976, the committee became the Accounting Standards Committee (ASC). The six accountancy bodies formed the Consultative Committee of Accountancy Bodies (CCAB).

Prior to the issue of any accounting standard by the ASC, a great deal of preparatory work was done and an exposure draft (ED) was issued and copies were sent to those with a special interest in the topic for comment. The journals of the CCAB (i.e. the official magazines of each of the six accountancy bodies) also gave full details of the exposure drafts. After the period allowed for consultation ended, it was seen to be desirable, and an accounting standard on the topic was issued. The Standards issued by the ASC were called Statements of Standard Accounting Practice (SSAPs).

Because the ASC had to obtain approval from its six professional accountancy body members, it did not appear to be as decisive and independent as was desired. In 1990, a new body, the Accounting Standards Board (ASB), took over the functions of the ASC. The ASB is more independent of the accounting bodies and can issue its recommendations, known as financial reporting standards (FRSs), without approval from any other body. The ASB adopted the SSAPs in force but many have since been replaced by FRSs (of which 27 were in force in December 2007) and, as at December 2007, only 7 SSAPs remained in force. As with the ASC, the ASB issues exposure drafts – FREDs – on which comments are invited prior to the issue of a new standard.

In 1997, the ASB issued a third category of standard – the Financial Reporting Standard for Smaller Entities (FRSSE). SSAPs and FRSs had generally been developed with the larger company in mind. The FRSSE was the ASB's response to the view that smaller companies should not have to apply all the cumbersome rules contained in the SSAPs and FRSs. It is, in effect, a collection of some of the rules from virtually all the other accounting standards. Small companies can choose whether or not to apply the FRSSE or, as seems unlikely, continue to apply all the other accounting standards.

In addition to the FRSs and the FRSSE, the ASB also issues Urgent Issues Task Force Abstracts (UITFs). These are issued in response to an urgent need to regulate something pending the issue of a new or amended FRS. They have the same status as an FRS but, due to the perceived urgent need for them to be issued, no exposure drafts are issued. Forty-five UITFs had been issued by December 2007, of which 26 were still in force.

While there is no general law compelling observation of the standards, accounting standards have had statutory recognition since the Companies Act 1989. As a result, apart from entities exempted from certain standards or sections within standards – SSAPs 13 (*Research and development*) and 25 (*Segmental reporting*), and FRS 1 (*Cash flow statements*), for example, all contain exemption clauses based on company size – accounting standards must be complied with by all entities when preparing financial statements intended to present a 'true and fair view'. The Companies Acts state that failure to comply with the requirements of an accounting standard must be explained in the financial statements.

Historically, the main method of ensuring compliance with the standards by their members has always been through each professional body's own disciplinary procedures on their members. The ASB felt this was insufficient – such measures seek to control only individual accountants, not the organisations they work for. As a result, it created a Review Panel with power to prosecute companies under civil law where their financial statements contain a major breach of the standards.

In 2005, all companies listed on the stock exchange preparing consolidated (i.e. group) financial statements were required to switch from UK GAAP to International GAAP. All other companies were given the option of doing so, and many have. It is only a question of time before they all do so.

The ASB has been at pains to ensure that most of the provisions of the relevant international standards are incorporated in existing SSAPs or FRSs, the difference in the information required or in the manner of its presentation is often minimal. To this end, each FRS indicates the level of compliance with the relevant international standard(s), making it easier for companies to determine the potential impact on their financial statements should they adopt international standards instead of SSAPs and FRSs.

This book deals in outline with all UK accounting standards issued and still in force in April 2008. It does not deal with all the many detailed points contained in the standards and exposure drafts. It would be a far larger book if this was attempted. Students at the later stages of their professional examinations will need to get full copies of all standards and study them thoroughly. [You will find similar details and coverage of International Accounting Standards in *Business Accounting 2*.]

The remainder of this chapter deals with all the current UK accounting standards and related documents which are not covered in detail elsewhere in this book.

This changing regulatory environment clearly creates problems for students and authors alike. *Be guided by your teachers and lecturers and, most importantly, by the syllabus you are to be examined upon. It is likely that most exam bodies will continue to focus upon UK standards, at least in the short term.*

During this transition period, although this book focuses on UK accounting standards, reference to the equivalent international standard(s) will be made when appropriate and the manner in which the requirements of the equivalent international standard(s) differ on specific topics will also be shown. At the end of this chapter is a table listing the UK accounting standards and their international equivalent, in case you should need to refer to them by number or name.

The next section presents an overview of the history of international accounting standards.

11.3 International accounting standards

The Accounting Standards Board issues accounting standards for adoption in the UK and Ireland. Other countries also have their own accounting standards boards – for example, the FASB (Financial Accounting Standards Board) operates in the USA and Australia has the AASB (Australian Accounting Standards Board). However, many smaller countries could not justify the creation of their own accounting standards but needed some form of regulation over the financial statements produced. This led, in 1973, to the setting up of the International Accounting Standards Committee (IASC). The IASC was replaced in 2001 by the International Accounting Standards Board (IASB). At that time, like the ASB, the IASB adopted all the International Accounting Standards (IASs) that the IASC had issued. All new standards issued by the IASB are called International Financial Reporting Standards (IFRSs).

The work of the IASB is overseen by 22 trustees, six from Europe, six from North America, and six from Asia/Pacific. The remaining four trustees can be from anywhere so long as the geographical balance is maintained. The IASB has 12 full-time members and two part-time members. Its members must reflect an appropriate balance of auditors, financial statement preparers, users of financial statements and academics.

When the IASC was founded, it had no formal authority and the IASs were entirely voluntary and initially intended for use in countries that did not have their own accounting standards or which had considerable logistical difficulty in establishing and maintaining the infrastructure necessary to sustain a national accounting standards board.

Apart from providing standards for use in countries that do not issue their own accounting standards, the need today for the IASB is mainly due to:

1 The considerable growth in international investment, which means it is desirable to have similar methods the world over so that investment decisions are more compatible.
2 The growth in multinational firms which have to produce financial statements covering a large number of countries. Standardisation between countries makes the accounting work easier, and reduces costs.
3 The fact that it is desirable that the activities and efforts of the various national standard-setting bodies be harmonised.

Activity 11.1   Why do you think this switch in the UK and Ireland towards international accounting standards has occurred?

Let's look at the principles that underpin accounting standards.

11.4   Statement of Principles

In 1999, the Accounting Standards Board issued its *Statement of Principles*. The objective of this document is to assist the ASB, and all other users of financial statements (*see* Chapter 27), by clarifying the concepts that underlie its work and so, therefore, underpin the rules issued by the ASB relating to the preparation and presentation of financial statements. The *Statement of Principles* is not, however, an accounting standard. It does not contain any requirements on how financial statements should be prepared and does not override any standard.

When the ASB first started developing the *Statement of Principles*, it drew heavily upon the IASC's 1989 *Framework for the Preparation and Presentation of Financial Statements*. The *Statement of Principles* is very similar in content to the framework documents issued by the accounting standard-setters in Australia, Canada, New Zealand and the USA, so aiding the move towards internationalisation of accounting standards and harmonisation of accounting practice.

Objectives

'The objective of Financial Statements is to provide information about the financial position, performance and financial adaptability of an enterprise, that is useful to a wide range of users in making economic decisions.'

Information

The *Statement of Principles* emphasises that a key characteristic of the information contained in financial statements is that it be useful. A diagram was included in an early draft of the *Statement of Principles* which shows how these characteristics related to each other. The diagram is shown in Exhibit 11.1.

Exhibit 11.1 The qualitative characteristics of accounting information

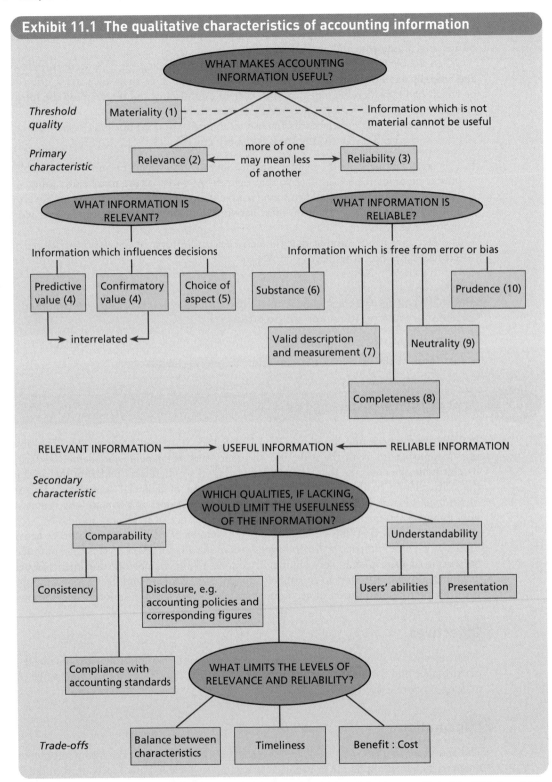

Qualitative characteristics of financial information

Financial statements should contain information that is 'useful'. Information is useful if it is *relevant*, *reliable*, *comparable* and *understandable*. The four terms are defined by the ASB as follows:

1 **Relevant.** Information is relevant if it has the ability to influence the economic decisions of users and is provided in time to influence those decisions.
2 **Reliable.** Information is reliable if:
   (*a*) it can be depended upon to represent faithfully what it either purports to represent or could reasonably be expected to represent, and therefore reflects the substance of the transactions and other events that have taken place;
   (*b*) it is complete and is free from deliberate or systematic bias and material error; and
   (*c*) in its preparation under conditions of uncertainty, a degree of caution has been applied in exercising the necessary judgements.
3 **Comparable.** Information is comparable if it enables users to discern and evaluate similarities in, and differences between, the nature and effects of transactions and other events over time and across different reporting entities.
4 **Understandable.** Information is understandable if its significance can be perceived by users that have a reasonable knowledge of business and economic activities and accounting and a willingness to study with reasonable diligence the information provided.

Where there is a conflict between these four characteristics, the objectives of financial statements must be met by arriving at a trade-off. For example, relevance is considered to be more important than reliability.

Notes indicated by the numbers in brackets in Exhibit 11.1 give further insights into these four characteristics.

Note 1

An item of information is material to the financial statements if its omission or mis-statement might influence an economic decision of a user of the financial statements. It follows that information which is not material is not useful and is therefore beyond the threshold for inclusion in the financial statements.

Note 2

To be useful, information must be relevant to the decision-taking needs of users. Relevance relates to the influence of the information on the user's evaluation of events – past, present or future. This evaluation can be influenced by the way items in financial statements are presented.

Note 3

As you saw earlier, reliability means information free from material error and bias and which can be relied on by users to conform with descriptions given.

It is clear that information may be very relevant but unreliable – e.g. a betting tip at a horse race. Reliability may not ensure relevance, e.g. reliable analysis of last year's performance may exclude important indicators of future potential, such as new management in position. *Relevance* and *reliability* are primary characteristics of accounting information.

They are broken down into further characteristics as follows.

Notes on relevance

Note 4

Predictive value means using an analysis of current or past performance to predict a future outcome. The same information can be used to confirm whether predictions in past periods have come true. Confirmatory value is this second part, i.e. checking past predictions.

Note 5

The term 'choice of aspect' implies that there may be significant choice for the preparer of accounts as to which aspects of transactions to represent. For example, a business might acquire a new building in a good position for trading and on which it owns the freehold. Another relevant piece of information is that the property is in an area proposed for a new motorway and could well be the subject of a compulsory purchase order. To be relevant to a user who wishes to value the business for future prospects, both aspects of the information are relevant. Note that a simple statement that the property was owned and showing its purchase price would be a valid description and measurement and therefore reliable – so far as it went.

Notes on reliability

Note 6

Substance indicates that information should represent the events it purports to represent. Sometimes complex legal arrangements may be entered into to obscure the ownership of assets. To be reliable, the true operation and ownership of the assets with respect to the substance must be reflected in the financial statements. Artificial legal transactions should not obscure the substance.

Note 7

Although the title indicates the intention, it is important to relate this aspect of reliability to Note 5 'choice of aspect'. 'Valid description and measurement' needs to be applied to the appropriate aspects of events.

Note 8

This indicates that incomplete information may make it false or misleading and thus not relevant.

Note 9

Neutrality implies freedom from bias. This indicates that financial statements should not be prepared with the intention of influencing decisions in any particular way.

Note 10

Prudence implies a degree of caution (anticipating losses) in the valuation of assets. In many cases this is subjective as it relates to the future, e.g. in predicting doubtful debts. This aspect should not be used to overestimate potential losses and thus misrepresent the affairs of an organisation.

In the second part of the chart, secondary characteristics which, if lacking, would limit the usefulness of the information are shown. Comparability and understandability have already been covered above. The other items shown are self-explanatory and are not discussed further in this text.

 Activity 11.2 Why do you think there is such an emphasis on the 'qualitative' aspects of information in the *Statement of Principles*?

We'll now look at each of the current UK accounting standards, in number order. However, because it underpins every other UK accounting standard, we'll start by looking at FRS 18: *Accounting policies.*

11.5 FRS 18: Accounting policies

Users of financial statements issued by organisations want to analyse and evaluate the figures contained within them. They cannot do this effectively unless they know which accounting policies have been used when preparing such statements. This FRS was issued to help continue the improvement in the quality of financial reporting that had been started in 1971 by the accounting standard it replaced, SSAP 2.

The FRS focuses upon **accounting policies** and considers the **estimation techniques** used in implementing them. It also looks in detail at the various accounting concepts.

Accounting policies

These are defined in FRS 18 as:

> *those principles, bases, conventions, rules and practices applied by an entity that specify how the effects of transactions and other events are to be reflected in its financial statements through:*
> *(i) recognising,*
> *(ii) selecting measurement basis for, and*
> *(iii) presenting*
> *assets, liabilities, gains, losses and changes to shareholders' funds.*

In other words, accounting policies define the processes whereby transactions and other events are reflected in the financial statements. The accounting policies selected should enable the financial statements to give a true and fair view and should be consistent with accounting standards, UITFs and company legislation.

When selecting an accounting policy, its appropriateness should be considered in the context of the four 'objectives' (or characteristics of information) you met when you learnt about the *Statement of Principles*:

1 *Relevance* – Does the accounting policy produce information that is useful for assessing stewardship and for making economic decisions?
2 *Reliability* – Does it reflect the substance of the transaction and other events that have occurred? Is it free of bias, i.e. neutral? Is it free of material error? If produced under uncertainty, has prudence been exercised?
3 *Comparability* – Can it be compared with similar information about the entity for some other period or point in time?
4 *Understandability* – Is it capable of being understood by users who have a reasonable knowledge of business and economic activities and accounting?

Estimation techniques

These are the methods adopted in order to arrive at estimated monetary amounts for items that appear in the financial statements.

Examples of accounting policies

1 The treatment of gains and losses on disposals of fixed assets – they could be applied to adjust the depreciation charge for the period, or they may appear as separate items in the financial statements.
2 The classification of overheads in the financial statements – for example, some indirect costs may be included in the trading account, or they may be included in administration costs in the profit and loss account.

3 The treatment of interest costs incurred in connection with the construction of fixed assets – these could be charged to profit and loss as a finance cost, or they could be capitalised and added to the other costs of creating the fixed assets – this is allowed by FRS 15: *Tangible fixed assets*.

The equivalent IASs to FRS 18 are IAS 1 (*Presentation of financial statements*) and IAS 8 (*Accounting policies, changes in accounting estimates and errors*). The differences in the requirements of these two standards and FRS 18 are minimal.

11.6 SSAP 4: Accounting for government grants

Many different types of grant are or have been obtainable from government departments. Where these relate to revenue expenditure, e.g. subsidies on wages, they should be credited to revenue in the period when the revenue is incurred. The principle is that the grants should be recognised in the profit and loss account so as to match the expenditure to which they are intended to contribute.

Where there are grants relating to capital expenditure, then SSAP 4 states that they should be credited to revenue *over the expected useful economic life of the asset*. This may be achieved by treating the amount of the grant as a deferred income, a portion of which is credited to the profit and loss account annually, over the life of the asset, on a basis consistent with depreciation. The amount of the deferred credit should, if material, be shown separately. It should not be shown as part of shareholders' funds.

The same effect as treating the grant as deferred income would be achieved by crediting the grant to the fixed asset account and depreciating only the net balance of the cost of the asset over its lifetime (depreciation is thus reduced by the grant). However, although this method is acceptable in principle, it is considered to be illegal under the Companies Act 1985 Schedule 4 para. 17, which requires the balance sheet value of a fixed asset to be its purchase price or production cost.

The equivalent IAS is IAS 20 (*Accounting for government grants and disclosure of government assistance*). There are no major differences between the requirements of SSAP 4 and IAS 20.

11.7 SSAP 5: Accounting for value added tax

All that needs to be noted here is that *Business Accounting UK GAAP 1* deals with SSAP 5. There is no need here to go into further detail at this stage of your studies. There is no equivalent international standard.

11.8 SSAP 9: Stocks and long-term contracts

Due to the many varying kinds of businesses and conditions in companies, there simply cannot be one system of valuation for stocks and long-term contracts. All that the standard can do is to narrow down the different methods that could be used. It does so, initially, by dealing with them as separate and distinct items.

Stocks

Stocks should be stated at the total of the lower of cost and net realisable value of the separate items of stock or of groups of similar items. Profit should not, except in the case of long-term contracts, be recognised in advance, but immediate account should be made for anticipated losses.

In the balance sheet (or in the notes), stocks should be sub-classified so as to indicate the amounts held in each of four main categories in a Companies Act balance sheet: *raw materials and consumables, work in progress, finished goods and goods for resale*, and *payments on account*.

Net realisable value consists of the expected selling price less any expenses necessary to sell the product. This may be below cost because of obsolescence, deterioration and similar factors. SSAP 9 also defines 'cost' and certainly in the case of a manufacturing business it will also include overhead expenses, so that prime cost could not be used. **Cost** is defined in SSAP 9 in relation to the different categories of stocks and work in progress as being:

> *that expenditure which has been incurred in the normal course of business in bringing the product or service to its present location and condition. This expenditure should include, in addition to cost of purchase* [as defined later] *such costs of conversion* [as defined later] *as are appropriate to that location and condition.*

Cost of purchase comprises purchase price including import duties, transport and handling costs and any other directly attributable costs, less trade discounts, rebates and subsidies.

Cost of conversion comprises:

(*a*) costs which are specifically attributable to units of production, i.e. direct labour, direct expenses and subcontracted work;

(*b*) production overheads (as defined later);

(*c*) other overheads, if any, attributable in the particular circumstances of the business to bringing the product or service to its present location and condition.

Production overheads based on the normal level of activity and including fixed production overheads, taking one year with another, should all be included. Obviously, neither selling nor general administration costs should be included in cost.

Notice that abnormal costs should not be included, as they should not have the effect of increasing stock valuation.

The last in, first out (LIFO) and base stock methods should not be used, as they do not provide an up-to-date valuation.

The standard does accept that replacement cost may, in certain circumstances, be acceptable. As a result, the lower of replacement cost or net realisation value may be used.

The equivalent international standard is IAS 2 (*Inventories*). There is no significant difference between the two standards.

Long-term contracts

Chapter 3 of this book deals with long-term contracts. The equivalent IASs are IAS 11 (*Construction contracts*) and IAS 18 (*Revenue*). As with IAS 2, there is no significant difference between the requirements of SSAP 9 and those of the international standards.

11.9 SSAP 13: Accounting for research and development

SSAP 13 divides research and development expenditure under three headings, except for the location or exploitation of oil, gas or mineral deposits, or where all expenditure will be reimbursed by a third party. The three headings are:

1 **Pure (or basic) research.** Experimental or theoretical work undertaken primarily to acquire new scientific or technical knowledge for its own sake rather than directed towards any specific aim or application.

2 **Applied research.** Original or critical investigation undertaken in order to gain new scientific or technical knowledge and directed towards a specific practical aim or objective.

3 **Development.** Use of scientific or technical knowledge in order to produce new or substantially improved materials, devices, products or services, to install new processes or systems prior to the commencement of commercial production or commercial applications, or to improve substantially those already produced or installed.

Expenditure incurred on pure and applied research can be regarded as part of a continuing operation required to maintain a company's business and its competitive position. In general, one particular period rather than another will not be expected to benefit and therefore it is appropriate that these costs should be written off as they are incurred.

The development of new and improved products is, however, distinguishable from pure and applied research. Expenditure on such development is normally undertaken with a reasonable expectation of specific commercial success and of future benefits arising from the work, either from increased revenue and related profits or from reduced costs. However, development expenditure should be written off in the year of expenditure, except in the following circumstances when it may be deferred to future periods:

(a) there is a clearly defined project; and
(b) the related expenditure is separately identifiable; and
(c) the outcome of such a project has been assessed with reasonable certainty as to:
    (i) its technical feasibility; and
    (ii) its ultimate commercial viability considered in the light of factors such as:
        – likely market conditions (including competing products);
        – public opinion;
        – consumer and environmental legislation;
(d) furthermore, a project will be of value only if:
    (i) the aggregate of the deferred development cost and any further development costs to be incurred on the same project together with related production, selling and administration costs is reasonably expected to be exceeded by related future revenues; and
    (ii) adequate resources exist, or are reasonably expected to be available, to enable the project to be completed and to provide any consequential increases in working capital.

The elements of uncertainty inherent in the considerations set out in points (a) to (d) are considerable. There will be a need for different persons having differing levels of judgement to be involved in assessing the technical, commercial and financial viability of the project. Combinations of the possible different assessments which they might validly make can produce widely differing assessments of the existence and amounts of future benefits.

If these uncertainties are viewed in the context of the concept of prudence, the future benefits of most development projects would be too uncertain to justify carrying the expenditure forward. Nevertheless, in certain industries it is considered that there are numbers of major development projects that satisfy the stringent criteria set out above.

The standard says that if the criteria are satisfied then expenditure may be deferred to the extent that its recovery can reasonably be regarded as assured. It is also required that where this policy is adopted, all projects meeting the criteria should be included.

If development costs are deferred, they should be amortised over the period of sale or use of the product.

At each accounting date the unamortised balance of development expenditure should be examined project by project to ensure that it still fulfils the criteria. Where any doubt exists as to the continuation of those circumstances the balance should be written off.

Fixed assets may be acquired or constructed to provide facilities for research and/or development activities. The use of such fixed assets will usually extend over a number of accounting periods and accordingly they should be capitalised and written off over their usual life.

The standard requires that accounting policy on research and development expenditure should be stated and explained. The total amount of research and development expenditure charged in the profit and loss account should be disclosed, analysed between the current year's expenditure and amounts amortised from deferred expenditure. Movement on deferred expenditure and the amount carried forward at the beginning and end of the period should be disclosed. Deferred development expenditure should be disclosed under intangible fixed assets in the balance sheet.

The equivalent international standard is IAS 38 (*Intangible assets*). It has broadly similar rules on this topic to those of SSAP 13.

11.10 SSAP 16: Current cost accounting

See Chapter 30 for an outline of this outdated and suspended SSAP.

11.11 SSAP 19: Accounting for investment properties

Under the accounting requirements of FRS 15: *Tangible fixed assets*, tangible fixed assets are generally subject to annual depreciation charges to reflect on a systematic basis the wearing out, consumption or other loss of value whether arising from use, effluxion of time or obsolescence through technology and market changes. Under those requirements it is also accepted that an increase in the value of such a fixed asset does not generally remove the necessity to charge depreciation to reflect on a systematic basis the consumption of the asset.

A different treatment is, however, required where a significant proportion of the fixed assets of an enterprise is held not for consumption in the business operations but as investments, the disposal of which would not materially affect any manufacturing or trading operations of the enterprise. In such cases, the current value of these investments and changes in that current value are of prime importance rather than a calculation of systematic annual depreciation. Consequently, for the proper appreciation of the financial position, a different accounting treatment is considered appropriate for fixed assets held as investments (called, in this standard, 'investment properties').

Investment properties may be held by a company which holds investments as part of its business such as an investment trust or a property investment company. Investment properties may also be held by a company whose main business is not the holding of such investments.

Where an investment property is held on a lease with a relatively short unexpired term, it is necessary to recognise the annual depreciation in the financial statements to avoid the situation whereby a short lease is amortised against the investment revaluation reserve while the rentals are taken to the profit and loss account.

This statement requires investment properties to be included in the balance sheet at open market value. The statement does not require the valuation to be made by qualified or independent valuers, but calls for disclosure of the names or qualifications of the valuers, the bases used by them and whether the person making the valuation is an employee or officer of the company. However, where investment properties represent a substantial proportion of the total assets of a major enterprise (e.g. a listed company) the valuation thereof would normally be carried out:

(*a*) annually by persons holding a recognised professional qualification and having recent post-qualification experience in the location and category of the properties concerned, and
(*b*) at least every five years by an external valuer.

The equivalent IAS is IAS 40 (*Investment property*). The main difference concerns the value used in the balance sheet. SSAP 19 requires annual revaluation. IAS 40 allows either revaluation or depreciation of net book value. Also, where revaluation is used, SSAP 19 gains or losses are recognised in the statement of total gains and losses. Only permanent deficits appear in the profit and loss account. IAS 40 recognises all gains and losses on revaluation in the profit and loss account.

11.12 SSAP 21: Accounting for leases and hire purchase contracts

Details of SSAP 21 were given in Chapter 2. The equivalent international standard is IAS 17 (*Leases*). There are some differences in the classification criteria of these two standards but the overall requirements are broadly similar.

11.13 SSAP 25: Segmental reporting

This standard was introduced to help interpret the requirement of the Companies Act 1985 that the information in the financial statements should be broken down (segmented) in two principal ways: by class of business and geographically. A **class of business** is a distinguishable component of an entity that provides a separate product or service. A **geographical segment** is an area comprising an individual country or group of countries in which an entity operates.

The main provisions of the standard can be summarised as follows. If an entity has two or more classes of business and operates in two or more geographical segments, then it should report for each class and segment:

(*a*) **turnover** – split between that to external activities and that to other segments;
(*b*) **result**, i.e. profit before taxation, minority interest and extraordinary items;
(*c*) **net assets.**

The equivalent international standard is IFRS 8 (*Operating Segments*). SSAP 25 exempts companies from disclosure if prejudicial to the company. IFRS 8 requires disclosure. Also, while SSAP 25 requires disclosure of net assets, IFRS 8 requires that assets and liabilities be disclosed.

11.14 Statements of Recommended Practice and UITF Consensus Pronouncements

In 1986 the Accounting Standards Committee (ASC) issued the first statement of recommended practice (SORP). It is important to note that SORPs are different from accounting standards. Provisions in standards must be carried out, unless there is sufficient and adequate evidence to prove otherwise and, in addition, any non-compliance must be clearly stated. A SORP simply sets out what is considered to be the best practice on a particular topic in respect of which it is not considered suitable to issue a standard at that time. Companies are simply encouraged to use the SORP. No action will be taken by the accounting bodies if a SORP is not followed.

A sub-category of SORPs was introduced, called 'franked SORPs'. Generally these refer to topics which are of limited application for a specific industry and they are not included in this text.

The ASB does not issue SORPs. In the event that the ASB's authority is required to standardise practice within a specialised industry, the ASB will issue an industry standard if the issue cannot be resolved under the existing accounting standards.

In 1991, the ASB set up a committee known as the Urgent Issues Task Force (UITF). This committee assists the ASB in areas where an accounting standard or Companies Act provision exists but where unsatisfactory or conflicting interpretations have developed or seem likely to do so. In these circumstances, the UITF issues a 'consensus pronouncement' (or 'abstract'). The ASB considers that compliance with consensus pronouncements forms an important element in deciding whether financial statements give a true and fair view. Consequently, they have the same status as accounting standards and *must* be observed. As of December 2007, 45 UITF abstracts had been issued, of which 26 were still in force. Wherever appropriate, UITFs are included in this book when the topic to which they relate is being discussed.

There is no IASB equivalent of the UITFs.

11.15 FRS 1: Cash flow statements

See Chapter 15. The equivalent international standard is IAS 7 (*Statement of cash flows*).

11.16 FRS 2: Accounting for subsidiary undertakings

See Chapter 26. The equivalent international standards are IAS 27 (*Consolidated and separate financial statements*) and IFRS 3 (*Business combinations*).

11.17 FRS 3: Reporting financial performance

See Chapter 12. The equivalent international standards are IAS 1 (*Presentation of financial statements*), IAS 8 (*Accounting policies, changes in accounting estimates and errors*) and IFRS 5 (*Non-current assets held for sale and discontinued*).

11.18 FRS 5: Reporting the substance of transactions

The purpose of FRS 5 is to ensure that the substance of an entity's transactions is reported in its financial statements. The commercial effect of the entity's transactions, and any resulting assets, liabilities, gains or losses, should be faithfully represented in its financial statements.

The standard does not apply to:

(*a*) forward contracts and futures;
(*b*) foreign exchange and interest rate swaps;
(*c*) contracts where a net amount will be paid or received based on a movement in a price or an index;
(*d*) expenditure commitments and orders placed, until the earlier of delivery or payment;
(*e*) employment contracts.

In determining the substance of a transaction, all its aspects and implications should be identified and greater weight given to those more likely to have a commercial effect in practice. Where a group or series of transactions achieves, or is intended to achieve, an overall commercial effect, the transactions should be viewed as a whole, not as individual transactions.

The substance of a transaction depends upon whether it has given rise to new assets or liabilities for the reporting entity and whether it has changed the entity's existing assets and liabilities. An entity has rights or other access to benefits (and therefore has an asset) if the entity is exposed to the risks inherent in the benefits, taking into account the likelihood of those risks having a commercial effect. Evidence that an obligation to transfer benefits (i.e. a liability) exists is shown if there is some circumstance in which the entity cannot avoid, legally or commercially, an outflow of benefits.

Where an asset or a liability results from a transaction, it should be recognised in the balance sheet if there is sufficient evidence of its existence (including, where relevant, any future inflow or outflow of benefit), and if it can be measured at a monetary amount with sufficient reliability.

Where transactions have no significant effect upon either the entity's rights or other access to benefits arising from a previously recognised asset, or to the entity's exposure to the risks inherent in those benefits, the entire asset should continue to be recognised. When the transactions transfer *all* the significant rights or other access to benefits *and all* the significant exposure to risk, the entire asset should cease to be recognised. Where a stage between nil and full effect is found, and it is a significant change, the description or monetary amounts relating to an asset should be changed and a liability recognised for any obligations to transfer benefits that are assumed. However, the standard also states that this partial case arises in only three situations:

(*a*) a transfer of only part of the item;
(*b*) a transfer of all of the item for only part of its life;
(*c*) a transfer of all of the item for all of its life but where the entity retains some significant right to benefits or exposure to risk.

Where a transaction is in substance a financing of a recognised asset (whether previously recognised or not), the finance should be shown deducted from the gross amount of the item it finances on the face of the balance sheet within a single asset caption of 'linked presentation'. The gross amounts of both the item and the finance should be shown on the face of the balance sheet. Profit on a linked presentation should be recognised on entering into the arrangement only to the extent that the non-returnable proceeds received exceed the previous carrying value of the item. Thereafter, any profit or loss arising should be recognised in the period in which it arises, both in the profit and loss account and in the notes.

Assets and liabilities should not be offset, except where they do not constitute separate assets and liabilities.

Where an entity has a quasi-subsidiary (i.e. a company, trust, partnership or other vehicle that is directly or indirectly controlled by the reporting entity, but that is not a subsidiary, and which gives rise to benefits for the reporting entity that are in substance no different from those that would arise were the vehicle a subsidiary), the substance of the transactions entered into by the quasi-subsidiary should be reported in the consolidated statements. The fact that a quasi-subsidiary has been included in the consolidated financial statements should be disclosed and a summary of the financial statements of the quasi-subsidiary should be provided in the notes.

Disclosure of a transaction in the financial statements should be sufficient to enable the user of those statements to understand its commercial effect. Where a transaction has resulted in the recognition of assets or liabilities whose nature differs from that of items usually included under the relevant balance sheet heading, the differences should be explained.

There is no directly equivalent international standard, though IAS 1 and IAS 39, for example, cover some of the issues contained in FRS 5.

11.19 FRS 6: Acquisitions and mergers

See Chapter 25. IFRS 3 (*Business combinations*) is the international standard which deals with this subject.

11.20 FRS 7: Fair values in acquisition accounting

See Chapter 22. IFRS 3 (*Business combinations*) is the international standard which deals with this subject.

11.21 FRS 8: Related party disclosures

This FRS requires disclosure of all material related party transactions. The FRS extends the disclosure requirements contained in the Companies Acts, thus providing guidance in an area that had previously not been covered adequately by either statute or the Stock Exchange Rules.

The equivalent international standard is IAS 24 (*Related party disclosures*). There are no major differences between the two standards other than that FRS 8 requires the controlling party to be named.

11.22 FRS 9: Associates and joint ventures

See Chapter 26. IAS 28 (*Investments in associates*) is the equivalent international standard on associates and IAS 31 (*Financial reporting of interests in joint ventures*) is the equivalent one dealing with joint ventures.

11.23 FRS 10: Goodwill and intangible assets

Although written with a focus upon goodwill arising from the acquisition of a subsidiary undertaking by a parent company that prepares consolidated accounts, the standard also applies to reporting entities acquiring a business or an investment that is accounted for using the equity method (*see* Section 29.8).

A brief summary of the FRS is as follows:

1 Positive purchased goodwill should be capitalised as an asset on the balance sheet.
2 Internally generated goodwill should not be capitalised.
3 An intangible asset acquired as part of the acquisition of a business should be capitalised separately from goodwill, initially at its fair value. Unless the asset has a readily ascertainable market value, the fair value should be limited to an amount that does not create or increase any negative goodwill arising on the acquisition.
4 An intangible asset acquired as part of the acquisition of a business whose fair value cannot be measured reliably should be included within the amount of the purchase price attributed to goodwill.
5 An intangible asset purchased separately should be capitalised at cost.
6 An internally developed intangible asset may be capitalised only if it has a readily ascertainable market value.
7 Where goodwill and intangible assets are regarded as having limited useful economic lives, they should be amortised on a systematic basis over those lives.
8 Where goodwill and intangible assets are regarded as having indefinite useful economic lives, they should *not* be amortised. A life of longer than 20 years can be used only if the durability of the acquired business or intangible asset can be demonstrated and the goodwill or intangible asset is capable of continued measurement over the period selected. Companies legislation requires goodwill to be amortised over a finite period. When no amortisation occurs, this departure from the legislation must be justified as being required in order to provide a true and fair view.
9 The useful economic lives of goodwill and intangible assets should be reviewed at the end of each reporting period and revised if necessary.
10 The straight line method of amortisation should be adopted, unless another method can be demonstrated to better reflect the expected pattern of depletion of the goodwill or intangible asset.

11 Intangible assets may be revalued but, if one is, all others of the same class must also be revalued. Any revalued intangible assets must be subject to sufficiently frequent further revaluations to ensure that the carrying value does not differ materially from the market value at the balance sheet date.

12 Goodwill should not be revalued, except when previous adjustments for impairment losses (that arose, for example, when part of an acquired business was held to have a lower value than had been adopted at the time of acquisition) are reversed and it causes the recoverable amount of the goodwill to rise above its current carrying value. (The same impairment-derived adjustment rules apply to intangible assets.)

13 When the fair value of the assets acquired exceed the fair value of the consideration given, the resulting negative goodwill should be recognised and separately disclosed on the face of the balance sheet immediately below the goodwill heading, followed by a sub-total showing the net amount of positive and negative goodwill.

Note: In the chapters dealing with consolidated financial statements, a figure for goodwill will often be calculated. It must be borne in mind that this is subject to the contents of FRS 10 just as much as for a company simply buying the business of a sole trader or partnership.

There are two equivalent international standards, IAS 38 (*Intangible assets*) and the relevant disclosure requirements contained in IFRS 3 (*Business combinations*). There are significant differences between FRS 10, IFRS 3 and IAS 38. For example, FRS 10 permits use of one indefinite life; IFRS does not; under UK GAAP goodwill can be amortised but IFRS prohibits this and requires annual impairment reviews instead; negative goodwill is recognised and shown in the balance sheet under UK GAAP but must be eliminated immediately under IFRS. IFRS 3 specifies disclosure requirements for business combinations and goodwill.

11.24 FRS 11: Impairment of fixed assets and goodwill

This FRS applies to all fixed assets and purchased goodwill that is recognised in the balance sheet except:

(*a*) fixed assets within the scope of any FRS addressing disclosures of derivatives and other financial instruments (this is covered by FRS 13: *Derivatives and other financial instruments: disclosures* – *see* Section 11.26 below);

(*b*) investment properties (*see* Section 11.11 above);

(*c*) an entity's own shares held by an ESOP (employee share ownership plan) and shown as a fixed asset in the balance sheet under UITF 13: *Accounting for ESOP trusts*; and

(*d*) costs capitalised while a field is being appraised under the Oil Industry Accounting Committee's SORP, *Accounting for oil and gas exploration and development activities*.

Investments in subsidiary undertakings, associates, and joint ventures *do* fall within the scope of FRS 11. However, smaller entities applying the FRSSE are exempt from the FRS.

A brief summary of the FRS is as follows:

1 An impairment review should be carried out if events or changes in circumstances indicate that the carrying amount of a fixed asset or of goodwill may not be recoverable.

2 Impairment is measured by comparing the carrying value of an asset with its recoverable amount (the higher of its net realisable value and its value in use).

3 Impairment losses are recognised in the profit and loss account except that impairment losses on revalued fixed assets are shown in the statement of total recognised gains and losses. Impairments on both unrevalued and revalued assets below the depreciated historical cost are recognised in the profit and loss account.

4 If the recoverable amount of a previously impaired asset or investment increases because of a change in economic conditions or in the expected use of the asset, the resulting reversal of

the impairment loss should be recognised in the current period to the extent that it increases the carrying amount up to the amount that it would have been had the original impairment not occurred. The reversal should be recognised in the profit and loss account unless it arises on a previously revalued fixed asset, in which case it should be recognised in the profit and loss account to the extent that the previous impairment loss (adjusted for subsequent depreciation) was recognised in the profit and loss account, any remaining impairment reversal balance being recognised in the statement of total recognised gains and losses.

IAS 36 (*Impairment of assets*) is the equivalent international standard. There is no significant difference between the requirements of the two standards.

11.25 FRS 12: Provisions, contingent liabilities and contingent assets

FRS 12 defines a provision as:

a liability that is of uncertain timing or amount, to be settled by the transfer of economic benefits.

A provision should be recognised only when it is probable that a transfer of economic benefits will have to occur and a reasonable estimate can be made of the amount involved.
It defines a contingent liability as:

either a possible obligation arising from past events whose existence will be confirmed only by the occurrence of one or more uncertain future events not wholly within the entity's control; or a present obligation that arises from past events but is not recognised because it is not probable that a transfer of economic benefits will be required to settle the obligation or because the amount of the obligation cannot be measured with sufficient reliability.

It defines a contingent asset as:

a possible asset arising from past events whose existence will be confirmed only by the occurrence of one or more uncertain events not wholly within the entity's control.

Neither contingent liabilities nor contingent assets should be recognised.
Smaller entities applying the FRSSE are exempt from FRS 12.
The equivalent IAS is IAS 37 (*Provisions, contingent liabilities and contingent assets*). There are no significant differences between the two standards.

11.26 FRS 13: Derivatives and other financial instruments: disclosures

A derivative is defined in the standard as:

a financial instrument that derives its value from the price or rate of some underlying item. Underlying items include equities, bonds, commodities, interest rates, exchange rates, and stock market and other indices.

Only banking and other similar institutions are within the scope of this standard. For all other entities, FRS 25 and FRS 29 replaced FRS 13 in 2007.
The disclosures required by the standard focus mainly upon the risks that arise in connection with financial instruments and how they have been managed. It requires a range of information to be presented concerning the risks arising from the entity's financial instruments, and its attitude and response to those risks. In effect, entities are required to publish in summary form details of their loans, investments and hedging transactions.

Smaller entities applying the FRSSE are exempt from FRS 13.

The requirements of FRS 13 are virtually the same as the equivalent requirements of IAS 32. IAS 39 (*Financial instruments: recognition and measurement*) is also relevant to the issues covered by FRS 13.

11.27 FRS 15: Tangible fixed assets

This FRS applies to all tangible fixed assets except investment properties (*see* Section 11.11 above). First, some definitions:

- **Depreciation.** The measure of the cost or revalued amount of the economic benefits of the tangible fixed asset that have been consumed during the period. Consumption includes the wearing out, using up or other reduction in the useful economic life of a tangible fixed asset whether arising from use, effluxion of time or obsolescence through either technology or demand for the goods and services produced by the asset.
- **Useful economic life.** The period over which the entity expects to derive economic benefit from that asset.
- **Residual value.** The net realisable value of an asset at the end of its economic life. Residual values are based on prices prevailing at the date of the acquisition (or revaluation) of the asset and do not take account of expected future price changes.
- **Recoverable amount.** The higher of net realisable value and the amount recoverable from its further use.

Depreciation should be provided in respect of all tangible fixed assets which have a finite useful economic life. It should be provided by allocating the cost (or revalued amount) less net realisable value over the periods expected to benefit from the use of the asset being depreciated. No depreciation method is prescribed, but the method selected should be that which produces the most appropriate allocation of depreciation to each period in relation to the benefit being received in that period through use of the asset. The depreciation should be calculated on the value as shown on the balance sheet and not on any other figure. It *must* be charged against the profit and loss account, *not* against reserves.

When the useful economic life of an asset is longer than 50 years, impairment reviews must be performed so as to ensure that the carrying amount of the asset is not overstated.

Useful economic lives should be reviewed at the end of every reporting period. If it is revised, the carrying amount at the date of the revision should be depreciated over the revised remaining useful economic life of the asset.

The depreciation method may be changed only when to do so will give a fairer presentation of the results and of the financial position. A change in depreciation method does not constitute a change in accounting policy. When the method is changed, the carrying amount should be depreciated over the remaining useful economic life of the asset, commencing with the period when the change occurred. Where a change of method occurs, the effect, if material, should be shown as a note attached to the financial statements.

UITF Abstract 5, issued in July 1992, introduced rules relating to situations where current assets are included in the balance sheet at the lower of cost and net realisable value. Specifically, it addressed the question of an appropriate transfer value when a current asset becomes a fixed asset through its being retained for use on a continuing basis. (This could arise, for example, when a motor dealer removes a second-hand car from sale and provides it as a company car to the company secretary.) To avoid entities being able to effect transfers from current assets to fixed assets at above net realisable value and subsequently to write down the value through a debit to a revaluation reserve, UITF 5 requires that all such transfers are done at the lower of cost and net realisable value, with any diminution in value at that point being charged in the profit and loss account.

Asset revaluation

Asset revaluation is permitted and, if a policy of revaluation is adopted, the valuations should be kept up to date. If one asset is revalued, all the assets of that class (i.e. those with a similar nature, function or use) must be revalued.

Revaluation losses caused by use of the asset should be recognised in the profit and loss account. Other revaluation losses should be recognised in the statement of total recognised gains and losses until the carrying amount of the asset is less than the amount the asset would be carried at had depreciated historical cost been adopted rather than asset revaluation.

For example, imagine an asset is revalued from a carrying amount of £20,000 down to £6,000 because the asset had become obsolete. Had it never been revalued, its carrying amount would have been £11,000. The carrying amount of the asset (£6,000) is, therefore, below £11,000 and so the loss on revaluation of £14,000 would be split with £9,000 being recognised in the statement of total recognised gains and losses and £5,000 being recognised in profit and loss.

Revaluation gains should be recognised in the statement of total recognised gains and losses unless they relate to an asset that had previously had revaluation losses charged to the profit and loss account. Where that is the case, the revaluation gain should also be charged to profit and loss, after adjusting for depreciation since the revaluation loss was recognised.

Depreciation should be charged irrespective of when the asset was revalued. An increased value arising from a revaluation does not mean that depreciation should not be charged. The new value is the one on which future depreciation should be based. Depreciation charged before revaluation should not be credited back to profit and loss.

According to paragraph 21 of FRS 3: *Reporting financial performance*, the profit or loss on the disposal of an asset should be accounted for in the profit and loss account of the period in which the disposal occurs as the difference between the net sale proceeds and the net carrying amount, whether carried at historical cost (less any provisions made) or at a valuation.

Land and buildings

Freehold land

As this normally lasts for ever there is no need to depreciate, unless subject to depletion or loss of value for reasons which may be applicable in certain circumstances, such as desirability of location, land erosion, extraction of minerals, dumping of toxic waste, etc.

It is rare to encounter circumstances under which freehold land should be subject to depreciation. The problem that most often occurs is the distinction between the cost/value of freehold land and the cost/value of the buildings upon it. FRS 15 states that the distinction should be made as only the buildings have a limited useful economic life and should be depreciated. Land has an unlimited life and should not be depreciated. Failure to separate the two elements of the cost/value will result in non-compliance with the standard.

Buildings

These have finite lives and should be depreciated.

Notes to the financial statements

The FRS requires that the following should be disclosed:

1 Methods of depreciation used.
2 Useful economic lives or the depreciation rates in use.
3 Total depreciation charged for the period.
4 Where material, the financial effect of a change in either useful economic lives or estimates of residual values.

5 The cost or revalued amount at both the start and end of the accounting period.

6 The cumulative amount of provisions for depreciation or impairment at the beginning and end of the financial period.

7 A reconciliation of the movements, separately disclosing additions, disposals, revaluations, transfers, depreciation, impairment losses, and reversals of past impairment losses written back in the period.

8 The net carrying amount at the beginning and end of the financial period.

The equivalent IASs are IAS 16 (*Property plant and equipment*) and IAS 23 (*Borrowing costs*). Differences between the requirements of FRS 15 and these standards are minimal. IFRS 5 (*Non-current assets held for sale and discontinued operations*) introduced new rules which the ASB are considering adopting for these two special cases.

11.28 FRS 16: Current tax

In brief, the FRS requires that:

1 Current tax for the period is recognised in the profit and loss account. The only exception is tax on gains and losses that have been recognised in the statement of total recognised gains and losses. Any such tax should be recognised in that statement, not in the profit and loss account.

2 Dividends received from UK companies are reported at the net amount received. Dividends received from other countries are reported gross only to the extent that they have suffered a withholding tax.

3 Income and expenses subject to non-standard rates of tax (or exempt from tax) should be included in the pre-tax results on the basis of the income or expenses actually receivable or payable, without any adjustment to reflect a notional amount of tax that would have been paid or relieved in respect of the transaction if it had been taxable, or allowable for tax purposes, on a different basis.

4 Current tax should be measured using tax rates and laws that have been enacted or substantively enacted by the balance sheet date.

IAS 12 (*Income taxes*) is the equivalent international standard. The main differences between them are that IAS 12 makes no reference to tax on dividends but it does require any tax expense on discontinuing operations to be disclosed and it does require that current tax be presented *separately* in the balance sheet.

11.29 FRS 17: Retirement benefits

The objective of FRS 17 is that the employer should recognise the expected cost of providing pensions on a 'systematic and rational basis' over the period during which he/she derives benefit from the employees' services. The main requirements are as follows:

1 Pension scheme assets are measured using market values.

2 Pension scheme liabilities are measured using a projected unit method and discounted at an AA corporate bond rate.

3 The pension scheme surplus (to the extent it can be recovered) or deficit is recognised in full on the balance sheet.

4 The movement in the scheme surplus/deficit is analysed into:
   (*a*) the current service cost and any past service costs; these are recognised in operating profit;
   (*b*) the interest cost and expected return on assets; these are recognised as other finance costs;
   (*c*) actuarial gains and losses; these are recognised in the statement of total recognised gains and losses.

IAS 19 (*Employee benefits*) is the equivalent international standard. The ASB are currently (December 2004) considering whether to adopt its requirements, which differ significantly in some aspects.

11.30 FRS 18: Accounting policies

This standard was covered in Section 11.5 above.

11.31 FRS 19: Deferred tax

This FRS is covered in Chapter 8. The equivalent international standard is IAS 12 (*Income taxes*), which is also the equivalent international standard for FRS 16. IAS 12 differs from FRS 19 by requiring deferred tax to be provided when assets are revalued and prohibiting the discounting of future deferred tax liabilities.

11.32 FRS 20: Share-based payment

This standard was issued in April 2004, replacing UITF 17. Its requirements are identical to those of IFRS 2 (*Share-based payment*), except that FRS 20 includes an exemption for entities applying the FRSSE.

Under FRS 20, share-based payments must be recognised as an expense, measured at fair value which should be based on market prices and should take into account the terms and conditions upon which the instruments were granted. The standard gives the accounting treatment to be adopted and disclosures to be made by entities making such payments.

FRS 20 identifies three types of share-based payment transaction:

(*a*) equity-settled share-based payment transactions. These are transactions in which the entity receives goods or services as consideration for equity instruments of the entity;
(*b*) cash-settled share-based payment transactions. These are transactions in which the entity acquires goods or services by incurring liabilities to the supplier of those goods or services for amounts that are based on the price (or value) of the entity's equity instruments;
(*c*) transactions in which the entity receives or acquires goods or services and the terms of the arrangement provide one or other of the parties to the transaction with a choice as to whether the transaction is settled in cash or by issuing equity instruments.

Examples of share-based payments include:

(*a*) all types of executive share option and share purchase plans and employee share option and share purchase schemes, including Save-As-You-Earn (SAYE) plans and similar arrangements;
(*b*) arrangements such as share appreciation rights, where a cash payment is made, the amount of which depends on the share price; and
(*c*) transactions with suppliers of goods or non-employee services that involve share-based payments being made in exchange for those goods or services.

11.33 FRS 21: Events after the balance sheet date

This standard was issued in May 2004, replacing SSAP 17. Its requirements are identical to those of IAS 10 (*Events after the reporting period*), except that FRS 21 includes an exemption for entities applying the FRSSE.

Obviously, any event which occurred during a financial period will have been taken into account when the financial statements were prepared. Generally, once financial statements have been approved and authorised for issue, it becomes impossible to alter them. However, during the period between the balance sheet date and the date when the financial statements are authorised for issue, events may arise which throw some light upon the valuation of assets or amounts of liabilities in those financial statements. FRS 21 directs its attention to such events during this period.

To clarify the period involved, entities must report the date on which their financial statements were authorised for issue. For companies, this *is not* the date when they are presented to the shareholders at the AGM. Rather, it is the date on which the directors authorised the financial statements to be issued.

Two terms are of particular importance in applying the requirements of FRS 21: 'adjusting events' and 'non-adjusting events'.

Adjusting events

These are events which provide evidence of conditions that existed at the balance sheet date for which the entity shall adjust the amounts recognised in its financial statements or recognise items that were not previously recognised. Examples include:

● The settlement after the balance sheet date of a court case that confirms the liability of the entity at the balance sheet date.
● The discovery after the balance sheet date of errors or frauds which show that the financial statements were incorrect.
● Information received after the balance sheet date that indicates that the value of an asset was impaired (i.e. less than previously believed) at the balance sheet date. The could arise in many ways, for example:
  (*a*) **Fixed assets.** The subsequent determination of the purchase price or of the proceeds of sale of assets purchased or sold before the year end.
  (*b*) **Property.** A valuation which provides evidence of a permanent diminution in value.
  (*c*) **Investments.** The receipt of a copy of the financial statements or other information in respect of an unlisted company which provides evidence of a permanent diminution in the value of a long-term investment.
  (*d*) **Stocks and work in progress:**
    (*i*) the receipt of proceeds of sales after the balance sheet date or other evidence concerning the net realisable value of stocks;
    (*ii*) the receipt of evidence that the previous estimate of accrued profit on a long-term contract was materially inaccurate.
  (*e*) **Debtors.** The renegotiation of amounts owing by debtors, or the insolvency of a debtor.

Non-adjusting events

These are events which arise after the balance sheet date and concern conditions which did not exist at that time. Consequently they do not result in changes in amounts in financial statements. They may, however, be of such materiality that their disclosure is required by way of notes to ensure that the financial statements are not misleading. Such disclosure should describe the nature of the event and an estimate of its financial effect (or a statement that it is not possible to do so).

Examples of non-adjusting events which may require disclosure include:

● a decline in market value of investments between the balance sheet date and the date when the financial statements are authorised for issue;
● a major business combination after the balance sheet date or disposing of a major subsidiary;

- announcing a plan to discontinue an operation, disposing of assets or settling liabilities attributable to a discontinuing operation or entering into binding agreements to sell such assets or settle such liabilities;
- major purchases and disposals of assets, or expropriation of major assets by government;
- the destruction of a major production plant by a fire after the balance sheet date;
- announcing, or commencing the implementation of, a major restructuring;
- major ordinary share transactions and potential ordinary share transactions after the balance sheet date;
- abnormally large changes after the balance sheet date in asset prices or foreign exchange rates;
- changes in tax rates or tax laws enacted or announced after the balance sheet date that have a significant effect on current and deferred tax assets and liabilities;
- entering into significant commitments or contingent liabilities, for example, by issuing significant guarantees;
- commencing major litigation arising solely out of events that occurred after the balance sheet date.

The standard makes it clear that dividends proposed or declared after the balance sheet date *are not* to be treated as a liability in the balance sheet. Rather, they are to be disclosed in a note to the financial statements.

11.34 FRS 22: Earnings per share

The objective of earnings per share (EPS) information is to provide a measure of the interests of each ordinary share of a parent entity in the performance of the entity over the reporting period. Basic earnings per share is a widely used stock market measure. The IAS tries to bring about a consistent method to aid comparability and reduce misunderstandings.

Under FRS 22, entities must calculate basic earnings per share amounts for profit or loss attributable to ordinary equity holders of the parent entity and, if presented, profit or loss from continuing operations attributable to those equity holders. Basic earnings per share is calculated by dividing profit or loss attributable to ordinary equity holders of the parent entity (the numerator) by the weighted average number of ordinary shares outstanding (the denominator) during the period.

When there are potential ordinary shares (for example if share options are exercised) they are treated as dilutive when, and only when, their conversion to ordinary shares would decrease earnings per share or increase loss per share from continuing operations. When there are dilutive ordinary shares, a diluted earnings per share must also be calculated.

Entities must present on the face of the income statement basic and, where applicable, diluted earnings per share for profit or loss from continuing operations attributable to the ordinary equity holders of the parent entity and for profit or loss attributable to the ordinary equity holders of the parent entity for the period for each class of ordinary shares that has a different right to share in profit for the period. Basic and diluted earnings per share must be presented with equal prominence for all periods presented.

The standard prescribes how to adjust the average number of shares when events occur to change the number of ordinary shares, such as bonus issues, share splits, and share consolidations. Students taking examinations which cover FRS 22 in detail should read the actual standard.

Basic EPS is calculated as follows:

		£	
			£
Profit on continuing activities after taxation			XXX
Less:	Minority interest (*see* chapters on group financial statements)[Note]	XXX	
	Preference dividends	XXX	
			(XXX)
Profit available to equity shareholders			XXX

$$EPS = \frac{\text{Profit available to equity shareholders}}{\text{Number of ordinary shares}} = \text{EPS in pence}$$

Note: **You will see later that minority interests exist only where the entity controls another entity which is partly owned by outsiders.**

Smaller entities applying the FRSSE are exempt from FRS 22. The equivalent international standard is IAS 33, which is the same as FRS 22 except that there is no equivalent to the FRSSE exemption.

11.35 FRS 23: The effect of changes in foreign exchange rates

This standard is covered in Chapter 1, Section 1.

11.36 FRS 24: Financial reporting in hyperinflationary economies

The results of an entity whose functional currency is the currency of a hyperinflationary economy must be restated in terms of the measuring unit current at the balance sheet date (i.e. the currency value at that date) before being translated into a different presentation currency. Comparative figures for prior periods are also restated into the measuring unit at the current balance sheet date. Balance sheet amounts not already expressed in terms of the measuring unit current at the balance sheet date are restated by applying a general price index. Any gain or loss as a result on the net monetary position must be included in net income and separately disclosed.

The equivalent international standard is IAS 29, which is the same as FRS 24.

11.37 FRS 25: Financial instruments: disclosure and presentation

A financial instrument is any contract that gives rise to a financial asset of one entity and a financial liability or equity instrument of another entity. Each financial instrument must be classified as either a financial liability or as an equity instrument. It is an equity instrument if, and only if, both the following conditions are met:

1 The instrument includes no contractual obligation:
  (*a*) to deliver cash or another financial asset to another entity; or
  (*b*) to exchange financial assets or financial liabilities with another entity under conditions that are potentially unfavourable to the issuer.
2 If the instrument will or may be settled in the issuer's own equity instruments, it is:
  (*a*) a non-derivative that includes no contractual obligation for the issuer to deliver a variable number of its own equity instruments; or
  (*b*) a derivative that will be settled by the issuer exchanging a fixed amount of cash or another financial asset for a fixed number of its own equity instruments. For this purpose, the issuer's own equity instruments do not include instruments that are themselves contracts for the future receipt or delivery of the issuer's own equity instruments.

If it does not meet these conditions, it is a financial liability.

An example of a type of financial instrument that you have encountered many times in *Business Accounting Essentials 1* and *2* is preference shares. They may be either financial liabilities or equity instruments. If they are not redeemable and dividends are at the discretion of the issuer, they are equity instruments and are included in equity in the balance sheet. In contrast, where they are redeemable for fixed or determinable amounts at a fixed or determinable future date, or where the holder has the option to redeem them, they are classified as a financial liability and included in liabilities in the balance sheet.

The equivalent international standard is IAS 32, which is the same as FRS 25. However, the disclosure requirements of FRS 29 (*Financial instruments: disclosure*) replaced those of FRS 25 in 2007 and the ASB is considering amendments to FRS 25 to change the classification of certain financial instruments from liabilities to equity; a similar change is proposed to IAS 32.

11.38 FRS 26: Financial instruments: recognition and measurements

The definition of a financial instrument is extremely wide and includes cash, debt, and equity investments, loans, trade receivable and payables certain provisions, and derivatives. FRS 26 covers the recognition, measurement and derecognition of financial instruments, along with riles or hedge accounting (relating to attempts to offset risk). FRS 26 is possibly the most complex of all standards and is beyond the scope of this book. The equivalent international standard is IAS 39.

11.39 FRS 27: Life assurance

This standard applies only to life assurance businesses and is outside the scope of this book. There is no equivalent international standard.

11.40 FRS 28: Corresponding amounts

This standard requires that corresponding amounts are shown for items in the primary financial statements and notes to the financial statements. Where corresponding amounts are not directly comparable with the amount to be shown in respect of the current financial year, they must be adjusted and the basis for adjustment disclosed in a note to the financial statements.

Entities applying the FRSSE are exempt from FRS 28. There is no equivalent international standard.

11.41 FRS 29: Financial instruments: disclosures

FRS 29 complements the principles for recognising, measuring and presenting financial assets and financial liabilities in FRS 25 *Financial Instruments: Presentation* and FRS 26 *Financial Instruments: Recognition and Measurement*. It regulates the disclosures that must be made in the financial statements of entities with financial instruments. These disclosures are intended to enable users to evaluate:

(*i*) the significance of financial instruments for the entity's financial position and performance; and

(*ii*) the nature and extent of risks arising from financial instruments to which the entity is exposed during the period and at the reporting date, and how the entity manages those risks.

The equivalent international standard is IFRS 7. FRS 29 is beyond the scope of this book.

11.42 FRSSE: Financial Reporting Standard for Smaller Entities

The FRSSE was first issued in November 1997 and has been updated regularly thereafter. It may be applied to all financial statements intended to give a true and fair view of the financial position and profit or loss (or income and expenditure) of all entities that are small companies or groups or entities (other than building societies) that would be classified as such were they incorporated under companies legislation.

Small companies are defined in the FRSSE according to the definition contained in Section 382 of the Companies Act 2006 as being those that in a year satisfy at least two of the following:

1 Turnover no greater than £5.6 million.
2 A balance sheet total no greater than £2.8 million.
3 An average of no more than 50 employees.

Other than in the case of newly incorporated companies, the condition must have been satisfied in two of the last three years. For small groups, the threshold limits are aggregate turnover not exceeding £5.6 million 'net' (i.e. after set-offs and other adjustments required by Schedule 4A of the Companies Act 1985) or £6.72 million 'gross' (i.e. before the set-offs and adjustments); aggregate balance sheet total not exceeding £2.8 million net, £3.36 million gross; and aggregate number of employees not exceeding 50. (Companies Act 1985, Sections 382 and 383.)

Application of the FRSSE is voluntary – reporting entities may choose instead to apply all the other accounting standards and UITFs. Those that do apply it are exempt from complying with the other accounting standards and UITFs.

The FRSSE contains a simplified, but lengthy, set of requirements derived from those included in all the other standards and UITFs. It would not be appropriate to describe these in detail here. For information concerning the precise contents of the FRSSE, reference should be made to the FRSSE itself or to a book specialising in accounting standards.

There is no equivalent international standard as of December 2007. However, the IASB is currently considering the introduction of a standard in this area and has issued an exposure draft.

11.43 Equivalent international standards

Exhibit 11.2

UK standard	International standard
SSAP 4 – Accounting for government grants	IAS 20
SSAP 5 – Accounting for value added tax	none
SSAP 9 – Stocks and long-term contracts	IAS 2; IAS 11 and IAS 18
SSAP 13 – Accounting for research and development	IAS 38
SSAP 19 – Accounting for investment properties	IAS 40
SSAP 21 – Accounting for leases and hire purchase contracts	IAS 17
SSAP 25 – Segmental reporting	IFRS 8
FRS 1 – Cash Flow Statements	IAS 7
FRS 2 – Accounting for Subsidiary Undertakings	IAS 27 and IFRS 3
FRS 3 – Reporting Financial Performance	IAS 1; IAS 8; and IFRS 5
FRS 5 – Reporting the Substance of Transactions	IAS 1; IAS 39 and others
FRS 6 – Acquisitions and Mergers	IFRS 3
FRS 7 – Fair Values in Acquisition Accounting	IFRS 3
FRS 8 – Related Party Disclosures	IAS 24
FRS 9 – Associates and Joint Ventures	IAS 28 and IAS 31
FRS 10 – Goodwill and Intangible Assets	IAS 38 and IFRS 3
FRS 11 – Impairment of Fixed Assets and Goodwill	IAS 36
FRS 12 – Provisions, Contingent Liabilities and Contingent Assets	IAS 37
FRS 13 – Derivatives and other Financial Instruments: Disclosures	IAS 32 and IAS 39
FRS 15 – Tangible Fixed Assets	IAS 16; IAS 23; and IFRS 5
FRS 16 – Current Tax	IAS 12
FRS 17 – Retirement Benefits	IAS 19

UK standard	International standard
FRS 18 – Accounting Policies	IAS 1 and IAS 8
FRS 19 – Deferred Tax	IAS 12
FRS 20 – Share-based Payment	IFRS 2
FRS 21 – Events after the Balance Sheet Date	IAS 10
FRS 22 – Earnings per share	IAS 33
FRS 24 – Financial reporting in hyperinflationary economies	IAS 29
FRS 25 – Financial instruments; disclosure and presentation	IAS 32
FRS 26 – Financial instruments; recognition and measurement	IAS 39
FRS 27 – Life assurance	none
FRS 28 – Corresponding amounts	none
FRS 29 – Financial instruments	IFRS 7
FRSSE – Financial Reporting Standard for Smaller Entities	none

Information on the latest developments in UK and international standards can be found in the ASB's quarterly publication, *Inside Track*. It can be found at **www.frc.org.uk/asb/publications/insidetrack.cfm**

Learning outcomes

You should now have learnt:

1 Accounting standards have statutory recognition and must, therefore, be complied with when preparing financial statements intended to present a true and fair view.

2 The *Statement of Principles* provides details of the concepts that underpin accounting standards.

3 As of December 2007, there were 35 accounting standards (7 SSAPs, 27 FRSs and 1 FRSSE), and 26 UITF abstracts in force.

4 About the main requirements of a range of accounting standards.

5 Which international standards address the issues contained in the UK accounting standards.

Answers to activities

11.1 Apart from the legal requirement that certain companies switch to international standards, international accounting standards are becoming increasingly adopted across the world. At the same time, there is an increasing internationalisation of business and a need for greater international uniformity in the regulations underpinning the preparation of company financial statements, particularly for multinational companies.

11.2 Most non-accountants assume that the information in financial statements is accurate, correct and free of bias. They believe this to be the case because they assume that all such information is based on firm facts – for example, what something cost is shown in the invoice and confirmed by the amount paid for it as shown in the bank statement. They do not realise that many of the figures shown are based on estimates and subject to the subjective interpretation of a situation by the person preparing the financial statements. They are unaware that accountants have many choices to make, so much so that it is unlikely that two accountants would ever produce identical financial statements for any but the smallest of organisations.

By placing an emphasis on the qualitative aspects of information, the *Statement of Principles* seeks to restrict diversity in the range of options open to the preparers of financial statements and so guide them towards a more uniform interpretation of the options available to them, thereby increasing the level of faith that users of those statements may have in the information they contain.

Review questions

11.1 In preparing its accounts for the year to 31 May 2007, Whiting plc had been faced with a number of accounting problems, the details of which were as follows:

(*i*)   The company had closed down its entire American operations which represented a significant part of Whiting plc's business.

(*ii*)   The corporation tax for the year to 31 May 2006 had been over-provided by £5,000.

(*iii*)   Land and buildings had been revalued at an amount well in excess of the historic cost (note: the current value is to be adjusted in the financial statements).

(*iv*)   A trade debtor had gone into liquidation owing Whiting plc an amount equivalent to 20 per cent of Whiting's turnover for the year. It is highly unlikely that any of this debt will ever be repaid.

(*v*)   During the year, the company changed its method of valuing stock. If the same method had been adopted in the previous year, the profits for that year would have been considerably less than had previously been reported.

Required:

(*a*) Being careful to give your reasons, explain how each of the above matters should be treated in the financial statements of Whiting plc for the year to 31 May 2007 if the company follows the requirements of FRS 3.

(*b*) Outline the provisions of FRS 10 (*Goodwill and intangible assets*) for the treatment of both non-purchased and purchased goodwill in the balance sheets of companies and groups of companies.

(*Association of Accounting Technicians*)

11.2   The directors are preparing the published accounts of Dorman plc for the year to 31 October 2005. The following information is provided for certain of the items which are to be included in the final accounts.

(*i*)   *Stocks of raw material, monolite:*

	£
Cost	26,500
Replacement cost	48,100

(*ii*)   *Stocks of finished goods:*

	Paramite £	Paraton £
Direct costs	72,600	10,200
Proportion of fixed factory overhead	15,300	4,600
Proportion of selling expenses	6,870	1,800
Net realisable value	123,500	9,520

(*iii*)   *Plant and machinery.* An item of plant was shown in the 2004 accounts at a net book value of £90,000 (£160,000 cost less accumulated depreciation £70,000). The plant was purchased on 1 November 2002 and has been depreciated at 25 per cent reducing balance. The directors now consider the straight line basis to be more appropriate: they have estimated that at 1 November 2004 the plant had a remaining useful life of six years and will possess zero residual value at the end of that period.

(*iv*)   *Freehold property.* The company purchased a freehold property for £250,000 11 years ago, and it is estimated that the land element was worth £50,000 at that date.

The company has never charged depreciation on the property but the directors now feel that it should have done so; the building is expected to have a total useful life of 40 years.

(*v*)   *Research expenditure* incurred in an attempt to discover a substitute for raw materials currently purchased from a politically sensitive area of the world amounted to £17,500 during the year.

(vi) *Development expenditure* on Tercil, which is nearly ready for production, amounted to £30,000. Demand for Tercil is expected significantly to exceed supply for at least the next four years.

(vii) *Accident.* On 1 December 2005 there was a fire in the warehouse which damaged stocks, other than the items referred to in (*i*) and (*ii*) above. The book value of these stocks was £92,000. The company has discovered that it was underinsured and only expects to recover £71,000 from the insurers.

(viii) *Investments.* Dorman purchased 30,000 ordinary shares in Lilleshall Ltd on 1 November 2004 for £96,000, and immediately succeeded in appointing two of its directors to Lilleshall's board. The issued share capital of Lilleshall consists of 100,000 ordinary shares of £1 each. The profits of Lilleshall for the year to 31 October 2005 amounted to £40,000. (Ignore taxation.)

Required:
Explain how each of the above items should be dealt with in the published financial statements of Dorman plc.

(*Institute of Chartered Secretaries and Administrators*)

11.3A In preparing the published financial statements of a company, briefly state the significant accounting/disclosure requirements you would have in mind in ensuring that the financial statements comply with best accounting practice as embodied in accounting standards concerning:

(*a*) Value added tax.
(*b*) Earnings per share.
(*c*) The disclosure requirements of each major class of depreciable assets.
(*d*) Research expenditure.
(*e*) Capital-based grants relating to fixed assets.
(*f*) Goodwill on consolidation.
(*g*) The disclosure requirements relating to generally accepted fundamental accounting concepts.
(*h*) The accounts of a subsidiary undertaking having similar activities to that of the parent undertaking.

(*Association of Accounting Technicians*)

11.4A Oldfield Enterprises Limited was formed on 1 January 2005 to manufacture and sell a new type of lawn mower. The bookkeeping staff of the company have produced monthly figures for the first ten months to 31 October 2005 and from these figures together with estimates for the remaining two months, Barry Lamb, the managing director, has drawn up a forecast profit and loss account for the year to 31 December 2005 and a balance sheet as at that date.

These statements together with the notes are submitted to the board for comment. During the board meeting discussion centres on the treatment given to the various assets. The various opinions are summarised by Barry Lamb who brings them, with the draft accounts, to you as the company's financial adviser.

Oldfield Enterprises Ltd
Draft Profit and Loss Account for the year to 31 December 2005

	£000	£000
Sales		3,000
Cost of sales		1,750
Gross profit		1,250
Administration overheads	350	
Selling and distribution overheads	530	
		880
Net profit before taxation		370

→

Draft Balance Sheet at 31 December 2005

Fixed assets – tangible	Cost £000	Depreciation and amortisation £000	Net £000
Leasehold land and buildings	375	125	250
Freehold land and buildings	350	–	350
Plant and machinery	1,312	197	1,115
	2,037	322	1,715
Fixed assets – intangible			
Research and development			375
Current assets			
Stock		375	
Debtors		780	
		1,155	
Current liabilities			
Creditors	250		
Bank overdraft	125	375	
			780
			2,870
Share capital			2,500
Net profit for year			370
			2,870

Notes:

(a) Administration overheads include £50,000 written-off research and development.

(b) The lease is for 15 years and cost £75,000. Buildings have been put up on the leasehold land at a cost of £300,000. Plant and machinery has been depreciated at 15 per cent. Both depreciation and amortisation are included in cost of sales.

Opinions put forward

Leasehold land and buildings:

The works director thinks that although the lease provides for a rent review after three years the buildings have a 50-year life. The buildings should therefore be depreciated over 50 years and the cost of the lease should be amortised over the period of the lease.

The managing director thinks that because of the rent review clause the whole of the cost should be depreciated over three years.

The sales director thinks it is a good idea to charge as much as the profits will allow in order to reduce the tax bill.

Freehold land and buildings:

The works director thinks that as the value of the property is going up with inflation no depreciation is necessary.

The sales director's opinion is the same as for leasehold property.

The managing director states that he has heard that if a property is always kept in good repair no depreciation is necessary. This should apply in the case of his company.

Plant and machinery:

The managing director agrees with the 15 per cent for depreciation and proposes to use the reducing balance method.

The works director wants to charge 25 per cent straight line.

Research and development:
The total spent in the year will be £425,000. Of this £250,000 is for research into the cutting character-istics of different types of grass, £100,000 is for the development of an improved drive system for lawn mowers and £75,000 is for market research to determine the ideal lawn mower characteristics for the average garden.

The managing director thinks that a small amount should be charged as an expense each year.

The works director wants to write off all the market research and 'all this nonsense of the cutting characteristics of grass'.

The sales director thinks that, as the company has only just started, all research and development expenditure relates to future sales so all this year's expenditure should be carried forward.

Stock:
Both the managing director and the works director are of the opinion that stock should be shown at prime cost.

The sales director's view is that stocks should be shown at sales price as the stock is virtually all sold within a very short period.

Required:
(*a*) You are asked to comment on each opinion stating what factors should be taken into account to determine suitable depreciation and write-off amounts.
(*b*) Indicate what amounts should, in your opinion, be charged to profit and loss and show the adjusted profit produced by your recommendations, stating clearly any assumptions you may make.

(*Association of Chartered Certified Accountants*)

11.5 The accountant of Hook, Line and Sinker, a partnership of seven people, has asked your advice in dealing with the following items in the partnership accounts for the year to 31 May 2007.

(*a*) (*i*) Included in invoices prepared and dated in June 2007 were £60,000 of goods despatched during the second half of May 2007.
(*ii*) Stocks of components at 31 May 2007 include parts no longer used in production. These components originally cost £50,000 but have been written down for purposes of the accounts to £25,000. Scrap value of these items is estimated to be £1,000. Another user has expressed interest in buying these parts for £40,000.
(*b*) After May 2007 a customer who accounts for 50 per cent of Hook, Line and Sinker sales suffered a serious fire which has disrupted his organisation. Payments for supplies are becoming slow and Hook, Line and Sinker sales for the current year are likely to be substantially lower than previously. This customer owed £80,000 to Hook, Line and Sinker at 31 May 2007.
(*c*) During the year to 31 May, Hook, Line and Sinker commenced a new advertising campaign using television and expensive magazine advertising for the first time. Sales during the year were not much higher than previous years as the partners consider that the effects of advertising will be seen in future years.

Expenditure on advertising during the year is made up of:

	£
Television	50,000
Advertisements in magazines	60,000
Advertisements in local papers	25,000

All the expenditure has been treated as expense in the accounts but the partners wish to carry forward three-quarters of the television and magazine costs as it is expected that this cost will benefit future years' profits and because this year's profits will compare unfavourably with previous years if all the expenditure is charged in the accounts.

→

→ (d) Three projects for the construction of sinkers have the following cost and revenue characteristics:

	Project A 75%	Project B 50%	Project C 15%
Degree of completion	£	£	£
Direct costs to date	30,000	25,000	6,000
Sales price of complete project	55,000	50,000	57,500
Overheads allocated to date	4,000	2,000	500
Costs to complete – Direct	10,000	25,000	40,000
– Overheads	2,000	2,000	3,000

No profits or losses have been included in the accounts.

(e) After considerable discussion with management, the sales of a newly developed special purpose hook have been given the following probabilities:

First year of production

Sales £	Probability
15,000	0.2
30,000	0.5
40,000	0.3

Second year of production

Increase over first year £	Probability
10,000	0.1
20,000	0.5
30,000	0.4

Second year sales may be assumed independent of first year levels.
Cost–volume–profit analysis shows that the breakeven point is £50,000.

Production of the special purpose hook started prior to the end of the accounting year and stocks of the finished product are included at cost amounting to £20,000. It has been decided that if there is less than 0.7 probability of breakeven being reached in the second year then stocks should be written down by 25 per cent.

(f) During the year it was discovered that some stock sheets had been omitted from the calculations at the previous year end. The effect is that opening stock for the current year, shown as £35,000, should be £42,000. No adjustment has yet been made.

Required:
Discuss the treatment of each item with reference to relevant accounting standards and accounting concepts and conventions. Recommend the appropriate treatment for each item showing the profit effect of each recommendation made.

(*Association of Chartered Certified Accountants*)

11.6 The chief accountant of Uncertain Ltd is not sure of the appropriate accounting treatment for a number of events occurring during the year 2005/6.

(i) A significant number of employees have been made redundant, giving rise to redundancy payments of £100,000 which have been included in manufacturing cost of sales.
(ii) One of Uncertain Ltd's three factories has been closed down. Closure costs amounted to £575,000. This amount has been deducted from reserves in the balance sheet.
(iii) The directors have changed the basis of charging depreciation on delivery vehicles. The difference between the old and new methods amounts to £258,800. This has been charged as a prior period adjustment.

(*iv*) During October 2006 a fire occurred in one of the remaining factories belonging to Uncertain Ltd and caused an estimated £350,000 of additional expenses. This amount has been included in manufacturing cost of sales.

(*v*) It was discovered on 31 October 2006 that a customer was unable to pay his debt to the company of £125,000. The £125,000 was made up of sales in the period July to September 2006. No adjustment has been made in the draft accounts for this item.

Uncertain Ltd
Draft Profit and Loss Account for the year ended 30 September 2006

	£	£
Sales		5,450,490
Manufacturing cost of sales		3,284,500
Gross profit		2,165,990
Administration expenses	785,420	
Selling expenses	629,800	
		(1,415,220)
		750,770
Corporation tax (50%)		(375,385)
		375,385

Notes: (1) A dividend of £125,000 is proposed.
(2) A prior period adjustment of £129,400 (£258,800 less corporation tax of £129,400) has been made to reserves.

Required:
(*a*) Write a report to the chief accountant of Uncertain Ltd with suggestions for appropriate treatment for each of the items (*i*) to (*iv*), with explanations for your proposals.
(*b*) Amend the draft profit and loss account to take account of your proposals.

(*Association of Chartered Certified Accountants*)

11.7 With reference to FRS 21: *Events after the balance sheet date* and FRS 12: *Provisions, contingent liabilities and contingent assets*:

(*a*) Define the following terms:
(*i*) post-balance sheet events
(*ii*) adjusting events
(*iii*) non-adjusting events
(*iv*) contingent asset/liability;
(*b*) Give FOUR examples of adjusting events, and FOUR examples of non-adjusting events; and
(*c*) State how
(*i*) a material contingent liability, and
(*ii*) material contingent assets should be accounted for in financial statements.

You can find a range of additional self-test questions, as well as material to help you with your studies, on the website that accompanies this book at **www.pearsoned.co.uk/wood**

The financial statements of limited companies: profit and loss accounts, related statements and notes

Learning objectives

After you have studied this chapter, you should be able to:

- state how the Companies Act 2006 defines company size
- explain the alternative presentation formats available under the Companies Acts that must be used when preparing profit and loss accounts for external reporting purposes
- explain how to present financial information under the most commonly used Companies Act format
- describe the differences between the most commonly used statutory financial statement format and the formats generally adopted for internal use
- describe the FRS 3 requirements that relate to the profit and loss account concerning:
  - continuing operations
  - acquisitions
  - discontinued operations
  - sale or termination of an operation
  - reorganisation and restructuring costs
  - profits and losses on disposal of fixed assets
  - exceptional and extraordinary items
  - prior period adjustments
- describe the impact of FRS 3 upon the Companies Act format
- describe the format of the statement of total recognised gains and losses
- describe the format of the note of historical cost profits and losses

Introduction

In this chapter, you'll learn about the way in which accounting standards and the Companies Acts govern the presentation of information in published company financial statements.

12.1 Background

When a company draws up its own financial statements, purely for internal use by directors and the management, it can adopt any format it wishes. It can, for example, switch the order of items in the balance sheet, combine items that are never combined when official formats are used, and use its own terminology in place of normal accounting terminology. There are no rules which must be followed when preparing accounting information for internal use. Drawing up a trading and profit and loss account and balance sheet for a company's own use is not, therefore, necessarily the same as drawing up such financial statements for other purposes.

If an organisation wishes to charge something in the trading account that, in theory, ought to be shown in the profit and loss account, there is nothing to prevent it from doing so. On the other hand, students sitting an exam and accountants preparing financial statements for publication must base their work on accounting theory and accounting rules and regulations, *not* on the internal reporting practices of an organisation.

When it comes to publication, i.e. when the financial statements are sent to the shareholders or to the Registrar of Companies, the Companies Acts lay down the information which must be shown, and also how it should be shown. Prior to 1981, provided the necessary information was shown, it was up to each company to decide how it wanted to present it. The provisions of the 1981 Act brought the UK into line with the Fourth Directive of the EC, and the freedom previously available to companies on how to show the information was removed. There are, however, some advantages to be gained from such standardisation.

> **Activity 12.1** What do you think these advantages may be?

12.2 Financial statement formats

The Companies Acts give companies the choice of two alternative formats (layouts) for balance sheets, and four alternative formats for profit and loss accounts. We are going to focus on the most commonly used of these formats. If you need to know the layouts prescribed by the other formats, they are readily available in the Companies Acts themselves.

We are going to approach this topic, first, by presenting you with a profit and loss account produced for use within a company (an 'internal' profit and loss account) which can easily be adapted to cover publication requirements under the Companies Acts, along with an 'internal' balance sheet.

> **Activity 12.2** The reason for taking this approach ought to be fairly obvious. What do you think it is?

All companies, even the smallest, have to produce financial statements for their shareholders that adhere to the requirements of the Companies Acts. 'Small' and 'medium-sized' companies can, however, file summarised financial statements with the Registrar of Companies, but they must still prepare a full set of financial statements for their shareholders. In addition, listed companies may send their shareholders summary financial statements in place of the full version, but each shareholder has the right to request a full version and many do.

The Companies Act 2006 definition of 'small-' and 'medium-sized' companies is that, for the financial year in question and the previous year, the company is defined as 'small-' or 'medium-sized' if it lies within the limits of at least two of the following three criteria:

	Small	*Medium-sized*
Turnover not more than	£5.6 million	£22.8 million
Balance sheet total not more than	£2.8 million	£11.4 million
Employees not more than	50	250

Of the four Companies Act formats which could be used, the format we will use in this book for the published profit and loss account is called Format 1.

12.3 Format 1

The Companies Acts show Format 1 as in Exhibit 12.1:

Exhibit 12.1

Profit and loss account – Format 1

1 Turnover
2 Cost of sales
3 Gross profit or loss
4 Distribution costs
5 Administrative expenses
6 Other operating income
7 Income from shares in group undertakings
8 Income from participating interests
9 Income from other fixed asset investments
10 Other interest receivable and similar income
11 Amounts written off investments
12 Interest payable and similar charges
13 Tax on profit or loss on ordinary activities
14 Profit or loss on ordinary activities after taxation
15 Extraordinary income
16 Extraordinary charges
17 Extraordinary profit or loss
18 Tax on extraordinary profit or loss
19 Other taxes not shown under the above items
20 Profit or loss for the financial year

It is presented as a list and does not show where subtotals should be placed. The important point is that items 1 to 20 have to be displayed in that order. If some items do not exist for the company in a given year, then those headings are omitted from the published profit and loss account. Thus, if the company has no investments, items 7, 8, 9, 10 and 11 will not appear in its published profit and loss account, and item 6 will be followed by item 12. The category reference numbers on the left-hand side of items are normally omitted from the published profit and loss account.

12.4 Financial statements for internal use

Exhibit 12.2 shows a trading and profit and loss account drawn up for internal use by a company. As mentioned earlier, there are no statutory rules concerning how financial statements are drawn up for internal use. However, as you learnt in Activity 12.2, if the internal financial statements were drawn up in a completely different fashion from those needed for publication quite a lot of work would be needed in order to reassemble the figures into a profit and loss account for publication.

Exhibit 12.2 Financial statement for internal use

Block plc
Trading and Profit and Loss Account for the year ended 31 December 2006

		£000	£000	£000
(1)	Turnover			800
	Less Cost of sales:			
	Stock 1 January 2006		100	
	Add Purchases		525	
			625	
	Less Stock 31 December 2006		(125)	
				(500)
(2)	Gross profit			300
(3)	Distribution costs			
	Salaries and wages	30		
	Motor vehicle costs: Distribution	20		
	General distribution expenses	5		
	Depreciation: Motors	3		
	Machinery	2		
			60	
(4)	Administrative expenses			
	Salaries and wages	25		
	Motor vehicle costs: Administration	2		
	General administration expenses	7		
	Auditors' remuneration	2		
	Depreciation: Motors	3		
	Machinery	1		
(5)			40	
				(100)
				200
(6)	Other operating income			30
				230
(7)	Income from shares in group undertakings		20	
(8)	Income from participating interests		10	
(9)	Income from shares from non-related companies		5	
(10)	Other interest receivable		15	
				50
				280
(11)	Amounts written off investments		4	
	Interest payable			
	Loans repayable within five years	10		
	Loans repayable in ten years	6		
(12)			16	
				(20)
	Profit on ordinary activities before taxation			260
(13)	Tax on profit on ordinary activities			(95)
(14)	(20) Profit on ordinary activities after taxation			165
	Retained profits brought forward from last year			60
				225
	Transfer to general reserve		40	
	Proposed ordinary dividend		100	
				(140)
	Retained profits carried forward to next year			85

In Exhibit 12.2, the internal profit and loss account has been prepared using a format which makes it much easier to get the figures for the published profit and loss account. Examination questions on this topic sometimes ask for both (*a*) internal and (*b*) published financial statements. You should find things are easier if the internal and published financial statements follow a similar format.

To help you see how this internal format follows the one for publication, the line numbers from the Companies Act format are shown in brackets. Do *not* include these numbers when preparing 'internal' financial statements.

12.5 Financial statements for publication

Note that there are no items in Exhibit 12.2 that would appear under items 15 to 19 in Companies Act Format 1 and that, as a result, items 14 and 20 are represented by the same figure. Exhibit 12.3 redrafts Exhibit 12.2 into a form suitable for publication according to Format 1. However, as before, the category reference numbers to the left-hand side of Exhibit 12.3 are for your benefit only; they do not have to be included. You will see that one difference between the two exhibits is that the detail between each entry has been removed. Such detail could, of course, be included as notes to the published financial statement. The other main difference is that none of the lines after the profit on ordinary activities after taxation line appears in a profit and loss account for publication.

Exhibit 12.3 Financial statements for publication presented according to Format 1

Block plc
Profit and Loss Account for the year ending 31 December 2006

	£000	£000
1 Turnover		800
2 Cost of sales		(500)
3 Gross profit		300
4 Distribution costs	60	
5 Administrative expenses	40	
		(100)
		200
6 Other operating income		30
		230
7 Income from shares in group undertakings	20	
8 Income from participating interests	10	
9 Income from other fixed asset investments	5	
10 Other interest receivable and similar income	15	
		50
		280
11 Amounts written off investments	4	
12 Interest payable and similar charges	16	
		(20)
Profit or loss on ordinary activities before taxation		260
13 Tax on profit or loss on ordinary activities		(95)
14 Profit or loss on ordinary activities after taxation		165
Earnings per share 25p		

Note: **Transfers to reserves, dividends paid and retained profit from the previous year are not shown. They would normally appear in a note to the financial statements concerning movements on the reserves. (Movements in Shareholders' Funds.)**

When internal financial statements are prepared in the format shown in Exhibit 12.2, they could be published just as they are, because all the items are shown in the correct order. The Companies Act does not force companies to publish detailed financial statements (for example, such as shown in Exhibit 12.2). Rather, it states the *minimum* information which must be disclosed. A company can show more than the minimum if it wants to but normally, as above, companies usually prefer to do so in notes to the financial statement, if at all.

 Activity 12.3 Why would most companies *not* want to publish detailed financial statements?

Now, let's look at Format 1 in more detail.

12.6 Definition of items in Format 1

Format item 1

Turnover is defined as the amounts derived from the provision of goods and services falling within the company's ordinary activities, net after deduction of VAT and trade discounts.

Format items 2, 4 and 5

The figures for cost of sales, distribution costs and administrative expenses must include any depreciation charges connected with these functions. For example, in the case of Block plc, depreciation charges are included in both distribution costs and administration expenses, but not in cost of sales.

Format item 6

This is operating income which does not fall under item 1. Such items as rents receivable or royalties receivable might be found under this heading.

Format item 7

In Chapter 19, you will be introduced to the concept of parent and subsidiary undertakings. A parent is able to exert a dominant influence over (i.e. control) the activities of the subsidiary usually but, not necessarily, as a result of its owning a majority of the voting rights in the subsidiary. Together, the parent company and all its subsidiaries are a 'group'. Any dividends received by a company from its investments in shares in any member of the group have to be shown separately.

 Activity 12.4 Why do you think dividends of this kind must be shown separately?

Format item 8

The term 'participating interest' means one where the parent company has a long-term holding of shares or their equivalent in an undertaking for the purpose of securing a contribution to the investor's own activities by the exercise of control or influence arising from or related to that interest. Where the equity stake exceeds 20 per cent, there is a presumption of such influence unless the contrary is shown.

Format item 12

This includes bank interest on loans and overdrafts, debenture interest, etc.

The profit and loss account produced will not appear precisely as presented in Exhibit 12.1. As can be seen in Exhibit 12.3, the published profit and loss account for Block plc contains no items in categories 15, 16, 17, 18, 19 or (although the amount it represents is shown under item 14) 20. In addition, after item 14, there are several more lines that must be included where they have values, those of transfer to reserves and proposed dividends. Although not included in Format 1, they are required according to the detailed rules accompanying the format. This also applies to line 20, 'Profit or loss for the financial year' shown in Exhibit 12.1, when that line is included.

It would also have been possible to amalgamate items, for instance 4 and 5 could have been shown together as 'Net operating expenses £100,000'. In this case, included in the notes appended to the financial statements would be an item showing the composition of the figure of £100,000.

In the notes attached to the profit and loss account, the Companies Acts require that the following be shown separately:

1 Interest on bank loans, overdrafts and other loans:
   (a) repayable within 5 years from the end of the accounting period;
   (b) finally repayable after 5 years from the end of the accounting period.
2 Amounts set aside for redemption of share capital and for redemption of loans.
3 Rents from land, if material.
4 Costs of hire of plant and machinery.
5 Auditors' remuneration, including expenses.

Where a company carries on business of two or more classes differing substantially from each other, a note is required of the amount of turnover for each class of business, and the division of the profit and loss before taxation between each class. Information also has to be given of the turnover between geographical markets.

Notes are also required concerning numbers of employees, wages and salaries, social security costs, and pension costs.

Three further disclosure requirements of the Companies Act are expanded by FRS 3:

1 The effect must be stated of any amount relating to any preceding financial year included in any item in the profit and loss account.
2 Particulars must be given of any extraordinary income or charges arising in the financial year.
3 The effect of any transaction of exceptional size or incidence that falls within the ordinary activities of the company must be stated.

12.7 Layout of the profit and loss account

If Block plc had items relevant to the other Format 1 categories, the profit and loss account would have been presented as shown in Exhibit 12.4. Note that the lines added have been included simply to show what the statement would look like. Where a category has no value, it would normally be omitted from the statement, as was the case in Exhibit 12.3. In addition, Exhibit 12.4 shows the extra lines that must be included but are not included in Format 1 in the Companies Act. It is also worthwhile noting that the four lines in Format 1 that relate to *extraordinary items* are virtually eliminated as a result of the definition of the term that was introduced in FRS 3: *Reporting financial performance*. As a result of its issuing FRS 3, the

Accounting Standards Board does not expect any company to identify an item as 'extraordinary' in its financial statements and so items 15 to 18 are unlikely to be seen in any future published profit and loss accounts.

See Section 12.11 for more on FRS 3 and extraordinary items.

Exhibit 12.4

Block plc
Profit and Loss Account for the year ending 31 December 2026

	£000	£000
1 Turnover		800
2 Cost of sales		(500)
3 Gross profit		300
4 Distribution costs	60	
5 Administrative expenses	40	
		(100)
		200
6 Other operating income		30
		230
7 Income from shares in group undertakings	20	
8 Income from participating interests	10	
9 Income from fixed asset investments	5	
10 Other interest receivable and similar income	15	
		50
		280
11 Amounts written off investments	4	
12 Interest payable and similar charges	16	
		(20)
Profit or loss on ordinary activities before taxation		260
13 Tax on profit or loss on ordinary activities		(95)
14 Profit or loss on ordinary activities after taxation		165
15 Extraordinary income	0	
16 Extraordinary charges	0	
17 Extraordinary profit or loss	0	
18 Tax on extraordinary profit or loss	0	
		0
		165
19 Other taxes not shown under the above items		0
20 Profit or loss for the financial year		165

Earnings per share	25p

12.8 Allocation of expenses

It will be obvious under which heading most expenses will be shown, whether they are:

(*a*) cost of sales;
(*b*) distribution costs; or
(*c*) administrative expenses.

However, as the Companies Acts do not define these terms, some items are not so easy to allocate with certainty. Some companies may choose one heading for a particular item, while another company will choose another. For example:

1 **Discounts received.** These are for prompt payment of amounts owing by us. Where they are for payments to suppliers of goods they could be regarded either as a reduction in the cost of goods or, alternatively, as a financial recompense, i.e. the reward for paying money on time. If regarded in the first way they would be deducted from cost of sales, whereas the alternative approach would be to deduct them from administrative expenses. However, these discounts are also deducted when paying bills in respect of distribution costs or administrative expenses, and it would also be necessary to deduct from these headings if the cost of sales deduction approach is used. As this raises complications in the original recording of discounts received, it would be more suitable in this book if all cash discounts received are deducted in arriving at the figure of administrative expenses.
2 **Discounts allowed.** To be consistent in dealing with discounts, this should be included in administrative expenses.
3 **Bad debts.** These could be regarded as an expense connected with sales: after all, they are sales which are not paid for. The other point of view is that for a debt to become bad, at least part of the blame must be because the proper administrative procedures in checking on customers' creditworthiness has not been thorough enough. In this book bad debts will be treated as being part of administrative expenses.

12.9 FRS 3: Reporting financial performance

Accounting is not a static subject. Changes occur over the years as they are seen to be necessary, and also get general agreement as to their usefulness. Since the advent of SSAPs and FRSs the number of changes that practitioners and students have had to learn has increased at a very fast rate. A prime example of this is the introduction of FRS 3, which necessitates changes to the formats of profit and loss accounts when certain events have occurred.

This standard replaced SSAP 6: *Extraordinary items and prior year adjustments*, temporarily amended SSAP 3: *Earnings per share* (FRS 14: *Earnings per share* was issued five years after FRS 3), and also made changes as a result to various other accounting standards.

Suppose that you are considering the affairs of a business over the years. The business has not changed significantly, there have been no acquisitions, no discontinued operations, no fundamental reorganisation or restructuring of the business, nor have there been any extraordinary items affecting the financial statements. In these circumstances, when comparing the financial statements over the years, you are comparing like with like, subject to the problem of the effect of inflation or deflation.

On the other hand, suppose that some of the things mentioned have occurred. When trying to see what the future might hold for the company, simply basing your opinions on what has happened in the past can be very confusing.

To help you to distinguish the past and the future, and to give you some idea as to what changes have occurred, FRS 3 requires that the following are highlighted in the profit and loss account if the amounts involved are material:

1 *What the results of continuing operations are, including the results of acquisitions.* Obviously acquisitions affect future results, and are therefore included in continuing operations.
2 *What the results have been of discontinued operations.* This should help distinguish the past from the future.

3 *The profits or losses on the sale or termination of an operation, the costs of fundamental reorganisation or restructuring* and *the profits and losses on the disposal of fixed assets.* The profits and losses concerning these matters are not going to happen again, and so this also helps us distinguish the past from the future.

You can see how FRS 3 requires these items to be shown on the face of the profit and loss account in Exhibit 12.5. Not only is the turnover split to show the figures relevant to continuing operations, acquisitions, and discontinued operations, the operating profit is split along the same lines. In addition, any profit or loss on the disposal of the discontinued operations is also shown. Exhibit 12.5 is restricted to the first six categories of Format 1 as this is the part of the statement affected by these FRS 3 requirements. Once again, we will use Block plc for the example.

Exhibit 12.5

Block plc
Profit and Loss Account for the year ending 31 December 2006 (extract)

	£000	£000
1 Turnover		
Continuing operations	520	
Acquisitions	110	
	630	
Discontinued operations	170	
		800
2 Cost of sales		(500)
3 Gross profit		300
4 Distribution costs	60	
5 Administrative expenses	40	
		(100)
Operating profit		
Continuing operations	160	
Acquisitions	60	
	220	
Discontinued operations (loss)	(20)	
		200
Profit on disposal of discontinued operations (a)		10
		210
6 Other operating income		20
Profit or loss on ordinary activities before interest		230

The item marked **(a)** can be described as an exceptional item. It is material in amount, falls within the ordinary activities of the firm, and needs to be shown so that the financial statements will give a 'true and fair view'.

It is exceptional in that it is not the ordinary daily occurrence, but remember that it falls within the ordinary activities of the company. FRS 3 requires that three categories of exceptional items be shown separately on the face of the profit and loss account after operating profit and before interest, and included under the appropriate heading of continued or discontinued operations:

1 Profits or losses on the sale or termination of an operation.
2 Costs of a fundamental reorganisation or restructuring having a material effect on the nature and focus of the reporting entity's operations.
3 Profits or losses on the disposal of fixed assets.

Other exceptional items should be credited or charged in arriving at the profit or loss on ordinary activities by inclusion under the heading to which they relate. The amount of each exceptional item should be disclosed in a note, or on the face of the profit and loss account, if necessary in order to give a true and fair view.

12.10 Other statements and notes required by FRS 3

Statement of total recognised gains and losses

The *statement of total recognised gains and losses* is one of two new primary statements introduced by FRS 3. It shows the extent to which shareholders' funds have increased or decreased from all the various gains and losses recognised in the period, and enables users to consider all recognised gains and losses of a reporting entity in assessing its overall performance; an example of what would be included in the statement would be unrealised gains on fixed asset revaluations. Exhibit 12.6 presents an example of the statement using the data from Block plc:

Exhibit 12.6

Block plc
Statement of Total Recognised Gains and Losses

	2006
	£000
Profit for the financial year*	165
Unrealised surplus on revaluation of properties	12
Unrealised (loss)/gain on trade investment	(8)
	169
Currency translation differences on foreign currency investments	(5)
Total recognised gains and losses relating to the year	164
Prior period adjustment	(19)
Total gains and losses recognised since last annual report	145

*See Exhibit 12.4.

Note: Only the profit figure can be found in the profit and loss account. The others have been inserted to demonstrate what the statement looks like. As with all these statements, including the profit and loss account, comparative figures would also be shown.

Note of historical cost profits and losses

Where assets have been revalued, which obviously affects depreciation, the revalued figures may have a material effect upon the results shown in the financial statements. If this is the case, FRS 3 requires that there should also be shown as a note what the profit and loss account would have been if the account had been shown using historical (i.e. not revalued) figures.

The note should also show how the reported profit on ordinary activities (using revalued assets) can be reconciled with that calculated using historical figures, and should also show the retained profit figure for the financial year reported on the historical cost basis. The note should be presented immediately following the profit and loss account or the statement of total recognised gains and losses. An example of the note is presented in Exhibit 12.7:

Exhibit 12.7

Block plc
Note of Historical Cost Profits and Losses

	2006 £000
Reported profit on ordinary activities before taxation[Note 1]	260
Realisation of property revaluation gains of previous years	12
Difference between a historical cost depreciation charge and the actual depreciation charge of the year calculated on the revalued amount	1
Historical cost profit on ordinary activities before taxation	273
Historical cost profit for the year retained after taxation, minority interests, extraordinary items and dividends (273 – 95 – 100)	78

Notes:
(1) See Exhibit 12.4.
(2) As with the statement of total recognised gains and losses, only the profit figure can be identified in the profit and loss account. Also, comparative figures should be shown.

Reconciliation of movements in shareholders' funds

The profit and loss account and the statement of total recognised gains and losses reflect the performance of a reporting entity in a period, but there are other changes that can occur in shareholders' funds that these two statements do not disclose, and which can be important in understanding the change in the financial position of the entity – for example, a new share issue or goodwill written off. For this reason, FRS 3 also gave the *reconciliation of movements in shareholders' funds* the status of a primary statement, its purpose being to highlight these other changes in the financial position. When shown as a primary statement (there *is* an option to show it as a note), the reconciliation should be shown separately from the statement of total recognised gains and losses. Exhibit 12.8 presents an example of the statement.

Exhibit 12.8

Block plc
Reconciliation of Movements in Shareholders' Funds

	2006 £000
Profit for the financial year[Note 1]	165
Dividends	(100)
	65
Other recognised gains and losses relating to the year (net)	(1)
New share capital subscribed	20
Goodwill written off	(25)
Net addition to shareholders' funds	59
Opening shareholders' funds (originally £321,000 before deducting prior period adjustment of £19,000)	302
Closing shareholders' funds	361

Notes:
(1) See Exhibit 12.4.
(2) The figures can be found in the other statements except for the new share capital, the goodwill written off and the opening shareholders' funds amounts. As before, comparative figures should also be presented.

12.11 FRS 3 and extraordinary items

You have just seen that FRS 3 requires that some of the exceptional items are highlighted on the face of the profit and loss account, whilst others can be put under appropriate headings with notes giving more detail attached to the financial statements.

In Exhibit 12.3 all of these exceptional items will have been dealt with by the time that item 14, 'Profit for the year on ordinary activities after taxation', has been reached. Any extraordinary items are shown as items 15, 16, 17 and 18.

Before FRS 3, the distinction between what was an exceptional item and what was an extraordinary item was not as well defined as it could have been. This led to directors of companies sometimes manipulating the figures for their own ends while keeping within the necessary legal boundaries.

They did this because the profit per item 14 was widely used to assess how well a company was being managed. It was a vital part of calculating the earnings per share (EPS) which is a main indicator to many people of the company's performance. If a favourable item could be called an 'exceptional item' it would increase the size of the profit as shown by item 14. On the other hand, should an item be unfavourable, and therefore lower the figure of profit shown by item 14, then perhaps it could be (and it often was) included instead as an 'extraordinary item'. In this way, the profit per item 14 could be shown at a higher figure than was really justified. Such actions could and did affect the Stock Exchange value of companies' shares.

FRS 3 put an end to this by being more strict about what is, or is not, an extraordinary item, and thus to be shown after item 14 in the profit and loss account. Extraordinary items:

(a) should be material items possessing a high degree of abnormality which arise from events or transactions that fall outside the ordinary activities of the business; and

(b) are not expected to recur;

(c) do not include exceptional items; and

(d) do not include items relating to a prior period merely because they relate to a prior period.

Extraordinary items fall *outside* the 'ordinary' activities of a company, whereas exceptional items fall *within* them. 'Ordinary activities' are any activities undertaken by a reporting entity as part of its business and such related activities in which the reporting entity engages in furtherance of, incidental to or arising from these activities. Ordinary activities include the effects on the reporting entity of any event in the various environments in which it operates. It is little wonder that the ASB did not believe that anything could ever be categorised as an extraordinary item after the introduction of FRS 3.

12.12 FRS 3 and prior period adjustments

Prior period adjustments are material adjustments applicable to prior periods arising from changes in accounting policies or from the correction of fundamental errors. They do not include normal recurring adjustments or corrections of accounting estimates (such as, for example, the estimated scrap value of a fixed asset) made in prior periods.

Prior period adjustments are accounted for by restating the comparative figures (i.e. the equivalent figures for the previous accounting period) for the preceding period in the primary statements and notes and adjusting the opening balance of reserves for the cumulative effect. The cumulative effect of the adjustments is also noted at the foot of the statement of total recognised gains and losses of the current period (*see* Exhibit 12.6). Where practicable, the effect of prior period adjustments on the results for the preceding period is disclosed.

12.13 FRS 3 and comparative figures

Comparative figures should be shown for all items in the primary statements and the notes to the statements required by FRS 3. The comparative figures in the 'continuing operations' category of the profit and loss account should include only the results of those operations included in the current period's 'continuing operations' category.

12.14 IAS 1: *Presentation of financial statements*

While there are differences between FRS 3 and IAS 1 – there is no international equivalent of the *statement of realised gains and losses*, for example – the presentation of information under both standards is similar.

Learning outcomes

You should now have learnt:

1 How the Companies Act defines company size.

2 There are set formats for the preparation of published financial statements.

3 Financial statements prepared for internal use need not comply with these set formats but are often based upon them.

4 FRS 3: *Reporting financial performance* amended the Companies Act format for the profit and loss account by requiring further details to be disclosed concerning:
   (a) continuing and discontinued operations;
   (b) restructuring; and
   (c) disposal of fixed assets.

5 In addition, by defining extraordinary items out of existence, FRS 3 effectively made obsolete a number of the categories contained in the Companies Act profit and loss accounts format relating to extraordinary items.

6 FRS 3 introduced two additional primary financial statements:
   (a) the statement of total recognised gains and losses;
   (b) the reconciliation of movements in shareholders' funds (may be shown as a note).

7 It also introduced a new note – the note of historical cost profits and losses.

Answers to activities

12.1 Combined with the regulations enshrined in accounting standards that govern how data will be processed and selected for inclusion as information in the financial statements, the standardisation brought about by the Companies Act 1981 makes meaningful comparison between the financial statements of different companies feasible.

12.2 For the same reason that many small companies use the percentage rates provided by the tax rules relating to capital allowances when setting their depreciation rates – it saves them redoing the calculation – many small companies use the Companies Act formats as the basis for their internal financial statements, adding more detail when they feel it is appropriate to do so.

12.3 Because doing so may give their competitors information which would lead to the company losing some of its competitive advantage.

12.4 The parent company can decide how much it wishes to receive as dividends from its subsidiaries. Unless this amount is shown separately, the total amount received from all investments by way of dividends may mislead anyone who does not know where they came from.

Advice: **It is important for you to know that the published profit and loss account of a company must show certain items in a given order.**

The contents of FRS 3 are likely to attract quite a lot of exam questions. Some may come in the form of the directors of a company wanting to classify something as extraordinary, and therefore shown after item 14, 'Profit or loss on ordinary activities after taxation'.

Review questions

12.1 From the following selected balances of Filo plc as at 31 March 2005 draw up (*i*) a detailed trading and profit and loss account for internal use, and (*ii*) a profit and loss account for publication.

	£
Profit and loss account as at 31 March 2004	210,000
Stock 1 April 2004	160,000
Purchases	2,920,000
Sales	4,960,000
Returns inwards	214,000
Returns outwards	70,000
Carriage inwards	26,000
Wages and salaries (*see* Note (*b*))	270,000
Rent and business rates (*see* Note (*c*))	25,000
General distribution expenses	54,000
General administrative expenses	42,000
Discounts allowed	68,000
Bad debts	9,000
Debenture interest	18,000
Motor expenses (*see* Note (*d*))	15,000
Interest received on bank deposit	8,000
Income from shares in undertakings in which the company has a participating interest	6,000
Motor vehicles at cost: Administrative	90,000
Distribution	140,000
Equipment at cost: Administrative	30,000
Distribution	24,000
Royalties receivable	5,000
Dividends paid	240,000

Notes:
(*a*) Stock at 31 March 2005 £208,000.
(*b*) Wages and salaries are to be apportioned: Distribution costs ¼, Administrative expenses ¾.
(*c*) Rent and business rates are to be apportioned: Distribution costs 60 per cent, Administrative expenses 40 per cent.
(*d*) Apportion motor expenses in the proportions 2:3 between distribution costs and administrative expenses.
(*e*) Depreciate motor vehicles 25 per cent and equipment 20 per cent on cost.
(*f*) Accrue auditors' remuneration of £16,000.
(*g*) Accrue corporation tax for the year on ordinary activity profits £489,000.
(*h*) A sum of £30,000 is to be transferred to general reserve.

12.2 From the following selected balances of State plc as at 31 December 2008, prepare (*i*) a detailed trading and profit and loss account for the year ended 31 December 2008 for internal use and (*ii*) a profit and loss account for the same period for publication.

	£
Stock 1 January 2008	140,000
Sales	1,860,000
Purchases	1,140,000
Carriage inwards	8,000
Returns inwards	9,000
Returns outwards	5,000
Discounts allowed	11,000
Discounts received	14,000
Wages (putting goods into saleable condition)	88,000
Salaries and wages: Sales and distribution staff	62,000
Salaries and wages: Administrative staff	74,000
Motor expenses (see Note (*c*))	24,000
Rent and business rates (see Note (*d*))	28,000
Investments in undertakings in which the company has a participating interest (market value £74,000)	100,000
Income from shares in undertakings in which the company has a participating interest	5,000
General distribution expenses	12,000
General administrative expenses	6,000
Bad debts	2,000
Interest from government securities	3,000
Haulage costs: Distribution	4,000
Debenture interest payable	2,000
Profit and loss account: 31 December 2007	94,000
Motor vehicles at cost: Distribution and sales	60,000
Administrative	26,000
Plant and machinery at cost: Distribution and sales	50,000
Administrative	30,000
Production	60,000
Directors' remuneration	36,000
Dividends paid	60,000

Notes:
(*a*) The production department puts goods bought into a saleable condition.
(*b*) Stock at 31 December 2008 £160,000.
(*c*) Apportion motor expenses: distribution ³/₄, administrative ¹/₄.
(*d*) Apportion rent and business rates: distribution 40 per cent, administrative 60 per cent.
(*e*) Write £26,000 off the value of investments in undertakings in which the company has a participating interest.
(*f*) Depreciate motor vehicles 25 per cent on cost, plant and machinery 15 per cent on cost.
(*g*) Accrue auditors' remuneration £14,000.
(*h*) Accrue corporation tax on ordinary activity profits £104,000.
(*i*) A sum of £25,000 is to be transferred to debenture redemption reserve.

→

12.3 The following information has been extracted from the books of account of Rufford plc for the year to 31 March 2006:

	Dr £000	Cr £000
Administration expenses	97	
Deferred taxation		24
Depreciation on office machinery (for the year to 31 March 2006)	8	
Depreciation on delivery vans (for the year to 31 March 2006)	19	
Distribution costs	33	
Dividends received (from a UK listed company on 31 July 2005)		14
Factory closure expenses (closed on 1 April 2005)	12	
Interest payable on bank overdraft (repayable within five years)	6	
Interim dividend (paid on 30 September 2005)	21	
Interest receivable		25
Purchases	401	
Retained profit at 31 March 2005		160
Sales (net of VAT)		642
Stock at 1 April 2005	60	

Additional information:

1 Administrative expenses include the following items:

	£000
Auditors' remuneration	20
Directors' emoluments	45
Travelling expenses	1
Research expenditure	11
Hire of plant and machinery	12

2 It is assumed that the following tax rates are applicable for the year to 31 March 2006:

Corporation tax	50%
Income tax	30%

3 There was an overprovision for corporation tax of £3,000 relating to the year to 31 March 2005.

4 Corporation tax payable for the year to 31 March 2006 (based on the profits for that year) is estimated to be £38,000. The company, in addition, intends to transfer a further £9,000 to its deferred taxation account.

5 A final dividend of £42,000 for the year to 31 March 2006 is expected to be paid on 2 June 2006.

6 Stock at 31 March 2006 was valued at £71,000.

7 As a result of a change in accounting policy, a prior period charge of £15,000 (net of tax) is to be made.

8 The company's share capital consists of 420,000 ordinary shares of £1 each. There are no preference shares, and no change had been made to the company's issued share capital for some years.

Required:

(*a*) In so far as the information permits, prepare the company's published profit and loss account for the year to 31 March 2006 in the vertical format in accordance with the Companies Act and with related accounting standards.

(NB: A statement of the company's accounting policies is not required.)

(*b*) Prepare balance sheet extracts in order to illustrate the balances still remaining in the following accounts at 31 March 2006:

(*i*) corporation tax;

(*ii*) proposed dividend; and

(*iii*) deferred taxation.

(NB: A detailed balance sheet is not required.)

(*Association of Accounting Technicians*)

12.4A From the following balances in the books of Breaker plc you are to draw up (*i*) a detailed trading and profit and loss account for the year ending 31 March 2004 for internal use, and (*ii*) a profit and loss account for publication:

	£
Plant and machinery, at cost (*see* Note (*c*))	105,000
Bank interest receivable	3,000
Discounts allowed	7,000
Discounts received	6,000
Hire of motor vehicles: Sales and distribution	14,000
Hire of motor vehicles: Administrative	5,000
Licence fees receivable	13,000
General distribution expenses	26,000
General administrative expenses	19,000
Wages and salaries: Sales and distribution	177,000
Administrative	98,000
Directors' remuneration	41,000
Motor expenses (*see* Note (*e*))	11,000
Ordinary dividend paid	80,000
Stock 31 March 2003	208,000
Sales	1,450,000
Purchases	700,000
Returns outwards	22,000
Returns inwards	29,000
Profit and loss account as at 31 March 2003	88,000

Notes:
(*a*) Stock at 31 March 2004 £230,000.
(*b*) Accrue auditor's remuneration £8,000.
(*c*) Of the plant and machinery, £70,000 is distributive in nature, while £35,000 is for administration.
(*d*) Depreciate plant and machinery 25 per cent on cost.
(*e*) Of the motor expenses, $^4/_5$ is for sales and distribution and $^1/_5$ for administration.
(*f*) Corporation tax on ordinary profits is estimated at £143,000.
(*g*) A sum of £25,000 is to be transferred to general reserve.

→

→ **12.5A** The following balances have been extracted from the books of Mitchell plc on 31 July 2002. From them draw up (*i*) a detailed trading and profit and loss account for internal use, for the year ending 31 July 2002, also (*ii*) a profit and loss account for publication for the year to that date.

	£
Purchases	1,310,000
Sales	1,790,000
Returns inwards	29,000
Returns outwards	57,000
Carriage inwards	10,000
Wages – productive	109,000
Discounts allowed	11,000
Discounts received	15,000
Stock 31 July 2001	317,000
Wages and salaries: Sales and distribution	41,000
Wages and salaries: Administrative	62,000
Motor expenses: Sales and distribution	26,000
Motor expenses: Administrative	8,000
General distribution expenses	7,000
General administrative expenses	6,000
Rent and business rates (*see* Note (*c*))	17,000
Directors' remuneration	35,000
Profit and loss account: 31 July 2001	141,000
Advertising	19,000
Bad debts	3,000
Hire of plant and machinery (*see* Note (*b*))	14,000
Motor vehicles at cost: Sales and distribution	45,000
Administrative	18,000
Plant and machinery: Distribution	13,000
Debenture interest payable	7,000
Income from shares in group undertakings	8,000
Income from shares in undertakings in which the company has a participating interest	5,000
Preference dividend paid	20,000
Profit on disposal of investments	14,000
Tax on profit on disposal of investments	3,000
Ordinary dividend paid	110,000

Notes:
(*a*) Stock at 31 July 2002 £303,000.
(*b*) The hire of plant and machinery is to be apportioned: productive £12,000, administrative £2,000.
(*c*) Rent and business rates to be apportioned: distribution $^3/_4$, administrative $^1/_4$.
(*d*) Motors are to be depreciated at $33^1/_3$ per cent on cost; plant and machinery to be depreciated at 10 per cent on cost.
(*e*) Auditors' remuneration of £15,000 to be accrued.
(*f*) Corporation tax on profit from ordinary activities for the year is estimated at £29,000, excluding tax on disposal of investments.
(*g*) Transfer £50,000 to general reserve.

12.6A Bunker plc is a trading company; it does not carry out *any* manufacturing operations. The following information has been extracted from the books of account for the year to 31 March 2010:

	£000
Auditors' remuneration	30
Corporation tax: based on the accounting profit for the year to 31 March 2010	7,200
overprovision for the year to 31 March 2009	200
United Kingdom corporation tax relief on	
overseas operations: closure costs	30
Delivery expenses	1,200
Dividends: final (proposed – to be paid 1 August 2010)	200
interim (paid on 1 October 2009)	100
Fixed assets at cost:	
Delivery vans	200
Office cars	40
Stores plant and equipment	5,000
Investment income (amount received from listed companies)	1,600
Office expenses	800
Overseas operations: closure costs of entire operations on 1 April 2009	350
Purchases (net of value added tax)	24,000
Sales (net of value added tax)	35,000
Stocks at cost:	
at 1 April 2009	5,000
at 31 March 2010	6,000
Storeroom costs	1,000
Wages and salaries:	
Delivery staff	700
Directors' emoluments	300
Office staff	100
Storeroom staff	400

Additional information:
1 Depreciation policy:
 Depreciation is provided at the following annual rates on a straight line basis: delivery vans 20 per cent; office cars 7.5 per cent; stores plant and equipment 10 per cent.
2 The following taxation rates may be assumed:
 corporation tax 35 per cent; income tax 25 per cent; value added tax 15 per cent.
3 The investment income arises from investments held in fixed asset investments.
4 It has been decided to transfer an amount of £150,000 to the deferred taxation account.
5 There were 1,000,000 ordinary shares of £1 each in issue during the year to 31 March 2010. There were no preference shares in issue.

Required:
In so far as the information permits, prepare Bunker plc's published profit and loss account for the year ending 31 March 2010 in accordance with the minimum requirements of the Companies Act 1985 and related accounting standards.

Note: A statement of accounting policies is NOT required, but where appropriate, other formal notes SHOULD be attached to your profit and loss account. Detailed workings should also be submitted with your answer.

(Association of Accounting Technicians)

→ **12.7A** Fresno Group plc have prepared their financial statements for the year ended 31 January 2004. However, the financial accountant of Fresno Group plc had difficulty in preparing the statements required by FRS 3: *Reporting financial performance*, and approached you for help in preparing those statements. The financial accountant furnished you with the following information:

(*i*)
Fresno Group plc
Profit and Loss Account extract for year ended 31 January 2004

	£ million
Operating profit – continuing operations	290
Profit on sale of property in continuing operations	10
Profit on ordinary activities before taxation	300
Tax on ordinary activities	(90)
Profit after taxation	210

Note: Dividends of £15 million were paid during the year.

The financial accountant did not provide for the loss on any discontinued operations in the profit and loss account. (However, you may assume that the taxation provision incorporated the effects of any provision for discontinued operations.)

(*ii*) The shareholders' funds at the beginning of the financial year were as follows:

	£ million
Share capital – £1 ordinary shares	350
Merger reserve	55
Revaluation reserve	215
Profit and loss reserve	775
	1,395

(*iii*) Fresno Group plc regularly revalues its fixed assets and at 31 January 2004, a revaluation surplus of £375 million had been credited to revaluation reserve. During the financial year, a property had been sold on which a revaluation surplus of £54 million had been credited to reserves. Further, if the company had charged depreciation on a historical cost basis rather than the revalued amounts, the depreciation charge in the profit and loss account for fixed assets would have been £7 million. The current year's charge for depreciation was £16 million.

(*iv*) The group has a policy of writing off goodwill on the acquisition of subsidiaries directly against a merger reserve. The goodwill for the period amounted to £250 million. In order to facilitate the purchase of subsidiaries, the company had issued £1 ordinary shares of nominal value £150 million and share premium of £450 million. The premium had been taken to the merger reserve. All subsidiaries are currently 100 per cent owned by the group.

(*v*) During the financial year to 31 January 2004, the company had made a decision to close a 100 per cent owned subsidiary, Reno plc. However, the closure did not take place until May 2004. Fresno Group plc estimated that as at 31 January 2004 the operating loss for the period 1 February 2004 to 31 May 2004 would be £30 million and that in addition redundancy costs, stock and plant write-downs would amount to £15 million. In the event, the operating loss for the period 1 February 2004 to 31 May 2004 was £65 million, but the redundancy costs, stock and plant write-downs only amounted to £12 million.

(*vi*) The following information relates to Reno plc for the period 1 February 2004 to 31 May 2004.

Reno plc

	£ million
Turnover	175
Cost of sales	(195)
Gross loss	(20)
Administrative expenses	(15)
Selling expenses	(30)
Operating loss before taxation	(65)

Required:

(a) Prepare the following statements in accordance with current statutory requirements and FRS 3: *Reporting financial performance* for Fresno Group plc for the year ending 31 January 2004:
  (i) statement of total recognised gains and losses;
  (ii) reconciliation of movements in shareholders' funds;
  (iii) analysis of movements on reserves;
  (iv) note of historical cost profits and losses.

(b) Explain to the financial accountant:
  (i) how the decision to close the subsidiary, Reno plc, affects the financial statements of Fresno Group plc for the year ended 31 January 2004;
  (ii) how the subsidiary, Reno plc, should be dealt with in the financial statements of Fresno Group plc for the year ended 31 January 2005.

(Association of Chartered Certified Accountants)

You can find a range of additional self-test questions, as well as material to help you with your studies, on the website that accompanies this book at **www.pearsoned.co.uk/wood**

The financial statements of limited companies: balance sheets

Learning objectives

After you have studied this chapter, you should be able to:

- describe the most commonly used format available under the Companies Acts that may be used when preparing balance sheets for external reporting purposes
- present information under the most commonly used of the Companies Acts formats
- describe the differences between the statutory format and formats generally adopted for internal use
- describe the exemption of some 'small' companies from having their financial statements audited
- describe the exemptions available to small and medium-sized companies in respect of filing modified financial statements
- describe the option available to public limited companies to send members a summary financial statement

Introduction

In this chapter, you'll learn about the format normally adopted for balance sheets prepared for publication. You will also be reminded of the fundamental accounting concepts that you covered in *Business Accounting UK GAAP 1* and introduced to the rules relating to the preparation of modified financial statements for small and medium-sized companies.

13.1 Balance sheet formats

The Companies Acts set out two formats for the balance sheet. The method we will follow is that contained in Format 1, because this is the one used by most UK companies.

Format 1 is shown in Exhibit 13.1. Monetary amounts have been included to make it easier to follow and understand.

Exhibit 13.1

Balance Sheet – Format 1

	£000	£000	£000
A CALLED-UP SHARE CAPITAL NOT PAID*			10
B FIXED ASSETS			
I Intangible assets			
1 Development costs	20		
2 Concessions, patents, licences, trade marks			
and similar rights and assets	30		
3 Goodwill	80		
4 Payments on account	5		
		135	
II Tangible assets			
1 Land and buildings	300		
2 Plant and machinery	500		
3 Fixtures, fittings, tools and equipment	60		
4 Payments on account and assets in course			
of construction	20		
		880	
III Investments			
1 Shares in group undertakings	15		
2 Loans to group undertakings	10		
3 Participating interests	20		
4 Loans to undertakings in which the company has			
a participating interest	5		
5 Other investments other than loans	30		
6 Other loans	16		
7 Own shares	4		
		100	
			1,115
C CURRENT ASSETS			
I Stock			
1 Raw materials and consumables	60		
2 Work in progress	15		
3 Finished goods and goods for resale	120		
4 Payments on account	5		
		200	
II Debtors			
1 Trade debtors	200		
2 Amounts owed by group undertakings	20		
3 Amounts owed by undertakings in which the			
company has a participating interest	10		
4 Other debtors	4		
5 Called-up share capital not paid*	–		
6 Prepayments and accrued income†	–		
		234	
III Investments			
1 Shares in group undertakings	40		
2 Own shares	5		
3 Other investments	30		
		75	
IV Cash at bank and in hand		26	
		535	

	£000	£000	£000
D PREPAYMENTS AND ACCRUED INCOME†		15	
		550	
E CREDITORS: AMOUNTS FALLING DUE WITHIN ONE YEAR			
1 Debenture loans	5		
2 Bank loans and overdrafts	10		
3 Payments received on account	20		
4 Trade creditors	50		
5 Bills of exchange payable	2		
6 Amounts owed to group undertakings	15		
7 Amounts owed to undertakings in which the company has a participating interest	6		
8 Other creditors including taxation and social security	54		
9 Accruals and deferred income‡	–		
		(162)	
F NET CURRENT ASSETS (LIABILITIES)			388
G TOTAL ASSETS LESS CURRENT LIABILITIES			1,513
H CREDITORS: AMOUNTS FALLING DUE AFTER MORE THAN ONE YEAR			
1 Debenture loans	20		
2 Bank loans and overdrafts	15		
3 Payments received on account	5		
4 Trade creditors	25		
5 Bills of exchange payable	4		
6 Amounts owed to group undertakings	10		
7 Amounts owed to undertakings in which the company has a participating interest	5		
8 Other creditors including taxation and social security	32		
9 Accruals and deferred income‡	–		
		116	
I PROVISIONS FOR LIABILITIES AND CHARGES			
1 Pensions and similar obligations	20		
2 Taxation, including deferred taxation	40		
3 Other provisions	4		
		64	
J ACCRUALS AND DEFERRED INCOME‡		20	
			(200)
			1,313
K CAPITAL AND RESERVES			
I Called-up share capital			1,000
II Share premium account			100
III Revaluation reserve			20
IV Other reserves:			
1 Capital redemption reserve		40	
2 Reserve for own shares		10	
3 Reserves provided for by the articles of association		20	
4 Other reserves		13	
			83
V Profit and loss account			110
			1,313

*†‡ These items may be shown in any of the positions indicated.

It should be noted that various items can be shown in alternative places, i.e.:

(a) *called-up share capital not paid*, either in position A or position CII 5;
(b) *prepayments and accrued income*, either CII 6 or as D;
(c) *accruals and deferred income*, either E9 or H9, or in total as J.

Items preceded by letters or roman numerals *must* be disclosed on the face of the balance sheet, e.g. B Fixed assets, KII Share premium account, whereas those shown with arabic numerals (1, 2, 3, 4, etc.) may be combined where they are not material or when the combination facilitates assessment of the company's affairs. Where they are combined, the details of each item should be shown in the notes accompanying the financial statements. The actual letters, roman numerals or arabic numbers do *not* have to be shown on the face of the published balance sheets and, in virtually all cases, they are not.

13.2 Further details for Format 1

The following also apply to balance sheets prepared according to the Format 1 layout.

BI Intangible assets are assets not having a 'physical' existence compared with tangible assets which do have a physical existence. For instance, you can see and touch the tangible assets, such as land and buildings, plant and machinery, etc., but you cannot touch goodwill.

For each of the fixed assets, whether it is an intangible asset, tangible asset, or investment, full details must be given in the notes accompanying the financial statements of (a) cost, at beginning and end of financial year, (b) any effect on that item of acquisitions, disposals, revaluations, etc. during the year, and (c) full details of depreciation, i.e. accumulated depreciation at start of year, depreciation for year, effect of disposals on depreciation in the year and any other adjustments.

All fixed assets, including property and goodwill, must be depreciated over the period of the useful economic life of each asset. Prior to this, many companies had not depreciated property because of rising money values of the asset. Costs of research must not be treated as an asset, and development costs may be capitalised only in special cases. Any hire purchase owing must not be deducted from the assets concerned. Only goodwill which has been purchased can be shown as an asset; internally generated goodwill must not be capitalised.

See Chapter 17 for further information on goodwill in consolidated financial statements.

Where an asset is revalued, normally this will be fixed assets being shown at market value instead of cost. Any difference on revaluation must be debited or credited to a revaluation reserve – *see* KIII in Format 1.

Investments shown as CIII will be in respect of those not held for the long term.

Two items which could previously be shown as assets – (a) preliminary expenses (these are the legal expenses etc. in forming the company), and (b) expenses of and commission on any issue of shares or debentures – must not now be shown as assets. They can be written off against any share premium account balance; alternatively they should be written off to the profit and loss account.

Full details of each class of share capital, and of authorised capital, will be shown in notes accompanying the balance sheet.

13.3 Choice of formats

The Acts leave the choice of a particular format for the balance sheet and the profit and loss account to the directors. Once adopted, the choice must be adhered to in subsequent years except in the case that there are special reasons for the change. If a change is made, then full reasons for the change must be stated in the notes attached to the financial statements.

13.4 Fundamental accounting principles

The Companies Acts set out the accounting principles (or 'valuation rules' as they are called in the Fourth Directive of the EC) to be followed when preparing company financial statements.

The following principles are stated in the Acts. The reader is referred to Chapter 10 of *Business Accounting Essentials 1* for a fuller discussion of some of them.

1 A company is presumed to be a going concern.
2 Accounting policies must be applied consistently from year to year.
3 The prudence concept must be followed.
4 The accruals concept must be observed.
5 Each component item of assets and liabilities must be valued separately. As an instance of this, if a company has five different types of stock, each type must be valued separately at the lower of cost and net realisable value, rather than be valued on an aggregate basis.
6 Amounts in respect of items representing assets or income may *not* be set off against items representing liabilities or expenditure. Thus an amount owing on a hire purchase contract cannot be deducted from the value of the asset in the balance sheet.

13.5 True and fair view

If complying with the requirements of the Companies Acts would cause the financial statements not to be 'true and fair' then the directors must set aside such requirements. This should not be done lightly, and it would not be common to find such instances.

13.6 Small and medium-sized company reporting requirements

Small and medium-sized companies (for a definition, *see* Section 12.2) do not have to file a full set of financial statements with the Registrar of Companies. If they wish, they can send a full set of financial statements, but what they *have* to file is a minimum of 'modified financial statements'. They still have to send a full set to their own shareholders who request them – the modified financial statements refer only to those filed with the Registrar.

In addition, there is no longer an audit requirement for small companies with a turnover of not more than £5.6 million and a balance sheet total of not more than £2.8 million, unless 10 per cent or more of shareholders sign a formal notice requesting an audit and lodge this at the registered office.

Activity 13.1 Why do you think these small companies are exempted from having their financial statements audited?

13.7 Modified financial statements of small companies

1 Neither a profit and loss account nor a directors' report has to be filed with the Registrar.
2 A modified balance sheet showing only those items to which a letter or roman numeral are attached (*see* Format 1, Exhibit 13.1) has to be filed. As a result, for example, the total for CI Stock has to be shown but not the figures for each of the individual items comprising this total.

13.8 Modified financial statements of medium-sized companies

1 The profit and loss account per Format 1 does not have to show item 1 (Turnover), item 2 (Cost of sales) or item 6 (Other operating income). It will therefore begin with the figure of gross profit or loss.
2 The analyses of turnover and profit normally required as notes to the financial statements need not be given.
3 The balance sheet, however, must be given in full.

Note: **Review questions on published company financial statements including notes required by law are at the end of Chapter 14.**

13.9 Summary financial statements

A public limited company (plc) may send a summary financial statement to members in place of the full statements, but any member who requests the full statements must be sent them. The summary statement must:

(*a*) state that it is only a summary of information in the company's financial statements and the directors' report;
(*b*) contain a statement by the company's auditors of their opinion as to whether the summary financial statement is consistent with those financial statements and that report and complies with the requirements of the section in the Companies Act (CA 2006 Section 427 (unquoted company) or 428 (quoted company)) that permits the distribution of this summary financial statement and the regulations made under it;
(*c*) state whether the auditors' report on the financial statements was unqualified or qualified, and if it was qualified set out the report in full together with any further material needed to understand the qualification;
(*d*) state whether the auditors' report on the annual accounts contained a statement under either:
  (*i*) CA 2006 Section 498(2)(a) or (b) – accounting records or returns inadequate or financial statements not agreeing with records or returns; or
  (*ii*) CA 2006 Section 498(3) – failure to obtain necessary information and explanations and, if so, set out the statement in full.

13.10 Website publication

A quoted company must make its annual accounts and reports available on a website.

Activity 13.2 Why do you think companies are allowed to send their shareholders summary financial statements rather than the full statements?

Learning outcomes

You should now have learnt:

1 There are set formats for the preparation of published financial statements.

2 Financial statements for internal use need not comply with these set formats.

3 Accounting standards have statutory recognition and must, therefore, be complied with when preparing financial statements intended to present a true and fair view.

4 Some small companies are exempted from having their financial statements audited.

5 Small and medium-sized companies may file modified financial statements with the Registrar if they wish.

6 Public limited companies may send a summary financial statement to members in place of the full statements, but any member who requests the full statements must be sent them.

Answers to activities

13.1 Having financial statements audited is estimated as costing an average of £1,200. While this appears a small amount of money, it can be relatively expensive for small companies, particularly when they are newly formed and are making little or no profit. However, although this is a good reason for such companies not incurring the expense of having an audit, as the sole reason for not having an audit it goes against the principles upon which the need for an audit was based. A far more realistic explanation is that errors and misleading items in the financial statements of small companies have far less of an impact than in the case of larger organisations and, on a purely cost/benefit basis, it is unlikely that the costs of having an audit will be sufficiently offset by any amendments or clarifications that an audit may bring.

13.2 Many shareholders are not accountants and have no understanding of many of the items in full financial statements. Rather than sending them information they will not understand, shareholders may be sent simplified information containing those parts of the financial statements that they are both more likely to understand and more likely to be interested in having. This saves the companies (and their shareholders) money which, in itself, is a good thing. It also increases the possibility that shareholders will look at the financial statements in the first place.

Review questions

13.1 The following balances remained in the books of Exit Ltd on 31 March 2004, *after* the profit and loss account and appropriation account had been drawn up. You are to draft the balance sheet as at 31 March 2004 in accordance with the Companies Acts.

	Dr £	Cr £
Ordinary share capital: 10p shares		400,000
Preference share capital: £1 shares		150,000
Calls account (ordinary shares)	10,000	
Development costs	52,000	
Goodwill	184,000	
Land and buildings – at cost	320,000	
Plant and machinery – at cost	80,000	
Provision for depreciation: Buildings		30,000
Provision for depreciation: Plant and machinery		50,000
Shares in undertakings in which the company has a participating interest	120,000	
Stock: Raw materials	5,000	
Stock: Finished goods	40,000	
Debtors: Trade	35,000	
Amounts owed by undertakings in which the company has a participating interest	12,000	
Prepayments	8,000	
Debentures (*see* Note 1)		40,000
Bank overdraft (repayable on demand)		19,000
Creditors: Trade (payable within 1 year)		21,000
Bills payable (*see* Note 2)		15,000
Share premium		55,000
Capital redemption reserve		16,000
General reserve		25,000
Profit and loss account		45,000
	866,000	866,000

Notes:
1 Of the debentures, £15,000 is repayable in 7 months' time, while the other £25,000 is repayable in 6 years' time.
2 Of the bills payable, £12,000 is in respect of a bill to be paid in 10 months' time and £3,000 for a bill payable in 16 months' time.
3 The depreciation charged for the year was: Building £10,000, Plant and machinery £14,000.

→

Part 2 ● Companies

13.2 After the profit and loss account has been prepared for the year ending 30 April 2007 and various transfers made from the profit and loss reserve, the following balances remain in the books of Tickers plc. Prepare a balance sheet in accordance with the Companies Acts.

	£	£
Ordinary share capital		100,000
Share premium		60,000
Revaluation reserve		23,000
General reserve		30,000
Foreign exchange reserve		7,000
Profit and loss		35,000
Patents, trade marks and licences	6,000	
Goodwill	42,000	
Land and buildings	280,000	
Provision for depreciation: Land and buildings		80,000
Plant and machinery	90,000	
Provision for depreciation: Plant and machinery		47,000
Stock of raw materials: 30 April 2007	24,000	
Work in progress: 30 April 2007	9,000	
Finished goods: 30 April 2007	21,000	
Debtors: Trade	84,000	
Debtors: Other	3,000	
Prepayments and accrued income	2,000	
Debentures (redeemable in 6 months' time)		50,000
Debentures (redeemable in 4½ years' time)		40,000
Bank overdraft (repayable in 3 months)		3,000
Trade creditors (payable in next 12 months)		26,000
Trade creditors (payable after 12 months)		2,000
Bills of exchange (payable within 12 months)		5,000
Corporation tax (payable in 9 months' time)		38,000
National insurance (payable in next month)		1,000
Pensions contribution owing		8,000
Deferred taxation		6,000
	561,000	561,000

13.3 The following trial balance has been extracted from the books of Baganza plc as at 30 September 2007:

	£000	£000
Administrative expenses	400	
Called up share capital (1,200,000 ordinary shares of £1 each)		1,200
Cash at bank and in hand	60	
Corporation tax (overpayment for the year to 30 September 2006)		20
Deferred taxation (at 1 October 2006)		460
Distribution costs	600	
Dividends received (on 31 March 2007)		249
Extraordinary item (net of tax)		1,500
Freehold property:		
at cost	2,700	
accumulated depreciation (at 1 October 2006)		260
Interim dividend (paid on June 2007)	36	
Investments in United Kingdom companies	2,000	
Plant and machinery:		
at cost	5,200	
accumulated depreciation (at 1 October 2006)		3,600
Profit and loss account (at 1 October 2006)		2,022
Purchases	16,000	
Research expenditure	75	
Stock (at 1 October 2006)	2,300	
Tax on extraordinary item		360
Trade creditors		2,900
Trade debtors	2,700	
Turnover		19,500
	£32,071	£32,071

Additional information:

1 The stock at 30 September 2007 was valued at £3,600,000.
2 Depreciation for the year to 30 September 2007 is to be charged on the historic cost of the fixed assets as follows:
   Freehold property: 5 per cent
   Plant and machinery: 15 per cent
3 The basic rate of income tax is assumed to be 27 per cent.
4 The directors propose a final dividend of 60p per share.
5 The company was incorporated in 2000.
6 Corporation tax based on the profits for the year at a rate of 35 per cent is estimated to be £850,000.
7 A transfer of £40,000 is to be made to the deferred taxation account.

Required:

In so far as the information permits, prepare Baganza plc's profit and loss account for the year ending 30 September 2007, and a balance sheet as at that date in accordance with the Companies Act 2006 and appropriate accounting standards.

However, formal notes to the accounts are not required, although detailed workings should be submitted with your answer, which should include your calculation of earnings per share.

(*Association of Accounting Technicians*)

→

13.4A The trial balance of Jeremina plc as at 31 March 2002 is as follows:

	Dr £	Cr £
Preference share capital: 50p shares		200,000
Ordinary share capital: £1 shares		300,000
General reserve		25,000
Exchange reserve		15,000
Profit and loss as on 31 March 2001		21,000
Stock 31 March 2001	184,000	
Sales		1,320,000
Returns inwards	34,000	
Purchases	620,000	
Carriage inwards	6,000	
Wages (putting goods into a saleable condition)	104,000	
Wages: Warehouse staff	40,000	
Wages and salaries: Sales staff	67,000	
Wages and salaries: Administrative staff	59,000	
Motor expenses (see note (ii))	29,000	
General distribution expenses	17,000	
General administrative expenses	12,000	
Debenture interest	2,000	
Royalties receivable		5,000
Directors' remuneration	84,000	
Bad debts	10,000	
Discounts allowed	14,000	
Discounts received		11,000
Plant and machinery at cost (see note (iii))	240,000	
Provision for depreciation: Plant and machinery (see note (iv))		72,000
Motor vehicles at cost (see note (ii))	120,000	
Provision for depreciation: Motors (see note (iv))		48,000
Goodwill	200,000	
Development costs	24,000	
Trade debtors	188,000	
Trade creditors		45,000
Bank overdraft (repayable on demand)		7,000
Bills of exchange payable (all due within 1 year)		7,000
Debentures (redeemable in 3 years' time)		30,000
Preference dividend	12,000	
Ordinary dividend	40,000	
	2,106,000	2,106,000

Notes:
(i) Stock of finished goods on 31 March 2002 £163,000.
(ii) Motor expenses and depreciation on motors to be apportioned: Distribution $^4/_5$, Administrative $^1/_5$.
(iii) Plant and machinery depreciation to be apportioned: Cost of sales $^7/_{10}$, Distribution $^1/_5$, Administrative $^1/_{10}$.
(iv) Depreciate the following fixed assets on cost: Motor vehicles 20 per cent, Plant and machinery 15 per cent.
(v) Accrue corporation tax on profits of the year £38,000. This is payable on 31 December 2002.

You are to draw up:
(a) a detailed trading and profit and loss account for the year ending 31 March 2002 for internal use, and
(b) a profit and loss account for publication, also a balance sheet as at 31 March 2002.

13.5A You are presented with the following information relating to Plott plc for the year to 31 March 2011:

	£000
Bank overdraft	500
Called-up share capital (issued and fully paid)	2,100
Corporation tax (based on the profit for the year to 31 March 2011)	900
Creditors	300
Debtors	200
Deferred taxation (credit)	80
Fixed assets: at cost	3,800
accumulated depreciation (at 31 March 2011)	1,400
Fixed asset investments: at cost	100
Profit and loss account (at 1 April 2010: credit)	1,200
Proposed dividend	420
Retained profit (for the year to 31 March 2011)	585
Share premium account	315
Stocks: at cost (at 31 March 2011)	400
Trade creditors	2,000
Trade debtors	5,300

Additional information:

1 The above information has been obtained after the compilation of the company's profit and loss account for the year to 31 March 2011.

2 Details of fixed assets for the year to 31 March 2011 are as follows:

	£000
(a) At cost	
At 1 April 2010	3,400
Additions	600
Disposals	200
(b) Accumulated depreciation	
At 1 April 2010	1,200
Additions	500
Disposals	300

3 The market value of the fixed asset investments at 31 March 2011 was £110,000. There were no purchases or sales of fixed asset investments during the year.

4 Stocks comprise finished goods. The replacement cost of these goods is similar to the value indicated in the balance sheet.

5 Assume that the basic rate of income tax is 25 per cent.

6 The authorised share capital of the company consists of 2,500,000 ordinary shares of £1 each.

Required:

In so far as the information permits, prepare Plott plc's balance sheet as at 31 March 2011 in accordance with the *minimum* requirements of the Companies Act 2006 and related accounting standards.

Notes:

1 Where appropriate, formal notes must be attached to your balance sheet; and
2 Detailed working should be submitted with your answer.

(Association of Accounting Technicians)

→

→ **13.6A** The following information has been extracted from the books of Quire plc as at 30 September 2011.

	£000	£000
Bank overdraft		2,400
Called-up share capital (ordinary shares of £1 each)		4,000
Deferred taxation		200
Delivery expenses	2,800	
Fixed assets: at cost	3,500	
accumulated depreciation (at 1 October 2010)		1,100
Debentures held	100	
Debenture interest (net)		40
Interest payable	400	
Interim dividend paid	60	
Office expenses	3,000	
Other creditors		180
Other debtors	160	
Profit and loss account (at 1 October 2010)		820
Purchases	12,000	
Sales		19,000
Stocks (at 1 October 2010)	500	
Trade creditors		100
Trade debtors	5,320	
	£27,840	£27,840

The following additional information is to be taken into account:

1 Stocks at 30 September 2011 were valued at £400,000.
2 All items in the above trial balance are shown net of value added tax.
3 At 30 September 2011, £130,000 was outstanding for office expenses, and £50,000 had been paid in advance for delivery van licences.
4 Depreciation at a rate of 50 per cent is to be charged on the historic cost of the tangible fixed assets using the reducing balance method: it is to be apportioned as follows:

	%
Cost of sales	60
Distribution	30
Administration	10
	100

There were no purchases or sales of fixed assets during the year to 30 September 2011.
5 The following rates of taxation are to be assumed:

	%
Corporation tax	35
Income tax	25
Value added tax	17.5

The corporation tax payable based on the profits for the year to 30 September 2011 has been estimated at £80,000.
6 A transfer of £60,000 is to be made from the deferred taxation account.
7 The directors propose to pay a final ordinary dividend of 3p per share.

Required:
In so far as the information permits, prepare Quire plc's profit and loss account for the year ending 30 September 2011, and a balance sheet as at that date in accordance with the MINIMUM requirements of the Companies Act 2006 and related accounting standards.

Note: Formal notes to the accounts are NOT required, but detailed workings should be submitted with your answer.

(Association of Accounting Technicians)

12.7A The following trial balance has been extracted from the books of Patt plc as at 31 March 2010:

	Dr £000	Cr £000
Bank overdraft		25
Called-up share capital (ordinary shares of £1 each)		1,440
Creditors		55
Debtors	50	
Fixed assets: at cost	300	
accumulated depreciation (at 1 April 2009)		120
Marketing expenses	100	
Office expenses	200	
Profit and loss account (at 1 April 2009)		200
Production expenses	2,230	
Purchases (net of VAT)	3,700	
Sales (amounts invoiced, net of VAT)		7,000
Stocks (at 1 April 2009)	130	
Trade creditors		160
Trade debtors	2,290	
	£9,000	£9,000

Additional information:

1 Following the preparation of the above trial balance, the following additional matters need to be taken into account:
(a) stock at 31 March 2010 was valued at £170,000;
(b) at 31 March 2010, £20,000 was owing for office expenses, and £15,000 had been paid in advance for marketing expenses;
(c) a customer had gone into liquidation owing the company £290,000; the company does not expect to recover any of this debt;
(d) the company decides to set up a provision for doubtful debts amounting to 5 per cent of the outstanding trade debtors as at the end of each financial year; and
(e) depreciation is to be charged on the fixed assets at a rate of 20 per cent on cost; it is to be apportioned as follows:

	%
Marketing	20
Office	10
Production	70
	100

Note: There were no acquisitions or disposals of fixed assets during the year to 31 March 2010.

2 Corporation tax (based on the accounting profit for the year at a rate of 35 per cent) is estimated to be £160,000. The basic rate of income tax is assumed to be 25 per cent.
3 The directors are to recommend the payment of a dividend of 10p per ordinary share.

Required:
In so far as the information permits, prepare Patt plc's profit and loss account for the year ending 31 March 2010, and a balance sheet as at that date in accordance with the Companies Act 2006 and related accounting standards.

Notes:
(i) Where appropriate, formal notes should be attached to your profit and loss account and balance sheet. However, a statement of accounting policies is NOT required.
(ii) Detailed workings should also be submitted with your solution. They should be clearly designated as such, and they must not form part of your formal notes.

(Association of Accounting Technicians)

Published financial statements of limited companies: accompanying notes

Learning objectives

After you have studied this chapter, you should be able to:

- describe the additional notes to published financial statements that are required by the Companies Acts
- describe the requirement to include a directors' report with the published financial statements

Introduction

In this chapter, you'll learn about the notes that must be included when company financial statements are published and about the report that must be prepared by the directors to accompany the financial statements.

14.1 Notes to accompany the financial statements

Companies may include as many notes as they wish when they publish their financial statements. However, there are some notes that the Companies Acts require. These are currently under review following publication of the Companies Act 2006. However, changes to previous requirements are unlikely to be significant. The principal requirements are:

1 Information about related undertaking unless doing so would be prejudicial to the business

2 Particulars of staff

(a) Average number employed by the company (or by the group), divided between categories of workers, e.g. between manufacturing and administration
(b) (i) Wages and salaries paid to staff
(ii) Social security costs of staff
(iii) Other pension costs for employees.

3 The directors' report

The directors' report for a financial year must state:

(a) the names of the persons who, at any time during the financial year, were directors of the company, and

(b) the principal activities of the company in the course of the year.

Except in the case of small companies, the report must state the amount (if any) that the directors recommend should be paid by way of dividend.

Unless the company is subject to the small companies' regime, the directors' report must contain a business review. The purpose of the business review is to inform members of the company and help them assess how the directors have performed their duty to promote the success of the company.

The business review must contain a fair review of the company's business, and a description of the principal risks and uncertainties facing the company. The review required is a balanced and comprehensive analysis of the development and performance of the company's business during the financial year, and the position of the company's business at the end of that year, consistent with the size and complexity of the business.

In the case of a quoted company the business review must, to the extent necessary for an understanding of the development, performance or position of the company's business, include the main trends and factors likely to affect the future development, performance and position of the company's business; and information about:

● environmental matters (including the impact of the company's business on the environment);
● the company's employees; and
● social and community issues,

including information about any policies of the company in relation to those matters and the effectiveness of those policies; and information about persons with whom the company has contractual or other arrangements which are essential to the business of the company (unless such disclosure would, in the opinion of the directors, be seriously prejudicial to that person and contrary to the public interest). If the review does not contain information of each kind mentioned above, it must state which of those kinds of information it does not contain.

The review must, to the extent necessary for an understanding of the development, performance or position of the company's business, include:

● analysis using financial key performance indicators (i.e. factors by reference to which the development, performance or position of the company's business can be measured effectively); and
● where appropriate, analysis using other key performance indicators, including information relating to environmental matters and employee matters. (Medium-sized companies need not comply with these requirements so far as they relate to non-financial information.)

The review must, where appropriate, include references to, and additional explanations of, amounts included in the company's annual accounts.

The disclosure of information about impending developments or matters in the course of negotiation is not required if the disclosure would, in the opinion of the directors, be seriously prejudicial to the interests of the company.

The directors' report must also contain a statement to the effect that, in the case of each of the persons who are directors at the time the report is approved:

● so far as the director is aware, there is no relevant audit information of which the company's auditor is unaware; and
● he has taken all the steps that he ought to have taken as a director in order to make himself aware of any relevant audit information and to establish that the company's auditor is aware of that information.

The director's report must be approved by the board of directors and signed on behalf of the board by a director or the secretary of the company. If the report is prepared in accordance with the small companies regime, it must contain a statement to that effect in a prominent position above the signature.

> **Activity 14.1** Why do you think the directors' report is audited?

The directors of a quoted company must also prepare a directors' remuneration report for each financial year of the company, disclosing within the report details of individual directors' remuneration packages, the company's remuneration policy, and the role of the board and remuneration committee in this area.

The directors' remuneration report must be approved by the board of directors and signed on behalf of the board by a director or the secretary of the company. It should include:

1 Aggregate amounts of:
   (a) emoluments, including pension contributions and benefits in kind. Distinction to be made between those emoluments as fees and those for executive duties;
   (b) pensions for past directors;
   (c) compensation for loss of office.
2 The chairman's emoluments and those of the highest-paid director, if paid more than the chairman. In both cases, pension contributions are to be excluded.
3 Number of directors whose emoluments, excluding pension contributions, fall within each bracket of £5,000.
4 Total amounts waived by directors and the number concerned.

The disclosures under 2 and 3 above are not needed for a company being neither a parent nor subsidiary undertaking where its directors' emoluments under 1 do not exceed £60,000. The disclosures under 2 and 3 are also not necessary for directors working wholly or mainly overseas.

An illustration is now given in Exhibit 14.1:

Exhibit 14.1

Name	Fee (as directors)	Remuneration (as executives)	Pension contributions
A (Chairman)	£5,000	£85,000	£20,000
B	£2,500	£95,000	£30,000
C	£2,500	£55,000	£15,000
D	£1,500	£54,000	£12,500
E	£1,500	£30,000	£10,000

Note to accounts:
Directors' remuneration: the amounts paid to directors were as follows:

Fees as directors	£13,000
Other emoluments, including pension contributions	£406,500

Emoluments of the Chairman – excluding pension contributions – amounted to £90,000, and those of the highest-paid director to £97,500. Other directors' emoluments were in the following ranges:

£30,001 – £35,000	1
£55,001 – £60,000	2

4 Various charges to be shown as notes

1 Auditors' remuneration, including expenses.
2 Hire of plant and machinery.
3 Interest payable on:
   (*a*) bank loans, overdrafts and other loans repayable by instalments or otherwise within five years;
   (*b*) loans of any other kind.
4 Depreciation:
   (*a*) amounts of provisions for both tangible and intangible assets;
   (*b*) effect on depreciation of change of depreciation method;
   (*c*) effect on depreciation of revaluation of assets.

5 Income from listed investments

6 Rents receivable from land, after deducting outgoings

7 Taxation (see also FRS 16: *Current tax*)

1 Tax charges split between:
   (*a*) UK corporation tax, and basis of computation;
   (*b*) UK income tax, and basis of computation;
   (*c*) irrecoverable VAT;
   (*d*) tax attributable to franked investment income.
2 If relevant, split between tax on ordinary and tax on extraordinary activities.
3 Show, as component part, charge for deferred tax.
4 Any other special circumstances affecting tax liability.

8 Extraordinary and exceptional items and prior period adjustments

See FRS 3: *Reporting financial performance*, which is dealt with in Chapter 12.

9 Redemption of shares and loans

Show amounts set aside for these purposes.

10 Earnings per share (listed companies only)

See FRS 14: *Earnings per share*, which is dealt with in Section 11.29.

11 Statement showing movements on reserves

Activity 14.2 Why do you think these notes are required rather than leaving it up to companies to provide the information they believe to be worthwhile including?

Let's look at how all these requirements are enacted by working through two examples.

14.2 Illustrative company financial statements: worked example 1

F Clarke Ltd are specialist wholesalers. This is their trial balance at 31 December 2004.

	Dr £	Cr £
Ordinary share capital: £1 shares		1,000,000
Share premium		120,000
General reserve		48,000
Profit and loss account as at 31.12.2003		139,750
Stock: 31.12.2003	336,720	
Sales		5,090,370
Purchases	2,475,910	
Returns outwards		121,220
Returns inwards	136,200	
Carriage inwards	6,340	
Carriage outwards	43,790	
Warehouse wages (average number of workers 59)	410,240	
Salespeople's salaries (average number of workers 21)	305,110	
Administrative wages and salaries	277,190	
Plant and machinery	610,000	
Motor vehicle hire	84,770	
Provisions for depreciation: plant and machinery		216,290
General distribution expenses	27,130	
General administrative expenses	47,990	
Directors' remuneration	195,140	
Ordinary dividend	375,000	
Rents receivable		37,150
Trade debtors	1,623,570	
Cash at bank and in hand	179,250	
Trade creditors (payable before 31.3.2005)		304,570
Bills of exchange payable (payable 28.2.2005)		57,000
	7,134,350	7,134,350

Notes:
(a) Stock at 31.12.2004: £412,780, consists of goods for resale.
(b) Plant and machinery is apportioned: distributive 60 per cent; administrative 40 per cent.
(c) Accrue auditors' remuneration: £71,000.
(d) Depreciate plant and machinery: 20 per cent on cost.
(e) Of the motor hire, £55,000 is for distributive purposes.
(f) Corporation tax on profits, at a rate of 35 per cent, is estimated at £238,500 and is payable on 1.10.2005.
(g) Pension contributions for staff amounted to £42,550 and social security contributions to £80,120. These figures are included in wages and salaries in the trial balance. No employee earned over £30,000.
(h) Plant of £75,000 had been bought during the year.
(i) Directors' remuneration has been as follows:

	£
Chairman	46,640
Managing Director	51,500
Finance Director	46,000
Marketing Director	43,000
	187,140

In addition each of them drew £2,000 as directors' fees. Pensions are the personal responsibility of directors.

Required:

Subject to the limits of the information given you, draw up a profit and loss account for the year ending 31 December 2004, and a balance sheet as at that date. They should be in published form and accompanied by the necessary notes prescribed by statute.

Answer to worked example 1

Workings

	£		£	£
Turnover: Sales	5,090,370	Cost of sales:		
Less Returns in	(136,200)	Opening stock		336,720
	4,954,170	*Add* Purchases	2,475,910	
		Less Returns out	(121,220)	
			2,354,690	
		Add Carriage in	6,340	2,361,030
				2,697,750
		Less Closing stock		(412,780)
				2,284,970
Distribution costs:		Administrative expenses:		
Warehouse wages	410,240	Wages and salaries		277,190
Salespeople's salaries	305,110	Motor hire		29,770
Carriage out	43,790	General expenses		47,990
General expenses	27,130	Directors' remuneration		150,140
Motor hire	55,000	Auditors' remuneration		71,000
Depreciation: plant	73,200	Depreciation: plant		48,800
				624,890
Marketing Director's remuneration	45,000			
	959,470			

F Clarke Ltd
Profit and Loss Account for the year ending 31 December 2004

	£	£
Turnover		4,954,170
Cost of sales		(2,284,970)
Gross profit		2,669,200
Distribution costs	959,470	
Administrative expenses	624,890	
		(1,584,360)
		1,084,840
Other operating income		37,150
Profit on ordinary activities before taxation		1,121,990
Tax on profit on ordinary activities		(238,500)
Profit on ordinary activities after taxation		883,490

F Clarke Ltd
Balance Sheet as at 31 December 2004

	£	£	£
Fixed assets			
Tangible assets: Plant and machinery			271,710
Current assets			
Stock: Finished goods and goods for resale		412,780	
Debtors: Trade debtors		1,623,570	
Cash at bank and in hand		179,250	
		2,215,600	
Creditors: amounts falling due within one year			
Trade creditors	304,570		
Bills of exchange payable	57,000		
Other creditors including taxation and social security	309,500		
		(671,070)	
Net current assets			(1,544,530)
Total assets less current liabilities			1,816,240
Capital and reserves			£
Called-up share capital			1,000,000
Share premium account			120,000
Other reserves:			
General reserve			48,000
Profit and loss			648,240
			1,816,240

NOTES TO THE ACCOUNTS

1 Employees
Average number of workers was:

Warehousing	59
Sales	21
	80

Remuneration of employees was:

	£
Wages and salaries	869,870
Social security costs	80,120
Pension contributions	42,550
	992,540

2 Directors' remuneration
The amounts paid to directors were as follows:

	£
Fees as directors	8,000
Other emoluments	187,140

Emoluments of the Chairman amounted to £46,640, and those of the highest-paid director £51,500. Other directors' emoluments were in the following ranges:

£40,001–45,000	1
£45,001–50,000	1

3 Operating profit is shown after charging

	£
Auditors' remuneration	71,000
Hire of motors	84,770

4 Fixed assets
Plant and machinery

	£	£
Cost at 1.1.2004	535,000	
Additions	75,000	
		610,000
Depreciation to 31.12.2003	216,290	
Charge for the year	122,000	
		(338,290)
		271,710

5 Trade and other Creditors

	£	£
Auditors' remuneration	71,000	
Trade accounts payable	304,570	
		375,570

6 Retained profits

Balance at 31.12.2003	139,750	
Profit for the year	883,490	
	1,023,240	
Dividends paid	(375,000)	
Balance at 31.12.2004		648,240

Note: **The retained profit information would be shown in a note on movements in shareholders funds.**

14.3 Illustrative company financial statements: worked example 2

The trial balance of Quartz plc on 31 December 2003 was as follows:

	Dr £000	Cr £000
Preference share capital: £1 shares		200
Ordinary share capital: £1 shares		1,000
Exchange reserve		75
General reserve		150
Profit and loss account 31.12.2002		215
Sales		5,095
Purchases	2,196	
Carriage inwards	38	
Stock 31.12.2002	902	
Wages (adding value to goods)	35	
Wages: warehousing	380	
Wages and salaries: administrative	120	
Wages and salaries: sales	197	
Motor expenses	164	
Bad debts	31	
Debenture interest	40	
Preference dividend	20	
Ordinary dividend	500	
Bank overdraft interest	19	
General distribution expenses	81	
General administrative expenses	73	
Directors' remuneration	210	
Investments in undertakings in which the company has a participating interest	340	
Income from shares in undertakings in which the company has a participating interest		36
Discounts allowed and received	55	39
Buildings: at cost	1,200	
Plant and machinery: at cost	330	
Motor vehicles: at cost	480	
Provisions for depreciation:		
Land and buildings		375
Plant and machinery		195
Motors		160
Goodwill	40	
Patents, licences and trade marks	38	
Trade debtors and creditors	864	392
Bank overdraft (repayable any time)		21
Debentures 10 per cent		400
	8,353	8,353

Notes:
(a) Stock at 31.12.2003: £1,103,000 at cost.
(b) Motor expenses and depreciation on motors to be apportioned: distribution 75 per cent; administrative 25 per cent.

(c) Depreciation on buildings and plant and machinery to be apportioned: distribution 50 per cent; administrative 50 per cent.

(d) Depreciate on cost: motor vehicles 25 per cent; plant and machinery 20 per cent.

(e) Accrued corporation tax on profits of the year £266,000. This is payable 1 October 2004.

(f) During the year new vehicles were purchased at a cost of £60,000.

(g) During June 2003 one of the buildings, which had originally cost £130,000, and which had a written-down value at the date of the sale of £80,000, was sold for £180,000. Depreciation on buildings to be charged against the year's profits £60,000. The buildings are revalued by B & Co., Chartered Surveyors, at £1,500,000 at 31.12.2003 (and this figure is to be included in the financial statements).

(h) Directors' remuneration was as follows:

	£
Marketing	42,000
Chairman	37,000
Managing	61,000
Finance	50,000
	190,000

In addition each director drew £5,000 fees.

(i) Of the goodwill, 50 per cent is to be written-off to reserves during this year, and 50 per cent in the following year.

(j) The debentures are to be redeemed in five equal annual instalments, starting in the following year 2004.

(k) The investments are in listed companies with a market value at 31 December 2003 of £438,000.

(l) Accrue auditors' remuneration, including expenses, £7,000.

You are required to prepare a profit and loss account and a balance sheet as at 31 December 2003. It should:

(a) conform to the requirements of the Companies Acts;

(b) conform to the relevant accounting standards;

(c) give the notes necessary to the accounts.

Answer to worked example 2

Workings

	£000		Dist. £000	Admin. £000
Cost of sales:		Wages	577	120
Opening stock	902	Motor expenses	123	41
Add Purchases	2,196	General	81	73
Add Carriage in	38	Depreciation: plant	33	33
	3,136	motors	90	30
Less Closing stock	(1,103)	buildings	30	30
	2,033	Directors	47	163
Wages (added value)	35	Auditors' remuneration		7
	2,068	Discounts (net) 55–39		16
		Bad debts		31
			981	544

Quartz plc
Profit and Loss Account for the year ended 31 December 2004

	£000	£000
Turnover		5,095
Cost of sales		(2,068)
Gross profit		3,027
Distribution costs	981	
Administrative expenses	544	
		(1,525)
		1,502
Income from shares in undertakings in which the company has a participating interest		36
		1,538
Interest payable and similar charges		(59)
Profit on ordinary activities before taxation		1,479
Tax on profit on ordinary activities		(266)
Profit for the year on ordinary activities after taxation		1,213

Quartz plc
Balance Sheet as at 31 December 2003

	£000	£000	£000
Fixed assets			
Intangible assets			
Patents, licences and trade marks		38	
Goodwill		20	
		58	
Tangible assets			
Buildings	1,500		
Plant and machinery	69		
Vehicles	200		
		1,769	
Investments			
Shares in undertakings in which the company has a participating interest		340	
			2,167
Current assets			
Stock	1,103		
Trade debtors	864		
		1,967	
Creditors: amounts falling due within one year			
Debenture loans	80		
Bank overdraft	21		
Trade creditors	392		
Other creditors	273		
		(766)	
Net current assets			1,201
			3,368
Creditors: amounts falling due after more than one year			
Debenture loans			(320)
			3,048
Net assets			
Capital and reserves			
Called-up share capital			1,200
Revaluation reserve			735
Profit and loss account			888
Other reserves			225
			3,048

NOTES TO THE ACCOUNTS

1 Share capital called up

	£
200,000 10 per cent preference shares of £1 each	200,000
1,000,000 ordinary shares of £1 each	1,000,000
	1,200,000

2 Accounting policies

Goodwill of £20,000 has been written-off against reserves. The directors intend to write-off the remaining £20,000 next year.

3 Tangible assets

	Buildings £000	Plant £000	Vehicles £000
Cost at 1.1.2004	1,330	330	480
Disposals (at cost)	(130)	–	–
Adjustment for revaluation	735		
	1,935	330	480
Depreciation at 1.1.2004	425	195	160
Provided in year	60	66	120
Disposals	(50)		
	435	261	280
Net book values	1,500	69	200

4 Investments

The market value of investments at 31 December 2003 was £438,000.

5 Ten per cent debenture loans

These are redeemable in five equal annual instalments, starting next year. Interest of £40,000 is charged in this year's accounts.

6 Trade and other accounts payable

	£
Auditors' remuneration	7,000

7 Other reserves

	£
Exchange reserve	75,000
General reserve	150,000
	225,000

8 Directors' remuneration

The amounts paid to directors were as follows:

	£	£
Fees as directors	20,000	
Other emoluments	190,000	210,000

Emoluments of the chairman amounted to £42,000 and those of the highest-paid director £66,000. Other directors' emoluments were in the following ranges:

£45,001–£50,000	1
£50,001–£55,000	1

9 Operating profit is shown after charging

	£
Auditors' remuneration	7,000
Bank overdraft interest	19,000

Learning outcomes

You should now have learnt:

1 The Companies Acts require that additional notes be prepared and included with the published financial statements.

2 In some cases, the contents of these notes have been extended through the issuing of an accounting standard. For example, SSAP 25: *Segmental reporting* extended the disclosure required of many entities concerning segmental performance.

3 Along with the notes to the financial statements, a directors' report must be presented which summarises the activities and performance of the entity, along with specific details on a number of matters, including directors' shareholdings and information concerning significant changes in fixed assets.

4 The notes to the financial statements and the directors' report are both audited and the views of the auditors on their content are included in the auditors' report which is attached to companies' published annual reports.

Answers to activities

14.1 The directors' report contains a review of the company's performance, activities and future intentions. It also contains many other qualitative and quantitative items of information considered likely to influence the economic decisions of the users of financial statements. The audit report indicates whether, in the opinion of the auditors, the directors' report presents a true and fair view of the items contained within it. If the directors' report was not audited, unscrupulous directors could paint pictures concerning the company that gave an overly favourable impression of its performance, so biasing the judgement of those taking economic decisions based on its content.

14.2 These items are all of a type considered to be important and likely to influence the economic decisions of the users of financial statements. They are subject to review by the auditors of the company in the same way as the financial statements.

Review questions

14.1 The following trial balance of X Limited, a non-listed company, has been extracted from the books after the preparation of the profit and loss account and various transfers from profit and loss for the year ending 31 March 2007.

	£000	£000
Ordinary share capital – authorised, allotted and		
called-up fully paid shares of £1 each		1,000
12% debentures (repayable in 9 years)		500
Deferred taxation		128
Provisions for depreciation:		
Plant and machinery at 31 March 2007		650
Freehold properties at 31 March 2007		52
Vehicles at 31 March 2007		135
Investments (listed), at cost	200	
Trade debtors and prepayments	825	
Corporation tax		270
Proposed final dividend		280
Tangible fixed assets:		
Freehold properties at 31 March 2007	1,092	
Plant and machinery at 31 March 2007	1,500	
Vehicles at 31 March 2007	420	
Profit and loss account – balance at 31 March 2007		356
Share premium account		150
Trade creditors and accruals		878
Research and development costs	35	
Stocks:		
Raw materials	200	
Work in progress	50	
Finished goods	250	
Bank balance	439	
Revaluation reserve on freehold properties		612
	5,011	5,011

You are also provided with the following information:

1 Investments
The listed investments consist of shares in W plc quoted on the Stock Exchange at £180,000 on 31 March 2007. This is not considered to be a permanent fall in the value of this asset.

2 Trade debtors and prepayments
The company received notice, during April 2007, that one of its major customers, Z Limited, had gone into liquidation. The amount included in trade debtors and prepayments is £225,000 and it is estimated that a dividend of 24p in the £ will be paid to unsecured creditors.

3 Taxation
(a) Corporation tax
The figure in the trial balance is made up as follows:

	£000
Based on profits for the year	174
Tax on exceptional item (*see* Note 4)	96
	270

(b) Deferred taxation
A transfer of £50,000 was made from the profit and loss account during the year ended 31 March 2007.

4 Tangible fixed assets

(a) In arriving at the profit for the year, depreciation of £242,000 was charged, made up of freehold properties £12,000, plant and machinery £150,000 and vehicles £80,000.

(b) During the year to 31 March 2007, new vehicles were purchased at a cost of £200,000.

(c) During March 2007, the directors sold one of the freehold properties which had originally cost £320,000 and which had a written-down value at the date of the sale of £280,000. A profit of £320,000 on the sale, which was regarded as exceptional, has already been dealt with in arriving at the profit for the year. The estimated corporation tax liability in respect of the capital gain will be £96,000, as shown in Note 3. After this sale, the directors decided to have the remaining freehold properties revalued, for the first time, by Messrs V & Co, Chartered Surveyors and to include the revalued figure of £1,040,000 in the 2007 accounts.

5 Research and development costs

The company carries out research and development and accounts for it in accordance with the relevant accounting standard. The amount shown in the trial balance relates to development expenditure on a new product scheduled to be launched in April 2007. Management is confident that this new product will earn substantial profits for the company in the coming years.

6 Stocks

The replacement cost of the finished goods, if valued at 31 March 2007, would amount to £342,000.

You are required to prepare a balance sheet at 31 March 2007 to conform to the requirements of the Companies Acts and relevant accounting standards in so far as the information given allows. The vertical format must be used.

The notes necessary to accompany this statement should also be prepared.

Workings should be shown, but comparative figures are not required.

(*Chartered Institute of Management Accountants*)

14.2 The following information has been extracted from the books of account of Billinge plc as at 30 June 2006:

	Dr £000	Cr £000
Administration expenses	242	
Cash at bank and in hand	157	
Cash received on sale of fittings		3
Corporation tax (over-provision for the previous year)		10
Deferred taxation		60
Depreciation on fixtures, fittings, tools and equipment (1 July 2005)		132
Distribution costs	55	
Factory closure costs	30	
Fixtures, fittings, tools and equipment at cost	340	
Profit and loss account (at 1 July 2005)		40
Purchase of equipment	60	
Purchases of goods for resale	855	
Sales (net of VAT)		1,500
Share capital (500,000 authorised, issued and fully paid ordinary shares of £1 each)		500
Stock (at 1 July 2005)	70	
Trade creditors		64
Trade debtors	500	
	£2,309	£2,309

Additional information:
1 The company was incorporated in 2000.
2 The stock at 30 June 2006 (valued at the lower of cost or net realisable value) was estimated to be worth £100,000.
3 Fixtures, fittings, tools and equipment all related to administrative expenses. Depreciation is charged on them at a rate of 20 per cent per annum on cost. A full year's depreciation is charged in the year of acquisition, but no depreciation is charged in the year of disposal.
4 During the year to 30 June 2006, the company purchased £60,000 of equipment. It also sold some fittings (which had originally cost £20,000) for £3,000 and for which depreciation of £15,000 had been set aside.
5 The corporation tax based on the profits for the year at a rate of 35 per cent is estimated to be £100,000. A transfer of £40,000 is to be made to the deferred taxation account.
6 The company proposes to pay a dividend of 20p per ordinary share.
7 The standard rate of income tax is 30 per cent.

Required:
In so far as the information permits, prepare Billinge plc's profit and loss account for the year ending 30 June 2006, and a balance sheet as at that date in accordance with the Companies Acts and appropriate accounting standards.

(*Association of Accounting Technicians*)

14.3A Cosnett Ltd is a company principally involved in the manufacture of aluminium accessories for camping enthusiasts. Its trial balance at 30 September 2005 was:

	£	£
Issued ordinary share capital (£1 shares)		600,000
Retained profit at 1 October 2004		625,700
Debentures redeemable 2009		150,000
Bank loan		25,000
Plant and machinery at cost	1,475,800	
Accumulated depreciation to 30 September 2005		291,500
Investments in UK companies at cost	20,000	
Turnover		3,058,000
Dividends from investments		2,800
Loss arising on factory closure	86,100	
Cost of sales	2,083,500	
Political and charitable contributions	750	
Distribution costs	82,190	
Salaries of office staff	42,100	
Directors' emoluments	63,000	
Rent and rates of offices	82,180	
Hire of plant and machinery	6,700	
Travel and entertainment expenses	4,350	
General expenses	221,400	
Trade debtors	396,100	
Trade creditors and accruals		245,820
Stocks	421,440	
Bank	17,950	
Interim dividend paid	21,000	
Interest charged	19,360	
Provision for deferred taxation		45,100
	5,043,920	5,043,920

→

→ *You are provided with the following additional information*:

(*a*) The company's shares are owned, equally, by three brothers: John, Peter and Henry Phillips; they are also the directors.

(*b*) The bank loan is repayable by five annual instalments of £5,000 commencing 31 December 2005.

(*c*) The investments were acquired with cash, surplus to existing operating requirements, which will be needed to pay for additional plant the directors plan to acquire early in 2006.

(*d*) On 1 January 2005 the company closed a factory which had previously contributed approximately 20 per cent of the company's total production requirements.

(*e*) Trade debtors include £80,000 due from a customer who went into liquidation on 1 September 2005; the directors estimate that a dividend of 20p in the £ will eventually be received.

(*f*) Trade creditors and accruals include:
  (*i*) £50,000 due to a supplier of plant, of which £20,000 is payable on 1 January 2006 and the remainder at the end of the year;
  (*ii*) accruals totalling £3,260.

(*g*) The mainstream corporation tax liability for the year is estimated at £120,000.

(*h*) The directors propose to pay a final dividend of 10.5p per share and to transfer £26,500 to the deferred tax account.

Required:

The profit and loss account of Cosnett Ltd for the year to 30 September 2005 and balance sheet at that date together with relevant notes attached thereto. The accounts should comply with the minimum requirements of the Companies Acts and accounting standards so far as the information permits.

(*Institute of Chartered Secretaries and Administrators*)

14.4A The following trial balance has been extracted from the books of Arran plc as at 31 March 2007:

	£000	£000
Administrative expenses	95	
Called-up share capital (all ordinary shares of £1 each)		200
Cash at bank and in hand	25	
Debtors	230	
Deferred taxation (at 1 April 2006)		60
Distribution costs	500	
Fixed asset investments	280	
Income from fixed asset investments		12
Interim dividend paid	21	
Overprovision of last year's corporation tax		5
Land and buildings at cost	200	
Land and buildings: accumulated depreciation at 1 April 2006		30
Plant and machinery at cost	400	
Plant and machinery: accumulated depreciation at 1 April 2006		170
Profit and loss account (at 1 April 2006)		229
Profit on exceptional item		50
Purchases	1,210	
Sales		2,215
Stocks at 1 April 2006	140	
Trade creditors		130
	£3,101	£3,101

Additional information:
1 Stocks at 31 March 2007 were valued at £150,000.
2 Depreciation for the year to 31 March 2007 is to be charged against administrative expenses as follows:

	£000
Land and buildings	5
Plant and machinery	40

3 Assume that the basic rate of income tax is 30 per cent.
4 Corporation tax of £180,000 is to be charged against profits on ordinary activities for the year to 31 March 2007.
5 £4,000 is to be transferred to the deferred taxation account.
6 The company proposes to pay a final ordinary dividend of 30p per share.

Required:
In so far as the information permits, prepare the company's profit and loss account for the year ending 31 March 2007 and a balance sheet as at that date in accordance with the Companies Acts and related accounting standards. (*Note*: Profit and loss account and balance sheet notes are not required, but you should show the basis and computation of earnings per share at the foot of the profit and loss account, and your workings should be submitted.)

(*Association of Accounting Technicians*)

14.5A The following trial balance has been extracted from the books of account of Greet plc as at 31 March 2008

	Dr £000	Cr £000
Administrative expenses	210	
Called-up share capital (ordinary shares of £1 fully paid)		600
Debtors	470	
Cash at bank and in hand	40	
Corporation tax (overprovision in 2007)		25
Deferred taxation (at 1 April 2007)		180
Distribution costs	420	
Exceptional item		60
Fixed asset investments	560	
Investment income		72
Plant and machinery: at cost	750	
accumulated depreciation (at 31 March 2008)		220
Profit and loss (at 1 April 2007)		182
Purchases	960	
Stock (at 1 April 2007)	140	
Trade creditors		261
Turnover		1,950
	£3,550	£3,550

Additional information:
1 Stock at 31 March 2008 was valued at £150,000.
2 The following items *are already included* in the balances listed in the above trial balance:

	Distribution costs £000	Administrative expenses £000
Depreciation (for the year to 31 March 2008)	27	5
Hire of plant and machinery	20	15
Auditors' remuneration	–	30
Directors' emoluments	–	45

→ **3** The following rates of taxation are to be assumed:

	%
Corporation tax	35
Income tax	27

4 The corporation tax charge based on the profits for the year is estimated to be £52,000.
5 A transfer of £16,000 is to be made to the credit of the deferred taxation account.
6 The exceptional item relates to the profit made on the disposal of a factory in Belgium following the closure of the company's entire operations in that country.
7 The company's authorised share capital consists of 1,000,000 ordinary shares of £1 each.
8 A final ordinary payment of 50p per share is proposed.
9 There were no purchases or disposals of fixed assets during the year.
10 The market value of the fixed assets investments as at 31 March 2008 was £580,000. There were no purchases or sales of such investments during the year.

Required:
In so far as the information permits, prepare the company's published profit and loss account for the year ending 31 March 2008 and a balance sheet as at that date in accordance with the Companies Acts and with related accounting standards.

Relevant notes to the profit and loss account and balance sheet and detailed workings should be submitted with your answer, but a statement of the company's accounting policies is not required.

(*Association of Accounting Technicians*)

14.6 The accountant of Scampion plc, a retailing company listed on the London Stock Exchange, has produced the following draft financial statements for the company for the year to 31 May 2002.

Profit and Loss Account for year ending 31 May 2002

	£000	£000
Sales		3,489
Income from investments		15
		3,504
Purchases of goods and services	1,929	
Value added tax paid on sales	257	
Wages and salaries including pension scheme	330	
Depreciation	51	
Interest on loans	18	
General administration expenses		
– Shops	595	
– Head office	25	
		3,205
Net profit for year		299
Corporation tax at 40%		120
Profit after tax for year		179

Balance Sheet at 31 May 2002

	£000	£000
Fixed assets		
Land and buildings		1,178
Fixtures, fittings, equipment and motor vehicles		194
Investments		167
		1,539
Current assets		
Stock	230	
Debtors	67	
Cash at bank and in hand	84	
	381	
Current liabilities		
Creditors	487	
		(106)
		1,433
Ordinary share capital (£1 shares)		660
Reserves		703
Loans		70
		1,433

You discover the following further information:

(*i*)   Fixed assets details are as follows:

	Cost	Depreciation	Net
	£000	£000	£000
Freehold land and buildings	1,212	34	1,178
Fixtures, fittings and equipment	181	56	125
Motor vehicles	137	68	69

Purchases of fixed assets during the year were freehold land and buildings £50,000, fixtures, fittings and equipment £40,000, motor vehicles £20,000. The only fixed asset disposal during the year is referred to in note (*x*). Depreciation charged during the year was £5,000 for freehold buildings, £18,000 for fixtures, fittings and equipment and £28,000 for motor vehicles. Straight-line depreciation method is used assuming the following lives: Freehold buildings 40 years, fixtures, fittings and equipment 10 years and motor vehicles 5 years.

(*ii*)   A dividend of 10 pence per share is proposed.

(*iii*)   A valuation by Bloggs & Co Surveyors shows the freehold land and buildings to have a market value of £1,350,000.

(*iv*)   Loans are:
£20,000 bank loan with a variable rate of interest repayable by 30 September 2002;
£50,000 12 per cent debenture repayable 2006;
£100,000 11 per cent debenture repaid during the year.
There were no other loans during the year.

(*v*)   The income from investments is derived from fixed asset investments (shares in related companies) £5,000 and current asset investment (government securities) £10,000.

(*vi*)   At the balance sheet date the shares in related companies (cost £64,000) are valued by the directors at £60,000. The market value of the government securities is £115,000 (cost £103,000).

(*vii*)   After the balance sheet date but before the financial statements are finalised there is a very substantial fall in share and security prices. The market value of the government securities had fallen to £50,000 by the time the directors signed the accounts. No adjustment has been made for this item in the accounts.

→

→ (*viii*) Within two weeks of the balance sheet date a notice of liquidation was received by Scampion plc concerning one of the company's debtors. £45,000 is included in the balance sheet for this debtor and enquiries reveal that nothing is likely to be paid to any unsecured creditor. No adjustment has been made for this item in the accounts.

(*ix*) The corporation tax charge is based on the accounts for the year and there are no other amounts of tax owing by the company.

(*x*) Reserves at 31 May 2001 were:

	£
Revaluation reserve	150,000
Share premium account	225,000
Profit and loss account	149,000

The revaluation reserve represents the after-tax surplus on a property which was valued in last year's balance sheet at £400,000 and sold during the current year at book value.

Required:
A profit and loss account for the year ending 31 May 2002 and a balance sheet at that date for Scampion plc complying with the Companies Acts in so far as the information given will allow.
    Ignore advance corporation tax.

(*Association of Chartered Certified Accountants*)

14.7A The Companies Acts and accounting standards require a great deal of information to be disclosed in a company's annual report and accounts.

Required:
List the disclosure requirements for the following items:
(*a*) employees;
(*b*) directors' emoluments; and
(*c*) fixed assets.

(*Association of Accounting Technicians*)

You can find a range of additional self-test questions, as well as material to help you with your studies, on the website that accompanies this book at **www.pearsoned.co.uk/wood**

Cash flow statements

Learning objectives

After you have studied this chapter, you should be able to:

● explain the purpose of cash flow information

● explain the difference between cash flow and profit

● prepare a cash flow statement for a company following the two formats given in FRS 1

● explain the differences between the requirements of FRS 1 and IAS 7

Introduction

In this chapter, you'll build on what you learnt in Chapter 37 of *Business Accounting UK GAAP 1* relating to cash flow statements. You will learn more about the nine standard headings within a cash flow statement prepared on the basis of FRS 1 and be reminded of the layouts as given in FRS 1 and shown how to use them in practice. You'll also be shown the layout of cash flow statements prepared on the basis of IAS 7.

15.1 Background

Chapter 37 of *Business Accounting UK GAAP 1* introduced cash flow statements and this chapter moves on to consider in more detail the two accounting standard relating to these statements – FRS 1: *Cash flow statements*.

FRS 1 requires that a cash flow statement be prepared according to prescribed formats for all companies other than those exempt from doing so, either because they are 'small', as defined by the Companies Act (*see* Section 12.2), or because they are subsidiary undertakings and the group they belong to is publishing group financial statements in the European Union. The standard requires that the statement be included as a primary statement within the financial statements, i.e. it has the same status as the profit and loss account and the balance sheet.

15.2 FRS 1: Standard headings

The objective of FRS 1 is to ensure that reporting entities report the cash generation and cash absorption for a period by highlighting the significant components of cash flow in a way that facilitates comparison of the cash performance of different businesses; and that they provide information that assists in the assessment of their liquidity, solvency and financial adaptability. For this reason, the statement must show the flows of cash and cash equivalents for the period under the headings:

1 operating activities
2 dividends from joint ventures and associates
3 returns on investments and servicing of finance
4 taxation
5 capital expenditure and financial investment
6 acquisitions and disposals
7 equity dividends paid
8 management of liquid resources
9 financing.

The first seven headings should be in the order shown. The other two can be combined under a single heading provided that each of their cash flows are shown separately and separate sub-totals are given. Operating cash flows can be presented by either the *direct* method (showing the relevant constituent cash flows) or the *indirect* method (calculating operating cash flows by adjustment to the operating profit reported in the profit and loss account).

The standard indicates in which section various items are to be located and these are described in Sections 15.4–15.11. Further guidance concerning where items appear in the statement can be seen in the examples presented later in this chapter.

The standard requires that either adjoining the statement, or in a separate note, reconciliations are presented between operating profit and net cash flow from operating activities for the period, and between the movement in cash in the period and the movement in net debt. Neither reconciliation forms part of the statement. The reconciliation to net debt should identify the cash flows of the entity, the acquisition or disposal of subsidiary undertakings (excluding cash balances), other non-cash changes, and the recognition of changes in the market value and exchange rate movements.

15.3 FRS 1 and cash flow

Cash flow is defined in paragraph 2 of FRS 1 as 'an increase or decrease in an amount of cash'. Anything that falls outside this definition is not a cash flow and should not appear in the statement (though it could appear in the notes).

Cash is defined as 'cash in hand and deposits repayable on demand with any qualifying financial institution, less overdrafts from any qualifying financial institution repayable on demand'.

'Deposits repayable on demand' are deposits that can be withdrawn at any time without notice and without penalty or if a maturity or period of notice of not more than 24 hours or one working day has been agreed.

Cash includes cash in hand and deposits denominated in foreign currencies.

15.4 FRS 1: Operating activities and cash flows

Operating activities are generally the cash effects of transactions and other events relating to operating or trading activities. The net cash flow from operating activities represents the net increase or decrease in cash resulting from the operations shown in the profit and loss account in arriving at operating profit.

The reconciliation between operating profit and net cash flow from operating activities for the period should disclose separately the movements in stocks, debtors, and creditors related to operating activities, and other differences between cash flows and profits. It should also show separately the difference between dividends received and results taken into account for equity accounted entities.

In the cash flow statement, **operating cash flows** may be shown using either the indirect method or the direct method. Using the **indirect method**, it would be laid out in a manner similar to that shown in Exhibit 15.1.

Exhibit 15.1

	£
Operating profit	12,000
Depreciation charges	500
Loss on sale of tangible fixed assets	10
Increase in stocks	(200)
Increase in debtors	(100)
Increase in creditors	300
Net cash inflow from operating activities	12,510

FRS 1 requires that a reconciliation be shown between the net cash flow from operating activities and the operating profit as shown in the profit and loss account, which is precisely what is produced if the *indirect* method is adopted. Consequently, by adopting the indirect method, as the detailed information is to be included in a reconciliation, the main part of the statement may only include a single line 'net cash flow from operating activities'. Thus, instead of being included in the body of the cash flow statement, the details shown in Exhibit 15.1 would be included in the notes to the statement. When the indirect method is adopted, no details of the equivalent *direct* method analysis is required.

On the other hand, when the **direct method** is adopted for preparation of the statement, the reconciliation (i.e. the *indirect* method analysis) must also be prepared and included as a note to the statement. The direct method would produce an analysis in the cash flow statement similar to that shown in Exhibit 15.2.

Exhibit 15.2

Operating activities	£
Cash received from customers	120,000
Cash payments to suppliers	(40,000)
Cash paid to and on behalf of employees	(60,000)
Other cash payments	(7,490)
Net cash inflow from operating activities	12,510

It is generally easier for an entity to adopt the indirect method – the figures are readily available from the profit and loss account and balance sheet data. The direct method, on the other hand, requires that the Cash Book is analysed. Despite there being much more work involved in preparing it, in Appendix III to FRS 1, the ASB encourages the use of the direct method when the potential benefits to users outweigh the costs of doing so – it does help provide a far clearer view of cash flow than the bookkeeping adjustments to profit that are undertaken under the indirect method.

Note: In an examination, if sufficient information on cash flows is provided for you to adopt the *direct* method, you should assume that is the approach to take – however, you would still need to adopt the *indirect* method when completing the reconciliation if that was also required by the question.

15.5 FRS 1: Dividends from joint ventures and associates

This category was added to the statement following the issue of FRS 9: *Associates and joint ventures* in 1997. It was felt appropriate to show these dividends as a separate item as they were not part of operating income and they have a different nature from that of dividends from a company's returns on investment.

15.6 FRS 1: Returns on investment and servicing of finance

This section concerns receipts resulting from the ownership of an investment and payments to providers of finance, non-equity shareholders, and minority interests.

Generally, the standard endeavours to classify all cash flows according to the substance of the transaction that gave rise to them. As a result, this section of the statement excludes any item that may be classified under one of the other headings. For example, payments to *non-equity* shareholders (e.g. holders of preference shares in the entity) are included in this section, but payments to *equity* shareholders appear in the 'equity dividends paid' section.

Among the cash inflows included in this section are interest and dividends received (other than dividends from equity accounted entities whose results are included as part of operating profit). Cash outflows in this section include interest paid; finance costs, as defined under FRS 4: *Capital instruments* – see Chapter 11; the interest element of finance lease rental payments, as defined under SSAP 21: *Accounting for leases and hire purchase contracts* – see Chapter 2; and dividends paid to minority interests and to non-equity shareholders of the entity.

15.7 FRS 1: Taxation

This section includes cash flows to and from taxation authorities in respect of the reporting entity's revenue and capital profits. Other tax cash flows should be included under the same heading as the cash flow which gave rise to them – property taxes, such as rates, and VAT, for example, are seen as relating to 'operating activities'. Thus, the net amount of VAT paid to or received from the tax authorities is included under that section. The exception to this arises when VAT is irrecoverable, in which case it is added to the originating transaction value and not distinguished from it within the cash flow statement.

15.8 FRS 1: Capital expenditure and financial investment

Capital expenditure means *buying and selling fixed assets*. **Financial investment** means *buying and selling shares held as investments*. Included in this section are cash flows relating to the acquisition or disposal of any fixed asset other than those required to be classified under the 'acquisitions and disposals' section of the statement, and those relating to any current asset investment not included in the 'management of liquid resources' section.

The heading can be reduced to 'capital expenditure' if there are no cash flows relating to financial investment.

The cash inflows include:

(a) receipts from the sale or disposal of property, plant or equipment; and
(b) receipts from the repayment of the reporting entity's loans to other entities and sales of debt instruments of other entities (other than receipts forming part of an acquisition or disposal or a movement in liquid resources and classified as falling within either of those two sections of the statement).

The cash outflows include:

(a) payments to acquire property, plant or equipment; and

(b) loans made by the reporting entity and payments to acquire debt instruments of other entities (other than payments forming part of an acquisition or disposal or a movement in liquid resources and classified as falling within either of those two sections of the statement).

15.9 FRS 1: Acquisitions and disposals

It is quite normal for businesses to buy and sell other businesses or interests in other businesses. This category of cash flow records the cash-related results of these activities. Included in this section are those cash flows relating to the acquisition or disposal of any trade or business, or of an investment in an entity that is or, as a result of the transaction, becomes or ceases to be either an associate, a joint venture or a subsidiary undertaking.

15.10 FRS 1: Equity dividends paid

This section includes the dividends paid on the reporting entity's or, in a group, the parent's equity shares.

15.11 FRS 1: Management of liquid resources

The FRS defines liquid resources as 'current asset investments held as readily disposable stores of value'. A 'readily disposable investment' is one that is disposable without curtailing or disrupting the entity's business and is either readily convertible into known amounts of cash or traded in an active market. In other words, this heading is concerned with short-term investments.

Cash inflows in this section include withdrawals from short-term deposits not qualifying as cash and inflows from the disposal or redemption of any other investments held as liquid resources.

Cash outflows in this section include payments into short-term deposits not qualifying as cash and outflows to acquire any other investment held as a liquid resource.

Each entity must explain what it includes in liquid resources and declare any change in its policy.

Activity 15.1 Imagine you are running a business and you have £500,000 that you won't need for three months. How will you invest it?

15.12 FRS 1: Financing

This category reports the cash flow effects of changes to share capital and long-term borrowings. Receipts and repayments of the principal amounts (i.e. the advance, not the interest) from or to external providers of finance are entered in this section. Examples include receipts from issuing and payments towards the redemption of shares and other equity instruments, debentures, loans, notes, bonds, and from long-term and short-term borrowings (other than overdrafts); the capital element of finance lease rental payment; and payments of expenses or commission on any issue of equity shares.

The amount of any financing cash flows received from or paid to an equity accounted entity should be disclosed separately.

15.13 FRS 1: Material transactions not resulting in any cash flows

FRS 1 also requires that details of material transactions that do not result in any cash flows should be included in a note if it is necessary for an understanding of the underlying transactions. A possible example would be an operating lease. It would involve the acquisition of an asset, but the reporting entity is paying rent, not purchasing the asset.

Activity 15.2 Why do you think that such items not affecting cash flows should still be reported in a note?

15.14 FRS 1: Exceptional and extraordinary items

Cash flows relating to items classed as exceptional or extraordinary in the profit and loss account should be shown under the appropriate standard headings, according to their nature. They should be identified in the cash flow statement or a note to it and the relationship between the cash flows and the originating exceptional or extraordinary item should be explained.

Where the cash flows themselves are exceptional because of their size or incidence but the underlying event that gave rise to them is not, sufficient disclosure should be given to explain their cause and effect.

15.15 An example of the FRS 1 layout using the indirect method

As you learnt in *Business Accounting 1*, FRS 1 permits cash flow statements to be prepared either under the indirect method or the direct method. The following example of a cash flow statement prepared under the indirect method from *Business Accounting 1* is included here to remind you of the format. We will then look at two examples of cash flow statements prepared under FRS 1, one using the indirect method and the other using the direct method.

Each of the nine headings of the cash flow statement can be shown as one line in the statement and the detail in a note. (The numbers are shown in Exhibit 15.3 in order to make it clear what the nine headings are. The numbers shown would not normally be included.)

The reconciliation to net debt does not form part of the statement, nor does the reconciliation of operating profit to net cash flow from operating activities. Either can be shown in a separate note (as the reconciliation of operating profit to net cash flow from operating activities is shown below) or adjoining the statement (as in the case of the reconciliation of the movement of cash to net debt below).

Exhibit 15.3

X Limited
Cash Flow Statement for the year ending 31 December 2007

	£000	£000
1 **Net cash inflow/(outflow) from operating activities** (*see* Note 1)		XXX
2 *Dividends from joint ventures and associates*		XXX
3 *Returns on investments and servicing of finance*		
Interest received	XXX	
Interest paid	(XXX)	
Preference dividends paid	(XXX)	
Net cash inflow/(outflow) from returns on investments and servicing of finance		XXX
4 *Taxation*		XXX
5 *Capital expenditure and financial investment*		
Payments to acquire intangible fixed assets	(XXX)	
Payments to acquire tangible fixed assets	(XXX)	
Receipts from sales of tangible fixed assets	XXX	
Net cash inflow/(outflow) from capital expenditure and financial investment		(XXX)
6 *Acquisitions and disposals*		
Purchase of subsidiary undertaking	(XXX)	
Sale of business	XXX	
Net cash inflow/(outflow) from acquisitions and disposals		XXX
7 *Equity dividends paid*		(XXX)
8 *Management of liquid resources*		
Cash withdrawn from 7-day deposit	XXX	
Purchase of government securities	(XXX)	
Sale of corporate bonds	XXX	
Net cash inflow/(outflow) from management of liquid resources		XXX
9 *Financing*		
Issue of ordinary share capital	XXX	
Repurchase of debenture loan	(XXX)	
Expenses paid in connection with share issues	(XXX)	
		XXX
Increase/(decrease) in cash in the period		XXX

Reconciliation of net cash flow to movement in net debt/funds

	£000	£000
Increase/(decrease) in cash in the period	XXX	
Cash inflow/(outflow) from increase/decrease in debt and lease financing	XXX	
Cash inflow/(outflow) from decrease/increase in liquid resources	XXX	
Change in net debt resulting from cash flows		XXX
Loans and finance leases acquired with subsidiary		(XXX)
New finance leases		(XXX)
Exchange rate translation differences		XXX
Movement in net debt in the period		XXX
Net debt at 1 January 2007		XXX
Net debt at 31 December 2007		XXX

→

Note to the cash flow statement:

1 *Reconciliation of operating profit to net cash inflow/(outflow) from operating activities*

	£000
Operating profit	XXX
Depreciation charges	XXX
(Profit)/Loss on sale of tangible fixed assets	XXX
(Increase)/Decrease in stocks	XXX
(Increase)/Decrease in debtors	XXX
Increase/(Decrease) in creditors	XXX
Net cash inflow/(outflow) from operating activities	XXX

15.16 Two further examples

Exhibits 15.4 and 15.5 further illustrate how a cash flow statement is prepared under FRS 1, this time using numbers to add clarity. Some key points to remember include:

1 It is amounts paid rather than charged or accrued that are included. Thus for both tax and dividends, it is the actual payments and receipts that occurred during the period that are included in the statement, not the amounts provided for that will be paid or received in a future period.
2 Profit on sale of fixed assets is already included in the sale amount and should not be included a second time.
3 Care should be taken to identify and eliminate non-cash adjustments to the original profit before tax figure, for example depreciation and bad debt provisions.
4 If the layout presented in Exhibits 15.4 and 15.5 is followed, the entries in the 'Financing' section will have the opposite signs to the others, i.e. income will be shown with negative values, rather than positive as is the case in the other sections of the statement.

Exhibit 15.4

From the following profit and loss and balance sheet information, prepare a cash flow statement as required by FRS 1 *using the indirect method.*

Profit and Loss Account for the year ending 31 December 2004

	£000	£000
Sales		10,000
Cost of goods sold		(6,000)
		4,000
Expenses		
Depreciation	600	
Interest	150	
Other expenses	2,100	
		(2,850)
Profit for the year before tax		1,150
Tax		(200)
Profit for the year after tax		950

Note: During the year, a dividend of £150,000 was paid.

Balance Sheet as at 31 December

	2004		2003	
	£000	£000	£000	£000
Fixed assets at cost		6,000		6,000
Less accumulated depreciation		3,000		2,400
Net book value		3,000		3,600
Current assets				
Stock	500		450	
Trade debtors	200		250	
Cash	1,610		150	
		2,310		850
Less Current liabilities				
Trade creditors	310		300	
Taxation	200		150	
		(510)		(450)
		4,800		4,000
Financed by:				
Ordinary share capital		2,000		2,000
Revenue reserves		2,800		2,000
		4,800		4,000

Outline solution

Cash Flow Statement (using the indirect method) for the year ending 31 December 2004

	£000
Net cash inflow from operating activities	1,910
Dividends from joint ventures and associates	–
Returns on investments and servicing of finance	
Interest paid	(150)
Taxation	(150)
Capital expenditure and financial investment	
Acquisitions and disposals	–
Equity dividends paid	(150)
Management of liquid resources	–
Financing	–
Increase in cash in the period	1,460

Note to the cash flow statement:

1 Reconciliation of operating profit to net cash inflow from operating activities:

Operating profit	1,300
Depreciation charges	600
Increase in stocks	(50)
Decrease in debtors	50
Increase in creditors	10
Net cash inflow from operating activities	1,910

Working:
Operating profit = Retained profit (800) + Interest (150) + Dividend (150) + Tax (200) = 1,300.

Exhibit 15.5

From the summarised cash account and the fixed asset schedule of Thistle Ltd for 2002, prepare a cash flow statement as required by FRS 1 *using the direct method*.

Summarised Cash Account

	£000		£000
Opening balance	500	Wages	1,350
Cash from cash sales	3,500	Other expenses	600
Cash from credit sales	5,750	Cash paid to suppliers	4,320
Cash from issue of shares	1,200	Tax paid	100
Cash from sale of building	970	Cash paid on finance lease	700
		Final dividend for 2001	100
		Interim dividend 2002	50
		Closing balance	4,700
	11,920		11,920

Fixed Asset Schedule

	Plant £000	Buildings £000	Total £000
Cost at 1.1.2002	10,000	15,000	25,000
Acquisitions	4,730	–	4,730
Disposals	–	(5,000)	(5,000)
Cost at 31.12.2002	14,730	10,000	24,730
Accumulated depreciation at 1.1.2002	3,500	6,000	9,500
Charge for year	650	1,500	2,150
Disposals	–	(4,500)	(4,500)
Accumulated depreciation at 31.12.2002	4,150	3,000	7,150

Other information:
(a) The tax charge for the year was £400,000. The opening balance on the tax liability was £100,000.
(b) Other expenses include insurance, which is paid a year in advance, on 30 June. In 2001, insurance of £300,000 was paid. The amount paid in 2002 was £400,000.
(c) Accrued wages were £75,000 at 1.1.2002, and £95,000 at 31.12.2002.
(d) Stocks were £1,500,000 at 1.1.2002, and £1,700,000 at 31.12.2002.
(e) All £700,000 paid on the finance lease in 2002 represented capital. This was the first year of the lease and interest was not paid until the second payment, which was made in 2003. Interest of £403,000 was included in the 2003 payment and was accrued in the 2002 financial statements.
(f) Opening and closing trade debtors and trade creditors were:

	1.1.2002	31.12.2002
Trade debtors	300,000	450,000
Trade creditors	500,000	475,000

(g) 600,000 £1 ordinary shares were issued at a premium on 1.3.2002.
(h) Retained profits for the year to 31.12.2002 were £752,000.

8 management of liquid resources
9 financing.

4 The headings in the FRS 1 cash flow statement should be in that order and the statement should include a total for each heading.

5 Cash flow is an increase or decrease in cash resulting from a transaction.

6 Operating activities are generally the cash effects of transactions and other events relating to operating and trading activities.

7 Under FRS 1, operating cash flows can be shown using either the *indirect* method or the *direct* method.

8 FRS 1 requires that reconciliations are presented between operating profit and net cash flow from operating activities for the period, and between the movement in cash in the period and the movement in net debt.

9 The ASB recommends that companies applying FRS 1 use the *direct* method *if the benefits of doing so outweigh the costs*.

10 The differences between FRS 1 and IAS 7.

Answers to activities

15.1 Possible short-term investments include term deposits (e.g. 30- or 60-day deposit accounts), government stock (e.g. Treasury stock) and corporate bonds (e.g. loan stock issued by companies).

15.2 As the example of the operating lease given in the text indicates, it is a question of the substance of the transaction. The asset leased generated revenue through its use. Had it been purchased, the cash flow statement would have indicated that an additional asset was purchased. This information could then be used to explain changes in revenues. As it was leased not purchased, no such information is available to the user of the financial statements. By including a note about this, the user of the financial statements is able to draw similar conclusions concerning the asset to those that could be drawn if the asset had been purchased and, at the same time, is made aware that the company has adopted this approach which, in itself, has a direct impact upon cash flows.

15.3 In principle, the direct method is very easy to calculate. You just add up all the cash inflows and outflows relating to trading activities shown in the Cash Book. However, in practice, the volume of cash flows generated by any but the smallest business means that this can be a difficult and time-consuming task. It is not surprising that very few companies adopt this approach.

Review questions

15.1 List the nine headings in the cash flow statement, as required by FRS 1.

15.2A Give an example of the information to be included under each of the headings in an FRS 1-based cash flow statement and indicate why this information might be useful.

15.3 Prepare a cash flow statement for Lee Ltd for the year ended 31 December 2004 as required under FRS 1 using the direct method, together with note 1 to the statement. The profit and loss account, balance sheet and cash account for Lee Ltd for the year 2004 are given below. (Do not attempt to provide the reconciliation of net cash flow to net debt.)

→

→
Profit and Loss Account for the year ending 31 December 2004

	£	£
Sales		6,500
Less Cost of goods sold		(3,000)
		3,500
Less Expenses		
Wages	2,000	
Other costs	600	
Depreciation	500	
Interest	100	
		(3,200)
Profit for the year		300

Note: During the year, dividends of £50 were paid.

Balance Sheet as at 31 December

		2004		2003
	£	£	£	£
Fixed assets at cost		4,500		3,800
Less Accumulated depreciation		2,300		1,800
Net book value		2,200		2,000
Current assets				
Stock	400		500	
Trade debtors	150		200	
Cash	200		100	
		750		800
Less Current liabilities				
Trade creditors	325		300	
Accrued wages	25		50	
		(350)		(350)
		2,600		2,450
Financed by:				
Debentures		900		1,000
Ordinary share capital		1,000		1,000
Retained profits		700		450
		2,600		2,450

Cash Account for 2004

	£		£
Opening balance	100	Wages	2,025
Cash from customers	6,550	Other expenses	600
		Cash paid to suppliers	2,875
		Interest paid	100
		Cash purchase of fixed assets	700
		Cash paid to debenture holders	100
		Dividends paid	50
		Closing balance	200
	6,650		6,650

15.4A The balance sheets and additional information relating to Pennylane Ltd are given below. Prepare a cash flow statement for Pennylane Ltd for the year ended 31 December 2003 as required under FRS 1 using the indirect method, together with Note 1 to the statement. (Do not attempt to provide the reconciliation of net cash flow to net debt.)

Pennylane Ltd
Balance Sheets as at 31 December

	2003 £000	2002 £000
Fixed assets		
Tangible assets	400	325
Intangible assets	230	180
Investments	–	25
	630	530
Current assets		
Stocks	120	104
Debtors	400	295
90-day deposit	50	–
Cash in hand	10	4
	580	403
Creditors: amounts falling due within one year		
Trade creditors	122	108
Bank overdraft	188	185
Taxation	120	110
	430	403
Net current assets	150	–
Total assets less current liabilities	780	530
Creditors: amounts falling due after one year		
Long-term loan	(100)	–
Provisions for liabilities and charges: deferred taxation	(80)	(60)
	600	470
Capital and reserves		
Share capital (£1 ordinary shares)	200	150
Share premium account	160	150
Revaluation reserve	100	90
Profit and loss account	140	80
	600	470

Additional information:
(a) During the year interest of £75,000 was paid, and interest of £25,000 was received.
(b) The following information relates to tangible fixed assets.

At 31 December	2003 £000	2002 £000
Cost	740	615
Accumulated depreciation	(340)	(290)
Net book value	400	325

(c) The proceeds of the sale of fixed asset investments were £30,000.
(d) Plant, with an original cost of £90,000 and a net book value of £50,000, was sold for £37,000.
(e) Tax paid to Revenue and Customs during 2003 amounted to £110,000.
(f) Dividends of £80,000 were paid during 2003.

15.5 State the purposes of a cash flow statement.

(*Association of Chartered Certified Accountants*)

15.6 The following information has been extracted from the books of Nimmo Limited for the year to 31 December 2009:

Profit and Loss Account extracts for the year ending 31 December

	2009 £000	2008 £000
Profit before taxation	20,400	9,500
Taxation	(5,200)	(3,200)
Profit after taxation	15,200	6,300

Note:

Dividends paid	2009	2008
Preference	100	100
Ordinary	8,000	4,000
	8,100	4,100

Balance Sheets at 31 December

	2008 £000	2009 £000
Fixed assets		
Plant, machinery and equipment, at cost	17,600	23,900
Less Accumulated depreciation	9,500	10,750
	8,100	13,150
Current assets		
Stocks	2,000	9,000
Trade debtors	8,600	26,700
Prepayments	300	400
Cash at bank and in hand	600	–
	11,500	36,100
Current liabilities		
Bank overdraft	–	(16,200)
Trade creditors	(6,000)	(10,000)
Accruals	(800)	(1,000)
Taxation	(3,200)	(5,200)
Dividends	(3,000)	(6,000)
	(10,000)	(32,400)
	9,600	16,850
Share capital		
Ordinary shares of £1 each	5,000	5,000
10% preference shares of £1 each	1,000	1,000
Profit and loss account	3,000	10,100
	9,000	16,100
Loans		
15% debenture stock	600	750
	9,600	16,850

Additional information:

1 The directors are extremely concerned about the large bank overdraft as at 31 December 2009 and they attribute this mainly to the increase in trade debtors as a result of alleged poor credit control.
2 During the year to 31 December 2009, fixed assets originally costing £5,500,000 were sold for £1,000,000. The accumulated depreciation on these assets as at 31 December 2008 was £3,800,000.

Required:
Prepare a cash flow statement for the year to 31 December 2009.

Authors' note: **Use the FRS 1 indirect method but do not attempt to provide the reconciliation of net cash flow to net debt.**

(*Association of Accounting Technicians*)

15.7 The following summarised balance sheets relate to Track Limited:

Balance Sheets at 30 June

	2011 £000	2010 £000
Fixed assets at cost	650	500
Less Accumulated depreciation	300	200
	350	300
Investments at cost	50	200
Current assets		
Stocks	700	400
Debtors	1,550	1,350
Cash and bank	–	100
	2,250	1,850
Current liabilities		
Bank overdraft	(60)	–
Creditors	(920)	(800)
Taxation	(190)	(230)
	(1,170)	(1,030)
	1,480	1,320
Capital and reserves		
Called-up share capital (£1 ordinary shares)	750	500
Share premium account	200	150
Profit and loss account	530	670
	1,480	1,320

Additional information:
1 During the year to 30 June 2011, some fixed assets originally costing £25,000 had been sold for £20,000 in cash. The accumulated depreciation on these fixed assets at 30 June 2010 amounted to £10,000. Similarly, some of the investments originally costing £150,000 had been sold for cash at their book value.
2 The taxation balances disclosed in the above balance sheets represent the actual amounts agreed with the Inland Revenue. All taxes were paid on their due dates. Advance corporation tax may be ignored.
3 A dividend of £130,000 was paid during the year to 30 June 2011.
4 During the year to 30 June 2001, the company made a 1-for-2 rights issue of 250 ordinary £1 shares at 120p per share.

Required:
Prepare Track Ltd's cash flow statement for the year to 30 June 2011 in accordance with the requirements of FRS 1 using the indirect method. (Do not attempt to provide the reconciliation of net cash flow to net debt.)

(*Association of Accounting Technicians*)

15.8A You are presented with the following summarised information relating to Ward plc:

Profit and Loss Account for the year ending 30 June 2008

	£000
Net profit for the year before taxation	900
Taxation (see Note 1)	(636)
Profit for the year after taxation	264
Extraordinary item (after tax relief of £35,000)	(90)
Profit for the year after taxation and extraordinary item	174

Balance Sheet at 30 June 2008

	2008 £000	2007 £000
Fixed assets (see Note 2)	1,810	1,515
Investments	40	40
	1,850	1,555
Current assets		
Stocks	70	75
Debtors	60	100
Cash at bank and in hand	–	20
	130	195
Creditors: amounts falling due within one year		
Bank loans and overdrafts	(21)	–
Trade creditors	(100)	(130)
Other creditors including taxation and social security (see Note 3)	(465)	(400)
	(586)	(530)
Creditors: amounts falling due after more than one year		
Debenture loans	(50)	(200)
Provisions for liabilities and charges		
Taxation, including deferred taxation (see Note 4)	(229)	(120)
	£1,115	£900
Capital and reserves		
Called-up share capital	910	750
Profit and loss account	205	150
	£1,115	£900

Notes:
1 The taxation charge in the profit and loss account includes the following items:

	£000
Corporation tax based on the profit for the year	542
Overprovision of last year's corporation tax	(15)
Transfer to deferred taxation account	109
	£636

2 During the year to 30 June 2008, Ward sold an asset originally costing £150,000 for £5,000 in cash. The depreciation charged on this asset was £135,000. The total depreciation charged in the profit and loss account for the year to 30 June 2008 was £384,000.

3 Other creditors including taxation and social security includes the following items:

	2008 £000	2007 £000
Corporation tax	465	400

4 The deferred taxation balances include the following items:

	2008 £000	2007 £000
Opening balance	120	70
Transfer from the profit and loss account	109	50
	£220	£120

5 During 2007, a dividend was paid of £119,000.

Required:
In so far as the information permits, prepare Ward plc's statement of cash flow for the year ending 30 June 2008 in accordance with FRS 1.

(*Association of Accounting Technicians*)

15.9A The accountant of a private company has been able to get the use of a computer to produce the spreadsheets shown below but as yet the computer lacks a program to print out final accounts. The accountant nevertheless expects to use the spreadsheet data to reconstruct a summary profit and loss account and a cash flow statement for the year ending 30 April 2006.

Movements of Assets during the year 2005/06 (£000)

	Balance sheet value last year	Depreciation or amortisation for year	Additions during year	Sales during year	Other changes	Balance sheet value this year
Goodwill	–	–	40	–	–	40
Property	760	(36)	–	–	–	724
Plant and vehicles	540	(84)	420	(60)	–	816
Stocks	230	–	–	–	24	254
Debtors	254	–	–	–	76	330
Bank and cash	50	–	–	–	14	64
	1,834	(120)	460	(60)	114	2,228

Movement of Liabilities and Reserves during the year 2005/06 (£000)

	Balance sheet value last year	New capital issued	Payments during year	Transfers to reserves and for provisions	Other changes	Balance sheet value this year
Ordinary shares (£1 each)	1,060	440	–	–	–	1,500
Deferred taxation	36	–	–	176	–	212
General reserve	152	–	–	32	–	184
Creditors	136	–	–	–	24	160
Provision for corporation tax	450	–	(450)	172	–	172
	1,834	440	(450)	380	24	2,228

→

→ *Notes*:
(*i*) Proceeds of £40,000 were received from the sale of plant and vehicles.
(*ii*) During the year the company redeemed 10,000 of its £1 ordinary shares for £125,000 wholly out of distributable profits and this transaction has not been included in the spreadsheets.

Required:
(*a*) Reconstruct the profit and loss account for the year ending 30 April 2006.
(*b*) Prepare a cash flow statement for the year to 30 April 2006.

***Authors' note*: Prepare the statement under the rules of FRS 1.**

(*Institute of Chartered Secretaries and Administrators*)

15.10 You are presented with the following forecast information relating to Baker Limited for the nine months to 30 September 2007.
Forecast profit and loss accounts (abridged) for the three quarters to 30 September 2007:

	March 2007 £000	June 2007 £000	Sept 2007 £000
Sales	250	300	350
Cost of goods sold	(200)	(240)	(280)
Gross profit	50	60	70
Depreciation	(3)	(20)	(4)
Administration, selling and distribution expenses	(37)	(40)	(42)
Forecast net profit	£10	–	£24

Forecast balances at	31 Dec 2006 £000	31 March 2007 £000	30 June 2007 £000	30 Sept 2007 £000
Debit balances				
Tangible fixed assets at cost	360	240	480	480
90 day deposit at cost	15	5	5	10
Stocks at cost	40	30	40	55
Trade debtors	50	65	75	80
Cash at bank and in hand	80	–	–	–
Credit balances				
Debentures (10%)	–	–	–	50
Trade creditors	80	120	140	150
Taxation	8	–	–	–

Additional information:
1 Sales of tangible fixed assets in March 2007 were expected to realise £12,000 in cash.
2 Administration, selling and distribution expenses were expected to be settled in cash during the month in which they were incurred.
3 Baker Limited includes as liquid resources term deposits of less than one year.
4 The directors have proposed that a dividend of £15,000 be paid on 28 February.

Required:
(*a*) calculate Baker Limited's forecast net cash position at 31 March, 30 June and 30 September 2007 respectively; and
(*b*) prepare a forecast statement of cash flow for the nine months ending 30 September 2007.

***Authors' note*: Prepare the forecast statement of cash flow under the rules of FRS 1.**

(*Association of Accounting Technicians*)

15.11A The following information has been extracted from the draft financial information of V Ltd:

Profit and Loss Account for the year ended 31 December 2003

	£000	£000
Sales		495
Raw materials consumed	(49)	
Staff costs	(37)	
Depreciation	(74)	
Loss on disposal	(4)	
		(164)
Operating profit		331
Interest payable		(23)
Profit before tax		308
Taxation		(87)
		221

Note: Dividend paid = £52,000

Balance Sheets

	31 December 2003		31 December 2002	
	£000	£000	£000	£000
Fixed assets (see below)		1,145		957
Current assets				
Stock	19		16	
Trade debtors	38		29	
Bank	31		37	
	88		82	
Current liabilities				
Trade creditors	(12)		(17)	
Taxation	(100)		(81)	
	(112)		(98)	
Working capital		(24)		(16)
		1,121		941
Long-term liabilities				
Long-term loans		(70)		(320)
		1,051		621
Share capital		182		152
Share premium		141		80
Revaluation reserve		170		
Profit and loss		558		389
		1,051		621

→

	Land & buildings £000	Machinery £000	Fixtures & fittings £000	Total £000
Fixed assets				
Cost or valuation:				
At 31 December 2002	830	470	197	1,497
Additions	–	43	55	98
Disposals	–	(18)	–	(18)
Adjustment on revaluation	70	–	–	70
At 31 December 2003	900	495	252	1,647
Depreciation				
At 31 December 2002	(90)	(270)	(180)	(540)
Charge for year	(10)	(56)	(8)	(74)
Disposals	–	12	–	12
Adjustment on revaluation	100	–	–	100
At 31 December 2003	0	(314)	(188)	(502)
Net book value				
At 31 December 2003	900	181	64	1,145
At 31 December 2002	740	200	17	957

(a) **You are required to** prepare a cash flow statement for V Ltd for the year ended 31 December 2003 in accordance with the requirements of Financial Reporting Standard 1 (FRS 1).

(b) It has been suggested that the management of long-term profitability is more important than short-term cash flow. Explain why this might be so.

(*Chartered Institute of Management Accountants*)

You can find a range of additional self-test questions, as well as material to help you with your studies, on the website that accompanies this book at **www.pearsoned.co.uk/wood**

Part

3

GROUPS

Introduction

This part is concerned with group financial statements: how they are prepared, how various transactions should be dealt with, and how their presentation is regulated by the Companies Acts and accounting standards.

16.6 Control by dominant influence

The issue of FRS 2 in 1992 introduced a further way of looking at whether or not one company has control of another. It states that if one company has 'the right to exercise a dominant influence' over another undertaking, then the company with the dominating influence is deemed to have control of the other. **It is not necessary to have over 50 per cent of the voting share capital of a company in order to be able to exercise a dominant influence.** A dominant influence means that the holder of it has a right to give directions with regard to the operating and financial policies of another undertaking, and that the directors of that latter undertaking are obliged to follow those directions, whether or not the directors consider that those directions are for the benefit of the undertaking.

In other words, if one undertaking can tell another undertaking what to do, both from an operating and a financial point of view, and the directors of that latter undertaking have to carry out such instructions, then such an undertaking will be a subsidiary undertaking. This is a much wider definition than merely looking at the amounts of the shareholdings.

> **Activity 16.2**
>
> How can an entity have a dominant influence when it does not own over 50 per cent of the voting share capital?

This topic is covered in more detail in Chapter 26.

16.7 The nature of a group

Wherever two or more companies are in the relationship of parent and subsidiary undertakings, a 'group' is said to exist. As you're already learnt in Section 16.4, in order to comply with legal requirements when such a group exists, besides the financial statements of the parent undertaking itself there must be a set of financial statements prepared in respect of the group as a whole. These group financial statements are usually known as **consolidated financial statements**, because the financial statements of all the companies have had to be consolidated together to form one set of financial statements.

Sometimes parent undertakings carry on trading as well as investing in their subsidiaries. There are, however, many parent undertakings that do not trade, all of their activities being concerned with investing in other companies.

16.8 Subsidiary undertakings which are not limited companies

At one time, group financial statements consolidated only financial statements of limited companies. In effect, subsidiaries had to be limited companies to 'merit' inclusion in the consolidated financial statements. This is no longer the case: in FRS 2 widened this so that a subsidiary undertaking does not need to be a limited company. Share of ownership or the dominant influence approach will determine whether or not an entity is a subsidiary undertaking. If so, its financial statements are included in the preparation of the consolidated financial statements, in a similar fashion to those of limited companies.

Other forms of entity – associate undertakings and joint ventures – are, by definition, *not* subsidiaries and are not consolidated. They are included in the financial statements according to the rules contained in FRS 9.

See Chapter 26 for further details of these rules.

Thus, the main changes to accounting for subsidiary undertakings introduced by FRS 2 were as follows:

1 The concept of 'dominant influence' widened the scope of which companies could be seen as subsidiary undertakings, rather than relying on share ownership.
2 Unincorporated businesses (i.e. not companies) were brought into its scope and came to be classed as subsidiary undertakings which have to have their financial statements consolidated with the rest of the group.

16.9 Teaching method

This topic is normally taught and learnt using one of two methods. One focuses on the journal entries required; this is quite abstract and, many feel, more difficult to understand than the other method. Accordingly, the method used in this book for teaching consolidated financial statements is the alternative approach of showing the adjustments needed on the face of the consolidated balance sheet, together with any workings required to explain the amounts included. This approach is adopted because:

1 We believe our job is to try to help you to understand the subject, and not just to be able to perform the necessary calculations. We believe that, given a clear explanation of what is happening, the necessary accounting entries are much easier to understand. Showing the adjustments on the face of the balance sheet gives a 'bird's-eye view' so that it is easier to see what is happening, rather than having to laboriously trace your way through a complex set of double-entry adjustments made in ledger accounts.
2 This would be a much lengthier and more costly book if all of the double entry accounts were shown. It is better for a first look at consolidated financial statements to be an introduction to the subject only, rather than both an introduction and a very detailed analysis of the subject. If you can understand the consolidated financial statements shown in this book, you will have a firm foundation which will enable you, in your future studies, to tackle the more difficult and complicated aspects of the subject.

Learning outcomes

You should now have learnt:

1 Ordinary shareholders generally have voting rights, a right in the net assets of the company, and a right to an interest in profits earned.

2 Preference shareholders do not usually have any voting rights.

3 Ordinary shareholders receive copies of the financial statements for the company whose shares they hold, but not for any company whose shares are owned by the company they hold their shares in.

4 Consolidated financial statements provide shareholders in parent undertakings with financial statements incorporating the relevant data for all companies in the group – not just the parent company's own accounts data.

5 The status of 'subsidiary undertaking' is dependent upon the existence of control over that undertaking by another entity.

6 'Control' is determined by whether 'dominant influence' can be exerted, not simply by the level of investment in the company.

Answers to activities

16.1 Preference shareholders have far less risk in their investment than ordinary shareholders. In exchange for the greater risk they experience, the ordinary shareholders get voting rights that permit them to influence the decision making of the company.

16.2 It could have a dominant influence by virtue of some agreement made with the company. For example, a bank may have dominant influence over the major decisions of a company in exchange for a loan it has granted to the company. Dominant influence is generally able to exist because of agreements between shareholders that result in one of the shareholders being granted the dominant influence.

Review questions

16.1 What determines whether or not one company is a subsidiary undertaking of another company?

16.2 How are incorporated businesses affected by the provisions of FRS 2?

16.3 What benefits accrue to the investor in a parent undertaking by the use of consolidated financial statements?

16.4 How did FRS 2 change the way in which consolidated financial statements should be drawn up?

You can find a range of additional self-test questions, as well as material to help you with your studies, on the website that accompanies this book at **www.pearsoned.co.uk/wood**

Consolidation of balance sheets: basic mechanics (I)

Learning objectives

After you have studied this chapter, you should be able to:

- explain the principle of cancellation that is adopted when preparing consolidated financial statements
- explain why goodwill may arise on consolidation
- calculate goodwill and include it in the consolidated balance sheet
- explain what is meant by the term 'minority interest'
- explain how the existence of reserves at the time of acquisition affects the preparation of consolidated financial statements

Introduction

In this chapter, you'll learn how to consolidate financial statements where a subsidiary is wholly owned or partially owned, how to calculate and include positive goodwill in the consolidated balance sheet, and how to consolidate subsidiaries with reserves. Finally, you'll be reminded about how to deal with negative goodwill in the consolidated financial statements.

17.1 Background

This chapter is concerned with the basic mechanics of consolidating balance sheets. The figures used will be quite small, as there is no virtue in obscuring the principles involved by using more realistic amounts. For the sake of brevity, some abbreviations will be used. As the consolidation of the financial statements of either two or three companies, but no more, will be attempted, then the abbreviations will be: P for the parent undertaking, S1 for the first subsidiary undertaking, and S2 for the second subsidiary undertaking. Where there is only one subsidiary undertaking it will be shown as S. Unless stated to the contrary, all the shares will be ordinary shares of £1 each.

It will make the problems of the reader far easier if relatively simple balance sheets can be used to demonstrate the principles of consolidated financial statements. To this end, the balance sheets which follow in the next few chapters will usually have only two sorts of assets, those of stock and cash at bank. This will save a great deal of time and effort. At this stage on this topic, if every time a consolidated balance sheet had to be prepared it included land, buildings, patents, motor vehicles, plant and machinery, stock, debtors and bank balances, then you'd find it far harder to understand the principles involved.

17.2 The principle of cancellation

The various financial statements of the parent undertaking and its subsidiary undertakings have to be brought together and consolidated into one set of financial statements for the whole of the group. Some items in one of the original sets of financial statements will also be found to refer to exactly the same transactions in the financial statements of one of the other entities.

Let us look at some of the more common examples:

1 An item which is a debtor in one balance sheet may be shown as a creditor in another balance sheet. For example, if P Ltd had sold goods to S Ltd, its subsidiary, but S Ltd had not yet paid for them, then the item would be shown as a debtor in the balance sheet of P Ltd and as a creditor in the balance sheet of S Ltd.
2 Sales by one of the group to another company in the group will appear as sales in one company's accounts and purchases in another company's financial statements.
3 Shares bought in one of the subsidiary undertakings by the parent undertaking will be shown as an investment on the assets side of the parent undertaking's balance sheet. In the balance sheet of the subsidiary, exactly those same shares will be shown as issued share capital.
4 Dividends paid by a subsidiary undertaking to its parent undertaking will be shown as paid dividends in the financial statements of the subsidiary, and as dividends received in the financial statements of the parent undertaking.

Consolidated financial statements are supposed to show how groups as a whole have dealt with the world outside. Transactions which are simply within the group do not represent dealings with the outside world. When all of the separate accounts of the companies within the group are put together such items need to be deleted, and will not appear in the consolidated financial statements of the group.

This therefore is the principle of cancellation. Similar things in different financial statements within the group should be cancelled out to arrive at the group's financial statements. None of the items listed above will therefore appear in the consolidated financial statements.

This can be shown in the form of the diagram in Exhibit 17.1:

Exhibit 17.1 Consolidation of financial statements of a group

This means that a consolidated balance sheet, where the subsidiaries are 100 per cent owned by the parent undertaking, will appear as follows:

Consolidated Balance Sheet as at . . .

	£	£
Fixed assets (*less* Cancelled items)		xxxx
Current assets (*less* Cancelled items)	xxxx	
Less Current liabilities (*less* Cancelled items)	(xxxx)	
		xxxx
		xxxx
Financed by:		
Share capital (of the parent undertaking only, as the purchase of shares in the subsidiaries have cancelled out)		xxxx
Reserves (*less* Cancelled items)		xxxx
		xxxx

17.3 Rule 1

In consolidation, the first rule, therefore, is that like things cancel out each other. In fact, **cancellation accounts** are what consolidated financial statements are all about. It also helps the reader to see the issue more clearly if the consolidated balance sheet is constructed immediately after P has bought the shares in S.

Exhibit 17.2

100 per cent of the shares of S bought at balance sheet value.

P has just bought all the shares of S. Before consolidation the balance sheets of P and S appear as follows:

P Balance Sheet

		£
Investment in subsidiary S	(A)	6
Bank		4
		10
Share capital		10

S Balance Sheet

		£
Stock		5
Bank		1
		6
Share capital	(B)	6

Now the consolidated balance sheet can be drawn up. The rule about like things cancelling out each other can now be applied. As can be seen, item (A) in P's balance sheet and item (B) in S's balance sheet are concerned with exactly the same thing, namely the 6 ordinary shares of S, and for the same amount, for the shares are shown in both balance sheets at £6. These are cancelled out when the consolidated balance sheet is drafted.

P & S Consolidated Balance Sheet

	£
Stock	5
Bank (£4 + £1)	5
	10
Share capital	10

However, sometimes the amount paid by the parent undertaking is not the same as the subsidiary's figure for share capital.

Exhibit 17.3

100 per cent of the shares of S bought for more than balance sheet value.

P Balance Sheet

		£
Investment in subsidiary S: 6 shares	(C)	9
Bank		1
		10
Share capital		10

S Balance Sheet

		£
Stock		5
Bank		1
		6
Share capital	(D)	6

Now (C) and (D) refer to like things, but the amounts are unequal. What has happened is that P has given £3 more than the book value for the shares of S. In accounting, where the amount paid (or 'consideration') for something exceeds the stated value, the difference is known as *goodwill*; and, when the consideration is less than the stated value, the difference is known as *negative goodwill*. (In practice, the accounting standards require that 'fair values', rather than book values are used – *see* Section 22.3; however, for the sake of clarity, unless otherwise indicated, the book values will be used throughout this book.) The consolidated balance sheet is therefore:

P and S Consolidated Balance Sheet

	£
Goodwill (C) £9 – (D) £6	3
Stock	5
Bank (£1 + £1)	2
	10
Share capital	10

Let's look at an example where negative goodwill has been created.

Exhibit 17.4

100 per cent of the shares of S bought for less than balance sheet value.

P Balance Sheet

		£
Investment in subsidiary S: 6 shares	(E)	4
Stock		5
Bank		1
		10
Share capital		10

S Balance Sheet

		£
Stock		5
Bank		1
		6
Share capital	(F)	6

P has bought all the shares of S, but has given only £4 for £6 worth of shares at balance sheet values. The £2 difference is negative goodwill. The uninitiated might look upon the £2 as being 'profit' but your knowledge of company financial statements should tell you that this difference could never be distributed as cash dividends. This negative goodwill is treated as a minus entry in the Goodwill section of the balance sheet under FRS 10: *Goodwill and intangible assets*.

Under FRS 10, the consolidated balance sheet appears as:

P and S Consolidated Balance Sheet

	£
Goodwill: negative goodwill (E) £4 – (F) £6	(2)
Stock (£5 + £5)	10
Bank (£1 + £1)	2
	10
Share capital	10

17.4 Cost of control

The expression **cost of control** could be used instead of 'goodwill'. This expression probably captures the essence of the purchase of the shares rather than calling it goodwill. It is precisely for the sake of gaining control of the assets of the company that the shares are bought. However, the expression 'goodwill' is more widely used and is correspondingly the one that will be used throughout the remainder of this book.

> See Section 23.4 for details of how to record entries in a 'cost of control' account.

> You can now attempt Review Questions 17.1, 17.2 and 17.3.

17.5 Rule 2

Rule 2 states that, although the whole of the shares of the subsidiary have not been bought, nonetheless the whole of the assets of the subsidiary (subject to certain intercompany transactions described later) will be shown in the consolidated balance sheet.

This rule comes about because of the choice made originally between two possible methods that could have been chosen. Suppose that P bought 75 per cent of the shares of S then the balance sheets could be displayed in one of two ways:

P and S Consolidated Balance Sheet – Method 1

	£
Goodwill	xxxx
Assets of P: 100 per cent	xxxx
Assets of S: 75 per cent	**xxxx**
	xxxx
Share capital of P	xxxx
	xxxx

P and S Consolidated Balance Sheet – Method 2

	£
Goodwill	xxxx
Assets of P: 100 per cent	xxxx
Assets of S: 100 per cent	xxxx
	xxxx
Share capital of P	xxxx
Minority interest (i.e. claims of outsiders which equal 25 per cent of the assets of S)	**xxxx**
	xxxx

It can be seen that both balance sheets show the amount of assets which P owns by virtue of its proportionate shareholding. On the other hand the second balance sheet gives a fuller picture, as it shows that P has control of all of the assets of S, although in fact it does not own all of them. The claims of outsiders come to 25 per cent of S and obviously they cannot control the assets of S, whereas P, with 75 per cent, can control the whole of the assets even though they are not fully owned by it. The second balance sheet method gives rather more meaningful information and is the method that is used for consolidated financial statements in accordance with FRS 2.

Assume that S has 6 shares of £1 each and that it has one asset, namely stock £6. P buys 4 shares for £1 each, £4. If the whole of the assets of S £6 are to be shown on the assets side of the consolidated balance sheet, and the cancellation of only £4 is to take place on the other side, then the consolidated balance sheet would not balance. Exhibit 17.5 shows this in detail before any attempt is made to get the consolidated balance sheet to balance.

Exhibit 17.5

P Balance Sheet

	£
Investment in subsidiary: 4 shares (bought today)	4
Stock	5
Bank	1
	10
Share capital	10

S Balance Sheet

	£
Stock	6
Share capital	6

As the two extra shares have not been bought by P, they cannot be brought into any calculation of goodwill. P has bought four shares with a balance sheet value of £1 each, i.e. £4, for precisely £4. There is therefore no element of goodwill or negative goodwill. On the other hand, the consolidated balance sheet per Rule 2 must show the whole of the assets of S. This gives a consolidated balance sheet as follows:

P and S Consolidated Balance Sheet

	£
Stock (£5 + £6)	11
Bank	1
Share capital	10

Quite obviously, if you now inserted the totals, they would differ by £2. What is this £2? On reflection it can be seen to be the £2 shares not bought by P. These shares belong to outsiders, they are not owned by the group. These outsiders also hold less than 50 per cent of the voting shares of S. In fact, if they owned more, then S would probably not be a subsidiary of P. The title given to the outside shareholders was used on the previous page and is the apt one of '**minority interest**'.

As the whole of the assets of S are shown in the consolidated balance sheet then part of these assets are owned by the minority interest. This claim against the assets is therefore shown in the capital section of the consolidated balance sheet. The consolidated balance sheet becomes:

P and S Consolidated Balance Sheet

	£
Stock (£5 + £6)	11
Bank	1
	12
Share capital	10
Minority interest	2
	12

This therefore is the convention of showing the whole of the assets of the subsidiary (less certain intercompany transactions) in the consolidated balance sheet, with the claim of the minority interest shown on the other side of the balance sheet.

Exhibit 17.6

Where less than 100 per cent of the subsidiary's shares are bought at more than book value.

P Balance Sheet

		£
Investment in subsidiary: 6 shares	(G)	8
Stock		11
Bank		1
		20
Share capital		20

S Balance Sheet

		£
Stock		7
Bank		3
		10
Share capital	(I)	10

P has bought 6 shares only, but has paid £8 for them. As the book value of the shares is £6, the £2 excess must therefore be goodwill. The cancellation is therefore £6 from (G) and £6 from (I), leaving £2 of (G) to be shown as goodwill in the consolidated balance sheet. The remaining £4 of (I) is in respect of shares held by the minority interest.

P and S Consolidated Balance Sheet

	£
Goodwill	2
Stock (£11 + £7)	18
Bank (£1 + £3)	4
	24
Share capital	20
Minority interest	4
	24

Exhibit 17.7

Where less than 100 per cent of the shares in the subsidiary are bought at less than book value.

P Balance Sheet

		£
Investment in subsidiary: 7 shares	(J)	5
Stock		13
Bank		2
		20
Share capital		20

→

➔

S Balance Sheet

		£
Stock		9
Bank		1
		10
Share capital	(K)	10
		10

Seven shares of S have now been bought for £5. This means that £5 of (J) and £5 of (K) cancel out with £2 of the share capital being represented by £2 of negative goodwill. The remaining £3 of (K) is in respect of the shares held by the minority interest and will be shown as such in the consolidated balance sheet.

P and S Consolidated Balance Sheet

	£
Goodwill: negative goodwill	(2)
Stock (£13 + £9)	22
Bank (£2 + £1)	3
	23
Shares	20
Minority interest	3
	23

You can now attempt Review Questions 17.6 and 17.7.

17.6 Taking over subsidiaries with reserves

So far, for reasons of simplification, the examples given have been of subsidiaries with share capital but no reserves. When reserves exist, as they do in the vast majority of cases, it must be remembered that they belong to the ordinary shareholders. This means that if P buys all the 10 shares of S for £15, and S at that point of time has a credit balance of £3 on its profit and loss account and a general reserve of £2, then what P acquires for its £15 is the full entitlement/ rights of the 10 shares measured by/shown as:

	£
10 shares	10
Profit and loss	3
General reserve	2
	15

This means that the £15 paid and the £15 entitlements as shown will cancel out each other and will not be shown in the consolidated balance sheet. This is shown by the balance sheets shown in Exhibit 17.8:

Exhibit 17.8

Where 100 per cent of the shares are bought at book value when the subsidiary has reserves.

P Balance Sheet

		£
Investment in subsidiary: 10 shares	(L)	15
Stock		11
Bank		2
		28
Share capital		20
Profit and loss		5
General reserve		3
		28

S Balance Sheet

		£
Stock		9
Bank		6
		15
Share capital	(M1)	10
Profit and loss	(M2)	3
General reserve	(M3)	2
		15

P and S Consolidated Balance Sheet

	£
Stock (£11 + £9)	20
Bank (£2 + £6)	8
	28
Share capital	20
Profit and loss	5
General reserve	3
	28

The cost of the shares (L) £15 is cancelled out exactly against (M1) £10 + (M2) £3 + (M3) £2 = £15. These are therefore the only items cancelled out and the remainder of the two balance sheets of P and S are then combined to be the consolidated balance sheet.

Exhibit 17.9

Where 100 per cent of the shares are bought at more than book value when the subsidiary has reserves.

P Balance Sheet

		£
Investment in subsidiary: 10 shares	(N)	23
Stock		7
Bank		5
		35
Share capital		20
Profit and loss		9
General reserve		6
		35

S Balance Sheet

	£
Stock	15
Bank	2
	17
Share capital (O1)	10
Profit and loss (O2)	4
General reserve (O3)	3
	17

P paid £23 (N) for the entitlements (O1) £10 + (O2) £4 + (O3) £3 = £17, so that a figure of £6 will be shown in the consolidated balance sheet for goodwill.

P and S Consolidated Balance Sheet

	£
Goodwill	6
Stock (£7 + £15)	22
Bank (£5 + £2)	7
	35
Share capital	20
Profit and loss	9
General reserve	6
	35

Exhibit 17.10

Where 100 per cent of the shares in the subsidiary are bought at below book value when the subsidiary has reserves.

P Balance Sheet

	£
Investment in subsidiary: 10 shares (Z)	17
Stock	10
Bank	8
	35
Share capital	20
Profit and loss	6
General reserve	9
	35

S Balance Sheet

	£
Stock	16
Bank	5
	21
Share capital (Q1)	10
Profit and loss (Q2)	8
General reserve (Q3)	3
	21

P has paid £17 (Z) for the benefits of (Q1) £10 + (Q2) £8 + (Q3) £3 = £21. This means that there will be negative goodwill of £21 − £17 = £4 in the consolidated balance sheet, while (Z), (Q1), (Q2) and (Q3), having been cancelled out, will not appear.

P and S Consolidated Balance Sheet

	£
Goodwill: negative goodwill	(4)
Stock (£10 + £16)	26
Bank (£8 + £5)	13
	35
Share capital	20
Profit and loss	6
General reserve	9
	35

Exhibit 17.11

Where less than 100 per cent of the shares are bought in a subsidiary which has reserves, and the shares are bought at the balance sheet value.

P Balance Sheet

		£
Investment in subsidiary: 8 shares	(R)	24
Stock		15
Bank		6
		45
Share capital		20
Profit and loss		17
General reserve		8
		45

S Balance Sheet

		£
Stock		21
Bank		9
		30
Share capital	(T1)	10
Profit and loss	(T2)	5
General reserve	(T3)	15
		30

The items (R) and the parts of (T1), (T2) and (T3) which are like things need to be cancelled out. The cancellation takes place from the share capital and reserves of S as follows:

	Total at acquisition date £	Bought by P 80 per cent £	Held by minority interest £
Share capital	10	8	2
Profit and loss	5	4	1
General reserve	15	12	3
	30	24	6

The amount paid by P was £24, and as P acquired a total of £24 value of shares and reserves the cancellation takes place without there being any figure of positive or negative goodwill. The consolidated balance sheet therefore appears:

P and S Consolidated Balance Sheet

	£
Stock (£15 + £21)	36
Bank (£6 + £9)	15
	51
Share capital	20
Profit and loss	17
General reserve	8
Minority interest	6
	51

Activity 17.1   What are the two rules of consolidation?

17.7 Partial control at a price not equal to balance sheet value

In Exhibit 17.11, the amount paid for the 80 per cent of the shares of S was equal to the balance sheet value of the shares in that it amounted to £24. This is unusual. As the price is normally different from balance sheet value. If an amount paid is greater than the balance sheet value then the excess will be shown as goodwill in the consolidated balance sheet; while if a smaller amount than balance sheet value is paid then the difference is negative goodwill and will be shown as such in the consolidated balance sheet. Using the balance sheet figure of S in Exhibit 17.11, if P had paid £30 for 80 per cent of the shares of S then the consolidated balance sheet would show a goodwill figure of £6. If, instead, only £21 had been paid then the consolidated balance sheet would show £3 negative goodwill.

When the acquisition of two subsidiaries brings out in the calculations a figure of goodwill in respect of the acquisition of one subsidiary, and a figure for negative goodwill in respect of the acquisition of the other subsidiary, the two figures should be shown separately in the consolidated balance sheet, followed by the net figure. For instance if P had acquired two subsidiaries S1 and S2 where the calculations showed a figure of £10 for goodwill on the acquisition of S1 and a figure of £4 negative goodwill on the acquisition of S2, then the consolidated balance sheet would show a figure for goodwill of £10 and a figure for negative goodwill of £4.

The final exhibit in this chapter is a composite one, bringing in most of the points already shown.

Exhibit 17.12

Where two subsidiaries have been acquired, both with reserves, full control being acquired of one subsidiary and a partial control of the other subsidiary.

P Balance Sheet

		£
Investment in subsidiaries:		
S1 10 shares	(U)	37
S2 7 shares	(V)	39
Stock		22
Bank		2
		100
Share capital		40
Profit and loss		50
General reserve		10
		100

S1 Balance Sheet

		£
Stock		19
Bank		11
		30
Share capital	(W1)	10
Profit and loss	(W2)	12
General reserve	(W3)	8
		30

S2 Balance Sheet

		£
Stock		42
Bank		18
		60
Share capital	(X1)	10
Profit and loss	(X2)	30
General reserve	(X3)	20
		60

With the acquisition of S1 P has paid £37 for (W1) £10 + (W2) £12 + (W3) £8 = £30, giving a figure of £7 for goodwill. With the acquisition of S2 P has given £39 for $^7/_{10}$ of the following: (X1) £10 + (X2) £30 + (X3) £20 = £60 × $^7/_{10}$ = £42, giving a figure of £3 for negative goodwill. The two figures should be shown separately in the consolidated balance sheet.

P and S1 and S2 Consolidated Balance Sheet

		£
Goodwill		7
Negative goodwill		(3)
		4
Stock (£22 + £19 + £42)		83
Bank (£2 + £11 + £18)		31
		118
Share capital		40
Profit and loss		50
General reserve		10
Minority interest:		
$^3/_{10}$ of (X1)	3	
$^3/_{10}$ of (X2)	9	
$^3/_{10}$ of (X3)	6	
		18
		118

Now work through Review Questions 17.10 and 17.11.

Learning outcomes

You should now have learnt:

1 Some items in the financial statements of one of the group companies will refer to exactly the same transactions as in the financial statements of one of the other group companies and they will need to be cancelled out when the consolidated financial statements are prepared (*Rule 1*).

2 Where the consideration exceeds the balance sheet value acquired, goodwill arises.

3 Where the consideration is less than the balance sheet value acquired, the negative goodwill is treated as a negative entry in the Goodwill section of the balance sheet under FRS 10.

4 The treatment of goodwill is governed by FRS 10. (*See* Chapter 11.)

5 Minority interests exist when less than 100 per cent of the share capital of a subsidiary is owned at the balance sheet date.

6 All the assets of a subsidiary are included in the consolidated financial statements, even where less than 100 per cent of the share capital has been acquired (*Rule 2*).

7 When a subsidiary has reserves at the date of acquisition, those reserves are treated as part of the capital acquired and the calculation of goodwill includes the relevant proportion of the reserves.

8 When goodwill arises in respect of consolidation of one subsidiary and negative goodwill arises on another, the two amounts should be shown separately in the consolidated financial statements.

Answer to activity

17.1 Rule 1: items in the financial statements of one of the group companies that refer to exactly the same transactions as in the financial statements of one of the other group companies (e.g. a debtor balance in one company's ledger that corresponds to an equal creditor balance in another group company's ledger) need to be cancelled out when the consolidated financial statements are prepared.

Rule 2: all the assets of a subsidiary are included in the consolidated financial statements, even where less than 100 per cent of the share capital has been acquired.

Review questions

Note: In each of these review questions, the amounts have been kept low, so as to enable you to demonstrate an understanding of, and ability to apply, the principles involved.

17.1 The following balance sheets were drawn up immediately after Pai Ltd had acquired control of Filho Ltd. You are to draw up a consolidated balance sheet.

Pai Balance Sheet

	£
Investment in Filh Ltd: 2,200 Ordinary £1 shares	3,200
Stock	1,500
Bank	1,300
	6,000
Share capital – £1 Ordinary shares	6,000

Filho Balance Sheet

	£
Stock	1,600
Bank	600
	2,200
Share capital – £1 Ordinary shares	2,200

17.2 Prepare a consolidated balance sheet from the following balance sheets of Pop Ltd and Son Ltd which were drawn up immediately after Pop Ltd had acquired the share capital of Son Ltd.

Pop Balance Sheet

	£
Investment in Son Ltd: 30,000 £1 Ordinary shares	25,000
Fixed assets	45,000
Stock	12,000
Debtors	6,000
Bank	2,000
	90,000
Share capital – £1 Ordinary shares	90,000

Son Balance Sheet

	£
Fixed assets	20,000
Stock	5,000
Debtors	3,000
Bank	2,000
	30,000
Share capital – £1 Ordinary shares	30,000

→

17.3 Draw up a consolidated balance sheet from the following balance sheets which were drawn up as soon as Pa Ltd had acquired control of Sonny Ltd.

Pa Balance Sheet

	£
Investment in Sonny Ltd: 90,000 Ordinary £1 shares	90,000
Fixed assets	89,000
Stock	54,000
Debtors	34,000
Bank	8,000
	275,000
Share capital – Ordinary £1 shares	275,000

Sonny Balance Sheet

	£
Fixed assets	72,000
Stock	14,000
Debtors	3,000
Bank	1,000
	90,000
Share capital – Ordinary £1 shares	90,000

17.4A Papi Ltd acquired all the shares in Son and Sister Ltd and then the following balance sheets were drawn up. You are to prepare a consolidated balance sheet.

Papi Balance Sheet

	£
Investment in Son and Sister Ltd – Ordinary £1 shares	70,000
Fixed assets	120,000
Stock	32,000
Debtors	26,000
Bank	2,000
	250,000
Share capital – Ordinary £1 shares	250,000

Son and Sister Balance Sheet

	£
Fixed assets	38,000
Stock	9,000
Debtors	2,000
Bank	1,000
	50,000
Share capital – Ordinary £1 shares	50,000

17.5A Draw up a consolidated balance sheet from the balance sheets of Parental Ltd and Sibling Ltd that were drafted immediately after the shares in Sibling Ltd were acquired by Parental Ltd.

Parental Balance Sheet

	£
Investment in Sibling Ltd: 180,000 Ordinary £1 shares	120,000
Fixed assets	60,000
Stock	14,000
Debtors	37,000
Bank	4,000
	235,000
Share capital – Ordinary shares of 50p each	235,000

Sibling Balance Sheet

	£
Fixed assets	110,000
Stock	28,000
Debtors	41,000
Bank	1,000
	180,000
Share capital – Ordinary £1 shares	180,000

17.6 Parent Ltd acquires 60 per cent of the shares in Siblings Together Ltd. Balance sheets are then drafted immediately. You are to draw up the consolidated balance sheet.

Parent Balance Sheet

	£
Investment in Siblings Together Ltd: 12,000 Ordinary £1 shares	25,000
Fixed assets	80,000
Stock	18,000
Debtors	24,000
Bank	3,000
	150,000
Share capital – Ordinary shares of 25p each	150,000

Siblings Together Balance Sheet

	£
Fixed assets	14,000
Stock	3,000
Debtors	1,000
Bank	2,000
	20,000
Share capital – Ordinary £1 shares	20,000

→

17.7 Parents United Ltd acquires 95 per cent of the shares of Son and Friends Ltd. The following balance sheets are then drafted. You are to draw up the consolidated balance sheet.

Parents United Balance Sheet

	£
Investment in Son and Friends Ltd: 15,200 Ordinary £1 shares	13,200
Fixed assets	39,000
Stock	15,600
Debtors	10,200
Bank	2,000
	80,000
Share capital – Ordinary £1 shares	80,000

Son and Friends Balance Sheet

	£
Fixed assets	9,600
Stock	4,300
Debtors	1,700
Bank	400
	16,000
Share capital – Ordinary £1 shares	16,000

17.8A Papa and Mamae Ltd buys $66^2/_3$ per cent of the shares in Son and Daughter Ltd. You are to draw up the consolidated balance sheet from the following balance sheets constructed immediately control had been achieved.

Papa and Mamae Balance Sheet

	£
Investment in Son and Daughter: 12,000 Ordinary £1 shares	10,800
Fixed assets	58,000
Stock	10,200
Debtors	15,900
Bank	5,100
	100,000
Share capital – Ordinary £1 shares	100,000

Son and Daughter Balance Sheet

	£
Fixed assets	8,000
Stock	5,000
Debtors	4,000
Bank	1,000
	18,000
Share capital – Ordinary £1 shares	18,000

17.9A After Pop and Mum Ltd acquired 75 per cent of the shares of Sons and Cousins Ltd the following balance sheets are drawn up. You are to draw up the consolidated balance sheet.

Pop and Mum Balance Sheet

	£
Investments in Sons and Cousins Ltd: 15,000 Ordinary £1 shares	18,000
Fixed assets	45,000
Stock	8,000
Debtors	13,000
Bank	6,000
	90,000
Share capital – Ordinary shares of 10p each	90,000

S Balance Sheet

	£
Fixed assets	12,000
Stock	3,000
Debtors	4,000
Bank	1,000
	20,000
Share capital – Ordinary £1 shares	20,000

17.10 Immediately after Pai and Family Ltd had acquired control of Son One Ltd and Son Two Ltd the following balance sheets were drawn up. You are to draw up a consolidated balance sheet.

Pai and Family Balance Sheet

	£
Investments in subsidiaries:	
Son One Ltd (10,000 Ordinary £1 shares)	16,000
Son Two Ltd (12,000 Ordinary £1 shares)	18,000
Fixed assets	73,000
Current assets	33,000
	140,000
Share capital – Ordinary £1 shares	110,000
Profit and loss account	30,000
	140,000

Son One Balance Sheet

	£
Fixed assets	11,000
Current assets	4,000
	15,000
Share capital – Ordinary £1 shares	10,000
Profit and loss account	2,000
General reserve	3,000
	15,000

→

→

Son Two Balance Sheet

	£
Fixed assets	19,000
Current assets	6,000
	25,000
Share capital – Ordinary £1 shares	15,000
Profit and loss account	6,000
General reserve	4,000
	25,000

17.11 Immediately after Parental Time's Ltd had acquired control of Offspring One Ltd and Offspring Two Ltd the following balance sheets were drawn up. You are to draw up a consolidated balance sheet.

Parental Time's Balance Sheet

	£
Investment in subsidiaries:	
Offspring One Ltd (50,000 Ordinary £1 shares)	110,000
Offspring Two Ltd (50,000 Ordinary 50p shares)	20,000
Fixed assets	210,000
Current assets	60,000
	400,000
Share capital – Ordinary £1 shares	300,000
Profit and loss account	40,000
General reserve	60,000
	400,000

Offspring One Balance Sheet

	£
Fixed assets	80,000
Current assets	40,000
	120,000
Share capital – Ordinary £1 shares	60,000
Profit and loss account	35,000
General reserve	25,000
	120,000

Offspring Two Balance Sheet

	£
Fixed assets	50,000
Current assets	10,000
	60,000
Share capital – Ordinary 50p shares	40,000
Profit and loss account	15,000
General reserve	5,000
	60,000

17.12A Immediately after Pa, Ma and Co Ltd had achieved control of Sub 1 Ltd and Sub 2 Ltd the following balance sheets are drawn up. You are to draw up the consolidated balance sheet.

Pa, Ma and Co Balance Sheet

	£
Investments in subsidiaries:	
Sub 1 Ltd 16,000 £1 Ordinary shares	30,000
Sub 2 Ltd 24,000 £1 Ordinary shares	38,000
Fixed assets	81,000
Current assets	27,000
	176,000
Share capital – Ordinary £1 shares	100,000
Profit and loss account	56,000
General reserve	20,000
	176,000

Sub 1 Balance Sheet

	£
Fixed assets	37,000
Current assets	11,000
	48,000
Share capital – Ordinary £1 shares	16,000
Profit and loss account	18,000
General reserve	14,000
	48,000

Sub 2 Balance Sheet

	£
Fixed assets	29,000
Current assets	13,000
	42,000
Share capital – Ordinary £1 shares	28,000
Profit and loss account	9,000
General reserve	5,000
	42,000

→

→ **17.13A** The following balance sheets of Parents Forever Ltd, Sonny 1 Ltd and Sonny 2 Ltd were drawn up as soon as Parents Forever Ltd had acquired the shares in both subsidiaries. You are to draw up a consolidated balance sheet.

Parents Forever Balance Sheet

	£
Investments in subsidiaries:	
Sonny 1 Ltd 28,000 Ordinary £1 shares	70,000
Sonny 2 Ltd 30,000 Ordinary £1 shares	50,000
Fixed assets	91,000
Current assets	27,000
	238,000
Share capital – Ordinary £1 shares	160,000
Profit and loss account	58,000
General reserve	20,000
	238,000

Sonny 1 Balance Sheet

	£
Fixed assets	62,000
Current assets	23,000
	85,000
Share capital – Ordinary £1 shares	40,000
Profit and loss account	30,000
General reserve	15,000
	85,000

Sonny 2 Balance Sheet

	£
Fixed assets	36,000
Current assets	5,000
	41,000
Share capital – Ordinary £1 shares	30,000
Profit and loss account	9,000
General reserve	2,000
	41,000

You can find a range of additional self-test questions, as well as material to help you with your studies, on the website that accompanies this book at **www.pearsoned.co.uk/wood**

Consolidation of balance sheets: basic mechanics (II)

Learning objectives

After you have studied this chapter, you should be able to:

- explain the implications when the date of acquisition and the group balance sheet date do not coincide
- explain that the calculation of goodwill is performed as at the date of acquisition
- describe the difference in treatment between pre- and post-acquisition reserves of subsidiary undertakings

Introduction

In this chapter, you'll learn that goodwill is calculated on the basis of the financial position at the date of acquisition and that it does not change thereafter. You'll also learn that reserves acquired when an entity is acquired are not available for distribution and you'll learn how to show post-acquisition profits and losses in the consolidated balance sheet and how to calculate any minority interest when there are post-acquisition profits or losses.

18.1 Background

In the previous chapter, the consolidated balance sheets were drawn up immediately the shares in the subsidiary had been acquired. **Even though the consolidation is normally performed at the end of the parent company's accounting period and, thus, frequently some time after the acquisition, it must also be prepared *as at* the time *the acquisition occurred*.** A similar thing must be done with the profit and loss account of the subsidiary and any of the balances on the other reserve accounts which have changed since the date of acquisition.

18.2 Goodwill in later years' financial statements

Goodwill is calculated at the date of acquisition and remains unchanged as the years go by. It is important to remember this. Say, for instance, that the calculation of goodwill was made on an acquisition made on 31 December 2003 and that the goodwill figure was £5,000. Even if the calculation were made one year later, on 31 December 2004, the calculation must use the reserves etc. as on 31 December 2003 as this is when they were acquired, and so the figure of goodwill will always be £5,000. This would be true no matter how much time passed before anyone performed the calculation.

However, in examinations, the goodwill figure may still have to be calculated, even though the consolidated balance sheet being drawn up is 5, 10 or 20 years after the company became a subsidiary. This has to be done because the previous financial statements and notes which show the figure to use are not available to an examinee.

18.3 Capital reserves

As you would expect, when companies purchase their own shares, previous holders of the shares have, effectively, had their investment returned to them and so cease to be shareholders in the company. The company has, in effect, returned some of its capital to those ex-shareholders. Unless special permission has been granted by the court, it is illegal for any company to return its capital to its shareholders in any other way. If a parent undertaking were to pay money to acquire a company as a subsidiary, and then distributed as dividends the assets it had bought, this would be the same as returning its capital to its shareholders and is, therefore, not allowed.

Let's look at an example. P pays £15 to acquire 100 per cent of the shares of S, and the share capital of S consists of £10 of shares and £5 profit and loss account. Thus, to acquire a capital asset (i.e. ownership of S), the holding company has parted with £15. If the balance of the profit and loss account of S were merely added to those of P in the consolidated balance sheet, the £5 balance of S could be regarded as being distributable as cash dividends to the shareholders of P. As this £5 of reserves has been bought as a capital asset, a dividend payment that was in part funded by this £5 of reserves would amount to a return of capital to the shareholders of P.

To prevent this, the balance of the profit and loss account of S on acquisition is capitalised, i.e. it is brought into the balance sheet through the calculation of goodwill and is not shown in the consolidated balance sheet as a profit and loss account balance. On the other hand, the whole of any profit made by S since acquisition will clearly belong to P's shareholders as P owns 100 per cent of the shares of S.

 Activity 18.1   Why do you think it would be a 'bad' thing to distribute as dividends the reserves acquired at the time of acquisition?

Exhibit 18.1

Where the parent undertaking holds 100 per cent of the subsidiary undertaking's shares.

P acquires the shares on 31 December 2004. The balance sheets one year later are as follows:

P Balance Sheet as at 31 December 2005

		£
Investment in subsidiary: 10 shares bought 31.12.2004	(A)	18
Stock		11
Bank		3
		32
Share capital		20
Profit and loss		12
		32

S Balance Sheet as at 31 December 2005

		£	£
Stock			14
Bank			2
			16
Share capital	(B)		10
Profit and loss:			
As at 31.12.2004	(C)	5	
Profit for 2005	(D)	1	
			6
			16

The shares were acquired on 31 December 2004, therefore the calculation of the goodwill is based on the financial position of those firms at that date. Thus P obtained the following for (A) £18 at 31 December 2004: shares (B) £10 and profit and loss (C) £5 = £15. Goodwill therefore amounted to £3. The profit made by S during 2005 was obviously made after acquisition and does not therefore come into the goodwill calculation. The figure of (D) £1 is a reserve which belongs wholly to P, as P in fact owns all of the shares of S. This (D) £1 is added to the reserves shown in the consolidated balance sheet.

P Consolidated Balance Sheet as at 31 December 2005

	£
Goodwill	3
Stock (£11 + £14)	25
Bank (£3 + £2)	5
	33
Share capital	20
Profit and loss (P £12 + S £1)	13
	33

Exhibit 18.2

Where the parent holds 100 per cent of the shares of the subsidiary and there is a post-acquisition loss.

P Balance Sheet as at 31 December 2005

		£	£
Investment in subsidiary:			
10 shares bought 31.12.2004	(E)		19
Stock			10
Bank			4
			33
Share capital			20
Profit and loss:			
As at 31.12.2004		7	
Add Profit 2005		6	
			13
			33

S Balance Sheet as at 31 December 2005

		£	£
Stock			9
Bank			2
			11
Share capital	(F)		10
Profit and loss			
As at 31.12.2004	(G)	4	
Less Loss 2005	(I)	(3)	
			1
			11

In calculating goodwill, the items (F) £10 and (G) £4 are cancelled against the amount paid (E) £19, thus the goodwill is £5. The loss (I) has been incurred since acquisition. A profit since acquisition, as in Exhibit 18.1, adds to the reserves in the consolidated balance sheet, therefore a loss must be deducted.

P Consolidated Balance Sheet as at 31 December 2005

	£
Goodwill	5
Stock (£10 + £9)	19
Bank (£4 + £2)	6
	30
Share capital	20
Profit and loss (£13 − (I)£3)	10
	30

Exhibit 18.3

Where the parent acquires less than 100 per cent of the shares of the subsidiary and there is a post-acquisition profit.

P Balance Sheet as at 31 December 2005

		£	£
Investment in subsidiary: 8 shares bought 31.12.2004	(J)		28
Stock			7
Bank			3
			38
Share capital			20
Profit and loss			
As at 31.12.2004		10	
Add Profit 2005		8	
			18
			38

S Balance Sheet as at 31 December 2005

		£	£
Stock			28
Bank			2
			30
Share capital	(K)		10
Profit and loss			
As at 31.12.2004	(L)	15	
Add Profit 2005	(M)	5	
	(N)		20
			30

P has given (J) £28 to take over 80 per cent of (K) + (L), i.e. 80 per cent of (£10 + £15) = £20. Therefore goodwill is £8. The profit for 2005 (M) £5 is also owned 80 per cent by P = £4, and as this has been earned since the shares in S were bought, the whole of this belongs to the shareholders of P and is also distributable to them, therefore it can be combined with other profit and loss account balances in the consolidated balance sheet.

The minority interest is 20 per cent of (K) £10 + (N) £20 = £6. It must be pointed out that, although the holding company splits up the profit and loss account balances into pre-acquisition and post-acquisition, there is no point in the minority interest doing likewise. It would, however, amount to exactly the same answer if they did, because 20 per cent of (K) £10 + (L) £15 + (M) £5 still comes to £6, i.e. exactly the same as 20 per cent of (N) £20 + (K) £10 = £6.

P Consolidated Balance Sheet as at 31 December 2005

	£
Goodwill	8
Stock (£7 + £28)	35
Bank (£3 + £2)	5
	48
Share capital	20
Profit and loss (P £18 + £4)	22
Minority interest (shares £2 + profit and loss £4):	6
	48

If there had been a post-acquisition loss, then this would have been deducted from P's profit and loss account balance of £18 when the consolidated balance sheet was drawn up.

Learning outcomes

You should now have learnt:

1 Goodwill must be calculated on the basis of the fair values at the date of acquisition of the consideration given and the net assets acquired.

2 Once calculated, there is no point in recalculating the goodwill on an acquisition at a future balance sheet date as the value determined will not alter.

3 Pre-acquisition reserves of a subsidiary are part of the capital acquired and are cancelled out on consolidation; they are not treated as reserves of the group.

4 Pre-acquisition reserves acquired are not available for distribution to the shareholders of the parent company.

5 The group's share of a subsidiary undertaking's post-acquisition profits and losses are included on consolidation with the reserves of the rest of the group.

6 The minority interest amount does not distinguish between pre- and post-acquisition reserves.

Answer to activity

18.1 The £5 reserves acquired by P on acquisition of S were not earned by P and do not represent profits made by P. As such, it would be inappropriate to distribute them in this way.

Review questions

Note: In all these review questions, the share capital of all the companies comprises ordinary shares of £1 each.

18.1 Pop Ltd buys 100 per cent of the shares of Sibling Ltd on 31 December 2002. The balance sheets of the two companies on 31 December 2003 are as shown. You are to draw up a consolidated balance sheet as at 31 December 2003.

Pop Balance Sheet as at 31 December 2003

	£	£
Investment in subsidiary:		
120,000 shares bought 31.12.2002		150,000
Fixed assets		96,000
Current assets		30,000
		276,000
Share capital		100,000
Profit and loss account:		
As at 31.12.2002	102,000	
Add Profit for 2003	64,000	
		176,000
		276,000

Sibling Balance Sheet as at 31 December 2003

	£	£
Fixed assets		106,000
Current assets		46,000
		152,000
Share capital		120,000
Profit and loss account:		
As at 31.12.2002	12,000	
Add Profit for 2003	20,000	
		32,000
		152,000

18.2 Dad and Mum Ltd bought 60 per cent of the shares of Child 1 and 2 Ltd on 31 March 2004. The balance sheets of the two companies on 31 March 2005 are as follows. You are to draw up a consolidated balance sheet as at 31 March 2005.

Dad and Mum Balance Sheet as at 31 March 2005

	£	£
Investment in Child 1 and 2 Ltd:		
105,000 shares bought 31.3.2004		130,000
Fixed assets		154,000
Current assets		22,000
		306,000
Share capital		100,000
Profit and loss account:		
As at 31.3.2004	74,000	
Add Profit for 2005	92,000	
		166,000
General reserve		40,000
		306,000

Child 1 and 2 Balance Sheet as at 31 March 2005

	£	£
Fixed assets		128,000
Current assets		61,000
		189,000
Share capital		150,000
Profit and loss account:		
As at 31.3.2004	30,000	
Less Loss for 2005	(6,000)	
		24,000
General reserve (unchanged since 2001)		15,000
		189,000

→

→ **18.3A** Papai Ltd bought 51 per cent of the shares in Sons and Co Ltd on 31 October 2007. From the following balance sheets you are to draw up the consolidated balance sheet as at 31 October 2008.

Papai Balance Sheet as at 31 October 2008

	£	£
Investment in Sons and Co Ltd: 40,800 shares		60,000
Fixed assets		74,000
Current assets		36,000
		170,000
Share capital		125,000
Profit and loss account:		
As at 31.10.2007	19,000	
Add Profit for 2008	26,000	
		45,000
		170,000

Sons and Co Balance Sheet as at 31 October 2008

	£	£
Fixed assets		91,000
Current assets		19,000
		110,000
Share capital		80,000
Profit and loss account:		
As at 31.10.2007	7,000	
Add Profit for 2008	8,000	
		15,000
General reserve (unchanged since 2007)		15,000
		110,000

18.4 Pops Ltd buys shares in Sub 1 and Sub 2 on 31 December 2007. You are to draft the consolidated balance sheet as at 31 December 2008 from the following:

Pops Balance Sheet as at 31 December 2008

	£	£
Investment:		
Subsidiary 1: 90,000 shares		110,000
Subsidiary 2: 40,000 shares		60,000
Fixed assets		100,000
Current assets		53,000
		323,000
Share capital		200,000
Profit and loss account:		
As at 31.12.2007	55,000	
Add Profit for 2008	48,000	
		103,000
General reserve		20,000
		323,000

Subsidiary 1 Balance Sheet as at 31 December 2008

	£	£
Fixed assets		123,000
Current assets		62,000
		185,000
Share capital		120,000
Profit and loss account:		
As at 31.12.2007	30,000	
Add Profit for 2008	25,000	
		55,000
General reserve (same as 31.12.2007)		10,000
		185,000

Subsidiary 2 Balance Sheet as at 31 December 2008

	£	£
Fixed assets		48,000
Current assets		9,000
		57,000
Share capital		50,000
Profit and loss account:		
As at 31.12.2007	8,000	
Less Loss for 2008	(5,000)	
		3,000
General reserve (same as 31.12.2007)		4,000
		57,000

18.5A P Ltd bought 40,000 shares in S1 Ltd and 27,000 shares in S2 Ltd on 31 December 2002. The following balance sheets were drafted as at 31 December 2003. You are to draw up a consolidated balance sheet as at 31 December 2003.

P Balance Sheet as at 31 December 2003

	£	£
Investments in subsidiaries		
S1 Ltd 40,000 shares		49,000
S2 Ltd 27,000 shares		30,500
Fixed assets		90,000
Current assets		80,500
		250,000
Share capital		200,000
Profit and loss account:		
As at 31.12.2002	11,000	
Add Profit for 2003	16,000	
		27,000
General reserve		23,000
		250,000

→

S1 Balance Sheet as at 31 December 2003

	£	£
Fixed assets		38,200
Current assets		19,200
		57,400
Share capital		50,000
Profit and loss account:		
As at 31.12.2002	3,000	
Less Loss for 2003	(1,600)	
		1,400
General reserve (as at 31.12.2002)		6,000
		57,400

S2 Balance Sheet as at 31 December 2003

	£	£
Fixed assets		31,400
Current assets		14,600
		46,000
Share capital		36,000
Profit and loss account:		
As at 31.12.2002	4,800	
Add Profit for 2003	3,400	
		8,200
General reserve (as at 31.12.2002)		1,800
		46,000

18.6A The following information relates to Heather Limited and its subsidiary, Thistle Limited.

1 *Heather Limited*
Retained profits as at 31 March 2008 £700,000.
80,000 ordinary shares were purchased in Thistle Limited on 1 April 2001 for £150,000.
2 *Thistle Limited*
Retained profits as at 1 April 2001 £50,000.
Retained profits as at 31 March 2008 £120,000.
There were no other capital or revenue account balances at either of these dates.
Issued share capital: 100,000 ordinary shares of £1 each.
3 Goodwill arising on consolidation is written off immediately on acquisition against reserves.

Required:
Make the following calculations:

(*a*) the goodwill arising on the acquisition of Thistle Limited;
(*b*) the retained profits to be shown in the Heather Group balance sheet as at 31 March 2008;
(*c*) the minority interest in the Heather Group as at 31 March 2008.

(*Association of Accounting Technicians*)

You can find a range of additional self-test questions, as well as material to help you with your studies, on the website that accompanies this book at **www.pearsoned.co.uk/wood**

Intercompany dealings: indebtedness and unrealised profit in stocks

Learning objectives

After you have studied this chapter, you should be able to:

- explain how to treat intragroup indebtedness upon consolidation
- explain how to treat unrealised intragroup profits upon consolidation

Introduction

In this chapter, you'll learn how to deal with intragroup debts and unrealised profits in stocks sold between companies in a group, and so learn how to reduce the values shown in individual group financial statements so as to eliminate intragroup items prior to preparation of consolidated financial statements.

19.1 Intragroup debts

When a subsidiary owes money to its parent, the amount owing will be shown as a debtor in the parent's balance sheet and as a creditor in the subsidiary's balance sheet. The Companies Acts require that such debtor and creditor balances are shown separately in the company balance sheets from other debtor and creditor balances. When this type of situation exists it is really just 'two sides of the same coin'. That is, the debtor balance and the creditor balance of the two companies can be paired up and so cancel each other out when consolidated financial statements are prepared. As a result, neither amount is included in the consolidated financial statements.

The same treatment applies to debts owed by the parent to the subsidiary, or to debts owed by one subsidiary to another subsidiary. The treatment is exactly the same whether or not the subsidiary is 100 per cent owned.

Let's look at an example.

Exhibit 19.1

Where the subsidiary owes money to the parent.

P Balance Sheet

		£	£	£
Investment in subsidiary: 10 shares				10
Stock			13	
Debtors:				
Owing from subsidiary	(A)	4		
Other debtors		7		
			11	
Bank			1	
			25	
Less: Creditors			(9)	
				16
				26
Share capital				20
Profit and loss				6
				26

S Balance Sheet

		£	£
Stock			6
Debtors			13
Bank			3
			22
Less: Creditors			
Owing to parent	(B)	4	
Other creditors		8	
			(12)
Net assets			10
Share capital			10

P & S Consolidated Balance Sheet

	£
Stock (£13 + £6)	19
Debtors (£7 + £13)	20
Bank (£1 + £3)	4
	43
Less: Creditors (£9 + £8)	(17)
	26
Share capital	20
Profit and loss	6
	26

19.2 Unrealised profit in stock

Some companies in a group may not trade with each other. If so, the stocks held at the balance sheet date will not include goods bought from another member of the group.

It is also possible that companies within a group may have traded with each other but, at the balance sheet date, all such goods have been sold to individuals and organisations unconnected with the group. The result is that none of the companies in the group will have any such goods included in their year-end stock.

However, when companies in a group have traded with each other, and one or more of the companies has stock at the balance sheet date which has been bought from another group member, adjustments to the stock figure must be made before consolidation is carried out.

If the goods have been traded between members of the group at cost price, the goods would be included in the purchasing company's stock in its balance sheet. In this case, the consolidated balance sheet will not be altered. Because the goods were transferred at cost price it would not be correct to add together all of the stock figures in the group company balance sheets and show the total in the consolidated balance sheet, as the total will represent the total cost to the group of the unsold goods within the group.

However, goods are usually sold between companies within a group at prices above the original cost price paid by the selling company. If one or more of the companies in a group has goods in its stock at the balance sheet date which have been bought from another group member at above cost price, the goods would be included at the higher price in the purchasing company's stock-in-trade in its balance sheet.

 If the amount at which the stock is included in the balance sheet of each company is the amount the stock cost that company, why would the total derived not represent the total cost of the unsold goods within the group?

When you have a situation like that described in Activity 19.1. In this case, you can't simply add together all of the stock figures in the group company balance sheets and show the total in the consolidated balance sheet. The total derived would not represent the total cost of the unsold goods held within the group because it would include the unrealised profit which the selling company added to the cost of the goods when it sold them to the other group company which has those goods in stock at its balance sheet date.

Suppose that the parent, P, owns all the shares in S, the subsidiary, and that P sold goods for £20 to S which had cost P £12. Also assume that S had sold none of these goods by the balance sheet date. In the balance sheet of S, the goods will be included in stock at £20, while the profits made by P will include the £8 profit recorded in buying the goods for £12 and selling them for £20. Although this is true reflection of what occurred from each company's point of view, it most certainly is not true from the perspective of the group. The goods have not passed to anyone outside the group. Therefore, the profit of £8 has not been realised by the group and so must be eliminated from both sets of financial statements before consolidation takes place.

 Why do you think this intragroup profit must be eliminated upon consolidation?

If you are finding this difficult to understand, think back to when you were studying departmental accounts in *Business Accounting UK GAAP 1* and what you needed to do when departments sold goods to each other at above or below cost.

 What could be the benefit to a group if companies within the group were to sell goods to other companies in the group at below cost?

19.3 Realisation of profits

Going back to basic accounting concepts, the realisation concept states that profit should not be recognised until goods have been passed to the customer. You have just learnt that, as consolidated financial statements are concerned with an overall picture of a group, any profits on intragroup sales of goods that have not yet been sold to customers unconnected with the group are unearned and so must be eliminated before consolidation is performed. You saw an example of this in the previous section. Let's now consider some more complex examples.

If P had sold goods which had cost £12 to S, a 100 per cent owned subsidiary, for £20, and S had sold $^3/_4$ of the goods for £22 by the balance sheet date, the situation would obviously be different. P will have included a profit in its profit and loss account for these sales of £8. In addition, S will have shown a profit in its profit and loss account for the sales made of £7, i.e. £22 – $^3/_4$ of £20. The two profit and loss accounts show total profits of £8 + £7 = £15 on these goods.

However, looking at the group as a whole, these goods cost the group £12. Three-quarters of them have been sold to entities unconnected with the group, so that the cost of goods sold outside the group is $^3/_4$ of £12 = £9. As these were sold by S, the profit realised by the group is £22 – £9 = £13. This is £2 less than that shown by adding up the separate figures for each company in the group which, of course, is $^1/_4$ of the profit P charged S. (This is as you would expect because $^1/_4$ of the goods sold by P to S are still held in stock by S.)

Thus, the group figures would be overstated by £2 if the separate figures were merely added together without any adjustment. In addition, the stock would be overvalued by £2 if the stock figures of the two companies were simply added together. The original cost to the group of the goods held in stock by S was $^1/_4$ of £12 = £3. The adjustment needed in the consolidation process involves deducting £2 from the profit and loss balance of P and £2 from the stock of S. Doing so will remove the unrealised intragroup profits. This adjustment can be shown in tabular form as:

		£
(a)	Cost of goods to P	12
(b)	Sold to S for	20
(c)	Sold by S, $^3/_4$ for	22
(d)	Stock of S at balance sheet date at cost to S $^1/_4$ of (b)	5
(e)	Stock of S at balance sheet date at cost to P $^1/_4$ of (a)	3
(f)	Excess of S balance sheet value of stock over cost to group (d) – (e)	2

(g) Profit shown in P profit and loss account (b) – (a) = £8
(h) Profit shown in S profit and loss account (c) £22 – $^3/_4$ of (b) = £7
(i) Profit shown in the profit and loss accounts of P and S = (g) + (h) = £15
(j) Actual profit made by the group dealing with outsiders (c) £22 less [$^3/_4$ of (a) £12] £9 = £13
(k) Profit recorded by individual companies exceeds profit made by the group's dealing with outsiders (i) – (j) = £2

This analysis confirms that the action needed before preparing the consolidated balance sheet is to deduct (f) £2 from the combined stock figure, and to deduct (k) £2 from the combined profit and loss account figure.

Let's apply what you've just learnt by looking at another example.

Exhibit 19.2

Where the stock of one company includes goods bought from another company in the same group.

P Balance Sheet as at 31 December 2003

		£	£
Investment in subsidiary:			
10 shares bought 31.12.2002			16
Stock			24
Bank			6
			46
Share capital			20
Profit and loss account:			
As at 31.12.2002		8	
Profit for 2003	(C)	18	
			26
			46

S Balance Sheet as at 31 December 2003

		£	£
Stock	(D)		22
Bank			3
			25
Share capital			10
Profit and loss account:			
As at 31.12.2002		6	
Profit for 2003		9	
			15
			25

During the year, P sold goods to S for £28. P paid £16 when it purchased the goods. The sale to S therefore resulted in a profit to P of £12. Of these goods, two-thirds had been sold by S at the balance sheet date. The stock of S (D) therefore includes £4 unrealised profit ($1/3 \times £12$). P's profit for the year of (C) £18 also includes £4 unrealised profit. When consolidating the two balance sheets, £4 therefore needs to be deducted from each of those figures.

P Consolidated Balance Sheet as at 31 December 2003

	£
Stock (S £22 − £4 + P £24)	42
Bank (P £6 + S £3)	9
	51
Share capital	20
Profit and loss accounts (S £9 + P £8 + £18 − £4)	31
	51

Note: In Exhibit 19.2, the subsidiary was wholly owned by the parent. The final figures would have been exactly the same if the subsidiary had sold the goods to the parent instead of vice versa.

19.4 Partially-owned subsidiaries and unrealised profits

In Exhibit 19.2 the subsidiary was 100 per cent controlled and the unrealised profit in stock was £4. A few years ago there were three possible methods of dealing with the adjustments needed – two of the methods took into account the actual percentage of shares owned. However, FRS 2 requires that intragroup profits or losses are eliminated in full. As a result, those two proportional elimination methods can no longer be used.

This means that if in Exhibit 19.2, S had been 75 per cent owned by P the full intergroup profit of £4 would still be deducted from the stock amount in the consolidated balance sheet, and the full £4 would also be deducted from the profit and loss account of P when it is consolidated.

 Activity 19.4 Why do you think the rules were changed upon the introduction of FRS 2?

Learning outcomes

You should now have learnt:

1 Intra-group indebtedness must be eliminated upon consolidation, irrespective of the proportion of the holding in the subsidiary undertaking(s) involved.

2 Unrealised intra-group profits must be eliminated upon consolidation, irrespective of the proportion of the holding in the subsidiary undertaking(s) involved.

Answers to activities

19.1 Because the original cost when they were first purchased by a group company was lower. For example, imagine S1 bought £10 of goods from a company that was not part of the group and then sold them to S2 for £12. At the end of the accounting period, S2 still had all those goods in stock so its stock figure in the balance sheet is £12, which is £2 more than the goods cost the group.

19.2 If it wasn't eliminated, groups could show far greater profits than they are actually making. For example, imagine S1 bought £10 of goods from a company that was not part of the group and then sold them to S2 for £12. At the end of the accounting period, S2 still had all those goods in stock so its stock figure in the balance sheet is £12. S1 would include a profit of £2 on these goods in its profit for the period. S2 would include the £12 in its purchases and in its closing stock, resulting in no effect upon its profit. On consolidation, the group would include the £2 profit made by S1 in the group profit for the period.

19.3 They could show far less profit by selling within the group at below cost, so delaying paying tax on some of their profits for a further 12 months.

19.4 By definition, subsidiaries are members of a group because the parent company can exercise a dominant influence over them. Unscrupulous parent companies could, therefore, require less than 100 per cent subsidiaries to purchase goods at above or below cost from other companies in the group and could require them not to sell those goods. Prior to the release of FRS 2, this power could be abused to manipulate profits of the group, as the minority share of the profits and losses could have been included in the profits or losses of the subsidiary and thus the group, making the group appear more or less profitable than it actually was. The change made when FRS 2 was issued eliminated the possibility of including such unrealised profits and losses in the consolidated financial statements.

Review questions

Note: Unless otherwise indicated, the share capital of the companies in these review questions comprises ordinary shares of £1 each.

19.1 Prepare a consolidated balance sheet from the following details as at 31 March 2006.

Pa Balance Sheet as at 31 March 2006

	£	£
Investment in subsidiary: 100,000 shares bought 31.3.2005		55,000
Fixed assets		280,000
		335,000
Stock	44,000	
Debtors	38,000	
Bank	8,000	
	90,000	
Less: Creditors	(11,000)	
		79,000
		414,000
Share capital		175,000
Profit and loss:		
As at 31.3.2005	112,000	
Profit for 2006	97,000	
		209,000
General reserve		30,000
		414,000

Daughter Balance Sheet as at 31 March 2006

	£	£
Fixed assets		55,000
Stock		23,000
Debtors		16,000
Bank		2,000
		96,000
Less: Creditors		(6,000)
		90,000
Share capital: 100,000 shares of 25p each		25,000
Profit and loss:		
As at 31.3.2005	20,000	
Profit for 2006	45,000	
		65,000
		90,000

During the year, Pa sold goods which had cost £1,900 to Daughter for £2,800. None of these goods had been sold by the balance sheet date.

At the balance sheet date Pa owes Daughter £5,000.

→ **19.2** Draw up a consolidated balance sheet as at 31 December 2007 from the following:

Parent Balance Sheet as at 31 December 2007

	£	£
Investment in subsidiary: 110,000 shares bought 31.12.2006		110,000
Fixed assets		248,000
		358,000
Stock	44,000	
Debtors	58,000	
Bank	16,000	
	118,000	
Less: Creditors	(12,000)	
		106,000
		464,000
Share capital		350,000
Profit and loss:		
As at 31.12.2006	168,000	
Less Loss for 2007	(54,000)	114,000
		464,000

Child Balance Sheet as at 31 December 2007

	£	£
Fixed assets		178,000
Stock	54,000	
Debtors	76,000	
Bank	4,000	
	134,000	
Less: Creditors	(6,000)	128,000
		306,000
Share capital		180,000
Profit and loss:		
As at 31.12.2006	72,000	
Profit for 2007	54,000	
		126,000
		306,000

At the balance sheet date, Child owes Parent £3,200.

During the year Parent sold goods which had cost £6,000 to Child for £9,600. One quarter of these goods had been sold by Child by the balance sheet date.

19.3 Prepare a consolidated balance sheet from the following details as at 31 March 2003.

Pops for Filhos Balance Sheet as at 31 March 2003

	£	£
Investment in subsidiaries:		
Sibling A 60,000 shares bought 31.3.2002		75,000
Sibling B 63,000 shares bought 31.3.2003		85,000
		160,000
Fixed assets		94,000
Stock	42,000	
Debtors	16,000	
Bank	11,000	
	69,000	
Less Creditors	(14,000)	
		55,000
		309,000
Share capital		200,000
Profit and loss		
As at 31.3.2002	44,000	
Add Profit for 2003	37,000	
		81,000
General reserve		28,000
		309,000

Filho A Balance Sheet as at 31 March 2003

	£	£
Fixed assets		50,000
Stock	12,000	
Debtors	17,000	
Bank	7,000	
	36,000	
Less Creditors	(8,000)	
		28,000
		78,000
Share capital		60,000
Profit and loss:		
As at 31.3.2002	25,000	
Less Loss for 2003	(12,000)	
		13,000
General reserve (as at 31.3.2002)		5,000
		78,000

→

→

Filho B Balance Sheet as at 31 March 2003

	£	£
Fixed assets		70,000
Stock	26,000	
Debtors	22,000	
Bank	8,000	
	56,000	
Less Creditors	(14,000)	42,000
		112,000
Share capital		70,000
Profit and loss:		
As at 31.3.2002	20,000	
Add Profit for 2003	22,000	
		42,000
		112,000

At the balance sheet date, Filho B owed Filho A £3,000 and Pops for Filhos owed Filho B £2,000.
    During the year, Pops for Filhos had sold to Filho A for £4,000 goods costing £3,600. Of these goods, one-quarter had been sold by the year end. Pops for Filhos had also sold goods costing £600 to Filho B for £900, of which none had been sold by the year end.

19.4A   You are presented with the following information from the Seneley group of companies for the year to 30 September 2006:

	Seneley plc £000	Lowe Ltd £000	Wright Ltd £000
Tangible fixed assets	225	300	220
Investments			
Shares in group companies:			
Lowe Ltd	450	–	–
Wright Ltd	130	–	–
	580	–	–
Current assets			
Stocks	225	150	45
Trade debtors	240	180	50
Cash at bank and in hand	50	10	5
	515	340	100
Creditors: amounts falling due within one year			
Trade creditors	(320)	(90)	(70)
Net current assets	195	250	30
	1,000	550	250
Capital and reserves			
Called-up share capital	800	400	200
Profit and loss	200	150	50
	1,000	550	250

Additional information:
(a) The authorised, issued and fully paid share capital of all three companies consists of £1 ordinary shares.
(b) Seneley purchased 320,000 shares in Lowe Ltd on 1 October 2003, when Lowe's profit and loss account balance stood at £90,000.

(c) Seneley purchased 140,000 shares in Wright Ltd on 1 October 2005, when Wright's profit and loss account balance stood at £60,000.

(d) During the year to 30 September 2006, Lowe had sold goods to Wright for £15,000. These goods had cost Lowe £7,000, and Wright still had half of these goods in stock as at 30 September 2006. Minority interests are not charged with their share of any unrealised stock profits.

(e) Included in the respective trade creditor and trade debtor balances as at 30 September 2006 were the following intercompany debts:
● Seneley owed Wright £5,000
● Lowe owed Seneley £20,000
● Wright owed Lowe £25,000.

(f) Seneley does not amortise goodwill arising on consolidation.

Required:
Prepare the Seneley group's consolidated balance sheet as at 30 September 2006. Your workings should be submitted.

(*Association of Accounting Technicians*)

19.5A You are to draw up a consolidated balance sheet as at 31 December 2005 from the following:

Pa and Mum Balance Sheet as at 31 December 2005

	£	£
Investment in subsidiaries:		
Son 1 90,000 shares bought 31.12.2004		125,000
Son 2 56,000 shares bought 31.12.2004		85,000
		210,000
Fixed assets		170,000
Stock	43,000	
Debtors	38,000	
Bank	17,000	
	98,000	
Creditors	(16,000)	82,000
		462,000
Share capital		325,000
Profit and loss:		
As at 31.12.2004	53,000	
Less Loss for 2005	(16,000)	
		37,000
General reserve (as at 31.12.2004)		100,000
		462,000

Son 1 Balance Sheet as at 31 December 2005

	£	£
Fixed assets		72,000
Stock	34,000	
Debtors	21,000	
Bank	18,000	
	73,000	
Creditors	(6,000)	67,000
		139,000
Share capital		90,000
Profit and loss:		
As at 31.12.2004	23,000	
Add Profit for 2005	26,000	
		49,000
		139,000

→

Son 2 Balance Sheet as at 31 December 2004

	£	£
Fixed assets		80,000
Stock	24,000	
Debtors	26,000	
Bank	13,000	
	63,000	
Creditors	(8,000)	55,000
		135,000
Share capital		100,000
Profit and loss:		
As at 31.12.2004	27,000	
Less Loss for 2005	(4,000)	
		23,000
General reserve (as at 31.12.2004)		12,000
		135,000

At the balance sheet date, Son 1 owed Pa and Mum £2,500 and Son 2 £1,100, and Pa and Mum owed Son 2 £2,100.

Pa and Mum had sold goods which had cost £1,400 to Son 2 for £2,100, and of these goods one-half had been sold by Son 2 by the year end.

19.6 The following summarised information relates to the Pagg group of companies.

Balance Sheet at 31 March 2010

	Pagg plc £000	Ragg Ltd £000	Tagg Ltd £000
Tangible fixed assets at net book value	2,000	900	600
Investments			
800,000 ordinary shares in Ragg Ltd	3,000	–	–
300,000 ordinary shares in Tagg Ltd	1,000	–	–
	4,000	–	–
Current assets			
Stocks	1,300	350	100
Debtors	3,000	200	300
Cash	200	20	50
	4,500	570	450
Current liabilities			
Creditors	(4,000)	(270)	(400)
	6,500	1,200	650
Capital and reserves			
Called-up share capital (all ordinary shares of £1 each)	5,500	1,000	500
Profit and loss	1,000	200	150
	6,500	1,200	650

Additional information:
1 Pagg acquired its shareholding in Ragg Ltd on 1 April 2005. Ragg's profit and loss account balance at that time was £600,000.
2 The shares in Tagg Ltd were acquired on 1 April 2009 when Tagg's profit and loss account balance was £100,000.
3 All goodwill arising on consolidation is amortised in equal amounts over a period of 20 years commencing from the date of acquisition of each subsidiary company.

4 At 31 March 2010, Ragg had in stock goods purchased from Tagg at a cost to Ragg of £60,000. These goods had been invoiced by Tagg at cost plus 20 per cent. Minority interests are not charged with any intercompany profit.

5 Intercompany debts at 31 March 2010 were as follows: Pagg owed Ragg £200,000 and Ragg owed Tagg £35,000.

Required:
In so far as the information permits, prepare the Pagg group of companies' consolidated balance sheet as at 31 March 2010 in accordance with the Companies Acts and standard accounting practice.

Note: Formal notes to the accounts are NOT required, although detailed working must be submitted with your answer.

(Association of Chartered Certified Accountants)

19.7A You are presented with the following summarised information relating to Block plc for the year to 30 September 2008:

	Block plc £000	Chip Ltd £000	Knot Ltd £000
Fixed assets	8,900	3,240	2,280
Investments			
Shares in group companies:			
Chip Ltd	2,500	–	–
Knot Ltd	1,600	–	–
	4,100	–	–
Current assets			
Stocks	300	160	80
Trade debtors	1,600	130	50
Cash at bank and in hand	400	110	120
	2,300	400	250
Creditors: amounts falling due within one year			
Trade creditors	(300)	(140)	(130)
	15,000	3,500	2,400
Capital and reserves			
Called-up share capital (ordinary shares of £1 each)	10,000	3,000	2,000
Profit and loss	5,000	500	400
	15,000	3,500	2,400

Additional information:

1 Block purchased 80 per cent of the share capital of Chip on 1 October 2003 when Chip's profit and loss account balance was £200,000 credit.

2 On 1 October 2007 Block purchased 60 per cent of the share capital of Knot. Knot's profit and loss account balance at that date was £500,000 credit.

3 Goodwill is not amortised.

4 During the year to 30 September 2008, Block sold goods costing £200,000 to Chip for £300,000. Half of these goods remained in stock at the year end.

5 Intercompany debts at the year end were as follows:

	£000
Chip owed Block	20
Knot owed Chip	30

Required:
Prepare the Block plc group of companies' consolidated balance sheet as at 30 September 2008. Formal notes to the accounts are NOT required, although detailed working should be submitted with your answer.

(Association of Chartered Certified Accountants)

Consolidated financial statements: acquisition of shares in subsidiaries at different dates

Learning objectives

After you have studied this chapter, you should be able to:

● calculate goodwill when an interest in a subsidiary undertaking was acquired in blocks over a period of time
● calculate goodwill when a subsidiary undertaking was acquired part-way through its accounting period

Introduction

In this chapter, you'll learn how to deal with piecemeal acquisitions, i.e. those situations where a subsidiary is acquired through a series of transactions. You will also learn how to calculate goodwill and pre-acquisition profits when a subsidiary is acquired part-way through its accounting period. In order to focus on the principles involved, we will use the threshold of ownership of over 50 per cent of the share capital acquired to determine when the acquired company becomes a subsidiary.

20.1 Shares bought at different dates

Up to this point, the shares in subsidiaries have all been bought at one point in time for each company. However, it is a simple fact that shares are often bought in blocks at different times, and that the earlier purchases may not give the buyer a controlling interest. This is known as 'piecemeal acquisition'.

There used to be two possible methods of calculating pre-acquisition profits, and therefore goodwill. However, FRS 2 states that only one method should be used, and this is the method used in this book. FRS 2 requires that the consolidation be based on the fair values at the date the undertaking actually becomes a subsidiary, even though the acquisition has been made in stages.

> **Activity 20.1** Why do you think you are not allowed to calculate and then recognise goodwill in the financial statements at each stage of acquisition?

Let's look at an example of piecemeal acquisitions.

A company, S, has an issued share capital of 100 ordinary shares of £1 each. The only reserve of S is the balance on the profit and loss account which was £50 on 31 December 2004, and two years later on 31 December 2006, it was £80. P buys 20 shares on 31 December 2004 for £36, and a further 40 shares on 31 December 2006 for £79. The date that S became a subsidiary was therefore 31 December 2006. The calculation of goodwill becomes:

Overall	£	£
Paid 31.12.2004	36	
Paid 31.12.2006	79	
		115
Shares bought (20 + 40)	60	
Profit and loss account of subsidiary (60% of £80)	48	
		(108)
Goodwill on acquisition		7
Comprising: 31.12.2004: £36 – (20% of £100 + 50 = £30)	=	6
31.12.2006: £79 – (40% of £100 + 80 = £72)	=	7
		13
Post-first purchase profits 31.12.2004 to 31.12.2006 (20% of £30)		(6)*
		7

*This is also the amount of goodwill avoided by delaying acquisition until 31.17.2006.

20.2 Shares bought during an accounting period

In addition, it has been conveniently assumed so far that all shares have been bought exactly on the last day of an accounting period. In reality, this is seldom the case. Most shares are bought part-way through an accounting period. Unless specially audited financial statements are drawn up as at the date of acquisition there is no up-to-date profit and loss account as at the date of acquisition. As this amount is needed for the calculation of goodwill, some other method must be used to obtain it.

The approach adopted is that the profit and loss balance according to the last balance sheet before the acquisition of the shares is taken, and an addition made (or deduction, if a loss) corresponding to the proportion of the year's profits that had been earned before acquisition took place. This is then taken as the figure of pre-acquisition profits for goodwill and capital reserve calculations.

Let's look at an example:

Exhibit 20.1

Calculation of pre-acquisition profits, and goodwill, where the shares are bought part-way through an accounting period.

P bought 20 of the 30 issued ordinary shares of S for £49 on 30 September 2005. The financial statements for S are drawn up annually to 31 December. The balance sheet of S as at 31 December 2004 showed a balance on the profit and loss account of £24. The profit and loss account of S for the year ending 31 December 2005 disclosed a profit of £12.

	£	£
Shares bought		20
Profit and loss account:		
Balance at 31.12.2004	24	
Add Proportion of 2005 profits before acquisition $^9/_{12} \times £12$	9	
	33	
Proportion of pre-acquisition profits		
20 shares owned out of 30, $^2/_3 \times £33$		22
		42

Paid for shares £49
Therefore goodwill is £49 – £42 = £7

Note: It may seem odd but, despite its name, goodwill is something parent undertakings seek to avoid. When on the date of acquisition goodwill is nil or negative, this is 'good'; the parent has done well. If goodwill on that date is positive, the parent has paid more than the net assets are worth. Put crudely, this is 'bad'. Of course, parent undertakings do not acquire subsidiaries without reason. Positive goodwill will be considered 'acceptable' by the parent undertaking that allows it to arise. Future foreseen benefits make it seem worthwhile. Nevertheless, such future benefits carry a risk of non-arrival. Hence positive goodwill is not something a parent undertaking seeks.

Learning outcomes

You should now have learnt:

1 When an interest in a subsidiary undertaking is acquired in blocks over a period of time, goodwill is calculated as if all the blocks had been purchased at the date when control was achieved.

2 When a subsidiary undertaking is acquired part-way through its accounting period, in the absence of specially audited financial statements, the proportion of profit (or loss) applicable to that part of the financial period that preceded the acquisition date should be treated as being part of the pre-acquisition reserves for the calculation of goodwill upon consolidation.

Answer to activity

20.1 The subsidiary was actually acquired only when control passed to the parent company. As goodwill is to be calculated when that happens, it could be considered to be inappropriate to calculate and recognise parts of it at an earlier date. However, failure to calculate fair values of the net assets acquired and the goodwill arising each time the shareholding was increased would result in the true make-up of the final goodwill (i.e. the overall goodwill at the date of acquisition) not being known, by calculating goodwill after each transaction, it can be seen when each element of the overall goodwill arose. This might be useful, for example, if goodwill had dropped on the final transaction (good) or had suddenly risen (bad). Remember, goodwill is something a parent wishes to avoid.

Review questions

20.1 On 31 March 2003, Son Ltd had issued share capital of 75,000 ordinary £1 shares and reserves of £40,000. Two years later, the reserves had risen to £60,000 but the share capital was unchanged. Pa Ltd purchased shares in Son Ltd: (i) 20,000 shares on 31 March 2003 for £34,000 and (ii) 30,000 shares on 31 March 2005 for £48,000. Calculate the figure for goodwill that will appear in the consolidated balance sheet as at 31 March 2005.

20.2A On 31 October 2004, its balance sheet date, Sons and Daughters Ltd had issued share capital of 600,000 ordinary £1 shares and reserves of £340,000. Four years later, the share capital is unchanged but the reserves have risen to £420,000. Pai Ltd purchased 150,000 shares in Sons and Daughters Ltd on 31 October 2004 for £260,000. On 31 October 2008, it paid £650,000 for another 300,000 shares. Calculate the goodwill to be shown in the consolidated balance sheet as at 31 October 2008.

20.3 Pop and Mom Ltd bought 120,000 of the 200,000 issued ordinary £1 shares of Sonny Ltd for £300,000 on 31 July 2004. Sonny Ltd financial statements are drawn up annually to 31 December. The balance sheet of Sonny Ltd on 31 December 2003 showed a balance on the profit and loss account of £62,000. The profit and loss account of Sonny Ltd for the year ending 31 December 2004 showed a profit of £69,000. No other reserves appear in either balance sheet. Calculate the figure for the goodwill to be shown in the consolidated balance sheet as at 31 December 2004.

20.4A On 1 January 2008, Sons and Co Ltd had an issued share capital of 200,000 ordinary £1 shares. The balance on the profit and loss account was £20,000 and there was also a general reserve of £16,000. During the year ended 31 December 2008, Sons and Co Ltd made a profit of £24,000, none of which was distributed. Pop Ltd bought 175,000 shares on 1 April 2008 for £240,000. Calculate the figure of goodwill to be shown in the consolidated balance sheet as at 31 December 2008.

Chapter

21

Intra-group dividends

Learning objectives

After you have studied this chapter, you should be able to:

● explain how to treat intra-group dividends

● explain how to treat dividends from a newly acquired subsidiary undertaking that were proposed prior to the acquisition date

● explain how to treat dividends proposed by subsidiary undertakings at the balance sheet date

Introduction

In this chapter, you'll learn how to treat dividends that have been received from a subsidiary and dividends that have been proposed by a subsidiary but not received at the end of the accounting period. You'll learn how to deal with dividends paid by a subsidiary out of pre-acquisition profits as compared with dividends paid by a subsidiary out of post-acquisition profits. You will also learn how to treat dividends proposed by a subsidiary at the acquisition date. Finally, you will learn how to treat dividends paid by non-wholly-owned subsidiaries.

21.1 Dividends paid from post-acquisition profits

Intra-group dividends are dividends paid by one member of a group to another, i.e. from one company in the group to another in the same group. They will, therefore, be shown in the receiving company's profit and loss account as investment income, with a subsequent increase in the bank balance. From the point of view of the paying company's financial statements, the dividend will appear in the note on movements in Shareholders' Funds as a deduction from reserves (normally its profit and loss account), thus reducing the balance on the reserves used. Also, when paid, there will be a reduction in the bank balance of that company.

If the dividend has been proposed, but not paid by the end of the accounting period, the proposed dividend appears only as a note to the financial statements of the company intending to make the payment. It does not appear anywhere in the notes or financial statements of the recipient company. No set-off is therefore required on dividends proposed.

Activity 21.1

What would be the impact upon the consolidated financial statements if the dividend had been paid before the end of the subsidiary's accounting period rather than simply being proposed?

335

21.2 Dividends paid from pre-acquisition profits

In Chapter 18, you learnt of the company law principle that dividends should not be paid out of capital. To prevent this happening, any pre-acquisition profits are capitalised and brought into the goodwill calculation. A company cannot circumvent the principle by buying the shares of a company, part of the purchase price being for the reserves of the subsidiary, and then utilising those reserves by paying itself dividends, and consequently adding those dividends to its own profits and then declaring an increased dividend itself. The next two exhibits illustrate this. Exhibit 21.1 shows an example of dividends paid from post-acquisition profits. Exhibit 21.2 shows what occurs when dividends are paid from pre-acquisition profits.

Exhibit 21.1

Dividends paid from post-acquisition profits.

P buys 100 per cent of the shares of S on 31 December 2004. In 2005, S pays a dividend of 50 per cent to P. To simplify matters, the dividend is declared for 2005 and paid in 2005.

P Balance Sheet as at 31 December 2004

	£
Investment in subsidiary:	
10 shares bought 31.12.2004	23
Stock	3
Bank	1
	27
Share capital	20
Profit and loss account	7
	27

S Balance Sheet as at 31 December 2004

	£
Stock	16
Bank	6
	22
Share capital	10
Profit and loss account	12
	22

Consolidated Balance Sheet as at 31 December 2004
(immediately after acquisition)

	£
Goodwill (P £23 – S £10 – S £12)	1
Stock	19
Bank (P £1 + S £6)	7
	27
Share capital	20
Profit and loss account	7
	27

This consolidated balance sheet was drafted immediately after acquisition of S by P. The following balance sheets show the position one year later. Remember, the calculation of goodwill does not alter.

One year later, the balance sheets are as follows:

P Balance Sheet as at 31 December 2005

	£	£
Investment in subsidiary:		
10 shares bought 31.12.2004		23
Stock		11
Bank		_1_
		35
Share capital		20
Profit and loss account:		
As at 31.12.2004	7	
Add Profit for 2005 (including dividend of £5 from S)	_8_	
		_15_
		35

S Balance Sheet as at 31 December 2005

	£	£	£
Stock			19
Bank			_7_
			26
Share capital			10
Profit and loss account:			
As at 31.12.2004		12	
Profit for 2005	9		
Less Dividend paid (to P)	(_5_)		
		_4_	
			_16_
			26

    To assess whether a dividend is paid out of pre- or post-acquisition reserves, we use the LEFO principle: **L**ast profits **E**arned are **F**irst profits **O**ut. The dividend of £5, therefore, has been paid out of profits made since the acquisition by P. The dividend can, therefore, be treated as being from post-acquisition profits and can, therefore, be shown in the profit and loss account of P as investment income so increasing the profits of P available for dividend purposes.

Consolidated Balance Sheet as at 31 December 2005

	£
Goodwill (£23 − £10 − £12)	1
Stock (P £11 + S £19)	30
Bank (P £1 + S £7)	_8_
	39
Share capital	20
Profit and loss account:	
[P £7 + £8 + S (£16 − £12 = £4)]	_19_
	39

Exhibit 21.2

Dividends paid from pre-acquisition profits.

Once again, P buys 100 per cent of the shares of S on 31 December 2004 and S pays a dividend for 2005 of 50 per cent to P during 2005. However, in this case, S makes neither a profit nor a loss in 2005.

The balance sheets at 31 December 2004 are obviously the same as in Exhibit 21.1. However, the balance sheets a year later are now:

P Balance Sheet as at 31 December 2005

	£	£
Investment in subsidiary:		
(£23 originally calculated less dividend from pre-acquisition profits £5)		18
Stock		11
Bank		1
		30
Share capital		20
Profit and loss account:		
As at 31.12.2004	7	
Add Profit for 2005 (does not include the dividend from S)	3	
		10
		30

S Balance Sheet as at 31 December 2005

	£	£
Stock		15
Bank		2
		17
Share capital		10
Profit and loss account:		
As at 31.12.2004	12	
Add Profit for 2005*	0	
Less Dividend paid (to P)	(5)	
		7
		17

*For simplicity, the profit of S for 2005 is taken as being exactly nil.

Consolidated Balance Sheet as at 31 December 2005

	£
Goodwill	1
Stock	26
Bank	3
	30
Share capital	20
Profit and loss	10
	30

When a dividend is paid by a subsidiary out of pre-acquisition profits it is, in fact, a return of capital to the parent company. Accordingly, the dividend is deducted from the original cost of the investment – it is a return of the purchase money – rather than being treated as investment income of the holding company.

Note: Examiners are always trying to identify the better candidates and award them marks to match their abilities. A common 'trick' used by some examiners is to treat the receipt as investment income instead of a refund of capital. Thus, the balance sheet of P as at 31 December 2005 in Exhibit 21.2 would have read 'Profit and loss account £15' instead of 'Profit and loss account £10', and the investment would be shown at £23 instead of £18. The examiner wants the candidate to demonstrate an awareness of the error in the balance sheet by adjusting it to show the correct amounts before proceeding with the consolidation of the balance sheets of P and S.

21.3 Dividends proposed at date of acquisition of shares

Sometimes when a company is acquired, it has already proposed but not yet paid a dividend. As a result, the new parent will receive the dividend even though it was paid from profits earned before acquisition took place. Clearly, the dividend is from pre-acquisition reserves. The action taken is similar to that in Exhibit 21.2: in that the dividend received is deducted from the price paid for the shares so that the net effective price paid may be calculated.

Exhibit 21.3

Shares acquired in a subsidiary at a date when the acquired company has declared a proposed dividend which has not yet been paid.

Parent Balance Sheet as at 31 December 2003

	£	£
Investment in subsidiary:		
10 shares bought 31.12.2002	24	
Less Dividend from pre-acquisition profits	(6)	
		18
Stock		9
Bank		2
		29
Share capital		20
Profit and loss account:		
As at 31.12.2002	4	
Profit for 2003	5	
		9
		29

Subsidiary Balance Sheet as at 31 December 2003

	£	£
Stock		19
Bank		4
		23
Share capital		10
Profit and loss account:		
As at 31.12.2002	11	
Less Dividend paid during 2003	(6)	
	5	
Add Profit for 2003	8	
		13
		23

→

→
Consolidated Balance Sheet as at 31 December 2003

	£	£
Goodwill*		3
Stock		28
Bank		6
		37
Share capital		20
Profit and loss account: (P £9 + S £8)		17
		37

Calculation of goodwill	£	£
Paid		24
Less Shares acquired	10	
Profit and loss balance at 31.12.2002	11	
		(21)
Goodwill		3
or,		
Paid		24
Less Dividend from pre-acquisition reserves		(6)
		18
Shares acquired	10	
Profit and loss balance at 31.12.2002	11	
Less Dividend paid during 2003	(6)	
	5	
		(15)
Goodwill		3

Note: Goodwill is the same irrespective of how much of pre-acquisition dividends are paid.

Learning outcomes

You should now have learnt:

1 Intra-group dividends paid out of post-acquisition reserves will not appear in the consolidated financial statements, the entries in the individual company financial statements cancelling out upon consolidation.

2 Dividends from a newly acquired subsidiary that were declared prior to the date of acquisition are treated as repayment of capital and the investment in the subsidiary in the parent company balance sheet is reduced by the amount received.

3 Dividends proposed by the subsidiary undertaking that are unpaid at the balance sheet date will not appear in the financial statements of the parent and will appear only as a note to the financial statements of the subsidiary.

Answers to activities

21.1 If the dividend has been paid, so far as the balance sheets are concerned, the bank balance of the subsidiary has decreased while the bank balance of the parent has increased. The profit and loss account reserve of the subsidiary have been reduced while the profit and loss account reserve of the parent have risen. These all offset each other and have no impact upon the consolidated financial statements.

Review questions

Note: Unless otherwise indicated, the share capital of all the companies in these review questions comprises ordinary £1 shares.

21.1 The following balance sheets were drawn up as at 31 March 2005. The person drafting the balance sheet of Parent Ltd was not too sure of an item and has shown it as a suspense amount.

Parent Ltd Balance Sheet as at 31 March 2005

	£	£
Investment in subsidiary:		
50,000 shares bought 31.3.2004		68,000
Fixed assets		70,000
Current assets		9,000
		147,000
Share capital		100,000
Profit and loss:		
As at 31.3.2004	15,000	
Add Profit for 2005	24,000	
		39,000
Suspense*		8,000
		147,000

*The suspense item consists of the 2004 dividend received in June 2004 from Subsidiary Ltd

Subsidiary Ltd Balance Sheet as at 31 March 2005

	£	£
Fixed assets		36,000
Current assets		30,000
		66,000
Share capital		50,000
Profit and loss:		
As at 31.3.2004*	7,000	
Add Profit for year to 31.3.2005	9,000	
		16,000
		66,000

*The balance of £7,000 is after deducting the dividend for 2004 of £8,000.

Required:
Draw up the consolidated balance sheet as at 31 March 2005.

21.2A The following balance sheets of Pop Ltd and Son Ltd were drawn up as at 31 December 2007. Draw up the consolidated balance sheet as at that date.

Pop Ltd Balance Sheet as at 31 December 2007

	£	£
Investment in subsidiary:		
80,000 shares bought 31.12.2006		160,000
Fixed assets		200,000
Current assets		60,000
		420,000
Share capital		300,000
Profit and loss:		
As at 31.12.2006	74,000	
Add Profit for 2007*	46,000	
		120,000
		420,000

*The profit figure for 2007 includes the dividend of £25,000 received from Son Ltd for the year 2006.

Son Ltd Balance Sheet as at 31 December 2007

	£	£
Fixed assets		79,000
Current assets		47,000
		126,000
Share capital		80,000
Profit and loss:		
As at 31.12.2006*	16,000	
Add Profit for 2007	30,000	
		46,000
		126,000

*The balance of £16,000 is after deducting the dividend for 2006 of £25,000.

21.3 Draw up a consolidated balance sheet as at 31 October 2003 from the following information.

Pa and Ma Ltd Balance Sheet as at 31 October 2003

	£	£
Investment in subsidiary: 42,000 shares bought 31.10.2002		70,000
Fixed assets		60,000
Current assets		18,000
		148,000
Share capital		100,000
Profit and loss:		
As at 31.10.2002	35,000	
Add Profit for year to 31.10.2003	13,000	
		48,000
		148,000

Son and Daughter Ltd Balance Sheet as at 31 October 2003

	£	£
Fixed assets		42,000
Current assets		36,000
		78,000
Share capital		60,000
Profit and loss:		
As at 31.10.2002	7,000	
Add Profit for 2003	20,000	
	27,000	
Less Dividend paid 2003	(9,000)	
		18,000
		78,000

Note: The dividend of Son and Daughter is for 2003 but has not yet been brought into the ledgers of Pa and Ma Ltd as the accountant was unsure what entries should be made.

21.4A   The balance sheets of Pops Ltd and Sons Ltd are as follows:

Pops Ltd Balance Sheet as at 31 December 2008

	£	£
Investment in subsidiary: 195,000 shares bought 31.12.2007		380,000
Fixed assets		240,000
Current assets		92,000
		712,000
Share capital		600,000
Profit and loss:		
As at 31.12.2007	72,000	
Add Profit for 2008	40,000	
		112,000
		712,000

Sons Ltd Balance Sheet as at 31 December 2008

	£	£
Fixed assets		270,000
Current assets	120,000	
Less Current liabilities	(50,000)	
		70,000
Net assets		340,000
Share capital		300,000
Profit and loss:		
As at 31.12.2007	62,000	
Less Loss for 2008	(22,000)	
		40,000
		340,000

Required:
Prepare the consolidated balance sheet as at 31 December 2008.

21.5 The following are the summarised balance sheets of P Ltd and S Ltd at 31 December 2006.

	P Limited £	P Limited £	S Limited £	S Limited £
Tangible fixed assets (*see* Note (*a*))		320,000		360,000
Loan to S Ltd		50,000		
Investment in S Ltd		250,000		
Current assets				
Stocks	110,000		50,000	
Debtors	98,000		40,000	
Loan interest	2,000			
Bank	30,000		10,000	
		240,000		100,000
Creditors: amounts falling due within one year				
Trade creditors	190,000		28,000	
Loan interest	–		2,000	
		(190,000)		(30,000)
Total assets *less* current liabilities		670,000		430,000
Long-term liability – Loan from P Ltd		–		(50,000)
		670,000		380,000
Capital and reserves:				
Ordinary shares of £1 each, fully paid		500,000		200,000
8% preference shares of £1 each, fully paid		–		100,000
Reserves		170,000		80,000
		670,000		380,000

Notes:
(a) Tangible fixed assets
P Limited

	Cost £	Cumulative depreciation £	WDV £
Buildings	120,000	10,000	110,000
Plant and machinery	200,000	40,000	160,000
Motor vehicles	80,000	30,000	50,000
	400,000	80,000	320,000

Tangible fixed assets
S Limited

	Cost £	Cumulative depreciation £	WDV £
Buildings	300,000	100,000	200,000
Plant and machinery	120,000	30,000	90,000
Motor vehicles	130,000	60,000	70,000
	550,000	190,000	360,000

There were no additions or disposals of fixed assets by the group during the year.
(*b*) P Limited acquired its holding on 1 January 2006, when the balance on S Limited's reserves stood at £50,000. The investment consists of 150,000 ordinary shares of £1 each, fully paid, purchased for £250,000.
(*c*) P Limited included in its profit and loss account a dividend of £7,500 from S Limited in March 2006, in respect of the shares acquired on 1 January 2006. S Limited does not intend to pay an ordinary dividend for the year ended 31 December 2006.

Required:
Prepare a consolidated balance sheet for P Limited and its subsidiary S Limited at 31 December 2006.

Note: Ignore taxation.

(*Chartered Institute of Management Accountants*)

21.6 X plc acquired 80 per cent of the ordinary share capital of Y plc on 1 January 2006 for £300,000. The lists of balances of the two companies at 31 December 2006 were as follows:

	X plc £000	Y plc £000
Called-up share capital:		
400,000 ordinary shares of £1 each, fully paid	400	
300,000 ordinary shares of £0.50 each, fully paid		150
Reserves as at 1 January 2006	220	90
Retained profits for 2006	40	28
Trade creditors	130	80
Taxation	30	14
Depreciation provisions:		
Freehold property	12	6
Plant and machinery	40	12
Current account		14
	872	394
Tangible fixed assets:		
Freehold property, at cost	120	160
Plant and machinery, at cost	183	62
Investment in Y plc	300	
Stocks	80	70
Debtors	160	90
Bank	10	12
Current account	19	
	872	394

Notes:
(a) A remittance of £2,000 from Y plc to X plc in December 2006 was not received by X plc until January 2007.
(b) Goods, with an invoice value of £3,000, were despatched by X plc in December 2006 but not received by Y plc until January 2007. The profit element included in this amount was £400.
(c) Included in the stock of Y plc at 31 December 2006 were goods purchased from X plc for £10,000. The profit element included in this amount was £2,000.
(d) No interim dividend was paid in 2006 by either company.
(e) Current accounts are the intragroup balances outstanding.
(f) Goodwill is not amortised.
(g) Y plc has proposed a dividend of £10,000 be paid. It is unpaid at 31 December 2006 and is not provided for in the above trial balances.

Required:
Prepare a consolidated balance sheet for X plc and its subsidiary Y plc as at 31 December 2006.

(*Chartered Institute of Management Accountants*)

→

→ **21.7A** P plc acquired 80 per cent of the ordinary share capital of S plc for £150,000 and 50 per cent of the issued 10 per cent cumulative preference shares for £10,000, both purchases being effected on 1 May 2007. There have been no changes in the issued share capital of S plc since that date. The following balances are taken from the books of the two companies at 30 April 2008:

	P plc £000	S plc £000
Ordinary share capital (£1 shares)	300	100
10% cumulative preference shares (50p shares)	–	20
Share premium account	20	10
General reserve	68	15
Profit and loss account	65	45
Trade creditors	35	22
Taxation	50	30
Depreciation		
Freehold property	40	15
Plant and machinery	100	48
	678	305
Freehold property at cost	86	55
Plant and machinery at cost	272	168
Investment in S plc	160	–
Stocks	111	65
Debtors	30	15
Cash	19	2
	678	305

The following additional information is available:

(a) Stocks of P plc include goods purchased from S plc for £20,000. S plc charged out these stocks at cost plus 25 per cent.

(b) Proposed dividend of £10,000 by S plc includes a full year's preference dividend. No interim dividends were paid during the year by either company.

(c) Creditors of P plc include £6,000 payable to S plc in respect of stock purchases. Debtors of S plc include £10,000 due from P plc. The holding company sent a cheque for £4,000 to its subsidiary on 29 April 2008 which was not received by S plc until May 2008.

(d) At 1 May 2007 the balances on the reserves of S plc were as follows:

	£000
Share premium	10
General reserve	20
Profit and loss account	30

(e) Goodwill is not amortised.

Required:

(a) Prepare a consolidated balance sheet for P plc and its subsidiary S plc at 30 April 2008. Notes to the accounts are not required. Workings must be shown.

(b) Explain what is meant by the term 'cost of control' and justify your treatment of this item in the above accounts.

(*Chartered Institute of Management Accountants*)

You can find a range of additional self-test questions, as well as material to help you with your studies, on the website that accompanies this book at **www.pearsoned.co.uk/wood**

Consolidated balance sheets: sundry matters

Learning objectives

After you have studied this chapter, you should be able to:

- calculate goodwill on the purchase of preference shares
- treat unrealised profits and losses on intragroup asset sales
- describe the effect of 'fair value' on the calculation of goodwill and on the preparation of the consolidated financial statements

Introduction

In this chapter, you'll learn how to calculate goodwill on preference shares and how to treat it in the consolidated financial statements. You'll also learn what to do with profits and losses on the sale of fixed assets between companies in the same group. Finally, you will learn more about what is meant by 'fair value' and how to calculate and incorporate it into consolidated financial statements.

22.1 Preference shares

You've already learnt that preference shares do not carry voting powers under normal conditions, nor do they possess a right to the reserves of the company. Contrast this with ordinary shares which, when bought by a parent undertaking, will give it voting rights and also a proportionate share of the reserves of the company.

The absence of any right to a share of the reserves for preference shareholders and the absence of voting rights for holders of preference shares means that preference shareholders cannot control a company, either by their holding a majority of the voting share capital (even if share capital comprised 99% preference shares and 1% ordinary shares) or (as a result of their preference shareholding) being in a position to exert significant influence on the decision making of the company, which is, of course, impossible. As a result, the calculation of goodwill on the purchase of preference shares is very simple indeed.

If 9 preference shares of £1 each are bought for £12 then goodwill will be £3, while if 20 preference shares of £1 each are bought for £16, the negative goodwill will be £4. The amount of goodwill on the purchase of preference shares is not shown separately from that calculated on the purchase of ordinary shares. Instead the figures will be amalgamated to throw up one figure only on the consolidated balance sheet. (Note the use of the nominal value of the preference shares when calculating goodwill.)

Preference shares owned by minority shareholders are simply shown as part of the minority interest figure in the consolidated balance sheet, each share being shown at nominal value.

22.2 Sale of fixed assets between members of the group

There is obviously nothing illegal in one company in a group selling some of its fixed assets to another company in the group. If the sale is at the original price paid for the fixed assets by the first company, then no adjustment will be needed in the consolidated balance sheet. However, such sales are usually at a price which differs from their original cost. Any intragroup unrealised profit or loss arising in this way must be eliminated in a similar fashion to that taken for the unrealised profit in trading stock as described in Chapter 19.

Not surprisingly, if a fixed asset is to be shown at its cost to the group in the consolidated balance sheet rather than at the cost paid by one group company to another, the depreciation figure on that asset must be adjusted to that based on the original cost of the asset to the group, rather than on the amount paid by the group company that now owns it.

Let's look at an example:

Exhibit 22.1

Parent and Co Ltd Balance Sheet as at 31 December 2006

	£	£
Investment in S:		
50 shares bought 31.12.2005		95
Fixed assets	78	
Less Depreciation	(23)	
		55
Current assets		20
		170
Share capital		100
Profit and loss:		
As at 31.12.2005	30	
For the year 2006	40	
		70
		170

Subsidiary and Co Ltd Balance Sheet as at 31 December 2006

	£	£
Fixed assets	80	
Less Depreciation	(20)	
		60
Current assets		35
		95
Share capital		50
Profit and loss:		
As at 31.12.2005	20	
For the year 2006	25	
		45
		95

During the year, Parent and Co Ltd had sold to Subsidiary and Co Ltd for £28 a fixed asset which had cost it £20. Of the figure of £20 depreciation in the balance sheet of Subsidiary and Co Ltd, £7 refers to this asset and £13 to the other assets. The rate of depreciation is 25 per cent straight-line. The £8 profit is included in the figure of £40 profit for 2006 in the balance sheet of Parent and Co Ltd.

Summarising all this:

(a) Parent and Co Ltd sold a fixed asset to Subsidiary and Co Ltd for £28 which had cost £20.

(b) Entries made in Parent and Co Ltd's accounts:

	£	£
Dr Bank	28	
Cr Fixed assets		20
Cr Profit and loss		8

(c) Entries made in Subsidiary and Co Ltd's accounts:

	£	£
Dr Fixed assets	28	
Cr Bank		28
Dr Depreciation [expense included in profit and loss]	7	
Cr Accumulated depreciation (£28 × 25%) [provision]		7

This means that the £8 needs to be removed from the asset costs in the consolidated balance sheet and from the profit and loss account balance. In addition the figure of depreciation needs adjusting downwards, from the £7 as shown on the balance sheet of Subsidiary and Co Ltd, to the figure of £5, i.e. 25 per cent depreciation based on the cost of the asset to the group. This in turn means that the figure of profit for Subsidiary and Co Ltd, £25, needs increasing by £2, as, instead of the expense of £7 depreciation, there will now be a reduced expense of £5. The consolidated balance sheet becomes:

Consolidated Balance Sheet as at 31 December 2006

	£	£
Goodwill		25
Fixed assets	150	
Less Depreciation	(41)	
		109
Current assets		55
		189
Share capital		100
Profit and loss: (Parent and Co: £70 – £8 + Son and Co £25 + £2)		89
		189

22.3 Fair values in acquisition accounting

Under acquisition accounting (also known as 'purchase method accounting'), the consolidation process is looked at from the point of view that the parent undertaking acquires shares in a company and thereby achieves control of that company. In addition, it is recognised that the reserves are also taken over. (The topic of acquisition accounting is developed further in Chapter 25.)

The consolidated balance sheet should give a picture of the group that is not clouded by the consolidation method adopted.

An entity is acquired to obtain control of its assets. The consolidated balance sheet should give the same picture as that which would have been recorded if, instead of buying shares, the assets themselves had been bought.

When FRS 6: *Acquisitions and mergers* and FRS 7: *Fair values in acquisition accounting* were issued in 1994, the way in which acquisitions were accounted for in the UK was standardised. One of the areas of greatest diversity before they were issued concerned the revaluation of assets and liabilities to 'fair values'. 'Fair value' is defined *as the amount for which an asset or liability could be exchanged in an arm's-length transaction* (i.e. in an exchange between strangers).

Generally, acquiring companies set their own 'fair values' on the assets and liabilities acquired, and then follow the FRS 10 (*Goodwill and intangible assets*) rules that the amount to be attributed to purchased goodwill should be the difference between the 'fair value' of the consideration given and the aggregate of the 'fair values' of the separable net assets acquired. This should apply to all the assets, including those attributable to minority interests.

Under acquisition accounting, the investment is shown at cost (which equals the 'fair value' given) in the parent company's own financial statements. On consolidation, if the fair value of the net assets (excluding goodwill) acquired is *less than* the fair value of the purchase consideration, FRS 10 requires that the difference is treated as goodwill and capitalised and, normally, amortised. If the fair value of the net assets (excluding goodwill) acquired *exceeds* the fair value of the purchase consideration, the difference is treated as negative goodwill. This is similar to the treatment that has been adopted throughout the previous few chapters, the only difference being that fair values should always be used rather than the values as shown in the balance sheet of the acquired company.

FRS 7 requires that upon acquisition, all assets and liabilities that existed in the acquired entity at that date are recorded at fair values reflecting their condition at that date. In addition, it seeks to ensure that all changes to the acquired assets and liabilities and the resulting gains and losses *that arise after control of the acquired entity has passed to the acquirer*, are reported as part of the post-acquisition financial performance of the reporting group.

FRS 7 contains a number of rules governing the determination of appropriate fair values:

1 The fair value of *tangible fixed assets* should be based upon either *market value* (if assets similar in type and condition are bought and sold on an open market) or *depreciated replacement cost* (reflecting the acquired business's normal buying process and the sources of supply and purchase prices available to it). However, the fair value should not exceed the recoverable amount (i.e. the greater of the net realisable value and the value in use) of the asset.
2 The fair value of *intangible assets* should be based on their *replacement cost*, which is normally their estimated market value.
3 *Stocks*, including commodity stocks, that the acquired entity trades on a market in which it participates as both a buyer and seller should be valued at *current market prices*.
4 *Other stocks and work in progress* should be valued at the lower of *replacement cost* and *net realisable value*. As with the use of *depreciated replacement cost* for *tangible fixed assets*, *replacement cost* for stock should be the cost at which it would have been replaced by the acquired entity, reflecting the acquired business's normal buying process and the sources of supply and prices available to it. The standard suggests that this is synonymous with 'the current cost of bringing the stocks to their present location and condition'.
5 *Quoted investments* should be valued at *market price*.
6 *Monetary assets and liabilities*, including accruals and provisions, should take into account their timing and the amounts expected to be received and paid. The *fair value* should be determined by reference to *market prices*, or by discounting to present value.
7 *Contingencies* should be measured at *fair values* where these can be determined, using reasonable estimates of the expected outcome if necessary.

The 'cost of acquisition' is defined in FRS 7 as *the amount of cash paid and the fair value of other purchase consideration given by the acquirer, together with the expenses of the acquisition*.

The effect of the use of fair values can be seen from what would occur if fair values were used by the acquiring company in arriving at the price it wished to pay, but then were never incorporated into the financial statements. For instance, if P buys all the 10 £1 shares of S for £18 when the reserves are £5, then the goodwill calculation if fair values are not used is:

	£	£
Cost		18
Less Shares	10	
Less Reserves	5	
		(15)
Goodwill		3

However, P might have bought the shares of S because it thought that the fair value of the net assets of S was £17.

 Activity 22.1 What would be wrong with P recording goodwill as £3 in this case?

The revaluation upwards of the fixed assets by £2, and the consequent reduction of the goodwill figure by £2 brings the figures into line with how P views them. Where there are depreciation charges on the revalued assets, they also need to be adjusted.

Let's look at an example of the amendments made when balance sheet values are adjusted to fair values.

Exhibit 22.2

P Balance Sheet as at 31 December 2006

	£	£
Investment in subsidiary:		
30 shares bought 31.12.2005		56
Fixed assets	80	
Less Depreciation for the year	(16)	
		64
Current assets		26
		146
Share capital		100
Profit and loss account:		
As at 31.12.2005	20	
Add Profit 2006	26	
		46
		146

S Balance Sheet as at 31 December 2006

	£	£
Fixed assets	50	
Less Depreciation for the year	(10)	
		40
Current assets		14
		54
Share capital		30
Profit and loss account:		
As at 31.12.2005	3	
Add Profit 2006	21	
		24
		54

At the time when P bought the shares in S, the assets in S were shown at a value of £33 in the balance sheet of S. However, P valued the fair values of the fixed assets of S as being worth £20 more than that shown in S's balance sheet. The consolidated balance sheet will therefore show them at this higher figure. In turn the depreciation on these fixed assets, which is at the rate of 20 per cent, will be increased accordingly, by £4. The consolidated balance sheet is therefore:

P and S Consolidated Balance Sheet as at 31 December 2006

	£	£
Goodwill		3
Fixed assets (£80 + £70)	150	
Less Depreciation (£16 + £14)	(30)	
		120
Current assets		40
		163
Share capital		100
Profit and loss account:		
(P £46 + S £21 – increased depreciation £4)		63
		163

22.4 IFRS 3: Business combinations

The international accounting standard which deals with the issues contained in FRS 7 is IFRS 3 (*Business combinations*). The principles contained in both standards are broadly similar which is hardly surprising given that IFRS 3 was issued in March 2004.

Learning outcomes

You should now have learnt:

1 Goodwill on the purchase of preference shares is the difference between their nominal value and the amount paid.

2 Unrealised profit on the sale of fixed assets between companies in a group must be eliminated upon consolidation.

3 'Fair values' at the time of acquisition should be used in the calculation of goodwill, rather than the value shown in the balance sheet of the subsidiary, and the consolidation of the subsidiary undertaking should also be based on those fair values.

4 Fair value is dependent upon the nature of the item being valued. However, the general rule is that it represents the amount for which an asset or liability could be exchanged in an arm's-length transaction, i.e. in an exchange between strangers.

Answer to activity

22.1 In P's eyes, it is giving £18 for physical assets worth £17 and the goodwill figure is correspondingly £18 − £17 = £1. Assuming that the difference is in the recorded value of fixed assets, then the consolidated balance sheet will not be showing a true and fair view if it shows goodwill £3 and assets £15. The assets should be valued at £17 and goodwill recorded as £1.

Review questions

Note: **Unless indicated otherwise, assume that the issued share capital of all the companies in these review questions comprises ordinary £1 shares.**

22.1 From the following balance sheets and further information you are to draw up a consolidated balance sheet as at 31 December 2003.

Parent Ltd Balance Sheet as at 31 December 2003

	£	£
Investment in Subsidiary:		
400,000 shares bought 31.12.2002		650,000
Fixed assets	450,000	
Less Depreciation	(200,000)	
		250,000
Current assets		90,000
		990,000
Share capital		800,000
Profit and loss:		
As at 31.12.2002	150,000	
Add Profit for 2003	40,000	
		190,000
		990,000

Subsidiary Ltd Balance Sheet as at 31 December 2003

	£	£
Fixed assets		370,000
Less Depreciation		(102,000)
		268,000
Current assets		240,000
		508,000
Share capital		400,000
Profit and loss:		
As at 31.12.2002	60,000	
Add Profit for 2003	48,000	
		108,000
		508,000

During the year Parent Ltd had sold to Subsidiary Ltd for £70,000 a fixed asset which had cost it £60,000. Subsidiary Ltd has written off 20 per cent of the amount it paid, i.e. £14,000 as depreciation for 2003.

22.2A From the following balance sheets and supplementary information you are to draw up a consolidated balance sheet as at 31 March 2004.

→

Pop and Mom Ltd Consolidated Balance Sheet as at 31 March 2004

	£	£
Investment in Son Ltd: 30,000 shares bought 31.3.2003		74,000
Fixed assets	174,000	
Less Depreciation	(29,000)	
		145,000
Current assets		56,000
		275,000
Share capital		210,000
Profit and loss:		
As at 31.3.2003	28,000	
Add Profit for 2004	37,000	
		65,000
		275,000

Son Ltd Balance Sheet as at 31 March 2004

	£	£
Fixed assets	90,000	
Less Depreciation	(36,000)	
		54,000
Current assets		20,000
		74,000
Share capital		30,000
Profit and loss:		
As at 31.3.2003	18,000	
Add Profit for 2004	10,000	
		28,000
General reserve (as at 31.3.2003)		16,000
		74,000

During the year Pop and Mom Ltd sold a fixed asset to Son Ltd. It had cost Pop and Mom Ltd £2,000 and it was sold to Son Ltd for £3,000. Son Ltd had written off £600 as depreciation during 2004.

22.3

Parental Times Ltd Balance Sheet as at 31 March 2005

	£	£
Investment in Subsidiary: 80,000 shares bought on 31.3.2004		160,000
Fixed assets	110,000	
Less Depreciation for year	(22,000)	
		88,000
Current assets		37,000
		285,000
Share capital		200,000
Profit and loss:		
As at 31.3.2004	51,000	
Add Profit for 2005	34,000	
		85,000
		285,000

Siblings Ltd Balance Sheet as at 31 March 2005

	£	£
Fixed assets	90,000	
Less Depreciation for year	(9,000)	
		81,000
Current assets		43,000
		124,000
Share capital		80,000
Profit and loss:		
As at 31.3.2004	24,000	
Add Profit for 2005	20,000	
		44,000
		124,000

When Parental Times Ltd bought the shares of Siblings Ltd it valued the fixed assets at £120,000 instead of the figure of £90,000 as shown in the balance sheet of Siblings Ltd.

Draw up a consolidated balance sheet as at 31 March 2005.

22.4A

Parent Undertakings Ltd Balance Sheet as at 31 December 2008

	£	£
Investment in Subsidiary: 40,000 shares bought 31.12.2007		68,000
Fixed assets	80,000	
Less Depreciation for year	(8,000)	
		72,000
Current assets		12,600
		152,000
Share capital		110,000
Profit and loss:		
As at 31.12.2007	32,000	
Add Profit for 2008	10,000	
		42,000
		152,000

Sons and Co Ltd Balance Sheet as at 31 December 2008

	£	£
Fixed assets	60,000	
Less Depreciation for year	(6,000)	
		54,000
Current assets		8,000
		62,000
Share capital		40,000
Profit and loss:		
As at 31.12.2007	10,000	
Add Profit for 2008	12,000	
		22,000
		62,000

When Parent Undertakings Ltd took control of Sons and Co Ltd it valued the fixed assets at 31.12.2007 at £75,000 instead of £60,000 as shown.

Draw up the consolidated balance sheet as at 31 December 2008.

Chapter
23

Consolidation of the financial statements of a group of companies

Learning objectives

After you have studied this chapter, you should be able to:

● explain how a company that is the subsidiary of another is also a subsidiary of its parent's own parent undertaking
● consolidate groups that include subsidiaries of subsidiaries

Introduction

In this chapter, you'll learn how to deal with situations where there are layers of subsidiaries beneath one overall parent company. You will learn about the exemption that wholly owned subsidiaries have from preparing consolidated financial statements; and you will learn more about how to treat dividends when preparing consolidated financial statements.

23.1 Subsidiaries that control other companies

So far, we have considered the case of parent undertakings having a direct interest in their subsidiary undertakings. That is, in each example and review question, the parent undertaking itself bought over 50 per cent of the voting shares in the subsidiary. In a straightforward case, where the parent company, P1, has bought shares in subsidiaries S1 and S2, it could be represented by a diagram (Exhibit 23.1).

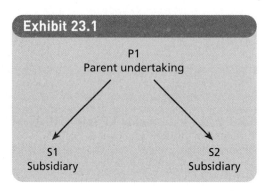

Exhibit 23.1

P1
Parent undertaking

S1
Subsidiary

S2
Subsidiary

Suppose instead that another parent undertaking, P2, bought 100 per cent of the shares in S3, and that S3 then bought 100 per cent of the shares in S4. Because P2 controls S3 completely, and S3 controls S4 completely, P2 controls both S3 and S4. This is shown as Exhibit 23.2.

If another parent undertaking, P3, owned S5 100 per cent, but S5 only owned 80 per cent of S6, then we can say that P3 owns 100 per cent of 80 per cent of S6 = 80 per cent (Exhibit 23.3). Similarly if another parent undertaking, P4, owned 75 per cent of S7, and S7 owns 80 per cent of S8, then P4 owns 75 per cent × 80 per cent = 60 per cent of S8 (Exhibit 23.4).

As can be seen in Exhibits 23.2, 23.3 and 23.4, the eventual ownership by the overall parent of each subsidiary's subsidiary exceeds 50 per cent.

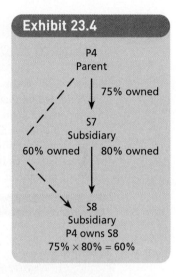

There will be cases where the ownership of the subsidiary of a subsidiary by the parent is less than 50 per cent. Exhibit 23.5 shows an example of this where parent undertaking P5 owns 80 per cent of S9, and S9 owns 60 per cent of S10. This means that P5 owns 80% × 60% = 48% of S10. Exhibit 23.6 similarly shows that parent undertaking P6 owns 60 per cent of S11 and S11 owns 55 per cent of S12. Therefore P6 owns 60% × 55% = 33% of S12.

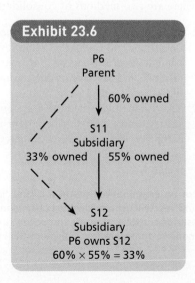

It might look as though S10 is not a subsidiary of P5, because P5 owns less than 50 per cent of S10. However, P5 controls S9 as its ownership is over 50 per cent and, in turn, S9 controls S10 as it owns more than 50 per cent. In effect, therefore, P5 controls S10 and so S10 is its subsidiary even though P5 only controls 48 per cent of the share capital of S10, *because it is able to exert a dominant influence over S10.*

Activity 23.1 Would P6 be considered the ultimate parent company of S12?

23.2 Legal exemptions from preparing consolidated financial statements

Section 228 of the Companies Act 1985 exempts a wholly-owned subsidiary from preparing consolidated financial statements. For instance, in Exhibit 23.2 the subsidiary S3 would not have to prepare consolidated financial statements; neither would S5 in Exhibit 23.3.

In each of cases S7, S9 and S11 in Exhibits 23.4, 23.5 and 23.6, there are minority shareholders. In practice, therefore, those subsidiary companies may have to prepare consolidated financial statements (for example, consolidating S7 and S8 in Exhibit 23.4) if sufficient of the minority interests demand it.

See also Chapter 26 for FRS 2-related exemptions.

Activity 23.2 Why do you think wholly-owned subsidiaries are normally exempted from preparing consolidated financial statements?

23.3 Methods of consolidating financial statements

There are two methods of consolidating the financial statements.

1 The 'indirect' or 'single-stage' method follows the reasoning already given in this chapter, i.e. computing the parent's interest in the subsidiaries and their subsidiaries and taking that percentage of the capital and reserves of these companies into the consolidation process. For instance, in Exhibit 23.5 the capital and reserves would give 100% of P5 + 80% of S9 + 48% of S10.

2 The 'multi-stage' method first consolidates the balance sheets of the subsidiary and its subsidiary, and when that is done it is then consolidated with the balance sheet of the holding company. This recognises the fact that subsidiaries with minority interests have to produce consolidated financial statements and is more generally used in practice than the indirect method.

For an examination, method 1 (the 'indirect' method) is to be preferred. It is a quicker method, and you will usually be short of time in an examination. Also, examination questions almost always ask for consolidation for the entire group only. As a result, there will be no need to do the intermediate consolidation. This book will therefore use method 1 only, the indirect method.

23.4 The indirect method consolidation technique

The consolidation technique you learnt in previous chapters is very similar to the **indirect method** described in the previous section, but two points need stressing:

1 The entry for the cost of investment in the cost of control account:
   (a) *For subsidiaries*: debit the total cost of investment to the cost of control account.
   (b) *For subsidiaries of subsidiaries*: debit only **the proportion of the cost concerned with the parent's share in the subsidiary which controls the subsidiary** to the cost of control account. Debit the minority interest account with the balance.

   If P invests £20,000 to buy 80 per cent of the shares of S1 and S1 then invests £10,000 to buy 60 per cent of the shares of S2, the entries in the cost of control account of the P group would be:

Cost of Control

	£	
Cost of shares in S1	20,000	
Cost of shares in S2 (80%)	8,000	

   The remaining proportion of investment by S1 is then debited to a minority interest account.

Minority Interest

	£	
Cost of shares in S2 (20%)	2,000	

2 The apportionment of share capital and reserves to the cost of control account and to the minority interest account:
   (a) *Cost of control*: take only the group's ultimate share of the subsidiary of subsidiary's share capital and reserves.
   (b) *Minority interest*: include the balance of the subsidiary of subsidiary's share capital and reserves.

   In the illustration given in 1(b) where P bought 80 per cent of S1, and S1 bought 60 per cent of S2, the ultimate share of the group is 80% × 60% = 48%. Therefore, in the consolidated financial statements 48 per cent should come into group calculations and 52 per cent shown in minority interest workings.

   The double entry from the cost of control account when preparing the consolidated financial statements is:

   Dr (appropriate) Reserve account
      Cr Cost of control account

23.5 A worked example

Example 1

P Ltd owns 80 per cent of the ordinary share capital of S1 Ltd. In turn S1 Ltd owns 75 per cent of the ordinary share capital of S2 Ltd. Both investments had been acquired on 31 December 2004, one year previous to the following balance sheets:

Review questions

Note: In all these review questions, unless otherwise indicated, assume that the share capital of all the companies comprises ordinary £1 shares.

23.1 From the following balance sheets, you are to draft a consolidated balance sheet for the group of Parent Ltd and its two subsidiaries, Sub 1 and Sub 2.

Parent Ltd Balance Sheet as at 31 December 2004

	£	£
Investment in Sub 1: 45,000 shares bought 31.12.2003		115,000
Fixed assets		495,000
Current assets		125,000
		735,000
Share capital		500,000
Profit and loss:		
As at 31.12.2003	75,000	
Add Profit for 2004	110,000	
		185,000
General reserve		50,000
		735,000

Sub 1 Ltd Balance Sheet as at 31 December 2004

	£	£
Investment in Sub 2: 7,000 shares bought 31.12.2003		30,000
Fixed assets		110,000
Current assets		25,000
		165,000
Share capital		50,000
Profit and loss:		
As at 31.12.2003	35,000	
Add Profit for 2004	80,000	
		115,000
		165,000

Sub 2 Ltd Balance Sheet as at 31 December 2004

	£	£
Fixed assets		12,000
Current assets		6,000
		18,000
Share capital		10,000
Profit and loss:		
As at 31.12.2003	2,000	
Add Profit for 2004	6,000	
		8,000
		18,000

23.2A From the following balance sheets prepare a consolidated balance sheet for the group of Parenting Ltd, Sub A and Sub B.

Parenting Ltd Balance Sheet as at 31 March 2003

	£	£
Investment in Sub A: 40,000 shares bought 31.3.2002		97,500
Fixed assets		500,000
Current assets		100,000
		697,500
Share capital		500,000
Profit and loss:		
As at 31.3.2002	107,500	
Add Profit for year ended 31.3.2003	90,000	
		197,500
		697,500

Sub A Balance Sheet as at 31 March 2003

	£	£
Investment in Sub B: 17,500 shares bought 31.3.2002		32,500
Fixed assets		40,000
Current assets		10,000
		82,500
Share capital		50,000
Profit and loss:		
As at 31.3.2002	15,000	
Add Profit for year ended 31.3.2003	10,000	
		25,000
General reserve (as at 31.3.2003)		7,500
		82,500

Sub B Balance Sheet as at 31 March 2003

	£	£
Fixed assets		26,250
Current assets		13,750
		40,000
Share capital		25,000
Profit and loss:		
As at 31.3.2002	2,500	
Add Profit for year ended 31.3.2003	12,500	
		15,000
		40,000

→

→ **23.3** On 1 April 2001, Machinery Limited bought 80 per cent of the ordinary share capital of Components Limited. On 1 April 2003, Machinery Limited was itself taken over by Sales Limited who purchased 75 per cent of the ordinary shares in Machinery Limited.

The balance sheets of the three companies at 31 October 2005 prepared for internal use showed the following position:

	Sales Ltd		Machinery Ltd		Components Ltd	
	£	£	£	£	£	£
Fixed assets						
Freehold land at cost		89,000		30,000		65,000
Buildings at cost	100,000		120,000		40,000	
Less						
Accumulated depreciation	(36,000)		(40,000)		(16,400)	
		64,000		80,000		23,600
Plant and equipment at cost	102,900		170,000		92,000	
Less						
Accumulated depreciation	(69,900)		(86,000)		(48,200)	
		33,000		84,000		43,800
		186,000		194,000		132,400
Investments						
Shares in Machinery at cost		120,000				
Shares in Components at cost				128,000		
Current assets						
Stocks	108,500		75,500		68,400	
Debtors	196,700		124,800		83,500	
Cash at bank	40,200		–		25,400	
		345,400		200,300		177,300
		651,400		522,300		309,700
Current liabilities						
Creditors	240,000		200,700		71,200	
Bank overdraft	–		69,400		–	
Corporation tax	57,400		47,200		24,500	
		(297,400)		(317,300)		(95,700)
		354,000		205,000		214,000
Ordinary shares		200,000		120,000		100,000
10% preference shares		–		–		40,000
Revenue reserves		154,000		85,000		74,000
		354,000		205,000		214,000

Additional information:
(a) All ordinary shares are £1 each, fully paid.
(b) Preference shares in Components Ltd are 50p each fully paid.
(c) All creditors are payable within one year.
(d) Items purchased by Machinery Ltd from Components Ltd and remaining in stock at 31 October 2005 amounted to £25,000. The profit element is 20 per cent of selling price for Components Ltd.
(e) Depreciation policy of the group is to provide for:
   (i) buildings – at the rate of 2 per cent on cost each year;
   (ii) plant and equipment – at the rate of 10 per cent on cost each year including full provision in the year of acquisition.
   These policies are applied by all members of the group.
   Included in the plant and equipment of Components Ltd is a machine purchased from the manufacturers, Machinery Ltd, on 1 January 2004 for £10,000. Machinery Ltd recorded a profit of £2,000 on the sale of the machine.

(f) Intra-group balances are included in debtors and creditors respectively and are as follows:

			£
Sales Ltd	Creditors – Machinery Ltd		45,600
	– Components Ltd		28,900
Machinery Ltd	Debtors – Sales Ltd		56,900
Components Ltd	Debtors – Sales Ltd		28,900

(g) A cheque drawn by Sales Ltd for £11,300 on 28 October 2005 was received by Machinery Ltd on 3 November 2005.

(h) At 1 April 2001, reserves in Machinery Ltd were £28,000 and in Components Ltd £20,000. At 1 April 2003 the figures were £40,000 and £60,000 respectively.

Required:

Prepare a group balance sheet at 31 October 2005 for Sales Ltd and its subsidiaries complying, so far as the information will allow, with the accounting requirements of the Companies Acts and UK accounting standards.

(*Association of Chartered Certified Accountants*)

23.4A Bryon Ltd has held 1,500,000 shares in Carlyle Ltd for many years. At the date of acquisition, the reserves of Carlyle Ltd amounted to £800,000. On 31 March 2006 Carlyle Ltd bought 400,000 shares in Doyle Ltd for £600,000 and a further 400,000 shares were purchased on 30 June 2006 for £650,000.

At 30 September 2006 the balance sheets of the three companies were:

	Bryon Ltd		Carlyle Ltd		Doyle Ltd	
	£	£	£	£	£	£
Freehold land and buildings						
– cost		950,000		1,375,000		300,000
Plant and equipment						
Cost	500,000		10,000,000		750,000	
Depreciation	(280,000)		(7,500,000)		(500,000)	
		220,000		2,500,000		250,000
		1,170,000		3,875,000		550,000
Investments						
1,500,000 shares in						
Carlyle Ltd		1,600,000				
800,000 shares in						
Doyle Ltd				1,250,000		
Stocks	50,000		2,050,000		850,500	
Debtors	325,000		2,675,000		1,700,000	
Cash at bank	25,500		–		16,500	
		400,500		4,725,000		2,567,000
		3,170,500		9,850,000		3,117,000
Creditors under 1 year	291,500		2,385,750		1,395,800	
Bank overdraft	–		1,450,850		–	
		(291,500)		(3,836,600)		(1,395,800)
		2,879,000		6,013,400		1,721,200
10% debenture		–		(2,000,000)		–
		2,879,000		4,013,400		1,721,200
Ordinary shares of						
£1 each		2,000,000				1,200,000
50p each				1,000,000		
8% redeemable preference						
shares of £1 each		–		2,000,000		–
Reserves		879,000		1,013,400		521,200
		2,879,000		4,013,400		1,721,200

→

→ Dividends on the preference shares were paid for one-half year on 1 April 2006; the next payment date was 1 October 2006.

Profits for the year in Doyle Ltd were £310,000 before making any adjustments for consolidation, accruing evenly through the year.

The directors of Bryon Ltd consider that the assets and liabilities of Carlyle Ltd are shown at fair values, but fair values for Doyle Ltd for the purposes of consolidation are:

	£	£
Freehold land and building		500,000
Plant and equipment – Valuation	968,400	
– Depreciation	639,600	
		328,800

Other assets and liabilities are considered to be at fair values in the balance sheet.

Additional depreciation due to the revaluation of the plant and equipment in Doyle Ltd amounts to £40,000 for the year to 30 September 2006.

Included in stocks in Carlyle Ltd are items purchased from Doyle Ltd during the last three months of the year, on which Doyle Ltd recorded a profit of £80,000.

On 30 September 2006 Carlyle Ltd drew a cheque for £100,000 and sent it to Doyle Ltd to clear the current account. As this cheque was not received by Doyle Ltd until 3 October, no account was taken of it in the Doyle Ltd balance sheet.

Required:
Prepare a balance sheet as at 30 September 2006 for Bryon Ltd and its subsidiaries, conforming with the Companies Acts so far as the information given will permit.

Ignore taxation.

(Association of Chartered Certified Accountants)

You can find a range of additional self-test questions, as well as material to help you with your studies, on the website that accompanies this book at **www.pearsoned.co.uk/wood**

Consolidated profit and loss accounts

Learning objectives

After you have studied this chapter, you should be able to:
- prepare consolidated profit and loss accounts for groups with wholly-owned subsidiaries
- prepare consolidated profit and loss accounts for groups with partly-owned subsidiaries

Introduction

In this chapter, you'll learn how to prepare consolidated profit and loss accounts for groups with wholly-owned subsidiaries, partly-owned subsidiaries, or both.

24.1 The consolidated profit and loss account

So far, we've been looking at how to prepare the consolidated balance sheet. However, consolidated financial statements comprise all the financial statements that must be prepared by individual companies, not just the balance sheet.

The consolidated profit and loss account is drawn up to show the overall profit (or loss) of the companies in the group, treating the group as a single entity. If all of the subsidiaries are owned 100 per cent, and there are no intragroup dividends or unrealised profits in stock, then it is simply a case of adding together all the amounts contained in each of the individual company profit and loss accounts to form the consolidated profit and loss account. However, such a simple situation is rarely found in practice.

Activity 24.1 Why can't we simply add together all of the separate profit and loss accounts to form the consolidated profit and loss account when the subsidiaries are partly owned and there are no intragroup dividends or unrealised profits on stock?

Exhibit 24.1 shows the framework for preparing a consolidated profit and loss account giving details of the adjustments needed. As similar principles are applied to those used when preparing a consolidated balance sheet, you will see that it is done in much the same way as was shown in Chapters 19–23.

Note: This exhibit looks very complicated. It isn't. All we have done is summarised most of the equivalent balance sheet adjustments into one exhibit, rather than distancing them out over four or five chapters. If you find it difficult to understand, refer back to the equivalent balance sheet adjustments. This should help you follow what is being done.

Exhibit 24.1

Specimen Profit and Loss Account for the Year ending . . .

	£000	£000	
Turnover	(a)	200	Parent plus
Cost of sales	(b)	(120)	subsidiaries
Gross profit		80	less cancellation
Distribution costs	10		of intra-group
Administrative expenses	20		items
		(30)	
Profit on ordinary activities before taxation		50	
Tax on profit on ordinary activities	(c)	(14)	
Profit on ordinary activities after taxation		36	
Minority interest	(d)	(4)	
Profit for the financial year		32	

Notes:
(a) Turnover. Intragroup sales to be deducted.
(b) Cost of sales: (i) Intragroup purchases. This is the same figure as for (a), as the price at which sales are made by one group company is the same figure at which the other group company has bought them. (ii) Adjust for unrealised profit in stock, by reducing closing stock. As cost of sales = opening stock + purchases − closing stock, any reduction in closing stock will increase 'cost of sales'. The balance sheet stock figure will be reduced by unrealised profits.
(c) Tax on profit on ordinary activities. This is the sum of tax for all companies within the group.
(d) Minority interest:
  (i) If ordinary shares only are issued by subsidiary: deduct the minority interest's percentage of the subsidiary's profits *after* taxation.
  (ii) If preference shares are also issued by the subsidiary this figure is found by:
  Minority interest percentage of preference share capital × total preference dividend paid
    plus
  Minority interest percentage of ordinary share capital × balance of profits (i.e. after tax and preference dividend) for the year, e.g.
    Total preference shares £1,000: Minority interest £400.
    Total ordinary shares £2,000: Minority interest £500.
    Total preference dividend paid £150.
    Profit of subsidiary after tax: £950.

Therefore, the minority interest is:		£
Share of preference dividend: 40% × £150	=	60
Share of balance of after-tax profits: 25% × (£950 − £150)	=	200
		260

Let's look at two more examples. One shows the consolidation of the profit and loss account when the subsidiary is wholly owned (Exhibit 24.2) and the other shows it where there is a minority interest in the subsidiary company (Exhibit 24.3).

Exhibit 24.2 Where the subsidiary is wholly owned

P Ltd owns 100 per cent of the share capital of S Ltd. The profit and loss accounts of these companies for the year ending 31 December 2004 are:

Profit and loss accounts	P Ltd		S Ltd	
	£000	£000	£000	£000
Turnover		400		280
Cost of sales		(270)		(190)
Gross profit		130		90
Distribution costs	20		10	
Administrative expenses	30		15	
		(50)		(25)
Profit on operating activities before taxation		80		65
Tax on profit on ordinary activities		(17)		(11)
Profit on ordinary activities after taxation		63		54

Notes:
(a) P Ltd had sold goods which cost £10,000 to S Ltd for £15,000.
(b) At the balance sheet date, 40 per cent of the goods in (a) had not been sold by S Ltd.
(c) Of the £7,000 retained profits from last year for S Ltd, £3,000 is in respect of post-acquisition profits.

The consolidated profit and loss account is:

P Group Ltd
Consolidated Profit and Loss Account for the year ending 31 December 2004

	£000	£000
Turnover (W1)		665
Cost of sales (W2)		(447)
Gross profit		218
Distribution costs	30	
Administrative expenses	45	
		(75)
Profit on ordinary activities before taxation		143
Tax on profit on ordinary activities		(28)
Profit on ordinary activities after taxation		115

Workings:
Letters (a) to (d) refer to the descriptions given above and in Exhibit 24.1.
(W1) P 400 + S 280 − 15 intercompany sales = 665 (a).
(W2) P 270 + S 190 − 15 intercompany purchases + the unrealised profit in stock (40% × 5 = 2)
= 447 (b) (i) and (ii).

Note: The difference between the total retained profit found of £115 and the total of the two retained profits shown in the individual company profit and loss accounts (£63 + £54 = £117) is £2. This represents £2 unrealised profit [b(ii)].

Activity 24.2 Why was the £2 unrealised profit in the stock held by S Ltd added to the consolidated figure for cost of sales in Working 2?

Exhibit 24.3 Where there is a minority interest in the subsidiary

P2 Ltd owns 80 per cent of shares in S2 Ltd. Profit and loss accounts of the companies for the year ending 31 December 2002 are as follows:

Profit and loss accounts	P2 Ltd		S2 Ltd	
	£000	£000	£000	£000
Turnover		640		330
Cost of sales		(410)		(200)
Gross profit		230		130
Distribution costs	35		20	
Administrative expenses	70		55	
		(105)		(75)
Profit on operating activities before taxation		125		55
Tax on profit on ordinary activities		(26)		(10)
Profit on ordinary activities after taxation		99		45

Notes:
(a) S2 Ltd had sold goods which cost £20,000 to P2 Ltd for £30,000.
(b) At the balance sheet date, 30 per cent of the goods in (a) had not been sold by P2 Ltd.
(c) Of the £35,000 retained profits of S2 Ltd brought forward, £15,000 is post-acquisition profits.

P2 Group Ltd
Consolidated Profit and Loss Account for the year ending 31 December 2002

	£000	£000
Turnover (W1)		940
Cost of sales (W2)		(583)
Gross profit		357
Distribution costs	55	
Administrative expenses	125	
		(180)
Profit on ordinary activities before taxation		177
Tax on profit on ordinary activities		(36)
Profit on ordinary activities after taxation		141
Minority interest (W3)		(9)
Profit for the financial year		132

Workings:
Letters (a) to (d) refer to the descriptions given above and in Exhibit 24.1.
(W1) P2 640 + S2 330 − intercompany sales 30 = 940 (a).
(W2) P2 410 + S2 200 − intercompany purchases 30 + unrealised profit in stock (30% × 10 = 3) = 583 (b) (i) and (ii).
(W3) 20 per cent × 45: profit after taxation of S2 Ltd = 9 (d) (i).

Activity 24.3 Explain the difference between the consolidated retained profits figure of £132 and the total of £144 found if you add together the profits for the year of P2 Ltd and S2 Ltd.

Note: If you remember the adjustments made to reconcile the consolidated profit figure in Activity 24.3, you should have no difficulty preparing consolidated profit and loss accounts.

Learning outcomes

You should now have learnt:

1 When consolidating profit and loss accounts for groups with wholly-owned subsidiaries with no intragroup transactions or indebtedness, it is simply a case of adding together all the separate profit and loss accounts to form the consolidated profit and loss account.

2 When consolidating profit and loss accounts, adjustments for unrealised profits on intragroup transactions and for intragroup indebtedness must be made where they exist (as per Chapters 19, 21 and 22).

3 When consolidating profit and loss accounts for groups with partly-owned subsidiaries, the approaches detailed in Chapters 17 and 23 should be followed.

Answers to activities

24.1 You need to deduct the minority interest in the profits or losses of the subsidiary when combining the figures for profits and/or losses of the companies for the period.

24.2 It was added because it was deducted from the purchases of S Ltd when the cost of sales figure for S Ltd was calculated. As it represents unrealised profit, it needs to be added back, so increasing the cost of sales of the group to the correct figure – i.e. one that does not include any unrealised profit.

24.3 The difference of £12 comprises: £3 (unrealised profit in stock) + £9 (minority interest share of this year's profit of S2).

Review questions

Note: **Unless otherwise indicated, assume that the share capital of all the companies in these review questions comprises ordinary £1 shares.**

24.1 The following information relates to the Brodick group of companies for the year to 30 April 2007:

	Brodick plc £000	Lamlash Ltd £000	Corrie Ltd £000
Turnover	1,100	500	130
Cost of sales	(630)	(300)	(70)
Gross profit	470	200	60
Administrative expenses	(105)	(150)	(20)
Dividend from Lamlash Ltd	24	–	–
Dividend from Corrie Ltd	6	–	–
Profit before tax	395	50	40
Taxation	(65)	(10)	(20)
Profit after tax	330	40	20

→

→ *Additional information:*

(a) The issued share capital of the group was as follows:
  Brodick plc: 5,000,000 ordinary shares of £1 each;
  Lamlash Ltd: 1,000,000 ordinary shares of £1 each; and
  Corrie Ltd: 400,000 ordinary shares of £1 each.

(b) Brodick plc purchased 80 per cent of the issued share capital of Lamlash Ltd in 2000. At that time, the retained profits of Lamlash amounted to £56,000.

(c) Brodick plc purchased 60 per cent of the issued share capital of Corrie Ltd in 2004. At that time, the retained profits of Corrie amounted to £20,000.

Required:

In so far as the information permits, prepare the Brodick group of companies' consolidated profit and loss account for the year ending 30 April 2007 in accordance with the Companies Acts and related UK accounting standards. (*Note:* Notes to the profit and loss account are not required, but you should append a statement showing the make-up of the 'retained profits carried forward', and your workings should be submitted.)

(*Association of Accounting Technicians*)

24.2 You are presented with the following summarised information for Norbreck plc and its subsidiary, Bispham Ltd:

Profit and Loss Accounts for the year to 30 September 2007

	Norbreck plc £000	Bispham Ltd £000
Turnover	1,700	450
Cost of sales	(920)	(75)
Gross profit	780	375
Administration expenses	(300)	(175)
Income from shares in group company	120	–
Profit on ordinary activities before taxation	600	200
Tax on profit on ordinary activities	(30)	(20)
Profit on ordinary activities after taxation	570	180

Balance Sheets at 30 September 2007

	Norbreck plc £000	Bispham Ltd £000
Fixed tangible assets	1,280	440
Investments: Shares in group company	400	–
	1,680	440
Current assets		
Stocks	300	250
Debtors (including, for Norbreck plc, the dividend proposed by the subsidiary)	280	150
Cash at bank and in hand	40	10
	620	410
Creditors (amounts falling due within one year)		
Trade creditors	(80)	(160)
Other creditors, taxation and social security	(160)	(70)
	(240)	(230)
Net current assets	380	180
Total assets *less* current liabilities	2,060	620
Provisions for liabilities and charges		
Taxation, including deferred taxation	(460)	(20)
	1,600	600
Capital and reserves		
Called-up share capital (ordinary shares of £1 each)	900	400
Reserves (including profit and loss account)	700	200
	1,600	600

Additional information:

(a) Norbreck plc acquired 80 per cent of the shares in Bispham Ltd on 1 October 2004. Bispham's profit and loss account balance as at that date was £10,000.

(b) Goodwill arising on acquisition is capitalised. There is no impairment adjustment to be made to the amount; and it is not amortised. During the year, Norbreck paid dividends of £360,000 and Bispham paid dividends of £150,000.

Required:

Prepare Bispham plc's consolidated profit and loss account for the year ending 30 September 2007 and a consolidated balance sheet as at that date.

Note: Formal notes to the account are not required, although detailed workings should be submitted with your answer. You should also append to the consolidated profit and loss account your calculation of earnings per share and a statement showing the make-up of 'retained profits carried forward'.

(Association of Accounting Technicians)

→

24.3A The following figures for the year to 30 April 2006 have been extracted from the books and records of three companies which form a group:

	Old plc £	Field Ltd £	Lodge Ltd £
Revenue reserves at 1 May 2005	30,000	40,000	50,000
Stocks at 1 May 2005	90,000	150,000	80,000
Sales	1,250,000	875,000	650,000
Purchases	780,000	555,000	475,000
Distribution expenses	125,000	85,000	60,000
Administration expenses	28,000	40,000	72,000
Interim dividends:			
Paid 31 July 2005, ordinary	45,000	35,000	15,000
Paid 31 October 2005, preference		4,000	
Share capital – fully paid ordinary shares of £1 each	450,000	350,000	200,000
8% preference shares of £1 each		100,000	
Stocks at 30 April 2006	110,000	135,000	85,000

Profits are deemed to accrue evenly throughout the year.

Other information:
(a) Corporation tax of the following amounts is to be provided on the profits of the year:

Old plc	£125,000
Field Ltd	£75,000
Lodge Ltd	£20,000

(c) Field Ltd sells goods for resale to both Old plc and Lodge Ltd. At 30 April 2006, stocks of goods purchased from Field Ltd are:

in Old plc	£40,000
in Lodge Ltd	£28,000

The net profit percentage for Field Ltd on sales of these goods is 25 per cent.
Old plc had £36,000 of these goods in stock at 1 May 2005.
Total sales in the year by Field Ltd to Old plc were £150,000 and to Lodge Ltd £120,000.

(d) Old plc acquired the whole of the ordinary shares in Field Ltd many years ago. Old plc acquired 120,000 shares in Lodge Ltd on 1 August 2005.

Required:
A consolidated profit and loss account for Old plc and its subsidiaries for the year ended 30 April 2006, together with any relevant notes.

(*Association of Chartered Certified Accountants*)

24.4A The following are the trial balances of ATH Ltd, GLE Ltd, and FRN Ltd as at 31 December 2008.

	ATH Ltd £	GLE Ltd £	FRN Ltd £
Ordinary share capital (shares of £1 each, fully paid)	100,000	30,000	20,000
Profit and loss account – balance at 31.12.2007	15,600	6,000	1,900
Current liabilities	20,750	15,900	18,350
Sales	194,000	116,000	84,000
Dividend received from GLE Ltd	1,200		
	331,550	167,900	124,250
Fixed assets	45,000	29,000	25,000
Current assets	46,000	27,500	17,500
24,000 ordinary shares in GLE Ltd at cost	33,700	–	–
20,000 ordinary shares in FRN Ltd at cost	21,250	–	–
Cost of goods sold	153,000	87,000	63,000
General expenses	32,600	22,900	18,750
Dividend for 2008, paid on 31.12.2008	–	1,500	–
	331,550	167,900	124,250

ATH Ltd acquired the shares in FRN Ltd on 31 December 2006, when the credit balance on the profit and loss account of FRN Ltd was £700, and acquired the shares in GLE Ltd on 31 December 2007. No dividend was paid by either ATH Ltd or GLE Ltd for the year 2007.

The sales of GLE Ltd for 2008 (£116,000) include £1,000 for goods sold to FRN Ltd and this amount has been debited to purchases account in the books of FRN Ltd.

All these goods were sold by FRN Ltd during 2008.

Required:
A consolidated trading and profit and loss account for the year 2008 and a consolidated balance sheet as on 31 December 2008 (not necessarily in a form for publication).

Ignore depreciation of fixed assets and taxation.

(*Institute of Chartered Secretaries and Administrators*)

You can find a range of additional self-test questions, as well as material to help you with your studies, on the website that accompanies this book at **www.pearsoned.co.uk/wood**

Chapter

25

Consolidated financial statements: acquisitions and mergers

Learning objectives

After you have studied this chapter, you should be able to:

- explain when merger accounting should be used
- explain the difference between the acquisition and the merger methods of preparing consolidated financial statements

Introduction

In this chapter, you'll learn about the two accounting methods used to combine the accounting information when two companies join together to form one new overall organisation: acquisition accounting and merger accounting. Much of the content of this chapter has been covered earlier, but here it is presented all in one place and should serve as good revision and a reminder of what you should know.

25.1 Methods used to account for the combination of companies

When two limited companies join together to form one new overall organisation, it is obvious that the shares of both companies must come under common ownership. There are two main methods of achieving this, each of which has its own distinct set of accounting entries and procedures: 'acquisition accounting', which would normally be applied (and which has been assumed throughout Chapters 16 to 24); and 'merger accounting', which can be appropriate only under very specific circumstances. Under UK accounting standards, acquisition accounting is dealt with in FRS 2: *Accounting for subsidiary undertakings*, FRS 6: *Acquisitions and mergers* and FRS 7: *Fair values in acquisition accounting*. FRS 6 also deals with the merger accounting approach. The equivalent international accounting standards are IAS 27: *Consolidated and separate financial statements* and IFRS 3: *Business combinations*.

Examples of combinations where it would be appropriate to adopt acquisition accounting

Merger accounting is very rare in the UK since FRS 6 was issued in 1994. Acquisition accounting is the norm, even where it does not ideally suit the circumstances of the business combination. However, there are many instances when it is always preferable to use acquisition accounting rather than merger accounting.

Exhibit 25.1 FRS 6 requirements to be met if merger accounting is to be used

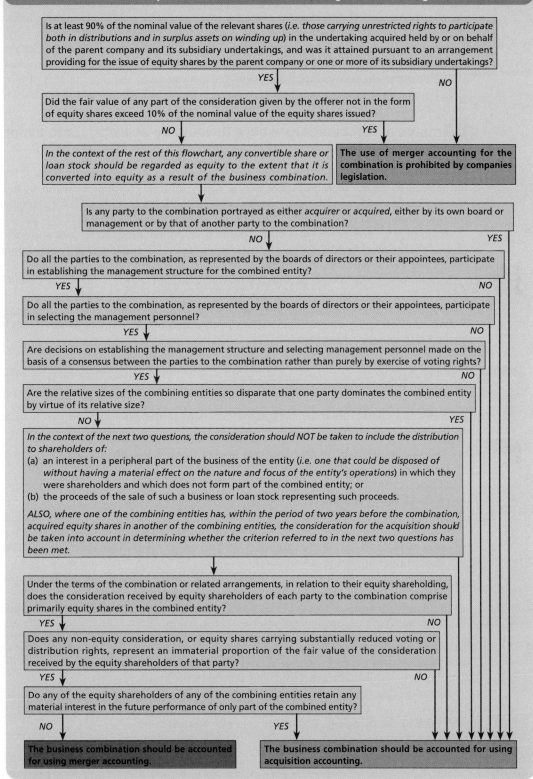

A common approach to the formation of new business combinations is for one company, A, to purchase all the shares of another company, B, often by A making a cash payment to the shareholders of B. In accepting the cash, the shareholders of B sever their links with the company. Company A's shareholders now control both companies.

Another common approach is where company A issues debentures (loan stock) to company B's shareholders in exchange for their shareholdings in B: the new debenture holders have no voting power in the new group, which would be controlled by the shareholders of A.

In both of these cases, **acquisition accounting** should *always* be used.

Examples of combinations where it would be appropriate to adopt merger accounting

When company A does not pay cash or issue debentures to the old shareholders of company B but instead issues the shareholders of B new equity (ordinary voting) shares in A, the result is that shareholders of A and B have 'merged' into one and, between them, have a joint interest in the new group. This is often referred to as a 'pooling of interest'.

A variation on this is the 'new entity' method of combination. Here, a new company, C, is formed to take over A and B, giving the old shareholders of A and B new (ordinary voting) shares in C. Once again, the two sets of shareholders have 'merged' into one.

In both these cases, **merger accounting** may be used, but *only if a number of conditions contained in FRS 6 are met*. Otherwise, acquisition accounting must be used.

Exhibit 25.1 shows the conditions to be met if merger accounting is to be used under FRS 6.

Note: **Under IFRS 3 (*Business combinations*), only acquisition accounting (which it calls 'purchase method accounting') is permitted.**

25.2 Acquisition accounting method

As mentioned above, this is the method that has been adopted in Chapters 16–24. In the books of the parent undertaking:

(a) shares purchased in a subsidiary are shown at cost less dividends received out of pre-acquisition profits;

(b) dividends out of pre-acquisition profits cannot be regarded as available for distribution as dividends by the parent.

In the consolidated financial statements:

(c) assets *and* liabilities of the subsidiary at the date of acquisition are shown in the balance sheet at their fair value at that date;

(d) the difference at the date of acquisition between the fair value of the purchase consideration and the fair value of the net assets acquired is treated as goodwill;

(e) only post-acquisition profits of the subsidiary attributable to members of the group should be included in the consolidated reserves of the group.

The idea underlying these rules is to stop capital receipts, i.e. dividends from pre-acquisition profits, being paid out as dividends. Clearly, they also prevent reserves attributable to minority shareholders from being treated as if they belong to the group.

The consolidation of balance sheets using the *acquisition* method is now shown in Exhibit 25.2. You should know this well by now but, if you do find any items in the Exhibit hard to follow, refer back to the chapter in which that item was first explained.

Exhibit 25.2

A Ltd made an offer of £270,000 for the whole of the share capital of B Ltd and it was accepted. Payment was made in cash. The fair value placed on the tangible fixed assets of B Ltd for the purposes of the merger was £148,000. The balance sheets of the two companies immediately before the merger on 31 December 2003 were:

	A Ltd £000	A Ltd £000	B Ltd £000	B Ltd £000
Tangible fixed assets		400		120
Current assets	450		200	
Less Current liabilities	(130)		(90)	
		320		110
		720		230
Ordinary shares £1		500		150
Revenue reserves		220		80
		720		230

The balance sheets of A Ltd and of the group immediately following the merger were:

Balance Sheet at 31 December 2003

		A Ltd £000	A Ltd £000		Group £000	Group £000
Fixed assets						
Intangible (goodwill)		–		(W2)	12	
Tangible		400		(W3)	548	
Investments		270			—	
			670			560
Current assets	(W1)	180		(W4)	380	
Less Current liabilities		(130)			(220)	
			50			160
			720			720
Share capital			500			500
Reserves			220			220
			720			720

Workings (£000):

(W1) Original current assets 450 – cash paid 270 = 180

(W2) Paid for shares   270

Less Net assets of B at takeover date   230

Add Increase in value of fixed assets of B to a 'fair value' 148 – 120 =   28

                                                                                    (258)

Goodwill (intangible fixed asset)   12

(W3) Fixed assets A Ltd 400 + B Ltd 148 = 548

(W4) A Ltd (after payment) 180 + B Ltd 200 = 380

Now, let's look at how merger accounting is performed and, thus, at how it differs from acquisition accounting.

25.3 Merger accounting method

1 Shares issued by the parent to 'pay' for the acquisition of another company are merely the means of achieving the merger in a technical sense. No payment is received for the shares issued and all shares issued are issued at their nominal value *not* their market value. Consequently, no

share premium arises. The newly issued shares are shown in the parent's balance sheet (A Ltd) at nominal value, as an addition to issued share capital.

2   As mentioned in (1), no share premium arises so the cost of the investment in the parent's balance sheet (A Ltd) is the nominal value of shares issued. If the nominal value of the shares is not the same as the Stock Exchange or similar market valuation then, obviously, the 'true' value of the subsidiary is not shown in the 'cost' of the investment.

3   Under merger accounting, all reserves are treated as if the 'new' organisation always existed. As a result, all dividends received by the parent (A Ltd) from the subsidiary (B Ltd) can be distributed in full by the parent, irrespective of whether they were earned pre- or post-merger. All the subsidiary's reserves are included in the consolidated balance sheet.

4   The assets of the subsidiary are not revalued at 'fair value' at the date of merger. It would not make sense to revalue B Ltd's assets while leaving A Ltd's assets valued at the old amounts. Sometimes, however, under the 'new entity' method of merger, described in Section 25.1, both companies revalue their assets.

5   Where the total nominal value of the shares issued by the parent, A Ltd, is more than the total nominal value of the shares of B Ltd, the difference is deducted from group reserves. If the total is less, then the shortfall becomes a *non-distributable* group reserve.

6   Any existing balance on the share premium account or capital redemption reserve of the new subsidiary undertaking should be brought into the consolidated balance sheet by being shown as a *movement on other reserves*.

7   Merger expenses should be charged to the profit and loss account of the combined entity at the effective date of the merger, as *reorganisation or restructuring expenses*.

Let's look at an example.

Exhibit 25.3

Taking the same companies, A Ltd and B Ltd, as in Exhibit 25.2 but, instead of a cash offer of £270,000, the offer is 200,000 ordinary shares of £1 each which, at that time, had at a stock exchange value of £270,000.

The balance sheets of A Ltd and the group immediately after the merger are now:

	A Ltd		Group	
	£000	£000	£000	£000
Fixed assets				
Tangible	400		520	
Investments	200		–	
		600		520
Current assets	450		650	
Less Current liabilities	(130)		(220)	
		320		430
		920		950
Share capital		700		700
Reserves		220		250
		920		950

Workings:

Reserve	A Ltd	220	
	B Ltd	80	
			300

Less Excess of nominal value shares issued by A Ltd over those
        exchanged of B Ltd, i.e. 200 – 150   (50)
                                                                              250

Spend a couple of minutes comparing these balance sheets with those shown after the merger in Exhibit 25.2. You should note how merger accounting makes the group appear more wealthy than acquisition accounting. Let's now consider some of the other apparent advantages to a group that adopts merger accounting.

25.4 The advantages of merger accounting to a group

Merger accounting has a number of advantages from the perspective of the investing group:

1 The subsidiary's pre-acquisition reserves and pre-acquisition results are included in the consolidated financial statements, as well as those relating to the post-acquisition period. Consequently, the group can appear to the casual reviewer as more profitable than it was. However, as the amounts relating to pre- and post-merger must be disclosed in the notes to the financial statements, this is not as great an advantage as it may appear.

2 The parent undertaking can appear misleadingly successful if it is in receipt of pre-acquisition dividends which it treats as revenue income. (The investment is normally recorded at the nominal value of the holding company shares issued, plus any other consideration given, and for obvious reasons, is not normally reduced to account for the pre-acquisition distribution.)

3 Because they do not have to be included at their fair values at the date of the merger, assets are likely to be undervalued (compared with equivalent situations where *acquisition accounting* has been applied), providing an opportunity for instant earnings by selling assets so realising unrealistically high gains on sale and, therefore, resulting in misleadingly higher returns on capital.

4 Lower depreciation charges (because the assets are at lower balance sheet values) and an absence of goodwill will result in a correspondingly higher return on capital employed than would be the case were the acquisition accounting approach adopted.

5 Most importantly, all the pre-acquisition distributable reserves of the companies involved are available for distribution to the group's shareholders (though this may be subject to a reduction if the nominal value of the new shares exceeds the nominal value of the shares received).

However, despite these apparent advantages, the merger method has only been used infrequently in the UK and, following the issue of FRS 6 in 1994, current and future adoption of merger accounting in the UK is likely to be very rare indeed. Indeed, once all UK entities adopt IFRS 3, merger accounting will cease to be used.

25.5 Final points concerning FRS 6

According to FRS 6, when *merger accounting* is used, it is not necessary to adjust values of the subsidiaries' assets and liabilities to fair values. However, adjustments must still be made if they are necessary to achieve uniformity of accounting policies across the group.

Remember that *in a merger* there is no such thing as *pre-acquisition profits*. The distribution of pre-acquisition profits is not restricted in the way it is under *acquisition accounting*.

Finally, while *acquisition accounting* will generally give rise to goodwill (positive or negative), *merger accounting* never does – not because a difference cannot arise between the consideration given and the value received, but because such differences arising under the merger accounting approach do not conform to the fair-value-based definition of goodwill given in FRS 10.

Activity 25.1 Given a choice, why would most companies prefer to adopt acquisition accounting?

25.6 IFRS 3: Business combinations

The main difference between IFRS 3 and FRS 6 is that the international standard prohibits the use of merger accounting. This can only be a positive step towards the portrayal of a true and fair view in consolidated financial statements. While companies listed on the Stock Exchange must now comply with IFRS 3, there are still many smaller unlisted companies in the UK for which FRS 6, *not* IFRS 3 applies. As a result, it will be some time before merger accounting ceases to be used in the UK.

Learning outcomes

You should now have learnt:

1 Under FRS 6, merger accounting should be used only when certain conditions are met, and must be used when they are.

2 Otherwise, acquisition accounting should be used.

3 IFRS 3 prohibits use of merger accounting.

4 Under merger accounting, assets and liabilities do not require to be stated at their fair values on acquisition.

5 Goodwill can arise only under acquisition accounting.

6 No distinction is made between pre- and post-acquisition reserves under merger accounting.

7 Double entry follows the rules of the accounting equation.

Answer to activity

25.1 It may not be so much that they would prefer to adopt acquisition accounting as that they have little choice but to do so. Merger accounting really does involve companies merging. Effectively, they must lose their independent identities to merge – the last question on the flowchart shown in Exhibit 25.1 highlights this point. Other questions on the flowchart provide further evidence of this. It is most unlikely that doing so would be desirable to all parties and is, in itself, sufficient to prevent merger accounting from being a feasible option, *if they truly had a choice*. Nevertheless, if the companies involved really were engaged in a merger, they would probably prefer to adopt merger accounting as the advantages of doing so appear far greater than the advantages of adopting acquisition accounting.

Review questions

25.1 Large plc, a manufacturer and wholesaler, purchased 600,000 of the 800,000 issued ordinary shares of a smaller company, Small Ltd, on 1 January 2005 when the retained earnings account of Small Ltd had a credit balance of £72,000.

The latest accounts of the two companies are:

Summary Profit and Loss Accounts for the year to 30 September 2006 (£000s)

	Large plc	Small Ltd
Credit sales	10,830	2,000
Cost of sales and production services	(3,570)	(1,100)
Gross profit	7,260	900
Administrative and marketing expenses (including depreciation, audit fee and directors' remuneration)	(2,592)	(180)
Operating profit	4,668	720
Dividend received from Small Ltd	180	–
Net profit before tax	4,848	720
Taxation	2,304	200
	2,544	520

Summary Balance Sheets at 30 September 2006 (£000)

	Large plc	Small Ltd
Intangible assets:		
Research and development:		
– pure research	20	–
– applied research	30	–
– development	180	–
Goodwill – purchased (at cost less amounts written-off)	48	–
– unpurchased	50	–
Fixed assets at cost less depreciation	3,920	728
Investment in Small Ltd	525	–
Current account with Large plc	–	75
Stock	594	231
Debtors	2,250	370
Bank	99	24
	7,716	1,428
Less Current account with Small Ltd	(75)	(–)
Creditors for goods and services	(297)	(156)
	7,344	1,272
Share capital	6,000	800
Retained earnings	1,344	472
	7,344	1,272

Notes:
The intangible asset section of the balance sheet of Large plc has not yet been amended prior to consolidation to take account of the provisions of the Companies Acts or the recommendations contained in accounting standards regarding intangible assets.

The stock of Large plc contained goods valued at £108,000 purchased from Small Ltd at production cost plus 50 per cent.

Required:
(a) Prepare the consolidated profit and loss account of Large plc and its subsidiary Small Ltd for the year to 30 September 2006 using the acquisition (purchase) method of consolidation.
(b) Prepare the consolidated balance sheet of Large plc and its subsidiary Small Ltd at 30 September 2006 using the acquisition method of consolidation.
(c) What would the reserves of the group be if the merger method of consolidation were used instead of the acquisition method? Briefly explain why there is a difference between the values of the reserves arising from the two methods of consolidation.

(Institute of Chartered Secretaries and Administrators)

Chapter

26

Standards covering subsidiary and associated undertakings and joint ventures

Learning objectives

After you have studied this chapter, you should be able to:

- explain the importance of the control concept
- describe the circumstances under which a parent/subsidiary relationship is recognised
- describe the conditions whereby companies are exempt from preparing consolidated financial statements
- describe the conditions under which a subsidiary should not be included in the consolidated financial statements
- describe what to do when a company has investments in associated undertakings but does not prepare consolidated financial statements because it has no investments in subsidiary undertakings

Introduction

In this chapter, you'll learn about the various accounting standards that regulate the preparation of accounting information relating to subsidiaries and associate undertakings. These regulations have changed considerably in recent years and are now more standardised than in the past, enabling far greater comparability than was previously the case.

26.1 Background

Over the last few years, the whole field of accounting relating to consolidated financial statements and groups in general has undergone considerable changes. FRS 2 was introduced to clarify and extend business operations for which consolidated financial statements are needed, and to define those situations where exemptions from their preparation should apply; FRS 9 updated the requirements concerning associates, and introduced regulations relating to joint ventures; and FRS 10 replaced SSAP 22 as the accounting standard relating to goodwill. The relevant international accounting standards relating to FRS 2 are IAS 27 and IFRS 3. For FRS 9, they are IAS 28 and IAS 31.

This chapter considers the UK standards and then looks briefly at the equivalent international standards.

26.2 FRS 2: Accounting for subsidiary undertakings

While the application of FRS 2 must comply with the requirements of the Companies Acts, FRS 2 redefines those legal requirements by reducing the number of alternatives available and making the requirements and definitions more precise, thereby improving the standardisation and hence comparability of financial statements.

The main differences between current regulations and those of 10–15 years ago are:

(*a*) the definitions of parents and subsidiaries are now based upon control, rather than on ownership;

(*b*) instead of 'company', the term 'undertaking' is used in the regulations. This means that un-incorporated bodies are now covered;

(*c*) there are now more exemptions available to companies and groups that do not wish to prepare consolidated financial statements.

In the remainder of this chapter, the more important provisions of the standards applicable to groups are discussed. As Chapters 16–25 have already incorporated the mechanics of implementing FRS 2, those points will not be looked at again. While this chapter is concerned with the other important aspects of FRS 2 and of FRS 9, it does not cover every detail. Such detail would be needed only at a later stage in your studies.

Activity 26.1 Why do you think control is now the key factor in determining the relationship between related companies, rather than ownership?

26.3 Parent and subsidiary relationship

As you have learnt over the last six chapters, the main test as to the existence of a parent/subsidiary relationship is one of control. A group consists of all the various enterprises, including unincorporated businesses as well as companies, under the control of the parent. In fact, control and ownership usually go together, but the exceptions to this general premise (whereby control could exist even when ownership was less than 50 per cent) led to a tightening up of the definition of control so that ownership became one of, rather than only indicator of a parent/subsidiary relationship.

FRS 2 states that an undertaking is a parent undertaking of another undertaking (this being the subsidiary undertaking) if any of the following can apply to it:

1 It holds a majority of the voting rights (i.e. shares carrying a right to vote) in the undertaking.
2 It is a member of the undertaking and has the right to appoint or remove directors holding a majority of the voting rights at meetings of the board on substantially all matters.
3 It has the right to exercise a 'dominant influence' over the undertaking.

    This could be by virtue of provisions in the undertaking's memorandum or articles, or by a control contract which must be in writing and be legally valid. 'Dominant influence' means that influence that can be exercised to achieve the operating and financial policies desired by the holder of the influence, not withstanding the rights or influence of any other party. In other words, it has the right to give directions as to the functioning of the operating and financial policies of the undertaking, whether or not they are to the benefit of that undertaking.
4 It is a member of the undertaking and alone controls a majority of the voting rights by agreement with other members.
5 It has a 'participating interest' (i.e. an interest in the shares of the undertaking which is held for the long term for the purpose of securing a contribution to its activities by the exercise of

control or influence arising from that interest – this would normally be a holding of more than 20 per cent of the shares of the undertaking) and either (*a*) it exercises a dominant influence over the undertaking, or (*b*) it and the undertaking are managed on a unified basis (i.e. where the whole of the operations of the undertakings are integrated and they are managed as a single unit).

6 A parent undertaking is also treated as the parent undertaking of the subsidiary undertakings of its subsidiary undertakings.

Points 2 to 5 are the more recent tests introduced by FRS 2.

26.4 Exemption from preparing consolidated financial statements

The Companies Act 2006 contains provisions which exempt some groups from having to prepare consolidated financial statements. Exactly the same provisions are contained in FRS 2. The main points contained in the Act are:

1 Small and medium-sized groups can claim exemption from the requirement to prepare consolidated financial statements on the grounds of size. In order to do so, they must comply with at least two of the following criteria:

	Small	*Medium-sized*
Aggregate turnover not more than	£5.6 million net/ £6.72 million gross	£22.8 million net/ £27.36 million gross
Aggregate gross assets not more than	£2.8 million net/ £3.36 million gross	£11.4 million net/ £13.68 million gross
Aggregate employees not more than	50	250

(This exemption does not apply to groups whose members include a plc, a bank, an insurance company, or an authorised person under the Financial Services and Markets Act 2000.)

However, they must choose between filing *full* consolidated financial statements or filing *individual* company financial statements.

2 Except for companies who have any of their securities listed on any stock exchange in the European Union, any parent undertaking that is itself a wholly-owned subsidiary whose immediate parent is established in the European Union *does not have to prepare consolidated financial statements*.

Individual company financial statements must still be prepared for the parent and they must include the name of its own parent undertaking; the country where its own parent is incorporated, if it is not the UK; and the fact that it is exempt from preparing group financial statements. As well as this, a copy of the audited consolidated financial statements of its own parent must be filed with its own individual company financial statements. (This exemption can be overturned by the minority shareholders who can require that consolidated financial statements are prepared.)

3 If all of the subsidiary undertakings are permitted or required to be excluded from consolidation under the Companies Acts, consolidated financial statements are not required.

26.5 Exemption from the inclusion of a subsidiary in consolidated financial statements

There are three grounds for exclusion of a subsidiary given in FRS 2:

(*a*) where severe long-term restrictions substantially hinder the rights of the parent undertaking over the assets or management of the subsidiary undertaking;

(b) where the interest in the subsidiary undertaking is held exclusively for subsequent resale; and

(c) where activities are so different from those of other undertakings to be included in the consolidation that their inclusion would be incompatible with the obligation to give a true and fair view.

A subsidiary that is excluded on the grounds of long-term restriction (i.e. (a) above) should be treated as a fixed asset investment. However, if the parent still exercises significant influence it should be treated as an associated undertaking.

Subsidiaries excluded on the grounds that they are being held exclusively for resale should be included as current assets at the lower of cost and net realisable value.

Where exclusion is due to the activities of the subsidiary being so different from those of other undertakings to be included in the consolidation that their inclusion would be incompatible with the obligation to give a true and fair view, they should be accounted for using the equity method.

26.6 IAS 27: Consolidated and separate financial statements

The international standard is similar to FRS 2, any differences between them being likely to be eliminated as UK and international standards converge.

26.7 FRS 9: Associates and joint ventures

FRS 9 encompasses **associate undertakings** and **joint ventures**, which it defines as entities in which the reporting entity holds an interest on a long-term basis and which are jointly controlled by the reporting entity and one or more other venturers under a contractual arrangement.

FRS 9 introduced the '**gross equity**' method of accounting, a form of equity accounting (which you will learn about in the next section) applicable to joint ventures under which the investor's share of the aggregate gross assets and liabilities of the joint venture is shown on the face of the balance sheet and the investor's share of the joint venture's turnover is noted in the profit and loss account.

Previous to FRS 9, B Ltd would be considered as an associate of A Ltd if A Ltd could *significantly* influence the financial and operating decisions of B Ltd. FRS 9 amended this definition of an associate to include entities only where the investing entity *exercises* a significant influence, rather than one that is *in a position to exercise* significant influence. At the same time, the amount of disclosure required in the financial statements was increased.

> **Activity 26.2** Why do you think this change in the definition of an associate was made?

26.8 Equity accounting

When a company has invested in an associate undertaking, ordinary investment accounting (which includes only the income from dividends in the investing company's profit and loss account) is not appropriate. Instead, the investing company's full share of the profit (whether or not distributed as dividends) or loss, is incorporated in the investing company's financial statements. This approach is known as '**equity accounting**'.

Equity accounting is, therefore, a modified form of consolidation that requires similar adjustments to be made as apply under FRS 2: *Accounting for subsidiary undertakings* for full consolidations prepared under the principles of acquisition accounting.

When the equity method is used to account for an associate, in the consolidated profit and loss account, the investing company includes its full share of the earnings of the associate, whether or not the associate has distributed the earnings as dividends. In the consolidated balance sheet, the investment is shown at cost, adjusted each year by the share of retained profits belonging to the investor, subject to an adjustment for any goodwill arising on acquisition that has been written off.

We will shortly see how this is carried out. You will learn that there are major differences between equity accounting and consolidation accounting of a subsidiary's results. For example, under acquisition accounting, the group would take credit for the whole of the turnover, cost of sales, etc. and then make a one-line adjustment to remove any minority interest. Under equity accounting, the associated undertaking's turnover, cost of sales, etc. are not amalgamated with those of the group. Instead, only the items concerned with the group's share of the associated undertaking's profit or loss are included.

As it would be quite rare for a company with investments in associate undertakings not to have subsidiaries, we will use an example that demonstrates how to include the relevant equity accounting-based information into a set of consolidated financial statements.

Effect upon the consolidated profit and loss account

Take out:
(a) dividends received or receivable from the associate.

Include instead the group's share of the associate's:
(b) pre-tax profit
(c) taxation charge
(d) post-acquisition retained profits brought forward.

Effect upon the consolidated balance sheet

Rather than   the cost of the investment
Show instead   the cost of the investment
                 plus
                 the group's share of associate's post-acquisition retained profit.

Exhibit 26.1 shows how an associated undertaking's results are incorporated into a set of consolidated financial statements.

Exhibit 26.1

A Ltd is a holding company with subsidiaries. It also has 25 per cent of the equity share capital of B Ltd. This was bought for £100,000 three years ago when B Ltd had reserves (retained profits) of £20,000.

Profit and Loss Accounts for the year ending 31 December 2003

	A Ltd & Subsidiaries (consolidated)		B Ltd (associated co.)	
	£000	£000	£000	£000
Turnover		540		200
Cost of sales		(370)		(130)
Gross profit		170		70
Distribution costs	20		3	
Administrative expenses	40		7	
		(60)		(10)
		110		60
Dividends received from B Ltd	(A)	10		–
Profit on ordinary activities before taxation		120	(B)	60
Tax on profit on ordinary activities		(28)	(C)	(16)
Profit on ordinary activities after taxation		92		44

Note: During 2003, A Ltd paid a dividend of £60,000; B Ltd paid a dividend of £40,000 on 31 December 2003.

Balance Sheet as at 31 December 2003 (abbreviated)

	£000	£000
Fixed assets	145	130
Investment in B Ltd at cost	100	–
Net current assets	180	114
	425	244
Share capital (ordinary shares)	350	200
Reserves (A = 43 + 92 – 60 = 75; B = 40 + 44 – 60 = 44)	75	44
	425	244

Note: **Retained profits at 31 December 2002 were £43,000 (A Ltd group) and £40,000 (B Ltd).**

We can now prepare the entries to incorporate B Ltd into the consolidation. As you have just learnt, the adjustments to be made are:

Take out: (A) Dividends received

Include: (B) Group share of pre-tax profit
   (C) Group share of taxation
   (D) Group's share of post-acquisition retained profit brought forward.

The answer is:

A Ltd Group
Consolidated Profit and Loss Account for the year ending 31 December 2003

	£000	£000
Turnover		540
Cost of sales		(370)
		170
Distribution costs	20	
Administrative expenses	40	
		(60)
		110
Share of profit of associated undertaking (W1)	(B)	15
Profit on ordinary activities before taxation		125
Tax on profit on ordinary activities (W2)	(C)	(32)
Profit on ordinary activities after taxation		93

Consolidated Balance Sheet as at 31 December 2003

	£000
Fixed assets	145
Investment in B Ltd (W4)	106
Net current assets	180
	431
Share capital	350
Reserves (W5)	81
	431

Workings:
(W1) 25% of profit before taxation of B Ltd × £60 = £15
(W2) A £28 + 25% of B £16 = £32
(W3) Retained profits at 31 December 2002 = A £43 + 25% of B's post-acquisition profits
       (£40 – £20) £20 = £48

(W4)	Cost of 25% share in B =		100
	Add Retained profits B c/d	44	
	Less Pre-acquisition profits	(20)	
	Post-acquisition profits	24	
	25% share		6
			106
(W5)	Reserves A		75[Note]
	Add 25% of post-acquisition profit of B (*see* W4)		6
			81

Note: This is after dividends paid during 2003.

26.9 Investing companies without subsidiaries

If no consolidated financial statements are produced by an investing company and that company is not exempt from preparing consolidated statements, or would not be if it had subsidiaries, a separate profit and loss account (or a supplement to the investing company's own profit and loss account) should be prepared showing the information that would have been included in respect of the associated undertaking had consolidated financial statements been prepared. Similar requirements apply to the balance sheet. An example of a supplementary statement incorporating the results of associated undertakings is shown in Exhibit 26.2:

Exhibit 26.2 Profit and loss account of a company without subsidiaries

Profit and Loss Account

	£000	£000
Turnover		2,000
Cost of sales		(1,400)
Gross profit		600
Distribution costs	175	
Administrative expenses	125	
		(300)
Profit on ordinary activities before taxation		300
Tax on profit on ordinary activities		(85)
Profit on ordinary activities after taxation		215

Supplementary statement incorporating results of associated undertakings:

	£000
Share of profits less losses of associated undertakings	50
Less Tax	(15)
Share of profits after tax of associated undertakings	35
Profit on ordinary share activities after taxation (as above)	215
Profit attributable to members of the investing company	250

Note: The earnings per share figure would be based on £250,000.

26.10 The control concept

The control concept underlies the presentation of consolidated financial statements for a group as a single economic entity. While the list given in Section 26.3 can be used to identify a parent/subsidiary relationship, it may result in more than one undertaking being classified as the parent. However, FRS 2 states that **control can only be held by one parent**, and that the control that identifies undertakings as parent and subsidiary undertakings should be distinguished from shared control, for example as in a joint venture. If more than one undertaking is identified as the parent, their interests in the subsidiary are, in effect, interests in a joint venture, and no parent/subsidiary relationship exists.

On the other hand, one or more of these parents may exercise a non-controlling but significant influence over the company in which it has invested. In that case it would be appropriate to account for it as an associate undertaking.

26.11 IAS 28 and IAS 31

While FRS 9 deals with both associate undertakings and joint ventures, each of these topics has its own international standard: IAS 28 (*Investments in associates*) and IAS 31 (*Financial reporting of interests in joint ventures*).

The definition of associate differs slightly, in that IAS 28 requires that only the power to exercise significant influence exists, whereas FRS 9 requires that significant influence is exercised.

The definition of joint venture also differs between IAS 31 and FRS 9. IAS 31 requires that joint control exists. FRS 9 requires that neither party can exercise sole control over the financial or operating decisions of the venture.

IAS 31 permits proportionate consolidation. FRS 9 does not. Equity accounting is permissible under IAS 31 and the gross equity method is required by FRS 9.

These differences are likely to be eliminated as the convergence of UK and international standards proceeds.

Learning outcomes

You should now have learnt:

1 The existence of a parent/subsidiary relationship depends upon whether the 'parent' undertaking can exercise *dominant* influence over the 'subsidiary' undertaking.

2 The existence of a parent/associate relationship depends upon whether the 'parent' undertaking actually exercises *significant* influence over the 'associate' undertaking.

3 There are some circumstances where groups are exempted from the preparation of consolidated financial statements.

4 Equity accounting is used when including associate undertakings in consolidated financial statements.

5 When a company has investments in associated undertakings but does not prepare consolidated financial statements because it has no investments in subsidiary undertakings, it should prepare a supplement to its financial statements detailing the information that would have been included in respect of the associated undertaking had consolidated financial statements been prepared.

6 Subsidiary undertakings can have only one parent; however, more than one parent may have a significant influence over an associated undertaking.

Answers to activities

26.1 Control is far more all-encompassing. Control in some cases can be exercised with very little ownership. It depends entirely upon the circumstances and may, in fact, depend on contractual agreements, as between lender and borrower, rather than equity ownership. By shifting the emphasis from ownership to control, the substance of the relationship is identified as the main deciding factor. As a result, parent/subsidiary relationships (and parent/associate relationships) are much more realistically defined, thus providing a more meaningful basis for the preparation of group financial statements.

26.2 Associate undertakings are those over which a *significant* influence is exerted. They are only marginally different, in terms of control by the investing undertaking, from subsidiaries, for which a *dominant* influence is the key. Associate undertakings are clearly part of the group of companies in which they are given the status of 'associate undertaking'. Hence, it is appropriate to include their results under the group operating profit.

Review questions

26.1 Q plc has three subsidiaries: L Ltd, M Ltd, and N Ltd. All three were acquired on 1 January at the start of the financial year which has just ended. Q has a 55 per cent, 70 per cent and 95 per cent holding respectively and holds a majority of the voting equity in L and M. It has changed the composition of both these companies' boards since they were acquired. However, despite its 95 per cent holding in N Ltd, it has only a 45 per cent holding of the voting equity and has so far failed in all its attempts to have a director appointed to the board. How should these three investee companies be treated in the Q group consolidated financial statements?

26.2 At the end of 2005, a parent company, P plc, with one subsidiary had a holding representing 10 per cent of the equity of R Ltd, a clothing company. It had cost £80,000 when purchased at the start of 2004. At the time of that investment, R Ltd had net assets of £560,000 which increased to £840,000 by the end of that year. At the start of the current year, the investment was increased by a further 11 per cent of the equity at a cost of £110,000.

Required:
(a) How would the investment be shown in the financial statements if it were treated as a *trade investment,* i.e. as neither an associate nor as a subsidiary?
(b) How would the investment be shown in the financial statements if it were treated as an *associated undertaking*?

26.3A Relevant balance sheets as at 31 March 2004 are set out below:

	Jasmin (Holdings) plc £000	Kasbah plc £000	Fortran plc £000
Tangible fixed assets	289,400	91,800	7,600
Investments			
Shares in Kasbah (at cost)	97,600		
Shares in Fortran (at cost)	8,000		
	395,000		
Current assets			
Stock	285,600	151,400	2,600
Cash	319,000	500	6,800
	604,600	151,900	9,400
Creditors: amounts falling due within one year	(289,600)	(238,500)	(2,200)
Net current assets	315,000	(86,600)	7,200
Total assets less current liabilities	710,000	5,200	14,800
Capital and reserves:			
Called-up share capital			
Ordinary £1 shares	60,000	20,000	10,000
10% £1 Preference shares		4,000	
Revaluation reserve	40,000		1,200
Profit and loss reserve	610,000	(18,800)	3,600
	710,000	5,200	14,800

→

→ You have recently been appointed chief accountant of Jasmin (Holdings) plc and are about to prepare the group balance sheet at 31 March 2004. The following points are relevant to the preparation of those accounts.

(*i*) Jasmin (Holdings) plc owns 90 per cent of the ordinary £1 shares and 20 per cent of the 10 per cent £1 preference shares of Kasbah plc. On 1 April 2003 Jasmin (Holdings) plc paid £96 million for the ordinary £1 shares and £1.6 million for the 10 per cent £1 preference shares when Kasbah's reserves were a credit balance of £45 million.

(*ii*) Jasmin (Holdings) plc sells part of its output to Kasbah plc. The stock of Kasbah plc on 31 March 2004 includes £1.2 million of stock purchased from Jasmin (Holdings) plc at cost plus one-third.

(*iii*) The policy of the group is to revalue its tangible fixed assets on a yearly basis. However, the directors of Kasbah plc have always resisted this policy, preferring to show tangible fixed assets at historical cost. The market value of the tangible fixed assets of Kasbah plc at 31 March 2004 is £90 million. The directors of Jasmin (Holdings) plc wish to follow the requirements of FRS 2 'Accounting for Subsidiary Undertakings' in respect of the value of tangible fixed assets to be included in the group accounts.

(*iv*) The ordinary £1 shares of Fortran plc are split into 6 million 'A' ordinary £1 shares and 4 million 'B' ordinary £1 shares. Holders of 'A' shares are assigned 1 vote and holders of 'B' ordinary shares are assigned 2 votes per share. On 1 April 2003 Jasmin (Holdings) plc acquired 80 per cent of the 'A' ordinary shares and 10 per cent of the 'B' ordinary shares when the profit and loss reserve of Fortran plc was £1.6 million and the revaluation reserve was £2 million. The 'A' ordinary shares and 'B' ordinary shares carry equal rights to share in the company's profit and losses.

(*v*) The fair values of Kasbah plc and Fortran plc were not materially different from their book values at the time of acquisition of their shares by Jasmin (Holdings) plc.

(*vi*) Goodwill arising on acquisition is amortised over five years.

(*vii*) Kasbah plc has paid its preference dividend for the current year but no other dividends are proposed by the group companies. The preference dividend was paid shortly after the interim results of Kasbah plc were announced and was deemed to be a legal dividend by the auditors.

(*viii*) Because of its substantial losses during the period, the directors of Jasmin (Holdings) plc wish to exclude the financial statements of Kasbah plc from the group accounts on the grounds that Kasbah plc's output is not similar to that of Jasmin (Holdings) plc and that the resultant accounts therefore would be misleading. Jasmin (Holdings) plc produces synthetic yarn and Kasbah plc produces garments.

Required:
(a) List the conditions for exclusion of subsidiaries from consolidation for the directors of Jasmin (Holdings) plc and state whether Kasbah plc may be excluded on these grounds.
(b) Prepare a consolidated balance sheet for Jasmin (Holdings) Group plc for the year ending 31 March 2004. (All calculations should be made to the nearest thousand pounds.)
(c) Comment briefly on the possible implications of the size of Kasbah plc's losses for the year for the group accounts and the individual accounts of Jasmin (Holdings) plc.

(*Association of Chartered Certified Accountants*)

26.4A Huge plc acquired a holding of 600,000 of the 800,000 ordinary £1 shares of Large plc on 1 October 2005 when the revenue reserves of Large stood at £320,000.

On 1 October 2006, the directors of Medium plc agreed to appoint the commercial manager of Huge as one of its directors to enable Huge to participate in its commercial, financial and dividend policy decisions. In exchange, Huge agreed to provide finance to Medium for working capital. On the same day, Huge acquired its holding of 100,000 of the 400,000 ordinary £1 shares of Medium when the revenue reserves of Medium were £150,000. Three months later, the directors of Small plc, who supplied materials to Large, heard of the arrangement between Huge and Medium and suggested that they would be pleased to enter into a similar relationship. The board of Huge were interested in the proposal and showed their good faith by acquiring a 10 per cent holding in Small which at that time had a debit balance of £2,000 on its profit and loss account.

Balance Sheets of the four companies on 30 September 2007

	Huge £000	Large £000	Medium £000	Small £000
Property, plant and machinery	2,004	780	553	85
Investment in Large	650			
Investment in Medium	180			
Investment in Small	12			
Current a/c Medium	40			
Current a/c Small		10		
Stocks	489	303	72	28
Debtors	488	235	96	22
Bank/cash	45	62	19	5
	3,908	1,390	740	140
Less Liabilities due in one year: Creditors	(318)	(170)	(90)	(10)
	3,590	1,220	650	130
Ordinary share capital	2,400	800	400	80
Revenue reserves	1,190	420	210	40
Current a/c Huge			40	
Current a/c Large				10
	3,590	1,220	650	130

Required:

(a) Identify which of the four companies should be included in a group consolidation, explaining how and why the treatment of one company in the consolidation may be different from another. Mention any appropriate accounting standards or legislation applicable.

(b) Prepare the consolidated balance sheet of the group at 30 September 2007 using the acquisition method of accounting.

(Institute of Chartered Secretaries and Administrators)

You can find a range of additional self-test questions, as well as material to help you with your studies, on the website that accompanies this book at **www.pearsoned.co.uk/wood**

Part

4

FINANCIAL ANALYSIS

Introduction

This part considers how accounting information is traditionally analysed and used.

Chapter

27

Accounting ratios

Learning objectives

After you have studied this chapter, you should be able to:

- describe various groups of accounting ratios, where they would be used, why they would be of interest, and to whom they would be of interest
- calculate a number of commonly used accounting ratios
- describe some of the difficulties that may arise in the calculation and interpretation of accounting ratios
- describe the dangers of overtrading and how ratio analysis can be used to detect it

Introduction

This chapter revises what you learnt in *Business Accounting Essentials 1* concerning ratios and introduces some that are more commonly used. You will also learn about one of the main causes of small business failure, overtrading, and of how ratios can be used to minimise the risk of its occurring undetected.

27.1 Background

Without ratios, financial statements would be largely uninformative to all but the very skilled. By using ratios, financial statements can be interpreted and usefully applied to satisfy the needs of the reader, whether skilled or not.

The subject of accounting ratios and their use when analysing financial statements was introduced in *Business Accounting UK GAAP 1*. This chapter takes that material forward, re-examining it for reinforcement, and then developing it so as to increase the depth of your knowledge and understanding.

Information can be defined as 'data organised for a purpose'. Information in financial statements is organised to enable users of the financial statements to draw conclusions concerning the financial well-being and performance of the reporting entity. In the case of the financial statements of companies, independent auditors review the manner in which the data has been presented and provide a filter mechanism attesting to the reliability of the information presented.

For partnerships and sole traders, there is generally no such independent review. However, as the financial statements are generally subject to review by the tax authorities, there is some justification in assuming that they are a reasonable reflection of reality and, in fact, many are prepared by qualified accountants who are governed by the ethical standards of their professional body and so, while not required to do so by the business involved will, nevertheless, strive to produce financial statements that represent a 'true and fair view' of the performance and financial position of the business.

Yet, being 'reasonably assured' of the reliability of such financial statements is not generally sufficient for tax authorities. As a result, they often review the financial statements of partnerships and sole traders to determine whether there may be cause to doubt their reliability. One of the key instruments at their disposal is ratios, and they use ratio analysis to compare those found in the entity under review with those typically existing in that sector of the economy. Hence, through ratio analysis, factors characteristics and deviations from the norm can be identified that would not otherwise be apparent.

Activity 27.1 What sort of 'deviations from the norm' do you think they may be looking for?

As you learnt in *Business Accounting UK GAAP 1*, ratio analysis can also be used to review trends and compare entities with each other. A number of financial analysis organisations specialise in this service, providing detailed ratio analysis of the financial statements of plcs to anyone who subscribes to their service, thereby enabling analysts to see, at a glance, how one company is performing, or how its financial structure compares with that of others of a similar nature.

This is fine for analysts, academic researchers and business competitors who can afford the services of such an organisation. However, there are a vast number of other stakeholders interested in analysing financial statements, including shareholders, lenders, customers, suppliers, employees and government agencies, not all of whom would either want this information, nor wish to pay for it. In many cases, each stakeholder group will be interested in different things, and so there is no definitive, all-encompassing list of points for analysis that would be useful to all the groups even if some organisation endeavoured to do so.

Nevertheless, it is possible to construct a series of ratios that together will provide all these groups with something that they will find relevant, and from which they can choose to investigate further, if necessary.

Ratio analysis is, therefore, a first step in assessing the performance and financial position of an entity. It removes some of the mystique surrounding the financial statements and makes it easier to pinpoint items which would be interesting to investigate further.

Exhibit 27.1 shows some categories of ratios and indicates some of the groups that would be interested in them. You will recall a similar list in *Business Accounting Essentials 1*. However, note that the term 'solvency' has been substituted for 'liquidity' in the list here. 'Solvency' is a broader term and more clearly indicative of precisely what we are trying to identify when we consider the ratios that fall within its group. **Despite 'solvency' being the more appropriate term, many examiners use the term 'liquidity' when referring to this group of ratios.**

Exhibit 27.1

Ratio category	Examples of interested groups
Profitability	Shareholders, management, employees, creditors, competitors, potential investors
Solvency	Shareholders, suppliers, creditors, competitors
Efficiency	Shareholders, potential purchasers, competitors
Shareholder	Shareholders, potential investors
Capital structure	Shareholders, lenders, creditors, potential investors

Let's now revise the main features of each category of ratios.

27.2 Profitability

These measures indicate whether the company is performing satisfactorily. They are used, among other things, to measure the performance of management, to identify whether a company may be a worthwhile investment opportunity, and to determine a company's performance relative to its competitors.

There are a large number of these ratios. You will recall that we covered three in *Business Accounting Essentials 1* – *gross profit : sales*, *net profit : sales* and *return on capital employed*. We shall review them once more and add some others that are commonly used.

Gross profit : Sales

If gross profit is £120,000 and sales are £480,000, the ratio would be 25 per cent. (This should not be confused with the gross margin : cost of sales ratio which compares the gross profit to the cost of sales which, in this case, would have a value of 33.33 per cent.)

Net profit after tax : Sales

If net profit is £38,400 and sales are £480,000, the ratio would be 8 per cent. It indicates how much safety there is in the price, i.e. current prices could be reduced by up to 8 per cent without causing the company to make a loss. Of course, it is much more complex than this. As any student of economics knows only too well, if a commodity's price falls, generally demand for it rises. This could result in costs increasing (if unexpected demand has to be met in a hurry) or falling (as bulk discounts become available that were not previously obtainable owing to the lower level of demand). Nevertheless, as a general guide, it is a sensible indicator of safety, as well as an indicator of success.

While a high value for this ratio may suggest successful performance, it is not always the case. It is possible for selling prices to be so high that demand is reduced causing overall profitability to be significantly lower than it could be were a lower price being used. In this circumstance, the ratio would produce a high percentage, but performance would certainly not be as good as it ought to have been.

Return on capital employed

An adequate return on capital employed is what many investors seek and is, therefore, one of the main reasons why people invest their money in a business in the first place. As a result, this is an extremely important ratio. First, let's remind ourselves of what we learnt in *Business Accounting UK GAAP 1*.

(i) Sole traders

In this chapter, we will use the average of the capital account as the figure for capital employed, i.e. (opening balance + closing balance) ÷ 2.

In businesses C and D in Exhibit 27.2 the same amount of net profit has been made, but the capitals employed are different.

Exhibit 27.2

Balance Sheets

	C £	D £
Fixed + Current assets − Current liabilities	<u>10,000</u>	<u>16,000</u>
Capital accounts		
Opening balance	8,000	14,000
Add Net profit	<u>3,600</u>	<u>3,600</u>
	11,600	17,600
Less Drawings	(<u>1,600</u>)	(<u>1,600</u>)
	<u>10,000</u>	<u>16,000</u>

Return on capital employed (ROCE) is:

$$ROCE = \frac{Net\ Profit}{Capital\ employed} \times 100$$

therefore

C	D
$\dfrac{3,600}{(8,000 + 10,000) \div 2} \times \dfrac{100}{1} = 40\%$	$\dfrac{3,600}{(14,000 + 16,000) \div 2} \times \dfrac{100}{1} = 24\%$

The ratio illustrates that what is important is not simply how much profit has been made but how well the capital has been employed. Business *C* has made far better use of its capital, achieving a return of £40 net profit for every £100 invested, whereas *D* has received only a net profit of £24 per £100.

(ii) Limited companies

There is no universally agreed definition of **capital employed** for companies. The main ones used are:

(*a*) return on capital employed by ordinary shareholders;
(*b*) return on capital employed by all long-term suppliers of capital.

Let's now look at each of these:

(*a*) In a limited company this is known as 'return on owners' equity' (ROOE) or, more commonly, 'return on shareholders' funds' (ROSF).
   From now on, we shall use the second of these terms, 'return on shareholders' funds', but you will need to remember that when you see 'return on owners' equity', it is the same as ROSF.
   The word 'return' is the net profit for the period. The term 'shareholders' funds' means the book value of all things in the balance sheet that describe the owners' capital and reserves. As the 'owners' are the holders of the *ordinary* share capital, shareholders funds = ordinary share capital + all reserves.

(*b*) This is often known as 'return on capital employed' (ROCE). The word 'return' in this case means net profit + any preference share dividends + debenture and long-term loan interest. The word 'capital' means ordinary share capital + reserves + preference shares + debentures and other long-term loans.

Now, let's calculate ROSF and ROCE for P Ltd and Q Ltd. Q Ltd has issued debentures, so its ROSF and ROCE will not be the same. P Ltd's capital employed is sourced solely from shareholders' funds, so its ROSF and ROCE will be identical.

Balance Sheets as at 31 December

	P Ltd		Q Ltd	
	£	£	£	£
	2008	*2009*	*2008*	*2009*
Fixed assets	5,200	5,600	8,400	9,300
Net current assets	2,800	3,400	1,600	2,700
	8,000	9,000	10,000	12,000
10% debentures	–	–	(1,200)	(1,200)
	8,000	9,000	8,800	10,800
Share capital (ordinary)	3,000	3,000	5,000	5,000
Reserves	5,000	6,000	3,800	5,800
	8,000	9,000	8,800	10,800

Profit and Loss Accounts for years to 31 December 2009

	P Ltd	Q Ltd
	£	£
Net profit	2,200	3,800
Dividends	(1,200)	(1,800)
	1,000	2,000

Return on Shareholders' Funds (ROSF)

P Ltd	Q Ltd
$\dfrac{2,200}{(8,000+9,000) \div 2} \times \dfrac{100}{1} = 25.9\%$	$\dfrac{3,800}{(8,800+10,800) \div 2} \times \dfrac{100}{1} = 38.8\%$

Return on Capital Employed (ROCE)

P Ltd	Q Ltd
Same as ROSF[(Note 1)] = 25.9%	$\dfrac{3,800 + 120^{(\text{Note 2})}}{(10,000+12,000) \div 2} \times \dfrac{100}{1} = 35.6\%$

Note 1: The return on capital employed by all long-term sources of capital (in Q Ltd's case, the shareholders' funds and the debentures) is the same as the ROSF in the case of P Ltd, as it has no debentures.

Note 2: The debenture interest (i.e. 10% of £1,200 = £120) must be added back, as it was an expense in calculating the £3,800 net profit.

To summarise: return on capital employed is one of the more awkward ratios to deal with. Unlike for example, the current ratio, there is no widely agreed definition for ROCE – even the ones given here are but examples of how it may be defined. Hence, care must be taken when comparing this ratio as calculated for one company and as reported by another 'so as to confirm that like is being compared with like'. Using the services of financial analysis organisations which use the same formulae to calculate the ratios of all the companies they consider is one way around this difficulty. Another is to ensure that the formula used by the companies with which comparison is being made is known and, where necessary, the ratio result is recalculated in order to bring it into line with the internally calculated ratio.

Note: A problem you face as a student is that you will never be quite sure what an examiner wants if the exam paper refers to this ratio. You should always write down the formula you are using on your exam script.

To avoid confusion, unless otherwise indicated by, for example, the examiner, for companies use the definition of ROCE given above. The ratio compares the profit earned (usually *before* interest and tax) to the funds used to generate that return (often the total of shareholders' funds at the beginning of the accounting period plus long-term creditors – most simply defined as total assets minus current liabilities). If the profit before interest and tax was £40,000 and the opening capital employed shown in the balance sheet was £800,000 the return on capital employed would be 5 per cent.

In theory, the higher the ratio, the more profitably the resources of the company have been used.

Return on share capital

In theory, the higher this ratio is, the more profitably the shareholders' investment in the company has been used. It is often used to compare a company's performance across accounting periods, rather than to make comparisons with the ROSC of other companies. As with ROCE, there are a number of different ways in which return on share capital may be calculated. One is to compare profit on ordinary activities before tax with share capital and reserves. For example, if profit on ordinary activities before tax was £40,000 and the share capital and reserves at the start of the accounting period were £720,000 the return on share capital (ROSC) would be 5.56 per cent.

Net profit after tax : Total assets

Net profit after tax is compared with the total of all assets other than current assets, plus working capital (i.e. current assets less current liabilities). If working capital is £20,000 and all non-current assets total £820,000, total assets are £840,000. If net profit after tax is £30,000 the ratio is £30,000/£840,000 i.e. 3.57 per cent.

There are problems with the validity of this ratio: it is really concerned with the operating profit generated by the net assets. However, some items of expenditure, e.g. interest on debentures, will have been charged against the profit in arriving at the figure for profit after tax. Strictly speaking, these other payments to investors and creditors ought to be excluded from this ratio and so should be added back to arrive at the profit figure used in the ratio, otherwise the profit may be significantly understated, giving a less healthy view than would be appropriate to present.

In addition, intangible assets, such as goodwill, are included in the value of total assets used in the ratio. Many would argue that this is inappropriate, as there is not an agreed view on how such assets should be valued.

These issues result in variations of this ratio being used – some add back expenditure, some exclude all intangible assets, some don't – which may not be apparent if only the ratio result is available. As a result, intercompany comparisons may be misleading.

Net operating profit : Operating assets

This is an alternative to the *net profit after tax : total assets* ratio. It takes the net profit before interest, taxes and dividends, and before inclusion of any investment income. This is then compared with the assets other than intangibles and investments outside the company. Working capital would be included, but bank overdrafts would be excluded from the current liabilities on the basis that they are not generally short term in nature. Assume that net operating profit before interest, tax and dividends is £36,000 and tangible fixed assets excluding investments made outside the company are £600,000, working capital is £20,000 and there is a bank overdraft of £5,000. The ratio is:

$$\frac{£36,000}{£625,000} = 5.76\%$$

27.3 Solvency

Being solvent means having sufficient resources to meet your debts when due. Your resources must be sufficiently liquid to do so, hence the frequent use of the term 'liquidity' when referring to this group of ratios. As you learnt in *Business Accounting UK GAAP 1*, the solvency of individuals is often performed through credit checks undertaken by credit rating agencies. Many lenders, such as banks, use a checklist of questions concerning financial status before they will lend or grant credit to a private individual. For companies, information can be purchased that indicates their solvency, i.e. whether they are liable to be bad credit risks. Such information is usually based, at least in part, upon ratio analysis of their financial statements.

When it comes to the solvency of a business, both its own ability to pay its debts when due *and* the ability of its debtors to pay the amount they owe to the business are of great importance. Ratio analysis that focuses upon solvency (or liquidity) of the business generally starts with a look at two ratios that are affected most by these two aspects of liquidity: the **current ratio** and the **acid test ratio**.

Current ratio

The **current ratio** compares total current assets to total current liabilities and indicates whether there are sufficient short-term assets to pay the short-term liabilities. This ratio is so sector-dependent that it would be and is inappropriate to suggest a ratio result that may be seen generally as being the 'norm'. Consequently, no such guidance will be given here. Rather, a set of issues to consider is offered below:

1 What is the norm in this industrial sector?
2 Is this company significantly above or below that norm?
3 If so, can this be justified after an analysis of the nature of these assets and liabilities, and of the reasons for the amounts of each held?

The ratio may be expressed as either a ratio to 1, with current liabilities being set to 1, or as a 'number of times', representing the relative size of the amount of total current assets compared with total current liabilities.

Example

If total current assets are £40,000 and total current liabilities are £20,000 the current ratio could be expressed as either:

$$£40,000 : £20,000 = 2 : 1$$

or as:

$$\frac{£40,000}{£20,000} = 2 \text{ times}$$

Acid test ratio

As with the current ratio, there is no point in suggesting a norm for the ratio result to expect. The only difference in the items involved between the two ratios is that the acid test ratio (or 'quick' ratio) does not include stock. Otherwise, it is identical to the current ratio, comparing current assets, excluding stock, with current liabilities. Stock is omitted as it is considered to be relatively illiquid, because it depends upon prevailing and future market forces and may be impossible to convert to cash in a relatively short time.

Many companies operate with acid test ratios below 1:1; that is, they have insufficient liquid assets to meet their short-term liabilities. The great majority of companies in this situation have no problem paying their creditors when due. Consideration of a simple example should explain how this is possible.

> **Activity 27.2**
>
> The only difference between the current and acid test ratios is that stock is omitted from the acid test ratio. Why is it appropriate to remove stock from the analysis?

Example

If total current assets, including stock of £22,000 are worth £40,000 and total current liabilities stand at £20,000, the acid test ratio will be £18,000 : £20,000 = 0.9 : 1 (or 0.9 times). This means that at the balance sheet date, had all current liabilities been due for payment, it would not have been possible to do so without converting some other assets (e.g. stock, or some fixed assets) into cash even though it would be unlikely that they could be converted quickly into cash without offering a discount on their true value. In other words, the company would have had to pay a premium in order to meet its obligations, clearly something it would not be able to do indefinitely.

However, the reality is generally that the current liabilities shown in the balance sheet are due for payment at varying times over the coming financial period and some, for example a bank overdraft, may not in reality ever be likely to be subject to a demand for swift repayment.

The current assets, on the other hand, are within the control of the company and can be adjusted in their timing to match the due dates for payment to creditors. They can be renewed many times before one or other of the current liabilities is due for payment. For example, debtors may be on a 10-day cycle while trade creditors are paid only after 90 days' credit has expired. Clearly, in this case, cash receipts from nine times the balance sheet debtors' figure could be received and available to meet the trade creditor figure shown in the balance sheet when it falls due.

As with the current ratio, the acid test ratio should be compared with the norms for the industrial sector, and then the underlying assets and liabilities should be considered to determine whether there is any cause for concern in the result obtained.

> **Activity 27.3**
>
> If stock is removed from the analysis when calculating the acid test ratio, why isn't the figure for debtors also removed? Debtors can be just as difficult to turn into cash.

27.4 Efficiency ratios

Profitability is affected by the way that the assets of a business are used. If plant and equipment are used for only a few hours a day, the business is probably failing to utilise these assets efficiently. This may be because there is limited demand for the product produced. It could be due to the business restricting supply to maximise profitability per item produced. On the other hand, it could be that there is a shortage of skilled labour and that there is no one to operate the plant and machinery the rest of the time. Alternatively, it could be that the plant and machinery are unreliable, breaking down a lot, and that the limited level of use is a precautionary measure designed to ensure that production targets are met.

In common with all accounting ratios, it is important that the results of efficiency ratio computations are not treated as definitively good or bad. They must be investigated further through consideration both of the underlying variables in the ratios, and of the broader context of the business and its relation to the industrial sector in which it operates.

Efficiency ratios include:

Asset turnover

Asset turnover is a measure of how effectively the assets are being used to generate sales. It is one of the ratios that would be considered when interpreting the results of profitability ratio analyses like ROCE, but is of sufficient importance to be calculated and analysed irrespective of its relevance to other ratios. The calculation involves dividing sales by total assets less current liabilities.

As a general guide, where a company's asset turnover is significantly lower than that of its competitors, it suggests there may be overinvestment in assets which could, in turn, make the company vulnerable to takeover by a company interested in selling off any surplus assets while otherwise retaining the business in its current form. However, considerable care must be taken when interpreting this ratio: the assets may be much newer than those of other companies; the company may use a lower rate of depreciation than its competitors; or the company may purchase its plant and machinery, whereas the industry norm is to lease them. On the other side of the ratio, the result may be high because, for example, selling prices are being suppressed in order to maximise volume.

Stock turnover

Included in virtually every case where accounting ratios are being calculated, stock turnover measures the number of times (approximately) that stock is replenished in an accounting period. If average stock is £100,000 and cost of goods sold is £800,000, the stock turnover ratio would be 8 times. The ratio can also be expressed as a number of days – the number of days stock held. In this example, 365 would be divided by 8, producing a result of 45.6 days.

There are two major difficulties in computing the stock turnover ratio: if cost of sales is not available, it is tempting to use sales instead. This should not be done. Sales are expressed at selling prices; stock is expressed at cost price. Use of sales instead of cost of sales in the equation will not be comparing like with like.

In addition, there are at least three possible stock values that could be used: opening, closing and the average of these figures. The average figure is the more commonly used, but use of any of the three can be justified.

Whichever approach is taken, the result will, at best, be a crude estimate. Due to seasonality of the business, stock as shown in the balance sheet may not be representative of the 'normal' level of stock. However, it is still useful for comparing trends over time and should be used mainly for that purpose. The result it produces needs to be handled with care. A rising stock turnover may indicate greater efficiency; or it may be an indicator that stocks are being run down and that there may be problems in meeting demand in future. A falling stock turnover may indicate lower efficiency, perhaps with a build-up of obsolete stocks; or it could indicate that higher stock volumes are being held because stock purchasing has become more efficient and the higher stock levels are financially beneficial for the company. In addition, it is important not to overlook that any change in the ratio may have nothing to do with stock but, instead, may be due to changes in factors relating to the sales for the period.

Debtor days

Debtor days indicates how efficient the company is at controlling its debtors. If debtors are £50,000 and sales £800,000, debtors are taking, on average, 22.8 days credit, i.e.

$$\frac{£50,000}{£800,000} \times 356 = 22.8$$

Strictly speaking, the two figures are not comparable. Debtors includes the VAT on sales; the figure for sales excludes VAT. However, the adjustment is not difficult to make if required for clarity.

As with stock, the amount shown in the balance sheet for debtors may not be representative of the 'normal' level of debtors. Nevertheless, this is generally a useful ratio to calculate and comparison with that of other companies in the same industrial sector may be very interesting. However, as with stock turnover, its strength lies in trend analysis between periods.

Creditor days

The creditor days ratio indicates one aspect of how the company uses short-term financing to fund its activities, and further investigation will reveal whether or not the result found is due to efficiency. It is calculated by dividing creditors by purchases, and multiplying the result by 365. The purchases figure is not usually available in published financial statements, the cost of sales amount being used in its place. As with stock turnover and debtor days, its strength lies in trend analysis between periods.

27.5 Shareholder ratios

Shareholder ratios are those most commonly used by anyone interested in an investment in a company. They indicate how well a company is performing in relation to the price of its shares and other related items including dividends and the number of shares in issue. The ratios usually calculated are described below.

Dividend yield

Dividend yield measures the real rate of return by comparing the dividend paid to the market price of a share. It is calculated as:

$$\frac{\text{Gross dividend per share}}{\text{Market price per share}}$$

Earnings per share (EPS)

EPS is the most frequently used of all the accounting ratios and is generally felt to give the best view of performance. It indicates how much of a company's profit can be attributed to each ordinary share in the company. FRS 14: *Earnings per share* provides the formula to be used when calculating this ratio:

$$\frac{\text{Net profit or loss attributable to ordinary shareholders}}{\text{The weighted average number of ordinary shares outstanding during the period}}$$

Dividend cover

Dividend cover compares the amount of profit earned per ordinary share with the amount of dividend paid, thereby showing the proportion of profits that could have been distributed and were. It differs from EPS only in having a different denominator. The formula is:

$$\frac{\text{Net profit or loss attributable to ordinary shareholders}}{\text{Net dividend on ordinary shares}}$$

Price earnings (P/E) ratio

The P/E ratio relates the earnings per share to the market price of the shares. It is calculated as:

$$\frac{\text{Market price}}{\text{Earnings per share}}$$

and is a useful indicator of how the stock market assesses the company. It is also very useful when a company proposes an issue of new shares, in that it enables potential investors to better assess whether the expected future earnings make the share a worthwhile investment.

27.6 Capital structure

There are a number of ratios that can be used to assess the way in which a company finances its activities. One, creditor days, was referred to in the last section. The ratios discussed in this section differ in that they are longer-term in nature, being concerned more with the strategic rather than with the operational level of corporate decision making. Some of the more commonly analysed ratios of this type are described below.

Net worth : Total assets

This ratio indicates the proportion of fixed and current assets that are financed by net worth (the total of shareholders' funds, i.e. share capital plus reserves). If fixed assets are shown at a value of £500,000, current assets £100,000 and net worth is £300,000, then 50 per cent of total assets are financed by shareholders' funds. As with many accounting ratios, it is the trend in this ratio between periods that is important.

Fixed assets : Net worth

This ratio focuses on the longer-term aspects of the net worth: total assets ratio. By matching long-term investment with long-term finance it is possible to determine whether borrowing has been used to finance some long-term investment in assets. Where this has occurred, there may be a problem when the borrowing is to be repaid (as the fixed assets it was used to acquire cannot be readily converted into cash). Again, this ratio is of most use when the trend over time is analysed.

Fixed assets : Net worth + long-term liabilities

This ratio focuses on whether sufficient long-term finance has been obtained to meet the investment in fixed assets.

Debt ratio

This ratio compares the total debts to total assets and is concerned with whether the company has sufficient assets to meet all its liabilities when due. For example, if total liabilities are £150,000 and total assets are £600,000 the debts represent 25 per cent of total assets. Whether this is good or bad will, as with all accounting ratios, depend upon the norm for the industrial sector in which the company operates and on the underlying items within the figures included in the ratio.

Capital gearing ratio

This ratio provides the proportion of a company's total capital that has a prior claim to profits over those of ordinary shareholders. Prior claim (or prior charge) capital includes debentures, other long-term loans, and preference share capital and is any capital carrying a right to a fixed return. Total capital includes ordinary share capital and reserves, preference shares and long-term liabilities.

Debt : Equity ratio

This is the ratio of prior charge capital to ordinary share capital and reserves.

Borrowing : Net worth

This ratio indicates the proportion that borrowing represents of a company's net worth. If long-term liabilities are £100,000 and current liabilities are £50,000 then total borrowing is £150,000. If net worth is £300,000, the ratio is 1 : 2, or 50 per cent.

This and the debt : equity ratio indicate the degree of risk to investors in ordinary shares in a company. The higher these ratios are, the greater the possibility of risk to ordinary shareholders – both in respect of expectations of future dividends (especially in times of depressed performance where much of the profits may be paid to the holders of prior charge capital), and from the threat of liquidation should there be a slump in performance that leads to a failure to meet payments to holders of prior charge capital. Whether these risks may be relevant can be investigated by reference to the next ratio.

Interest cover

This ratio shows whether enough profits are being earned to meet interest payments when due. It is calculated by dividing profit before interest and tax by the interest charges. Thus, the interest cover is 20 times if profit before interest and tax is £400,000 and the total interest charges are £20,000. In this case, there would be little cause for immediate concern that there was any risk of the company's failing to meet its interest charges when due. However, just because a company is making profits does not guarantee that there will be sufficient cash available to make the interest charge payments when due.

27.7 Overtrading

A very high proportion of new businesses fail within the first two years of trading. This can occur because there was insufficient demand for the goods or services provided, because of poor management, or for any of a number of other reasons of which possibly the most common to arise is **overtrading**. However, unlike the other common causes of business failure, overtrading often arises when a business is performing profitably. Furthermore, overtrading can just as easily affect established businesses as new businesses.

Overtrading occurs when poor control over working capital results in there being insufficient liquid funds to meet the demands of creditors. As the cash dries up, so do the sources of supply of raw materials and other essential inputs – suppliers will not continue to supply a business that fails to settle its bills when due. Overtrading is generally the result of sales growth being at too fast a rate in relation to the level of trade debtors, trade creditors and stock.

Take an example where, over a twelve-month period, profits increased by 20 per cent, sales doubled from £1 million to £2 million; trade debtors doubled from £80,000 to £160,000; trade creditors quadrupled from £60,000 to £240,000; stock quadrupled from £50,000 to £200,000;

and the bank balance moved from positive £20,000 to an overdraft of £80,000. No changes occurred during the period in long-term financing of the business, though £100,000 was spent on some new equipment needed as a result of the expansion.

Working capital was 2.5 : 1; now it is 1.125 : 1 and the acid test ratio is now 0.5 : 1 from 1.67 : 1. Liquidity appears to have deteriorated significantly (but may have been high previously compared with other businesses in the same sector). Debtor days are unchanged (as the ratio of sales to debtors is unaltered). However, creditor days have probably doubled (subject to a slight reduction due to some cheaper purchasing costs as a result of the higher volumes involved). If the bank overdraft is currently at its limit, the business would be unable to meet any requests from creditors for immediate payment, never mind pay wages and other regular expenses.

This situation can be addressed by raising long-term finance, or by cutting back on the expansion – clearly, the first option is likely to be the more acceptable one to the owners of the business.

Signals suggesting overtrading include:

(*a*) significant increases in the volume of goods sold;
(*b*) lower profit margins;
(*c*) deteriorating debtor, creditor and stock turnover ratios;
(*d*) increasing reliance on short-term finance.

27.8 Summary of ratios

Profitability

Gross profit : Sales
$$\frac{\text{Gross profit}}{\text{Sales}}$$

Net profit after tax : Sales
$$\frac{\text{Net profit after tax}}{\text{Sales}}$$

Return on capital employed
$$\frac{\text{Profit before interest and tax}}{\text{Total assets} - \text{Current liabilities}}$$

Return on share capital
$$\frac{\text{Profit before tax}}{\text{Share capital} + \text{Reserves}}$$

Net profit after tax : Total assets
$$\frac{\text{Net profit after tax}}{\text{Fixed and other non-current assets} + \text{Working capital}}$$

Net operating profit : Operating assets
$$\frac{\text{Net profit before interest, tax, dividends, and investment income}}{\text{Tangible fixed assets} - \text{Outside investments} + \text{Working capital} + \text{Bank overdraft}}$$

Solvency

Current ratio
$$\frac{\text{Current assets}}{\text{Current liabilities}}$$

Acid test ratio
$$\frac{\text{Current assets} - \text{Stock}}{\text{Current liabilities}}$$

Efficiency

Asset turnover
$$\frac{\text{Sales}}{\text{Total assets} - \text{Current liabilities}}$$

Stock turnover $$\frac{\text{Cost of goods sold}}{\text{Average stock}}$$

Debtor days $$\frac{\text{Debtors}}{\text{Sales}} \times 365$$

Creditor days $$\frac{\text{Creditors}}{\text{Purchases}} \times 365$$

Shareholder ratios

Dividend yield $$\frac{\text{Gross dividend per share}}{\text{Market price per share}}$$

Earnings per share $$\frac{\text{Net profit or loss attributable to ordinary shareholders}}{\text{Weighted average number of ordinary shares outstanding during the period}}$$

Dividend cover $$\frac{\text{Net profit or loss attributable to ordinary shareholders}}{\text{Net dividend on ordinary shares}}$$

Price/earnings ratio $$\frac{\text{Market price}}{\text{Earnings per share}}$$

Capital structure

Net worth : Total assets $$\frac{\text{Shareholders' funds}}{\text{Total assets}}$$

Fixed assets : Net worth $$\frac{\text{Fixed assets}}{\text{Shareholders' funds}}$$

Fixed assets :
Net worth + long-term liabilities $$\frac{\text{Fixed assets}}{\text{Shareholders' funds + Long-term liabilities}}$$

Debt ratio $$\frac{\text{Total liabilities}}{\text{Total assets}}$$

Capital gearing ratio $$\frac{\text{Prior charge capital}}{\text{Total capital}}$$

Debt : Equity ratio $$\frac{\text{Prior charge capital}}{\text{Ordinary share capital and reserves}}$$

Borrowing : Net worth $$\frac{\text{Total borrowing}}{\text{Shareholders' funds}}$$

Interest cover $$\frac{\text{Profit before interest and tax}}{\text{Interest charges}}$$

Note: If you wish to read more about the topic of ratios, there are many worthwhile books available, such as Ciaran Walsh's *Key Management Ratios*, published by FT Prentice Hall. However, don't forget that there is no 'correct' formula for many of the financial ratios you have learnt about in this chapter. If you do read further on this topic *do not* make changes to these formulae. These are generally accepted formulae and ones your examiners will recognise.

Learning outcomes

You should now have learnt:

1 There are many different categories of accounting ratios and many different ratios within each category.

2 Ratios that are of interest to one group of readers of financial statements may not be of interest to another.

3 Ratios may be used to review reliability of financial statements.

4 Ratios may be used to review trends between periods for the same company.

5 Ratios may be used to compare a company with others in the same industrial sector.

6 Some ratios are in wide use for which there is no agreed 'correct' formula to calculate them. This makes comparison between analysis reported elsewhere of limited value unless the formula used can be identified.

7 The ratios derived can be misleading if taken at face value. It is essential that they are placed in context and that interpretation goes beyond a superficial comparison to general norms.

8 Used casually, accounting ratios can mislead and result in poor-quality decision making.

9 Used carefully, accounting ratios can provide pointers towards areas of interest in an entity, and provide a far more complete picture of an entity than that given by the financial statements.

10 Overtrading can be financially disastrous for a business and ratios can be used to help detect it.

Answers to activities

27.1 Lower levels of gross profit than the industry norm, which might indicate goods were being taken out of the business for the owner's own use but not being recorded as drawings. Alternatively lower levels of gross profit than the industry norm may indicate sales for cash were not all being recorded. Revenue and Customs uses ratios to detect anything that might indicate the possibility that a proprietor is understating the profit earned.

27.2 Stock is sometimes very difficult to convert into cash, particularly at the value placed upon it in the balance sheet. Because it can be difficult to generate liquid funds through the sale of stock, it is inappropriate to consider it when looking at the issue of whether an organisation is able to pay its debts quickly.

27.3 Debtors can be very difficult to turn into cash. However, there are three aspects of debtors that make them less problematic than stock in this context. Firstly, specialist financial agencies called 'factors' will take over debts in many instances in exchange for a percentage of the amount owing. Through this medium, organisations can convert some of their debtors into cash quickly and at relatively little cost. Secondly, debtors can be pursued through the courts. Thus, when an organisation urgently needs money owing from debtors that is already overdue, it can threaten legal action, thereby accelerating the receipt of the money due. Finally, most debtors do eventually pay their debts; stock may never be sold.

In the context of the cash it will generate, stock is usually sold at above the value placed upon it in the balance sheet while, apart from overestimation of doubtful debts, debtors never realise more than the value shown for them in the balance sheet. However, so far as the acid test ratio is concerned, the key difference is that money owing by debtors will generally be received more quickly than money tied up in stock.

Review questions

27.1 Five categories of accounting ratios were described in this chapter. What are they?

27.2A Why should different groups of people be interested in different categories of accounting ratios?

27.3 Describe two ratios from each of the five groups of ratios, including how to calculate them.

27.4A What is the purpose in using each of the following ratios:

(a) current ratio
(b) net profit after tax : sales
(c) asset turnover
(d) interest cover
(e) dividend cover?

27.5 If you wished to assess the efficiency of a company, which of these ratios would you use:

(a) stock turnover
(b) interest cover
(c) return on capital employed
(d) acid test ratio
(e) dividend yield?

27.6A A company has capital of 1 million ordinary shares of £1 each. It pays a dividend of 6 per cent out of its profits after tax of £480,000 on sales of £4 million. The market price of the shares is £2.40. What is the:

(a) net profit after tax : sales
(b) dividend yield
(c) earnings per share
(d) price earnings ratio?

27.7 In respect of each of the following events, select all the effects resulting from that event that are shown in the list of effects:

(i)   a bad debt written off;
(ii)   an increase in the bank overdraft;
(iii) a purchase of six months' stock;
(iv)   payment of all amounts due to trade creditors that had been outstanding for longer than 90 days;
(v)   an offer of 5 per cent discount to all customers who settle their accounts within two weeks.

Effects
(a) increased current ratio
(b) reduced current ratio
(c) increased acid test ratio
(d) reduced acid test ratio.

27.8A Using the following balance sheet and profit and loss accounts, calculate and comment on ten accounting ratios (ignore taxation):

Balance Sheet as at 31 March 2006 (£000)

Fixed assets
Equipment at cost		600
Less Depreciation to date		(200)
		400

Current assets
Stock	300	
Debtors	60	
Bank	–	
	360	

Less Current liabilities
Creditors	160	
Dividends payable	12	
Bank overdraft	168	
		(340)
		20
		420

Long-term liabilities		
5% debentures		(100)
Net assets		320

Financed by:
Share capital – ordinary shares of 50p each		250
Reserves		
General reserve		40
Profit and loss		30
		320

Profit and Loss Account for period ending 31 March 2006 (£000)

Sales		2,000
Less Cost of sales		
Opening stock	250	
Add Purchases	1,450	
	1,700	
Less Closing stock	(300)	
		(1,400)
Gross profit		600
Less Depreciation	80	
Other expenses	477	
		(557)
Net operating profit		43
Less Debenture interest		(5)
Net profit		38

Note: The note on Movements in Shareholders' Funds shows that retained profits at 1 April 2005 were £24,000; that £20,000 has been transferred from profit and loss to the general reserve; and that a dividend of £12,000 was paid during the year. (The balance sheet reflects these items.)

→

27.9 Study the following financial statements for two very similar privately owned department stores which each comprise of one store in the city centre of a major UK city and then answer the questions which follow.

Summary of Financial Statements

Balance Sheets	A £000s	A £000s	B £000s	B £000s
Fixed assets				
Building at cost	300		440	
Less Depreciation to date	(255)		(220)	
		45		220
Equipment at cost	140		180	
Less Depreciation to date	(119)		(90)	
		21		90
		66		310
Current assets				
Stock	200		240	
Debtors	205		140	
Bank	4		2	
	409		382	
Less Current liabilities				
Creditors	(245)		(252)	
		164		130
Net assets		230		440
Financed by:				
Capital accounts				
Balance at start of year		240		430
Add Net profit		60		90
		300		520
Less Drawings		(70)		(80)
		230		440
Trading and Profit and Loss Accounts				
Sales		1,800		2,700
Less Cost of goods sold				
Opening stock	300		280	
Add Purchases	1,300		2,250	
	1,600		2,530	
Less Closing stock	(200)		(240)	
		(1,400)		(2,290)
Gross profit		400		410
Less Depreciation	22		40	
Other expenses	318		280	
		(340)		(320)
Net profit		60		90

Required:

(a) Calculate the following ratios:
- (i) gross profit as percentage of sales;
- (ii) net profit as percentage of sales;
- (iii) expenses as percentage of sales;
- (iv) stockturn;
- (v) rate of return of net profit on capital employed (use the average of the capital account for this purpose);
- (vi) current ratio;
- (vii) acid test ratio;
- (viii) debtor : sales ratio;
- (ix) creditor : purchases ratio.

(b) Drawing upon all your knowledge of accounting, comment upon the differences and similarities of the accounting ratios for A and B. Which business seems to be the most efficient? Justify your opinion.

27.10A Study the following financial statements of two companies and then answer the questions which follow. Both companies are stores selling carpets and other floor coverings; each company has a single store in the same 10-year old custom-built shopping complex located on the outskirts of a major UK city.

Trading and Profit and Loss Accounts

	R Ltd £000s	R Ltd £000s	T Ltd £000s	T Ltd £000s
Sales		2,000		1,400
Less Cost of goods sold				
Opening stock	440		144	
Add Purchases	1,550		996	
	1,990		1,140	
Less Closing stock	(490)		(240)	
		(1,500)		(900)
Gross profit		500		500
Less Expenses				
Depreciation	27		14	
Wages and salaries	180		160	
Directors' remuneration	210		210	
Other expenses	23		16	
		(440)		(400)
Net profit		60		100

Note: The note on Movements in Shareholders' Funds shows that the profit and loss balances at the start of the year were £60,000 (R Ltd) and £20,000 (T Ltd): that dividends paid during the year were £50,000 (R Ltd) and £40,000 (T Ltd); and that both companies made transfers from profit and loss to general reserve at the end of the year; £20,000 (R Ltd) and £20,000 (T Ltd).

→

→

Balance Sheets

	R Ltd		T Ltd	
	£000s	£000s	£000s	£000s
Fixed assets				
Building at cost	300		100	
Less Depreciation to date	(150)		(50)	
		150		50
Equipment at cost	60		30	
Less Depreciation to date	(40)		(20)	
		20		10
Motor vans	40		35	
Less Depreciation to date	(16)		(14)	
		24		21
		194		81
Current assets				
Stock	490		240	
Debtors	680		320	
Bank	80		127	
	1,250		687	
Less Current liabilities				
Creditors	(324)		(90)	
		926		597
		1,120		678
Financed by:				
Issued share capital		1,000		500
Reserves				
General reserve	70		120	
Profit and loss	50		58	
		120		178
		1,120		678

Required:
(a) Calculate the following ratios for each of R Ltd and T Ltd:
   (i) gross profit as percentage of sales;
   (ii) net profit as percentage of sales;
   (iii) expenses as percentage of sales;
   (iv) stockturn;
   (v) rate of return of net profit on capital employed
       (for the purpose of this question only, take
       capital as being total of share capitals + reserves
       at the balance sheet date);
   (vi) current ratio;
   (vii) acid test ratio;
   (viii) debtor: sales ratio;
   (ix) creditor: purchases ratio.
(b) Comment briefly on the comparison of each ratio as between the two companies. State which
    company appears to be the more efficient, giving what you consider to be possible reasons.

27.11 The directors of L Ltd appointed a new sales manager towards the end of 2002. This manager
devised a plan to increase sales and profit by means of a reduction in selling price and extended
credit terms to customers. This involved considerable investment in new machinery early in 2003 in
order to meet the demand which the change in sales policy had created.

The financial statements for the years ended 31 December 2002 and 2003 are shown below. The sales manager has argued that the new policy has been a resounding success because sales and, more importantly, profits have increased dramatically.

Profit and loss accounts

	2003	2002
	£000	£000
Sales	2,800	900
Cost of sales	(1,680)	(360)
Gross profit	1,120	540
Selling expenses	(270)	(150)
Bad debts	(140)	(18)
Depreciation	(208)	(58)
Interest	(192)	(12)
Net profit	310	302

Balance sheets

	2003		2002	
	£000	£000	£000	£000
Fixed assets				
Factory		441		450
Machinery		1,791		490
		2,232		940
Current assets				
Stock	238		30	
Debtors	583		83	
Bank	–		12	
	821		125	
Current liabilities				
Creditors	(175)		(36)	
Bank	(11)		–	
	(186)		(36)	
Current assets *less* Current liabilities		635		89
		2,867		1,029
Borrowings		(1,600)		(100)
		1,267		929
Share capital		328		300
Profit and loss		939		629
		1,267		929

Note: the balance on profit and loss at the end of 2002 was £327,000.

(a) **You are required to** explain whether you believe that the performance for the year ended 31 December 2003 and the financial position at that date have improved as a result of the new policies adopted by the company. You should support your answer with appropriate ratios.

(b) All of L Ltd's sales are on credit. The finance director has asked you to calculate the immediate financial impact of reducing the credit period offered to customers. Calculate the amount of cash which would be released if the company could impose a collection period of 45 days.

(*Chartered Institute of Management Accountants*)

You can find a range of additional self-test questions, as well as material to help you with your studies, on the website that accompanies this book at **www.pearsoned.co.uk/wood**

Interpretation of financial statements

Learning objectives

After you have studied this chapter, you should be able to:

- explain the importance of trend analysis when analysing financial statements
- explain that there is no such thing as a generally 'good' or 'bad' value for any ratio
- describe the need to compare like with like if attempting to assess the quality of the result found from ratio analysis
- explain the pyramid of ratios that can be used in order to enhance the view obtained from ratio analysis
- explain that different groups of users of financial statements have access to different sources of information that may help in developing an understanding of and explanation for the results of ratio analysis

Introduction

In this chapter, you'll learn more about ratio analysis and how to use it effectively. You'll revisit how to perform comparisons between organisations and the need for effective and appropriate comparators if valid and worthwhile conclusions are to be made. You'll also learn about the interlinked relationships between ratios and look in greater detail at return on capital employed.

28.1 Background

When shareholders receive the financial statements of the company they have invested in, many simply look to see whether the business has made a profit, and then put the document away. (This is one reason why the introduction of an option to send shareholders abbreviated financial statements, rather than the far more costly to produce full set of financial statements, was introduced a few years ago.) They are aware of only one thing – that the company made a profit of £x. They do not know if it was a 'good' profit. Nor do they know whether it was any different from the profit earned in previous years. (Even if they had noticed the previous period's profit figure in the comparative column, they would be unaware of the equivalent figures for the periods that preceded it.) In addition, they would have no perception of how the performance compared with that of other companies operating in the same sector.

As explained in the previous chapter, ratio analysis can be used to assess company performance and financial position. However, as you learnt in *Business Accounting Essentials 1*, such analysis is relatively useless unless a similar task is undertaken on the financial figures for previous periods, so providing a view of the changes that have occurred over time. Trend analysis of this type is very important in the interpretation of financial statements, for it is only then that the position found can be truly placed in context and statements made concerning whether things are improving, etc.

Of similar importance if financial statements are to be usefully interpreted is comparison of the position shown with that of other companies operating in the same sector, both now and over a period of time.

28.2 Sector relevance

Analysis and interpretation of any phenomenon is all very well if conducted in isolation from the rest of the world. However, it can be of only limited use without comparators with which to develop an understanding of what is being examined. Even when this is done, it is important that the comparators are valid – there is not much point in comparing the performance of a Rolls-Royce with that of a bicycle. Like must be compared with like. Racing bike to racing bike, mountain bike to mountain bike, Premier League football team to Premier League football team, and so on. **For companies, the easiest way to ensure that like is being compared with like is to compare companies that operate in the same business sector.**

The importance of ensuring that any comparison undertaken between companies involves companies in the same sector can best be illustrated through an extreme example: that of the contrast between service companies and manufacturing companies.

Stating the obvious, a firm of consultants which advises its clients on marketing strategies will have far fewer tangible assets than a company with the same turnover and the same capital employed which manufactures forklift trucks. The firm of consultants will need premises, but these could easily be rented ready for use, whereas a manufacturing company would need to make major adjustments to the premises before using them. In addition, the firm of consultants would need very little in the way of machinery, possibly just some computer equipment and office equipment.

In comparison, the manufacturing company would need a great deal of machinery as well as lorries and various types of buildings, and so on. The manufacturing firm would also have stocks of materials and unsold forklift trucks. The consultancy would not have any stock.

Activity 28.1 What effect would these types of differences have on the ratios of the two businesses?

With wider use and increasing levels of personal ownership of PCs with broadband internet access, an increasing number of employees are working from home, especially in the service sector. This trend is set to continue with a resultant reduction in the need for many service industry organisations to maintain offices of the size required in the past.

All of this has an effect on the ratios of performance calculated from the financial statements of manufacturers and service industry firms. The figure of return on capital employed for a service firm, simply because of the far lower amount of tangible assets needed, may appear to be quite high. For a manufacturing firm the opposite may well be the case.

If this distinction between these completely different types of organisation is understood, then the interpreter of the financial statements is able to judge them appropriately. Failure to understand the distinction will bring forth some very strange conclusions.

28.3 Trend analysis

Looking internally at one organisation, sensible comparisons can clearly be made between the situation it was in at various points in time.

Activity 28.2 What two key things does an inward-looking analysis of this type NOT tell you? (*Hint*: think about the overall context.)

In *Business Accounting UK GAAP 1*, an example was shown of two companies, G and H. The example is now reintroduced and further developed. Exhibit 28.1 presents four ratios derived from the financial statements of G over this and the previous four years.

Exhibit 28.1

	Year:	1	2	3	4	5 (now)
Gross profit as % of sales		40	38	36	35	34
Net profit as % of sales		15	13	12	12	11
Net profit as % of capital employed		13	12	11	11	10
Current ratio		3.0	2.8	2.6	2.3	2.0

All other thing being equal, you would expect it more likely that all four of these ratios would rise over time. However, it is clear that they are all decreasing, but there is no other information available which might clarify whether or not this should be cause for concern. For example, the industry may be becoming more competitive, causing margins to shrink, and the falling current ratio may be due to an increase in efficiency over the control of working capital.

A company with this trend of figures could provide an explanation for the decline in margins and for the reduction in liquidity in its annual report. A reader of the financial statements could then decide to accept the explanation and put the calculations away. However, there is no guarantee that an explanation of this kind actually indicates a beneficial situation, irrespective of whether or not it is accurate.

In order to gain a better understanding of the analysis, comparison with other comparable companies in the same sector is needed. Exhibit 28.2 presents the information from Exhibit 28.1 for company G plus information on another company of a similar size operating in the same sector, company H.

Exhibit 28.2

	Years					
		1	2	3	4	5 (current)
Gross profit as % of sales	G	40	38	36	35	34
	H	30	32	33	33	34
Net profit as % of sales	G	15	13	12	12	11
	H	10	10	10	11	11
Net profit as % of capital employed	G	13	12	11	11	10
	H	8	8	9	9	10
Current ratio	G	3	2.8	2.6	2.3	2.0
	H	1.5	1.7	1.9	1.0	2.0

This form of presentation can be difficult to digest and interpret. As an alternative, these results may be compared through graphs, as shown by the example in Exhibit 28.3 which compares the trend in gross profit as a percentage of sales of the two companies. (Note that the vertical axis does not show the percentage below 30 as there is no percentage below that amount in Exhibit 28.2. Omitting the lower figures on the graph in these circumstances allows for a more informative display of the information.)

Exhibit 28.3 The trend of gross profit as a percentage of sales

Now, you should see the importance of placing trends in context. The companies have identical ratios for the current period – does that make them equally desirable as investments? Given one year's financial statements it appears so, but the five-year trend analysis reveals a different picture.

From these figures, G appears to be the worse investment for the future, as the trend for it appears to be downwards, while that of H is upwards. It suggests that the explanation made earlier for the falling margins may not be valid. If the trend for G is continued it could be in a very dangerous financial situation in a year or two's time. H, on the other hand, is strengthening its position all the time.

While it would be ridiculous to state without reservation that H will continue on an upward trend, or that G will continue downwards, a consistent trend of this type does suggest that the situation may well continue into the foreseeable future. It is certainly cause for further investigation.

28.4 Comparisons over time

As shown in the previous section, one of the best ways of using ratios is to compare them with the ratios for the same organisation in respect of previous years. Take another example, the net profit percentage of a company for the past six years, including the current year 2008:

	2003	2004	2005	2006	2007	2008 (now)
Net profit %	5.4	5.2	4.7	4.8	4.8	4.5

This could be presented in a graph as shown in Exhibit 28.4.

Exhibit 28.4

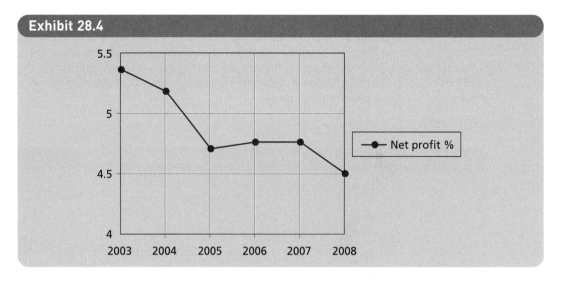

It is obvious that there is a long-term decline in the net profit percentage. This prompts us to examine why this should be so. Without measuring against past years our understanding of the direction in which the business seems to be heading would be much diminished.

We would not only look at the long-term changes in net profit percentages, but also compare similar long-term figures in relation to other aspects of the business.

Of course, other factors outside an organisation, particularly changes in the economy may make the interpretation of trends an extremely complex process. For example, the use of the historical cost accounting concept during periods of high inflation can make effective comparison of monetary amounts over time very problematic.

28.5 Comparisons with other businesses

We've already looked at some of the benefits of undertaking comparisons with other businesses in Section 28.3. Now, we'll consider it in more detail. No one can say in isolation that a business is very profitable. A business may have made an average net profit over the last few years of £6 million which, to most people, may seem profitable. On the other hand, if businesses of a similar size in the same industry are making £20 million a year, then the business making £6 million a year cannot be said to be very profitable.

Ideally, we would like to be able to compare the results of one business with those of similar businesses in the same industry. Then, and only then, would we be able to judge how well, or how badly, that business was doing.

The size of a business can have an important effect upon ratios. Just as we would not try to compare a chemist's shop with a building firm, it would also be wrong to judge a small independent supermarket against Sainsbury's, which owns hundreds of supermarkets.

Interfirm comparisons are also sometimes misleading because of the different accounting treatment of various items, and the location and ages of assets. Some industries have, however, set up interfirm comparisons with guidelines to the companies to ensure that the figures have been constructed using the same bases so that the information is comparable. The information does not disclose data which can be traced to any one firm, ensuring that full confidentiality is observed.

The information available may take the form shown in Exhibit 28.5:

Exhibit 28.5 Published ratios for the widget industry (extract)

	Solvency		Efficiency			
	Current	Acid test	Asset T/O	Stock T/O	Debtor days	Creditor days
2006	2.4	0.7	5.4	8.2	56.4	80.4
2007	2.2	0.8	5.7	9.3	52.6	66.8

The equivalent figures for the company being assessed can then be tabulated alongside the industry figures to enable comparisons to be made, as in Exhibit 28.6.

Exhibit 28.6

	Company ratios		Industry ratios	
	2006	2007	2006	2007
Current ratio	2.9	2.8	2.4	2.2
Acid test ratio	0.5	0.6	0.7	0.8
Asset turnover	5.2	5.3	5.4	5.7
Stock turnover	4.4	4.7	8.2	9.3
Debtor days	65.9	65.2	56.4	52.6
Creditor days	58.3	56.8	80.4	66.8

The financial status of the company is now much clearer. What appeared to be a situation of improving liquidity and efficiency is now shown to be an increasingly poorer liquidity and efficiency position compared with the industry as a whole.

However, it should be borne in mind that the industry figures probably include many companies that are either much larger or much smaller than the company being assessed. To obtain a more complete picture, information is needed concerning companies of a similar size, such as in the comparison between G and H earlier in this chapter (*see* Section 28.3). This information may be available from the source of the interfirm comparison. If not, other sources would need to be used, for example the published financial statements of appropriate companies.

The other information missing from the above comparison is data from previous periods. While not so relevant to the current position, it can be useful in explaining why a situation has developed, and in determining whether the current position is likely to persist.

Activity 28.3 When an organisation operates in more than one sector, how do you identify other appropriate organisations with which to make comparisons?

28.6 Pyramid of ratios

Once ratios have been analysed and compared, explanations must be sought for the results obtained. Sometimes it will be obvious why a certain result was obtained – for example, if a company has moved from traditional stock-keeping to a just-in-time system during the period, its stock turnover will bear no resemblance to that which it had in the previous period.

For those inside the company – its directors and management – the management accounting records are available to assist in finding explanations, as are the company's staff. Outsiders – shareholders, analysts, lenders, suppliers, customers, etc. – do not have access to all this internal information (though some of these user groups will have access to more internal information than others – banks, for example, can usually obtain copies of a company's confidential internal accounting information upon request). They must, instead, fall back upon other sources of information, such as newspaper reports and industry publications.

One source of additional information available to everyone is a result of the fact that most ratios can be further subdivided into secondary ratios which, themselves, can also be subdivided, so building into a **pyramid of ratios**. By following through the pyramid of a given ratio, the source of the original ratio can often be isolated, enabling a far more focused investigation than would otherwise be possible.

For example, one of the most important ratios is the return on the capital employed (ROCE). This ratio has not happened by itself. If the ratio of net profit to sales had not been a particular figure and the ratio of sales to capital employed had not been a particular figure, then the ROCE would not have turned out to be the figure that it is.

Thus, the ROCE comes about as a result of all the other ratios which have underpinned it. It is the final summation of all that has happened in the various aspects of the business. The ROCE pyramid of ratios is shown in Exhibit 28.7.

Exhibit 28.7

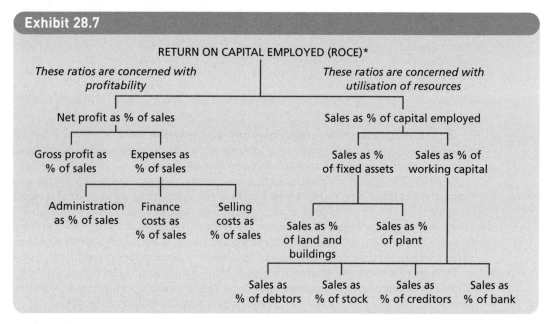

Note: The formula for ROCE used here is a (very) simplified version of the formula listed in Section 27.8. Nevertheless, to all intents and purposes, it is the same formula.

By itself, the pyramid of ratios does not tell you everything. It comes into full effect when compared with similar ratios from previous years, or with similar pyramids of ratios in respect of other businesses. If the ROCE has been falling over the past year, a study of the pyramid of ratios for each of the previous two years may enable you to pinpoint exactly where the changes have been made to bring about the worsening position. Investigation of these matters may then give you some indication of the action to take.

28.7 Return on capital employed: company policy

The pyramid of ratios in Exhibit 28.7 illustrates the interdependence of each ratio. This can be examined in greater detail by investigating the policies of two companies to achieve their desired return on capital employed.

The first part of the pyramid tells us that the ROCE is dependent on both net profit as a percentage of sales and also sales as a percentage of capital employed. This means that:

$$\text{ROCE} = \frac{\text{Net profit}}{\text{Capital employed}}$$

which by splitting the equation between profitability ratios and resource utilisation ratios means also that:

$$\text{ROCE} = \frac{\text{Net profit}}{\text{Sales}} \times \frac{\text{Sales}}{\text{Capital employed}}$$

This interrelationship of the subsidiary ratios can be illustrated through an example. At the same time, it can be seen that the result of computing a primary ratio is dependent upon the items comprising it; and that there is no guarantee that a value of x will be 'good', and y 'bad'. Whether the result obtained is 'good' or 'bad' depends on the underlying factors that give rise to the result obtained (what, for example, is the company's policy on depreciation and replacement of assets, as this can significantly affect the ROCE?), the sector in which the business operates and its relative size. Without knowledge of these items, comparison of the ratio analysis of two companies is likely to be misleading at best.

Two companies, both in the grocery business, may decide to aim for the same ROCE of 10 per cent. This can be achieved in completely different ways by the two companies.

A Ltd is a large company operating a supermarket. It seeks to attract customers by offering low prices and makes a net profit of only 1.25 per cent on sales. Its sales for the year are £8,000,000 on which its net profit is £100,000. Its capital employed is £1,000,000. The ROCE is, therefore, 10 per cent (i.e. £100,000 net profit on capital employed of £1,000,000). This can also be expressed as:

$$\text{ROCE} = \frac{\text{Net profit}}{\text{Sales}} \times \frac{\text{Sales}}{\text{Capital employed}}$$

$$= \frac{£100,000}{£8,000,000} \times \frac{£8,000,000}{£1,000,000}$$

$$= 10\%$$

B Ltd by comparison is a small local retailer. It seeks a higher margin per £100 sales, but because of higher prices it will achieve a lower volume of business. It makes a net profit of 5 per cent on sales. Its sales for the year amount to £200,000 on which it makes a net profit of £10,000. The capital employed is £100,000. The ROCE is therefore 10 per cent (i.e. £10,000 on capital employed of £100,000). This can also be expressed as:

$$\text{ROCE} = \frac{\text{Net profit}}{\text{Sales}} \times \frac{\text{Sales}}{\text{Capital employed}}$$

$$= \frac{£10,000}{£200,000} \times \frac{£200,000}{£100,000}$$

$$= 10\%$$

It can be seen that two companies, despite different sizes of business and operating different pricing policies, can have the same ROCE.

Learning outcomes

You should now have learnt:

1 Ratios on their own are frequently misleading – they should not be considered in isolation from similar computations:
   (a) in previous periods; and/or
   (b) on similar-sized firms in the same sector.

2 The items in the financial statements are affected by company policy – for example, the rate of depreciation to use, and the policy of asset replacement; the policies adopted, therefore, directly affect the ratio analysis.

3 Companies of very different size and in very different sectors can have the same ratio results despite their being different in every respect.

4 The importance and impact of size, sector and company policies upon ratios mean that there is no such thing as a 'good' or 'bad' value that can be treated as a yardstick for any ratio.

5 All ratios are part of one or more pyramids of ratios.

6 When the results of ratio analysis are being investigated further, the relevant pyramid of ratios can be analysed in order to pinpoint the element giving rise to the situation being investigated.

Answers to activities

28.1 The service business will probably have a lower current ratio – it has no stock. Its creditor days are probably near zero. Its return on capital employed is probably much higher. Its asset turnover may be extremely high – it may not have very many fixed assets. Overall, trying to draw any sensible conclusions by comparing the ratios of these two businesses will be a waste of time.

28.2 It won't tell you whether the organisation is or was in a good position relative to its competitors or other organisations in the same sector. Nor will it tell you if changes in the ratios are actually moving in the appropriate direction for the sector in which the organisation operates.

28.3 In this case, you can try to identify other organisations with a similar range of activities. However, it would probably be more beneficial to separate out the data relating to each type of activity and then compare the reduced data against appropriate comparators.

Advice

Ratio analysis is a topic that causes more marks to be thrown away in exams than probably every other topic combined. No other accounting topic is as concerned with understanding rather than knowledge, and examiners increasingly expect you to be able to demonstrate understanding rather than simply your ability to prepare the financial statements or calculate the ratios.

There is no one set pattern to the questions, which depend upon the examiner's ingenuity and background experience. The usual shortcomings in the answers handed in by examinees, particularly on questions relating to this topic but also on questions in other areas, can be listed as follows:

1 Not following the instructions as laid down. If the question says 'list the' then the examiner expects a list as an answer, 'Discuss the' means exactly that, 'Write a report' needs a report as the answer, and so on. You will lose a lot of marks for not giving the examiner exactly what has been asked for.

2 Very often all the ratios etc. are calculated, but then the candidate does not offer any comments even though they have been asked for. *Make certain you cover this part of the question in an appropriate amount of detail.*

3 Even where students have written something about the ratios, they often repeat what the calculations are and offer nothing else, e.g. 'you can see that the gross profit ratio has increased from 18 to 20 per cent' and the answer has finished there. The examiner can already see from your calculations that the gross profit percentage has increased, and wants you to write about *why* it might have increased, what conclusions, if any, can be arrived at, or what further information may be needed to discover why it has changed.

4 Remember that when the examiner asks you 'what other information you would like to have' about a firm when trying to interpret the financial statements so as to give advice to someone then, ideally, you would like to know more about the plans for the future of the business, how it compares with others in the same industry, whether or not there are going to be changes in the management and so on. We should not limit ourselves to information about the past, we really need to know as much about the future as we possibly can.

5 Do not restrict your examination answers to what you have read in a textbook. Keep your eyes and ears open as you go shopping, visit factories, work, buy petrol at the filling station, go to the theatre, and so on. Reading a 'quality' newspaper helps, as there are quite a lot of items about business. Bring all of this sort of knowledge and experience into your answers. You will impress the examiners. They are extremely bored reading regurgitations of textbook learning with nothing added.

6 Quite a few questions will concern the type of business of which you will have first-hand experience, so you can introduce personal knowledge into your answer. A typical instance would be comparing two grocery businesses. One would be a large supermarket and the other would be a small corner shop. The policies of the two firms would be quite different. The supermarket would have decided on a policy of attracting new customers by lowering sales margins and yet boosting ROCE. The corner shop might have a policy of high margins, but remain open on Sundays and late at nights, and thus be a 'convenience shop', i.e. customers might well go there when other shops are closed or are too far away to be worth the extra cost in petrol, etc. when compared with the extra cost of shopping at the corner shop.

7 Last, but not least, *show your workings*. If you make a mistake in your calculations and do not show your workings you cannot be awarded any credit for a partially incorrect calculation. Consider how much longer it takes to show the detail contained in Section 28.7 above, rather than simply the result of the calculation – maybe 30 seconds. *Now consider whether you would rather spend five minutes in an exam showing the workings of ten ratio calculations, or six months studying to retake the exam you failed because you made a mistake in two of your calculations and lost five marks because the examiner could not tell why you got the answer wrong.*

Review questions

28.1 Adrian Frampton was considering the purchase of one of two businesses. However, Frampton had only been provided with limited information about the businesses, as follows:

Summarised Financial Information for the year ended 31 December 2009

Information	Business X	Business Y
Cost of goods sold	£400,000	£600,000
Administrative expenses	£50,000	£60,000
Average stock at cost	£40,000	£50,000
Working capital as at 31 December 2009	£90,000	£250,000
Selling and distribution expenses	£15,000	£35,000
Proprietor's capital at 1 January 2009	£200,000	£350,000
Gross profit percentage mark-up on cost	20	25

Additional information:

1 Average stock had been calculated by using the year's opening and closing stocks. Subsequently it was discovered that Business Y had overvalued its stock on 31 December 2009 by £10,000.
2 Business X's administrative expenses included a payment for rent of £15,000 which covered a three-year period to 31 December 2011.

→

3 A sum of £2,500 was included in the administrative expenses of Business Y in respect of a holiday taken by the owner and his family.

4 Cash drawings for the year ended 31 December 2009 were:

	£
Business X	20,000
Business Y	25,000

5 The owners of the businesses had stipulated the following prices for their businesses:

	£
Business X	190,000
Business Y	400,000

Required:

(a) Based on the information available prepare comparative trading and profit and loss accounts for the year ending 31 December 2009.

(b) Using the information provided and the accounting statements prepared in (a), calculate relevant accounting ratios in order to give Frampton a basis for assessing the performances of the two businesses. Comment on the results.

(c) What additional information is needed in order to assess more accurately
  (i) the liquidity of the businesses;
  (ii) the future prospects of the businesses?

(AQA (Associated Examining Board): GCE A-level)

28.2 Three companies have the capital structures shown below.

Company	A	B	C
	£000	£000	£000
Ordinary shares	600	400	50
12% debentures	–	200	550
	600	600	600

The return on capital employed was 20 per cent for each firm in 2004, and in 2005 was 10 per cent. Corporation tax in both years was assumed to be 55 per cent, and debenture interest is an allowable expense against corporation tax.

(a) Calculate the percentage return on the shareholders' capital for each company for 2004 and 2005. Assume that all profits are distributed.

(b) Use your answer to explain the merits and the dangers of high gearing.

(Edexcel: University of London GCE A-level)

28.3A Martha is the accountant of a trading business. During the past year she produced interim accounts for the six months ended 30 November 2005, and draft final accounts for the year ended 31 May 2006, as follows:

	Interim accounts £	Draft final accounts £
Sales (all on credit terms)	140,000	336,000
Cost of sales (Note 1)	42,000	112,000
Gross profit	98,000	224,000
Less Expenses	56,000	168,000
Net profit	42,000	56,000
Fixed assets	70,000	63,000
Current assets (Note 2)	42,000	71,000
Current liabilities (Note 3)	(22,000)	(30,000)
	90,000	104,000
Share capital	30,000	30,000
Retained earnings	60,000	74,000
	90,000	104,000

Notes:
1 Average stock was £14,000 during the first six months.
2 Current assets were:

	30 Nov 2005	31 May 2006
	£	£
Stock	16,000	25,000
Debtors	24,000	28,000
Bank	2,000	18,000
	42,000	71,000

3 Current liabilities consisted entirely of trade creditors.

Martha informs you that the business leased additional premises from 1 December 2005, and that sales arising therefrom totalled £70,000 for the six months to 31 May 2006, with an average mark-up on cost prices of 150 per cent being made on those goods.

Expenses relating to these additional premises totalled £21,000 for the period. Two-fifths of the closing stock of the business was located at these premises.

Prepare a report, using appropriate accounting ratios, to explain the changes in the financial situation of the business during the year ended 31 May 2006.

(Edexcel: University of London GCE A-level)

28.4 John Jones is considering purchasing shares in one of two companies and has extracted the following information from the balance sheet of each company.

	Company A Plc £000	Company B Plc £000
Authorised share capital		
£1 ordinary shares	600	1,000
8% £1 preference shares	400	
Issued share capital		
£1 ordinary shares	300	800
8% £1 preference shares	200	
Reserves		
Share premium	300	400
Retained earnings	400	200
Loan capital		
10% debentures (2010)		200
12% debentures (2016)	400	

Required:
(a) Define the term 'gearing' stating clearly what is meant by a low gearing ratio.
(b) Calculate the gearing factor for each company.
(c) Explain to John Jones the significance of gearing to an ordinary shareholder in each of the companies above.
(d) Assuming for each company a trading profit of £200,000 before interest and an ordinary dividend of 15 per cent, show the movement on shareholders' funds for a year for each company. You should ignore taxation.

(AQA (Associated Examining Board): GCE A-level)

→

→ **28.5A** The following are extracts from the balance sheets as at 31 March 2004 and 31 March 2005 of Glebe Ltd:

	31 March 2004		31 March 2005	
	£	£	£	£
Current assets				
Stocks	20,000		25,000	
Trade debtors	10,000		17,000	
Cash	5,000		3,000	
		35,000		45,000
Less				
Current liabilities				
Trade creditors	12,000		16,000	
Bank overdraft	7,000		34,000	
		(19,000)		(50,000)
		16,000		(5,000)

Required:
(a) Calculate for each of the two years two ratios that indicate the liquidity position of the company.
(b) (i) From the information given, give reasons for the changes which have occurred in the working capital.
(ii) What other information regarding the current assets and current liabilities would you consider necessary to assess the ability of the business to continue in operation?
(c) Discuss any other information available from a balance sheet that may affect an assessment of the liquidity of a business.

(AQA (Associated Examining Board): GCE A-level)

28.6 Colin Black is considering investing a substantial sum in the ordinary shares of Jacks Ltd. Having some accounting knowledge he has extracted the following information from the accounts for the last two financial years.

	As at 31 March 2008	As at 31 March 2009
	£	£
Issued share capital		
£1 ordinary shares, fully paid	100,000	150,000
Reserves		
Share premium	10,000	60,000
Retained earnings	140,000	160,000
Loan capital		
10% debentures 2010–16	40,000	40,000

	For year ended 31 March 2008	For year ended 31 March 2009
	£	£
Net profit after tax	60,000	70,000

Because he was disappointed with the result he obtained when he calculated the return on the equity capital employed, Colin Black has asked for your advice.

Required:
(a) Calculate the figures which prompted Colin Black's reaction.
(b) Prepare a memorandum to Colin Black pointing out other information to be considered when comparing the return on equity capital employed over two years as a basis for his investment decision.
(c) Explain why a company builds up and maintains reserves.

(AQA (Associated Examining Board): GCE A-level)

28.7A The following information has been extracted from the accounts of Witton Way Ltd:

Profit and Loss Account for the year to 30 April

	2005 £000	2006 £000
Turnover (all credit sales)	7,650	11,500
Less Cost of sales	(5,800)	(9,430)
Gross profit	1,850	2,070
Other expenses	(150)	(170)
Loan interest	(50)	(350)
Profit before taxation	1,650	1,550
Taxation	(600)	(550)
Profit after taxation	1,050	1,000

Note: Dividends paid in 2006 were £300,000 (2005: £300,000).

Balance Sheet at 30 April

	2005 £000	2006 £000
Fixed assets		
Tangible assets	10,050	11,350
Current assets		
Stocks	1,500	2,450
Trade debtors	1,200	3,800
Cash	900	50
	3,600	6,300
Creditors: Amounts falling due within one year	(2,400)	(2,700)
Net current assets	1,200	3,600
Total assets less current liabilities	11,250	14,950
Creditors: Amounts falling due after more than one year		
Loans and other borrowings	(350)	(3,350)
	10,900	11,600
Capital and reserves		
Called-up share capital	5,900	5,900
Profit and loss account	5,000	5,700
	10,900	11,600

Additional information: During the year to 30 April 2006, the company tried to stimulate sales by reducing the selling price of its products and by offering more generous credit terms to its customers.

Required:
(a) Calculate six accounting ratios specifying the basis of your calculations for each of the two years to 30 April 2005 and 2006 respectively which will enable you to examine the company's progress during 2006.
(b) From the information available to you, including the ratios calculated in part (a) of the question, comment upon the company's results for the year to 30 April 2006 under the heads of 'profitability', 'liquidity', 'efficiency' and 'shareholders' interests'.
(c) State what additional information you would require in order to assess the company's attempts to stimulate sales during the year to 30 April 2006.

(*Association of Accounting Technicians*)

→

→ **28.8** You are presented with the following information for three quite separate and independent companies:

Summarised Balance Sheets at 31 March 2007

	Chan plc £000	Ling plc £000	Wong plc £000
Total assets *less* current liabilities	600	600	700
Creditors: amounts falling due after more than one year			
10% debenture stock	–	–	(100)
	£600	£600	£600
Capital and reserves:			
Called-up share capital			
Ordinary shares of £1 each	500	300	200
10% cumulative preference shares of £1 each	–	200	300
Profit and loss account	100	100	100
	£600	£600	£600

Additional information:
1 The operating profit before interest and tax for the year to 31 March 2008 earned by each of the three companies was £300,000.
2 The effective rate of corporation tax for all three companies for the year to 31 March 2008 is 30 per cent. This rate is to be used in calculating each company's tax payable on ordinary profit.
3 An ordinary dividend of 20p for the year to 31 March 2008 was paid by all three companies, as were the preference dividends.
4 The market prices per ordinary share at 31 March 2008 were as follows:

	£
Chan plc	8.40
Ling plc	9.50
Wong plc	10.38

5 There were no changes in the share capital structure or in long-term loans of any of the companies during the year to 31 March 2008.

Required:
(a) In so far as the information permits, prepare the profit and loss account for each of the three companies (in columnar format) for the year ending 31 March 2008 (formal notes to the accounts are not required);
(b) show the change in profit and loss for each company over the year;
(c) calculate the following accounting ratios for each company:
  (i) earnings per share;
  (ii) price earnings;
  (iii) gearing (taken as total borrowings (preference share capital and long-term loans) to ordinary shareholders' funds); and
(d) using the gearing ratios calculated in answering part (c) of the question, briefly examine the importance of gearing if you were thinking of investing in some ordinary shares in one of the three companies assuming that the profits of the three companies were fluctuating.

(*Association of Accounting Technicians*)

28.9A The chairman of a family business has been examining the following summary of the accounts of the company since it began three years ago.

Balance Sheet (at 30 June) £000

	2004 Actual		2005 Actual		2006 Actual	
Freehold land and buildings		150		150		150
Plant	150		150		450	
Less: Depreciation	(15)		(30)		(75)	
		135		120		375
		285		270		525
Stock and work in progress	20		45		85	
Debtors	33		101		124	
Bank and cash	10		15		–	
	63		161		209	
Less: Creditors	(20)		(80)		(35)	
Taxation	(4)		(17)		(6)	
Overdraft	(–)		(–)		(25)	
		39		64		143
		324		334		668
Less: Loan		(–)		(–)		(200)
		324		334		468
Ordinary share capital (£1 shares)		300		300		400
General reserve		17		25		45
Deferred tax account		7		9		23
		324		334		468

Profit and Loss Account (for year to 30 June) £000

	2004 Actual		2005 Actual		2006 Actual	
Sales		260		265		510
Trading profit		53		50		137
Depreciation	15		15		45	
Loan interest	–		–		43	
		(15)		(15)		(88)
Net profit		38		35		49
Taxation (including transfer to or from deferred tax account)		(11)		(15)		(15)
Net profit after tax		27		20		34
Dividend (proposed*)		10		12		14*

The company's products are popular in the locality and in the first two years sales could have been higher if there had been extra machine capacity available.

On 1 January 2006, additional share and loan capital was obtained which enabled extra machinery to be purchased. This gave an immediate increase in sales and profits.

Although 2005/06 showed the best yet results, the chairman is not very happy; the accountant has suggested that a dividend should not be proposed this year (2006) because of the overdraft. The accountant has, however, proposed that the directors consider a dividend of £14,000 (£2,000) up on last year.

Naturally, the chairman is displeased and wants some explanations from the accountant regarding the figures in the accounts. He specifically asks:

➡

→ (*i*) Why, if profits are the best ever and considering the company has obtained extra capital during the year, has the company gone into overdraft? Can there really be a profit if there is no cash left in the bank to pay a dividend next year?

(*ii*) Why is the freehold still valued at the same price as in 2004? The real value seems to be about £225,000. Why is this real value not in the balance sheet?

Required:

Write a report to the chairman:

(a) commenting on the state and progress of the business as disclosed by the accounts and the above information, supporting your analysis by appropriate key accounting ratios, and

(b) giving reasoned answers, in the context of recognised accounting law, rules and practices, to each of the questions raised by the chairman.

(*Institute of Chartered Secretaries and Administrators*)

28.10 The following information is provided for Bessemer Ltd which operates in an industry subject to marked variations in consumer demand.

(*i*) Shareholders' equity at 30 September 2005:	£000
Issued ordinary shares of £1 each fully paid	5,000
Retained profits	1,650
	6,650

There were no loans outstanding at the balance sheet date.

(*ii*) Profit and loss account extracts: year to 30 September 2005:	£000
Net profit before tax	900
Less Corporation tax	270
	630

(*iii*) Changes in retained profits: year ending 30 September 2005	
Retained profit at 1 October 2004	1,620
Dividends paid during year ending 30 September 2005	(600)
	1,020
Profit after tax for year ending 30 September 2005	630
Retained profit at 30 September 2005	1,650

(*iv*) The directors are planning to expand output. This will require an additional investment of £2,000,000 which may be financed either by issuing 1,000,000 ordinary shares each with a nominal value of £1, or by raising a 12 per cent debenture.

(*v*) Forecast profits before interest charges, if any, for the year to 30 September:

	£000
2006	1,800
2007	500
2008	2,200

A corporation tax rate of 30 per cent on reported profit before tax may be assumed; the directors plan to pay out the entire post-tax profit as dividends.

Required:

(a) The forecast dividends for each of the next three years and year-end balance sheet extracts, so far as the information permits, assuming that the expansion is financed by:
   (*i*) issuing additional shares, or
   (*ii*) raising a debenture.

(b) Calculate the forecast return on shareholders' equity, for each of the next three years, under the alternative methods for financing the planned expansion.

(c) An assessment of the merits and demerits of the alternative methods of finance based on the calculations made under (a) and (b) and any other relevant methods of comparison.

(*Institute of Chartered Secretaries and Administrators*)

28.11A An investor is considering the purchase of shares in either AA plc or BB plc whose latest accounts are summarised below. Both companies carry on similar manufacturing activities with similar selling prices and costs of materials, labour and services.

Balance Sheets at 30 September 2007 (£000)

	AA plc		BB plc	
Freehold property at revaluation 2005		2,400		–
Plant, machinery and equipment:				
at cost	1,800		1,800	
depreciation	1,200		400	
		600		1,400
Goodwill		–		800
Stocks: finished goods		400		200
work in progress		300		100
Debtors		800		500
Bank deposit		–		400
		4,500		3,400
Less Liabilities due within one year				
Creditors	600		900	
Overdraft	200		–	
	800		900	
Liabilities due after one year	1,400		1,000	
		(2,200)		(1,900)
		2,300		1,500
Ordinary £1 shares		1,000		500
Reserves		1,300		1,000
		2,300		1,500

Profit and Loss Accounts – Year ending 30 September 2007 (£000)

	AA plc		BB plc	
Sales		2,500		2,500
Operating profit		400		600
Depreciation – plant, machinery and equipment	180		180	
Loan interest	150		160	
		(330)		(340)
		70		260
Bank interest		–		100
		70		360
Taxation		(20)		(90)
Profit after taxation		50		270
Note:				
Dividend proposed		40		130
Price/earnings ratio	30		5	
Market value of share	£1.50		£2.70	

Required:

(a) write a report to the investor, giving an appraisal of the results and state of each business, and

(b) advise the investor whether, in your opinion, the price/earnings ratios and market price of the shares can be justified in the light of the figures in the accounts, giving your reasons.

(Institute of Chartered Secretaries and Administrators)

→

→ **28.12** The following are the summarised accounts for B Limited, a company with an accounting year ending on 30 September.

Summarised Balance Sheets for	2005/6		2006/7	
	£000	£000	£000	£000
Tangible fixed assets – at cost				
Less Depreciation		4,995		12,700
Current assets:				
Stocks	40,145		50,455	
Debtors	40,210		43,370	
Cash at bank	12,092		5,790	
	92,447		99,615	
Creditors: amounts falling due within one year:				
Trade creditors	34,389		39,215	
Taxation	2,473		3,260	
	36,862		42,475	
Net current assets		55,585		57,140
Total assets less current liabilities		60,580		69,840
Creditors: amounts falling due after more than one year:				
10% debentures 2006/2009		(19,840)		(19,840)
		40,740		50,000
Capital and reserves:				
Called-up share capital of £0.25 per share		9,920		9,920
Profit and loss account		30,820		40,080
Shareholders' funds		40,740		50,000

Summarised Profit and Loss Accounts for	2005/6	2006/7
	£000	£000
Turnover	486,300	583,900
Operating profit	17,238	20,670
Interest payable	(1,984)	(1,984)
Profit on ordinary activities before taxation	15,254	18,686
Tax on profit on ordinary activities	(5,734)	(7,026)
Profit for the financial year	9,520	11,660

Notes:
	2005/6	2006/7
(1) Retained profit brought forward	23,540	30,820
(2) Dividends paid during the year	2,240	2,400

You are required to:
(a) calculate, for each year, two ratios for each of the following user groups, which are of particular significance to them: (i) shareholders; (ii) trade creditors; (iii) internal management;
(b) make brief comments upon the changes, between the two years, in the ratios calculated in (a) above.

(*Chartered Institute of Management Accountants*)

28.13A The following are the financial statements of D Limited, a wholesaling company, for the year ended 31 December:

Profit and Loss Accounts	2004 £000	2004 £000	2005 £000	2005 £000
Turnover – credit sales	2,200		2,640	
cash sales	200		160	
		2,400		2,800
Cost of sales		(1,872)		(2,212)
Gross profit		528		588
Distribution costs		(278)		(300)
Administration expenses		(112)		(114)
Operating profit		138		174
Interest payable		–		(32)
Profit on ordinary activities before tax		138		142

Balance Sheets as at 31 December	2004 £000	2004 £000	2005 £000	2005 £000
Tangible fixed assets		220		286
Current assets: Stocks	544		660	
Debtors	384		644	
Cash at bank	8		110	
	936		1,414	
Creditors: amounts falling due within one year:				
Trade creditors	(256)		(338)	
Net current assets		680		1,076
Total assets *less* current liabilities		900		1,362
Creditors: amounts falling due after more than one year:				
Debenture loans		–		(320)
Shareholders' funds		900		1,042

The following information should be taken into consideration.

1 You may assume that:
(*i*) the range of products sold by D Limited remained unchanged over the two years;
(*ii*) the company managed to acquire its products in 2005 at the same prices as it acquired them for in 2004;
(*iii*) the effects of any inflationary aspects have been taken into account in the figures.
2 Ignore taxation.
3 All calculations must be shown to one decimal place.

You are required, using the information above, to assess and comment briefly on the company, from the point of view of:
(*a*) profitability;
(*b*) liquidity.

(*Chartered Institute of Management Accountants*)

→

→ **28.14** G plc is a holding company with subsidiaries that have diversified interests. G plc's board of directors is interested in the group acquiring a subsidiary in the machine tool manufacturing sector. Two companies have been identified as potential acquisitions, A Ltd and B Ltd. Summaries of both these companies' accounts are shown below:

Profit and Loss Accounts for the year ending 30 April 2008

	A Ltd £000	B Ltd £000
Turnover	985	560
Cost of goods sold		
Opening stock	150	145
Materials	255	136
Labour	160	125
Factory overheads	205	111
Depreciation	35	20
Closing stock	(155)	(140)
	650	397
Gross profit	335	163
Selling and administration expenses	(124)	(75)
Interest	(35)	(10)
Profit before taxation	176	78
Taxation	(65)	(25)
Profit after taxation	111	53

Balance Sheets at 30 April 2008

	A Ltd £000	A Ltd £000	B Ltd £000	B Ltd £000
Fixed assets		765		410
Current assets				
Stock	155		140	
Debtors	170		395	
Bank	50		45	
	375		580	
Current liabilities				
Trade creditors	235		300	
Other	130		125	
	(365)		(425)	
Net current assets		10		155
Debentures		(220)		(70)
		555		495
Share capital		450		440
Profit and loss account		105		55
		555		495

You are required to prepare a report for the board of G plc assessing the financial performance and position of A Ltd and B Ltd. Your report should be prepared in the context of G plc's interests in these two companies and should be illustrated with financial ratios where appropriate. You should state any assumptions you make as well as any limitations of your analysis.

(*Chartered Institute of Management Accountants*)

28.15A J plc supplies and fits car tyres, exhaust pipes and other components. The company has branches throughout the country. Roughly 60 per cent of sales are for cash (retail sales). The remainder are credit sales made to car hire companies and large organisations with fleets of company cars (business sales). Business sales tend to be more profitable than retail and the company is keen to expand in this area. There is, however, considerable competition. Branch managers are responsible for obtaining business customers and have some discretion over terms of trade and discounts.

The company's computerised accounting system has recently produced the following report for the manager of the Eastown branch for the six months ended 30 September 2004:

	Eastown Branch	Average for all branches
Return on capital employed	22%	16%
Gross profit	38%	45%
Selling and promotion costs/sales	9%	6%
Wages/sales	19%	14%
Debtors turnover (based on credit sales only)	63 days	52 days
Stock turnover	37 days	49 days

The Eastown branch manager has only recently been appointed and is unsure whether his branch appears well managed. He has asked for your advice.

You are required to compare the performance of the Eastown branch with the average for all branches. Suggest reasons for the differences you identify.

(*Chartered Institute of Management Accountants*)

28.16A Company managers are aware that the readers of financial statements often use accounting ratios to evaluate their performance. **Explain** how this could lead to decisions which are against the company's best interests.

(*Chartered Institute of Management Accountants*)

You can find a range of additional self-test questions, as well as material to help you with your studies, on the website that accompanies this book at **www.pearsoned.co.uk/wood**

Part 5

ISSUES IN FINANCIAL REPORTING

Introduction

This part looks at the theories upon which accounting practice is based, considers issues affecting accounting and financial reporting and reviews the place of accounting information in the context of the environment in which business entities operate.

Accounting theory

Learning objectives

After you have studied this chapter, you should be able to:

- explain that there is no one overall accepted general theory of accounting
- describe some of the possible valuation alternatives to historical cost
- explain the difference between current purchasing power and current cost accounting
- describe the characteristics of useful information
- describe problems relating to the production of accounting information

Introduction

This chapter is in three parts: general accounting theory; accounting for changing price levels; and the objectives of financial statements. You will learn about asset valuation, the concept of wealth measurement, the needs of the users of accounting information, and the problems inherent in the production of accounting information.

Part I — General accounting theory

29.1 Background

To many students it will seem strange that a discussion of accounting theory has been left until this late stage of the book. Logically you could argue that it should have preceded all the practical work.

The reason for not dealing with theory at the beginning is simple. From a teaching point of view, it could easily have confused you, and made it more difficult to assimilate the basic rules of accounting. The terms used in theory, such as what is meant in accounting by capital, liabilities, assets, net profit and so on, would not then have been understood. Leaving it until now, if theory points out what is wrong with accounting methods, at least you know those methods. Theory taught in a vacuum is counterproductive for most students.

In the discussion which follows, we want you to remember that this is your first proper look at accounting theory. We do not intend it to be an exhaustive examination, but simply an introduction to give you an overall appreciation. If you carry your studies to a higher level you will have to study accounting theory in much greater depth.

29.2 An overall accepted theory?

It would not be surprising if you were expecting to read here exactly what the overall accepted theory of accounting is, and then proceed to examine the details later. Unfortunately, there is no such 'accepted' theory. This is much regretted by those accountants who have chosen an academic life. To practising accountants, accounting is what accountants do, and they feel theory has little place in that. Such a narrow view is to be deprecated. The reality, however, is that accounting theory provides a general frame of reference by which accounting practices can be judged and it also guides the way to the development of new practices and procedures.

The lack of an accepted theory of accounting does not mean that it has not been attempted; there have been numerous attempts. At first an inductive approach was tried – i.e. one that tried to create a theory from a few examples. For example, if you saw a white swan, you might induce the theory that all swans are white (which they are not). The practices of accountants were observed and analysed to see if any consistent behaviour could be detected. This was done in the hope that if a general principle was identified, everyone could be led towards applying it. The inductive approach failed.

It was impossible to find consistent patterns of behaviour amongst the mass of practices that had developed over the years. Also, such an approach would not have brought about any important improvements in accounting practices, as it looked at 'what accountants do' rather than 'what accountants should be doing'.

A different approach emerged in the 1950s. It was a **normative approach**, in that it aimed to improve accounting practice. It looked at what accountants should be doing rather than at what they did. However, it also included elements of the inductive approach in attempting to derive rules based on logical reasoning when given a set of objectives. The combination of these approaches has been promising, but the main problem has been a lack of a general agreement as to the objectives of accounting.

As you might expect, attention then switched towards a less ambitious approach. This is based, first, on identifying the users of financial statements, and then finding out what kind of information they require. Such an approach was used in *The Corporate Report*, sponsored by the government and published in 1975. We will look later at the user groups which were identified. The other important report using this approach was that of the Sandilands Committee (also sponsored by the government and published in 1975). This will also be considered more fully later.

 Activity 29.1 Should accountants give the user groups the information they are asking for, or the information for which they should be asking?

Another point which will be considered later is whether only one report should be issued for all user groups, or whether each group should have its own report.

Having had an overall look at how theory construction is proceeding, we can now turn to look at theory in more detail.

29.3 Measurement of income

The syllabus uses the word 'income', but the term 'net profit' means exactly the same. (In accounting, we use the term 'revenue' when describing receipts arising from sales transactions. In accounting, the term 'income' does *not* have this meaning.) In this book the calculation of net profit is done within fairly strict guidelines. Chapter 10 in *Frank Wood's Business Accounting 1* provided guidance on the overall concepts ruling such calculations. However, just because the business world and the accounting profession use this basic approach does not mean it is the only one available. We will now consider possible alternatives to the basic method.

Let's start by looking at the simplest possible example of the calculation of profit, where everyone would agree with the way it is calculated. John is starting in business, his only asset being cash £1,000. He rents a stall in the market for the day, costing him £40. He then buys fruit for cash £90, and sells it all during the day for cash £160. At the end of the day John's only asset is still cash: £1,000 − £40 − £90 + 160 = £1,030. Everyone would agree that his profit for that day was £30, i.e. £160 sales − £90 purchases − £40 expenses = £30. In this case his profit equals the increase in his cash.

Suppose that John now changes his style of trading. He buys the market stall, and he also starts selling nuts and dried fruit, of which he can keep an inventory from one day to another. If we now want to calculate profit we cannot do it simply in terms of cash, we will also have to place a value both on the inventory of fruit and nuts and on his stall, at both the beginning and the end of each day.

The argument just put forward assumes that we can all agree that profit represents an increase in wealth. It assumes that John will make a profit for a period if either:

(a) he is better off at the end of the period than he was at the beginning; or
(b) he would have been better off at the end than at the beginning had he not consumed some of the profits by taking drawings.

The Nobel prize-winning economist Sir John Hicks expressed the view that profit was the maximum value which a person could consume during a period and still be as well off at the end of the period as at the beginning. You will learn later about the rules governing the calculation of profit. In a sense, profit is very much the same as income – what you have left after you subtract all your expenses from your receipts is your 'income'. (Accountants call it 'net income' or 'net profit' but, for simplicity, let's just call it 'income' for the time being.)

In terms of a limited company, the Sandilands Committee, which will be mentioned in greater detail later, said that a company's profit for the year is the maximum value which the company can distribute as dividends during the year, and still be as well off at the end of the year as it was at the beginning. There are some important questions here which need answering. They are:

1 How can we measure wealth at the beginning and end of a period?
2 How do we measure the change in wealth over a period?
3 Having measured wealth over a period, how much can be available for consumption and how much should not be consumed?

There are two main approaches to the measurement of wealth of a business:

(a) by finding the values of the individual assets of a business and then subtracting from them the value of the individual liabilities of the business;
(b) by measuring the expectation of future benefits. (This involves calculating something known as the 'present value of expected future net cash flows'. You will be covering this topic in Chapters 45 and 46.)

From these, you can see that in order to measure wealth, you must first identify the value of your assets and liabilities or the value of your future net cash flows.

Activity 29.2 If you paid £1,000 for a computer, what value would you say it had?

Arriving at an acceptable value for an asset is not nearly as simple as it appears. Firstly, you need to know what the term 'value' means. It is rather more than just the amount paid or the amount something is sold for. You need to consider the context – a glass of water has a lot more value in a desert than in London. If you have studied any economics, you will know that the availability of something dictates its value to the purchaser. Also, from an accounting perspective, once you own something, the value you place on it may not be what you paid for it and the basis of valuation that you use needs to be acceptable in the context of accounting.

Let's now look at the different methods that can be used to value assets.

29.4 Asset valuation alternatives

1 Historical cost

This is the most commonly applied method and you have been and will continue to use it throughout your accounting studies. The principles underpinning it are quite simple. An asset is valued at what it cost, less an amount representing the effect of its use so far upon that value.

Taking the computer costing £1,000 as an example. Let's assume it was expected to be used for four years before being scrapped. As it would last four years, each year its value would reduce by a quarter of what was paid for it. That is, it would be reduced by £250 every year. At the end of two years, it would have a value of £500 (£1,000 − £250 − £250).

This seems quite simple, except that someone needs to decide by how much to reduce its value by each year. Why was four years chosen for the useful life of the computer? Why not three or five? Why was it assumed that it would lose value equally each year? This depreciation adjustment is just one example of how imprecise accounting can be in relation to arriving at a value for something. There is no one 'true' answer; the choice of method, expected length of use of the asset, etc., is quite arbitrary.

Let's look at a couple of other examples.

1 Inventory to be used during the period can be charged out at FIFO (first in, first out), LIFO (last in, first out), AVCO (average cost method) for inventory valuation, and so on. There is no one 'true' figure.

2 Suppose we buy a block of assets, e.g. we take over the net assets of another organisation. How do we allocate the cost exactly? There is no precise way, we simply use a 'fair value' for each asset. As you know, any difference between the cost and total of the fair values is treated as goodwill.

2 Adjusted historical cost

Because of the changes in the value or purchasing power of money, the normal historical cost approach can be very unsatisfactory. Take the case of a buildings account. In it we find that two items have been debited. One was a warehouse bought in 1970 for £100,000 and the other an almost identical warehouse bought in 1995 for £400,000. These two figures are added together to show cost of warehouses £500,000 – quite clearly a value which has little significance.

To remedy this defect, the original historical cost of an asset is adjusted for the changes in the value or purchasing power of money over the period from acquisition to the present balance sheet date. The calculations are effected by using a price index.

This method does not mean that the asset itself is revalued. What is revalued is the money for which the asset was originally bought. This method forms the basis of what is known as **current purchasing power** accounting, abbreviated as CPP. During the early 1980s when inflation in the UK was high, many companies produced financial accounting information based on CPP.

The method does not remove the problem of the 'true' cost. All it does is to assume the original historical cost was accurate and then adjust the value of the business (and, hence, the owner's wealth) to allow for the different timings.

To illustrate how it works, let's take an instance which works out precisely, just as the proponents of CPP would wish.

A machine which will last for five years, depreciated using the straight line method, was bought on 1 January 2004 for £5,000. On 1 January 2006 exactly the same kind of machine (there have been no technological improvements) is bought for £6,000. The price index was 100 at 1 January 2004, 120 at 1 January 2006 and 130 at 31 December 2006. The machines would appear in the balance sheet at 31 December 2006 as follows, the workings being shown in the box alongside.

	Historical cost £	Conversion factor £		Balance sheet CPP at 31 Dec 2006 £
Machine 1	5,000	130/100	6,500	
Machine 2	6,000	130/120	6,500	13,000
Less Depreciation				
Machine 1	3,000	130/100	3,900	
Machine 2	1,200	130/120	1,300	(5,200)
				7,800

You can see that the CPP balance sheet shows two exactly similar machines at the same cost, and each has been depreciated £1,300 for each year of use. In this particular case CPP has achieved exactly what it sets out to do, namely put similar things on a similar basis.

Underlying this method are the problems inherent in the price index used to adjust the historical cost figures. Any drawbacks in the index will result in a distortion of the adjusted historical cost figures.

Activity 29.3 To summarise, what are the potential flaws in this method?

3 Replacement cost

Replacement cost, abbreviated as RC, is the estimated amount that would have to be paid to replace the asset at the date of valuation. You will often see it referred to as an 'entry value' as it is the cost of an asset entering the business.

How do we 'estimate' the replacement cost? As we are not, in fact, replacing the asset we will have to look at the state of the market at the date of valuation. If the asset is exactly the same as those currently being traded, perhaps we can look at suppliers' price lists.

Even with exactly the same item, there are still problems. Until you have actually negotiated a purchase it is impossible to say how much discount you could get – you might guess but you could not be certain. Also, if the asset consists of, say, ten computers, how much discount could you get for buying ten computers instead of one?

And that's the 'easy' one! What do you do when you are trying to find out these figures for assets that are no longer available? Technological change has greatly speeded up in recent years. If there is a second-hand market, it may be possible to get a valuation. However, in second-hand markets the price is often even more subject to negotiation. It becomes even more complicated when the original asset was specially made and there is no exactly comparable item, new or second-hand.

The difficulties outlined above mean that solutions to valuation can be sought under three headings:

1 **Market prices.** There will often be a market, new or second-hand, for the assets. For instance, this is particularly true for motor vehicles. However, if your asset differs in some way from the one you found the price of, an adjustment may be necessary to the value, thus decreasing the reliability of the value you place on the asset.

2 **Units of service.** Where a market price cannot be found, a value can be placed based upon the units of service (or output) which the asset can provide.

For example, take a machine that it is estimated will be able to produce another 1,000 items before it is scrapped. A new but different machine would be expected to produce 5,000 of the same items before being scrapped. The old machine can be given a value equal to one-fifth of the cost of the new machine. However, if the costs of operating the two machines differ, this would need to be taken into account when arriving at the valuation figure for the old machine.

3 **Cost of inputs.** If the asset was made or constructed by the owner, it may be possible to calculate the cost of replacing it at the balance sheet date. Present rates of labour and materials costs could be worked out to give the replacement cost.

Activity 29.4 What flaw can you see in this method?

4 Net realisable value

Net realisable value means the estimated amount that would be received from the sale of the asset less the estimated costs on its disposal. The term **exit value** is often used as it is the amount receivable when an asset leaves the business.

A very important factor affecting such a valuation is the conditions under which the assets are to be sold. To realise in a hurry would often mean accepting a very low price. Look at the sale prices received from stock from bankruptcies – usually very low figures. The standard way of approaching this problem is to value as though the realisation were 'in the normal course of business'. This is not capable of a precise valuation, as economic conditions change and the firm might never sell such an asset 'in the normal course of business'.

The difficulties of establishing an asset's net realisable value are similar to those of the replacement value method when similar assets are not being bought and sold in the marketplace. However, the problems are more severe as the units of service approach cannot be used, since that takes the seller's rather than buyer's viewpoint.

5 Economic value (present value)

As any economist would be delighted to tell you, they would value an asset as the sum of the future expected net cash flows associated with the asset, discounted (adjusted) to its present value (what the cash flows would be worth today). For example, £20 in a year's time might only be able to buy goods that today could be purchased for £19. The technicalities of discounting are discussed in Chapters 45 and 46.

Certainly, if you really did know (not guess) the future net cash flows associated with the asset and you had the correct discount rate, your valuation would be absolutely correct. The trouble is that it is impossible to forecast future net cash flows with certainty, neither will we necessarily have chosen the correct discount rate. It is also very difficult to relate cash flows to a particular asset, since a business's assets combine together to generate revenue.

Before considering the next method, you may find it helpful to see four of these methods compared in the contexts of time and valuation base.

Exhibit 29.1 Four methods of valuation in the contexts of time and valuation basis

	Past	Present	Future
Entry value	Historical cost	Replacement cost	
Exit value		Realisable value	Present value

6 Deprival value

The final concept of value is based on ideas propounded in the USA by Professor Bonbright in the 1930s, and later developed in the UK for profit measurement by Professor W T Baxter.

Deprival value is based on the concept of the value of an asset being the amount of money the owner would have to receive to compensate him exactly for being deprived of it. We had better point out immediately that the owner does not have to be deprived of the asset to ascertain this value, it is a hypothetical exercise. This leads to a number of consequences.

(*a*) Deprival value cannot exceed replacement cost, since if the owner were deprived of the asset he could replace it for a lesser amount. Here we will ignore any costs concerned with a delay in replacement.

(*b*) If the owner feels that the asset is not worth replacing, its replacement cost would be more than its deprival value. The owner simply would not pay the replacement cost, so the value to the owner is less than that figure.

(*c*) If the asset's deprival value is to be taken as its net realisable value, that value must be less than its replacement cost. It would otherwise make sense for someone to sell the asset at net realisable value and buy a replacement at a lower cost. Again, delays in replacement are ignored.

(*d*) Take the case where an owner would not replace the asset, but neither would he sell it. It is possible to envisage an asset, such as a machine, which has become obsolete but might possibly be used, for example, when other machines break down. It is not worth buying a new machine, as the replacement cost is more than the value of the machine to the business. Such a machine may well have a very low net realisable value. The benefit to the business of keeping such a machine can be said to be its 'value in use'. This value must be less than its replacement cost, as pointed out above, but more than its net realisable value, for otherwise the owner would sell it.

It is probably easier to summarise how to find deprival value by means of the diagram in Exhibit 29.2:

Exhibit 29.2 Deprival value

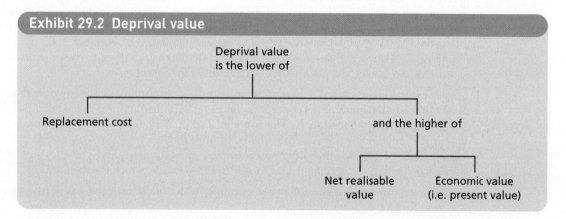

Deprival value is the lower of

Replacement cost

and the higher of

Net realisable value

Economic value (i.e. present value)

Deprival values can be illustrated by a few examples, using assets A, B and C.

	Asset A £	Asset B £	Asset C £
Replacement cost (RC)	1,000	800	600
Net realisable value (NRV)	900	500	400
Economic value (EV)	2,000	700	300

The deprival values can be explained as follows. (Check them against Exhibit 29.2.)

(a) *Asset A.* If the firm were deprived of asset A, what would it do? As economic value is greater than replacement cost it would buy another asset A. The deprival value to the business is therefore £1,000, i.e. replacement cost.

(b) *Asset B.* If deprived of asset B, what would the firm do? It would not replace it, as RC £800 is greater than its value to the business – its economic value £700. If deprived, the firm would therefore lose the present value of future cash flows, i.e. economic value £700. This then is the deprival value for asset B.

(c) *Asset C.* With this asset there would be no point in keeping it, as its economic value to the firm is less than the firm could sell it for. Selling it is the logical way, so the deprival value is net realisable value £400.

29.5 Capital maintenance

Let's go back to Sir John Hicks's definition of income (profit): 'A man's income is the maximum value which he can consume during a week, and still expect to be as well off at the end of the week as he was at the beginning.'

We've looked at the different ways assets may be valued so that they can be added together to find the wealth or 'well-offness' of a business at a particular date. Now, let's examine the problems of measuring the maintenance of wealth over a period. This is called *capital maintenance*.

Capital maintenance is the basic method of measuring maintenance of wealth used in accounting. If a business has a value (called its 'net worth') according to its financial statements of £100,000 on 1 January 2001, it must also have a value in its financial statements of £100,000 at 31 December 2001 to be as well off at the end of the period. Take the example of a company that has neither issued (sold) nor redeemed (bought back) any of its share capital (shares) and has paid no dividends. If it started with total equity according to its financial statements of £100,000 on 1 January 2002 and finished total equity in its financial statements of £170,000 on 31 December 2002, it must have made a profit of £70,000.

This approach is known as 'money capital maintenance'. It would be acceptable to everyone in a period when there is no change in price levels. However, most people would agree that it is not satisfactory when either prices in general, or specific prices affecting the business, are changing. In these two cases, to state that £70,000 profit has been made in 2002 completely ignores the fact that the £100,000 at 1 January 2002 and the £100,000 at 31 December 2002 do not have the same value. That is, the purchasing power of £100,000 has changed between the two dates.

From this we can see the possibilities of three different concepts.

1 **Money capital maintenance.** The traditional system of accounting as already described.
2 **Real capital maintenance.** This concept is concerned with maintaining the general purchasing power of the equity shareholders. This takes into account changes in the purchasing power of money (i.e. inflation) as measured by the retail price index.
3 **Maintenance of specific purchasing power of the capital of the equity.** This uses a price index which is related to the specific price changes of the goods in which the firm deals.

From these we can look at the following example, which illustrates three different figures of profit being thrown up for a company.

29.6 A worked example

A company has only class of share capital. Its net assets on 1 January 2005 are £1,000 and on 31 December 2005 they were £1,400. There have been no issues or withdrawal of share capital during the year. The general rate of inflation, as measured by the retail price index, is 10 per cent, whereas the specific rate of price increase for the type of goods in which the company deals is 15 per cent. The profits for the three measures are as follows:

	(a) Money maintenance of capital	(b) Real capital maintenance	(c) Maintenance of specific purchasing power
	£	£	£
Net assets 31 Dec 2005	1,400	1,400	1,400
Less What net assets would have to be at 31 Dec 2005 to be as well off on 1 Jan 2005			
(a) Money maintenance	(1,000)		
(b) Real capital £1,000 + 10%		(1,100)	
(c) Specific purchasing power maintenance £1,000 + 15%			(1,150)
Profit	400	300	250

Note that under the three methods:

(*a*) here the normal accounting method gives £400 profit;

(*b*) this case recognises that there has been a fall in the purchasing power of money;

(*c*) this takes into account that it would cost £1,150 for goods whose value at the start of the year was £1,000.

29.7 Combinations of different values and capital maintenance concepts

We have just looked at three ways of calculating profits based on historical cost allied with three capital maintenance concepts. This can be extended by using replacement cost or net realisable value instead. Each of these, when adjusted by each capital maintenance concept, will give three separate figures for profit. Together the three different means of valuation, multiplied by three different concepts of capital maintenance, will give us nine different profit figures.

At this stage in your studies it will be difficult to understand how such different profit measures could be useful for different purposes. We can leave this until your studies progress to more advanced examinations. However, we can use one simple example to illustrate how using only the traditional way of calculating profits can have dire consequences.

29.8 Another worked example

A company has net assets on 1 January 2007 of £100,000 financed purely by equity share capital. During 2007 there has been no injection or withdrawal of capital. At 31 December 2007 net assets have risen to £115,000. Both the retail price index and the specific price index for the goods dealt in have risen by 25 per cent. Taxation, based on traditional historical cost calculations (maintenance of money capital), is at the rate of 40 per cent. The profit may be calculated as follows:

	Maintenance of money capital	Maintenance of real capital and of specific purchasing power
	£	£
Net assets on 31 Dec 2007	115,000	115,000
Less Net assets needed to be as well off at 31 Dec 2007 as with £100,000 on 1 Jan 2007		
(a) Money capital	(100,000)	
(b) Both real capital and specific purchasing power £100,000 + 25%		(125,000)
Profit/loss	15,000	(10,000)

Tax payable is £15,000 × 40% = £6,000. Yet the real capital or that of specific purchasing power has fallen by £10,000. When tax is paid, that would leave us with net assets of £115,000 – £6,000 = £109,000. Because of price changes, £109,000 could not finance the amount of activity financed by £100,000 one year before. The operating capacity of the company would therefore be reduced.

Obviously it is not equitable for a company to have to pay tax on what is in fact a loss. It is only the traditional way of measuring profits that has thrown up a profit figure.

29.9 Operating capital maintenance concept

This approach looks at the output which could be generated by the initial holding of assets. A profit will only be made if the assets held at the end of the period are able to maintain the same level of output.

A simple example of this is that of a newspaper seller who sells newspapers on a street corner. The only costs the newspaper seller incurs are those of buying the newspapers. No other products are sold and the newspaper seller has no assets apart from the newspapers. In this case the operating capital consists solely of newspapers.

Under historical cost, a newspaper seller will recognise a profit if the revenue from the sale of newspapers is greater than the historical cost of the newspapers. Using the operating capital maintenance concept, the newspaper seller will recognise a profit only if the revenue from the sale is greater than the cost of buying the newspapers to replace the newspapers sold.

29.10 Summary

You should now be aware that there are a large number of alternative ways in which wealth can be measured. Accounting has tended always to use the simplest: historical cost. However, there have been occasions – during periods of high inflation, for example – when another method has been used. Another exception to historical cost is that net realisable value and replacement cost are both used when businesses need to value their unsold goods for resale at the end of periods.

Part II   Accounting for changing price levels

29.11 Background

As you have seen already in this chapter, changes in price levels can lead to both profit and asset valuation figures being far from reality if the original historical cost figures are used for their balance sheet amounts. This is not a recently observed phenomenon. As far back as 1938, Sir Ronald Edwards wrote several classic articles which were published in *The Accountant*. You can find these in the book *Studies in Accounting Theory*, edited by W T Baxter and S Davidson and published by the Institute of Chartered Accountants in England and Wales (ICAEW: London, 1977).

The greater the rate of change in price levels, the greater the distortion. The clamour for changes to simple historical cost accounting is noticeably greater when the inflation rate is high – at such times the deficiencies of historical cost financial statements are most obvious. If there were a period of deflation, however, the historical cost financial statements would be still misleading.

In certain countries the annual rate of inflation in recent years has been several hundred per cent. Historical cost financial statements in those countries would certainly be at odds with financial statements adjusted for inflation. In the UK the highest rate in recent years, based on the RPI, was 17.8 per cent for 1979, falling to less than 5 per cent in some years, particularly in recent years.

We can now look, in outline only, at suggestions made in the UK since 1968 as to methods which could be used to adjust financial statements for changing price levels.

29.12 Current purchasing power (CPP)

This proposal is something you have already read about. It is the adjustment of historical cost accounting figures by a price index figure to give figures showing what we called real capital maintenance. It will convey more of the problems and uncertainties facing the accounting profession in this regard, if we look at the history of the various proposals.

First came *Accounting for Stewardship in a Period of Inflation*, published in 1968 by the Research Foundation of the Institute of Chartered Accountants in England and Wales (ICAEW). Stemming from this came Exposure Draft No 8 (ED 8), published in 1973. ED 8 contained the proposal that companies should be required to publish, in addition to their conventional financial statements, supplementary statements which would be, in effect, their final financial statements amended to conform to CPP principles. In May 1974 a Provisional Statement of Standard Accounting Practice No 7 ([P]SSAP 7) was published. Notice the sign of uncertainty; it was a *provisional* standard – the only one yet published by the Accounting Standards Committee (ASC) or the Accounting Standards Board (ASB). Compared with ED 8, which said that a company should be *required* to publish CPP financial statements, [P]SSAP 7 simply *requested* them to publish such financial statements. Many companies would not accede to such a request.

[P]SSAP 7 stipulated that the price index to be used in the conversion of financial statements from historical cost should be the retail price index (RPI). As the actual price index relating to the goods dealt in by the firm might be quite different from RPI, the CPP financial statements could well be distant from the current values of the firm itself.

The exact nature of the calculations needed for CPP financial statements is not part of your syllabus, and we will not repeat the calculations here.

Many people, including the government, were completely dissatisfied with the CPP approach. After ED 8 was issued, the Government set up its own committee of inquiry into inflation accounting. The chairman of the committee was Sir Francis Sandilands. The report, known as the Sandilands Report, was published in September 1975.

29.13 Current cost accounting (CCA)

The Sandilands Committee's approach was quite different from ED 8 and [P]SSAP 7. The committee recommended a system called **current cost accounting** (CCA). This basically approved the concept of capital maintenance as the maintenance of operating capacity.

After the Sandilands Report appeared, the accounting bodies, as represented by their own Accounting Standards Committee (ASC), abandoned their proposals in [P]SSAP 7. A working party, the Inflation Accounting Steering Group (IASG), was set up to prepare a Statement of Standard Accounting Practice based on the Sandilands Report.

This group published ED 18: *Current cost accounting* in November 1976. It was attacked by many members of the ICAEW, whose members passed, in July 1977, a resolution rejecting compulsory use of CCA. However, the government continued its support, and in November 1977 the accounting profession issued a set of interim recommendations called the Hyde Guidelines (named after the chairman of the committee). The second exposure draft, ED 24, was issued in April 1979, followed by SSAP 16 in March 1980. SSAP 16 was to last three years to permit the evaluation of the introduction of CCA. After this, ED 35 was published in July 1984.

In November 1986 the CCAB Accounting Standards Committee published its handbook, *Accounting for the Effects of Changing Prices*. At the same time presidents of five of the leading accountancy bodies issued the following statement:

> The presidents of five of the leading accountancy bodies welcome the publication by the CCAB Accounting Standards Committee of its Handbook on *Accounting for the effects of changing prices*.
>
> The presidents endorse the CCAB Accounting Standards Committee's view that, where a company's results and financial position are materially affected by changing prices, historical cost accounts alone are insufficient and that information on the effects of changing prices is important for an appreciation of the company's results and financial position. The presidents join the Accounting Standards Committee in encouraging companies to appraise and, where material, report the effects of changing prices.
>
> The five bodies have proposed that SSAP 16, 'Current cost accounting', which was made non-mandatory by all the CCAB bodies in June 1985, should now be formally withdrawn. They take the view, however, that the subject of accounting for the effects of changing prices is one of great importance. Accordingly, they support the Accounting Standards Committee in its continuing work on the subject and agree that an acceptable accounting standard should be developed.
>
> *The Institute of Chartered Accountants in England and Wales; The Institute of Chartered Accountants of Scotland; The Institute of Chartered Accountants in Ireland; The Chartered Institute of Management Accountants; The Chartered Institute of Public Finance and Accountancy*

So once again the idea of forcing companies to produce financial statements adjusted for changing prices was rejected. The emphasis is now on encouragement, rather than trying to force companies to do it.

The reason why, at this early stage in your studies, we have given you some of the history behind the efforts to compel companies to produce CCA financial statements is to illustrate the conflicts that have taken place inside and outside the accountancy profession. Opinions on the merits of CCA financial statements are widely divided. You will study this in greater detail in the later stages of more advanced examinations, but it should be made clear at the outset that it is a controversial topic.

29.14 Handbook on *Accounting for the Effects of Changing Prices*

We can now look at the main outline of this handbook. The ASC encouraged companies to co-operate in an attempt to produce financial statements suitable for the effects of changing price levels. In doing this it did not try to recommend any one method, or even recommend one way only of publishing the results. The handbook says that the information may be presented:

(*a*) as the main financial statements; or
(*b*) in the notes to the financial statements; or
(*c*) as information supplemental to the financial statements.

The handbook first examines the problems.

Exhibit 30.1

Hillcrest Ltd
Balance Sheet as at 30 June (£000)

	2005		2004	
Fixed assets				
Plant and equipment				
Cost		800		800
Depreciation		(320)		(240)
Net book value		480		560
Current assets				
Stock	250		200	
Trade debtors	180		110	
Cash	105		75	385
	535		385	945
Current liabilities				
Trade creditors	(90)		(100)	
		445		285
		925		845
Long-term liabilities				
10% debentures		(310)		(310)
		615		535
Financed by				
Ordinary shares		200		200
Reserves		415		335
		615		535

Hillcrest Ltd
Profit and loss account for year ending 30 June 2005 (£000)

Sales		1,700
Cost of sales		
Opening stock	200	
Purchases	1,375	
	1,575	
Less Closing stock	(250)	
		(1,325)
Gross profit		375
Interest	31	
Depreciation	80	
Other expenses	184	
		(295)
Profit for the year		80

Exhibit 30.2

Price index for inventory at the end of each month:

March	2004	109
April	2004	112
June	2004	114
December	2004	116
March	2005	122
April	2005	126
June	2005	130

Average for the year ending 30 June 2005   126

Plant and equipment index			Debtors and creditors index		
June	2001	80	June	2004	110
June	2002	90	June	2005	200
June	2003	100			
June	2004	105			
June	2005	110	Average for	2005	155

In order to prepare current cost accounts, **the first step is to calculate current values for the assets.** Hillcrest Ltd's plant and equipment was purchased for £800,000 on 1 July 2001. The current value of the plant and equipment at 30 June 2005 is:

$$\text{Plant and equipment at cost} \times \frac{\text{Index at balance sheet date}}{\text{Index at date of purchase}}$$

$$= £800,000 \times \frac{110}{80}$$

$$= £1,100,000$$

The accumulated depreciation of £320,000 charged in the historical cost financial statements, representing 40 per cent of the asset which has been consumed, is also restated. The current value of the depreciation is:

$$£320,000 \times \frac{110}{80} = £440,000$$

On average, Hillcrest Ltd's stock was acquired three months before the year end. Hence, its current value, rounded to the nearest £000, at 30 June 2005 is:

$$£250,000 \times \frac{130}{122} = £266,393$$

Monetary assets, for example trade debtors and cash, and monetary liabilities, including trade creditors, are not restated. These items have a fixed monetary value which does not change. For example, if you borrow £1,000 today under an agreement to repay in 12 months' time, the monetary value of the amount borrowed will not change, that is you will repay £1,000. However, in times of rising prices, the market value of the amount will decrease. This gain will be dealt with later in this chapter.

29.15 Problems during a period of changing price levels

Obviously, the greater the rate of change, the greater will be the problems. We can now list some of them.

1 **Fixing selling prices.** If you can change your prices very quickly, an extreme case being a market trader, this problem hardly exists. For a company setting prices which it is expected to maintain for a reasonably long period, the problems are severe. It dare not price too highly, as early demand may be reduced by an excessive price; on the other hand, the company has to guess how prices are going to change over a period so that sufficient profit is made.
2 **Financial planning.** As it is so difficult to guess how prices are going to change over a period, planning the firm's finances becomes particularly trying. Obviously, it would be better if the plans were revised frequently as conditions changed.
3 **Paying taxation and replacing assets.** We have seen earlier how, during a period of inflation, traditional historical accounting will tend to overstate profits. Such artificial profits are then taxed. Unless various supplementary tax allowances are given, the taxation paid is both excessive and more than true profits, adjusted for inflation, can bear easily. This tends to lead to companies being short of cash, too much having been taken in tax. Therefore, when assets which have risen in price have to be replaced, adequate finance may not be available.
4 **Monetary assets.** If stocks of goods are held, they will tend to rise in money terms during a period of inflation. On the other hand, holding monetary assets, e.g. cash, bank and debtors, will be counterproductive. A bank balance of £1,000 held for six months, during which the purchasing power of money has fallen 10 per cent, will in real terms be worth only 90 per cent of its value six months before. Similarly, in real terms, debt of £5,000 owed continually over that same period will have seen its real value fall by 10 per cent.
5 **Dividend distribution.** Just as it is difficult to calculate profits, so is it equally difficult to decide how much to pay as dividends without impairing the efficiency and operating capability of the company. At the same time the shareholders will be looking to payment of adequate dividends.

29.16 Solutions to the problems

The handbook recommends the use of one of two concepts. These will now be examined fairly briefly, in as much detail as is needed at this stage of your examinations.

1 Profit under the operating capital maintenance concept

This has been mentioned previously, with a simple example given of a trader buying and selling newspapers. Under this concept several adjustments are needed to the profit calculated on the historical cost basis. Each adjustment is now considered.

Adjustment 1: holding gains and operating gains

Nearly all companies hold fixed assets and stocks. For each of these assets the opportunity cost will bear little relationship to its historical cost. Instead it is the asset's value to the business at date of consumption, and this is usually the replacement cost of the asset.

Accordingly the historical cost profit, which was based on money capital maintenance, can be divided into two parts.

1 Current cost profit, or operating gains. This is the difference between sales revenue and the replacement cost of the assets.

2 Holding gains. This is the replacement cost of the assets less the historical cost of those assets.

For example, a company buys an asset for £1,000 on 1 January 2004. It holds it for one year and sells it for £1,600 when the replacement cost is £1,200. There has been a historical cost profit of £600. This can be analysed as in Exhibit 29.3.

Exhibit 29.3

Profit for 2004

	£
Historical cost profit (£1,600 – £1,000)	600
Less Holding gain (£1,200 – £1,000)	(200)
Current cost profit (or operating gain)	400

To put it another way, the company makes £200 historical profit by simply holding the asset from when its replacement cost (i.e. original cost) was £1,000, until the date of sale when its replacement cost was £1,200. The actual current cost profit at point of sale must reflect conditions at the date of sale, i.e. the company has sold for £1,600 something which would currently cost £1,200 to replace. The current cost profit is therefore £400.

The holding gains are often described as a 'cost of sales adjustment' (COSA).

Adjustment 2: depreciation

Depreciation is to be adjusted to current replacement cost values. Without going into complicated examples, this means that if the historical cost of depreciation is £4,000 and the current cost of depreciation, based on current replacement cost values, is £7,000, then the adjustment should be £3,000 as follows:

	£
Depreciation based on historical cost	4,000
Adjustment needed to bring depreciation charge to CCA basis	3,000
CCA depreciation	7,000

Adjustment 3: monetary working capital adjustment

The monetary working capital needed to support the operating capability of the business will be affected by inflation. An adjustment will be needed to the historical profits in respect of this.

Adjustment 4: gearing adjustment

If we borrow £1,000 now, and have to pay back exactly £1,000 in five years' time, we will gain during a period of inflation. We will be able to put the £1,000 to use at current purchasing power. In five years' time, if £1 now is worth only 60p then, we will have gained because we will only be giving up £600 of current purchasing power now. The gearing adjustment is an attempt to adjust current cost operating profits for this factor.

2 Income statement based on the operating capital maintenance concept

A general idea of how such an income statement could appear can now be given.

Activity 30.1

If you replaced the £1,000 cost of the widgets in the above calculation of profit with the £1,100 it will cost to replace it, does it remind you of any of the alternatives to historical cost accounting you learnt about in Chapter 29?

From this simple example, one of the major criticisms of historical cost accounting is evident – its inability to reflect the effects of changing prices. Obviously, this criticism is dependent upon the level of inflation at the time.

An acceptable alternative to historical cost accounting has been sought by the accountancy profession in the UK for several years. The attempts of the Accounting Standards Committee (ASC) to introduce a system of inflation accounting, which are outlined in Chapter 29, failed.

The culmination of great effort and numerous exposure drafts and standards was the ASC handbook, *Accounting for the Effects of Changing Prices*, published in 1986. In Chapter 29, you started looking at some of the aspects covered in the handbook. In this chapter, we'll consider several of the issues dealt with in the handbook in the context of the preparation of a set of current cost accounts.

It is worth noting that the ASB recognises that the present system of historical cost accounting, modified by voluntary revaluations of certain assets, is unsatisfactory. The ASB aims to tackle the issue, and current values are once again on the agenda. It is unlikely, however, that a system of current cost accounting will be introduced without difficulty, particularly when inflation is at and has been at a low level in the UK for quite some time.

30.2 Valuation

Under historical cost accounting, assets and liabilities are recorded at their actual cost at the date of transaction. For example, when a new machine is purchased, the price per the invoice can be recorded in the books of the business. While this is a familiar and reasonably cheap method of recording the assets and liabilities of an entity, its main advantage is its objectivity. The historical cost of an item is an objective, verifiable fact that can easily be ascertained from the records of the business.

It is worth remembering that there is an element of subjectivity in the preparation of historical cost financial statements. Consider, for example, the choice of suitable depreciation method for an asset which is left to the discretion of the directors of the company. The size of the provision for doubtful debts is also dependent upon the exercise of judgement. Notwithstanding this, it is fair to say that historical values have a high degree of reliability.

Activity 30.2

Apart from the subjectivity in some of the adjustments made to the original figures, such as for depreciation, if you were asked for the main disadvantage of historical cost accounting, especially in times of rising prices, what would you say it was?

Current value accounting considers the following valuation methods which were covered in Chapter 29: economic value, value to the business (i.e. deprival value), replacement cost, net realisable value and recoverable amount.

To recap what you learnt in Chapter 29, the **economic value** of an asset is the sum of the future expected net cash flows associated with the asset, discounted to its present value. The value to the business, or **deprival value**, can be considered an appropriate valuation basis for accounting purposes. If a business is deprived of an asset, it can either replace it, or choose not to. If the asset is replaced, then its current value to the business is its net current **replacement cost**. This is normally its current cost, except where it has suffered a permanent diminution in value, in which case it will be written down to its **recoverable amount**. This may happen, for example, because there is no longer a market for the product the asset (e.g. equipment) is used to create. Alternatively, if the business chooses not to replace the asset which has diminished in value, it could sell it and its current cost becomes its **net realisable value**, i.e. the price at which it can be sold.

How are these values determined by a business? The replacement cost of an asset can be approximated using a relevant index. Indices published, for example, by the UK Government Statistical Service, are usually specific to a class of asset. A company may prepare its own index based on experience. The index will indicate the change in value of the asset or class of asset. Where it is not appropriate to use an index, a valuer may be relied upon. This is normal practice, for example, when revaluing property.

Consider the following example. A machine was purchased on 1 January 2002 for £75,000 when the relevant specific price index was 90. Its current value at 31 December 2004, when the relevant specific price index is 120, is:

$$\frac{\text{Index at accounting date}}{\text{Index at date of purchase}} \times £75,000 = \frac{120}{90} \times £75,000 = £100,000$$

Replacement does not necessarily mean replacement of the asset with a similar asset. Rather, it focuses on replacement of the service potential of the asset and its contribution to the business.

Net realisable value is the price at which the asset could be sold in an arm's-length transaction. A problem may arise where no market exists for the asset. The main problem with current values is the level of subjectivity involved in ascertaining valuations. A business may need to spend considerable time and effort ascertaining current values for its assets and liabilities.

Let's now look in detail at the principles of current cost accounting.

30.3 Current cost financial statements

In order to prepare current cost financial statements, a number of adjustments to the historical cost figures must be made. Specifically, **adjustments are needed relating to:**

- **fixed assets**
- **depreciation**
- **stock**
- **cost of sales**
- **monetary working capital**
- **gearing.**

Other than the gearing adjustment, no adjustment is made to monetary assets, such as debtors, bank and cash, or to monetary liabilities such as creditors or long-term loans.

We shall use Hillcrest Ltd to show how these adjustments are made.

The directors of Hillcrest Ltd are interested in preparing current cost accounts to reflect changing prices. They have prepared a historical cost balance sheet and profit and loss account (Exhibit 30.1). The relevant price indices for plant and machinery, stock, accounts receivable, and accounts payable are given in Exhibit 30.2.

Current cost reserve

Having revalued both plant and equipment and stock to their current values, the following revaluation gains are recorded:

	Plant & equipment (£)	Stock (£)	Total (£)
Current book value	660,000*	266,393	
Historical book value	(480,000)	(250,000)	
Surplus on revaluation	180,000	16,393	196,393

*Note: At current cost less accumulated depreciation, i.e. £1,100,000 – £440,000

The total gain of £196,393 is not a gain which has been realised through a transaction, for example, sale of goods at a profit. In addition, Hillcrest Ltd cannot distribute this revaluation gain as a dividend if it wishes to maintain its operating capacity. In this example the gain of £196,393 will be credited to a non-distributable reserve called the current cost reserve. The balance sheet incorporating these revaluations is shown in Exhibit 30.3:

Exhibit 30.3

Hillcrest Ltd
Balance Sheet (with some items restated to current cost) as at 30 June 2005 (£000)

Plant and equipment		
Current value		1,100
Depreciation		(440)
Net book value		660
Current assets		
Stock	266	
Debtors	180	
Cash	105	
	551	
Current liabilities		
Trade creditors	(90)	461
		1,121
Long-term liabilities		
10% debentures		(310)
		811
Financed by		
Ordinary shares		200
Reserves		415
Current cost reserve		196
		811

Exhibit 30.3, however, does not incorporate the effect of changing prices on the profit for the year. The reserves figure of £415,000 includes historical cost profit of £80,000 for the year ended 30 June 2005. We will now consider adjustments necessary in order to calculate the current cost profit for Hillcrest Ltd for the year.

30.5 Cost of sales adjustment

In calculating the profit for an accounting period, the cost of the goods sold (or cost of sales) is charged against revenue. In Exhibit 30.1, revenue of £1,700,000 is recorded at invoiced prices during the year to 30 June 2005. Likewise, purchases of £1,375,000 are recorded at their actual cost prices during the year. If we assume that activity occurs evenly throughout the year, a reasonable assumption unless trade is seasonal, then these figures will reflect the average prices for the period. The opening and closing stock valuations, in times of rising prices, will not reflect average prices under the historical cost convention. It is therefore necessary to adjust these figures in order to calculate the current cost of sales. This is carried out using an averaging method.

Using the price index for stock, the current cost of sales for Hillcrest Ltd is:

		£
Opening stock at average prices: $£200,000 \times \dfrac{130}{109} =$		238,532
Purchases (assume occur evenly through year)	=	1,375,000
		1,613,532
Closing stock at average prices: $£250,000 \times \dfrac{130}{122} =$		(266,393)
Current cost of sales	=	1,347,139

The cost of sales adjustment is the difference between the current cost of sales of £1,347,139 and the historical cost of sales of £1,325,000 i.e. £22,139. This is charged to the historical cost income statement as an adjustment in order to arrive at the current cost profit. A corresponding amount will be credited to the current cost reserve.

30.6 Depreciation adjustment

Depreciation charged to profit and loss should be based on the value of the asset as stated in the balance sheet. Hence, an adjustment is necessary where depreciation has been based on the historical cost of an asset.

Consider the following example in which the depreciation charge is based on the value of the asset at the year end. A fixed asset is purchased on 1 January 2003 for £10,000 when the relevant price index is 100. It is planned to depreciate this asset on a straight line basis at 20 per cent per annum. At the end of 2003, when the index has moved to 110, the current value of the asset is:

$$£10,000 \times \frac{110}{100} = £11,000$$

and depreciation based on current cost of the asset is:

$$£10,000 \times \frac{110}{100} \times 20\% = £2,200$$

The net book value of the asset as stated in the current cost balance sheet is:

	£
Asset at current value	11,000
Accumulated depreciation	(2,200)
	8,800

At the end of 2004 the relevant index is 120, and the current value of the asset is:

$$£10,000 \times \frac{120}{100} = £12,000$$

and the depreciation charge based on current cost is:

$$£10,000 \times \frac{120}{100} \times 20\% = £2,400$$

As a result, at the end of 2004, the net book value of the asset in the current cost balance sheet is:

	£
Asset at current value	12,000
Accumulated depreciation	(4,600)
	7,400

While 40 per cent of the value of the asset has been consumed at 31 December 2004, it is noted that £4,600 is not 40 per cent of £12,000. This is due to an undercharge of £200 depreciation in 2003 in current value terms. **As the original cost of the asset is altered to reflect current values, the aggregate depreciation must also be adjusted.**

The term given to depreciation relating to earlier years is **backlog depreciation.** Backlog depreciation is not charged against this period's profit. As we saw in the Hillcrest example, only an adjustment for this year's depreciation is charged against profit. **Backlog depreciation is charged to the current cost reserve.**

For Hillcrest Ltd, depreciation charged at 10 per cent on the current value of the plant and equipment of £1,100,000 is £110,000. Comparing this with the historical cost depreciation charge in the historical cost income statement of £80,000 gives an additional, i.e. backlog depreciation adjustment of £30,000. This is a charge in arriving at current cost profit for the year, the corresponding credit going to the current cost reserve.

30.7 Monetary working capital adjustment

The effect of changing prices on stock values has already been considered. In addition, during inflationary periods, the market value of monetary assets, e.g. trade debtors, trade creditors and cash, will change. In order for a business to maintain its operating capacity, this change needs to be reflected in the financial statements. **The monetary working capital adjustment represents the increase (or decrease) in finance necessary to provide an appropriate level of monetary working capital due to price changes, rather than a change in the volume of working capital.**

Cash is usually excluded from the calculation as the amount of cash held by a business may not relate to its operating activities. For example, cash may be held in order to make a capital investment. However, in the case of a bank, cash balances which are required to support daily operations are included in the **monetary working capital adjustment.**

Calculation of the monetary working capital adjustment is similar to the calculation of the cost of sales adjustment.

The index for debtors should reflect changes in the cost of goods or services sold which are included in debtors. Likewise, the index for creditors should reflect changes in the cost of goods or services purchased which are included in creditors. A single index may be appropriate, and in some businesses, a fair approximation may be the index used for stock. Consider the following example:

	31 December 2004	31 December 2005
	£	£
Trade debtors	9,000	12,000
Trade creditors	(7,500)	(11,000)
Monetary working capital	1,500	1,000

Relevant indices applicable to the business are:

31 December 2004	100
31 December 2005	200
Average for the year	150

The monetary working capital at 31 December 2004 in the historical cost financial statements is £1,500 (£9,000 – £7,500). Stating this at average values for the year gives:

$$£1,500 \times \frac{150}{200} = £2,250$$

The monetary working capital at 31 December 2005 in the historical cost financial statements is £1,000 (£12,000 – £11,000). Stating this at average values for the year gives:

$$£1,000 \times \frac{150}{200} = £750$$

The historical cost financial statements show a decrease in monetary working capital over the year of £500. However, at average values for the year, the monetary working capital is reduced by £1,500 (£2,250 – £750).

Activity 30.3 What does the difference between the change under the historical cost convention and under the current cost convention of £1,000 (£1,500 – £500) – the monetary working capital adjustment – represent?

Now, let's do the same thing for Hillcrest Ltd. The monetary working capital adjustment is calculated as follows:

	2005 £	2004 £
Trade debtors	180,000	110,000
Trade creditors	(90,000)	(100,000)
Net monetary working capital	90,000	10,000

Hence, the increase in monetary working capital in historical cost terms is £80,000 (£90,000 – £10,000).

Restating opening monetary working capital at average prices gives (to the nearest £000):

$$£10,000 \times \frac{155}{110} = £14,000$$

The value of closing monetary working capital at average prices is (to the nearest £000):

$$£90,000 \times \frac{155}{200} = £70,000$$

The increase in monetary working capital which is due to change in volume is £56,000 (£70,000 – £14,000). The increase due to price changes – the monetary working capital adjustment – is £24,000 (£80,000 – £56,000).

30.8 Current cost operating profit

Hillcrest Ltd's current cost operating profit, having applied the above adjustments, is given in Exhibit 30.4:

Exhibit 30.4

Hillcrest Ltd
Current Cost Operating Profit for year ending 30 June 2005 (£000)

Revenue		1,700
Profit for the year		80
Add Interest		31
		111
Adjustments		
Cost of sales adjustment	22	
Monetary working capital adjustment	24	
Additional depreciation adjustment	30	
		(76)
Current cost operating profit		35

From the point of view of a business and maintenance of its operating capacity, the current cost operating profit is relevant. However, maintenance of financial capital is also relevant where a business is not financed solely by equity. In this case, account should be taken of the capital structure of the business.

30.9 Gearing adjustment

If a company is financed by debt, and prices increase, whilst the monetary value of the loan has not changed, the market value has reduced. This gain for shareholders is recorded by making a gearing adjustment. The gearing adjustment is calculated in the following way.

Firstly, a gearing proportion is calculated. This is:

Average net borrowings for the year (L) : Shareholders' interest (S) + L

For Hillcrest Ltd, its net borrowings for the two years to 30 June 2005 are:

	2005	2004
	£	£
Debentures	310,000	310,000
Cash	(105,000)	(75,000)
Net borrowing	205,000	235,000

Hence, average net borrowings for the year to 30 June 2005 are:

$$\frac{£205,000 + £235,000}{2} = £220,000$$

Shareholders' interest for both years are:

	2005	2004
	£	£
Ordinary shares	200,000	200,000
Reserves	415,000	335,000
	615,000	535,000

Average shareholders' interest (S) for the year to 30 June 2005 is:

$$\frac{£615,000 + £535,000}{2} = £575,000$$

The gearing proportion is:

$$\frac{L}{L + S} = \frac{£220,000}{£220,000 + £575,000} = 27.67\%$$

To calculate the gearing adjustment, this proportion is applied to the sum of the current cost adjustments for the year, that is:

	£
Cost of sales adjustment	23,000
Depreciation adjustment	30,000
Monetary working capital adjustment	24,000
	77,000

The gearing adjustment for Hillcrest Ltd (to the nearest £000) is:

$$27.67\% \times £77,000 = £21,000$$

Exhibit 30.5 shows the current cost reserve having made the above adjustments:

Exhibit 30.5

Current cost reserve	£000
Surplus on revaluation of plant and equipment	180
Additional depreciation adjustment	30
Surplus on revaluation of stock	16
Cost of sales adjustment	22
Monetary working capital adjustment	24
Gearing adjustment	(21)
Balance at 30 June 2005	251

The current cost profit for the year ending 30 June 2005 is given in Exhibit 30.6:

Exhibit 30.6

Hillcrest Ltd
Current Cost profit and loss account for year ending 30 June 2005

		£000
Sales		1,700
Operating profit		111
Adjustments		
Cost of sales adjustment	22	
Monetary working capital adjustment	24	
Additional depreciation adjustment	30	
		(76)
Current cost operating profit		35
Gearing adjustment	21	
Less Interest	(31)	
		(10)
Current cost profit for the year		25

The balance sheet for Hillcrest Ltd for 30 June 2005, based on current costs, is given in Exhibit 30.7:

Exhibit 30.7

Hillcrest Ltd
Current Cost Balance Sheet as at 30 June 2005

		£000
Plant and equipment		
Cost		1,100
Depreciation		(440)
Net book value		660
Current assets		
Stock	266	
Debtors	180	
Cash	105	
	551	
Current liabilities		
Creditors	(90)	461
		1,121
Long-term liabilities		
10% debentures	310	
		(310)
		811
Financed by		
Ordinary shares		200
Reserves (335 + 25)		360
Current cost reserve		251
		811

Learning outcomes

You should now have learnt:

1 During inflationary periods, one of the main criticisms of historical cost accounting is its inability to reflect changing prices.

2 Deprival value is a suitable valuation basis for accounting purposes.

3 One of the major difficulties with current cost accounting is the level of subjectivity which can be involved in converting historical costs to current costs.

4 Relevant price indices, specific to an asset or class of assets, can approximate replacement cost.

5 The purpose of the cost of sales adjustment is to restate historical cost of sales in current cost terms by including opening and closing stock at average prices.

6 The depreciation adjustment ensures that the depreciation charge in the current cost profit and loss account is based on the current value of the asset as stated in the current cost balance sheet.

7 The monetary working capital adjustment reflects the change in the market value of monetary assets and liabilities, usually trade debtors and trade creditors, in the current cost financial statements.

→

8 Gains or losses for shareholders, which arise due to debt financing in times of changing prices, are accounted for in the gearing adjustment.

9 Surpluses and deficits on revaluations are credited or charged to the current cost reserve, which is a non-distributable reserve.

Answers to activities

30.1 Substituting the £1,100 it would cost to replace the stock in place of the £1,000 the stock cost would produce a profit of £100. This is an example of the concept of 'maintenance of specific purchasing power' you learnt about in Section 29.5.

30.2 The main disadvantage of historical cost accounting, particularly in times of changing prices, is its relevance to decision making. This was demonstrated in the widget example in the previous section, when any business that relied purely on the historical cost-based profit calculation to determine how much profit was available for distribution could find it impossible to replace all the stock it had sold.

30.3 The change in working capital due to price changes during the year.

Review questions

30.1 State whether you consider the following statements to be true or false:

(a) During inflationary periods, historical cost financial statements do not reflect a true and fair view.
(b) The preparation of historical cost financial statements does not involve subjectivity.
(c) Current cost accounting involves estimating future events.
(d) An index number must relate to a specific asset in order to be useful in converting historical cost accounts to current cost accounts.
(e) Where no market exists for an asset, conversion from historical cost to current cost can be difficult.

30.2A State whether you consider the following statements to be true or false:

(a) The current cost of plant and machinery is likely to be its net realisable value.
(b) A company should distribute dividends from the current cost reserve.
(c) The market value of a monetary asset, for example trade debtors, will decrease during inflationary periods.
(d) A gearing adjustment is necessary where a company is financed solely by equity capital.
(e) Backlog depreciation is charged to the current cost reserve.

30.3A What are the practical difficulties a company may encounter in ascertaining the current values of its assets?

30.4 Plant and equipment was purchased on 1 January 2003 for £30,000, when the relevant specific price index was 90. What is the current cost value of the asset at 31 December 2004 if the index at that date is 120?

30.5A The plant and equipment, details of which are given in Question 30.4, is depreciated on a straight line basis at 10 per cent per annum. The depreciation charge is based on year end values. What is the current cost depreciation charge for the year ended 31 December 2005, if the index at that date is 160?

30.6 Calculate backlog depreciation at 31 December 2005 for the plant and equipment, the details of which are given in Question 30.5A.

30.7A A company purchased equipment on 1 January 2004 for £40,000, at which date the relevant price index for equipment was 100. Depreciation is charged on a straight line basis at 25 per cent per annum. The index at 31 December 2004 had moved to 150, and at 31 December 2005 it was 200. Show the current cost balance sheet entries for equipment at 31 December 2004 and 31 December 2005. Calculate the adjustments to the current cost reserve in respect of this equipment.

30.8 The historical cost of sales figure for Pear Ltd for the year ended 31 December 2003 is calculated as follows:

	£
Opening stock	50,000
Purchases	450,000
	500,000
Closing stock	(70,000)
Cost of sales	430,000

Price indices for inventory are as follows:

Index at date of purchase of opening stock	80
Index at date of purchase of closing stock	120
Average index for 2003	100
Index at 31 December 2003	130

Required:
Assuming that purchases occur evenly throughout the year, calculate the cost of sales adjustment for Pear Ltd for 2003.

30.9A The balance sheet of Seafield Ltd at 31 December 2004 shows the following balances:

	31 December 2004	31 December 2003
	£	£
Trade debtors	35,000	30,000
Trade creditors	25,000	23,000

The relevant price indices for trade debtors and trade creditors are:

31 December 2003	120
31 December 2004	180
Average for the year ending 31 December 2004	150

Required:
Using the above information, calculate the monetary working capital adjustment at 31 December 2004 for Seafield Ltd.

30.10 If the relevant price indices for trade debtors and trade creditors are as follows, calculate the monetary working capital adjustment for Seafield Ltd, using the details given in Question 30.9A.

31 December 2003	200
31 December 2004	280
Average for the year ending 31 December 2004	240

30.11A The information given below has been extracted from the accounting records of Cedarwood Ltd for the year ending 30 June 2004. Prepare a statement showing the current cost operating profit to 30 June 2004.

	£
Revenue	2,500,000
Historical cost operating profit	1,400,000

Current cost adjustments

	£
Additional depreciation adjustment	500,000
Cost of sales adjustment	750,000
Monetary working capital adjustment	25,000

30.12 The balance sheet for Cremore Ltd at 31 December 2003 is given below (£000):

		2003		2002
Plant and equipment				
Cost		800		800
Depreciation		(320)		(160)
		480		640
Current assets				
Inventory	210		130	
Accounts receivable	100		60	
Cash	145		50	
	455		240	
Current liabilities				
Trade creditors	(80)		(60)	
		375		180
		855		820
Long-term liabilities				
10% debentures		(200)		(200)
		655		620
Financed by				
Ordinary shares		250		250
Reserves		370		340
Current cost reserve		35		30
		655		620

Required:
Using the above information, calculate the gearing adjustment percentage:

$$\frac{L}{L+S}$$

30.13A The following information has been extracted from the accounting records of Sycamore Ltd for the year ended 30 June 2003.

	£
Revenue	9,000,000
Historical cost trading profit	4,000,000
Interest paid	500,000
Corporation tax charge for the year	1,500,000
Ordinary dividend proposed	600,000
Additional depreciation adjustment	200,000
Cost of sales adjustment	800,000
Monetary working capital adjustment	370,000
Gearing adjustment: $\frac{L}{L+S}$	20%

Required:
Prepare a current cost profit and loss account for Sycamore Ltd for the year ending 30 June 2003.

30.14 During a period of inflation, many accountants believe that financial reports prepared under the historical cost convention are subject to the following major limitations:

1 Stocks are undervalued;
2 depreciation is understated;
3 gains and losses on net monetary assets are undisclosed;
4 balance sheet values are unrealistic; and
5 meaningful periodic comparisons are difficult to make.

Required:
Explain briefly the limitations of historical cost accounting in periods of inflation with reference to each of the items listed above.

(*Association of Accounting Technicians*)

30.15A You are presented with the following information relating to Messiter plc:

Year to 31 December	2004	2005
	£m	£m
Profit and loss account		
Revenue, all on credit terms	1,300	1,400
Cost of sales	650	770
Gross profit	650	630
Profit before taxation	115	130
Balance sheets at 31 December:		
Fixed assets at cost	850	850
Less Accumulated depreciation	510	595
Net book value	340	255
Stock at cost	105	135
Trade debtors	142	190

Required:
(a) Using the historical cost financial statements and stating the formulae you use, calculate the following accounting ratios for both 2004 and 2005:
  (*i*)   Gross profit percentage;
  (*ii*) Net profit percentage;
  (*iii*) Stock turnover, stated in days;
  (*iv*) Trade debtors collection period, stated in days; and
  (*v*)   Fixed asset turnover.

(b) Using the following additional information:
  (*i*) Restate the revenue for 2004 and 2005 incorporating the following average retail price indices:

Year to 31.12.2004	85
Year to 31.12.2005	111

  (*ii*) Calculate the additional depreciation charge required to finance the replacement of fixed assets at their replacement cost. The company's depreciation policy is to provide 10 per cent per annum on original cost, assuming no residual value.
    The replacement cost of fixed assets at 31 December was as follows:

	£ millions
2004	1,140
2005	1,200

  (*iii*) Based upon these two inflation adjustments, why may it be misleading to compare a company's results for one year with that of another without adjusting for changes in general (RPI) or specific inflation?

(*Association of Accounting Technicians*)

Chapter

31

Social accounting

Learning objectives

After you have studied this chapter, you should be able to:

● explain the term 'social accounting'
● describe the implications of social accounting for the accounting function
● describe some of the difficulties in the measurement of qualitative factors
● describe the conflict between shareholders' interests and social considerations

Introduction

In this chapter you'll learn about some of the issues underlying the development of social accounting, five general areas to which social accounting has been applied, and the extent to which social accounting is becoming part of company reporting.

31.1 Background

Over time, the objective of financial statements has changed. In addition to reporting to share-holders of the company, directors are aware of a wide range of other user groups who are interested in accounting information. These user groups include employees of the company and, more controversially, the public at large. The controversy arises when considering whether or not organisations are responsible for 'social actions', that is actions which do not have purely financial implications.

31.2 Costs and measurement

One of the problems associated with actions of this type is the difficulty of identifying costs and measuring the effects of (often intangible) factors that contribute to the 'value' of an organisation. It is obvious that employee loyalty and commitment to quality performance increase this value, but how are such intangibles to be measured using objective and verifiable techniques?

Activity 31.1 How would you value employee loyalty?

Some of the input costs of 'social' activities can be evaluated reasonably accurately. Providing 'social' information required under the Companies Act 2006 is not particularly difficult – it requires information regarding employees to be presented in the financial statements, including numbers of employees, wages and salaries data, and details regarding the company's policy on disabled persons. Also, even where 'social' actions are required by legislation, they can often be costed reasonably accurately. For example, there are a large number of European Union directives which have been implemented in the UK relating to social and environmental policies, including the monitoring and control of air and water pollution.

The costs of complying with these disclosure requirements and operational control measures can be high and, as the number of regulations increases, these costs will become a basic and essential part of financial statements. It will become increasingly important that not only the costs are reported, but also the benefits, and this is where the difficulties arise – how can the benefits of controlling pollution from a factory be evaluated? Indeed, should an attempt be made to evaluate them at all? Would they be better reported in qualitative or non-financial quantitative terms?

As soon as a company seeks to incorporate social criteria alongside other, more traditional performance measures, problems of objectivity, comparability and usefulness arise. For example, social criteria for a paper manufacturer may include environmental issues concerning reforestation; and an oil extraction company would include the environmentally safe disposal of oil rigs at the end of their useful economic lives among its social criteria.

However, issues of this type become problematical when viewed using conventional capital appraisal techniques. Not only may the measurable financial payback be so long as to be immaterial – as in the case of an environmental project such as reforestation – it may be virtually non-existent, as in the case of the disposal of obsolete oil rigs. Assessment of issues of this type require different techniques from those traditionally used, and organisations' accounting information systems will need to take this into account, not just in terms of using more qualitative value criteria, but also in selecting the information which is sought in order to assist in the decision-making process.

31.3 The pressure for social actions and social accounting

Despite the existence of many environmental laws, much of the pressure for social actions comes from pressure groups like Greenpeace. These groups can have an enormous impact upon an organisation's profitability, in ways that governments have singularly failed to do. For example, an air pollution law may concentrate on monitoring the quality of air around a factory, rather than on measuring emissions from the factory, making it far more difficult to enforce action against the factory, as it can always argue that another factory is the cause of any pollution found. Also, powerful cartels can influence legislation to create enormous delays in introducing socially responsible legislative controls. On the other hand, a pressure group can stop demand for a company's products, make it difficult for it to send its products to its customers, and may give it so much negative publicity that it can find its public image materially and irreversibly altered in a very short time.

While pressure groups are not a new phenomenon, their power is now far greater than it has ever been. Organisations need to be aware of the social, particularly the environmental, issues inherent in and/or related to their activities, and must be in a position to assess how best to approach these issues. They can only do so if they identify all the variables, both quantitative and qualitative, and both the inputs (costs) and the outputs (effects) of these variables, and determine methods with which to determine what actions to take.

Social accounting is concerned with how to report upon the application of the social policies adopted by an organisation, and upon how they have impacted upon the organisation and its environment. An organisation that does so effectively will not only be providing user groups with rich information from which to form a view concerning its social ethos, it will also be enhancing its ability to take decisions appropriate for its own longer-term survival and prosperity.

31.4 Corporate social reporting

The reporting of the social effects of a company's activities became an issue in the UK in the 1970s. The reporting of non-financial information usually takes the form of narrative disclosure, sometimes supported by a statistical summary. As much social reporting is non-mandatory, comparison with other companies is difficult, if not pointless and misleading. This is partially due to a positive bias in what is reported – most companies tend to report only 'good news' in their social reports. It is also due to the lack of standards governing what to include and how to present social reports.

Environmental issues have been firmly on the political agenda since the early 1980s and large corporations have responded to public demands for more information about 'green issues'. Oil companies, in particular, produce a notable amount of additional information in their annual reports. This environmental information usually includes details about the company's waste disposal practices, attitudes towards pollution and natural resource depletion, as well as the overall corporate environmental policy. However, many continue to avoid any non-mandatory social reporting, and many instances have been reported of organisations claiming to be socially responsible, when they were, in fact, anything but.

In 2003, the UK government announced that all listed companies would need to include an Operating and Financial Review in their annual reports from January 2005. In November 2005 this statutory requirement was removed, with effect from January 2006. While this false start set back the move towards a greater amount of CSR in the UK, it is unlikely to be long before CSR becomes a formal part of the annual report: the pressure for CSR is now too strong for it to be ignored. The latest move in the direction in the UK is the requirement that UK listed companies prepare an Enhanced Business Review from October 2008.

31.5 Types of social accounting

Social accounting can be divided into five general areas:

(a) national social income accounting;
(b) social auditing;
(c) financial social accounting in profit-oriented organisations;
(d) managerial social accounting in profit-oriented organisations;
(e) financial and/or managerial social accounting for non-profit organisations.

31.6 National social income accounting

National social income accounts have now been in existence for many years. The measure of the nation's productivity recorded in the accounts – basically in sales terms – gives an income called the gross national product, usually referred to as GNP.

To an outsider, an increase in GNP would seem to indicate a betterment or progress in the state of affairs existing in the country. This is not necessarily so. The following example illustrates this point.

A new chemical factory is built in a town. Fumes are emitted during production which cause houses in the surrounding areas to suffer destruction of paintwork and rotting woodwork, and it also causes extensive corrosion of bodywork on motor vehicles in the neighbourhood. In addition it also affects the health of the people living nearby. An increase in GNP results because the profit elements in the above add to GNP. These profit elements include:

● to construction companies and suppliers of building materials: profit made on construction of plant;

- to house paint dealers and paint manufacturers, painters and decorators, joiners and carpenters: profit made on all work effected in extra painting, woodwork, etc.;
- to garages and car paint manufacturers: profit made on all extra work needed on motor vehicles;
- to chemists and medical requirement manufacturers: profit made on dealing with effects on residents' health, because of extra medical purchases, etc.

However, in real terms one can hardly say that there has been progress. Obviously the quality of life has been seriously undermined for many people.

As national income accounts do not record the 'social' well-being of a country, other national measures have been proposed. The one most often mentioned is a system of 'social indicators'. These measure social progress in such ways as:

- national life expectancies
- living conditions
- levels of disease
- nutritional levels
- amount of crime
- road deaths.

Thus if national life expectancies rose, or road deaths per 100,000 people decreased, etc. there could be said to be social progress, while the converse would apply were the opposite signals found to be occurring.

The main difficulty with this approach is that (given present knowledge and techniques) it cannot be measured in monetary terms. Because of this, the national social income accounts cannot be adjusted to take account of social indicators. On the level of an individual organisation, however, social indicators similar to the above are used in Planning, Programming, Budgeting Systems (PPBS). This will be discussed in more detail in Section 31.10.

31.7 Social auditing

While national social accounting would measure national social progress, many individuals and organisations are interested in their own social progress. This form of social progress is usually called 'social responsibility'.

To identify activities to be measured, a 'social audit' is required, investigating:

(a) which of their activities contribute to, or detract from, being socially responsible;
(b) measurement of those activities;
(c) a report on the results disclosed by the investigation.

An example of this might be to discover how the organisation had performed in respect of such matters as:

- employment of women
- employment of disabled people
- occupational safety
- occupational health
- benefits at pensionable age
- air pollution
- water pollution
- charitable activities
- help to developing countries.

Social audits may be carried out by an organisation's own staff or by external auditors. The reports may be for internal use only or for general publication.

31.8 Financial social accounting in profit-oriented organisations

Financial social accounting is an extension to normal financial accounting. The objective may either be to show how the social actions have affected financial performance, or otherwise to put a social value on the financial statements of the organisations. The two main types of financial social accounting envisaged to date are those of human resource accounting and how the organisation has responded to governmental or professional bodies' regulations concerning environmental matters.

Human resource accounting

One of the main limitations of 'normal' financial accounting is the lack of any inclusion of the 'value' of the workforce to an organisation. The value may be determined by:

(a) capitalising recruitment and training costs of employees and apportioning value over employees' period of employment; or

(b) calculating the 'replacement cost' of the workforce and taking this as the value of human resources; or

(c) extending either of the above to include the organisation's suppliers and customers.

It is contended that such measurements have the benefits that (1) financial statements are more complete, and (2) managerial decisions can be made with a fuller understanding of their implications.

For instance, suppose that a short-term drop in demand for a company's goods led to a manufacturer laying off part of the workforce. This might mean higher profits in the short term, because of wages and salaries saved. In the long term, it could do irreparable damage, as recruitment could then be made difficult, or because of the effect on the morale of the rest of the workforce, or changes in attitudes of suppliers and customers.

Compliance costs of statutory/professional requirements

As the effects of organisations upon societies are more widely recognised there will be more and more regulations with which to comply. The costs of compliance will obviously then become a basic and essential part of financial statements.

31.9 Managerial social accounting in profit-oriented organisations

All that has been described has an effect upon the information systems of an organisation. They will have to be established on an ongoing basis, rather than be based purely on adjustments such as those made to the financial accounts at the year end.

The information will be used to affect the day-to-day decisions needed to run the organisation.

Activity 31.2 Why is an ongoing information system required in order to do this?

31.10 Financial and/or managerial social accounting for non-profit organisations

As profit is not a measure in these organisations it can be difficult to measure how well they are performing. Two approaches to measurement have been used, **planning, programming, budgeting systems (PPBS)** and **social programme measurement**.

Both of these approaches can be said to be part of what politicians in recent years have called 'value for money'. The general attitude is that while there may be a need for all sorts of social programmes, including health, there is a great need for ensuring that money is not wasted in doing this. The demand is that we should ensure that we get 'value for money' in that the outputs from such schemes should be worth the amount of money expended in carrying them out.

Planning, programming, budgeting systems (PPBS)

It has been said that in the past there was a great deal of confusion between planning and budgeting. Annual budgeting takes a short-term financial view. Planning, on the other hand, should be long term and also be concerned with strategic thinking.

PPBS enables management of non-profit organisations to make decisions on a better informed basis about the allocation of resources to achieve their overall objectives. PPBS works in four stages:

1 Review organisational objectives.
2 Identify programmes to achieve objectives.
3 Identify and evaluate alternative ways of achieving each specific programme.
4 On the basis of cost/benefit principles, select appropriate programme.

PPBS necessitates the drawing up of a long-term corporate plan. This shows the objectives which the organisation is aiming to achieve. Such objectives may not be in accord with the existing organisational structure.

For instance, suppose that the objective of a local government authority, such as a city, is the care of the elderly. This could include providing:

● services to help them keep fit
● medical services when they are ill
● old people's housing
● sheltered accommodation
● recreational facilities
● educational facilities.

These services will usually be provided by separate departments, e.g. housing, welfare, education. PPBS relates the total costs to the care of the elderly, rather than to individual departmental budgets.

Management is therefore forced by PPBS to identify exactly which services or activities should be provided, otherwise the worthiness of the programme could not be evaluated. PPBS also provides information which enables management to assess the effectiveness of their plans, such as giving them a base to decide whether, for every thousand pounds, they are giving as good a service as possible.

As the structure of the programme will not match up with the structure of the organisation, e.g. the services provided will cut across departmental borders, a specific individual must be made responsible for controlling and supervising the programme.

Social programme measurement

The idea that governmental social programmes should be measured effectively is, as yet, in its infancy.

A government auditor would determine whether the agency had complied with the relevant laws, and had exercised adequate cost controls. The auditor would determine whether or not the results expected were being achieved and whether there were alternatives to the programmes at a lower cost.

There should be cost/benefit analyses to show that the benefits are worth the costs they incur. However, the benefit side of the analysis is often very difficult to measure. How, for instance, do you measure the benefits of not dumping a particular substance or an obsolete oil rig into the sea?

As a consequence, most social programmes do not measure results (benefits). Instead they measure 'outputs', e.g. how many prosecutions for dumping waste: a high number of prosecutions is 'good', a low number 'bad'. This is hardly a rational way of assessing results, and quite a lot of research is going into better methods of audit.

31.11 Conflict between shareholders' interests and social considerations

Obviously, an organisation has to come to a compromise about how far it should look after the interests of its shareholders and how far it should bother about social considerations. For instance, a company could treat its employees so well in terms of pay, pensions and welfare that the extra costs would mean very low profits or even losses.

On the other hand there must be instances where, no matter what the effects on profits, the expenses just have to be incurred. If the company has a chemical plant which could easily explode, causing widespread destruction and danger to people, then there cannot be any justification for not spending the money either to keep the plant safe or to demolish it. The full severity of the law must bear down on transgressors of the law in such cases of wilful neglect.

All the facts of the particular case must be brought into account. Let us look at a typical case where the answer may seem obvious, but perhaps there may be other factors which may make the answer not so obvious. Workers in underdeveloped countries are usually paid far lower wages than those in the developed countries. What happens if a large multinational company pays its workers in a given country three or four times as much as home-based companies? Immediately everyone wants to work for the multinational company, which can afford high wages, and leave the home-based companies which cannot. Is that sensible? What chance is there for the development of the country's own home-based industries if the outside companies constantly take all the best brains and most able people?

In such a case it would probably make more sense for the multinational company to pay wages more in keeping with the particular economy, and to help that country in other ways such as by improving the health care generally for all, better education for all, and so on. Obviously a topic such as this will engender discussions and arguments for some considerable time.

31.12 Reports from companies

Companies, mainly those based in the USA, have begun to declare their philosophy towards such matters as the environment. This is usually included in the annual reports which accompany their financial statements.

For example, a company may have decided to have the following ten principles of environmental policy:

1 To comply with both governmental and community standards of environmental excellence.
2 To use only materials and packaging selected to be good for the health of consumers, and for the safety and quality of the environment.
3 To keep energy use per unit of output down to a low level.
4 To minimise waste.
5 To get to as low a level as possible the discharge of pollutants.
6 To use other firms which have shown commitment to environmental excellence.

7 To research fully the ecological effect of the company's products and packaging.

8 To carry on business operations in an open, honest and co-operative manner.

9 To make certain that on the board of directors there would be scientifically knowledgeable directors, and ensure that they were regularly provided with environmental reports.

10 To ensure that all the above principles are fully observed and that challenges posed by the environment are vigorously and effectively pursued.

Learning outcomes

You should now have learnt:

1 To whom organisations are responsible is a controversial area, and there is no exact definition of 'social accounting'.

2 Social indicators measure social progress, but as yet, given their inability to measure progress in monetary terms, they cannot be incorporated into social income accounts.

3 A social audit will test the social responsibility of an organisation, including compliance with regulations, for example legislation relating to employees.

4 If an organisation wishes to take account of social and environmental factors, these items need to be incorporated into its accounting information system.

5 There is a conflict between shareholders' interests, for example profit maximisation, and social considerations.

6 Corporate social reporting is the reporting of a company's activities and how they are related to social, including environmental, issues.

7 There are five areas into which social accounting can be divided:
   (a) national social income accounting;
   (b) social auditing;
   (c) financial social accounting in profit-oriented organisations;
   (d) managerial social accounting in profit-oriented organisations;
   (e) financial and/or managerial social accounting for non-profit organisations.

8 Social accounting is as yet in its infancy. There is obviously great difficulty in trying to put money values on the various aspects of being better off or worse off. There are also problems connected with exactly what 'better off' and 'worse off' mean. One person's worsening in some way may be someone else's betterment.

Answers to activities

31.1 There isn't a correct answer to this question but there are examples of values being placed on employee loyalty, for example, clocks for 25 years' service, gold watches for 50 years' service, etc. But, do acts like this actually place a value on employee loyalty? Hardly – what is the cost per year of a clock costing £25 that is presented to an employee for 25 years' loyal service to the organis-ation: £1 per year. Professional footballers who stay longer than the norm with one club are entitled to a testimonial match where all the proceeds are given to the loyal player. Similar schemes also exist in cricket though, in cricket, it is usually a 'benefit year' where lots of events are held for the benefit of an individual player. Yet, there have been cases where footballers have ended up out-of-pocket because the gifts they gave all the players who took part in the testimonial match (they don't get paid) and other expenses were greater than the income from the game – hardly a case of loyalty being rewarded.

Clearly, organisations don't tend to put a value on loyalty in such a way as to directly reward the loyal individual. They also cannot include a figure for employee loyalty in the balance sheet as an asset. However, when a business is sold, employee loyalty is one of the factors that will be taken into account when deciding what the business is worth.

Just about the only way a business can recognise loyalty and endeavour to give it a value is to publicise it. This can be done through the media (TV, radio, newspapers, Internet, etc.). It can also be done in the annual report, the document containing all the financial statements and accompanying reports that is sent to shareholders each year. The share price may rise slightly as a result but, even if it does, it is hardly the same as the company placing a value of the loyalty of its employees.

31.2 Being socially aware means that you monitor constantly the extent to which you are achieving your social-related goals. You can't simply check once a year whether you are putting too much pollution in the local river or whether your employees are being loyal and are happy, or whether your supplies are coming from companies that do not employ child labour. If an organisation becomes socially aware and adopts social accounting, its information system needs to be amended to reflect the change. It is not necessarily the case that its accounting information system will be affected – that depends upon whether the company's social policies are to be reported by the company along with its financial information.

Review questions

31.1 Describe how an increase in gross national product may not have a positive effect on the well-being of the country.

31.2 What types of measure could be used to measure social well-being? What difficulties would be discovered in trying to use accounting in measuring these?

31.3 What aspects of an organisation's activities could be measured in a social audit?

31.4 Describe how there could be conflicts between short-term and long-term benefits.

31.5 Describe how PPBS may conflict with departmental budgets.

31.6A Review a set of company financial statements for social disclosures. Consider the usefulness of such disclosures to different user groups.

31.7 Why has the traditional model of income measurement failed to account for the impact of business activities on the environment?

(*Association of Chartered Certified Accountants*)

You can find a range of additional self-test questions, as well as material to help you with your studies, on the website that accompanies this book at **www.pearsoned.co.uk/wood**

Chapter

32

Corporate governance

Learning objectives

After you have studied this chapter, you should be able to:

● explain why it is important for companies to adopt sound practices of corporate governance

● describe the background to the development of the *Combined Code on Corporate Governance*

● outline the nature of the contents of the *Combined Code on Corporate Governance*

Introduction

In this chapter, you'll learn about the increasingly important issue of **corporate governance**, the background to the development of a code on corporate governance that UK-listed companies must follow and on which they must report their compliance annually, and the nature of its contents.

32.1 The importance of corporate governance

Corporate governance has been defined as 'the exercise of power over and responsibility for corporate entities'. It is concerned with the manner in which directors carry out their stewardship responsibilities. If the directors of a company are failing to act in the interests of the shareholders, they are not performing the role to which they were appointed. Where this occurs, the shareholders need to be aware of it and take the steps necessary to ensure the directors do perform their role properly.

However, it is all very well saying this should happen. In the absence of any regulation that must be adhered to, it can take a long time for it to become clear to a company's shareholders that the directors are acting inappropriately. To this end, a set of guidelines has been developed over the last decade – the *Combined Code on Corporate Governance*.

More information on why corporate governance is important can be found in a briefing paper prepared by the ICAEW: *Briefing 03.02 Corporate governance: why should companies care?* It is available at **www.icaew.co.uk/index.cfm?route=111160**

32.2 The *Combined Code*

In 2003, in response to continuing public concerns about the actions and motivation of some company directors who appeared to have their own interests at heart, rather than those of the shareholders they were appointed to represent, a revised version of a document called the

Combined Code on Corporate Governance was published by the Financial Reporting Council. The latest version is the Combined Code 2006. It is available at **www.frc.org.uk/corporate/ combinedcode.cfm**

The *Combined Code* contains a set of guidelines which can be used to determine whether directors have adequately performed their primary task of corporate stewardship. That is, whether the directors have carried out their duties adequately and in an appropriate manner, and in the best interests of the shareholders that they represent.

32.3 The policing of effective corporate governance

The *Combined Code* is a voluntary *code of conduct* for the directors of all UK limited companies. It is neither a legally enforceable code nor has it the status of an accounting standard. However, compliance with the *Combined Code* is required by the listing rules of the Stock Exchange. As a result, when a company is listed on a UK Stock Exchange, the Directors' Report (which is included in the annual report of all UK companies) must include a statement indicating the extent to which requirements of the *Combined Code* have been observed. Along with the financial statements and notes, the Directors' Report is subject to review by a company's external auditors, thus minimising the possibility of spurious claims being made by the directors.

> **Activity 32.1** If corporate governance is so important, why do you think unlisted companies are not required to apply the *Combined Code*?

32.4 The development of the *Combined Code*

The development of the *Combined Code* began with the *Cadbury Report*. This was the report of a Committee set up in May 1991 by the Financial Reporting Council, the London Stock Exchange and the accountancy profession, under the chairmanship of Sir Adrian Cadbury, to consider the financial aspects of corporate governance. The *Cadbury Report* was published in December 1992.

Its main recommendation was that the boards of all the listed companies registered in the UK should comply with a code of practice and state in their financial accounts whether or not they have complied with it, identifying any areas of non-compliance. It also stated that non-executive directors should be appointed for specified terms and re-appointment should not be automatic, that such directors should be selected through a formal process and that both their selection and their appointment should be a matter for the board as a whole.

This was followed by the establishment of a committee chaired by Sir Richard Greenbury. The committee's main remit was to look into various aspects of directors' remuneration. The *Greenbury Report* was published in July 1995 and it recommended a Code of Best Practice based on the fundamental principles of accountability, transparency, and linkage of rewards to performance.

The *Cadbury Report* and the *Greenbury Report* were then reviewed together and the report on this review, *The Committee on Corporate Governance – Final Report* (often referred to as the *Hampel Report*) was published in January 1998. This report led to the first version of the *Combined Code* being published in June 1998.

Using that version as a starting point, the current version of the *Combined Code* was developed with reference to the *Turnbull Report on Internal Control* (2002–03), the *Smith Guidance on Audit Committees* (2003) and the *Higgs Report on Reviewing the Role and Effectiveness of non-Executive Directors* (2003) and contains elements of all three reports within it.

32.5 Justification for a *Combined Code*

Following the issue of the latest version of the *Combined Code* in 2003, the need for such a code was confirmed in a report called *Enterprise Governance: Getting the Balance Right*, prepared by the Professional Accountants in Business Committee of the International Federation of Accountants (IFAC) and was published by IFAC in 2004. It looked at 27 corporate case studies – 11 outstandingly successful companies and 16 companies that had failed. It found evidence of clear failures in corporate governance in the recent well known cases, including Enron, Worldcom and Vivendi. The report can be found at **www.ifac.org/MediaCenter/files/ EnterpriseGovernance.pdf**

The study analysed information for each company including:

● whether the role of the chairman and chief executive was split;
● how long the chairman, chief executive and financial director had been in place and where they had been recruited from;
● the executive remuneration package;
● the composition and background of the board;
● information about mergers and acquisitions;
● strategy development and implementation;
● the use of complex financial engineering techniques.

Corporate governance – key failure factors

High on the list of the key failure factors identified by the study was the culture and tone at the top level of the company. By their own poor example and failure to uphold high ethical standards, senior managers allowed a culture to flourish in which secrecy, rule-breaking and fraudulent behaviour became acceptable. Many examples were found of dominant, charismatic chief executives who went unchallenged by senior executives and board directors.

The study found that strategic factors were more important than good corporate governance. This confirmed what many commentators and business analysts had always felt to be the case – while poor corporate governance can ruin a company, good corporate governance cannot, on its own, ensure success.

32.6 The content of the *Combined Code*

The *Combined Code* comprises of two sections and three schedules:
Section 1: Companies
    A: Directors
    B: Remuneration
    C: Accountability and Audit
    D: Relations with Shareholders
Section 2: Institutional Shareholders
    E: Institutional Shareholders
Schedule A: Provisions on the design of performance related remuneration
Schedule B: Guidance on liability of non-executive directors: care, skill and diligence
Schedule C: Disclosure of corporate governance arrangements

It contains a set of main and supporting principles and all listed companies have to report on how it applies them. The form and content of this report are not prescribed, it being felt that companies should be free to explain their governance policies in the light of the principles, including any special circumstances which have led to a particular approach being adopted.

As you can see from the outline contents of the *Combined Code*, it also contains a set of provisions. Listed companies must either confirm they have complied with these provisions, or provide an explanation where they have not done so. However, companies outside the FTSE 350 (i.e. those companies that are not among the 350 largest companies) are exempt from some of the provisions.

Schedule C of the *Combined Code* contains guidance which suggests ways of applying the relevant principles and of complying with the relevant provisions on internal control (C.2 and part of C.3 in the Code); and on the provisions concerning audit committees and auditors (C.3 of the Code).

At times, the text of the *Combined Code* lacks the precision of, for instance, an accounting standard. For example, the main principle in Section 1 concerning directors states that 'Every company should be headed by an effective board, which is collectively responsible for the success of the company.' What precisely is meant by 'effective' is a matter of interpretation based on the detailed contents of the *Combined Code*.

The supporting principles concerning directors in Section 1 are similarly broadly presented:

'The board's role is to provide entrepreneurial leadership of the company within a framework of prudent and effective controls which enables risk to be assessed and managed. The board should set the company's strategic aims, ensure that the necessary financial and human resources are in place for the company to meet its objectives and review management performance. The board should set the company's values and standards and ensure that its obligations to its shareholders and others are understood and met'.

'All directors must take decisions objectively in the interests of the company'.

'As part of their role as members of a unitary board, non-executive directors should constructively challenge and help develop proposals on strategy. Non-executive directors should scrutinise the performance of management in meeting agreed goals and objectives and monitor the reporting of performance. They should satisfy themselves on the integrity of financial information and that financial controls and systems of risk management are robust and defensible. They are responsible for determining appropriate levels of remuneration of executive directors and have a prime role in appointing, and where necessary removing, executive directors, and in succession planning.'

While this may appear less likely to be effective than the heavily defined terminology of accounting standards, the nature of what is being dealt with in the *Combined Code* lends itself to this approach and there is no doubt that it is proving an effective instrument in improving corporate governance in the UK.

The full text of the *Combined Code* contains a list of related URLs which anyone wishing to look further into this topic would be well advised consulting.

Learning outcomes

You should now have learnt:

1 Why it is important for companies to adopt sound practices of corporate governance.
2 About the background to the development of the *Combined Code on Corporate Governance*.
3 About the nature of the content of the *Combined Code on Corporate Governance*.

Answer to activity

32.1 The *Combined Code* has been imposed upon listed companies following high profile incidences of financial irregularities that resulted in heightened public concerns about financial reporting, accounting procedures and the remuneration of directors. Unlisted companies are, by definition, much smaller enterprises where, typically, the directors own the majority, if not all the shares of the company. Many of these companies are exempt from an annual audit and, in the case of those that are externally audited, the only people likely to be affected by poor corporate governance are those same people who are failing in the performance of their stewardship role. Consequently, it makes little sense to require unlisted companies to apply the *Combined Code*.

Review questions

32.1 Define corporate governance.

32.2 If the *Combined Code* is a *voluntary* code of conduct for the directors of all UK limited companies, why is it that all listed UK companies must report annually on their compliance with it?

32.3 Briefly describe the development of the *Combined Code* from 1991 to the present day.

32.4 Briefly describe the main and supporting principles relating to directors contained in the *Combined Code*.

You can find a range of additional self-test questions, as well as material to help you with your studies, on the website that accompanies this book at **www.pearsoned.co.uk/wood**

Public sector accounting

33.1 The nature of the 'public sector'

The public sector has been defined as 'all organisations which are not privately owned or operated'. It consists of organisations the control of which is in the hands of 'public', as opposed to 'private' owners, and whose objectives involve the provision of services where profit is not a primary objective. The word 'public' as used in the phrase 'in the hands of the public' is often taken to mean 'government', either local or national.

Unlike the private sector of the economy, where there is a clear objective and motivation in making profits or a return on capital, the public sector has a multitude of demands and objectives.

> 'In the private sector, you are able to focus very clearly on the bottom line. You've got a clear objective. That's not always true in the public sector. In the public sector, you often have many conflicting objectives and grappling with those is part of the skill of public sector management and part of what makes it so interesting.' (Steve Bundred, Audit Commission Chief Executive, *Accountancy Age*, 2 September 2004, p 19.)

The public sector is concerned primarily with providing services to the general public which would not otherwise be available or provided adequately within the financial resources of all individual members of the public. Consequently, it exists primarily in order to:

- provide services which are beyond the private means of people using those services;
- provide a benefit to everyone within socially acceptable norms;
- achieve certain minimum standards of service, e.g. roads, education and training schemes;
- substitute central or local planning in place of consumer choice;
- ensure a consistent approach to certain practices or procedures;
- aid control and economic regulation in key areas.

These objectives within the public sector are significantly influenced by the central government. The relationship between central control and local democracy is an important political consideration and, while the concept of what the public sector provides is fairly universal, the means of control over the different organisations providing these services can differ.

33.2 Types of public sector organisations in the UK

Public sector organisations can be classified into five major groups in the UK:

- departments of central government
- nationalised industries, public corporations
- local authorities
- health authorities
- bodies set up for a specific purpose: universities; the Royal Mint; and HM Stationery Office.

33.3 The relevance of legislation

The nationalised industries and public corporations are required to meet certain criteria set by the government in the form of a return on capital. The other four category organisations are set other forms of performance targets. The obligation to provide public services by the different types of organisation is generally derived from statutes or legislation passed by Parliament. This legislation may be either 'general', i.e. applicable to the whole country, or 'local', relating to just one area.

For anyone looking at these organisations from an accounting perspective, a knowledge of certain aspects of this legislation is important. Not only will the relevant statutes set out the powers of the organisation for raising money to pay for the provision of services, but associated regulations may provide details of the accounting and audit requirements relating to the organisation.

33.4 The objectives of public sector organisations

'Many public bodies are effective monopolies, providing services to very vulnerable people or services that people can't choose to opt out of. So there's a necessity in the public sector to have other means to ensure effectiveness, stimulate innovation and drive improvement.' (Steve Bundred, Audit Commission Chief Executive, *Accountancy Age*, 2 September 2004, p 19.)

Each type of public sector organisation has its own accounting objectives which influence the form and content of its financial statements and accounting arrangements. Some of the underlying factors necessary to achieve those objectives are common to all public sector organisations.

Stewardship

The use of public money, particularly if it is acquired through taxation, demands that the accounts show that monies have been properly and lawfully used. This requires the publication of sufficient information which can be easily understood by the public.

Maintaining systematic records

All public sector organisations must maintain systematic records so that (i) financial require-ments can be estimated and (ii) the measurement of the use of these financial resources can be established and the relative efficiency and effectiveness of the organisation in using them can be assessed. Value for money is of the utmost importance, especially when taxation or charging levels are high or increasing rapidly. Accounting procedures must be directed towards ensuring that the maximum benefit is obtained from the limited resources.

Financial control

Total planned public expenditure in the year 2004–2005 was £488 billion, financed by receipts of £455 billion and borrowing of £33 billion. When amounts of this magnitude are involved, there is a significant need for effective financial control, particularly given the lack of any profit objective and the motivation and discipline that go with it. Even more than in the case of the private sector, financial control in the public sector must be exercised through a sound budgeting and accounting system. Such a control system will normally be supported by written internal regulations or instructions concerning expenditure and income procedures and their associated accounting arrangements and the control system used by one organisation is often virtually ident-ical to those in other similar public sector organisations.

> **Activity 33.1** Why do you think similar public sector organisations are likely to use virtually identical control systems?

In the rest of this chapter, we'll look at the accounting arrangements in place in central government, local government, and the national health service, focusing mainly on the system that operates in England and Wales.

33.5 Central government accounting

Central government services are administered through the various government departments which operate their accounting systems on a fund basis. The basic system is that all government income, from taxes and other revenues, is paid into a central Consolidated Fund and the various departments draw off this Fund to finance the services which they provide. Any deficit in the Consolidated Fund is financed from the National Loans Fund, and vice versa.

The funds available to finance public expenditure are allocated between the various govern-ment departments. The size of the allocation to an individual department depends on the political and social priorities of the government. Of particular importance in recent years has been the government's increase in the level of public expenditure coupled with achieving better value for money from every pound spent providing the various government services.

The amount of money available for public expenditure is subject to cash limits. Spending by a department in any year is stated in cash terms. That is, the prices prevailing in the November of the previous year plus an amount to cover forecast inflation in the next year. The total level of expenditure is controlled within this cash limited amount, and the Treasury is responsible for monitoring spending and reporting to the government on the level of spending by the various departments throughout the financial year.

Following an announcement in the 1993 budget speech a major change in government accounting took place from the 2001/2002 financial year when a system called 'Resource Accounting' was adopted. This resulted in a switch from a receipts-and-payments-based account-ing system (i.e. **cash-based accounting**) to a system based on normal commercial practice complete with accruals and movements in cash flows. This system was introduced by the Government Resources and Accounts Act 2000 and is part of a longer-term aim to publish fully audited 'Whole of Government Accounts' (WGA) covering the whole of the UK public sector based on generally accepted accounting principles (GAAP).

Under this Act, each department is required to prepare resource accounts for each financial year, in conformity with a Treasury direction, detailing the resources acquired or disposed of during the year and the use of resources by the department during the year.

The resource accounts are prepared on an accruals basis and must give a true and fair view of the state of affairs of the department, the net resource outturn, resources applied to objectives, recognised gains and losses, and cash flows for the financial year.

HM Treasury appointed the Permanent Head of Department as Accounting Officer of each government Department, with responsibility for preparing the department's accounts and for transmitting them to the *Comptroller and Auditor General* (who is head of the National Audit Office).

In preparing the accounts, the Accounting Officer is required to comply with the *Resource Accounting Manual* prepared by HM Treasury, and in particular to:

● observe the relevant accounting and disclosure requirements, and apply suitable accounting policies on a consistent basis;
● make judgements and estimates on a reasonable basis;
● state whether applicable accounting standards, as set out in the Resource Accounting Manual, have been followed, and disclose and explain any material departures in the accounts;
● prepare the accounts on a going-concern basis.

The responsibilities of an Accounting Officer, including responsibility (i) for the propriety and regularity of the public finances for which an Accounting Officer is answerable, and (ii) for keeping proper records and for safeguarding the Department's assets, are set out in the *Accounting Officers' Memorandum* issued by HM Treasury and published in *Government Accounting*.

33.6 Local government accounting

The Local Government Acts 1972 and 1985 contain the statutory provisions which broadly established the present structure of London and Metropolitan Boroughs, Unitary Authorities, County District and Parish Councils. Total planned expenditure on local government services in 2004–2005 was £44 billion with approximately 75 per cent on local education services.

The changing role of local government has accelerated in recent years particularly since 1979. In early 1994, the Financial Secretary to the Treasury told an audience of prominent local government and public sector figures that he would like to see their role diminish to that of a purchaser of services, which would almost wholly be provided by the private sector. The 'enabling' authority is seen as one mainly concerned with policy direction, the allocation of resources, determining standards and priorities and then monitoring the results. The widening of compulsory competitive tendering (CCT) was an important move in this direction, as is 'outsourcing', where local services are provided by a private company under contract, without the need for CCT and, more recently, Best Value measures (performance against a range of measurable criteria) in the provision of public services.

The role of the Chief Financial Officer

The Local Government Act 1972 abolished specific statutory reference to the need to appoint a 'treasurer' and to the 'making of safe and efficient arrangements for receipts and payments'. What it did do, however, was to impose wider but more general responsibilities for the financial administration of local authority affairs. The 1972 Act stated:

'A local authority shall appoint such officers as they think necessary for the proper discharge ... of their functions ... Every local authority shall make arrangements for the proper administration of their financial affairs and shall ensure that one of their officers has responsibility for the administration of those affairs.'

The Local Government Act 1988 strengthened the position of the 1972 Act by:

● requiring all Section 151 officers to have appropriate qualifications for the job;
● specifying those issues on which Section 151 officers must report to the council.

The title 'Chief Financial Officer' is widely used, but other titles also exist (e.g. 'Treasurer' and 'Director of Finances'). In practice it is for the members of an authority to determine the role of the Chief Financial Officer and to specify the terms and conditions of this appointment.

Government regulations place upon the 'responsible financial officer' (subject to instructions from the employer) the responsibility for determining the accounting system, form of accounts and supporting records. Further, that officer has a duty to ensure that the accounting systems are observed and that the accounts and supporting records are kept up to date.

The regulations contain several sections that are particularly relevant to the financial officer. In particular, the responsible officer is required to maintain an adequate and effective internal audit of the accounts of the body and have right of access at all times to such documents of the body which relate to the accounts of the body as they appear to him or her to be necessary for the purpose of the audit and shall be entitled to require from any officer of the body such information and explanation as is required for that purpose.

Local authority financial reporting

Local authorities prepare four main types of financial reports.

(*a*) an annual revenue budget and capital programme (budget);
(*b*) an information leaflet or mini-report to be sent to all council taxpayers with the council tax demand note;
(*c*) a statement of accounts (traditionally referred to as an 'abstract of accounts') (They are legally required to publish this.);
(*d*) an annual report.

The form and content of these reports is largely standardised, and must comply with four types of external requirements:

● statutory requirements, including Acts of Parliament and Accounts and Audit regulations;
● government directions in the form of codes of practice and notes of guidance;
● professional standards, including statements of standard accounting practice (SSAPs), statements of recommended practice (SORPs) and financial reporting standards (FRSs) and the CIPFAs *Code of Practice on Local Authority Accounting in the United Kingdom* (which specifies the form and content of the individual financial statements which comprise the statement of accounts);
● generally accepted accounting principles, consistently applied.

The Accounting Code of Practice

The CIPFA/LASAAC (Local Authority, Scotland, Accounts Advisory Committee, Accounting Code of Practice (ACOP)) is recognised by the Accounting Standards Board as a SORP (Statement of Recommended Accounting Practice) and, since its introduction in 1991, has been regularly updated, most recently in 2008.

A typical Statement of Accounts published by a district or borough council is drawn-up under UK GAAP and may contain the following sections:

(a) an explanatory foreword setting out the main financial features of the year;

(b) a Statement of Accounting Policies;

(c) a Statement of the respective responsibilities of the Local Authority and its Chief Financial Officer;

(d) a Statement setting out the main features of the system of internal financial control and arrangements for internal audit;

(e) the Income and Expenditure Account and Notes;

(f) a Statement of Movements on the General Fund balance

(g) a Statement of Recognised Gains and losses

(h) the Balance Sheet and Notes;

(i) the Cash Flow Statement and Notes;

(j) a Statement summarising the collection of Council Tax and Business Rates and the appropriation of that money to the relevant providers of local services.

County Councils publish sections (a) to (i) only, but would also include the accounts of the Superannuation Fund (revenue account and net assets statement covering employees of all local authorities in its area). Police and Fire Authorities prepare separate income and expenditure accounts and balance sheets.

Audit arrangements in local government

Local authority audits in England and Wales are overseen by the Audit Commission. A slightly different system operates in Scotland where Audit Scotland (**www.audit-scotland.gov.uk**) oversees the audits on behalf of and reports to the Audit Commission. In Northern Ireland, the Northern Ireland Audit Office (**www.niauditoffice.gov.uk/**) oversees the audits and reports to the Department of the Environment. As when we looked at central government auditing, we will focus on the system in England and Wales.

Auditing is to a national legislative standard (Audit Commission Act 1998) and a detailed Code of Practice issued by the Audit Commission, which was last revised in 2005. The Audit Commission is an independent public body responsible for ensuring that public money is spent economically, efficiently, and effectively in the areas of local government, housing, health, criminal justice and fire and rescue services.

The audit is usually performed by the District Audit Service. However, 30 per cent of these audits are performed by private sector auditing firms.

This audit is every bit as thorough as a private sector company audit and the impact on those responsible for the stewardship of a local authority who are found to have been acting inappropriately can be very severe indeed. The highest profile case involved the Audit Commission's role as auditor of Westminster Council which resulted in a 15-year battle conducted by the District Auditor to recover amounts lost to the council from Dame Shirley Porter, former leader of the council, for her role in what was referred to as 'the homes for votes scandal'.

The 'homes for votes scandal'

Between 1987 and 1989, Dame Shirley Porter who was then the leader (i.e. in charge of the stewardship) of Westminster Council kept council homes empty and sold them cheaply in the hope of boosting support for her political party in eight marginal wards (districts). By doing so, she hoped to prevent the Labour party winning control of the council. This policy was found to have cost the council £27,023,376! The case was finally settled after three appeals by a payment of £12.3 million in 2004.

When the auditors are satisfied that nothing material has been done, an unqualified audit opinion is issued, similar to the example shown in Exhibit 33.1:

Exhibit 33.1 An unqualified audit opinion

Opinion:

'In our opinion, the financial statements present fairly the financial position of the XYZ Borough Council as at 31 March 2008 and its income and expenditure for the year then ended.'

The website for the Audit Commission is **www.audit-commission.gov.uk/**.

33.7 National Health Service accounting

The National Health Service is almost wholly dependent upon central government funding (planned NHS expenditure in 2004–05 was £69 billion). Some of that funding is derived from employers' and employees' National Insurance contributions, but the bulk of it comes from general taxation. Some diagnostic services and treatments are free to patients requiring them. For other items such as spectacles, dentistry and drugs prescribed by doctors, most patients bear at least part of the cost, but there are important exemptions. In recent years, charges have been introduced for certain previously free items such as eye tests, though consultations with NHS doctors and specialists, as well as NHS hospital treatment, remain free.

Unlike local government, the NHS has no independent source of revenue equivalent to business rates or the community charge. Instead, its finances are determined by the Cabinet (i.e. the leaders of the government) in the annual public expenditure allocation process. Individual health authorities are permitted to and do raise limited amounts of money through fund-raising activities, but the amounts are insignificant compared to their overall funding needs.

NHS provision in England and Wales is through 28 Strategic Health Authorities whose catchment areas are based on geographical boundaries broadly equivalent to County Council areas. Within this structure, the bulk of health service provision is the responsibility of Primary Care Trusts (PCTs), which typically bring together primary care (GPs, dentists, pharmacists and opticians) and the commissioning of other services, especially treatment in local hospitals.

Internal financial controls are the primary responsibility of each PCT board. The accountable officer responsible for internal financial controls on a daily basis is the Chief Executive of the Trust, who has responsibility for (i) maintaining a sound system of internal control that supports the achievement of the organisation's objectives and (ii) reviewing its effectiveness. The system of internal control is based on an ongoing risk management process designed to identify the principal risks to the achievement of the organisation's objectives; to evaluate the nature and extent of those risks; and to manage them efficiently, effectively and economically. By its nature, this form of internal control is designed to *manage* rather than *eliminate* the risk of failure to achieve objectives. It can, therefore, only provide reasonable, rather than absolute assurance of effectiveness.

The system of internal control is underpinned by compliance with the requirements of *Controls Assurance Standards* on:

● governance
● financial management
● risk management.

NHS broad financial arrangements

Financial directives are issued by the Health Secretary and set down, in broad terms, the re-sponsibilities and requirements for financial control. These are minimum statutory requirements, including standing financial instructions, that form the basis upon which authorities develop their own financial control policies.

The purpose of the accounts of organisations within the NHS is to satisfy the 'primary requirements of public accountability for the use of NHS financial resources'. The annual accounts are used as the basis for the summarised accounts which the NHS executive is required to prepare and submit to the *Comptroller and Auditor General* who examines these accounts, certifies them and lays copies of them, together with his report, before Parliament. (This part of the process is different in Scotland, as you will see in Section 33.8.)

Four main financial statements are required to be published by a Primary Care Trust:

1 An operating cost statement showing gross commissioning and providing costs and net cost of each after deduction of miscellaneous income.
2 A balance sheet.
3 A cash flow statement (based on FRS 1).
4 A statement of realised gains and losses.

As a general rule, health authorities and NHS Trusts are expected to prepare their annual accounts in accordance with accounting standards issued or adopted by the Accounting Standards Board (ASB). However, the government considers certain principles under ASB pronouncements to be inappropriate to trusts and alternative treatments are prescribed. The annual accounts must be accompanied by a statement of accounting practice and must be certified by the director of finance and acknowledged by the chairman prior to audit. The required date for completion of the annual accounts is the 30th June after financial year to which they relate.

In addition to the annual accounts, health authorities and NHS trusts are required to complete a set of financial returns to provide various analyses of expenditure which are not obtainable from the annual accounts.

Audit arrangements

In England and Wales, audit arrangements are overseen by the *Comptroller and Auditor General*. Audit arrangements for individual trusts and health authorities are, as with local government, provided by the Audit Commission through its District Audit Service and subject to similar regulations and code of practice.

33.8 The National Audit Office (NAO)

The NAO (**www.nao.org.uk**) audits the financial statements of all government departments and agencies, and those of many other public bodies, and reports to Parliament on the spending of central government funds, specifically in the context of value for money. There are separate national audit offices for Scotland, Northern Ireland, and Wales.

33.9 Public sector auditing in Scotland

You have already learnt that the audit arrangement for local government in Scotland is slightly different from that which exists in England and Wales. For the rest of the public sector, the differences are considerably greater. In the rest of the UK, the audits of government Departments are the responsibility of the *Comptroller and Auditor General*. In Scotland, Audit Scotland conducts the audits on behalf of the *Auditor General* (**www.audit-scotland.gov.uk/about/ags**) who reports to the Scottish Parliament.

The role of the *Auditor General* is to:

● examine how public bodies spend public money
● make sure they manage their finances to the highest standards
● make sure they achieve value for money.

Public bodies that the *Auditor General* reviews include:

● Departments of the Scottish Government
● NHS boards
● further education colleges
● Scottish Water
● government agencies and non-departmental public bodies such as Scottish Enterprise, the Scottish Prison Service and Historic Scotland.

Learning outcomes

You should now have learnt:

1 What distinguishes the public sector from the private sector.

2 About the accounting arrangements in place in central government, local government, and the National Health Service.

3 About the structure of public sector auditing in the UK for central government, local government, and the National Health Service.

4 There are some differences between the structure of public sector auditing in Scotland and that which exists in the rest of the UK.

Answer to activity

33.1 The public sector organisations will all have similar regulations governing what they do, and performance targets set using the same criteria. As in any situation where organisations are ultimately owned by one entity, efforts will be made to achieve economies of scale (i.e. savings) and benefit from the increased efficiency and effectiveness that a control system developed using the resources of all organisations within the group can bring.

Review questions

33.1 What is the public sector?

33.2 Briefly describe the role of the Accounting Officer of a central government department.

33.3 Briefly describe the differences between the structure of local authority auditing in Northern Ireland compared to England and Wales.

33.4 Briefly describe the differences between the structure of public sector auditing in Scotland compared to the rest of the UK.

You can find a range of additional self-test questions, as well as material to help you with your studies, on the website that accompanies this book at **www.pearsoned.co.uk/wood**

Accounting for management control

Learning objectives

After you have studied this chapter, you should be able to:

● describe some of the deficiencies of financial accounting if it were used for management control purposes

● describe the need to avoid potential conflicts between alternative or competing objectives that may be adopted within an organisation

● explain that decision making should comprise more than just the financial figures involved

● explain that the information needs of organisations are, in part at least, a function of their size

● describe the difference between the three areas in which management operates, and their different information needs

● explain that accounting information is only one part of the overall system in which organisations operate

● describe how the accounting system is affected by the surrounding environment both inside and outside the organisation in which it operates

Introduction

In this chapter, you'll learn about the deficiencies of financial accounting information for decision-making. You'll also learn about the impact of organisational objectives, people and organisation size on decision-making and about the three-part role of management. Finally, you will learn about the manner in which the accounting system interacts with its environment and about the relationship between quantitative and qualitative data and formal and informal information systems.

34.1 The part played by financial accounting

So far your studies have been concerned primarily with the recording function of accounting, often called bookkeeping, and the drafting of the financial statements of different types of organisations, such as partnerships and limited companies. The term generally used for your studies up to this point is **'financial accounting'**. Much of financial accounting is concerned with legal requirements, such as complying with the provisions of accounting standards and the Companies Acts when drafting financial statements, or keeping an accounting record of a customer's legal indebtedness, i.e. a debtor's account.

With companies, the annual report represents the information given to the shareholders by the directors of their running of the company during a particular year. In other words, it is a description of the directors' 'stewardship' of the company. The financial statements are also given to other interested parties, such as the company's bankers, creditors, inspectors of taxes, etc.

While financial accounting is necessary from a legal point of view, it cannot be said to be ideal from the point of view of controlling the activities of a firm. Your studies would therefore be incomplete if you had seen only the 'stewardship' function of accounting as represented by financial accounting. The use of accounting for controlling the activities of an organisation is probably more important. In this chapter, we shall briefly consider accounting for 'management control'.

The word 'management' has nothing at all to do with whether or not an entity is a limited company, a plc or small a family-run business. It means the people who are managing the affairs of the organisation, whether they are directors, partners, sole traders or 'managers' classified as those employees who are in charge of other employees.

34.2　Deficiencies of financial accounting for management control

Before starting to examine accounting for management control, let's look first at the deficiencies of financial accounting when used to control the activities of an organisation.

The first major deficiency of financial accounting is that it deals with events that have already occurred. It deals with the past, not the future. It is possible to control something while it is happening, and control can be arranged for something that is going to happen but, when it has already happened without being controlled, the activity has ended and we are too late to do anything about it. For example, if a company incurs a loss and we do not realise it until long after it has happened, the loss obviously cannot be prevented.

What we really want to do is to control affairs so that a loss is not incurred if at all possible, and to be able to call on accounting techniques to help us do so. However, it certainly does not mean that we are not interested in the past. We can learn lessons from the past which can be very useful in understanding what is going on now, and what is likely to be happening in the future.

The second major deficiency of financial accounting is that it is concerned with the whole of the organisation. Thus the trading account of a business may show a gross profit of £60,000 but, while it is better to know that than to have no idea at all of what the gross profit is, it does not tell management much about past transactions. Suppose, for example, that it manufactures three products – watches, pens and cigarette lighters. Some possibilities of how much of the gross profit was attributable to each of the products are shown in Exhibit 34.1:

Exhibit 34.1

| | Various possibilities of profits and loss for each product (£s) | | | |
	1	2	3	4
Watches	20,000	5,000	30,000	(30,000)*
Pens	20,000	70,000	28,000	65,000
Lighters	20,000	(15,000)*	2,000	25,000
Total gross profit	60,000	60,000	60,000	60,000

*Losses are shown in brackets

These are only some of the possible figures of gross profit and loss for each product which could result in an overall gross profit of £60,000. The figure of total gross profit alone provides very few clues as to what lessons can be learnt. If, say, possibility number 2 was, in fact, the real situation, it would stimulate further discussion and investigation as to why these results had occurred. It could, perhaps, result in the closing down of the section of the business which makes cigarette lighters if, after investigation, it was found to be in the interests of the business to cease manufacturing them. (As you will learn later, simply because it is making a gross loss may not necessarily mean it would be wrong to continue manufacturing cigarette lighters.) Many more lessons can therefore be learnt if the business's activities can be examined piece by piece instead of looking at the overall, summarised results.

For these and a number of other reasons, **financial accounting is of little use by itself for management control purposes**. It does not mean that it is of no use at all for control purposes – for example, the financial accounting system may reveal that the debtors at a point in time are £50,000, something that management need to know if they are to control their finances properly – but much of the financial accounting information produced is of little use in controlling the business.

> **Activity 34.1**
>
> Imagine we bought a building in 1990 for £40,000 that is now worth £120,000. If we rented a similar building now it might cost us £30,000 a year. What use would you make of the knowledge that the building originally cost £40,000 when deciding whether or not to rent a similar building now, or buy another one for £120,000?

Let's consider in more detail what management control seeks to do, and why.

34.3 Objectives of the organisation

If we want to discuss management control we must first of all ask ourselves what is its purpose? We can only have control if it is for a particular purpose, otherwise how can we possibly determine what we may need to control, never mind start doing anything at all.

It might seem obvious that the objectives of an organisation should be spelled out clearly and unambiguously. In fact, the writing down of a formal set of objectives for an organisation is very often overlooked. It is often, instead, assumed in such cases that the objectives are obvious. As a result, in many cases, the employees of the organisation could be pulling in many different directions, as they all have different ideas of the objectives of the organisation.

Some of the possible objectives an organisation may have include:

● To ensure that the maximum profit is made. This still is not clear; do we mean profits in the long term or the short term?
● To obtain a minimum specific share of the market for its goods or services.
● To have the greatest share of the market for its goods or services.
● To achieve the highest possible level of quality in the goods being manufactured or services offered.
● To ensure that our customers are fully satisfied with our goods and services.
● To ensure full employment for its employees.
● To ensure that its employees' welfare is maintained at a high level, in terms of such things as back-up facilities and adequate pension schemes.
● To ensure that its employees receive the best training and are kept fully up to date with the latest technology for our sort of business.
● To cause as little damage as possible ecologically.
● To progressively take over all its major competitors.

> **Activity 34.2**
>
> What other objectives can you think of? Try to think of another two. If you can, try to make them objectives which cannot be identified or demonstrated using information provided by financial accounting.

You should now be beginning to see for yourself that there are many things which it would be useful to know about an organisation that cannot be provided by financial accounting.

If you look at the above list of possible objectives, you will see that some simply cannot be achieved at the same time – they contradict, or are incompatible with, one another. Let's look at how this problem of conflict between objectives can be addressed.

34.4 Conflicts between objectives

Most organisations have more than one objective, some compatible with some others and some not. By that we mean that pursuit of one objective may impact upon the organisation's ability to achieve some of its other objectives, and that, as a result, no objective can be considered completely on its own.

Take, for example, the objective of maximising profit being pursued at the same time as the objective of causing as little damage as possible ecologically. If any funds have to be spent in order to achieve the second objective, the first objective is automatically undermined. There would be an additional level of conflict if the ecological expenditure was being made voluntarily rather than being forced on the organisation by the authorities. Even where it was being forced on the organisation, it would raise a conflict as the firm would want to do so in the cheapest possible way so as to maintain its objective of profit maximisation. Cheapness may be achieved by relaxing controls so that a small but noticeable level of ecological damage occurred which just happened to be within the limit set by the government, thus enabling maximisation of the profit objective within the constraints of the ecological objectives.

Similarly, maintaining a very high quality of goods could mean lower profits if a large number of items manufactured are scrapped because they are not up to standard. Lowering the quality could possibly increase profits but would result in non-attainment of the quality objective.

> **Activity 34.3**
>
> Both these examples have something in common relating to the timeframe in which the actions taken can be justified. What is it?

It is thus essential to ensure that the objectives are very clearly spelled out *and prioritised*. In effect, the objectives should be stated in terms of Objective A being sought, subject to the constraint that Objective B must be achieved, etc. Otherwise people will easily misunderstand them and because of this the firm may not proceed in the direction that is desired. It is also essential that an appropriate timeframe is considered when resolving conflicting objectives.

34.5 People and management control

The *most* important resource of any organisation is the people who work for it. A danger exists that a great deal of care and attention may be given to designing a management control system and operating it, but it is a complete failure because the people in the organisation did not use it effectively. Systems and figures do not themselves do anything. It is the people in the organisation who take (or do not take) the necessary action that determine if a successful outcome is to result.

Figures thrown up by control systems are only part of the evidence available when a decision has to be made as to the necessary action to take. A department may be incurring losses now, but the sales manager may state that he believes sales will increase soon and that the department will then rapidly become profitable. If decision makers use accounting figures as the only criteria on which action should be based, there would be some very poor decisions taken by management.

Many very successful products have incurred losses at first, but have eventually proved successful because the organisation had faith in the product and persevered with it.

One important feature of any effective management control system is that it is integrated into the operations of the existing systems and used in an appropriate way. For example, if exactly the same system of management control was used in three different organisations, A may find that its control system was useless because no one acted on the data produced. In B, the control system might have damaged the organisation because management used the data as though it were the only criterion in gauging the actions it should take. In C, it might be very effective because the management saw the data as a useful guide in planning and control and had also made certain that the rest of the organisation took the same view.

How human beings use and react to a management control system is, therefore, at the heart of the problem of ensuring that management control systems are effective.

34.6 Different sizes of organisations and the decision-making process

Part of this book is about information which is intended to be used by the management of an organisation. For a small and simple organisation the information needs of management may be limited and can be obtained by direct observation – using the eyes to look and the voice to ask questions.

For example, a person managing a greengrocer's stall in a street market can often operate the business effectively without the assistance of any formal records or analysis. What he buys is determined by the goods available in the local wholesale market and his personal knowledge of what his customers are prepared to buy at a given price. His records will probably centre around the recording of cash – the details of his sales and his expenditure. However, apart from the essential requirement of maintaining an appropriate level of cash, these records do not help him in the day-to-day management of his business operations.

In contrast, if we look at the buyer responsible for buying fresh fruit and vegetables for a large supermarket chain, certain differences emerge. The basic decision about what to buy at a given price remains the same. However, a large organisation has a much wider choice of where and how to buy than a small one. The buyer from the large organisation may, for example, be able to enter into contracts directly with growers and to enter forward contracts for the supply of produce (for example, a farmer agrees at the start of the summer to sell all his summer output of potatoes and peas to a frozen foods manufacturer at a fixed price).

In a large supermarket chain, the buyer will not be in regular direct contact with each of the many different sales outlets and therefore relies upon written information to keep him in touch with demand. He does not have to listen to complaining customers! Similarly because there will be many more potential sources of supply than exist for a smaller business, he needs more formal information to keep him in touch with market prices than would be the case were he employed by a smaller organisation.

One of the other features about large organisations which distinguishes them from smaller ones is that responsibility for running the business is shared between many different people. In order to ensure that the operations of the organisation are carried out efficiently and effectively, there needs to be some criterion to measure the performance of the managers. In a small organisation, the poorly informed proprietor will either, at best, make a poor living or at the other extreme, go out of business. Thus success or failure is clearly the sole proprietor's own responsibility. In a large organisation, the same things can happen overall, but the situation may be obscured by a swings and roundabouts effect of some good sections making up for some bad. A management control system should help identify the problems and problem areas within an organisation.

34.7　The management process

The way that management operates in an organisation can be divided into three distinct activities:

(a) forecasting and planning;
(b) controlling operations;
(c) evaluating performance.

(a) Forecasting and planning

Forecasting and planning is the process by which senior management decides on major overall issues concerning what the business is going to do and how it is going to do it. It involves an assessment of information about the future which is produced through a process known as 'forecasting'. When a forecast has been prepared, senior management can plan how to achieve the organisation's objectives. 'Planning' is the process of co-ordinating the resources available to attain an objective.

(b) Controlling operations

Controlling operations involves management in a number of processes and requires several different kinds of information. The plans produced by senior management must be converted into an operating pattern which matches the parts into which the organisation is divided. This process breaks down the overall plan into detailed operating plans each of which relates to the management structure of the company. This process is called 'budgeting'.

When actual events occur, the information recording those events needs to be measured in such a way that it can be compared with the plan. This provides feedback on the success of the plan.

Controlling operations effectively also requires that information is provided in a form designed to help managers take the decisions which their jobs require. For example, information about the profit from one product as compared to another will enable a decision about how many of each product to make.

(c) Evaluating performance

Evaluating performance involves the analysis and assessment of actual results. This is partly, but not exclusively, a process of comparison with plans. The information on which plans were based may have been inaccurate. Thus, the analysis of performance, while involving comparison of actual results with planned results, needs considerable judgement as to what the plans should have been had all the information now available been known when the plans were drawn up.

The three activities we have described are by no means independent of each other. In reality, they follow a distinct sequence. One way of looking at this is in the form of a cycle in which information is circulating continually from one activity to another, as shown in Exhibit 34.2.

In this diagram, information is shown flowing around from one activity to another. Thus, for example, forecasts for a period may be improved before the period they apply to ends by taking account of the analysis of what happened during the previous period *and* during the period to which the forecast relates.

As shown in Exhibit 34.2, forecasting and planning relate to the future. Controlling operations relates to concurrent events – the here and now. Evaluating performance can only be concerned with the past.

Exhibit 34.2

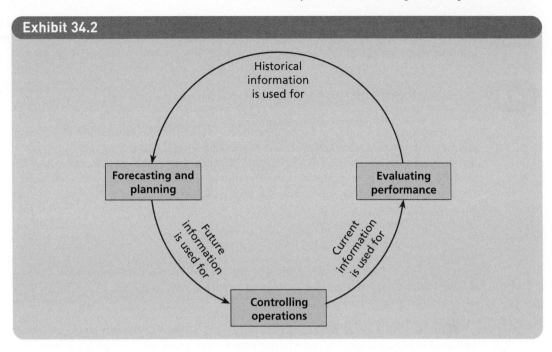

The diagram we have just considered only looks at internal information. Exhibit 34.3 recognises that information is being fed into the process from outside the organisation, both from the general environment in which the organisation operates and as a result of interactions between the organisation and its operating environment.

Exhibit 34.3

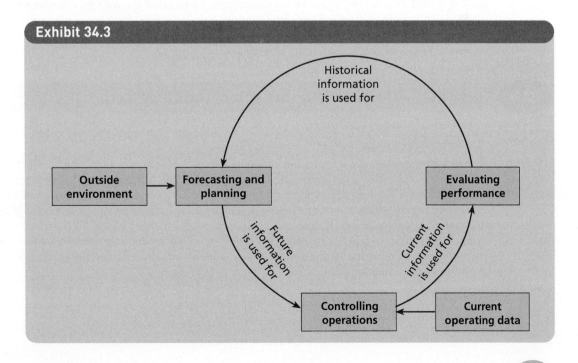

Senior management has to take into account all the information it can about the external environment, such as competition, economic cutbacks, etc. Controlling operations also receives information about actual business events, e.g. sales activity, purchasing activity, etc.

34.8 Types of management information

No attempt has been made so far to describe the nature of the information which management requires. Information may come in many shapes and forms. Accounting and, therefore, this book is concerned with information that is capable of being expressed in numerical terms. That is, with information that can be quantified. Information of a more general nature, such as information about people's feelings or views, may be very useful to management but cannot be quantified. Such information is, therefore, usually part of the informal rather than the formal information system of an organisation.

Activity 34.4 Apart from what is said above, what do you think is the main difference between formal and informal information systems?

Within the body of quantified information, it is normal to identify that part which can be measured in money terms. This part of the information system is called the 'accounting information system'. The accounting information system is a very important element of the organisation's information system since the organisation is basically an economic unit which must survive in conditions of economic scarcity and competition. In other words, an organisation which does not meet its economic objectives will eventually fail or be taken over, hence the central importance of accounting information.

However, other quantified information may be very important for management. For example, if you are a farmer you will measure the yield of milk from your cows in the first instance in litres. A production manager will be very concerned to monitor the tonnages produced on his machines. A supermarket will want to know how long customers have to queue at the check-out (and whether customers are being lost because it takes too long). None of these items is of interest to those preparing accounting information.

34.9 Quantitative methods in the information system

A management information system is the specialist information system designed for the management of an organisation.

A modern management information system collects all the data together (into what is called a 'database') and, after appropriate processing, provides the information which is important to each manager. Such an information system will include some information that originated in the accounting information system. As these systems have become more sophisticated (largely as a result of the impact of widespread computerisation), the distinction between accounting information and other types of management information has tended to become less meaningful. The techniques of quantitative analysis (or statistics) apply to all the data in this system, whether or not they are accounting data.

Learning outcomes

You should now have learnt:

1 Financial accounting fulfils a stewardship function by reporting past performance and financial position.

2 Financial accounting information is of only limited use for management control purposes, for which other forms of data and information are required.

3 It is important that organisational objectives are clearly defined and that the financial accounting information system is designed to meet and support those objectives in the most efficient and effective way.

4 Management is concerned with three areas of activity:
   (a) forecasting and planning;
   (b) control;
   (c) evaluating performance.

5 The financial accounting information system does not exist in a vacuum, it interacts with, and is affected by, the environment in which it is operating and must be designed accordingly.

Answers to activities

34.1 The original cost is now completely irrelevant for decision-making purposes, whether at this time or at some point in the future. Yet, in many cases, it is the £40,000 that will appear in the current year's balance sheet and, in that case, the £40,000 is included in the amounts used to calculate ROCE and other key profitability and efficiency ratios. This is one of the reasons why FRS 15 allows fixed assets such as buildings to be revalued on a regular basis.

34.2 (i) To be identified as the most innovative company in the field and (ii) to have the lowest rate of staff turnover in the industry are two, neither of which can be identified or demonstrated through the use of information provided by financial accounting.

34.3 Lowering the standard of pollution control or the quality of product could possibly increase profits in the short term, but it could mean lower profits in the long term if customers deserted the organisation because it had a reputation for causing pollution or its goods were considered to be second-rate. Short-termism can be very counterproductive and often leads to the wrong decisions being taken, from a long-term perspective. However, conflicting objectives can often become compatible objectives when a long-term view is taken. For example, in the ecology example, by eliminating pollution an organisation may be able to enhance its reputation sufficiently to recoup the additional cost through increased revenues and, thus, maximise its profits in the long term.

34.4 At its simplest, an informal information system is one that operates without rules and procedures. Information gets passed through it virtually accidentally, in the same way as you may learn what someone did last weekend during a casual conversation. An informal information system has no firm structure. It does not have a hierarchy and information does not undergo any uniform or routine transformation as it passes around the information system. Information is not constrained by the nature of the information system and can be both qualitative and quantitative.

A formal information system is everything an informal information system is not. It has rules, procedures, a hierarchy, a routing system for data and information flow and set procedures for data and information processing. The data and information within it tends to be quantitative, though this is changing as computer systems become capable of greater storage. One key aspect of the formal information system is that nothing gets into it that isn't identified beforehand as an appropriate form of input. Formal information systems also tend to be fairly inflexible and slow to change compared with informal ones. Thus, for example, if the VAT rate changes and the information system cannot be easily or quickly amended to accept the new VAT rate, it may be some time before the necessary changes can be made and the information adjusted to reflect the change.

Review questions

34.1 'Financial accounting looks behind, whilst management accounting looks ahead.' To what extent does this quotation accurately reflect the role of the two branches of accountancy?

(*Edexcel: GCE A-level*)

34.2 'Financial accounting is non-dynamic, backward looking, conservative, as objective as possible, and subject to statutory and other regulation. Management accounting is future oriented, is dynamic, produces forward looking figures, should not be too concerned with objectivity, and is not generally subject to external regulation.' (Prof. Michael Bromwich)
   Justify this statement, giving examples to illustrate your answer.

(*Edexcel: GCE A-level*)

34.3 What are some of the deficiencies of financial accounting?

34.4 Why is it important that the employees of an organisation should clearly understand what the objectives of the organisation are?

34.5 How can there be a conflict between the various objectives of an organisation?

34.6 Describe how the management process is carried out.

You can find a range of additional self-test questions, as well as material to help you with your studies, on the website that accompanies this book at **www.pearsoned.co.uk/wood**

Part

6

COSTING

Introduction

This part looks at what constitutes cost and at four techniques used to derive cost.

Elements of costing

Learning objectives

After you have studied this chapter, you should be able to:

- explain why information must fit the purpose for which it is prepared
- discuss why the costs of obtaining information should be less than the benefits of having the information
- describe the flow of costs through financial accounts
- describe the flow of costs through a manufacturing business
- classify expenses appropriately
- explain the importance of an effective costing system
- explain the importance of cost allocation in the context of control

Introduction

In this chapter, you'll learn how costs flow through financial accounts and through a manufacturing business's accounting system into its manufacturing account. You will also be introduced to, and reminded of, terminology relating to costs and expenses and learn the difference between them through an exercise in cost classification.

35.1 Management accounting

So far you have learnt about bookkeeping and the preparation of financial statements. These are the two principal components of financial accounting. As you learnt in Chapter 34, the information as produced by financial accounting is usually historic, backward-looking and produced (mainly) for the use of decision makers external to the organisation.

There is a second side to accounting. This one is generally forward-looking and capable of being used to aid managerial control, forecasting and planning. Similarly to financial accounting, it also consists of two components. One where costs are recorded, the other where the data is processed and converted into reports for managers and other decision makers. The cost recording component is called 'cost accounting' and the processing and reporting component is called 'management accounting', which is also the name used to refer to this side of accounting. It is also sometimes referred to as 'managerial accounting'.

Cost accounting data also feeds into financial accounting, where it is used to derive the cost and expenditure figures that appear in the trading and profit and loss account. However, the two branches of accounting use the data and information differently. Referring once more to the third exhibit in Chapter 34, reproduced here as Exhibit 35.1, you can follow the flow of data and information within it and see how and where management accounting information is used.

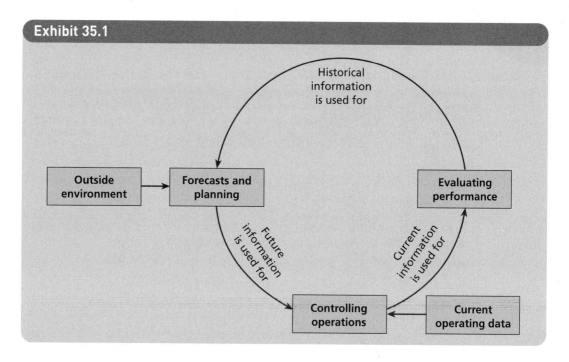

Exhibit 35.1

Management accounting produces the financial forecasts that guide planning. It embeds controls into the flow of operating data and uses them to control activities within the context of the plans. It evaluates performance and uses the information that is produced to underpin the forecasts that guide planning.

As you can see, while it frequently looks backwards to gather information, the main focus of management accounting is on producing information (i) for control over current operations and (ii) to forecast and plan for the future.

Activity 35.1 Which aspects of this exhibit also relate to financial accounting?

For financial accounting and management accounting to operate effectively, they both need the raw data that is then built up and processed into the information they produce. As mentioned earlier, the process whereby this data is gathered is known as cost accounting.

35.2 Costs for different purposes

Cost accounting underpins both the management accounting system and the financial accounting system of an organisation. Without cost accounting, such systems could not exist as they would be unable to determine with any accuracy the costs and expenditures relating to each aspect of their activities. Before entering into any detailed review of costs, it is better if we **ask ourselves first of all what use we are going to make of information about costs.** By doing so, the context and motivations for cost accounting will be revealed, thus making it easier to understand the nature of the costs themselves.

Let's do so, first, by referring to something which is not accounting, and then relating it to accounting. Suppose you had a job in a local business and that your employer has just left you a message asking you to measure the distance between Manchester and London. As you thought about this request, the following thoughts might go through your head:

1 *How* does he want the distance measured? Some possibilities are:
   (a) from the southern outskirts of Manchester to the northern outskirts of London;
   (b) from the accepted geographical centre of London to the accepted geographical centre of Manchester;
   (c) to the centres of the two cities calculated as mathematically precise points;
   (d) by road – this could be just major roads, just minor roads, or could be a mixture of both – the main requirement being the quickest route by road;
   (e) by canal;
   (f) by train;
   (g) by air; allowance may or may not be made for the distance covered by the aircraft which would include climbing to an altitude of 5,000 feet or perhaps 40,000 feet, or might ignore the distance travelling in achieving an altitude.

2 The *cost* of obtaining the information. Measuring distances (or measuring costs) is not costless itself. Using very sophisticated instruments to get accurate measurement can be very expensive indeed. On the other hand it might just be a matter of measuring the distance on a map with a rule and converting it into miles – this would cost hardly anything at all.

3 What is the *purpose* for which the measurement will be used? This has been deliberately left as the last point, but in fact it should have been the first question that came into your mind. Illustrations of the use could have been as follows:
   (a) he is going to drive from Manchester to London by car and wants a rough idea of the mileage so that he can gauge what time to set off if he is to arrive before it gets dark in London;
   (b) he might conceivably want to walk it;
   (c) he might be submitting a tender for the building of a motorway by the shortest possible route, cutting tunnels through ranges of hills;
   (d) perhaps he wants to send goods by canal;
   (e) maybe he wants to arrive as close as possible to an underground station;
   (f) he might be an amateur pilot who wants to fly from Manchester Airport to London Airport.

You may also wonder about how accurate an answer is required.

The lesson to be learnt from all this is that the measurement required depends entirely on the use that is to be made of it, i.e. of the data. Too often, businesses make measurements of financial and other data without looking first at the use that is going to be made of it. In fact, it is sometimes said that 'information' is useful data that is provided for someone to use for a specific purpose and that, unless it is suitable for that purpose, it is worthless.

Thus, data given to someone which is not relevant to the purpose for which it is required is simply *not* information. Data which is provided for a particular purpose, and which is completely wrong for the purpose, is worse than having no data at all. At least when there is no data, the decision maker knows that the best that can be done is to guess.

Activity 35.2 Apart from the obvious fact that it is irrelevant, why is useless data such a bad thing?

Having discovered what information is required, you need to look at the costs involved if the information is to be obtained. You need to consider the following:

1 *What is the data on costs wanted for?*
It might be needed for the preparation of the financial statements, for management control or for decision-making. Different data on costs are wanted for different purposes.

For example, the cost of each item of stock held at the end of the financial year is needed for the preparation of the financial statements; the cost of each item in stock is needed for management control to verify whether items are being manufactured or purchased at an appropriate price; and the cost of each unit of stock held is required to decide what price to sell it at. Three very different uses of three very similar items.

2 *How are the costs to be measured?*
Only when the purpose for which costs are to be used has been identified can the measurement process be selected. Sometimes, financial accounting needs a precision in calculating certain costs which is not needed in management accounting; sometimes the opposite is the case. It depends on the costs involved and why they are required.

3 *The cost of obtaining data should not exceed the benefits to be gained from having it.*
This does not refer to some cost data which is needed to comply with various provisions of the law but such exceptions are rare.

Let's look at some examples to illustrate the cost/benefit factor:
(a) Spending £100 to obtain cost data which will be used as a basis for pricing many of a company's products. If the costs used had been 'guessed' rather than actual figures, errors in the sales prices derived from those costs could have led to large losses as items were sold at prices lower than their actual cost while others were priced so high they could not be sold.
(b) Spending £10,000 to find data on sales which the sales manager will toss into the wastebasket, because it is not the sort of data she wants, is obviously money wasted.
(c) Spending a lot of time and money to find out that the stock values on a particular day were £2,532,198 when such precision was not needed. Perhaps the chairman was having an informal chat with the bank manager, and all he needed to know was an approximate stock valuation. The approximate figure could have been found easily and at little cost, so here the costs of obtaining the information have exceeded the benefits of having it.

When it is known what the costs are for, and how much may be spent on obtaining them, an appropriate method to be used to obtain them can be selected.

35.3 Past costs in trading companies

There are many classifications of cost. As we go through the rest of this chapter, we'll summarise briefly those that you already know about. The first of these is historical cost.

Historical cost

Historical costs underpin financial accounting as we know it today. Exhibit 35.2 shows a simplified view of costs flowing through the financial accounting system from original transaction to the ledgers to the financial statements and the calculation of profit. Income from sales has been included simply so as to enable profits to be shown.

Absorption and marginal costing

Learning objectives

After you have studied this chapter, you should be able to:

- explain why the costs relevant for decision making are often different from those used for the calculation of net profit
- explain the difference between fixed, variable, semi-variable and step-variable costs
- explain the difference between absorption and marginal costing
- discuss various factors underlying the pricing policy adopted by an organisation
- explain why marginal costing, not absorption costing, should be used when deciding how to utilise spare capacity through additional production
- explain what is meant by 'full cost pricing'
- explain the importance of contribution to pricing, production and selling decisions
- explain what is meant by activity-based costing (ABC)
- discuss the advantages and limitations of ABC

Introduction

In this chapter, you'll learn more about the nature of different types of costs, including fixed, variable and semi-variable costs. You will also learn how to arrive at a cost per unit that can then be used to set an appropriate selling price for a good or service. Two contrasting approaches – absorption (or 'full') costing and marginal costing – are reviewed; and the concept of **contribution** is introduced and its importance in pricing and production decisions is explored. Finally, you will learn about another approach to cost attribution: activity-based costing.

36.1 Allocation of indirect manufacturing costs

As you learnt in the previous chapter, all indirect manufacturing costs are allocated to the products manufactured. Indirect manufacturing costs, therefore, add to the value of work-in-progress and, so, to the value of finished goods stock. After apportioning all indirect manufacturing costs to the products produced, the production cost of any item comprises direct materials, direct labour, any direct expenses, plus a share of indirect manufacturing costs.

After a financial period has ended, it is possible to look back and accurately calculate the indirect costs. It is this figure that is used when calculating the valuation of closing stock. Consider a company which had produced 1,000 units, of which 200 units have not yet been sold, at a total production cost of £100,000. The closing stock valuation becomes:

$$\frac{\text{Unsold units}}{\text{Total units produced}} \times \text{Production cost of goods completed} = \frac{200}{1,000} \times £100,000$$

$$= £20,000 \text{ closing stock valuation}$$

The method we have just used above, which includes allocating all indirect manufacturing costs to products, is known as '**absorption costing**', sometimes called 'full costing'. While you proceed through the rest of this chapter, try to decide for yourself whether or not it would always be appropriate to use absorption costing in order to determine the cost of something produced (a good) or provided (a service).

36.2 Absorption costing: effect upon future action

Let's consider a decision you may have to make concerning a future action. Exhibit 36.1 concerns a decision about whether or not to take on an extra order, something that arises from time to time in all forms of business.

Exhibit 36.1

Donald Ltd's factory has been making 100,000 units annually of a particular product for the past few years. Last year, costs were:

	£
Direct labour	200,000
Direct materials	300,000
Indirect manufacturing costs	400,000
Production cost	900,000
Administration and other expenses	150,000
	1,050,000

The 100,000 units were sold for £12 each = £1,200,000

The production cost per unit can be seen to be $\dfrac{£900,000}{100,000} = £9$

The current year is following exactly the same pattern of production and costs. Suddenly, part-way through the year, a foreign buyer sends a request for 20,000 units if the price per unit can be cut from £12 to £8. A meeting is held and the managing director says, 'What a pity. This could have been our first export order, something we have been waiting to happen for several years. The selling price overseas has no bearing on our selling price at home. But it costs us £9 to produce a unit, so we would lose £1 per unit if we accepted this order. We just cannot afford to lose money in order to achieve some export sales. Our shareholders would not tolerate the annual profit of the company falling below £150,000.'

'I think you're wrong,' says John, the accountant. 'Let's look at this year's results (a) if we do not accept the order and (b) if the order is accepted':

36.4A Your company has been trading for three years. It has used a marginal costing approach to value its stock in its financial statements. The directors are interested to know what the recorded profits would have been if absorption costing had been used instead. **Using the following information, prepare a statement for each of the three years comparing both methods.**

(a) Fixed indirect manufacturing costs are £64,000 per year.
(b) Direct labour costs per unit over each of the three years were £16 per unit.
(c) Direct material costs over each of the three years were £12 per unit.
(d) Variable expenses which vary in direct ratio to production were £20 per unit.
(e) Sales are: Year 1: 36,000 units; Year 2: 40,000 units; Year 3: 60,000 units. All at £64 per unit.
(f) Production volumes were: Year 1: 40,000 units; Year 2: 48,000 units; Year 3: 51,000 units.

36.5 Greatsound Ltd manufactures and sells compact disc players, the cost of which is made up as follows:

	£
Direct material	74.80
Direct labour	18.70
Variable overhead	7.50
Fixed overhead	30.00
Total cost	131.00

The current selling price is £187.

Greatsound Ltd works a day shift only, at present producing 120,000 compact disc players per annum, and has no spare capacity.

Market research has shown that there is a demand for an additional 60,000 compact disc players in the forthcoming year. However, these additional sales would have a selling price of £150 each. One way of achieving the extra production required is to work a night shift. However, this would increase fixed costs by £2,500,000 and the labour force would have to be paid an extra 20 per cent over the day shift rate.

The company supplying the materials to Greatsound Ltd has indicated that it will offer a special discount of 10 per cent on total purchases if the annual purchases of materials increase by 50 per cent.

The selling price and all other costs will remain the same.

Assuming that the additional purchases will only be made if the night shift runs, **you are required to**:

(a) Advise Greatsound Ltd whether it should proceed with the proposal to commence the night shift, based on financial considerations.
(b) Calculate the minimum increase in sales and production required to justify the night shift.
(c) Give **four** other matters which should be taken into consideration when making a decision of this nature.

(AQA (Northern Examinations and Assessment Board): GCE A-level)

36.6A
(a) What is meant by the terms *contribution* and *marginal cost*?

(b) Barton & Co Ltd make and sell 2,000 units per month of a product 'Barco'. The selling price is £65 per unit, and unit costs are: direct labour £8; direct materials £17; variable overheads £11. Fixed costs per month are £29,400.

The company receives two export orders for completion in September 2002. Order A requests 600 items at a special total price of £20,000; order B requires 750 items at a total price of £34,000. Order A will require no special treatment, but order B will demand extra processing at a cost of £6 per item. The company has sufficient capacity to undertake *either* A *or* B in addition to its current production, but only by paying its direct labour force an overtime premium of 25 per cent.

Calculate the company's contribution and the profits for the month if:
(i) normal production only takes place
(ii) order A is accepted in addition to normal production
(iii) order B is accepted in addition to normal production.

(c) Use your answer to (b) to demonstrate that a company will normally accept an order which produces a *contribution* towards overheads.

(Edexcel: GCE A-level)

→

→ **36.7** Arncliffe Limited manufactures two types of product marketed under the brand names of 'Crowns' and 'Kings'. All the company's production is sold to a large firm of wholesalers.

Arncliffe is in something of a crisis because the chief accountant has been taken ill just as the company was about to begin negotiating the terms of future contracts with its customer. You have been called in to help and are given the following information relating to each product for the last year. This information has been prepared by a junior assistant.

Report on revenues/costs for the year just ended:

	Crowns £	Kings £
Revenue	60,000	25,000
Floor space costs (rent and rates)	10,000	5,000
Raw materials	8,000	2,000
Direct labour	20,000	10,000
Insurances	400	200
Machine running costs	12,000	3,000
Net profit	9,600	4,800

The junior assistant says in his report, 'As you can see, Crowns make twice as much profit as Kings and we should therefore stop manufacturing Kings if we wish to maximise our profits. I have allocated floor space costs and insurances on the basis of the labour costs for each product. All other costs/revenues can be directly related to the individual product.'

Further investigation reveals the following information:

(i) The wholesaler bought all the 20,000 Crowns and 10,000 Kings produced last year, selling them to his customers at £4 and £3 each respectively. The wholesaler is experiencing an increasing demand for Crowns and intends to raise his price next year to £4.50 each.
(ii) Crowns took 8,000 hours to process on the one machine the company owns, whereas Kings took 2,000 hours. The machine has a maximum capacity of 10,000 hours per year.
(iii) Because all production is immediately sold to the wholesaler no stocks are kept.

Required:
(a) Prepare the revenue/cost statement for the year just ended on a marginal cost basis, and calculate the rate of contribution to sales for each product.
(b) You are told that in the coming year the maximum market demand for the two products will be 40,000 Crowns and 36,000 Kings and that the wholesaler wishes to sell a minimum of 6,000 units of each product. Calculate the best product mix and resulting profit for Arncliffe Limited.
(c) Calculate the best product mix and resulting profit for Arncliffe Limited if another machine with identical running costs and capacity can be hired for £20,000 per annum. Floor space and insurance costs would not change and the maximum and minimum conditions set out in (b) above continue to apply.
(d) What points does Arncliffe Limited need to bear in mind when negotiating next year's contract with the wholesaler?

(Reproduced with the kind permission of OCR: from the University of Cambridge Local Examinations Syndicate)

36.8A Reed Ltd manufactures three products A, B and C. Budgeted costs and selling prices for the three months ending 30 September 2002 are as follows:

	A	B	C
Sales (units per month)	6,000	8,000	5,000
	£	£	£
Selling price per unit	45	44	37
Unit costs			
Direct labour	6	9	6
Direct materials*	20	24	16
Variable overhead	4	3	2
Fixed overhead	5	5	6

Labour costs are £3 per hour, and material costs are £4 per kilo for all products. The total fixed costs are of a general factory nature, and are unavoidable.

The company has been advised by its supplier that due to a material shortage, its material requirement for the month of September will be reduced by 15 per cent. No other changes are anticipated.

Required:
A A statement to show the maximum net profit for the three months ending 30 September 2002, taking into account the material shortage for the month of September.
B Explain how the fixed cost element is dealt with in marginal costing and in absorption costing. Briefly explain how this affects any closing stock valuation.

(Reproduced with the kind permission of OCR – University of Oxford Delegacy of Local Examinations: GCE A-level)

Authors' note: Assume that the materials used in each product are of the same kind.

36.9 Paul Wagtail started a small manufacturing business on 1 May 2008. He has kept his records on the double entry system, and has drawn up a trial balance at 30 April 2009 before attempting to prepare his first final accounts.

Extract from the Trial Balance of Paul Wagtail at 30 April 2009

	£	£
Purchases of raw materials	125,000	
Revenue		464,360
Selling expenses	23,800	
Insurance	4,800	
Factory repairs and maintenance	19,360	
Carriage on raw materials	1,500	
Heating and lighting	3,600	
Direct factory power	12,430	
Distribution expenses	25,400	
Production wages	105,270	
Factory supervisor's wages	29,600	
Administration expenses	46,700	
Plant and machinery at cost	88,000	
Delivery vehicles at cost	88,000	
Raw materials returned to supplier		2,100

At 30 April 2009, he has closing stock of raw materials costing £8,900. He has manufactured 9,500 completed units of his product, and sold 8,900. He has a further 625 units that are 80 per cent complete for raw materials and production labour, and also 80 per cent complete for factory indirect costs.

He has decided to divide his insurance costs and his heating and lighting costs 40 per cent for the factory and 60 per cent for the office/showroom.

He wishes to depreciate his plant and machinery at 20 per cent p.a. on cost, and his delivery vehicles using the reducing balance method at 40 per cent p.a.

He has not yet made up his mind how to value his stocks of work-in-progress and finished goods. He has heard that he could use either marginal or absorption costing to do this, and has received different advice from a friend running a similar business and from an accountant.

Required:
(a) Prepare Paul Wagtail's manufacturing, trading and profit and loss account for the year ending 30 April 2009 using *both* marginal and absorption costing methods, preferably in columnar format.
(b) Advise Paul Wagtail of the advantages and disadvantages of using each method.

(Reproduced with the kind permission of OCR – University of Oxford Local Delegacy Examinations: GCE A-level)

36.10A The figures given below are all that could be salvaged from the records after a recent fire in the offices of Firelighters Limited. The company manufactures a single product, has no raw materials or work in progress and values its stock at marginal cost (i.e. at variable manufacturing cost) using the FIFO basis. It is known that the unit closing stock valuation in 2010 was the same as in 2009.

	2010	2011
Selling price per unit	£10.00	£10.00
Variable manufacturing cost (per unit produced)	£4.00	£4.00
Variable selling cost (per unit sold)	£1.25	?
Quantity sold (units)	100,000	?
Quantity manufactured (units)	105,000	130,000
Contribution	?	£585,000
Fixed manufacturing costs	£105,000	£117,000
Other fixed costs	£155,000	?
Operating profit before interest charges	?	£292,000
Interest charges	£70,000	?
Opening finished stock (units)	?	?
Closing finished stock (units)	20,000	20,000
Net profit for the year	?	£210,000

Required:
Prepare a revenue statement for management showing contribution, operating profit and net profit for each year in as much detail as the information given above permits.

(Reproduced with the kind permission of OCR: from the University of Cambridge Local Examinations Syndicate)

36.11A Gainford Ltd is a manufacturing company which produces three specialist products – A, B and C. For costing purposes the company's financial year is divided into thirteen periods of four weeks. There is always sufficient raw material in stock to meet any planned level of production but there is a maximum number of labour hours available to the company. The production of each product requires a different physical layout of the factory equipment although the labour tasks are broadly similar. For this reason the company produces only one type of product at any time, and the decision as to which product to manufacture is taken before each four week period commences.
A forty-hour working week is in operation and the following factory staff are employed:

Grade 1   28 staff paid at a rate of £8 per hour
Grade 2   12 staff paid at a rate of £6 per hour

In addition, a limited number of qualified part-time staff can be employed when required. Both full-time and part-time staff are paid at the same rate. The next four-week period is number 7 and the following maximum part-time hours are available for that period:

Grade 1   2,240 hours
Grade 2   1,104 hours

The production costs and selling costs per unit for each product are:

	A	B	C
	£	£	£
Direct raw material	147	87	185
Direct labour: Grade 1	64	56	60
Grade 2	24	27	21
Variable overheads	15	10	15
Fixed overheads	12	12	12
Selling price of each product	400	350	450

There is a strong demand for all three products and every unit produced is sold.

Required:
(a) Explain the terms:
  (i) 'contribution'
  (ii) 'key factor'.
(b) Calculate the contribution and profit obtained when **each** product is sold.
(c) Prepare a statement from the available information, for period number 7 which will assist management to decide which product to produce in order to maximise contribution. This statement should include details of the:
  (i) total production labour hours available
  (ii) number of hours required to produce one unit of **each** type of product
  (iii) maximum production (in units) possible of **each** type of product
  (iv) product which will give the greatest contribution in period number 7.
(d) Outline the main steps in the manufacturing decision-making process which ought to be adopted by a business.

(AQA (Associated Examining Board): GCE A-level)

36.12A Vale Manufacturing started in business on 1 April 2003, and incurred the following costs during its first three years.

Year ending 31 March	2004	2005	2006
	£	£	£
Direct materials	60,000	49,900	52,200
Direct labour	48,000	44,000	45,000
Variable overheads	24,000	30,000	40,000
Fixed costs	40,000	40,600	41,300

Sales during the first three years were all at £20 per unit.

Production each year (units)	16,000	14,000	14,000
Sales each year (units)	14,000	14,000	15,000

Required:
(a) Prepare a statement showing the gross profit for each of the three years if the company used:
  (i) the marginal costing approach to valuing stock;
  (ii) the absorption costing approach to valuing stock.
(b) Advise the company of the advantages and disadvantages of using each method.

(Reproduced with the kind permission of OCR – University of Oxford Delegacy of Local Examinations: GCE A-level)

36.13 Frames Ltd make four different products: K, L, M and N. They have ascertained the cost of direct materials and direct labour and the variable overhead for each unit of product. An attempt is made to apportion the other costs in a logical manner. When this is done, 20 per cent is added for profit. The cost of direct labour and materials per unit is K: £28; L: £56; M: £120; N: £64. Variable overheads per unit are K: £8; L: £16; M: £26; N: £24. Fixed overhead costs of £3,800 are allocated per unit as K: £4; L: £8; M: £14; N: £12.

You are required to:
(a) Calculate the prices at which the units would be sold by Frames Ltd if the full cost system of pricing was adhered to.
(b) What would you advise the company to do if, because of market competition, prices had to be fixed at K: £66; L: £78; M: £140; N: £98?
(c) Assuming production of 100 units of each item per accounting period, what would be the net profit (i) if your advice given in your answer to (b) was followed; (ii) if the company continued to produce all of the items?
(d) What would you advise the company to do if, because of market competition, prices had to be fixed at K: £34; L: £96; M: £280; N: £78?

→ (e) Assuming production of 100 units of each item per accounting period, what would be the net profit (*i*) if your advice given in your answer to (*d*) was followed; (*ii*) if the company continued to produce all of the items?

36.14A Lenses Ltd makes six different products: P, Q, R, S, T and U. An analysis of costs ascertains the following:

Per unit	P	Q	R	S	T	U
	£	£	£	£	£	£
Direct labour and direct materials	45	51	114	147	186	342
Variable manufacturing expenses	18	33	30	63	66	69

Fixed costs of £34,200 are allocated per unit as P: £12; Q: £21; R: £21; S: £30; T: £48; U: £39. Using full cost pricing, 10 per cent is to be added per unit for profit.

You are required to:
(a) Calculate the prices that would be charged by Lenses Ltd if full cost pricing was adhered to.
(b) What advice would you give the company if a survey of the market showed that the prices charged could be P: £78; Q: £78; R: £198; S: £225; T: £240; U: £660?
(c) Assuming production of 600 units per period of each unit manufactured, what would be the profit of the firm (*i*) if your advice in (*b*) was followed, (*ii*) if the company continued to produce all of the items?
(d) Suppose that in fact the market survey had revealed instead that the prices charged could be P: £90; Q: £99; R: £225; S: £198; T: £435; U: £390, what would your advice have been to the company?
(e) Assuming that production of each item manufactured was 600 units per month, then what would have been the profit (*i*) if your advice in (*d*) had been followed, (*ii*) if the company chose to continue manufacturing all items?

36.15A
(a) What are the differences between marginal cost pricing and full cost pricing?
(b) How far is it true to state that marginal cost pricing is a short-term strategy?
(c) A.S. Teriod Ltd makes five different products – Ceres, Eros, Hermes, Icarus and Vesta. The various costs per unit of the products are respectively: direct labour, £14, £8, £22, £18 and £26; direct materials, £8, £10, £13, £12 and £17; variable overheads, £11, £9, £16, £15 and £19.

The fixed expenses for the month of February 2011 are estimated at £8,200, and this has been allocated to the units produced as Ceres £17, Eros £13, Hermes £19, Icarus £15 and Vesta £18. The company adds 20 per cent on to the total cost of each product by way of profit.

(*i*) Calculate the prices based upon full cost pricing.
(*ii*) Advise the company on which products to produce, if competition forces the prices to: Ceres £59, Eros £25, Hermes £80, Icarus £44 and Vesta £92.
(*iii*) Assuming that output for the month amounts to 100 units of each model, that fixed costs remain the same irrespective of output and that unused capacity cannot be used for other products: calculate the profit or loss if the company continued to produce the whole range at the new prices; AND if the company followed your advice in (*ii*) above.

(*Edexcel: GCE A-level*)

You can find a range of additional self-test questions, as well as material to help you with your studies, on the website that accompanies this book at **www.pearsoned.co.uk/wood**

Job, batch and process costing

Learning objectives

After you have studied this chapter, you should be able to:

- explain how indirect costs are apportioned among cost centres
- explain the difference between the accounting treatment of normal and abnormal losses
- explain the difference between scrap, by-products and joint products
- discuss some of the issues relating to cost allocation between joint products
- describe the system of job costing
- describe the system of process costing
- explain the appropriate treatment for under- and overabsorbed overheads

Introduction

In this chapter, you'll learn about the differences between costing for continuous production processes and costing for short-term production runs or one-off production activity. You'll learn more about attributing costs to cost centres, in this case, indirect costs such as service centre costs. Finally, you'll learn about how to deal with costs and revenues relating to by-products and joint products.

37.1 Background

The earlier chapters on costing have been concerned mainly with the business as a whole. You have seen the effects of and differences between applying marginal and absorption costing, and you have seen the flow of costs through manufacturing and retail businesses. Now we have to consider the actual use of these concepts in the application of costing in businesses. So far, things have been simplified so that the concepts could be seen and understood. For instance, it has been assumed in most of the *exhibits* that the businesses have been making only one kind of product, and that there has really been only one cost centre. Without stretching your imagination greatly, you will realise that businesses often manufacture many different items, and that most have a large number of cost centres.

Costing systems can usually be divided into two main types, (*a*) **job costing**, and (*b*) **process costing**. These two main types of costing system may adopt either an absorption or marginal costing approach, and may use FIFO or LIFO or AVCO methods of pricing issues from stock, etc.

It is important to realise that absorption costing and marginal costing *are not* costing *systems*. Rather, they are approaches to costing which are adopted when job or process costing systems are used.

37.2 Process costing or job costing?

Job costing is used when a finite number of units of a single product are made in one continuous batch. A job may be one single unit, as in the case of a bicycle manufacturer which produces bikes to the precise and very individual requirements of its customers. Alternatively, a job may comprise of many units. However, irrespective of the number of units involved, jobs are not often repeated and tend to all be uniquely different.

Process costing is used when production of identical products is continuous and lasts for a significant time. Unlike jobs, process products tend to be repeated as, for example, in a jam factory where the same five different jams are produced each week, each one being produced for an entire day.

Thus, process costing is relevant where production is a continuous flow, and is most applicable in industries where production is repetitive and continuous. For example, an oil refinery where crude oil is processed continually, emerging as different grades of petrol, paraffin, motor oil, etc. Another instance would be a salt works where brine (salt water) is pumped into the works, and the product is slabs or packets of salt. Salt works and oil refineries will have a repetitive and continuous flow of production and would, therefore, use process costing.

Exhibit 37.1

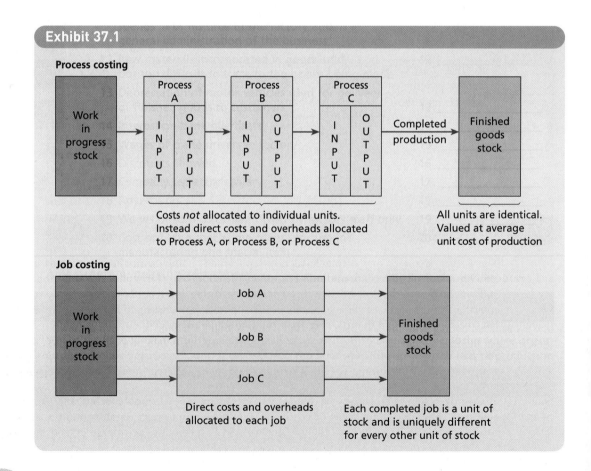

Contrasted with this would be production comprising of separate jobs for special orders which could be just one item or of a batch of items. For instance, where bodies of Rolls-Royce cars are made to each customer's specifications, each car can be regarded as a separate job. Compared with this would be a printer's business where books are printed, so that the printing of say 5,000 copies of a book can also be regarded as a job. **The 'job' can thus be one item or a batch of similar items.**

Two terms are used to describe this *specific order* form of costing. 'Job costing', when costs are to be attributed to an individual job (a customer order or task of relatively short duration); and '**batch costing**', when costs are to be attributed to a specific batch of a product (a group of similar items which is treated as a separate cost unit (a unit of product or service in relation to which costs are ascertained)).

The accounting treatment is the same. For our purposes, **in this chapter, we will only refer to job costing. If you are asked to perform batch costing, remember that the accounting approach is the same.** (Review Question 37.9 is on batch costing.)

We can compare process costing to job costing by using diagrams of the different types of costing. These are shown above in Exhibit 37.1.

Let's now look in detail at job costing.

37.3 Job costing

When job costing is used, each job is given a separate job number, and direct materials and direct labour used on the job are charged to the job. As a result, the job *is* the cost centre. The accumulation of the costs is done on a 'job cost sheet', which is simply a formal record of the costs incurred. (You will see examples of job cost sheets later in this chapter.) The materials will be charged to a job on a FIFO, LIFO, or AVCO basis. The direct labour costs will be found by recording the number of direct labour hours of each type of direct worker, and multiplying by the labour cost per hour for each type.

As the job is the cost centre, direct labour and direct materials can be charged directly to it. Indirect expenses, of course, cannot be charged directly to a job. Instead, they are charged to a service centre and the cost of the service centre is then apportioned between the various jobs to enable the cost of each job including indirect expenses to be calculated.

It is only after the end of the accounting period that the exact costs of each service centre for the period are known, but you need to know how much each job cost when it is finished, not several months later at the end of the accounting period.

Activity 37.1 How do you think this is done?

Let's consider an example. Suppose that four jobs are being done, each in a separate production department: A, B and C. There are also two service centres, G and H. Some of the indirect labour expenses and other indirect expenses can be allocated directly to departments – for instance the wages of the foremen (i.e. manager) of each of departments A, B and C; and items such as lubricating materials if each department used different lubricants. Other indirect labour and indirect expenses can be traced to the two service centres G and H. How will the costs accumulated in G and H be apportioned between departments A, B and C? One possibility is shown in Exhibit 37.2:

Exhibit 37.2

Indirect labour costs and other indirect expenses have been allocated to production departments A, B and C and service departments G and H as follows:

	Production departments (£s)			Service departments (£s)	
	A	B	C	G	H
Indirect labour	2,000	3,000	4,000	500	1,000
Other indirect expenses	1,000	2,000	3,000	1,500	2,000
	3,000	5,000	7,000	2,000	3,000

The problem is to apportion the costs of G and H to the production departments. Department G maintains the factory buildings while Department H maintains the factory machinery.

A study of the costs of Department G made it obvious how its costs should be apportioned. There was no doubt that the costs were in direct relationship to the floor space occupied by each department. But it must not be overlooked that Department H also needed the attention of Department G's workforce so that part of the costs of G must be apportioned to Department H.

These costs increase the total of the costs of Department H, which must then be apportioned between the three production departments. Floor space in square feet was A 2,000, B 4,000, C 3,000 and H 1,000. The £2,000 costs of Department G were therefore apportioned using the formula:

$$\frac{\text{Floor space in the department}}{\text{Total floor space}} \times £2,000$$

Therefore:

$$A \quad \frac{2,000}{10,000} \times £2,000 = \quad 400$$

$$B \quad \frac{4,000}{10,000} \times £2,000 = \quad 800$$

$$C \quad \frac{3,000}{10,000} \times £2,000 = \quad 600$$

$$H \quad \frac{1,000}{10,000} \times £2,000 = \quad \underline{200}$$
$$\underline{2,000}$$

Department H's costs have now increased by £200 to £3,200.

The apportionment of Department H's costs is far less straightforward. Apportionment based on the number of pieces of equipment (machines), volume of production, and type of equipment were all considered. However, let's suppose it was felt that there was a high relationship in this case between the value of the equipment in use and the costs of maintaining it. The more costly equipment was very complicated and needed a lot of attention. Consequently, it was decided to apportion Department H's costs between A, B and C on the basis of the value of equipment in each department: A £3,000; B £6,000; and C £7,000. The costs were therefore apportioned using the formula:

$$\frac{\text{Value of equipment in department}}{\text{Total value of equipment in all 3 departments}} \times £3,200$$

Therefore:

$$A \quad \frac{3,000}{16,000} \times £3,200 = \quad 600$$

$$B \quad \frac{6,000}{16,000} \times £3,200 = 1,200$$

$$C \quad \frac{7,000}{16,000} \times £3,200 = \underline{1,400}$$
$$\underline{3,200}$$

The costs and their apportionment can, therefore, be shown:

	Production departments (£s)			Service departments (£s)	
	A	B	C	G	H
Indirect labour	2,000	3,000	4,000	500	1,000
Other expenses	1,000	2,000	3,000	1,500	2,000
	3,000	5,000	7,000	2,000	3,000
Department G's costs apportioned	400	800	600	(2,000)	200
					3,200
Department H's costs apportioned	600	1,200	1,400		(3,200)
	4,000	7,000	9,000	–	–

This continuous method of apportioning service department overheads is sometimes called the **repeated distribution method.**

(See Review Question 37.7 for a discussion of this and another method, the elimination method.)

We have now identified the indirect expenses for each department. We now have another problem – how are these costs to be taken into the calculation of the cost of each job in these departments?

After investigation, Departments A and B are found to have a direct relationship between direct labour hours and indirect expenses but, in Department C, the guiding factor is machine hours.

If the total overheads of Departments A and B are divided by the total direct labour hours in those departments, this will give the indirect expenses rate per direct labour hour while, in Department C, the total indirect expenses will be divided by the total machine hours. The calculation of the indirect expenses rates are therefore:

	Production departments		
	A	B	C
Direct labour hours	5,000	4,000	
Machine hours			6,000
Indirect expenses rate per direct labour hour	$\frac{£4,000}{5,000}$	$\frac{£7,000}{4,000}$	
	= £0.8	= £1.75	
Indirect expenses rate per machine hour			$\frac{£9,000}{6,000}$
			= £1.5

(*Note*: **The indirect expenses rate is often referred to as the 'overhead rate'. As this is the term preferred by most examiners, we will use it from now on.**)

We can now calculate the costs of the four jobs being done in this factory:

Department A
Job A/70/144   Started 1.7.2002. Completed 13.7.2002
Cost of direct materials £130
Number of direct labour hours 100
Cost rate of direct labour per hour £0.9

Department B
Job B/96/121   Started 4.7.2002. Completed 9.7.2002
Cost of direct materials £89
Number of direct labour hours 40
Cost rate of direct labour per hour £1.1

Department C
Job C/67/198   Started 8.7.2002. Completed 16.7.2002
Cost of direct materials £58
Number of direct labour hours 50
Cost rate of direct labour per hour £1.0
Number of machine hours 40

Departments A and C
Job AC/45/34 Started in A 3.7.2002. Passed on to C 11.7.2002. Completed in C 16.7.2002
Cost of materials £115
Number of direct labour hours (in Dept A) 80
Number of direct labour hours (in Dept C) 90
Cost rate per direct labour hour Dept A £0.9
Dept C £1.0
Number of machine hours, Dept C 70

The job cost sheets for these four jobs are shown below. If an absorption costing approach had been used, indirect expenses (i.e. overheads) would include both fixed and variable indirect expenses. If a marginal costing approach had been used, the indirect expenses brought into the calculations of job costs would exclude fixed indirect expenses and, consequently, the overhead rate would be a variable one.

Job Cost Sheet. Job No. A/70/144

Started 1.7.2002 — Completed 13.7.2002

	Hours	Overhead Rates (£s)	£
Direct materials			130
Direct labour	100	0.9	90
Indirect manufacturing costs	100	0.8	80
Total job cost			300

Job Cost Sheet. Job No. B/96/121

Started 4.7.2002 — Completed 9.7.2002

	Hours	Overhead Rates (£s)	£
Direct materials			89
Direct labour	40	1.1	44
Indirect manufacturing costs	40	1.75	70
Total job cost			203

Job Cost Sheet. Job No. C/67/198

Started 8.7.2002 — Completed 16.7.2002

	Hours	Overhead Rates (£s)	£
Direct materials			58
Direct labour	50	1.0	50
Indirect manufacturing costs	40	1.5	60
Total job cost			168

Job Cost Sheet. Job No. AC/45/34

Started 3.7.2002 — Completed 16.7.2002

	Hours	Overhead Rates (£s)	£
Direct materials			115
Direct labour (Dept A)	80	0.9	72
Direct labour (Dept C)	90	1.0	90
Indirect manufacturing costs (Dept A)	80	0.8	64
Indirect manufacturing costs (Dept C)	70	1.5	105
Total job cost			446

37.4 Cost centres – job costing and responsibility

It must be pointed out that the use of a cost centre for job costing is not necessarily the same as tracing the costs down to the individual who is responsible for controlling them. There are two requirements here: (a) finding the cost of a job to check on its profitability and (b) controlling the costs by making someone responsible for them so that he/she will have to answer for any variations from planned results. As a result, many organisations keep separate records of costs to fulfil each of these functions when the appropriate cost centre to use for job costing is inappropriate for matching costs to the individuals responsible for those costs.

Now, let's look at process costing.

37.5 Process costing

Job costing treats production as comprising of a number of separate jobs, whereas process costing sees production as a continuous flow. **In process costing, no attempt is made to allocate costs to specific units being produced.**

There is, however, usually more than one process in the manufacture of goods. Take, for example, a bakery producing cakes. There are three processes: (A) the mixing of the cake ingredients, (B) the baking of the cakes, and (C) the packaging of the cakes. Each process is treated as a cost centre.

The costs for (A), (B) and (C) are, therefore, collected separately. Overhead rates are then calculated for each cost centre in a similar fashion to that in job costing.

In the case of the bakery, each accounting period would probably start and finish without any half-mixed or half-baked cakes, but many businesses which use process costing have processes which take rather longer to complete than baking cakes. A typical case would be the brewing of beer. At the beginning and end of each period there are stocks of partly processed units. It is a simple arithmetic exercise to convert unfinished units in production into 'equivalent units produced' (which is also known as **equivalent production**). For example, production during a particular period may be as in Exhibit 37.3:

Exhibit 37.3

Started and $^3/_4$ completed in previous period and $^1/_4$ completed in current period, 400 units: $400 \times ^1/_4$	100
Started and completed in current period	680
Started in current period and $^1/_8$ completed by end of period, 160 units: $160 \times ^1/_8$	20
Equivalent production	800 units

If the total costs of the cost centre amounted to £4,000 then the unit cost would be:

$$\frac{£4,000}{800} = £5$$

Process costing becomes more complicated if some of the part-produced items are, for example, complete in terms of materials, but incomplete in terms of labour; or $^2/_3$ complete for material and $^1/_4$ complete for labour. Although the situation is more complicated, the principles are no different from those described for calculating equivalent production when the proportion used of all items is the same.

We can now look at an example of process costing in Exhibit 37.4. So that we do not get involved in too many arithmetical complications, we will assume that there are no partly completed goods in any process either at the start or end of the period.

Exhibit 37.4

A bakery making cakes has three processes, process (A) the mixing of the cake ingredients, (B) the baking of the cakes, and (C) the packaging of the cakes.
  Activity in January was:

Direct materials used:	£
Process (A)	4,000
Process (B)	–
Process (C)	1,000
Direct labour:	
Process (A)	1,500
Process (B)	500
Process (C)	800
Indirect manufacturing costs:	
Variable:	
Process (A)	400
Process (B)	1,300
Process (C)	700
Fixed: (allocated to processes)	
Process (A)	600
Process (B)	500
Process (C)	400

100,000 cakes were made during January. The process cost accounts are:

Process (A)

	£		£
Direct materials	4,000	Transferred to process (B)	
Direct labour	1,500	100,000 units at £0.065	6,500
Variable factory indirect costs	400		
Fixed factory indirect costs	600		
	6,500		6,500

Process (B)

	£		£
Transferred from process (A)		Transferred to process (C)	
100,000 units at £0.065	6,500	100,000 units at £0.088	8,800
Direct labour	500		
Variable indirect manufacturing costs	1,300		
Fixed indirect manufacturing costs	500		
	8,800		8,800

Process (C)

	£		£
Transferred from process (B)		Transferred to finished goods	
100,000 units at £0.088	8,800	stock 100,000 units at £0.117	11,700
Direct materials	1,000		
Direct labour	800		
Variable indirect manufacturing costs	700		
Fixed indirect manufacturing costs	400		
	11,700		11,700

  Now, let's look at what is done when fewer units are produced during a process than was expected.

37.6 Normal and abnormal losses

There are some production losses that are a result of the production process which cannot be avoided and, as a result, the costs they represent cannot be eliminated from the total cost of the products produced. For instance, when printing books, losses of paper occur when paper is cut to the required size; when brewing beer there will be losses due to evaporation, when cutting steel the amount of cut steel will be less than the amount of steel before it was cut. **These losses are inevitable, even in the most efficient businesses. They are called 'normal losses' (sometimes called 'uncontrollable losses').**

On the other hand, there are losses which should be avoided if the production process is efficient. Such things as the incorrect cutting of cloth so that it is wasted unnecessarily, not mixing ingredients properly so that some of the product is unusable, and the use of inferior materials so that much of the product cannot pass quality inspection tests and is scrapped. **These are all examples of 'abnormal losses' (sometimes called 'controllable losses').**

The accounting treatments of these two very different types of losses are:

● **Normal losses.** These are not transferred from the process account but are treated as part of the process costs.
● **Abnormal losses.** These are transferred out of the process account and into an abnormal loss account. The double entry is:

Dr Abnormal loss account
Cr Process account

As a result, an abnormal loss is not included in the cost of items produced. Instead, it is treated as a period cost.

Activity 37.2   How do you think this is done?

37.7 Under/overabsorption of overheads

When an overhead rate is based on estimated annual indirect expenditure and estimated activity, it is not usually the same as it would have been had it been calculated at the end of the accounting period, when all costs are known. Either the costs themselves will differ from expectations, or the activity will not have proceeded as expected, or both.

For example, if £300,000 has been allocated for indirect costs to the year's production, but actual indirect costs were £298,000 then too much has been allocated. In other words, an overabsorption of indirect expenses has occurred amounting to £2,000. (Overabsorption is sometimes referred to as 'over-recovery'.)

If, on the other hand, £305,000 had been allocated but the actual costs were £311,000 then too little has been allocated. This would represent an underabsorption of indirect costs (i.e. overheads) amounting to £6,000. (Underabsorption is sometimes referred to as 'under-recovery'.)

At the closing balance sheet date, stock has been valued and this value includes something for indirect costs. In the case of an underabsorption, the question arises as to whether the closing inventory valuation should be amended to include something for the underabsorbed overheads. **The accounting answer is that no adjustment should be made to the inventory valuation.** Similarly, the stock valuation should not be reduced to take account of overabsorption of overheads.

Exhibit 37.5 shows how the indirect costs should be treated when there is an underabsorption of those costs which was caused by abnormal losses.

Exhibit 37.5

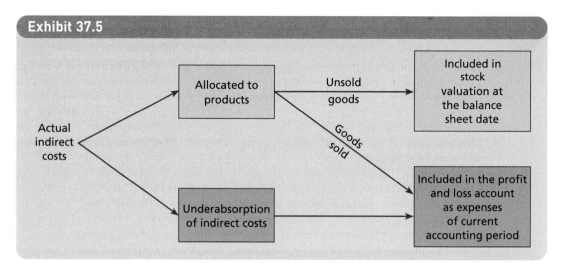

Any overabsorption is also included in the income statement, but as a credit.

37.8 Other kinds of businesses

Process costing is found most often in industries such as oil, canning, paint manufacture, steel, textiles and food processing.

37.9 The problem of joint costs

A manufacturing operation often results in only one product being produced. Any excess output other than the product itself is regarded as scrap, and the small cost that could be traced to it is ignored. For example, in the manufacture of a suit, when the cost is traced to the suit, the small unusable bits of cloth that are left over are ignored.

This is not always the case. **Where a group of separate products is produced simultaneously, each of the products having relatively substantial sales values, then the products are referred to as 'joint products'.** For example, crude oil taken to an oil refinery where it is processed into different grades of petrol, paraffin, motor oil, etc., all of which are joint products. The costs of the materials and processes, etc. must then be split between the joint products.

Many problems exist in doing so. Perhaps you will see why when you consider the problem of allocating the costs cutting up a cow for beef. From a cow there is rump steak, fillet steaks, T-bone steaks, sirloin, silverside, brisket, etc. If cutting up the cow cost £20, then how would you allocate the cost between all of these various joint products? This gives you some idea of the type of problems which can exist – in many industries this becomes increasingly problematic as the production technology in use increases in complexity.

Activity 37.3 How would you split the cost of cutting up the cow between joint products?

In fact, you could allocate the costs on any basis and none would be indisputably 'correct'. With joint products, there is no rational reason or basis for splitting their costs that cannot be argued against.

Sometimes, a minor (i.e. much lower value) but, nevertheless, distinguishable product is produced at the same time as the main product. One example is the sawdust that is created when wood is being converted into furniture. Such a product is known as a '**by-product**'. In most cases, the costs involved is to ignore them and simply credit any income derived from sale of the by-product against the cost of producing the main product(s).

Learning outcomes

You should now have learnt:

1 Neither marginal costing nor absorption costing are costing 'systems'; rather, they are approaches to costing which are used when job or processing costing systems are used.

2 The differences between job (and batch) costing and process costing.

3 Direct costs can be allocated directly to the relevant cost centre. However, indirect costs have to be apportioned among cost centres on an appropriate basis, as there is no way of knowing precisely how much indirect cost was incurred on each item produced.

4 How indirect costs can be apportioned across cost centres.

5 How to deal with normal and abnormal losses.

6 About the problems relating to cost allocation between joint products.

Answers to activities

37.1 The indirect expenses attributed to each service centre are estimated and then apportioned using an appropriate base to each job.

37.2 It is included in the costs charged to the profit and loss account at the end of the period.

37.3 Among the obvious choices, you could allocate the joint costs on the basis of the sale price of each of the joint products, or on the basis of the relative weight or volume of the joint products.

Review questions

Advice: Questions on job costing and process costing are usually fairly easy to answer and it is also relatively simple to gain quite high marks by tackling them. Don't forget, if a question refers to 'batch costing', this is accounted for using the same accounting procedures as job costing.

37.1 In a factory, four types of jobs are performed in separate production departments A, B, C and D. In addition there are three service departments, K, L and M. Costs have been allocated to the departments as follows:

	Production departments				Service departments		
	A	*B*	*C*	*D*	*K*	*L*	*M*
	£	£	£	£	£	£	£
Indirect labour	8,000	12,000	16,000	4,000	3,000	6,000	8,200
Other expenses	5,400	6,200	7,200	3,000	9,000	4,000	4,000

→

→ The expenses of the service departments are to be allocated between other departments as follows:

Dept K to Depts A 20 per cent: B 25 per cent: C 30 per cent: D 15 per cent: M 10 per cent.
Dept L to Depts A 35 per cent: C 45 per cent: D 20 per cent.
Dept M to Depts B 40 per cent: C 25 per cent: D 35 per cent.

In departments A and C the job costing is to use an overhead rate per direct labour hour, while in B and D a machine hour rate will be used. The number of direct hours and machine hours per department is expected to be:

	A	B	C	D
Direct labour hours	4,000	8,000	8,900	5,400
Machine hours	3,800	5,200	5,800	4,800

You are required to calculate:
(a) The overhead rates for departments A and C.
(b) The overhead rates for departments B and D.

(Keep your answer – it will be used as a basis for the next question.)

37.2 For the factory in Question 37.1, what would be the costs of the following jobs given that the direct labour costs per hour are: Dept A £5; B £4; C £6; D £7?

Job 351: Dept A	Direct materials cost	£760
	Number of direct labour hours	112
	Number of machine hours	80
Job 352: Dept B	Direct materials cost	£3,597
	Number of direct labour hours	256
	Number of machine hours	252
Job 353: Dept C	Direct materials cost	£2,000
	Number of direct labour hours	390
	Number of machine hours	300
Job 354: Dept D	Direct materials cost	£1,998
	Number of direct labour hours	180
	Number of machine hours	128
Job 355: Dept C	Direct materials cost	£1,680
	Number of direct labour hours	320
	Number of machine hours	300
	Job passed on to Dept B where additional direct materials cost	£204
	Number of direct labour hours	60
	Number of machine hours	40

37.3A A manufacturer is producing five types of job, each in a separate production department P, Q, R, S and T. In addition, there are two service departments F and G. Costs have been allocated to the departments as follows:

	Production departments				Service departments		
	P	Q	R	S	T	F	G
	£	£	£	£	£	£	£
Indirect labour	15,000	21,000	9,000	18,000	12,000	20,000	18,000
Other expenses	2,000	3,000	4,000	4,500	1,500	8,000	10,000

The expenses of the service departments are to be allocated between other departments as follows:

Dept F to Depts P 15 per cent; Q 10 per cent; S 40 per cent; T 20 per cent; G 15 per cent.
Dept G to Depts P 20 per cent; Q 15 per cent; R 30 per cent; S 25 per cent; T 10 per cent.

In departments R and T the job costing is to use an overhead rate per direct labour hour, while in the other production departments a machine hour rate will be used. The number of direct labour hours and machine hours per department is expected to be:

	P	Q	R	S	T
Direct labour hours	10,000	12,000	8,000	15,000	5,000
Machine hours	7,000	9,000	5,000	14,000	3,000

You are required to calculate:
(a) The overhead rates for departments R and T.
(b) The overhead rates for departments P, Q and S.

(Keep your answer – it will be used for Question 37.4A.)

37.4A For the company in Question 37.3A, what would be the costs of the following jobs, given that the direct labour rate per hour is Dept P £6; Q £9; R £8; S £11; T £10?

Job 701: Dept R	Direct materials cost	£345
	Number of direct labour hours	105
	Number of machine hours	87
Job 702: Dept T	Direct materials cost	£3,240
	Number of direct labour hours	540
	Number of machine hours	480
Job 703: Dept P	Direct materials cost	£1,560
	Number of direct labour hours	400
	Number of machine hours	280
Job 704: Dept S	Direct materials cost	£196
	Number of direct labour hours	620
	Number of machine hours	90
Job 705: Dept Q	Direct materials cost	£11,330
	Number of direct labour hours	860
	Number of machine hours	610
Job 706: Dept P	Direct materials cost	£1,480
	Number of direct labour hours	600
	Number of machine hours	540
	Then passed to Dept T for completion where direct materials cost	£32
	Number of direct labour hours	36
	Number of machine hours	6

37.5
(a) Define the term *equivalent production* and state when the principle is used.
(b) During May 2001, M Wurzel & Co. Limited's output was 4,000 finished items plus 600 partly finished items. There was no work-in-progress on 1 May 2001.

	Materials	Labour	Overheads	Total
Total cost (£)	8,172	7,120	5,196	20,488
WIP degree of completion %	90	75	55	–

Calculate for the month of May 2001:
(i)   the total equivalent production for each cost element;
(ii) the cost per complete unit;
(iii) the value of the work-in-progress.

(Edexcel: GCE A-level)

37.6A

(a) What is meant by the term *equivalent production*?

(b) At Earith Industries at the beginning of April there were no partially finished goods on hand. During the month, 6,000 completed units were produced, together with 800 units partially completed. Details of the partially finished items were:

	Total cost (£)	Percentage completed
Materials	12,540	75
Labour	8,476	65
Overheads	7,084	55

Calculate:

(i) the total equivalent production,

(ii) the cost per complete unit,

(iii) the total value of work-in-progress.

(*Edexcel: GCE A-level*)

37.7

(a) Explain the difference between the terms *overhead allotment*, *overhead apportionment* and *overhead absorption*.

(b) Why are *estimated* figures used in calculating overhead absorption rates?

(c) The following information relates to the Flyby Knight Plc for the six months ended 31 December 2001:

	Production Departments			Service Departments	
	A	B	C	X	Y
Overheads (£)	14,000	12,000	8,000	4,000	3,000
Overheads to be apportioned:					
Dept X (%)	35	30	20	–	15
Dept Y (%)	30	40	25	5	–

(i) Use the continuous apportionment (repeated distribution) method to apportion the service departments' overheads between each other.

(ii) Apportion the service departments' overheads calculated in (i) to the production departments.

(iii) Show how the overheads apportioned to the production departments would have differed if the elimination method had been used for the service departments.

(iv) State how far it is true to say that the elimination method produces an inaccurate answer, and is therefore not to be recommended.

(*Edexcel: GCE A-level*)

37.8A Kalmo Ltd offers a subcontracting service in assembly, painting and packing. Components are supplied by customers to the company, the required operations are then carried out, and the completed work returned to the customer. The company is labour intensive, with only a relatively small amount of materials purchased.

Currently, one factory overhead recovery rate is used which is a percentage of total direct labour costs. This is calculated from the following budgeted costs.

Department	Direct labour costs £	Direct labour hours	Machine hours	Factory overheads £
Assembly	450,000	150,000	6,000	180,000
Painting	500,000	140,625	–	225,000
Packing	250,000	100,000	8,000	75,000

The cost sheet for Job 131190 shows the following information:

Department	Direct labour costs £	Direct labour hours	Machine hours	Direct material costs £
Assembly	2,500	1,000	120	100
Painting	2,200	900	–	400
Packing	4,800	960	80	500

General administration expenses of 20 per cent are added to the total factory costs, and then a further 25 per cent of the total cost is added as profit, to arrive at the selling price.

Although the company has been using the blanket factory overhead recovery rate for a number of years, one of the directors has questioned this method, and asks if it would be possible to apply overhead recovery rates for each department.

Required:
(a) Calculate the current factory overhead recovery rate, and apply this to arrive at the selling price for Job 131190.
(b) In line with the director's comments, calculate overhead recovery rates for each department, using two alternative methods, and apply both to arrive at new selling prices for Job 131190.
(c) Briefly evaluate the methods you have used for the recovery of factory overheads, justifying which one you consider to be most appropriate.
(d) Outline how an unsatisfactory method of overhead absorption can affect the profits of a business.

(Reproduced with the kind permission of OCR (from *University of Oxford Delegacy of Local Examinations*): *GCE A-level*)

37.9
(a) What is meant by the term 'specific order costing'?
(b) In what ways does specific order costing differ from process costing?
(c) The Acme Shelving Co. Ltd manufactures shelving brackets in batches of 300. During May, Batch No. 23 was machined at a rate of 15 per hour. Sixty of the brackets failed to pass inspection, but of these, 40 were thought to be rectifiable. The remaining 20 were scrapped, and the scrap value was credited to the batch cost account. Rectification work took nine hours.

Batch No. 23

	£
Raw materials per bracket	1.60
Scrap value per bracket	0.86
Machinists' hourly rate	4.20
Machine hour overhead rate (running time only)	3.60
Setting up of machine: normal machining	21.00
rectification	18.00

Calculate:
(i) the cost of Batch No. 23 in total and per unit, if all units pass inspection;
(ii) the *actual* cost of Batch No. 23, in total and per unit, after crediting the recovery value of the scrapped components, and including the rectification costs;
(iii) the loss incurred because of defective work.

(*Edexcel: GCE A-level*)

37.10A Horden Products Ltd manufactures goods which could involve any or all of three production departments. These departments are simply entitled **A**, **B** and **C**. A direct wages cost percentage absorption rate for the recovery of production overheads is applied to individual job costs.

Details from the company's budgets for the year ended 31 March 2005 are as follows:

	Dept A	Dept B	Dept C
Indirect materials	£23,000	£35,000	£57,000
Indirect wages	£21,000	£34,000	£55,000
Direct wages	£140,000	£200,000	£125,000
Direct labour hours	25,000	50,000	60,000
Machine hours	100,000	40,000	10,000

→

The following information is also available for the production departments:

	Dept A	Dept B	Dept C
Area (square metres)	30,000	20,000	10,000
Cost of machinery	£220,000	£160,000	£20,000
Horse power of machinery	55	30	15

Other budgeted figures are:	£
Power	120,000
Rent, rates, light, heat	90,000
Insurance (machinery)	20,000
Depreciation	80,000

Machinery is depreciated on the basis of 20% on cost.

Job No. 347 passed through all three departments and incurred the following actual direct costs and times:

	Direct material £	Direct wages £	Direct labour hours £	Machine hours £
Dept A	152	88	35	60
Dept B	85	192	90	30
Dept C	52	105	45	10

A sum amounting to 30% of the production cost is added to every job to enable a selling price to be quoted.

Required:
(a) A statement to show the total production overheads per department and calculate the absorption rate which the company has adopted.
(b) Calculate the selling price to be quoted for Job No. 347.
(c) Using the available data, calculate absorption rates when based on:
  (i) direct labour hour rate;
  (ii) machine hour rate.
(d) Explain clearly the meaning of the following terms relating to overheads:
  (i) allotment;
  (ii) allocation;
  (iii) apportionment.

(AQA (Associated Examining Board): GCE A-level)

37.11A
(a) Explain the following terms as used in process costing:
  (i) normal losses
  (ii) abnormal losses
  (iii) equivalent production
  (iv) joint cost
  (v) split-off point.

(b) In process costing, it is neither the technology nor the costs incurred, but the market price of the item, which determines whether an item is classed as:
  (i) scrap or waste; and
  (ii) a joint product or a by-product.

  How far do you agree?

(Edexcel: GCE A-level)

BUDGETS

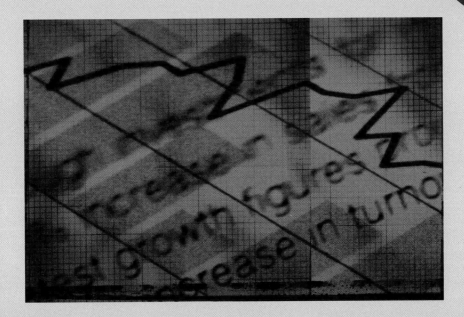

Introduction

This part looks at how management can institute a system to support planning, evaluation and control through the use of budgets.

Budgeting and budgetary control

Learning objectives

After you have studied this chapter, you should be able to:

- describe the budgetary process
- explain the importance of budgets for planning and control
- explain how to apply the economic order quantity approach to inventory control

Introduction

In this chapter, you'll learn about the need for budgeting, how production budgets can be set, both when production is to be at a constant level and when it is to vary according to demand. You will also learn about how to determine the most appropriate point in time to order new supplies and about alternatives to traditional methods of ensuring that sufficient but not too many raw materials and bought-in goods for resale are available for production and sale when required.

38.1 Background

In Chapters 34 and 35, you learnt that management control is needed if organisations are to achieve their objectives. Once the objectives of an organisation have been agreed, plans need to be drawn up so that the objectives can be met.

Don't assume that plans can only be expressed in monetary terms and values. For example, quality of the product might be best shown in engineering terms, or social objectives shown in a plan concerned with employee welfare. But some of the objectives, such as the attainment of a desired profit, or of the attainment of a desired growth in assets, can be expressed and measured in monetary terms and values.

When a plan is expressed quantitatively (i.e. in numbers – monetary amounts or quantities) it is known as a '**budget**' and the process of converting plans into budgets is known as '**budgeting**'. In this book, we are concerned primarily with budgets shown in monetary terms, i.e. 'financial budgets'.

A budget is like a lane on a motorway. You may enjoy being able to switch lanes and, at times, you may need to do so but, if you want to reach your destination at a specific time, you need to spend as much of the journey as possible in the lane that is most appropriate for the time you have available.

The budgeting process may be very formal, as it typically is in most large organisations. Sometimes it may be so formal a process that committees are set up to co-ordinate and review the task. On the other hand, in a very small organisation the owner may jot down his budget on a piece of scrap paper or the back of a used envelope. Some even manage without writing anything down at all, they have done the budgets in their heads and can remember them easily. In this book, we will focus upon budgeting in a formal manner.

38.2 Budgets and people

In no other part of accounting is there a greater need for understanding people than in the processes of budgeting. Budgets are prepared in order to try to guide the organisation towards its objectives. Yet, there is no doubt that some budgets are even more harmful to the organisation than if none were drawn up at all. The main cause of such a mismatch between a budget and the organisation is a failure to consider the human side of budgeting.

Activity 38.1 What does this statement concerning the harm budgets may bring to an organisation remind you of from earlier chapters?

Budgets are drawn up for control purposes, that is, they represent an attempt to control the direction in which the organisation is moving. Many people, however, look upon budgets, not as a guide, but as a straitjacket. Let's look at a few undesirable actions that can result from people regarding budgets as a straitjacket rather than a guide.

1 A sales manager refuses to let a salesman go to Sweden in response to an urgent and unexpected request from a Swedish firm. The reason: the overseas sales expenses budget has already been spent. The result: the most profitable order that the company would have received for many years is lost to a competitor.
2 The factory manager turns down requests for overtime work on a job because the budgeted overtime has already been exceeded. The result: the job is not completed on time and the company has to pay a large sum under a penalty clause in the contract.
3 Towards the end of the accounting period, a manager realises that she has not spent all of her budget for a particular item. She is worried that failing to do so will result in a cut in her budget for the next accounting period. As a result, she launches on a spending spree, buying many completely unnecessary items. The result: a lot of unusable and unnecessary equipment.
4 The staff training budget has been spent early in the year. As a result, the human resources manager will not let anyone go on courses for the rest of the year. The result: the company starts to fall behind in a fast-changing industry which is highly dependent on advanced technology, the staff concerned become disillusioned (as they know they need to 'keep up') and the better ones start to look for jobs in other companies which are more responsive to the need to allow personnel to keep in touch with changing technology.

Studies have shown that the more that managers are brought into the budgeting process, then the more successful budgetary control is likely to be. A manager on whom a budget is imposed is likely to pay less attention to the budget and use it less wisely in the control process compared to a manager who had an active part in the drafting of his budget.

Having sounded the warning that needs to be borne in mind constantly when budgeting, we can now look at the positive end of budgeting – the advantages of a good budgetary control system.

38.3 Budgets, planning and control

The methodology of budgetary control is probably accounting's major contribution to the process of management. Before we get down to the actual mechanics of preparing a budget, we will first look briefly at the main steps involved in drafting a budget.

When budgets are being prepared, two principal objectives must be uppermost in the mind of top management. Budgets exist in order to implement:

1 **Planning.** This means a properly co-ordinated and comprehensive plan *for the whole business*. Each part *must* interlock with the other parts.
2 **Control.** Just because a plan is set down on paper does not guarantee that the plan will be followed automatically and that there will be no deviations from it. Control is needed to ensure a plan is followed and control is exercised via the budgets, thus the term 'budgetary control'. To achieve real control, the responsibility of managers and budgets must be so linked that the manager responsible for a certain part of the plan is given a guide to help her produce the desired results and, also, that the actual results achieved are then compared against the expected results, i.e. actual compared with budget.

38.4 Preparation of estimates and the sales budget

The first budget that should be prepared is the sales budget. However, before doing so, the first thing to establish when preparing a budget is what limiting factors exist that affect it. For example, it may well be that sales cannot be pushed above a certain amount, or it might be that the company could sell as much as it can produce, but productive capacity is limited. There is no doubt that identification of the limiting factors is crucial if an achievable budget is to be set. There would not, for instance, be much point in budgeting for the sale of 1,000 units a year if production could not manufacture more that 700; or in budgeting to manufacture 2,000 units a year if only 1,300 of them could be sold.

The most difficult estimate to make when preparing a company's budget is that of sales volume and, then, sales revenue. This can be done using one of two methods:

(1) Make a statistical forecast on the basis of the economic conditions relating to the goods sold (e.g. how demand reacts to price changes) and what is known about the actions of competitors.

This approach has an *external* rather than an *internal* focus. When adopted, it tends to be performed at a high level in the organisation, with relatively little consultation involving employees actually engaged in the selling process.
(2) The alternative approach uses information gathered lower down in the organisation. This is usually done by asking each salesperson, or group of salespeople, to estimate the sales in their own areas, and then adding together all the estimates.

If you have studied, or are studying economics, you will find it very useful in helping you understand some of the issues mentioned above. In particular, a knowledge of elasticity of demand; whether the product is a complementary product (e.g. the price of egg-cups is linked to the demand for eggs); or whether it is a substitute (e.g. a rise in the price of butter may induce consumers to use butter substitutes instead), is very relevant. Factors such as whether the company has a monopoly dominance of its market; whether the company has many small customers, a few large customers, or just one large customer, are all of crucial importance. When estimating sales revenue all relevant economic factors must be considered.

The sales budget is, however, more than just a forecast of sales volume and sales revenue. **Budgets should show the actions that management is taking to influence future events.** If an increase in sales is desired, the sales budget may show extra sales, which may well also indicate that management is going to attempt to increase sales by means such as extra television advertising, making a better product, or giving retailers better profit margins.

Now, let's look at another key budget, the production budget.

38.5 The production budget

The production budget must be compatible with the sales budget. However, some other factors are also highly relevant, such as the level of stock of finished goods which will be held by the business.

If sales are at the same level over the year, production can be too and the stock figure can remain constant. For example, if a company sells 50 units every month, it can produce 50 units per month. In almost every business, a minimum stock level will have to be maintained, the quantity of stock being dependent on factors such as the amount of storage space, the estimated amount needed to cater for breakdowns in production or for delays in receiving raw materials, etc. The minimum level of stock to be held is a separate issue from the level of production. Consequently, whether the stock level was to be a minimum of 70 units, 100 units or any other level, production in the above example would be 50 units per month.

On the other hand, sales may not be constant. For example, sales may *average* 50 units per month, but the monthly figures may be as follows:

January	20 units	February	30 units	March	60 units
April	80 units	May	70 units	June	40 units

If production levels were kept at 50 units per month, there would be a shortage of 10 units in May – when 70 were demanded but only 60 were available for sale (10 left over from April plus 50 produced in May). An extra 10 units would need to be held to cover this shortfall. If production each month is to be the same, 10 units would need to be held in stock at the start of the year.

Any calculation of minimum stock levels must include these 10 units. For example, if minimum stock of 100 is required, stock at the beginning of the year would need to be 110 units, otherwise stock at the end of May would only be 90, not 100.

However, instead of producing the same number of units each month, the monthly production could be set to equal the sales figures. If a minimum stock level of 100 units is required, the number of units held at the beginning of the year would then be 100.

We can now compare the two levels of production in Sections 38.6 and 38.7.

38.6 Even production levels

The problem here is to find the stock level that the business would need on 1 January if (*a*) sales are as shown, (*b*) the stock must not fall below 100 units, and (*c*) production is to be 50 units per month.

The stock level can be found by trial and error. For example, if you decided to see what would happen if the business had 100 units in stock on 1 January, you would find that after adding production and deducting sales each month, the stock level would fall to 90 units in May. As 100 units of stock is the minimum, you would need to start off on 1 January with 110 units.

The method simply requires that you start off your calculation with an estimated figure of stock at the start of the period, which must not be less than the minimum stock level, and then find the lowest figure of stock during the period. If this is, for example, 10 units less than the minimum stock required, go back and add 10 units to the stock to be held at the start. If the lowest figure is 30 units less than required add 30 units to the opening stock, and so on. Let's look at this in Exhibit 38.1:

Exhibit 38.1

Units	January	February	March	April	May	June
Opening stock	110	140	160	150	120	100
Add Units produced	50	50	50	50	50	50
	160	190	210	200	170	150
Less Sales	(20)	(30)	(60)	(80)	(70)	(40)
Closing stock	140	160	150	120	100	110

Activity 38.2

Sales are expected to be: January 70, February 40, March 50, April 120, May 140 and June 70. The stock level must not fall below 120 units, which is the level at the end of May, and an even production flow of 80 units is required. What stock level would have to have been held on 1 January?

In many organisations, it is felt to be more important to ensure a smooth production flow than to bother unduly about stock levels. They simply assume that the minimum stock level is always attained. If the work is skilled, the labour force may take several years to become trained, and skilled labour in many industries does not take kindly to being sacked and re-employed as the demand for the goods they produce fluctuates. Of course, there are exceptions. For example, in the building industry, bricklayers may go to a builder until they have completed a contract such as building a college, a hospital or a housing estate, and then leave and look for another employer.

On the other hand, a skilled engineer concerned with the manufacture of, say, diesel engines would not expect to be fired and re-employed continuously. The bricklayer has a skill that is easily transferable to many other building employers in an area, whereas the diesel engineer may have only one firm within fifty miles of her home where she can perform her skills properly. A person employed as a labourer might work on a building site in one part of the year and in a brewery during the rest of the year.

Whether a business could carry on production with widely uneven production levels depends so much on the type of firm and the type of labour involved. A business would only sack skilled labour which it needed to rehire soon afterwards if it could persuade them to come back when required. If the people who had been sacked were likely to find other employment, and not return to their previous employer when required, they would probably be kept on the payroll instead of being temporarily sacked. Production could continue but inventory of finished goods would begin to pile up.

Many businesses do accept their social obligations by only laying off workers when no other reasonable alternative exists. In some organisations, there are probably more workers from time to time than are actually needed – this is known as 'organisational slack' so that there is a leeway between the increasing of production and having to take on extra workers.

38.7 Uneven production levels

Some organisations, by their very nature, have uneven production levels, and this is accepted by their labour force. An ice-cream firm would find its sales at their highest levels in summer, tailing off in winter. It is not really possible to build up a stock of ice-cream very much in the winter for summer sales. Even if it could be done, the costs of refrigerating large quantities of ice-cream for several months could hardly be economical. The large labour force used in the summer months probably includes quite a few students occupying their vacation periods profitably, who are not able to work at the job all the year round, even if they wanted to. Such a business will normally have a far stronger relationship between its current stock levels and current sales than one which has even production levels.

The calculation of the quantity to be produced in any one period is:

Units sold – Opening stock + Closing stock = Units produced

This can also be stated as:

Opening stock + Units produced – Units sold = Closing stock

Thus, if the opening stock is 80 units, units sold are expected to be 100, and the desired closing stock is 50 units, the quantity to be produced becomes:

	Units
Opening stock	80
Add Production	?
	?
Less Sales	(100)
Closing stock	50

Production will, therefore, be the missing figure, i.e. 70 units (80 + production 70 = 150 for sale less actually sold 100 = closing stock 50).

Exhibit 38.2 shows the units to be produced if the following information is known: stock required 1 January 40, at end of each month, January 60, February 110, March 170, April 100, May 60, June 20. Sales are expected to be January 100, February 150, March 110, April 190, May 70, June 50.

Exhibit 38.2

Units	*January*	*February*	*March*	*April*	*May*	*June*
Opening stock	40	60	110	170	100	60
Production required (?)	120	200	170	120	30	10
	160	260	280	290	130	70
Less Sales	(100)	(150)	(110)	(190)	(70)	(50)
Closing stock	60	110	170	100	60	20

Linked with the production budget will be a materials purchase budget. It may well be that an order will have to be placed in January, received in March and issued to production in April. The purchase of materials will have to be planned as scientifically as possible.

Activity 38.3 What is the relationship between the sales budget, the production budget and the materials purchase budget?

38.8 Stock control

In your earlier studies of accounting, you probably examined the different methods by which stocks are valued – see, for example, *Frank Wood's Business Accounting 1*, Chapter 29. Apart from valuation of stock, accountants are also interested in knowing if the quantity of stock being carried is greater than it need be.

Let's look at what makes this information interesting – holding excessive stock can have a detrimental effect upon the financial results of a business:

1 Money tied up in unnecessarily large stocks is not earning anything. If, therefore, an extra £1 million is tied up unnecessarily in this way, the money which could have been earned from utilising that extra £1 million somewhere else has been lost. If a 10 per cent return could have been earned on that money, the unnecessary stock has cost £100,000 a year, even before the cost of storing this excess stock is considered.
2 Too much stock needs extra storage space. Therefore the rent for the extra space, heating, lighting, insurance, wages of extra storekeepers, etc. is all money being spent for no benefit.

One thing that anyone should look for when examining the affairs of a business is to see if stocks are larger than they need be. For someone controlling a business, there are three commonly used methods of cutting down on unnecessarily high stocks:

1 **Economic order quantity (EOQ).** This is a mathematical method which finds the lowest amount of stock that should be ordered at a time so that the costs of purchasing and holding stock are minimised.

The formula for this is:

$$EOQ = \sqrt{\frac{2CO}{S}}$$

where:

C = consumption (usage) per annum in units
O = cost of placing one order
S = cost of storage and holding of one unit per year

S includes the costs of operating the stores where the stock is kept, transport and insurance, and also the costs concerned with interest on capital which has been invested in stock.

Exhibit 38.3 shows an example of the calculation.

Exhibit 38.3

Annual consumption = 800 units
Cost of reordering = £4
Storage and holding costs per unit = £1

$$EOQ = \sqrt{\frac{2 \times 800 \times 4}{1}} = \sqrt{\frac{6,400}{1}} = 80 \text{ units per order (i.e. 10 orders per year)}$$

2 **Just-in-time (JIT).** This has been seen as one of the major factors which have resulted in the success of Japanese manufacturers over the last 20 or so years. It is not just an approach which is concerned with stock levels, but that is part of it.

The JIT approach requires that delivery of materials should occur immediately before their use. If arrangements are made with suppliers for more frequent deliveries, then stock can be cut to a minimum. Getting suppliers to inspect the materials before they deliver them, and getting them to guarantee their quality, also cuts down on costs, including the need to keep larger stocks in case there are deficiencies.

This sort of service is obtained by giving more business to fewer suppliers, and also placing longer-term orders. This enables the supplier to plan ahead more effectively to give you a better service.

3 **Optimised production technology (OPT).** The object of this approach to the management of production is to distinguish between 'bottleneck' and 'non-bottleneck' resources. For example, the 'bottleneck' resource might be a machine which has a limited capacity. As a result, everything

else can only be operated at that same level. Rather than other parts of the business produce more than the 'bottleneck' machine can absorb, a lower overall level of activity takes place. This needs fewer units of stock.

Of course, if a 'bottleneck' can be eliminated it will be. The above applies when a bottleneck, for whatever reason, cannot be eliminated.

It is better to have a smooth-running business, operating within its 'bottleneck' capacities, than to have one which operates very irregularly. One run irregularly would have to have parts of the business shut down at times. One running smoothly, besides all the other economies, needs fewer units of stock.

Of these three methods, the existence of a formula which gives a precise and easily justified answer makes EOQ particularly easy to use and, for the same reason, examine. It is a useful aid to management in ensuring that they are making best use of their stock-related resources. Also, because of the precise nature of the calculation, it lends itself to incorporation within a computerised managerial decision support system.

38.9 Safety stock

Safety stock (often referred to as 'safety inventory') is a quantity of stock carried in excess of expected usage. It is held in order to reduce the possibility of running out of stock. For example, if 100 units of stock are expected to be sold in a period, but there is a possibility that as many as 110 units might be sold, an extra 10 units (i.e. 110 − 100) would be held. That is, 110 units would be held in stock. The 10 extra units are the 'safety stock'.

Learning outcomes

You should now have learnt:

1 Budgets are prepared in order to guide the firm towards its objectives.

2 They should be drawn up within the context of *planning* and *control*.

3 Budgets should be drawn up in consultation with those who will be affected by them.

4 While budgets are drawn up for control purposes, a budget should not be seen as a straitjacket.

5 There are a number of methods or techniques available to management wishing to ensure that excessive stock is not carried by their organisations. These include economic order quantity (EOQ), just-in-time (JIT) and optimised production technology (OPT).

Answers to activities

38.1 'Data which is provided for a particular purpose, and which is completely wrong for the purpose, is worse than having no data at all.' (Section 35.2)
'The wrong kind of costing can be even worse than having no costing at all.' (Section 36.12)

38.2

Units	January	February	March	April	May	June
Opening stock	140	150	190	220	180	120
Add Units produced	80	80	80	80	80	80
	220	230	270	300	260	200
Less Sales	(70)	(40)	(50)	(120)	(140)	(70)
Closing stock	150	190	220	180	120	130

38.3 The sales budget is used to set the levels of activity required in the production budget which, in turn, is used to set the quantities required to be obtained in the materials purchase budget.

Review questions

38.1 Using the data provided below, what production levels should be set for each month?

Units 2002	Jul	Aug	Sep	Oct	Nov	Dec
(a) Stock levels wanted at the						
end of each month	138	156	220	280	232	188
(b) Expected sales each month	160	184	218	264	296	204
(c) Stock at 1 July 2002 will be 148 units.						

38.2 For the year ended 31 December 2007, the quantities of units sold are expected to be:

January	330	July	210
February	540	August	290
March	310	September	510
April	450	October	330
May	360	November	450
June	300	December	570

The opening stock at 1 January 2007 will be 144 units. The closing stock desired at 31 December 2007 is 150 units.

Required:
(a) What will production be per month if an even production flow is required and stock levels during the year can fall to zero because that minimises the cost of holding stock?
(b) Given the same information plus the constraint that stock levels must never fall below 80 units, and that extra production will be undertaken in January 2007 to ensure this happens, what will be the January production figure?

38.3A
(a) For each of the following, state three reasons why a firm may wish to keep:
   (i) a minimum stock level of finished goods, and
   (ii) an even level of production in the face of fluctuating demand.
(b) The sales forecast for Douglas & Co for July–December 2007 is:

	J	A	S	O	N	D
Units	280	200	260	360	400	420

Produce a production budget showing monthly opening and closing stock figures if the firm wishes to maintain an even level of producing 300 units each month, and a minimum stock level of 150 units.
   What must the opening stock be at 1 July to achieve this?
(c) Under what circumstances, in budgetary control, may a firm's productive capacity prove to be its limiting or key factor?

(AQA (Associated Examining Board): GCE A-level)

You can find a range of additional self-test questions, as well as material to help you with your studies, on the website that accompanies this book at **www.pearsoned.co.uk/wood**

Cash budgets

Introduction

In this chapter, you'll learn how to prepare a cash budget, of the advantages of cash budgets and, in the context of business survival, of the relationship between profit, cash and a shortage of cash funds.

39.1 The need for cash budgets

It is no use budgeting for production and for sales if, during the budget period, the business runs out of cash funds. When talking about cash in budgets we are also usually including bank funds. For that reason, in this book we will not differentiate between cash and cheque payments or between cash and cheques received.

As cash is so important, a budget is created for it. As a result, any shortage of cash can be foreseen and action taken in good time to obtain a loan or a bank overdraft to cover the short-fall when it occurs. Bank managers do not like it when one of their customers needs a loan or a bank overdraft without prior warning. If a cash budget had been prepared, the customer would have known well in advance that there would be a need for additional cash funds on a particular date.

The finance needed may not be found by borrowing from a bank or finance house. It may well be a long-term need that can only be satisfied by an issue of shares or debentures. Such issues need planning well in advance, and a cash budget can reveal (*a*) that they will be needed, (*b*) how much is needed and (*c*) when it will be needed.

We can now look at a very simple case. Without being concerned in this first example with exactly what the receipts and payments are for (just to keep things simple at this stage) you can see the dangers that are inherent in not budgeting for cash.

Exhibit 39.1

Mr Muddlem had a meeting with his accountant on 1 July 2008. He was feeling very pleased with himself. He had managed to get some very good orders from customers, mainly because he was now allowing them extra time in which to pay their accounts. Sprite, the accountant, said, 'Can you afford to do all that you are hoping to do?'

Muddlem laughed, 'Why, I'll be making so much money I won't know how to spend it.'

'But have you got the cash to finance everything?' asked Sprite.

'If I'm making a good profit, of course I'll have the cash,' said Muddlem. 'I know the bank manager says that the bank overdraft cannot be more than £1,000, but I doubt if I'll ever need it.'

'Let's not rely on guesses,' says Sprite. 'Let's work it out.'

After an hour's work the following facts emerge.

(a) Present cash balance (including bank balance) £800.

(b) Receipts from debtors are expected to be: July £2,000; August £2,600; September £5,000; October £7,000; November £8,000; December £15,000.

(c) Payments are expected to be: July £2,500; August £2,700; September £6,900; October £7,800; November £9,900; December £10,300.

This is then summarised:

	July £	Aug £	Sep £	Oct £	Nov £	Dec £
Balance at the start of the month:	800	300	200			
Deficit at the start of the month:				(1,700)	(2,500)	(4,400)
Receipts	2,000	2,600	5,000	7,000	8,000	15,000
	2,800	2,900	5,200	5,300	5,500	10,600
Payments	(2,500)	(2,700)	(6,900)	(7,800)	(9,900)	(10,300)
Balance at end of the month	300	200				300
Deficit at the end of the month			(1,700)	(2,500)	(4,400)	

'I'm in an awkward position then,' says Muddlem. 'I just cannot borrow £4,400 and it would be stupid for me to try to reduce my sales; and, anyway, I don't really want to as these new sales are very profitable indeed. If only I'd known this, I could have borrowed the money from my brother only last week but he's invested it elsewhere now.'

'Come and see me tomorrow,' says Sprite. 'There may well be something we can do.'

Fortunately for Muddlem his luck was in. He arrived to see his accountant the following morning waving a cheque. 'My wife won £5,000 on a jackpot bingo last night,' he said.

'Thank goodness for that. At least in future you'll learn to budget ahead for cash requirements. You can't be lucky all the time,' says Sprite.

39.2 Timing of cash receipts and payments

In drawing up a cash budget, you need to be aware that all the payments made relating to units produced are very rarely made at the same time as production itself. For instance, raw materials might be bought in March, incorporated in goods being produced in April, and paid for in May. On the other hand, the raw materials may have been in stock for some time, bought in January, paid for in February, and used in production the following August.

In contrast, the direct labour part of a product is usually paid for at almost the same time as the unit is produced. Even here, a unit may be produced in one week and the wages paid one week later, so that a unit might be produced on, say, 27 June and the wages for the direct labour involved paid on 3 July.

Similarly, except for supermarkets and retail stores where most of the goods sold are paid for at the time of sale, the date of sale and the date of receipt of cash will not usually be the same. Goods might be sold in May and the money received in August, or even paid for in advance so that the goods might be paid for in February but the goods not shipped to the buyer until May. This is especially true, at least for part of the goods, when a cash deposit is left for custom-made goods which will take some time to manufacture. A simple example of this would be a made-to-measure suit on which a deposit would be paid at the time of order, the final payment being made when the completed suit is collected by the buyer.

Exhibit 39.2

A cash budget for the six months ended 30 June 2008 is to be drafted from the following information.

(a) Opening cash balance at 1 January 2008 £3,200.
(b) Sales, at £12 per unit, cash received three months after sale: in units.

2007			2008								
Oct	Nov	Dec	Jan	Feb	Mar	Apr	May	June	July	Aug	Sept
80	90	70	100	60	120	150	140	130	110	100	160

(c) Production: in units.

2008			2008								
Oct	Nov	Dec	Jan	Feb	Mar	Apr	May	June	July	Aug	Sept
70	80	90	100	110	130	140	150	120	160	170	180

(d) Raw materials used in production cost £4 per unit of production. They are paid for two months before being used in production.
(e) Direct labour, £3 per unit paid for in the same month as the unit is produced.
(f) Other variable expenses, £2 per unit, 3/4 of the cost being paid for in the same month as production, the other 1/4 paid in the month after production.
(g) Fixed expenses of £100 per month are paid monthly.
(h) A van is to be bought and paid for in April for £800.

Schedules of payments and receipts are as follows:

Payments (the month shown in brackets is the month in which the units are produced):

January	£	February	£
Raw materials: 130 (March) × £4	520	140 (April) × £4	560
Direct labour: 100 (January) × £3	300	110 (February) × £3	330
Variable: 100 (January) × 3/4 × £2	150	110 (February) × 3/4 × £2	165
90 (December) × 1/4 × £2	45	100 (January) × 1/4 × £2	50
Fixed	100	Fixed	100
	1,115		1,205

March	£	April	£
Raw materials: 150 (May) × £4	600	120 (June) × £4	480
Direct labour: 130 (March) × £3	390	140 (April) × £3	420
Variable: 130 (March) × 3/4 × £2	195	140 (April) × 3/4 × £2	210
110 (February) × 1/4 × £2	55	130 (March) × 1/4 × £2	65
Fixed	100		100
Motor van			800
	1,340		2,075

May	£	June	£
Raw materials: 160 (July) × £4	640	170 (August) × £4	680
Direct labour: 150 (May) × £3	450	120 (June) × £3	360
Variable: 150 (May) × 3/4 × £2	225	120 (June) × 3/4 × £2	180
140 (April) × 1/4 × £2	70	150 (May) × 1/4 × £2	75
Fixed	100		100
	1,485		1,395

Receipts: (the month shown in brackets is the month in which the sale was made):

				£
January	80	(October)	× £12	960
February	90	(November)	× £12	1,080
March	70	(December)	× £12	840
April	100	(January)	× £12	1,200
May	60	(February)	× £12	720
June	120	(March)	× £12	1,440

Cash Budget

	Jan £	Feb £	Mar £	Apr £	May £	June £
Balance from previous month	3,200	3,045	2,920	2,420	1,545	780
Add Receipts (per schedule)	960	1,080	840	1,200	720	1,440
	4,160	4,125	3,760	3,620	2,265	2,220
Less Payments (per schedule)	(1,115)	(1,205)	(1,340)	(2,075)	(1,485)	(1,395)
Balance carried next month	3,045	2,920	2,420	1,545	780	825

39.3 Advantages of cash budgets

These can be said to be:

1 Having to think ahead and plan for the future and express plans in figures, **focuses the mind** in a way that thinking in a general fashion about the future will not do – a general optimistic feeling that 'all will be well' often fails to stand up to scrutiny when the views of the future are expressed in a cash budget.

2 Seeing that money will have to be borrowed at a particular date will mean that **you can negotiate for a loan in advance**, rather than at the time when you have actually run out of cash. Bankers and other lenders do not like someone attempting to borrow money in a panic.

When borrowing money, you have to give the lender the confidence that the loan will be repaid at the agreed time, plus any interest and charges that may accrue. Last-minute borrowing, unsupported by any calmly thought-out plan, will not inspire such confidence, and will often lead to the loan's being refused as the lender may think that the risk is too great.

 Activity 39.1 What other disadvantages do you think there might be in waiting until the last minute to arrange a loan of this type?

3 Knowing about the need to borrow in advance also **widens the possible pool of lenders**. Such people as friends, relations and businesspeople or investors other than bankers rarely have large sums of cash quickly available. They need time to turn their own investments into cash before they can lend to you.

4 Alternatively, you may find that you will have cash funds surplus to requirements. Knowing this in advance **enables you to carefully investigate how you can invest this surplus cash until required**, thus earning interest or other investment income. Surplus cash lying in bank current accounts very often earns absolutely no interest at all, no matter how large the amount. Banks often offer deposit accounts linked to current accounts that automatically transfer funds from one to the other so that any surplus fund in the current account are moved immediately to the deposit account and reversed back to the current account when required.

There are also other sorts of short-term investments which banks and accountants can advise businesses to put their surplus cash into at appropriate times.

39.4 Profits and shortages of cash funds

As you've just learnt, making good profits does not mean there cannot be a shortage of cash funds. But, how can this happen? Let's look at how some businesses may have good profits and yet still be short of cash funds, possibly having bank overdrafts or loans which are getting steadily bigger.

1 A has increased its revenue by 50 per cent. It is making the same percentage gross profit and its expenses have hardly increased, yet its overdraft has got bigger. The reason is that it increased its sales by giving all of its customers four months to pay instead of the usual one month. This has attracted a lot of new customers.

This means that the accounts receivable balance is increasing by very large amounts, as they can wait another three months in which to pay their bills. Thus, the equivalent of three months' cash receipts have not come into the bank. Meanwhile, the business is making extra purchases for goods for the new customers, with a consequent outflow of more cash than usual, especially if it has not got longer credit terms from its suppliers. So, hardly any cash is coming in in the short term, while more cash than usual is going out.

The answer to this is: large increase in profits and fewer cash funds probably resulting in higher bank overdrafts or loans.

2 B has the same sales, purchases and expenses as usual. However, the proprietor is now taking much higher drawings than before. In fact, his drawings are exceeding the profits he is making.

Such a situation cannot go on for ever. He will start to find his cash funds in the business are decreasing, possibly meaning higher loans or overdrafts being needed.

3 C has just spent a lot of money on fixed assets. It will be several years before the business recoups the money it has paid out. In the meantime, only the depreciation provisions are charged against profits. However, the cash funds have been reduced by the whole amount paid for fixed assets.

The net result is that profits may be recorded but the business is hard-up for cash funds.

4 D is going through a bad patch in that sales are very difficult to make, but it does not want to get rid of any of its workforce. Production is kept going at normal rates, and the products not sold are simply kept in stock. Thus the stock is increasing at an alarming rate.

If stock is not being sold, then cash is obviously not being received in respect of such production. Meanwhile, all the expenses and wages are still being paid for. This can result in a severe shortage of funds if carried on for long unless further finance is received.

5 A long-term loan has been paid off but no extra finance from anywhere else has been received. Or, a partner retires and the balance due to him is paid out of the firm's funds, without a new partner being introduced. Or, a company buys back its shares without making a new issue of shares.

In the long term, there is a connection between profits and cash funds available, even though it may not be that marked. In the short term, you can see that there may be no relationship at all. This simple fact is one that surprises most people. It is because the calculation of profits follows one set of concepts, whereas the calculation of cash funds follows a completely different set of rules.

Go back to Section 27.7 for a discussion on overtrading.

Learning outcomes

You should now have learnt:

1 The difference between profit and cash funds.

2 When undertaking a cash budget, 'cash' includes both money held in the form of cash and amounts held in the bank.

3 The importance of cash funds to an organisation.

4 What is meant by the term 'cash budget'.

5 The importance of preparing and monitoring a cash budget.

6 How to prepare a cash budget.

7 The difference between profits and cash in the context of organisational survival.

Answer to activity

39.1 It is not only that you risk the loan being refused. Lenders will often realise that they have you at their mercy, and will charge much higher rates of interest and impose other conditions than they would otherwise have done.

Review questions

Advice: **Cash budgeting is an extremely important part of accounting. Questions on this topic are relatively easy to do, and high marks can be gained quite easily.**

39.1 Took comes to see you in March 2006. He is full of enthusiasm for a new product that he is about to launch on to the market. Unfortunately his financial recklessness in the past has led him into being bankrupt twice, and he has only just been discharged by the court from his second bankruptcy.

'Look here, laddie,' he says, 'with my new idea I'll be a wealthy man before Christmas.'

'Calm down,' you say, 'and tell me all about it.'

Took's plans as far as cash is concerned for the next six months are:

(a) Present cash balance (including bank) £200.
(b) Legacy under a will – being received on 1 April 2006, £10,000. This will be paid into the business bank account by Took.
(c) Receipts from debtors will be: April £800; May £8,000; June £16,000; July £24,000; August £18,000; September £10,000.
(d) Payments will be: April £200; May £10,000; June £22,000; July £40,000; August £24,000; September £14,000.

You are required:
(a) To draw up a cash budget, showing the balances each month, for the six months to 30 September 2006.
(b) The only person Took could borrow money from would charge interest at the rate of 70 per cent per annum. This is not excessive considering Took's past record. Advise Took.

39.2 Draw up a cash budget for F. Jack showing the balance at the end of each month, from the following information for the six months ended 31 December 2004:

(a) Opening cash (including bank) balance on 1 July 2004 £3,600
(b) Production in units:

585

	2004										2005
	March	April	May	June	July	Aug	Sep	Oct	Nov	Dec	Jan
	720	810	900	960	1,050	1,110	1,140	1,020	930	780	750

(c) Raw materials used in production cost £15 per unit. Of this, 90 per cent is paid in the month of production and 10 per cent in the month after production.

(d) Direct labour costs of £24 per unit are payable in the month of production.

(e) Variable expenses are £6 per unit, payable 40 per cent in the same month as production and 60 per cent in the month following production.

(f) Sales at £60 per unit:

2004									
Feb	Mar	Apr	May	Jun	July	Aug	Sep	Oct	Nov
780	600	960	870	1,200	900	1,050	1,200	1,170	1,200

Debtors to pay their accounts three months after that in which sales are made.

(g) Fixed expenses of £1,200 per month payable each month.

(h) Machinery costing £6,000 to be paid for in September 2004.

(i) Will receive a legacy of £7,500 in November 2004.

(j) Drawings will be £900 per month.

39.3 Herbert Limited make a single product, whose unit budget details are as follows:

	£	£
Selling price		30
Less Costs		
Direct material	9	
Direct labour	4	
Direct production expenses	6	
Variable selling expenses	4	
		(23)
Contribution		7

Additional information:

1 Unit sales are expected to be:

June	July	August	September	October
1,000	800	400	600	900

2 Credit sales will account for 60 per cent of total sales. Debtors are expected to pay in the month following sale for which there will be a cash discount of 2 per cent.

3 Stock levels will be arranged so that the production in one month will meet the next month's sales demand.

4 The purchases of direct materials in one month will just meet the next month's production requirements.

5 Suppliers of direct materials will be paid in the month following purchase.

6 Labour costs will be paid in the month in which they are incurred. All other expenses will be paid in the month following that in which they are incurred.

7 Fixed expenses are £2,000 per month and include £180 for depreciation.

8 The bank balance at 1 July 2009 is £3,900 favourable to the business.

Required:

(a) A cash budget for Herbert Limited for the three month period ending on 30 September 2009 showing the balance of cash at the end of each month.

(b) List and explain **three** ways in which the preparation of a cash flow budget could be of advantage to the management of Herbert Limited.

(AQA (Associated Examining Board): GCE A-level)

39.4A Mtoto Ltd operate as wholesale 'cash and carry' stores and in addition to its main store have two other depots. The company's summarised balance sheet as at 31 August 2011 was as follows.

	£	£	£
Fixed assets			
(at net book value)			549,600
Current assets			
Inventory		399,900	
Trade Accounts receivable		21,000	
		420,900	
Total assets			
Current liabilities			
Trade and other accounts payable	110,500		
Bank overdraft	240,000		
		(350,500)	
			70,400
			620,000
Equity			
Authorised and Issued Share Capital			
450,000 £1 Ordinary Shares fully paid			450,000
Retained earnings at 1 Sept 2010		300,000	
Less: Loss for year ending 31 Aug 2011		(130,000)	
			170,000
			620,000

● Over the past year the company has experienced increased competition and as a consequence reported a net trading loss for the year ended 31 August 2011.
● The company has decided that in the new financial year tighter control must be exercised over cash resources.

The following information is available:

1 All goods are purchased by the main store.

Purchases 2011

Actual		*Forecast*			
July	Aug	Sept	Oct	Nov	Dec
£	£	£	£	£	£
55,800	61,200	64,300	41,000	46,000	41,800

● Mtoto Ltd pays suppliers two months after the month of purchase.
● Forecast purchases are being reduced since the managing director regarded current stock levels as too high.
● In addition, shop-soiled stock which cost £20,000 is to be sold for cash in October. It is anticipated that this stock will be sold for £17,000. This sale is not included in the sales of Note 2 below.

2 All sales are on a cash basis only except for several important customers who trade only with Mtoto's main store.

Sales 2011

	Actual		*Forecast*			
	July	Aug	Sept	Oct	Nov	Dec
	£	£	£	£	£	£
Main store						
Cash sales	21,500	21,600	18,000	26,300	19,200	24,700
Credit sales	24,000	21,000	32,500	26,000	25,400	27,800
Depot 1	15,500	17,400	19,700	18,000	17,600	17,900
Depot 2	21,000	24,000	26,300	19,700	21,000	19,100

3 Mtoto Ltd pays £9,500 fixed overhead costs per month.

→ **4** Wages and salaries are paid each month through a centralised payroll system.

Wages and salaries 2011

	Actual		Forecast		
	Aug	Sept	Oct	Nov	Dec
	£	£	£	£	£
	16,000	17,000	19,000	13,000	12,000

In October, ten staff were made redundant and are to receive their redundancy compensation of £12,000 in December. This amount is not included in the above figures.

5 Other variable overhead charges are paid by Mtoto Ltd in the month following the month they are incurred.

Variable overhead charges 2011

	Actual		Forecast		
	Aug	Sept	Oct	Nov	Dec
	£	£	£	£	£
	5,600	6,800	6,100	7,400	6,900

6 Plant surplus to requirement is to be sold in September for £26,500 cash. The plant cost £55,000 and depreciation to date is £20,000.

Required:
(a) A detailed cash budget, on a month by month basis, for the first four months of the financial year ending 31 December 2011 for Mtoto Ltd.
(b) A report commenting on:
   (i) the current and forecast liquidity position.
   (ii) the action that Mtoto Ltd could take to attempt a return to a profit situation.

(AQA (Associated Examining Board): GCE A-level)

39.5 David Llewelyn has been advised by his bank manager that he ought to provide a forecast of his cash position at the end of each month. This is to ensure that his cash inputs will be sufficient to allow a bank loan to be repaid when due and to check that his outgoings are properly controlled. It is estimated that at 30 June 2010 his current account will be £5,000 in credit, whereas the amount owing in respect of the bank loan taken out on 1 July 2005 will be £15,000. Monthly deductions from the current account balance amount to £242 including interest charges on account of this loan. In addition to these outgoings, David has to allow for the following:

(i)   The payment of wages of £2,000 per month.
(ii)   Personal drawings of £500 per month.
(iii)   On average David earns a margin of 15 per cent (of sales) and expects to sell stock purchased in the previous month. Of the sales in any one month, 20 per cent are paid for within that month, 70 per cent the following month and the remainder two months after sale. Other receipts from debtors are expected to be £40,000 in July 2010, £32,000 in August 2010 and £4,000 in September 2010.
(iv)   Purchases of supplies will amount to £38,250 per month from July 2000 payable one month in arrears. In addition, purchases of £7,500 to increase stock will be delivered in September 2000 and must be paid for in October 2010. Creditors of £34,000 for purchases made in June 2000 are to be paid in July 2010.
(v)   Monthly payments to Revenue and Customs for the taxation of his employees' earnings will amount to £500 per month.
(vi)   Rent which has to be paid quarterly in advance amounts to £5,000 per annum. These payments commenced in January 2010.
(vii)   Business rates are to be paid in two instalments as due in October 2010 and in March 2011. This estimated expenditure will amount to £4,500 per annum.
(viii) Payment of Value Added Tax to H.M. Revenue and Customs of £5,000 in July 2010 and every third month thereafter (but see also (ix)).

(ix)   David intends to purchase a van for £8,150 in August 2010. He will then be entitled to deduct £1,050 from the VAT payment due to H.M. Revenue and Customs in October 2010.

Required:
A forecast cash flow statement in columnar form showing the estimated current account balance at the close of each of the four months ending 31 October 2010.

(*Welsh Joint Examining Board: GCE A-level*)

39.6 The managing director of Pumpkin Ltd was reviewing the results of the company for the financial year ended 31 March 2010. The following summarised information was available:

	£
Balances as at 1 April 2009	
Issued ordinary share capital:	
£1 fully paid shares	150,000
Share premium account	100,000
Balance of retained earnings	40,000
Balances as at 31 March 2010	
Net profit for year 2009/10	70,000
Fixed assets	300,000
Bank overdraft	150,000
Other net current assets	210,000

Note: There were no other accounts with balances. The balances as at 1 April 2009 had remained unchanged throughout the year.

The managing director was pleased that the company had made a good profit, but he was rather concerned that a healthy bank balance at the beginning of the year had now become a large bank overdraft.

Consequently he asked the company accountant to prepare forecast information for 2010/11 in order that the cash situation could be improved.

The following information was prepared by the accountant:

1 Company sales – March 2010

	£
Cash sales	30,000
Credit sales	65,000

In each month April to September (inclusive) the revenue per month would be:

	£
Cash sales	40,000
Credit sales	70,000

All credit sales are settled the month after the sale.

2 All goods purchased are from a single supplier. The goods are purchased on credit and each month's purchases are paid for three months after the month of purchase.

The following purchase schedule had been prepared for the first 9 months of 2010:

	January	February	March
Purchases	£60,000	£58,000	£61,000

Purchases in April, May and June
£55,000 in each month
Purchases in July, August and September
£45,000 in each month

Note: The company had successfully negotiated lower prices from its supplier commencing 1 July 2010.

3 Dividends would be paid as follows:
(*i*) Final ordinary dividend of 5p per share payable on 31 May 2010 in respect of financial year 2009/10.

→ (ii) Interim ordinary dividend of 2p per share payable on 31 July 2010 in respect of financial year 2010/11.

4 Selling and distribution expenses are expected to be 6 per cent of a given month's total sales. They are paid one month in arrears.

5 Administration charges would be incurred as follows:

2010 February, March, April	£10,000 per month
2010 May to September (inclusive)	£13,500 per month

Administration charges are settled two months after the month in which they were incurred.

6 The company had decided to make a bonus issue of shares of one share for every three held. The issue would be made on 30 April 2010. The bonus shares would not qualify for the final dividend of 2009/10, but would qualify for the interim dividend to be paid on 31 July 2010.

Required:
(a) Comment on the liquidity of the company as at 31 March 2010 and explain to the managing director why a company can apparently make a good profit but have no cash in the bank.
(b) Prepare a cash budget for each of the four months ending 31 July 2010.
(c) Comment on the forecast bank balance as shown by your cash budget. Identify ways in which the bank overdraft could be reduced over the last five months of 2010.

(AQA (Associated Examining Board): GCE A-level)

39.7A Belinda Raglan owns a clothing factory. Trading over the last two years has been very successful and she feels that having achieved good results it is now time to request an increase in the overdraft facility.

● In the past the bank has been willing to offer business overdraft facilities and at present there is an agreed limit of £15,000.
● On 1 May 2004 the overdraft stands at £5,000.
● In order to support her request for the increased facility, she has produced a forecast profit statement for the four months ended 31 August 2004 as follows:

	May		June		July		August	
	£000	£000	£000	£000	£000	£000	£000	£000
Revenue		74		28		116		168
Cost of sales		51		12		78		101
Gross profit		23		16		38		67
Less Rent	4		4		4		4	
Other expenses	8		3		10		14	
Depreciation	5		5		5		5	
		(17)		(12)		(19)		(23)
Net profit		6		4		19		44

Although Belinda thought these figures would be sufficient to satisfy the requirements of the bank, the manager has asked for a cash budget for the period concerned to be submitted.

The following additional information concerning the business is available.

(1) Rent is paid quarterly in advance on the first day of May, August, November and February.
(2) All other expenses are payable in the month in which they are incurred.
(3) Purchases for the period are expected to be – May £60,000; June £120,000; July £40,000 and August £43,000. These will be paid for in the month of purchase. Purchases will be unusually high in May and June because they will be subject to a special reduction of 3 per cent of the amounts quoted.
(4) 80 per cent of the sales are on a credit basis payable two months later. Sales in March and April were £88,000 and £84,000 respectively.
(5) A compensation payment of £10,000 to a former employee for an industrial injury, not covered by insurance, is due to be paid in May.

Required:
(a) Prepare a forecast cash budget on a month by month basis for the period May to August 2004.
(b) Discuss the advantages and disadvantages of cash budgeting.
(c) Draft notes, to be used by the bank manager for a letter to Ms Raglan, indicating why the request for an increased overdraft facility may be refused.

(AQA (Associated Examining Board): GCE A-level)

39.8A Ian Spiro, formerly a taxi-driver, decided to establish a car-hire business after inheriting £50,000. His business year would be divided into budget periods, each being four weeks.

He commenced business on a Monday the first day of Period 1, by paying into a business bank account £34,000 as his initial capital.

All receipts and payments would be passed through his bank account.

The following additional forecast information is available on the first four budget periods of his proposed business venture.

1 At the beginning of Period 1 he would purchase 6 saloon cars of a standard type; list price £6,000 each, on which he had negotiated a trade discount of 11 per cent.

2 He estimates that four of the cars will be on the road each Monday to Friday inclusive, and at weekends all six cars will be on the road. Hire charges as follows:

   Weekday rate £10 per day per car
   Weekend rate £18 per day per car

   He estimates that this business trading pattern will commence on the Monday of the second week of Period 1, and then continue thereafter.
   All hire transactions are to be settled for cash.
   Note: a weekend consists of Saturday and Sunday. All remaining days are weekdays.

3 An account was established with a local garage for fuel, and it was agreed to settle the account two periods in arrear. The forecast litre usage is as follows:

Period 1	Period 2	Period 3	Period 4
200	200	400	500

   The fuel costs £1.80 per litre.

4 Servicing costs for the vehicles would amount to £300 per period, paid during the period following the service. Servicing would commence in Period 1.

5 Each of his vehicles would be depreciated at 25 per cent per annum on a reducing balance basis.

6 Fixed costs of £200 per period would be paid each period.

7 He had agreed with a local firm to provide two cars on a regular basis, Monday to Friday inclusive, as chauffeur driven cars. The agreed rate was £60 a day (per car), payment being made in the following period.
   This contract would not commence until the first day of Period 2, a Monday.

8 Drawings: Periods 1 and 2: £400 a period.
            Periods 3 and 4: £800 a period.

9 Wages and salaries:
   (a) Initially he would employ 3 staff, each on £320 a budget period. Employment would commence at the beginning of Period 1.
   (b) On commencement of the contract the two additional staff employed as chauffeurs would each receive £360 a budget period. Payments are to be made at the end of the relevant period.

10 In anticipation of more business being developed he planned to buy a further three cars for cash in period 4. The cars would cost £6,500 each and it was agreed he would be allowed a trade discount of 10 per cent.

Required:
(a) A detailed cash budget for the first four budget periods.
(b) An explanation as to why it is important that a business should prepare a cash budget.
(c) Identify how a sole proprietor may finance a forecast cash deficit distinguishing between internal and external financial sources.

(AQA (Associated Examining Board): GCE A-level)

Chapter

40

Co-ordination of budgets

Learning objectives

After you have studied this chapter, you should be able to:

● explain the benefits of budgeting to an organisation
● explain the importance of effective co-ordination of budgets for the organisation
● prepare a master budget
● describe the benefits of operating a system of flexible budgeting

Introduction

In this chapter, you'll learn about the process of preparing a budget and of how budgets are co-ordinated and used to monitor and identify deviations between them and actual performance. You'll also learn about the importance of investigating these differences and of the benefits of adopting a system of flexible budgeting as compared with budgets being set that remain fixed during the entire period they cover.

40.1 Master budgets

Once prepared, all the various budgets have to be linked together to draw up a **master budget**, which is really a budgeted set of financial statements. We have looked at the sales, production and cash budgets. However, many more budgets are typically prepared, including:

● a selling budget
● an administration expense budget
● a manufacturing overhead budget
● a direct labour budget
● a purchases budget
● a capital expenditure budget

and so on. In this book, we do not wish to get entangled in too many details, but in a real business with a proper set of budgeting techniques there will be a great deal of detailed computations behind the figures that are incorporated in the budgets.

It may be that when all the budgets have been co-ordinated, or slotted together, the master budget shows a smaller profit than the directors are prepared to accept. This will mean recasting budgets to see whether a greater profit can be earned and, if at all possible, the budgets will then be altered. Eventually, there will be a master budget that the directors can agree to. This then gives the target for the results that the business hopes to achieve in financial terms.

Remember, there are other targets, such as employee welfare, product quality, etc., that cannot be expressed in financial terms but which will impact upon and influence the setting of budgets.

The rest of this chapter is concerned with the drawing up of budgets for an imaginary company, Walsh Ltd, culminating in the drawing up of the master budget.

Let's start with a look at the balance sheet of Walsh Ltd, as at 31 December 2004. This gives us our opening figures for stock of raw materials, stock of finished goods, cash (including bank) balance, creditors, debtors etc. Next, we'll produce budgets for the six months ending 30 June 2005.

Walsh Ltd
Balance Sheet as at 31 December 2004

Fixed assets		Cost	Depreciation to date	Net
		£	£	£
Machinery		4,000	1,600	2,400
Motor vehicles		2,000	800	1,200
		6,000	2,400	3,600
Current assets				
Stock: Finished goods (75 units)			900	
Raw materials			500	
Debtors (2004 October £540 + November £360 +				
December £450)			1,350	
Cash and bank balances			650	
			3,400	
Current liabilities				
Creditors for raw materials (November £120 + December £180)		300		
Creditors for indirect manufacturing expenses (December)		100	(400)	
				3,000
Net assets				6,600
Financed by				
Share capital: 4,000 shares £1 each				4,000
Profit and loss				2,600
				6,600

The plans for the six months ended 30 June 2005 are as follows:

(a) Production will be 60 units per month for the first four months, followed by 70 units per month for May and June.

(b) Production costs will be (per unit):

	£
Direct materials	5
Direct labour	4
Variable overhead	3
	12

(c) Fixed indirect manufacturing expenses are £100 per month, payable always one month in arrears.

(d) Sales, at a price of £18 per unit, are expected to be:

	January	February	March	April	May	June
No. of units	40	50	60	90	90	70

(e) Purchases of direct materials (raw materials) will be:

	January	February	March	April	May	June
	£	£	£	£	£	£
	150	200	250	300	400	320

(f) Creditors for raw materials bought are paid two months after purchase.

(g) Debtors are expected to pay their accounts three months after they bought the goods.

(h) Direct labour and variable indirect manufacturing expenses are paid in the same month as the units are produced.

(i) A machine costing £2,000 will be bought and paid for in March.

(j) 3,000 shares of £1 each are to be issued at par in May.

(k) Depreciation for the six months: machinery £450; motor vehicles £200.

We must first of all draw up the various budgets and then incorporate them into the master budget. Some of the more detailed budgets which can be dispensed with in this illustration will be omitted.

Materials Budget (£s)

	January	February	March	April	May	June
Opening stock	500	350	250	200	200	250
Add Purchases	150	200	250	300	400	320
	650	550	500	500	600	570
Less Used in production:						
Jan–April 60 × £5	(300)	(300)	(300)	(300)		
May and June 70 × £5					(350)	(350)
Closing stock	350	250	200	200	250	220

Production Budget (in units)

	January	February	March	April	May	June
Opening stock	75	95	105	105	75	55
Add Produced	60	60	60	60	70	70
	135	155	165	165	145	125
Less Sales	(40)	(50)	(60)	(90)	(90)	(70)
Closing stock	95	105	105	75	55	55

Production Cost Budget (£s)

	January	February	March	April	May	June	Total
Materials cost	300	300	300	300	350	350	1,900
Labour cost	240	240	240	240	280	280	1,520
Variable indirect							
manufacturing expenses	180	180	180	180	210	210	1,140
	720	720	720	720	840	840	4,560

Creditors Budget (£s)

	January	February	March	April	May	June
Opening balance	300	330	350	450	550	700
Add Purchases	150	200	250	300	400	320
	450	530	600	750	950	1,020
Less Payments	(120)	(180)	(150)	(200)	(250)	(300)
Closing balance	330	350	450	550	700	720

Debtors Budget (£s)

	January	February	March	April	May	June
Opening balances	1,350	1,530	2,070	2,700	3,600	4,320
Add Sales	720	900	1,080	1,620	1,620	1,260
	2,070	2,430	3,150	4,320	5,220	5,580
Less Received	(540)	(360)	(450)	(720)	(900)	(1,080)
Closing balances	1,530	2,070	2,700	3,600	4,320	4,500

Cash Budget (£s)

	January	February	March	April	May	June
Opening balance	650	550	210			1,050
Opening overdraft				(2,010)	(2,010)	
Received						
(see schedule)	540	360	450	720	3,900	1,080
	1,190	910	660	(1,290)	1,890	2,130
Payments						
(see schedule)	(640)	(700)	(2,670)	(720)	(840)	(890)
Closing balance	550	210			1,050	1,240
Closing overdraft			(2,010)	(2,010)		

Cash Payments Schedule (£s)

	January	February	March	April	May	June
Creditors for goods bought						
two months previously	120	180	150	200	250	300
Fixed indirect manufacturing						
expenses	100	100	100	100	100	100
Direct labour	240	240	240	240	280	280
Variable indirect manufacturing						
expenses	180	180	180	180	210	210
Machinery			2,000			
	640	700	2,670	720	840	890

Cash Receipts Schedule (£s)

	January	February	March	April	May	June
Debtors for goods sold						
three months previously	540	360	450	720	900	1,080
Shares issued					3,000	
					3,900	

Master Budget
Forecast Operating Statement for the six months ending 30 June 2005

	£	£	£
Revenue			7,200
Less Cost of goods sold:			
Opening stock of finished goods		900	
Add Cost of goods completed		4,560	
		5,460	
Less Closing stock of finished goods		(660)	
			(4,800)
Gross profit			2,400
Less			
Fixed indirect manufacturing expenses		600	
Depreciation: Machinery	450		
Motors	200		
		650	
			(1,250)
Net profit			1,150

Forecast Balance Sheet as at 30 June 2005

Fixed assets	Cost	Depreciation to date	Net
	£	£	£
Machinery	6,000	2,050	3,950
Motor vehicles	2,000	1,000	1,000
	8,000	3,050	4,950
Current assets			
Stock: Finished goods		660	
Raw materials		220	
Debtors		4,500	
Cash and bank balances		1,240	
		6,620	
Creditor: amounts falling due within 1 year			
Creditors for raw materials	720		
Creditors for indirect manufacturing expenses	100		
		(820)	5,800
Net assets			10,750
Represented by			
Called-up share capital			7,000
Profit and loss (2,600 + 1,150)			3,750
			10,750

40.2 Capital budgeting

You'll have noticed that the cash budget included £2,000 for the machine paid for in March. The other side of the double entry will also have been entered in a budget – the **capital expenditure budget**. This is where all the plans for the acquisition of fixed assets such as machinery, buildings, etc. are entered. Management will evaluate the various possibilities open to it, and will compare the alternatives. This is a very important part of budgeting. However, for the purposes of demonstrating how budgets are co-ordinated, we shall stick to the budgets we have demonstrated in this example. Suffice to say that the process for the capital expenditure budget and other budgets omitted from the detail of this example is broadly similar to those you have seen so far.

40.3 The advantages of budgeting

The process of preparing budgets, including the involvement of employees in all areas of the organisation, and finally producing a profit plan, is a regular feature in all but the smallest businesses. Very often, this is the one period each year when the various parts of management can really get together and work as a team rather than as separate parts of an organisation.

 Activity 40.1 What is it that you learnt about earlier in this book which involved all the functional areas and departments across the organisation that needs to be 'right' if appropriate budgets are to be agreed?

When budgeting is conducted under favourable conditions, there is no doubt that **an organisation which uses budgeting will tend to perform rather better than a similar business that does not**. Using budgeting means that managers can no longer give general answers affecting the running of the business. They have to express their plans in financial terms and they know that, in the end, their estimated figures are going to be compared with what the actual figures turn out to be.

It has often been said that **the act of budgeting is possibly of more benefit than the budgets that are produced**. However, the following benefits can be claimed for good budgeting:

1 **The strategic planning carried out by the board of directors or owners can be more easily linked to the decisions made by managers concerning how the resources of the business will be used to try to achieve the objectives of the business.** The strategic plan has to be converted into action, and budgeting provides the ideal device for converting such plans into financial terms.

2 **Standards of performance can be agreed for the various parts of the business.** If sales and production targets are set as part of a co-ordinated plan, then the sales department cannot really complain that production is insufficient if they had agreed previously to a production level and this is being achieved. Nor can production complain if its output exceeds the amount it budgeted for and the excess output remains unsold.

3 **The expression of plans in comparable financial terms.** Some managers think mainly in terms of, say, units of production, or of tonnes of inputs or outputs, or of lorry mileage, etc. The effect that the actions of each manager has upon financial results must be brought home to them. For instance, a transport manager might be unconcerned about the number of miles that his fleet of lorries covers until the cost of a large mileage is brought home to him, often during budgeting, and it may be then and only then that he starts to search for possible economies. It is possible in many cases to use mathematical formulae to find the best ways of loading vehicles, or to plan routes taken by vehicles so that fewer miles are covered and yet the same delivery service is maintained. This is just one example of many where the expression of the plans of a section of a business in financial terms sparks off a search for economies, when otherwise it may never have started at all.

4 **Managers can see how their work slots into the activities of the organisation.** It can help to get rid of the feeling of 'I'm only a number not a person', because they can identify their positions within the organisation and can see that their jobs really are essential to the proper functioning of the business.

5 **The budgets for an organisation cannot be set in isolation.** This means that the situation of the business, the nature of its products and its workforce, etc., must be seen against the economic background of the country. For instance, it is no use budgeting for extra labour when labour is in extremely short supply, without realising the implications, such as having to pay higher than normal wage rates. Increasing the sales target during a credit squeeze needs a full investigation of the effect of the shortage of money upon the demand for the firm's goods and so on.

 Activity 40.2 What disadvantages you learnt about earlier in this book may arise if an organisation's managers are not allowed to vary their activities from budget?

However, budgets can be mis-used. Too often they are set at one level of sales or production and remain unchanged throughout the budget period when, in fact, flexible budgets ought to be used – see Section 40.5. Sometimes, budgets are forced upon managers against their will. Instead, a 'selling job' should be conducted to try to convince managers that their budgets are not unreasonable. A trial run for part of a business is often much better than starting off with a fully detailed budget for the whole of the business.

Learning to use budgets is rather like learning to swim. Let a child get used to the water first and remove its fear of the water, then it will learn to swim fairly easily. For most children (but not all), if the first visit to a swimming pool meant being pushed into the deep end immediately, then reaction against swimming would probably set in. In organisations that introduce budgeting for the first time, it is best to let managers become used to the idea of budgeting during a trial period, without the fear of being dealt with severely if they don't adhere to their budgets. Most managers will then accept the idea and participate appropriately and effectively in the budgeting process.

40.4 The use of computers in budgeting

Years ago, budgeting was a task which most accountants hated. It was not the concept of budgeting that accountants disliked. Far from it: it suited their needs perfectly. Rather, it was the multitude of numerical manipulations that had to be performed time and time again that made the task both boring and formidable, never mind very prone to errors.

Everyone who has prepared financial statements from a trial balance and a list of adjustments knows the feeling when, after a lot of work, the balance sheet fails to balance. Searching through all the entries and workings to find the error(s) can be a daunting prospect. With budgets, the problem is even greater – you do not have anything to tell you if you have made an error. Imagine how much more complicated it is in a real business dealing with real figures, rather than with the simple sets of data which form your exercises. Also, imagine the thoughts going through the head of the accountant in the days before spreadsheets when the managing director said 'What would happen to net profit if we increased our prices by 5 per cent and took an extra month to settle our accounts payable?' The accountant would then have to plough his way through a large number of extra calculations.

Most of that is now a thing of the past. Computers are used instead. They either have software specially written for the task, or spreadsheets are used. By keying in the necessary data, the computer will automatically produce the budgets, and any 'what if'-based amended budgets within a very short space of time.

This enables management to see the results that would be expected from many separate propositions, thus enhancing the chance of choosing the best solution in setting the most acceptable budget. Also, as the accounting period unfolds, the changes that have occurred since the period started can be incorporated very easily so as to adjust (or 'flex') the budgets as the accounting period progresses.

Let's now look at how budgets may be adjusted using a process called 'flexible budgeting'.

40.5 Flexible budgets

So far in this book, budgets have been drawn up on the basis of one set of expectations, based on just one level of sales and production. Inevitably – no one can foretell the future with 100 per cent accuracy – when the actual results are compared with the budgeted results, they will not be identical. This occurs for two reasons:

1 While the actual and budgeted volumes of production and sales may be the same there may be a difference between the actual and the budgeted costs.
2 The volumes of actual and budgeted units of sales and production may vary. If they do, the costs and revenues will be different because of the different volumes of units involved.

The differences between budget and actual are called '**variances**'. Variances coming under (1) above will probably be under the control of the relevant department. On the other hand, variances under (2) are caused because of variations in plans brought about by changing sales, and/or production levels.

Budgets are used for guiding activity and for control. A manager does not take kindly to being held responsible for a variance in her spending if she is working to a fixed budget and the variance is caused by a type (2) occurrence. To avoid this, budgets are created for several levels of volume, to show what costs etc. should arise at each level of activity.

For example, if a budget had been fixed at a volume of 500 units and the actual volume is 550, the production manager would undoubtedly feel aggrieved if his costs for producing 550 units were compared with the costs he should have incurred for 500 units. Budgets which do allow for changing levels of activity are called **flexible budgets**.

To draft a full set of flexible budgets is outside the scope of this book, but an instance of one department's flexible budget for manufacturing overhead is shown in Exhibit 40.1:

Exhibit 40.1

Data Ltd
Budget for Manufacturing Overhead, Department S*

Units	400	450	500	550	600
	£	£	£	£	£
Variable indirect manufacturing expenses	510	550	600	680	770
Fixed indirect manufacturing expenses	400	400	400	400	400
Total indirect manufacturing expenses (A)	910	950	1,000	1,080	1,170
Direct labour hours (B)	200	225	250	275	300
Overhead rates (A) divided by (B)	£4.55	£4.22	£4.00	£3.92	£3.90

*In real life, this would be in greater detail and, using a spreadsheet, would be capable of showing the flexed budget for *any* level of activity.

Notice that the variable costs in Exhibit 40.1 do not vary in direct proportion to production. Once 500 units production have been exceeded, they start to climb rapidly. The flexible budget makes far greater sense than a fixed budget. For instance, if a fixed budget had been agreed at 400 units, with variable overhead £510. If production levels rose to 600 units, the manager would think the whole system unfair if he were expected to incur only £510 variable overhead (the figure for 400 units). On the contrary, if the comparison was on a flexible budget then costs at 600 units production would, instead, be compared with £770 (the budgeted variable overhead at 600 units).

Learning outcomes

You should now have learnt:

1 There are a number of budgets that together comprise the master budget and they must all reconcile to each other and to the master budget.

2 Budget preparation is often an iterative process as the master budget is focused more and more tightly to the objectives of the organisation.

3 How to prepare a master budget.

4 Flexible budgeting permits managers to adjust their budgets in the light of variations in plan, often involving items over which they have no control.

Answers to activities

40.1 The various objectives of each of the functional areas and departments need to be compatible with each other and with the overall goals of the organisation. (Section 34.3)

40.2 Budgets that are too rigorously applied generate a situation of inflexibility that can be extremely counterproductive. There must be scope for managers to depart from budget when it is in the best interests of the organisation to do so. (Section 38.2)

Review questions

Note: In many ways, preparing a set of budgeted financial statements is very much like preparing financial statements from single-entry records. However, financial statements prepared from single-entry records are based on facts and concern the past; whereas budgeted financial statements are based on estimates and concern the future.

40.1 Richard Toms has agreed to purchase the business of Norman Soul with effect from 1 August 2007. Soul's budgeted working capital at 1 August 2007 is as follows:

	£	£	£
Current assets			
Inventory at cost	13,000		
Accounts receivable	25,000		
		38,000	
Current liabilities			
Accounts payable	10,000		
Bank overdraft	20,000		
		(30,000)	
			8,000

In addition to paying Soul for the acquisition of the business, Toms intends to improve the liquidity position of the business by introducing £10,000 capital on 1 August 2007. He has also negotiated a bank overdraft limit of £15,000. It is probable that 10 per cent of Soul's accounts receivable will in fact be bad debts and that the remaining debtors will settle their accounts during August subject to a cash discount of 10 per cent. The opening creditors are to be paid during August. The sales for the first four months of Toms' ownership of the business are expected to be as follows: August £24,000, September £30,000, October £30,000 and November £36,000. All sales will be on credit and debtors will receive a two-month credit period. Gross profit will be at a standard rate of 25 per cent of selling price. In addition, in order to further improve the bank position and to reduce his opening stock, Toms intends to sell on 1 August 2007 at cost price £8,000 of stock for cash. In order to operate within the overdraft limit Toms intends to control stock levels and to organise his purchases to achieve a monthly rate of stock turnover of 3. He will receive one month's credit from his suppliers.

General cash expenses are expected to be £700 per month.

Required:

(a) An stock budget for the four months ending 30 November 2007 showing clearly the stock held at the end of each month.

(b) A cash budget for the four months ending 30 November 2007 showing clearly the bank balance at the end of each month.

(AQA (Associated Examining Board): GCE A-level)

40.2A A company's estimated pattern of costs and revenues for the first four months of 2007 is as follows:

Cost and Revenues: January–April 2007 (£000)				
Month	*Sales*	*Materials*	*Wages*	*Overheads*
January	410.4	81.6	16.2	273.6
February	423.6	84.8	16.8	282.4
March	460.8	93.6	18.3	306.7
April	456.3	91.2	18.6	304.5

1 One-quarter of the materials are paid for in the month of production and the remainder two months later: deliveries received in November 2006 were £78,400, and in December 2006 £74,800.
2 Customers are expected to pay one-third of their debts a month after the sale and the remainder after two months: sales expected for November 2006 are £398,400, and for December 2006, £402,600.
3 Old factory equipment is to be sold in February 2007 for £9,600. Receipt of the money is expected in April 2007. New equipment will be installed at a cost of £38,000. One-half of the amount is payable in March 2007 and the remainder in August 2007.
4 Two-thirds of the wages are payable in the month they fall due, and one-third a month later: wages for December 2006 are estimated at £15,900.
5 £50,000 of total monthly overheads are payable in the month they occur, and the remainder one month later: total overheads for December 2006 are expected to be £265,200.
6 The opening bank balance at 1 January 2007 is expected to be an overdraft of £10,600.

Required:
(a) Using the information above, prepare the firm's cash budget for the period January–April 2007.
(b) Provide a statement to show those items in part (a) which would appear in a budgeted balance sheet as at 30 April 2007.

(*Edexcel: GCE A-level*)

40.3 F. Tain is opening his first boutique on 1 July 2002. He is investing £30,000 as capital. His plans are as follows:

(i)   On 1 July 2002 to buy and pay for premises £60,000; shop fixtures £4,000; motor van £8,000.
(ii) To employ two assistants, each to get a salary of £130 per month, to be paid at the end of each month. (PAYE tax, National Insurance contributions, etc., are to be ignored.)
(iii) To buy the following quantities of goods for resale (shown in units):

	July	Aug	Sep	Oct	Nov	Dec
Units	600	660	840	1,050	1,200	990

(iv) To sell the following number of units of these goods:

	Jul	Aug	Sep	Oct	Nov	Dec
Units	360	540	720	900	1,170	1,260

(v)   Based on similar ventures in shops selling other products, he has decided to sell all goods at the same price – £30. Two-thirds of the sales are for cash, the other one-third being on credit. These latter customers are expected to pay their accounts in the third month following that in which they received their goods.
(vi) The goods will cost £7 each for July to October inclusive, and £8 each thereafter. Creditors will be paid in the second month following purchase. (Value stock on FIFO basis.)
(vii) The other expenses of the shop will be £450 per month payable in the month following that in which they were incurred.
(viii) Part of the premises will be sub-let as an office at a rent of £8,000 per annum. This is paid in equal instalments in March, June, September and December.
(ix) His cash drawings will be £1,400 per month.
(x)   Depreciation is to be provided on premises at 5 per cent per annum straight-line; shop fixtures at 15 per cent per annum and on the motor van at 25 per cent per annum, both using the reducing balance method.

You are required to:
(a) Draw up a cash budget for the six months ended 31 December 2002, showing the balance of cash at the end of each month.
(b) Draw up a forecast trading and profit and loss account for the six months ending 31 December 2002, and a forecast balance sheet as at that date.

→ **40.4A** M. Lamb is going to set up a new business on 1 April 2005. She estimates that her first six months in business will be as follows:

(*i*) She will put £60,000 into a bank account for the business on 1 April 2005.

(*ii*) On 1 April 2005, she will buy machinery for £8,000, a motor van for £6,400 and premises for £35,000, paying for them immediately out of the business bank account.

(*iii*) All purchases will be on credit. She will buy £10,000 of goods on 1 April and will pay for these in May. She will purchase another £12,000 of goods in April and £16,000 of goods each month during May, June, July, August, and September. Other than the first £10,000 purchase in April, all other purchases will be paid for two months after purchase.

(*iv*) Sales (all on credit) will be £26,000 for April and £28,000 for each month after that. Debtors will pay for the goods in the second month after purchase.

(*v*) Stock on 30 September 2005 will be £8,000.

(*vi*) Wages and salaries will be £2,100 per month and will be paid on the last day of each month.

(*vii*) General expenses will be £200 per month, payable in the month following that in which they were incurred.

(*viii*) She has an endowment assurance policy maturing on 15 July 2005. She will receive £17,500 on that date and it will be paid into the business bank account immediately.

(*ix*) Insurance covering the 12 months to 31 March 2006 will be paid by cheque on 30 September 2005, £560.

(*x*) Business rates will be paid as follows: for the three months to 30 June 2005 by cheque on 31 May 2005: for the 12 months ended 30 June 2006 by cheque on 31 October 2005. Business rates are £1,440 per annum.

(*xi*) She will make drawings of £1,800 per month by cheque.

(*xii*) She has substantial investments in public companies. Her bank manager will give her any overdraft that she may require.

(*xiii*) Depreciate premises 5 per cent per annum, van 25 per cent per annum, and machinery 20 per cent per annum, all using the straight line method.

You are required to:

(*a*) Draft a cash budget (includes bank) month by month showing clearly the amount of bank balance or overdraft at the end of each month.

(*b*) Draft the projected trading and profit and loss account for the first six months' trading, and a balance sheet as at 30 September 2005.

40.5A

(*a*) What is meant by the terms:
   (*i*) Budget
   (*ii*) Operating budget
   (*iii*) Master budget?

(b) The information below relates to the business of Madingley Ltd:

Balance Sheet as at 30 May 2010 (£000)

	Cost	Aggregate depreciation	Book value
Fixed assets			
Land and buildings	134.00	–	134.00
Plant and machinery	9.40	3.76	5.64
Fixtures and fittings	2.30	1.05	1.25
	145.70	4.81	140.89
Current assets			
Stock: Raw materials		91.70	
Finished goods		142.40	
Debtors		594.40	
Bank		12.40	
		840.90	
Current liabilities			
Creditors: Raw materials	82.20		
Overheads	127.40		
		(209.60)	631.30
Net assets			772.19
Financed by			
Share capital			500.00
Profit and loss account			272.19
			772.19

The following is a schedule of the budgeted income and expenditure for the six months ended 30 November 2010 (£000):

	Sales	Materials	Wages	Overheads
June	193.20	41.20	7.60	123.00
July	201.40	42.40	7.90	119.20
August	216.10	49.60	8.80	131.40
September	200.50	31.40	6.10	91.50
October	190.30	21.20	3.70	59.30
November	183.70	19.80	2.60	42.60

Notes:
(i) Generally, materials are paid for two months after receipt, and customers pay on average after three months.
(ii) Payments outstanding for materials at 1 June 2010 were: April £38,500; May £43,700.
(iii) Debtors were: March £194,300; April £203,600; May £196,500.
(iv) Wages are to be paid in the month in which they fall due.
(v) Overheads are to be paid one month after they are incurred: the figure for May was £127,400.
(vi) Stock of raw materials are to be kept at £91,700.
(vii) The stock of finished goods at 30 November 2010 is to be £136,200.
(viii) There is no stock of semi-finished items on 31 May 2010, and none are expected in stock on 30 November.
(ix) Forty per cent of the overheads are to be considered as fixed.
(x) Depreciation on plant and machinery is to be allowed at 10 per cent per annum on cost; the fixtures and fittings are thought to have a value at 30 November of £980.
(xi) There are no sales of finished goods or purchases of raw materials for cash planned during the period.

Prepare:
(a) A forecast operating statement for the period June to November 2010; and
(b) A forecast balance sheet as at 30 November 2010.

(Edexcel: GCE A-level)

→

→ **40.6** The following information has been extracted from the books of Issa Ltd for the financial year ended 31 December 2010.

**Trading and Profit and Loss Account
for the year ending 31 December 2010***

	£000		£000
Opening stock	90	Sales	750
Purchases	490		
	580		
Less Closing stock	80		
Cost of goods sold	500		
Gross profit	250		
	750		750
Administration expenses	60	Gross profit	250
Selling and distribution expenses	50		
Financial charges	20		
Depreciation of fixed assets	20		
Net profit	100		
	250		250

Balance Sheet as at 31 December 2010*

	£000	£000		£000	£000
Fixed assets at cost		750	£1 Ordinary shares fully paid		200
Less Aggregate			9% £1 Preference shares,		
depreciation		144	fully paid		100
		606			
Current assets			Share premium		150
Stock	80		Retained earnings		350
Trade debtors	75				
Less Provision for			*Current liabilities*		
doubtful debts	5	70	Trade creditors	50	
Balance at bank	100	250	Accrued expenses	6	56
		856			856

The company had commenced the preparation of its budget for the year ending 31 December 2011 and the following information is the basis of its forecast.

1 An intensive advertising campaign will be carried out in the first six months of 2011 at a cost of £15,000. It is anticipated that as a result of this, sales will increase to £900,000 in 2011.
2 The gross profit/sales ratio will be increased to 35 per cent.
3 A new stock control system is to be installed in 2011 and it is expected that the stock level will be reduced by £15,000 as compared to the 2010 closing stock.
4 Land and buildings which cost £50,000 (nil depreciation to date) will be sold in 2011 for £200,000 cash. Half of the proceeds will be used to buy ordinary shares in another company, Yates Ltd, at an agreed price of £4 per share. (Ignore share commission etc.)
5 The company planned to capitalise some of its reserves on 1 April 2011. New ordinary shares are to be issued on a 1 for 2 basis. Half the funds required will be drawn from the share premium account and the remainder will be taken from retained earnings.
6 Preference share dividends will be paid on 1 May 2011 and 1 November 2011. The company planned to pay an interim ordinary share dividend on the increased share capital of 2.5p per share on 1 July 2011. No final dividend is proposed.
7 Owing to inflation revenue expenses are expected to rise as follows:
Administration expenses will increase by 6 per cent.
Selling and distribution expenses will increase by 8 per cent.

The advertising campaign expenses are in addition to the increase above.
Financial charges will increase by 4 per cent.
These percentage increases are based on the figures for the year ended 31 December 2010.
8 With the projected sales increases trade debtors are expected to rise to £100,000 by 31 December 2011. The provision for doubtful debts is to be adjusted to 7½ per cent of forecast trade debtors.
9 Other forecast figures as at 31 December 2011.

	£000
Balance at bank	350.1
Trade creditors	56.0
Expense creditors	15.0

10 Depreciation of 10 per cent per annum on cost is to be provided on £600,000 of the company's non-current assets.

Required:
(a) A budgeted trading and profit and loss account for the year ending 31 December 2011.
   Show the full details of the trading account. Show the appropriations of retained profits in a note.
(b) A budgeted balance sheet as at 31 December 2011.
(c) What advantages accrue to a business by preparing a budget with respect to
   (i) forecast profitability;
   (ii) forecast liquidity?

(AQA (Associated Examining Board): GCE A-level)

*Authors' note: This profit and loss account and balance sheet are presented in the rarely used 'horizontal format'. They are presented in this way because examiners do, occasionally, use them. You should find it a simple process to identify or calculate the figures you are used to finding in vertical profit and loss accounts and balance sheets.

40.7 The balance sheet of Pies and Cakes Ltd at 30 June 2008 was expected to be as follows:

Balance Sheet 30 June 2008 (£)

Fixed assets	Cost	Depreciation to date	Net
Buildings	300,000	120,000	180,000
Plant and machinery	50,000	30,000	20,000
Motor vehicles	30,000	14,000	16,000
Office fixtures	2,500	1,100	1,400
	382,500	165,100	217,400

Current assets		
Stock: Finished goods (570 units at £12 each)		6,840
Raw materials		1,500
Debtors (June 2008 sales)		9,500
Cash and bank balances		35,500
		53,340

Current liabilities		
Creditors for raw materials (May £300 + June £240)	540	
Creditors payable for indirect manufacturing expenses	1,050	
	(1,590)	51,750
		269,150

Financed by	
Share capital	225,000
Profit and loss account	44,150
	269,150

→ The plans for the six months to 31 December 2008 can be summarised as:

(i) Production costs per unit will be:

	£
Direct materials	2
Direct labour	6
Variable indirect manufacturing expenses	4
	12

(ii) Sales will be at a price of £20 per unit for the three months to 30 September and at £21 subsequently. The number of units sold will be:

	Jul	Aug	Sept	Oct	Nov	Dec
Units	300	400	500	500	450	350

All sales will be on credit, and debtors will pay their accounts one month after they bought the goods.

(iii) Production will be consistent at 450 units per month.

(iv) Purchases of direct materials – all on credit – will be:

Jul	Aug	Sept	Oct	Nov	Dec
£	£	£	£	£	£
1,100	1,000	800	700	700	900

Creditors for direct materials will be paid two months after purchase.

(v) Direct labour is paid in the same month as production occurs.

(vi) Variable indirect manufacturing expenses are paid in the month following that in which the units are produced.

(vii) Fixed indirect manufacturing expenses of £450 per month are paid each month and never in arrears.

(viii) A machine costing £2,500 will be bought and paid for in July. A motor vehicle costing £10,000 will be bought and paid for in September.

(ix) Debentures of £25,000 will be issued and the cash received in November. Interest will not be charged until 2009.

(x) Provide for depreciation for the six months: Buildings £15,000; Motor vehicles £4,000; Office fixtures £220; Plant and machinery £5,000.

You are required to draw up as a minimum:
(a) Cash budget, showing figures each month.
(b) Debtors budget, showing figures each month.
(c) Creditors budget, showing figures each month.
(d) Raw materials budget, showing figures each month.
(e) Forecast operating statement for the six months.
(f) Forecast balance sheet as at 31 December 2008.

In addition, draw up any other budgets which show the workings behind the above budgets.

40.8 The following information relates to the actual sales of Griffton Ltd during the last four months of its financial year.

	March	April	May	June
Quantity (units)	900	900	900	1,000
Price each	£55	£55	£55	£55

The budgeted information below relates to the next financial year commencing 1 July 2002:

(i) The company forecasts that sales quantity will decrease in July by 10 per cent of the level in June. The reduced quantity will remain for August and September, but will then increase by 10 per cent in October, and remain fixed for the next three months.

The sales price will remain at £55 each until 1 September when it will be increased to £60 per unit, this price will be effective for a minimum of six months.

50 per cent of sales are on a cash basis and attract a 2 per cent cash discount, the remaining 50 per cent of sales are paid two months in arrears.

The company arranges its purchases of raw materials such that the closing stock at the end of each month exactly meets the requirement for the following month's sales. Each unit sold requires 2 kg of material at £15 per kg; this price is fixed until December 2003.

(ii) As a separate exercise, the managing director asks for stock levels to be reviewed, and asks you about the use of economic order quantities at some time in 2003. The following budgeted data would apply to this exercise:

Material	2,000 kg per month
Price	£15 per kg
Stock holding costs	20% p.a. on average stock value
Ordering costs	£10 per order

Required:
A. Draw up monthly budgets for the four-month period commencing 1 July 2002 for:
   (a) Debtors in £s;
   (b) Raw material purchases in kg.
B. From the budgeted information given in note (ii) calculate the economic order quantity for the company. Briefly outline the limitations of this ordering method.

(Reproduced with the kind permission of OCR: from *University of Oxford Delegacy of Local Examinations: GCE A-level*)

***Authors' note*: EOQ was covered in Section 38.8.**

40.9 Bedford Ltd is a manufacturing business with several production departments. Benjamin Kent, the manager of the machining department, submitted the following figures for the firm's annual budget for his department:

Units produced (normal production level)	64,000

	£
Raw materials	294,400
Direct labour	236,800
Power	38,400
Repairs and maintenance (25% variable at this level of budgeted cost)	51,200
Insurance	1,300
Heating and lighting	1,250
Indirect wages (15% variable at this level of budgeted cost)	64,000
Total cost	687,350

Total capacity for machining department	80,000 units

Actual production for the period is 68,000 units, and costs are:

Materials	310,750
Labour	249,100
Power	39,800
Repairs and maintenance	53,050
Insurance	1,350
Heating and lighting	1,200
Indirect wages	65,250
Total cost	720,500

Benjamin is being criticised for overspending £33,150 compared with his normal budget. It is appreciated that he has made a saving on heating and lighting, but concern is being expressed over the spending on materials and labour. Benjamin feels that he has been able to control the department's costs efficiently.

→

Required:

A. Construct a flexible budget for 60 per cent, 70 per cent, 75 per cent, 85 per cent and 90 per cent of production capacity, calculate any savings or overspending by Benjamin's department and comment on its efficiency.

B. Describe the operation of an efficient system of budgetary control.

(Reproduced with the kind permission of OCR: from *University of Oxford Delegacy of Local Examinations: GCE A-level*)

40.10A The summarised balance sheet of Newland Traders at 30 May 2007 was as follows:

	£000	£000
Fixed assets at cost		610
Less depreciation		264
		346
Current assets		
Stock	210	
Debtors	315	
Cash at bank and in hand	48	
	573	
Current liabilities		
Creditors	(128)	445
		791
Financed by		
Issued capital		600
General reserve		150
Profit and loss account		41
		791

Selling and materials prices at 30 May 2007 provide for a gross profit at the rate of 25 per cent of sales.

The creditors at 30 May 2007 represent the purchases for May 2007, and the debtors represent the sales for April of £150,000 and May of £165,000.

Estimates of sales and expenditure for the six months to 30 November 2007 are as follows:

(i) Sales for the period at current prices will be £800,000. Sales for the months of September and October will each be twice those of the sales in each of the other months.

(ii) Stock at the end of each month will be the same as at 30 May 2007 except that at 30 November 2007 it will be increased to 20 per cent above that level.

(iii) Creditors will be paid one month after the goods are supplied and debtors will be paid two months after the goods are supplied.

(iv) Wages and expenses will be £20,000 a month and will be paid in the month in which they are incurred.

(v) Depreciation will be at the rate of £5,000 a month.

(vi) There will be capital expenditure of £80,000 on 1 September 2007. Depreciation, in addition to that given in (v) above, will be at the rate of 10 per cent per annum on cost.

(vii) There will be no changes in issued capital, general reserve or prices of sales or purchases.

Required:

(a) Sales and purchases budgets and budgeted trading and profit and loss account for the six months ending 30 November 2007.

(b) A budgeted balance sheet as at 30 November 2007.

(c) A cash flow budget for the six months ended 30 November 2007 indicating whether or not it will be necessary to make arrangements for extra finance and, if so, your recommendation as to what form it should take.

Show all your calculations.

(*Welsh Joint Education Committee: GCE A-level*)

40.11A Len Auck and Brian Land trade as partners in Auckland Manufacturing Company making components for minicomputers. To cope with increasing demand the partners intend to extend their manufacturing capacity but are concerned about the effect of the expansion on their cash resources during the build-up period from January to April 2006.

The following information is available.

(a) The balance sheet of Auckland Manufacturing Company at 31 December 2005 is expected to be:

	£	£
Fixed assets		
Plant and machinery at cost		65,000
Less depreciation		28,000
		37,000
Current assets		
Stock – raw materials	10,500	
– finished goods	18,500	
Debtors	36,000	
Cash at bank	4,550	
	69,550	
Current liabilities		
Creditors	(27,550)	42,000
Net assets		79,000
Partners' capital accounts		
Len Auck		40,000
Brian Land		39,000
	£	79,000

(b) Creditors at 31 December 2005 are made up of:

Creditors for materials supplied in November and	
December at £13,000 per month	26,000
Creditors for overheads	1,550
	27,550

(c) New plant costing £25,000 will be delivered and paid for in January 2006.

(d) Raw material stock is to be increased to £12,000 by the end of January 2006, thereafter raw material stock will be maintained at that level. Payment for raw materials is made two months after the month of delivery. Finished goods stock will be maintained at £18,500 throughout the period. There is no work-in-progress.

(e) Sales for the four months are expected to be:

	£
January	18,000
February	22,000
March	22,000
April	24,000

Sales for several months prior to 31 December had been running at the rate of £18,000 per month. It is anticipated that all sales will continue to be paid for two months following the month of delivery.

(f) The cost structure of the product is expected to be:

	%
Raw materials	50
Direct wages	20
Overheads, including depreciation	17½
Profit	12½
Selling price	100

→

→ (g) Indirect wages and salaries included in overheads amount to £900 for the month of January and £1,000 per month thereafter.

(h) Depreciation of plant and machinery (including the new plant) is to be provided at £700 per month and is included in the total overheads.

(i) Wages and salaries are to be paid in the month to which they relate; all other expenses are to be paid for in the month following the month to which they relate.

(j) The partners share profits equally and drawings are £400 per month each.

(k) During the period to April an overdraft facility is being requested.

Required:

(a) A forecast profit and loss account for the four months January to April 2006 and a balance sheet as at 30 April 2006.

(b) A month by month cash forecast for the four months showing the maximum amount of finance required during the period.

(c) A calculation of the month in which the overdraft facility would be repaid on the assumption that the level of activity in April is maintained.

For the purposes of this question, taxation and bank interest may be ignored.

(*Association of Chartered Certified Accountants*)

You can find a range of additional self-test questions, as well as material to help you with your studies, on the website that accompanies this book at **www.pearsoned.co.uk/wood**

STANDARD COSTING AND VARIANCE ANALYSIS

Introduction

This part looks at how budgetary control can be exercised in a timely manner through the establishment of estimates for cost and income and the subsequent monitoring of those estimates against the actual costs and income as they arise.

Standard costing

Learning objectives

After you have studied this chapter, you should be able to:

● explain the difference between a standard costing system and an actual cost system

● explain the advantages of adopting a standard costing system

● distinguish between ideal standards and attainable standards

● explain the importance of selecting appropriate standards

Introduction

In this chapter, you'll learn about standard costing, its benefits, and the difference between 'ideal' and 'attainable' standards and the importance of recognising the difference between them.

41.1 Comparison with actual costs

A cost accounting system can be of two types. One which uses *actual* costs or one that uses something called '**standard costs**'. The difference is not in the systems themselves but in the *kind* of costs that are used. In the costing systems already shown, we have seen that they have consisted of the actual costs for direct materials and direct labour, and that overhead has been charged by reference to a predetermined overhead rate. Standard costing uses instead the costs that *should have been incurred*. **So standard costing has costs that *should* have been incurred, while other systems use costs that *have* been incurred.**

In a cost accounting system that uses 'actual costs', costs are traced through the records as product costs. On the other hand, **standard costing** uses standards of performance and of costs and prices derived from studying operations and on estimates of future costs and prices. Each unit being produced is given a standard material cost, a standard direct labour cost and a standard overhead cost. As with any form of management accounting, this does not have to be carried out in full. For example, some companies will use *standard* labour and *standard* overhead costs but *actual* material costs. In the rest of this chapter, we will consider organisations that use standard costs for everything.

As with all management accounting tools, the benefits flowing from using standard costing should exceed the costs of doing so. Advantages that may arise as a result of having a standard costing system include:

1 **Usually a standard costing system is simpler and needs less work than a costing system based on actual costs.** This is because once the standards have been set they are adhered to, and the standard costs remain unchanged for fairly long periods. Costing systems based on actual costs need constant recalculations of cost. For example, the average cost method of pricing issues of materials needs a recalculation of the price each time there are further receipts, whereas standard cost of materials will remain at a constant figure. This can bring about a reduction in the costs of clerical work.

2 **The unit costs for each identical product will be the same, whereas this may not be the same with actual costing systems.** For instance, in an actual cost system two people making identical units may be paid at different wage rates, the materials issued to one person may have come from a slightly later lot of raw materials received which cost more than the previous lot and therefore the issue price may be higher, and so on. In a standard costing system the same amount would be charged for each of these people until such time as the standards were altered.

3 **A standard cost system provides a better means of checking on the efficiency with which production is carried on,** in that the differences between the standard costs and the actual costs, i.e. the **variances**, throw up the changes in efficiency.

4 **Standard costing increases the speed of reporting.** This is certainly important, as generally the later that information is received the less useful it is. Standard costing has a great deal of predetermined data when compared with an actual costing system; therefore entering up job order sheets, job sheets and many other tasks can be speeded up if the actual costs do not have to be awaited.

By definition, the costs that flow through a standard costing system are standard costs. As actual costs will normally be different from the equivalent standard costs, the difference (i.e. 'variance') if adverse (i.e. actual costs have exceeded standard costs) is debited to profit or loss. If the variance is a favourable one (i.e. actual costs have been less than the standard costs) it is credited to profit or loss. This must be done, as all the costs used for the calculation of gross profit, etc. have been standard costs, and if the variances were not included in the income statement, the profit for the period that it shows would not be the profit actually made.

41.2 Setting standards

Standard costing is a classic case of the use of the principle of 'management by exception'. Put roughly, this means that **when things are going according to plan leave them alone, and concentrate instead on the things that are deviating from planned results.** With standard costing, the actual results that conform to the standards require little attention. Instead, management's interest is centred on the exceptions to standards. The approach whereby this information is given to management is known as 'exception reporting'.

Getting the standard costs, quantities and prices 'right' is, therefore, of prime importance. If the 'wrong' standards are used, not only will a lot of time and money have been wasted, but they may bring worse results than if no standard had been set at all.

 Activity 41.1 What does this last statement remind you of from earlier chapters?

Standards may be unsuitable because they were not set properly, or because conditions have changed greatly since they were set.

Standards can be of two types:

1 **Ideal standards.** These are based on maximum levels of efficiency. They thus represent standards of performance that can rarely, if ever, be attained. Adoption of this type of standard is never appropriate. Quite apart from the unrealistic view it gives of everything, it is misleading and can be demotivating if the standards set are perceived to be unachievable by those employees who are meant to be striving to achieve them.

2 **Attainable standards.** It is simple for someone to say that individuals will be motivated to attain standards that they are capable of, that they will not exert very much effort to exceed standards, and that standards outside their capabilities will not motivate them. From this follows the easy conclusion that standards should be neither 'too easy' nor 'too difficult' but should be 'just right'. The difficult part of this is in saying what the 'just right' figures are. There is no doubt that the work of behavioural scientists in this area has brought about a far greater insight into such problems. In a very large firm, such specialists may be members of the team setting the standards.

The standards for materials and for labour can be divided between those which are concerned with (*a*) prices and (*b*) quantities. Standard overhead costs are divided between standard variable overhead costs and standard fixed overhead costs. The standard fixed overhead costs will be used in absorption costing only, as marginal costing does not bring the fixed costs into its figures.

Activity 41.2

Think back to Activity 41.1. What message have you taken from these four statements:

1 'Data which is provided for a particular purpose, and which is completely wrong for the purpose, is worse than having no data at all.' (Section 35.2)
2 'The wrong kind of costing can be even worse than having no costing at all.' (Section 36.12)
3 'Some budgets that are drawn up are even more harmful to a firm than if none were drawn up at all.' (Section 38.2)
4 'If the "wrong" standards are used, not only will a lot of time and money have been wasted, but it may bring worse results than if no standard had been set at all.' (Section 41.1)

Learning outcomes

You should now have learnt:

1 Standard costing is based upon costs that should have been incurred, while other costing systems are based upon actual costs, i.e. costs that have been incurred.

2 About the benefits of standard costing.

3 Under a standard costing system, management focuses upon the exceptions to the standards.

4 It is essential that the standards adopted are appropriate and attainable.

Answers to activities

41.1 'Data which is provided for a particular purpose, and which is completely wrong for the purpose, is worse than having no data at all.' (Section 35.2)

'The wrong kind of costing can be even worse than having no costing at all.' (Section 36.12)

'Some budgets that are drawn up are even more harmful to a firm than if none were drawn up at all.' (Section 38.2)

41.2 In order to obtain maximum benefit from costing systems and management accounting systems, it is vital that appropriate data and management accounting techniques are used and that they are used in an appropriate and effective manner. Failure to do this is both directly wasteful of resources and can be not just counterproductive, but harmful to the organisation.

Review questions

Note: **This chapter gives background information only. You will not find many computational questions limited to its contents.**

41.1 Rimham plc prepares its budgets annually and as the accountant you are responsible for this task. The following standard data is available:

Material content	Product X kg	Product Y kg	Product Z kg
Material 1	–	18	24
Material 2	4	14	–
Material 3	12	10	6
Material 4	8	–	18

Material prices	Price per kg £
Material 1	0.1
Material 2	0.15
Material 3	0.25
Material 4	0.05

Labour content	Product X hours	Product Y hours	Product Z hours
Department A	2.5	1.5	3
Department B	2.5	1.5	3

Labour rates	Rate per hour £
Department A	1.6
Department B	1.2

Additional budgeted information

Direct labour hours	635,000
Production overheads	£1,143,000

● Production overheads are absorbed on the direct labour hour rate method.
● Administration and selling overheads are absorbed as a percentage of production cost at the rates of 50 per cent and 25 per cent, respectively.
● Profit is estimated at 12½ per cent on budgeted selling price.
● Sales, at standard selling price, for the following year are budgeted as follows:

Product	£
X	800,000
Y	1,280,000
Z	2,400,000

● In order to meet the needs of an expansion programme the company considers it necessary to increase stock as follows:

Material 1	90,000 kg
Material 2	36,000 kg
Material 3	42,000 kg
Material 4	54,000 kg
Finished goods	
Product X	5,000 units
Product Y	10,000 units
Product Z	10,000 units

You are required to prepare the following:
(a) A schedule giving a detailed standard cost and standard selling price per unit for **each** product.
(b) The sales budget in units.
(c) The production budget in units.
(d) The direct material purchases budget in both units and value.

(*Northern Examinations and Assessment Board: GCE A-level*)

41.2A Define the terms:

(*i*) standard costing
(*ii*) standard cost
(*iii*) standard hours
(*iv*) variance.

(*Edexcel Foundation, London Examinations: GCE A-level*)

You can find a range of additional self-test questions, as well as material to help you with your studies, on the website that accompanies this book at **www.pearsoned.co.uk/wood**

Materials and labour variances

Learning objectives

After you have studied this chapter, you should be able to:

● explain the difference between a favourable and an adverse variance
● calculate materials usage and price variances
● calculate labour efficiency and wage rate variances
● explain the similarity between the calculation of the materials usage variance and the labour efficiency variance
● explain the similarity between the calculation of the materials price variance and the wage rate variance
● suggest possible explanations for variances

Introduction

In this chapter, you'll learn about two of the main groups of variances, those relating to materials and labour, and how to calculate them.

42.1 Background

Variance analysis is a means of assessing the difference between budgeted and actual amounts. These can be monetary amounts or physical quantities.

Properly used, variance analysis can improve the operating efficiency of a business by, first of all, setting up the predetermined standard cost structures and, then, measuring actual costs against them to assess efficiency.

Variance analysis makes use of the principle of management by exception. When things are going according to plan they can be left alone. Management can then concentrate on the things that deviate from the planned results and, as mentioned in Chapter 41, can adopt exception reporting in order to do so.

42.2 Adverse and favourable variances

The difference between standard cost and actual cost has already been stated to be a variance. Remember these are classified:

● **Adverse**: actual cost amount *greater* than standard cost amount
● **Favourable**: actual cost amount *less* than standard cost amount.

The use of the words 'adverse' and 'favourable' should not be confused with their meaning in ordinary language. They are technical terms. Whether a variance is 'good' or 'bad' can only be determined after the causes of the variance have been fully investigated and ascertained. For example, the actual cost of a unit of a product may be less than the standard cost because more units than expected were produced, resulting in lower unit costs – a good thing. Alternatively actual cost may be lower because the standard cost was based on an error by the person who calculated it – a bad thing.

42.3 Computation of variances

There is a big difference between the *computation* of the variances and their *analysis*. The computation simply requires the use of straightforward formulae. In contrast, the analysis of a variance is a matter requiring a good deal of judgement which, by its very nature, cannot be done in a mechanical fashion.

We can now look at the computation of some variances. There are many variances which can be computed, but we will concentrate on a few of the more important ones. In order that sense can be made of the computations and a reasonable job of analysis done, it will be assumed that the standards set were calculated on a rational basis – i.e. they were appropriate.

Note: In the computations of variances which follow, exhibits are used to illustrate the variances which have been calculated. The lines drawn on the exhibits represent:

Representing standard costs — — — — — — — — — — — —

Representing actual costs ·······································

Where actual costs and standard costs are the same — — — — — — —

The shaded part(s) in each exhibit represent the variance. The value of each variance can be confirmed by multiplying price by quantity, i.e. it is the area of the shaded rectangle.

1 Materials price variances

Favourable variance

Material J	
Standard price per metre	£4
Standard usage per unit	5 metres
Actual price per metre	£3
Actual usage per unit	5 metres

Usage is the same as standard, therefore the only variance is that of price calculated:

	£
Actual cost per unit £3 × 5	15
Standard cost per unit £4 × 5	20
Variance (favourable)	5

Exhibit 42.1 shows the £5 variance (represented by the shaded area). This is the £1 difference in price multiplied by a quantity of 5, therefore the variance is £5. **The variance extends to the price line and not the quantity line, so it is a price variance.**

Exhibit 42.1

Adverse variance

Material K

Standard price per metre	£9
Standard usage per unit	8 metres
Actual price per metre	£11
Actual usage per unit	8 metres

Exhibit 42.2

Variance computed:	£
Actual cost per unit £11 × 8 units	88
Standard cost per unit £9 × 8 units	72
Variance (adverse)	16

The variance is shown in Exhibit 42.2 – £2 times a quantity of 8, i.e. £16. Notice that the shaded area is outside the lines marked – – – – – representing standard costs.

Note: **In the exhibits, when the variance is outside the standard cost area as marked by the standard cost lines, it will be an adverse variance. When it is inside the standard cost area as marked by the standard cost lines, it will be a favourable variance.**

2 Materials usage variances

Favourable variance

Material L

Standard price per tonne	£5
Standard usage per unit	100 tonnes
Actual price per tonne	£5
Actual usage per unit	95 tonnes

Cost is the same as standard, therefore the only variance is that of usage calculated:

	£
Actual cost per unit £5 × 95	475
Standard cost per unit £5 × 100	500
Variance (favourable)	25

Exhibit 42.3

Adverse variance

Material M

Standard price per centimetre	£8
Standard usage per unit	11 cm
Actual price per centimetre	£8
Actual usage per unit	13 cm

Exhibit 42.4

Variance computed:	£
Actual cost per unit £8 × 13	104
Standard cost per unit £8 × 11	88
Variance (adverse)	16

Here again the variances for materials L and M are shown in exhibits by means of shaded areas. **The variances extend to the quantity lines and are, therefore, usage variances.** With material L, the variance is shown inside the standard cost area, and is, therefore, a favourable variance, whereas material M shows an adverse variance as it is outside the standard cost area.

3 Combinations of materials price and usage variances

Most variances are combinations of both materials price and usage variances. Sometimes one variance will be favourable while the other is adverse; sometimes both will be adverse variances; and at other times both will be favourable variances.

Favourable and adverse variances combined

Material N

Standard price per metre	£6
Standard usage per unit	25 m
Actual price per metre	£7
Actual usage per metre	24 m

The net variance is calculated as:

	£
Actual cost per unit £7 × 24	168
Standard cost per unit £6 × 25	150
Variance (adverse)	18

Exhibit 42.5

As Exhibit 42.5 shows, this is in fact made up of two variances. The first variance, shown as the shaded portion A, is an adverse price variance (i.e. it is outside the standard cost lines, therefore actual cost has exceeded standard cost). The second variance, shown as the shaded portion B, is a favourable usage variance (i.e. it is inside the standard cost lines, therefore actual usage has been less than standard usage).

The adverse price variance can therefore be seen to be £1 by a quantity of 24 = £24. The favourable usage variance can be seen to be a length of 1 metre by a price of £6 = £6. The net (adverse) variance is therefore made up:

	£
Adverse material price variance	24
Favourable materials usage variance	6
Net (adverse) variance	18

Both adverse variances combined

Material O

Standard price per kg	£9
Standard usage per unit	13 kg
Actual price per kg	£11
Actual usage per unit	15 kg

The net variance is computed:

	£
Actual cost per unit £11 × 15	165
Standard cost per unit £9 × 13	117
Variance (adverse)	48

Exhibit 42.6

Exhibit 42.6 shows the shaded area A which is definitely a price variance of £2 × 13 = £26 adverse. Shaded area B is definitely a usage variance of 2 × £9 = £18 adverse. This makes up £44 of the variance, but there is the double-shaded area, C, of 2 × £2 = £4. This is really an area which is common to both usage and price. Sometimes, although not very often, this would be treated as a separate variance, but as detail is necessarily limited, in this book we will just add it to the price variance, making it £26 + £4 = £30, the usage variance being left at £18.

Both favourable variances combined

Material P

Standard price per tonne	£20
Standard usage per unit	15 tonnes
Actual price per tonne	£19
Actual usage per unit	13 tonnes

The net variance is computed:

	£
Actual cost per unit £19 × 13	247
Standard cost per unit £20 × 15	300
Variance (favourable)	53

Exhibit 42.7

Exhibit 42.7 shows the shaded area A which is definitely a price variance of £1 × 13 = £13 favourable. Shaded area B is a usage variance of 2 × £19 = £38 favourable. The double-shaded area C of £1 × 2 = £2, making up the total variance of 53, would normally be added to the usage variance to make it £38 + £2 = £40.

42.4 Materials variances – analysis

1 Price variances

The price variance is a simple one in that it is obvious that the purchasing department has not been able to buy at the anticipated price. How far this is completely outside the powers of the purchasing department depends entirely on the facts. It may simply be that the rate of inflation is far greater than it had been possible to foresee, or that special forms of extra taxes have been introduced by the government. No one can surely blame the purchasing department for not knowing the secrets of the government's budget each year.

On the other hand, it may have been that poor purchasing control has meant that orders for materials have been placed too late for the firm to manage to get the right price in the market, or that materials which ought to have been bought in bulk have, in fact, been bought in small lots at uneconomic prices. If there are regular suppliers, a short-term gain by buying a cheaper lot from somewhere else could act against the business's benefit in the long run if its regular suppliers took umbrage.

Buying the cheapest materials does not always result in the greatest possible profit being attained.

Activity 42.1 Why do you think this is the case?

In the end, after all the variance analysis has been undertaken, there must be someone to whom the responsibility for the price variance can be traced and who is then accountable for it. However, as Activity 42.1 illustrated, care must be taken not to give praise blindly or to criticise unfairly.

2 Usage variances

There are many reasons for excessive use of materials. Inferior materials can bring about a lot of waste, so can workers who are not as skilled as they ought to be. Perhaps the machinery is not suitable for the job, or there might even be deliberate wastage of material, e.g. wood wasted so that it can be taken home by workers as fuel, etc. The theft of material obviously aggravates a usage variance. Here again responsibility must be traced.

Activity 42.2 When you prepare one of these variance diagrams, there are two simple rules you can use to identify the type (price or usage) and nature (favourable or adverse) of the variance. What are they?

42.5 Key questions of variances

Before we look at the computation or analysis of any further variances this is a convenient point to raise some fundamental questions about variances. They are:

1 Why do we wish to calculate this particular variance?
2 When it has been calculated, what action are we going to take based on it?
3 If we are not going to make an effective use of the variance, then why bother to calculate it?

42.6 Formulae for materials variances

We have deliberately waited until now to give you the formula for calculating each variance. We wanted you to understand what the variances were, rather than simply give you the formula to calculate them. They are as follows:

> **Materials price variance** = (Standard price – Actual price per unit) × Quantity purchased
> = (SP – AP) × QP
>
> **Materials usage variance** = (Standard quantity required – Actual quantity) × Standard price
> = (SQ – AQ) × SP

42.7 Inventory records under standard costing

It is worth noting at this point that when a business adopts a standard costing system it avoids the difficulties involving FIFO, LIFO or average stock methods. In a standard costing system all materials received and issued are valued at the standard cost in the inventory account. There is no recording problem associated with changing prices during the period since they are separately recorded as variances.

Provided that standards are reviewed sufficiently often this system should ensure that the values of inventories are maintained close to their current value.

42.8 Disposition of variances

The question arises as to how the variances are to be brought into the financial statements of the business. There are, in fact, several methods of dealing with them.

They can be treated entirely as costs (if adverse variances) which are period costs and are, therefore, not included in the valuation of closing stocks of finished goods or work in progress. Alternatively they may be brought in as product costs and therefore used in the valuation of closing stocks. Another variation is to treat those variances which are controllable as period costs, but to treat the uncontrollable variances as product costs.

All of these methods are acceptable for the financial statements which are prepared for external reporting.

Before you read further, attempt Review Questions 42.1 and 42.2A.

42.9 Costing for labour

Before looking at labour variances, we first need to consider the range of basis upon which labour may be paid. There is no exact definition of 'wages' and 'salaries'. In general, it is accepted that wages are earnings paid on a weekly basis, while salaries are paid monthly.

The methods can vary widely between employers and also as regards different employees in the same organisation. The main methods are:

1 Fixed amount salaries or wages – these are an agreed annual amount.
2 Piece rate – based on the number of units produced by the employee.
3 Commission – a percentage based on the amount of sales made by the employee.
4 Basic rate per hour – a fixed rate multiplied by number of hours worked.

Arrangements for rewarding people for working overtime (time exceeding normal hours worked) will vary widely. The rate will usually be in excess of that paid during normal working hours. People being paid salaries will often not be paid for overtime.

In addition, bonuses may be paid on top of the above earnings. Bonus schemes will also vary widely and may depend on the amount of net profit made by the company, or on the amount of work performed or production achieved, either by the whole company or else the department in which the employee works.

It is important that the nature of payment to the employees is known before attempting to interpret the results of labour variance calculations. There will be significant differences in the possible explanations when employees are on salaries as opposed to basic rate as opposed to overtime, etc.

42.10 Labour variances

The computation of labour variances is similar to that of material variances. With labour variances the analysis can be broken down into:

(*a*) wage rate variances
(*b*) labour efficiency variances.

Note: **As you read and work through this section, you will notice great similarity between the labour variance formulae and the materials variance formulae. In actual fact, the only difference is a terminological one. The wage rate formula is identical in method to the materials price formula; and the labour efficiency formula is similarly identical to the materials usage formula. This is something that students frequently fail to grasp. In effect, it means that you need learn only one of the pairs of formulae, along with the terminology for the other pair. You can then complete any variance computation using both pairs of formulae.**

Because the computation of labour variances is so similar to those of materials variances only a few examples will be given.

1 Wage rate variance

Product A	
Standard hours to produce	100
Actual hours to produce	100
Standard wage rate per hour	£0.9
Actual wage rate per hour	£1.0

Exhibit 42.8

As the actual and standard hours are the same, then the only variance will be a wage rate variance, computed as follows:

		£
Actual cost per unit £1.0 × 100		100
Standard cost per unit £0.9 × 100		90
Variance (adverse)		10

Exhibit 42.8 illustrates this in that the variance is represented by the shaded area. This is £0.1 by a quantity of 100, therefore the variance is £10. The variance extends to the wage rate line and it is thus a wage rate variance, and as the shaded area is outside the standard cost lines, indicated by lines marked ━━━━━━, then it is an adverse variance.

2 Labour efficiency variance

Product B

Standard hours to produce	400
Actual hours to produce	370
Standard wage rate per hour	£1.0
Actual wage rate per hour	£1.0

Exhibit 42.9

As the actual and standard wage rates are the same, then the only variance will be a labour efficiency variance, computed as follows:

	£
Actual cost per unit £1.0 × 370	370
Standard cost per unit £1.0 × 400	400
Variance (favourable)	30

Exhibit 42.9 illustrates this in that the variance is represented by the shaded area. This is a quantity of 30 by a rate of £1.0, therefore the variance is £30. The variance extends to the time line, therefore this is an efficiency variance, as the job has been completed in a different number of hours from standard. As the shaded area is inside the standard cost lines indicated by lines marked − − − − − −, it is a favourable variance.

3 Combined wage rate and efficiency variance

Product C

Standard hours to produce	500
Actual hours to produce	460
Standard wage rate per hour	£0.9
Actual wage rate per hour	£1.1

Exhibit 42.10

The net variance can be computed as:

	£
Actual cost per unit £1.1 × 460	506
Standard cost per unit £0.9 × 500	450
Variance (adverse)	56

Exhibit 42.10 shows that this is made up of two variances. The first variance, shown as the shaded portion A, is an adverse wage rate variance (it is outside the standard cost lines, therefore it is an adverse variance because actual cost for this has exceeded standard cost). The second variance, shown as the shaded portion B, is a favourable labour efficiency variance (it is inside the standard cost lines, therefore actual hours have been less than standard hours).

The adverse wage rate variance can, therefore, be seen to be £0.2 by a quantity of 460 = £92. The favourable efficiency variance is a quantity of 40 by a price of £0.9 = £36. The net adverse variance is, therefore, made up of:

	£
Adverse wage rate variance	92
Favourable labour efficiency variance	36
	56

42.11 Labour variances – analysis

Labour wage rates will probably be set in conjunction with the trade unions involved, so that this variance may not really be subject to control at any other level other than at the bargaining table with the unions involved. Nevertheless such a variance could arise because a higher grade of labour was being used than was necessary, even taking into account trade union needs. It might reflect a job running behind schedule that had to be finished off quickly even though higher grade labour was used. It might have been a rush job that also meant bringing in a higher grade of labour as well. The staffing policy of the firm may have come adrift because the firm had not recruited sufficient numbers of the various grades of labour.

Labour efficiency variances can be caused by a great number of things. Using unsuitable labour, unsuitable machinery, workers trying to slow work up so that more overtime rates of pay are earned, the day after a bank holiday, or the day before it, can affect performance. The morale of workers, the physical state of workers, using poor materials which slows up production, hold-ups because of bottlenecks in production, and so on. The possibilities are almost endless. At the same time, if the variance was worth calculating, some form of action should follow. Otherwise, there is no point at all in calculating such variances.

42.12 Formulas for labour variances

Wage rate variance $= $(Standard wage rate per hour – Actual wage rate) $\times$ Actual hours worked

$= (SR - AR) \times AH$

Labour efficiency variance $=$ (Standard labour hours for actual production – Actual labour hours worked) $\times$ Standard wage rate per hour

$= (SH - AH) \times SR$

Don't forget, if you compare these formulae to the materials variance formulae, you will see that they are actually the same, only the terminology is different, i.e. 'wage rate' instead of 'price'; 'efficiency' instead of 'usage'.

Learning outcomes

You should now have learnt:

1 Variance analysis can improve the operating efficiency of a business by pinpointing items in need of investigation.

2 Adverse variances are not necessarily 'bad'. They result from more having been used or spent than was anticipated. Similarly, favourable variances are not necessarily 'good'. It is the reason for the variance, not the effect, that determines whether it is 'good' or 'bad'.

3 The materials usage variance formula is identical to the labour efficiency variance formula. Only the terminology differs.

4 The materials price variance formula is identical to the wage rate variance formula. Only the terminology differs.

Answers to activities

42.1 Buying cheaply may produce a favourable variance for the purchasing manager. This makes that individual appear efficient. However, doing so may result in poor quality materials being used, resulting in more wastage, a greater amount of labour time because the workers take longer to do the job with inferior materials, and a product made up of poor materials may well damage the image of the firm because its products do not last as long as they used to. This will make the production manager look inefficient. Clearly, it is not fair that the production manager takes the blame while the purchasing manager is congratulated for a job well done. This is one very good reason why it is important that overall variances are broken down into their constituent parts. Only then can blame be attributed to the correct individual and praise given to those that deserve it.

42.2 **Rule 1:** if the shaded box is horizontal, it is a price variance; if vertical, it is a usage variance.
Rule 2: if the shaded box lies inside the standard cost line, the variance is favourable; if it lies outside, it is adverse.

Review questions

Advice: **Work carefully through Review Questions 42.1 and 42.3. If you have any difficulty, repeat them after 24 hours. Questions on this topic rarely contain any surprises. Once you get used to doing them, you will find they are actually quite easy to answer.**

42.1 Calculate the materials variances from the following data.

(*i*)	Material A:	Standard price per tonne	£10	
		Standard usage per unit	30	tonnes
		Actual price per tonne	£9	
		Actual usage per unit	35	tonnes
(*ii*)	Material B:	Standard price per metre	£15	
		Standard usage per unit	60	metres
		Actual price per metre	£16	
		Actual usage per unit	54	metres
(*iii*)	Material C:	Standard price per metre	£24	
		Standard usage per unit	30	metres
		Actual price per metre	£28	
		Actual usage per unit	38	metres
(*iv*)	Material D:	Standard price per roll	£20	
		Standard usage per unit	31	rolls
		Actual price per roll	£18	
		Actual usage per unit	28	rolls
(*v*)	Material E:	Standard price per kilo	£4	
		Standard usage per unit	280	kg
		Actual price per kilo	£5	
		Actual usage per unit	310	kg
(*vi*)	Material F:	Standard price per litre	£75	
		Standard usage per unit	5,000	litres
		Actual price per litre	£66	
		Actual usage per unit	4,950	litres

42.2A Calculate the materials variances from the following data.

(i)	Material T:	Standard price per metre	£11	
		Standard usage per unit	176	metres
		Actual price per metre	£11	
		Actual usage per unit	171	metres
(ii)	Material U:	Standard price per tonne	£42	
		Standard usage per unit	50	tonnes
		Actual price per tonne	£45	
		Actual usage per unit	50	tonnes
(iii)	Material V:	Standard price per litre	£22	
		Standard usage per unit	79	litres
		Actual price per litre	£22	
		Actual usage per unit	83	litres
(iv)	Material W:	Standard price per foot	£8	
		Standard usage per unit	41	metres
		Actual price per foot	£10	
		Actual usage per unit	41	metres
(v)	Material X:	Standard price per tonne	£29	
		Standard usage per unit	60	tonnes
		Actual price per tonne	£30	
		Actual usage per unit	60	tonnes
(vi)	Material Y:	Standard price per kilo	£55	
		Standard usage per unit	84	kg
		Actual price per kilo	£55	
		Actual usage per unit	78	kg

42.3 Calculate the labour variances from the following data:

		Standard hours	Actual hours	Standard wage rate (£)	Actual wage rate (£)
(i)	Job J	440	432	6.00	6.00
(ii)	Job K	230	230	5.60	5.80
(iii)	Job L	400	480	5.70	5.70
(iv)	Job M	280	206	7.00	7.00
(v)	Job N	136	136	5.70	5.10
(vi)	Job O	60	68	5.60	5.60
(vii)	Job P	140	154	5.50	5.50
(viii)	Job Q	200	200	5.80	6.10

42.4A Calculate the labour variances from the following data:

		Standard hours	Actual hours	Standard wage rate (£)	Actual wage rate (£)
(i)	Job a	450	426	5.20	5.60
(ii)	Job b	660	680	4.90	4.70
(iii)	Job c	150	140	5.30	4.90
(iv)	Job d	510	520	5.10	5.40
(v)	Job e	420	450	5.20	4.80
(vi)	Job f	810	780	4.60	5.00

42.5 The company for which you are the accountant manufactures three related, but different, products. These are dishwashers, washing machines and refrigerators. Each product has a standard time per unit of production. These are:

→
dishwashers	10 hours
washing machines	12 hours
refrigerators	14 hours

In the month of March the actual production was:

dishwashers	150
washing machines	100
refrigerators	90

and the labour details were:

actual hours worked	4,100
standard hourly rate of pay	£4
actual wages incurred	£18,450

You are required to:
(a) Explain the term 'standard hour'.
(b) Calculate the standard hours produced in the month of March.
(c) Calculate the following variances, using the above data:
    (i)   total direct labour variance
    (ii) direct labour rate variance
    (iii) direct labour efficiency variance.
(d) Give **two** possible causes for **each** of the labour rate and efficiency variances in (c).

(AQA (Northern Examinations and Assessment Board): GCE A-level)

42.6A Central Grid plc manufactures tungsten parts which pass through two processes, machining and polishing, before being transferred to finished goods. The management of the company have in operation a system of standard costing and budgetary control. The standard cost and budget information for April 2008 has been established by the management accountant as follows:

Standard Cost and Budget Details for April 2008

	Machining	Polishing
Standard cost per unit		
Direct material	£5	–
Direct labour	£12	£4.50
Budgeted output – units	16,000	16,000
(*See* Note below)		
Budgeted direct labour hours	48,000	24,000

Note: Output passes through both processes and there is no opening or closing work in progress.

Additional information:
1 The actual production costs and details for April 2008 are as follows:
   (i)   The output that passed through the two processes was 12,000 units and there was no opening or closing work-in-progress.
   (ii) Direct material used at standard prices was £64,150.
   (iii) Direct material used at actual prices was £60,390.
   (iv) The direct wages bill and the direct labour hours clocked for the machining department were:

	£	Hours
Machining department	153,000	34,000

2 Variances for the polishing department have been calculated and reveal the following:

Labour efficiency variance	£3,000 Adverse
Labour rate variance	Nil

Required:
(a) Calculate the total direct materials variance and its analysis into:
  (i) direct materials usage variance
  (ii) direct materials price variance.
(b) Calculate the overall direct labour variance for the machining department and analyse this variance into:
  (i) direct labour efficiency variance
  (ii) direct labour rate variance.
(c) Identify the possible reasons for each of the variances calculated for the machining department in (a) and (b) above and also for the variances given for the polishing department.
(d) Discuss possible interrelationships between these variances.

(AQA (Associated Examining Board): GCE A-level)

42.7 Borrico Ltd manufactures a single product and they had recently introduced a system of budgeting and variance analysis. The following information is available for the month of July 2011:

1	Budget	Actual
	£	£
Direct materials	200,000	201,285
Direct labour	313,625	337,500
Variable manufacturing overhead	141,400	143,000
Fixed manufacturing overhead	64,400	69,500
Variable sales overhead	75,000	71,000
Administration costs	150,000	148,650

2 Standard costs were:
  Direct labour 48,250 hours at £6.50 per hour.
  Direct materials 20,000 kilograms at £10 a kilogram.

3 Actual manufacturing costs were:
  Direct labour 50,000 hours at £6.75 per hour.
  Direct materials 18,900 kilograms at £10.65 a kilogram.

4 Budgeted sales were 20,000 units at £50 a unit.
  Actual sales were
    15,000 units at £52 a unit
    5,200 units at £56 a unit

5 There was no work-in-progress or stock of finished goods.

Required:
(a) An accounting statement showing the budgeted and actual gross and net profits or losses for July 2011.
(b) The following variances for July 2011.
  (i) Direct materials cost variance, direct materials price variance and direct materials usage variance.
  (ii) Direct labour cost variance, direct labour rate variance and direct labour efficiency variance.
(c) What use can the management of Borrico Ltd make of the variances calculated in (b) above?

(AQA (Associated Examining Board): GCE A-level)

42.8A
(a) How does a system of standard costing enable a business to operate on the principle of management by exception?
(b) Some of the following materials and labour variances have been wrongly calculated, although the figures used are correct. Recalculate the variances, showing clearly the formulae you have used, and state whether the variances are adverse or favourable.

→

(i) Total Materials Variance
    (Standard price – Actual price)   (Standard quantity – Actual quantity)
    = (£8.42 – £8.24)   (1,940 litres – 2,270 litres)
    = (£0.18)   (–330 litres)
    = £59.40 adverse

(ii) Materials Price Variance
    (Standard price – Actual price)   Standard quantity
    = (£8.42 – £8.24)   1,940
    = £349.20 favourable

(iii) Materials Usage Variance
    (Standard quantity – Actual quantity)   Standard price
    = (1,940 – 2,270)   £8.42
    = £2,778.6 adverse

(iv) Total Labour Variance
    (Actual hours – Standard hours)   (Actual rate – Standard rate)
    = (860 – 800)   (£6.14 – £6.53)
    = (60 hours)   (–£0.39)
    = £23.4 adverse

(v) Wage Rate Variance
    (Standard rate – Actual rate)   Actual hours
    = (£6.53 – £6.14)   860
    = £335.4 favourable

(vi) Labour Efficiency Variance
    (Actual hours – Standard hours)   Standard rate
    = (860 – 800)   £6.53
    = £391.80 favourable

(Edexcel: GCE A-level)

42.9A Makers Ltd assembles computer games machines. Standard costs have been prepared as follows:

	Gamesmaster £	Gotchya £
Standard cost:		
Direct material: boards	5	10
components	20	30
Direct labour: assembly	5	5
testing	5	10
Overheads charged at 200%	20	30
	55	85
Profit margin	11	15
Standard selling price	66	100

The standard direct labour rate is £5 per hour.
During May 2005, 5,000 Gamesmasters were sold at £60 each and 2,000 Gotchyas at £110 each.

Actual costs were incurred as follows:

	£
5,050 Gamesmaster boards	26,000
5,060 sets Gamesmaster components	75,000
2,010 Gotchya boards	28,390
2,025 sets Gotchya components	56,409
10,000 assembly labour hours @ £4.90	49,000
7,000 testing labour hours at £5.10	35,700
Overheads	160,000
	430,499

There are no opening or closing inventories.

Required:
A schedule of direct materials and direct labour variances for the month.

(*Welsh Joint Education Committee: GCE A-level*)

42.10A The following diagram reflects costs under a standard costing system. Assume that all the variances are *unfavourable*. State, with reasons, which rectangle(s) represent:

(*i*)   the standard cost
(*ii*) the actual cost
(*iii*) the total labour cost variance
(*iv*) the efficiency variance
(*v*)   the wage rate variance.

(*Edexcel: GCE A-level*)

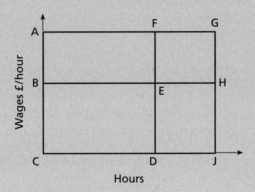

Overhead and sales variances

Learning objectives

After you have studied this chapter, you should be able to:

● calculate overhead expenditure variances, volume variances, efficiency variances and capacity variances

● calculate sales price, volume and mix variances

● describe the similarities between the variable production overhead efficiency variance and both the labour efficiency variance and the materials usage variance

● identify appropriate reasons why variances found have occurred

Introduction

In this chapter, you'll learn about another two groups of variances – those relating to overheads (both variable and fixed) and sales – and how to calculate them and interpret the results.

43.1 Management overheads

In Chapter 37, the problem of allocating overheads (i.e. indirect manufacturing expenses) to jobs or processes was introduced. First, these costs were collected in cost centres. The total costs of each cost centre were then apportioned to products or jobs as they passed through the cost centre.

Suppose a business collects costs into three manufacturing departments, with the result as shown in Exhibit 43.1:

Exhibit 43.1

| | Department | | |
	A	B	C
	£	£	£
Fixed overhead cost	50,000	40,000	20,000
Variable overhead cost	30,000	35,000	40,000
Total overhead	80,000	75,000	60,000
Direct labour hours	10,000	30,000	15,000
Machine hours	20,000	2,000	15,000

A decision has to be taken as to which activity, either labour hours or machine time, is the *dominant factor* in the department and will, therefore, provide the most appropriate basis for apportioning the overheads to products or jobs manufactured in each department.

(Note the focus on the 'dominant factor'. This is the key to appropriate selection of the apportionment basis to use.)

In the case of Department A, machine hours is the dominant factor. Overheads will, therefore, be charged on the basis £80,000/20,000 hours = £4 per machine hour. The business will record for each job or process the number of machine hours taken and the overheads will be allocated on this total of hours at £4 per hour.

In Department B, labour is the dominant factor. Overheads will be charged on a labour hour rate calculated at £75,000/30,000 hours = £2.50 per hour.

Department C does not exhibit any dominant activity and could be expressed in either a machine hour rate or a labour hour rate. Some businesses, where rates of pay in a department are stable and the mix of labour at different rates of pay stays the same, prefer to express the overheads as a percentage of labour cost. In Department C, if the direct labour cost was £75,000 it could be £60,000/£75,000 = 80 per cent. Thus the labour cost for all work going through Department C would be collected and overheads allocated at 80 per cent of the labour cost figure. Alternatively, either the direct labour hours or the machine hours could be used. Both give an overhead rate of £60,000/15,000 = £4 per hour.

43.2　Predetermined rates

The usual procedure, whether or not standard costing is being used, is to predetermine the overhead absorption rates using budgeted figures for both the overhead costs and the activity measure, whether it be machine or labour hours or something else, such as the direct labour cost. This process has a number of advantages. It not only allows appropriate current estimates to be made for things such as price quotations, but also avoids the problem of overhead rates that fluctuate at different times of the year due to seasonal factors.

For example, an ice-cream manufacturer is likely to be much more active in the summer months than in the winter. Because activity is low in winter, the overhead absorption rate is likely to rise steeply in the winter, as overhead costs will not all reduce proportionately – i.e. they will not all be purely variable in nature. It therefore makes more sense to view the overheads in this type of business on an annual cycle and recover the same amount of overhead throughout the year.

43.3　Variances in overhead recovery

In all situations where budgeted figures are used, there are almost certainly going to be variances at the end of a budget period. Let's take figures from Exhibit 43.1 for Department A as the budget, and compare them with actual performance. This is shown in Exhibit 43.2 on the next page.

The actual machine hours worked of 25,000 will have been used to allocate overheads to production at the rate of £4 per hour. As a result, £100,000 will have been allocated. Compared to actual overheads of £89,000 this represents an overabsorption of £11,000. The recovery would only have been exactly equal to actual overhead costs if 22,250 machine hours had been worked, i.e. 22,250 × £4 = £89,000.

Section 42.8 described the treatment of variances identified when standard costing is used. In a cost accounting system *not* using standard costing, any overabsorption or underabsorption of overheads would be either:

(*a*) transferred wholly to profit or loss for the period;
(*b*) allocated between closing stock and cost of goods sold; or
(*c*) carried forward to the next period.

Exhibit 43.2

	Department A	
	Budget figures	Actual figures
	£	£
Fixed overhead	50,000	52,000
Variable overhead	30,000	37,000
Total overhead	80,000	89,000
Machine hours	20,000	25,000
Machine hour rate £4		

The first would be used if the difference was felt to be due to below 'normal' levels of achievement that could and should have been avoided – i.e. if it represents an 'abnormal' loss or an 'abnormal' gain. For example, if the number of hours worked had dropped due to bad management planning. (This is what you learnt in Sections 37.6 and 37.7, when normal and abnormal losses were discussed.)

The second would be used if the differences were felt to be due to poor estimates of the original budgets. That is, if the activity levels achieved were 'normal' but the budget was based on something either above or below 'normal' activity. As a result, the overheads overabsorbed or underabsorbed represent costs that should be removed/added to the production cost for the period.

The third would apply only to interim financial statements, not those prepared at a period end.

Activity 43.1 Why?

Analysing the variances

The £11,000 variance found in Exhibit 43.2 between the amount recovered of £100,000 and the actual overhead cost of £89,000 can be analysed into a group of constituent variances in the normal manner of standard costing. In the example we have used, the variance can be due to either:

(a) the prices paid for goods and services were different from original estimates or standards – an 'expenditure' variance (sometimes called a 'budget' variance – both terms mean the same thing); or

(b) the volume of activity during the period was different from the original estimate – a 'volume' variance (for fixed overheads) or an 'efficiency' variance (for variable overheads).

Let's look at both these types of variances.

(a) Expenditure variance

An expenditure variance represents the difference between the actual cost of an overhead and its budgeted overhead cost after the level of activity used to calculate the total budgeted overhead cost is adjusted to the actual level of operational activity and the budgeted overhead cost recalculated.

From Exhibit 43.2 the budget figures need to be increased to take account of the fact that activity measured in machine hours has increased from 20,000 to 25,000 hours. **This will not, of** course, increase the fixed overhead – only the variable overheads, which we will assume increase by 25 per cent in line with the increase in the machine hours. (You can see from Exhibit 43.1 that the £4 overhead recovery rate comprised 5/8 (£2.50) for the fixed element and 3/8 (£1.50) for the variable element.) The adjusted budget figures are shown in Exhibit 43.3:

Exhibit 43.3

		Department A		
	a Original budget	b Adjusted budget	c Actual	b – c Variance
Fixed overhead	50,000	50,000	52,000	(2,000)
Variable overhead	30,000	37,500	37,000	500
	80,000	87,500	89,000	(1,500)

The actual expenditure of £89,000 exceeds the adjusted budget by £1,500. You can see from Exhibit 43.3 that this represents an adverse fixed overhead expenditure variance of £2,000 and a favourable variable expenditure variance of £500.

(b) Volume variance

Apart from the cost of the overheads, another factor was included in the calculations when the budgets were originally calculated – the estimated number of machine hours that would be worked. In the above example, we estimated that 20,000 machine hours would be worked. In fact, 25,000 machine hours were worked. This additional 5,000 hours would not matter if *all* the overheads were variable, since the rate per hour would be constant at different activities. However, where fixed costs are concerned, increasing the activity will increase the amount recovered above the level required and, if activity is below budget, insufficient fixed overhead will be recovered.

As you know, in this example the overhead rate of £4 per machine hour was split:

$$\text{Fixed} \qquad \frac{50,000}{80,000} \times £4 = £2.50$$

$$\text{Variable} \qquad \frac{30,000}{80,000} \times £4 = £1.50$$

As a result, when the actual machine hours increased from 20,000 to 25,000 we recovered $5,000 \times £2.50 = £12,500$ more than was actually incurred on the fixed overheads, i.e. there is a favourable variance (a volume variance) of £12,500.

An alternative way of viewing this is to compare the amount of overheads recovered at 25,000 hours with the flexible budget for this level of activity:

	Total		Fixed	Variable
Recovered 25,000 × £4 =		100,000	62,500	37,500
Budget variable cost 25,000 × £1.50	37,500			(37,500)
Fixed cost	50,000		(50,000)	
		(87,500)		
Volume variance		12,500	12,500	–

This volume variance shows that by increasing the utilisation of the fixed resources, considerable savings were made. (This is often the case.) The £12,500 is, therefore, a favourable variance in terms of the original machine-hours-rate-based budget.

Summary of variances

The analysis so far shows:

	£	£
Overhead recovered at actual level of activity (25,000 × £4)		100,000
Fixed overhead variance at this level of activity – adverse	2,000	
Variable overhead variance at this level of activity – favourable	(500)	
		1,500
		101,500
Volume variance – favourable		(12,500)
Actual level of expenditure overhead		89,000

This analysis has revealed that the variances to be investigated are the adverse fixed expenditure variance of £2,000 and the favourable variable expenditure variance of £500. The remaining £12,500 volume variance was due to the increase in activity and has been eliminated from further investigation after the budget was adjusted (i.e. flexed) for the change in activity.

However, while it does not apparently require further investigation, the volume variance does require to be dealt with. As it stands, £12,500 too much has been recovered. That is, production has been charged with £12,500 too much. If you are not operating a standard costing system and if it was due to an error in the estimation of 'normal' activity, you would need to deal with it using the second of the three approaches described earlier in this section – allocate it between closing inventories and the cost of goods sold. (We will return to this variance at the end of the next section.)

This is not the end of the analysis required of the variable variances. You need to do more than simply find the difference between what it should have cost at the actual level of activity (i.e. the flexed budget) and what it actually cost. You need to look at what was actually produced and use that information to identify precisely which variances are to be investigated.

43.4 Assessing variances

In an organisation manufacturing products that has adopted a standard costing system, the cost of the overheads are normally directly related to the products produced. For example, if a Superwidget is manufactured in Department A and it is estimated that it requires 2 machine hours to produce each Superwidget, the standard overhead cost per Superwidget will be 2 × £4 = £8.

If in the actual period, a Superwidget takes less than two hours to make there will be a favourable variance which will be costed at £4 per hour. Similarly, if more than two hours are taken, there will be an adverse (i.e. unfavourable) variance costed on the same basis.

Let's again use the example from Exhibit 43.1 and assume Department A manufactures only Superwidgets, that the original budget is to make 10,000 Superwidgets, and that the actual production of Superwidgets is 12,000. We can now flex the budget using the number of Superwidgets produced. This is shown in Exhibit 43.4.

Now that we are no longer using the machine hours to flex the budget, we can see another variance: 12,000 widgets should take 24,000 hours at the standard rate of 2 machine hours per Superwidget. Since the actual hours are 25,000, 1,000 times £4, i.e. £4,000 too much has been charged to production. In effect, this represents a favourable variance from the machine-hour-based flexed budget as actual costs do not include this £4,000. (This is quite complex as the number of machine hours worked is 1,000 higher than expected, so ought to be an adverse

Exhibit 43.4

	Department A		
	Original budget	*Flexed budget*	*Actual*
	£	£	£
Total overhead expenditure	80,000	96,000	89,000
Machine hours	20,000	24,000	25,000
Machine hours per Superwidget	2	2	
Number of units produced	10,000	12,000	12,000

variance. It would have been had the machine-hour-based overhead rate been used to flex the budget. It was not.) (Note: this is made up of both fixed *and* variable overhead.)

Using the flexed budget, we get a standard overhead recovery at the actual level of output (now based on units produced) of £96,000 (i.e. 12,000 Superwidgets at 2 machine hours each equals 24,000 machine hours at £4 per hour). Actual costs were £89,000. The total variance between the flexed budget figure of £96,000 and the actual expenditure of £89,000 is therefore £7,000. This can be broken down as shown below. (Note, the first two lines would not normally be included as the basis for the budgeted activity has been changed from machine hours to quantity produced. It is included here to illustrate the link between the effect of using the different overhead rate.)

	£
Overhead recovered at actual level of activity (25,000 × £4)	100,000
Variable overhead efficiency variance favourable	(4,000)
Standard cost of overheads for 12,000 actual Superwidgets produced × £8 =	96,000
Variable overhead expenditure variance – favourable (*see* below)	(500)
Variable overhead efficiency variance – adverse (*see* below)	1,500
Fixed overhead expenditure variance – adverse (*see* below)	2,000
Fixed overhead volume variance – favourable (*see* below)	(10,000)
Actual overhead expenditure	89,000

The £4,000 favourable variance represents the amount the overhead over-recovery would have increased had the original machine-hour-based overhead rate been used throughout rather than the output-based rate.

Compare this analysis with the one shown at the end of the *summary of variances* part of Section 43.3. The comparison should tell you three things. Firstly, the choice of the basis on which to flex a budget can significantly affect the information provided concerning the existence of variances and their cause. Secondly, if budgets are not flexed in a timely manner, variances can arise that need to be dealt with in the financial statements and in the valuation of stock that may be significantly greater than they should have been.

Finally, you can now see that the original £12,500 favourable volume variance comprised of favourable variances of £4,000 for the machine hours and a fixed volume variance of £10,000 and an adverse efficiency variance of £1,500. **You will see an alternative interpretation of the £12,500 variance in the next section.**

43.5 Formulae for variances

In this section, we will use the Superwidget example data. The formula for each overhead variance is as follows:

Variable overhead
expenditure variance = Actual cost − (Actual hours worked × Standard rate)

$$= AC − (AH × SR)$$
$$= £37,000 − (25,000 × £1.50) = £500 \text{ Favourable}$$

Variable overhead
efficiency variance = (Actual hours worked − Actual production in
standard hours) × Standard rate

$$= (AH − APSH) × SR$$
$$= (25,000 − 24,000) × £1.50 = £1,500 \text{ Adverse}^{Note\,2}$$

Fixed overhead
expenditure variance = Budgeted fixed production overheads − Actual fixed
production overheads

$$= BFPO − AFPO$$
$$= £50,000 − £52,000 = £2,000 \text{ Adverse}$$

Fixed overhead
volume variance[Note 1] = (Actual production in standard hours × Standard rate)
− Budgeted fixed production overheads

$$= (APSH × SR) − BFPO$$
$$= (24,000 × £2.50) − £50,000 = £10,000 \text{ Favourable}$$

The fixed overhead volume variance can be further divided into:

Fixed overhead
efficiency variance[Note 1] = (Actual hours worked − Actual production in
standard hours) × Standard rate

$$= (AH − APSH) × SR$$
$$= (25,000 − 24,000) × £2.50 = £2,500 \text{ Adverse}$$

Fixed overhead
capacity variance[Note 1] = (Actual hours worked − Budgeted hours to be worked)
× Standard rate

$$= (AH − BH) × SR$$
$$= (25,000 − 20,000) × £2.50 = £12,500 \text{ Favourable}$$

Note 1: The last three variances – the fixed overhead volume variance and its component variances, the fixed overhead efficiency and capacity variances – are only calculated when absorption costing is being used. When the basis of the costing system is marginal costing, only the first three are used (because you do not link fixed costs to the level of output). In a marginal-costing-based environment, the total standard overhead cost for the 12,000 Superwidgets would be 12,000 at £3.00 variable overhead cost per Superwidget (= £36,000) plus the budgeted fixed cost of £50,000.

Rather than simply calculating the fixed overhead volume variance, you should normally calculate the efficiency and capacity variances. However, you need to be aware that together they represent the fixed overhead volume variance and so you should be able to calculate it if required. Replacing the favourable fixed overhead volume variance of £10,000 in the Superwidgets example produces the following breakdown of costs and variances:

	£
Standard cost of overheads for 12,000 actual Superwidgets produced × £8 =	96,000
Variable overhead expenditure variance – *favourable*	(500)
Variable overhead efficiency variance – *adverse*	1,500
Fixed overhead expenditure variance – *adverse*	2,000
Fixed overhead efficiency variance – *adverse*	**2,500**
Fixed overhead capacity variance – *favourable*	**(12,500)**
Actual overhead expenditure	89,000

The formula for the variable overhead efficiency variance is the same formula as is used for the fixed overhead efficiency variance. As you will soon learn, it is also the same as the formula for the labour efficiency variance and the material usage variance.

Note 2: Efficiency variances are adverse when less is recovered than should have been.

43.6 A comprehensive example

The organisation in this example operates standard costing based on absorption costing. The data set out below refers to a cost centre for a particular period:

Budget

Variable overheads (extract) flexible budget

	Output	Cost
In units	*In standard hours*	*£*
9,800	49,000	98,000
9,900	49,500	99,000
10,000	50,000	100,000
10,100	50,500	101,000
10,200	51,000	102,000

Fixed overheads 150,000

Budgeted volume of production 10,000 units

Standard labour hours per unit = 5

Actual

Variable overhead	£104,000
Fixed overhead	£160,000
Direct labour hours worked	49,000 hours
Units of production	9,900 units

The 9,900 units of production is the equivalent of $9,900 \times 5 = 49,500$ standard direct labour hours.

Before calculating the variances, let's consider the data we've been given. The flexible budget shows that each unit of production has a standard variable overhead cost of £10. Alternatively, this can be expressed as £10 ÷ 5 = £2 per standard hour of labour. **It should not be assumed that this rate of £2 also applies to levels of production outside the range shown** – there may well be step costs, such as additional supervision, which **would alter** the standard variable overhead rate at levels of output outside the range shown.

The fixed costs are thought likely to remain fixed provided the range of output does not extend too far above or below the budgeted volume of production. The fixed standard rate is based on the budgeted volume of production and is therefore £150,000 ÷ 50,000 = £3 per standard hour of labour, or £150,000 ÷ 10,000 = £15 per unit.

The standard unit overhead cost is: £10 + £15 = £25 per unit or £2 + £3 = £5 per labour hour.

This budgeted volume of production is likely to be the level of output thought of as being 'normal' and acceptable in the long run. It is referred to as the normal volume of production or, more commonly, as the 'normal level of activity'.

Calculation of variances

Firstly, it is helpful to calculate the overall net variance which is to be analysed. This is found using the standard cost of the actual units produced:

		£
Actual total overhead costs		264,000
Standard cost of actual production 9,900 × £25 =		247,500
Total variance	Adverse	(16,500)

This is broken down into the five component variances as follows.

Variable overhead expenditure variance

		£
Actual cost		104,000
Actual hours worked at standard rate = 49,000 × £2		98,000
Variable expenditure variance	Adverse	(6,000)

Variable overhead efficiency variance

Actual hours worked	49,000			
Actual production in standard hours	49,500			
Variable efficiency variance	500	× £2	Favourable	1,000

Fixed overhead expenditure variance

Budgeted fixed production overheads		150,000
Actual fixed production overheads		160,000
Fixed expenditure variance	Adverse	(10,000)

Fixed overhead efficiency variance

Actual hours worked	49,000			
Actual production in standard hours	49,500			
Variable efficiency variance	500	× £3	Favourable	1,500

Fixed overhead capacity variance

Actual hours worked	49,000			
Budgeted hours to be worked	50,000			
Fixed volume variance	1,000	× £3	Adverse	(3,000)

Summary of variances

Variable expenditure	Adverse	(6,000)
Variable efficiency	Favourable	1,000
Fixed expenditure	Adverse	(10,000)
Fixed efficiency	Favourable	1,500
Fixed capacity	Adverse	(3,000)
	Net Adverse	(16,500)

Reconciliation of standard and actual cost

Standard cost of actual production 9,900 units × £25	(247,500)
Variable expenditure – adverse	(6,000)
Efficiency variance – favourable	1,000
Fixed expenditure – adverse	(10,000)
Fixed efficiency variance – favourable	1,500
Fixed capacity variance – adverse	(3,000)
Actual cost of overheads	(264,000)

43.7 Variances and management action

The calculation of variances and their explanation to managers is of no value unless the information so revealed is used when making decisions which change subsequent activities. The question then arises as to whether every variance needs some form of action. It is not possible to be dogmatic here. It really does depend on the circumstances. In some cases, a fairly large variance may be insignificant whereas, in others, even a small amount may call for urgent action.

There is no doubt that variance calculations of the *right* type, given to the *right* people at the *right* time, which have an effect upon subsequent operations, can make a significant positive impact.

On the other hand, much of the effort put into variance calculation in many organisations just goes to waste, as managers do not act appropriately on the information they have received. There are many reasons why this may occur, some obvious, some less so. However, it is often because a poor 'selling' job has been done by the management accountant on the managers concerned, in that either the information provided is not really what the managers require to enable them to tackle their jobs properly or, as often, because they have not been able to convince the managers that variance analysis is worthwhile. This is the major problem of variance analysis. Many managers and other decision makers view it as an accounting tool which is far too difficult to understand; so they ignore it.

43.8 Sales variances

The analysis of the difference between budgeted sales levels and actual sales levels can obviously have an important bearing on the depth of understanding of results. The main issues which are important in analysing sales are the sales price, volume, and mix. These are analysed using three variances, the:

(*a*) selling price variances
(*b*) volume variances
(*c*) mix variances.

The selling price variance measures the overall profit difference caused by budgeted unit selling price and actual unit selling price being different. If the budget was to sell 100 widgets at £5 each and the actual sales were 100 widgets of £4.50 each, there would be a profit reduction of £50 due to the adverse selling price variance of 50p per unit on the 100 units sold.

The volume variances in sales is measured in terms of the difference between the budgeted and the actual quantity sold. The impact of changes in volume of sales on profit can only be measured if we know the profitability of the units sold. This is considered at gross profit level. Thus, if the budget is to sell 100 widgets with a unit gross margin of £2 but only 90 are sold, this represents an adverse variance of 10 units at the margin of £2, i.e. a loss of profit of £20. If several products are being sold, the variance is calculated on the basis of the total units actually sold in the proportions originally budgeted.

Let's look at an example.

Exhibit 43.5

Product	Budget sales units	Budget %	Budget unit gross profit margin £	Total budget gross profit margin £	Actual sales units	Actual sales in budget %
X	200	33.3	1.00	200	250	240
Y	200	33.3	1.50	300	190	240
Z	200	33.3	3.50	700	280	240
	600	100.0		1,200	720	720

The **volume variance** is calculated by comparing actual sales in the same proportion of total sales as was used in the budget percentage mix with the original budget using the budgeted gross profit margins:

Product	Actual sales in same proportions as budget sales units*	Budget sales units	Difference in units	Budget unit gross profit margin £	Volume variances £
X	240	200	40	1.00	40.00
Y	240	200	40	1.50	60.00
Z	240	200	40	3.50	140.00
	720	600	120		240.00

*Note: Actual sales = 720 therefore, in budget proportions, 720 units would have been sold, $\frac{1}{3}X + \frac{1}{3}Y + \frac{1}{3}Z = 240 + 240 + 240$.

The **mix variance** arises where more than one product is being sold and the different products have different profit margins. If the proportions of the actual sales of the products vary from budget, the overall profit will vary as a consequence, even if the total sales revenue is the same as in the budget.

In the volume variance calculation, the original budget was compared with actual total overall sales volume split between the products in the budget mix. For the mix variance, the actual sales in the budget mix are compared with the actual sales and the differences evaluated at the budgeted gross profit margin.

Exhibit 43.6

Product	Actual units sold	Actual sales in same proportions as budget sales units	Difference in units	Budget unit gross profit margin £	Mix variance £
X	250	240	10	1.00	10
Y	190	240	(50)	1.50	(75)
Z	280	240	40	3.50	140
	720	720	–		75

The difference in mix between budget and actual has increased profit by £75 due to the influence of a higher proportion of sales of product Z which has a higher gross margin than the other products. That is, there is a favourable sales mix variance of £75.

In this example, we assumed the budget and actual selling prices per unit were identical. This is often not the case. Let's look at another example. This time, we will calculate the price variance, then the volume variance and, finally, the mix variance.

Exhibit 43.7

Product	Budget %	Units	Unit selling price £	Unit gross profit margin £	Total profit £	Units	Unit selling price £	Unit gross profit margin £	Total profit £
A	16.7	100	20	5	500	90	21	6	540
B	33.3	200	25	10	2,000	220	24	9	1,980
C	50	300	10	2	600	350	10	2	700
	100	600			3,100	660			3,220

Total variance =	Actual profit	3,220
	Budget profit	(3,100)
	Favourable variance	120

(i) Eliminate the price variance using the actual units sold as the basis.

	Actual units sold 1	Budget price 2 £	Actual price 3 £	Unit variance 3 − 2 = 4 £	Price variance 1 × 4 = 5 £
A	90	20	21	1	90
B	220	25	24	(1)	(220)
C	350	10	10	–	–
				Adverse price variance	(130)

(ii) Eliminate the volume variance using the unit budgeted gross profit to evaluate the variance.

	Actual units sold 1	Budget % 2	Actual sales in same proportions as budget sales units 3 £	Budget sales units 4 £	Difference in units 3 − 4 = 5 £	Budget unit gross margin 6 £	Volume variance 5 × 6 = 7 £
A	90	16.7	110	100	10	5	50
B	220	33.3	220	200	20	10	200
C	350	50	330	300	30	2	60
	660	100	660	600	60		
					Favourable volume variance		310

(iii) Calculate the mix variance.

	Actual units sold 1	Budget % 2	Actual sales in same proportions as budget sales units 3 £	Difference in units 1 − 3 = 4 £	Budget unit gross margin 5 £	Mix variance 4 × 5 = 6 £
A	90	16.7	110	(20)	5	(100)
B	220	33.3	220	–	10	–
C	350	50.0	330	20	2	40
	660		660			
					Adverse mix variance	(60)

Summary of variance:

	£
Adverse price variance	(130)
Favourable volume variance	310
Adverse mix variance	(60)
Favourable total sales variance	120

The gross profit margin may change for many reasons other than changes in sales volume. For example, if the cost of materials varies from budgets or wage rates change, the sales price may be raised in order to preserve the gross profit margin. This type of variance has, however, already been dealt with under materials and labour variances.

Learning outcomes

You should now have learnt:

1 How to calculate overhead and sales variances.

2 The similarities between the variable production overhead efficiency variance and both the labour efficiency variance and the materials usage variance.

3 How to identify appropriate reasons why variances found have occurred.

4 The calculation of variances and their explanation to managers is of no value unless the information so revealed is put to use in making decisions which change subsequent activities.

Answer to activity

43.1 Because they are period costs that must be charged to profit or loss during the accounting period.

Review questions

Advice: **Remember that the overhead variances consist of the difference between the standard costs at the actual level of activity and the actual costs. Remember also that the total sales variance comprises of three variances – price, volume and mix.**

It is important that you answer the parts of the questions that ask you to comment on exactly what might be behind the variances and what action is needed.

43.1 Calculate the appropriate overhead variances from the following data.

(a) Budgeted for £9,000 variable overhead expenditure and 1,500 labour hours of production activity.

Actual variable overhead expenditure	£8,400
Actual labour hours	1,500

(b) Budgeted for £60,000 variable overhead expenditure and 12,000 machine hours of production activity.

Actual variable overhead expenditure	£61,000
Actual machine hours	14,000

(c) Budgeted for £9,750 fixed overhead and the actual fixed overhead is found to be £9,400.
(d) Budgeted for £16,320 fixed overhead and the actual fixed overhead is found to be £16,400.
(e) Budgeted production of 17,000 units in 19,000 hours. Standard variable overhead rate is £4 per hour. In fact, 17,000 units are produced in 18,100 hours.
(f) Budgeted production of 11,500 units in 23,000 hours. Standard variable overhead rate is £6 per hour. In fact, 11,320 units are produced in 26,000 hours.

43.2A Calculate the overhead variances in the following cases:

(a) Budgeted for £19,000 fixed overhead. The actual fixed overhead turns out to be £18,109.
(b) Budgeted for production of 6,000 units in 300 machine hours. The variable overhead rate is £12 per machine hour. In fact, 6,000 units are produced in 280 machine hours.
(c) Budgeted for £28,000 variable overhead and 14,000 labour hours. Actual variable overhead is £28,000 and actual labour hours 13,800.
(d) Budgeted for £12,000 variable overhead and 6,000 machine hours. Actual variable overhead is £11,400 and actual machine hours 6,000.
(e) Budgeted for £84,100 fixed overhead. The actual fixed overhead turns out to be £88,700.
(f) Budgeted for production of 15,000 units in 20,000 machine hours. Standard variable overhead rate is £10 an hour. In fact, 14,600 units are produced in 20,000 machine hours.

43.3 Calculate the overhead variances of Mark & Son Ltd. The budget is prepared as:

(a) Total budgeted variable overhead: £120,000.
(b) Total budgeted fixed overhead: £48,000.
(c) Budgeted level of production activity: 60,000 direct labour hours to produce 50,000 units.

The actual results turn out to be:

(d) Actual variable overhead: £128,000.
(e) Actual fixed overhead: £46,000.
(f) Actual level of production activity was 59,000 direct labour hours which resulted in 52,000 units of production.

43.4A Calculate the overhead variances of Changes Ltd. The budget is prepared as:

(a) Total budgeted variable overhead; £80,000.
(b) Total budgeted fixed overhead; £120,000.
(c) Budgeted level of production activity: 60,000 direct labour hours to produce 240,000 units.

The actual results turn out to be:

(d) Actual variable overhead: £78,000.
(e) Actual fixed overhead: £104,000.
(f) Actual level of production activity was 64,000 direct labour hours which resulted in 236,000 units being produced.

43.5 The Morningside Company Ltd had the following results for the year to 31 December 2007. A single product – a woggley – was made by the company.

	Budget	Actual
Sales in units	140,000	168,000
Sales in £	350,000	403,200

The standard cost of manufacturing each unit was £2.20.

What are the price and volume variances on sales in 2007?

43.6A Felicidade PLC manufactures a detergent in one of its factories. The information for the year to 30 June 2005 was as follows:

	Budget	Actual
Sales in litres	80,000	75,000
Sales in £	480,000	480,000

The standard cost of manufacturing a litre was £3.10.

Calculate the price and volume variances for the year.

→

43.7 The following data was collected for Metal Chain Ltd for the year ended 31 October 2008.

Product	Budget selling price £	Budget sales units	%	Budget gross profit per unit £	Budget gross profit total £	Actual selling price £	Actual sales unit	%	Actual gross profit per unit £	Actual gross profit total £
A	6	1,000	25	2.00	2,000	8.20	1,224	34	1.90	2,325.60
B	9	2,000	50	2.50	3,000	11.60	2,160	60	2.30	4,830.00
C	8	1,000	25	2.20	2,200	10.90	216	6	2.20	475.20
		4,000	100		7,200		3,600	100		7,630.80

Calculate the price, volume and mix variances for the year.

43.8A The following information relates to The Melted Cheese Company Ltd for the year to 31 December 2011:

Product	Budget units	Sales %	Budget selling price per unit £	Budget gross profit per unit £	Actual units	Sales %	Actual unit selling price £	Actual unit gross profit £
X	800	14.3	60	10	1,000	20.8	58	8
Y	1,200	21.4	50	8	800	16.7	54	10
Z	3,600	64.3	80	20	3,000	62.5	78	18
	5,600	100.0			4,800	100.0		

Calculate the price, volume and mix variances for 2011.

43.9 Singleton has been operating for some years as a manufacturer of a single product, and after several years' growth has decided to form a company Singleton Ltd.

His accountant advised him that in an increasingly competitive world he really should achieve greater financial control of his business, and to assist Singleton in this objective the accountant prepared a simple manufacturing budget for the financial year ending 31 August 2009.

The following schedule provides the detail of the budget and the actual results for the year ended 31 August 2009. The actual results have been extracted from the ledger as at that date without any adjustments made.

	Budget £	Actual £
Raw materials consumed	80,000	90,000
Factory rent	10,000	12,500
Factory maintenance expenses	6,700	6,100
Heating and lighting	2,900	3,000
Direct labour wages	120,000	110,500
Direct expenses	5,800	6,000
Depreciation of plant and machinery	8,900	10,500
Wages, maintenance labour	18,000	24,000
Other factory overheads	12,700	9,600

Additional information:

1 At 31 August 2009 the following amounts were still owing:

	£
Direct labour wages	5,100
Heating and lighting	900
Other factory overhead	400

2 The factory rent paid covered the period from 1 September 2008 to 30 November 2009.
3 During the year the firm sold 90,000 units of its product at £4.50 a unit.
4 There was no work-in-progress. The stocks of finished goods were:

		£
1 September 2008		28,900
31 August 2009		35,000

Required:

(a) What is variance analysis and how can it contribute to the operating efficiency of Singleton's business?

(b) For the year ended 31 August 2009 prepare:
   (i) A manufacturing account and a schedule of the relevant variances;
   (ii) A trading account.

(c) Write a report to advise Singleton whether the principles of budgeting can be applied to:
   (i) Non-manufacturing costs;
   (ii) The control of cash resources.

Your report should indicate in each case the potential benefits that the firm could achieve through extending its use of budgeting.

(AQA (Associated Examining Board): GCE A-level)

43.10A Flint Palatignium Ltd calculates the prices of its output by adding a mark-up of 15 per cent to standard costs. These standard costs are arrived at by reference to budgeted outputs and estimated direct costs as follows:

	£ each	Standard price/rate
Materials	5.00	£1 per unit
Direct labour	2.50	£1.25 per hour
Overheads	7.50	£3.75 per direct labour hour
	15.00	
Mark-up	2.25	
Selling price	17.25	

Management accounts for April, 2008 provide an analysis of operations as follows:

	£
Sales – at standard price	534,750
Standard margin on sales	69,750
Favourable sales price variance	8,691
	78,441
Other favourable variances	
Material price	4,662
Labour rate	600
Overhead expenditure	147
	83,850
Adverse variances	
Material usage	(1,743)
Labour efficiency	(292)
Overhead capacity	(9)
Actual operating profit	81,806

Materials in stock are valued at standard cost. At 1 April, 1,000 units of material were held, whereas at 30 April the stock of this material increased to 1,750 units.

Required:

(i) A trading account for the month of April 2008 comparing the budgeted income and expenditure appropriate to actual output, to actual income and expenditure.

$\rightarrow$

→

(ii) An explanation of the value of standard costing and variance analysis to a service business whose custom is to negotiate fixed price contracts.

(Welsh Joint Education Committee: GCE A-level)

(*Note*: The following question covers material from both Chapters 42 and 43.)

43.11A HGW Limited produces a product called a Lexton. The standard selling price and the manufacturing costs of this product are as follows:

		£
Standard selling price per unit		86
Standard production costs:		
Direct material	1.5 kilos at £12 per kilo	18
Direct labour	4.4 hours at £7.50 per hour	33
Variable overheads	4.4 hours at £5 per hour	22
		73

The projected production and sales for March 2004 were 520 units.

On 1 April 2004 the following actual figures were determined.

Sales	550 units at £85 each
Production	550 units
Direct material	785 kilos at £12.40 per kilo
Direct labour	2,400 hours at £7.80 per hour
Overheads	£12,500 (overall variance £400 adverse)

There was no opening stock of the product Lexton.

Required:
(*a*) Prepare an actual profit and loss account for HGW Ltd for March 2004.
(*b*) Calculate the following variances and their respective sub-variances:
   (*i*) sales – price and volume
   (*ii*) direct materials – price and usage
   (*iii*) direct labour – rate and efficiency.
(*c*) Prepare a statement reconciling the actual profit calculated in part (*a*) with the budgeted profit on actual sales. (Use the variances calculated in part (*b*) and the given overhead variance.)
(*d*) Write a report to the management outlining the factors that need to be considered when standards are being established.

(AQA (Associated Examining Board): GCE A-level)

You can find a range of additional self-test questions, as well as material to help you with your studies, on the website that accompanies this book at **www.pearsoned.co.uk/wood**

Part

9

PLANNING, CONTROL AND DECISION MAKING

Introduction

This part looks at how accounting information may be used to guide decision making within an entity, at how the cost of investment is calculated, and at how organisations are beginning to use the information available to them to provide a richer view of the performance of the organisation than is possible from straightforward ratio analysis.

Breakeven analysis

Learning objectives

After you have studied this chapter, you should be able to:

● explain what is meant by 'breakeven'
● prepare breakeven graphs and contribution graphs
● explain the importance of contribution and fixed costs in identifying the breakeven level of sales
● use graphs to identify breakeven point, the margin of safety and the contribution for any level of activity
● use breakeven graphs to show the impact of changes in costs, volume and selling price upon profitability
● describe some of the limitations of breakeven charts
● use a formula in order to calculate the breakeven point
● explain the relevance of contribution to decision making

Introduction

In this chapter, you'll learn about breakeven analysis and, at the same time, about the relationship between costs, volume, selling price and profit.

44.1 Introduction

The level of activity achieved by a business is of great importance in determining both whether or not it makes a profit or loss, and the size of such profits or losses. Let's take an example to which the answer is obvious. If a business has fixed costs of £100,000 and its total revenue is £80,000 then, no matter how much the variable costs are, the business is bound to make a loss. A business has to cover both its fixed costs and its variable costs before it can make a profit. With revenue below the level of fixed costs, as in this case, a loss is bound to arise.

There is, therefore, a great deal of interest in exactly how much revenue (i.e. sales) has to be earned before a profit can be made. If revenue is below fixed costs, a loss will be incurred; if revenue is below total costs (i.e. fixed costs + variable costs) a loss will still be incurred. However, when revenue is greater than the combined total of the fixed and variable costs, a profit will have been made. The question is, at what level of sales does the business stop incurring a loss and, with the next unit of revenue, make a profit? That is, at what point does it break even and make neither a profit nor a loss?

Fixed costs stay unchanged over stated ranges in the volume of production, but variable costs change *in total* when the volume of production changes within a stated range. As revenue increases so do variable costs, so that the only item that remains unchanged is that of fixed costs. Let's look at an example showing the changing costs and revenues over differing volumes of production.

Apollo Ltd has fixed costs of £5,000. The variable costs are £2 per unit. The revenue (selling price) is £3 per unit. Looking at production in stages of 1,000 units we can see:

Exhibit 44.1

No. of units	Fixed cost	Variable cost	Total cost: Variable + Fixed	Revenue (Sales)	Profit	Loss
	£	£	£	£	£	£
0	5,000	nil	5,000	nil		5,000
1,000	5,000	2,000	7,000	3,000		4,000
2,000	5,000	4,000	9,000	6,000		3,000
3,000	5,000	6,000	11,000	9,000		2,000
4,000	5,000	8,000	13,000	12,000		1,000
5,000	5,000	10,000	15,000	15,000	nil	nil
6,000	5,000	12,000	17,000	18,000	1,000	
7,000	5,000	14,000	19,000	21,000	2,000	
8,000	5,000	16,000	21,000	24,000	3,000	
9,000	5,000	18,000	23,000	27,000	4,000	

With an activity level of 5,000 units, the business will break even. It will make neither a profit nor a loss. Above that it moves into profit; below that, it never makes a profit.

We could have calculated the breakeven point without drawing up a schedule of costs, etc. as in Exhibit 44.1. Instead we could have said that for one unit the revenue is £3 and the variable cost is £2, so that the remaining £1 is the amount out of which the fixed costs have to be paid, and that anything left over is profit.

The £1 is the 'contribution' towards fixed costs and profit. If the contribution was only just enough to cover fixed costs, there would be no profit, but neither would there be any loss. There are £5,000 fixed costs, so that with a contribution of £1 per unit there would have to be 5,000 units to provide a contribution of £5,000 to cover fixed costs. It could be stated as:

$$\text{Breakeven point} = \frac{\text{Fixed costs}}{\text{Selling price per unit} - \text{Variable costs per unit}}$$

i.e. in the case of Apollo Ltd

$$\frac{£5,000}{£3 - £2} = \frac{5,000}{1} = 5,000 \text{ units}$$

 Activity 44.1 If fixed costs were £7,000 and the contribution per unit were £2, what would be the breakeven level of sales?

44.2 The breakeven chart

The information given in Exhibit 44.1 can also be shown in the form of a chart. Many people seem to grasp the idea of breakeven analysis rather more easily when they see it in chart form. This is particularly true for anyone who is not used to dealing with accounting information. We will, therefore, plot the figures from Exhibit 44.1 on a chart which is shown as Exhibit 44.2.

The use of the chart can now be looked at. It would be extremely useful if you could draw the chart as shown in Exhibit 44.2 on a piece of graph paper. The larger the scale that you use, the easier it will be to take accurate readings. Plot the lines from the figures shown in Exhibit 44.1.

Exhibit 44.2

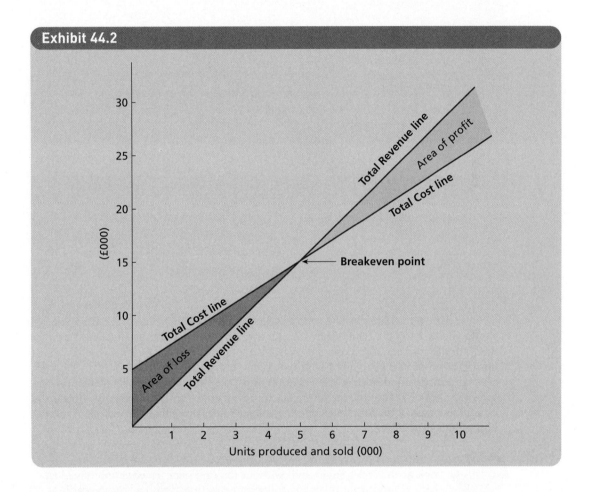

To find the **breakeven point** in terms of units of product, draw a line straight down from the breakeven point so that it meets the horizontal axis at right angles. This is shown in Exhibit 44.3 as line A which, when read off, gives units of production and sales as 5,000 units.

Exhibit 44.3

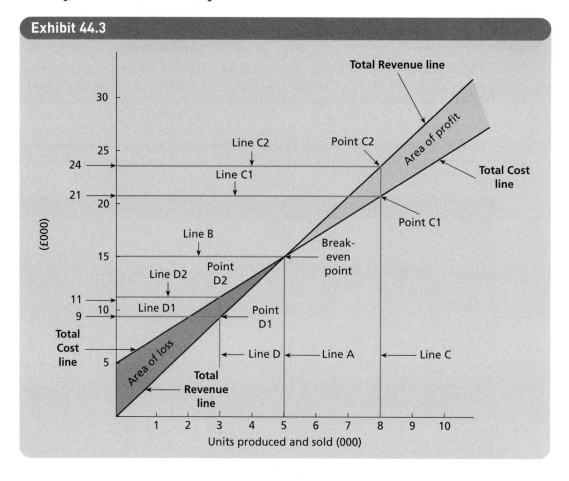

Now draw a line direct to the vertical £s axis so that it meets that at a right angle. This is line B and shows £15,000. This means that according to the chart the breakeven point is shown at 5,000 units where both costs and revenue are equal at £15,000. This is, of course, the same answer as given in the table in Exhibit 44.1.

As production and sales go above 5,000 units, the firm makes profits. When production and sales are above 5,000 units, the difference represents the '**margin of safety**'. **This is the number of units in excess of the breakeven point. If volume fell by more than the margin of safety, the business would incur losses.**

Activity 44.2

Look at the chart again and, without looking back at what you have just read, attempt to answer the following two questions by taking readings off your chart:

(*i*) What would the total costs of the firm be at (*a*) 2,000 units, (*b*) 7,000 units, (*c*) 8,500 units?

(*Remember*: take a line up from the product line for the figure needed then, from where the cost line is bisected, draw a line to the £s line to meet it at right angles.)

(*ii*) What is the revenue for (*a*) 3,000 units, (*b*) 6,000 units, (*c*) 7,500 units?

Before proceeding further, look at the answers to this activity.

Now we will try to find the amount of profit or loss at various levels by looking at the chart in Exhibit 44.3. First, let's calculate the profit made if 8,000 units are going to be made and sold. Draw a line up from the product line (horizontal axis) at right angles (shown as line C) until it bisects both the Total Cost line and the Total Revenue line, the points of intersection being shown as C1 for the Total Cost line and C2 for the Total Revenue line. Read off the amounts in £s by taking lines across to the £s vertical axis until they meet it at right angles. These are shown as lines C1 and C2. The line from C1 will give a reading of £21,000 and from C2 of £24,000. As the Total Revenue exceeds the Total Costs there is a profit. In this case, the profit is £3,000.

If we now try for 3,000 units, the line drawn up from the product line will meet the Total Revenue line at point D1 and the Total Cost line at D2. Reading off to the £s line D1 shows as £9,000 while D2 shows as £11,000. In this case, the Total Cost exceeds the Total Revenue by £2,000 and there is, therefore, a loss of £2,000.

Activity 44.3

Look at your chart again and use it to find the profit or loss recorded at

(a) 1,000 units, (b) 4,000 units, (c) 6,500 units and (d) 8,500 units.

Before proceeding, look at the answers to this activity at the end of the chapter.

44.3 Changes and breakeven charts

The effect of changes on profits can easily be shown by drawing fresh lines on the chart to show the changes, or intended changes, in the circumstances of the firm. Let's first consider some factors that can bring about a change in profits:

(a) the selling price per unit could be increased (or decreased);
(b) a possible decrease (or increase) in fixed costs;
(c) a possible decrease (or increase) in variable costs per unit;
(d) increase the volume of production and sales.

We will investigate these by starting with some basic information for a business and then seeing what would happen if each of the changes (a) to (d) were to happen.

The basic information is shown in Exhibit 44.4:

Exhibit 44.4

No. of units	Fixed cost	Variable cost	Total cost: Variable + Fixed	Revenue (Sales)	Profit	Loss
	£	£	£	£	£	£
100	2,000	400	2,400	900		1,500
200	2,000	800	2,800	1,800		1,000
300	2,000	1,200	3,200	2,700		500
400	2,000	1,600	3,600	3,600	nil	nil
500	2,000	2,000	4,000	4,500	500	
600	2,000	2,400	4,400	5,400	1,000	
700	2,000	2,800	4,800	6,300	1,500	
800	2,000	3,200	5,200	7,200	2,000	
900	2,000	3,600	5,600	8,100	2,500	

The table in Exhibit 44.4 shows that variable costs are £4 per unit and selling price £9 per unit. (These figures are found by dividing the variable cost and revenue values at any number of units by that number of units. For example, dividing £400 variable cost by 100 gives £4 variable cost per unit.)

We can draw a chart to incorporate this information before considering the changes being contemplated. This is shown in Exhibit 44.5:

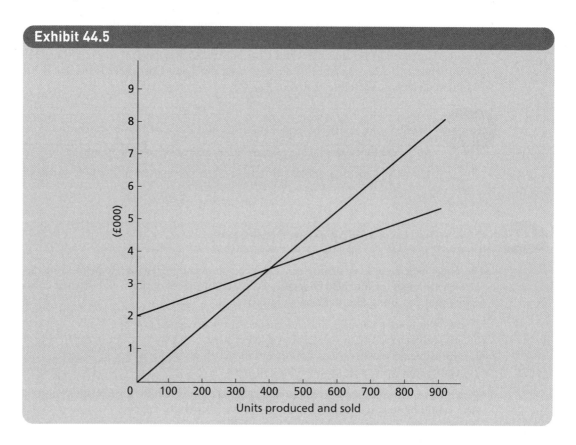

Exhibit 44.5

(a) Increase selling price

Taking the chart shown in Exhibit 44.5 as a base, we can now draw an extra line on it to represent an increase in selling price. Let us suppose that the selling price could be increased by £2 per unit. This can now be shown on a breakeven chart in Exhibit 44.6. The line shown as New Total Revenue can then be added. This would mean that the breakeven point would change as the increased revenue means that costs can be covered sooner. The dotted area shows the reduction in the loss area that would be incurred at the same volume of sales, while the shaded area shows the increase in profit at the various volumes of sales.

Exhibit 44.6

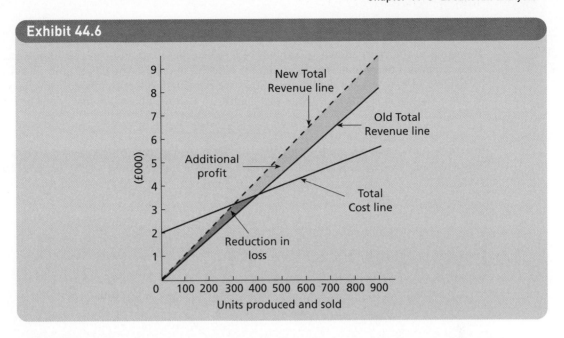

(b) Reduce fixed costs

We can now draw some more lines on the chart shown in Exhibit 44.6, this time to reflect a reduction of £800 in fixed costs. This can be seen in Exhibit 44.7, where a line entitled New Total Cost has been added. The reduction in loss if sales were at a low volume is represented by the dotted area, while the shaded area shows the additional profit at various volumes of activity. The change in profit or loss will be constant at £800 over these volumes.

Exhibit 44.7

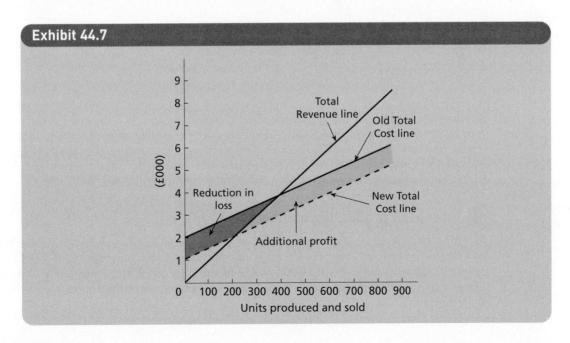

(c) Reduce variable costs

Reverting to the chart shown in Exhibit 44.6 (where the fixed costs are £2,000), we can see what happens if the variable costs per unit are reduced, in this case by £2 per unit. This is shown in Exhibit 44.8, where the dotted area shows the reduction in loss compared with the position if the costs had not changed, while the shaded area shows the additional profit at different levels of activity.

Exhibit 44.8

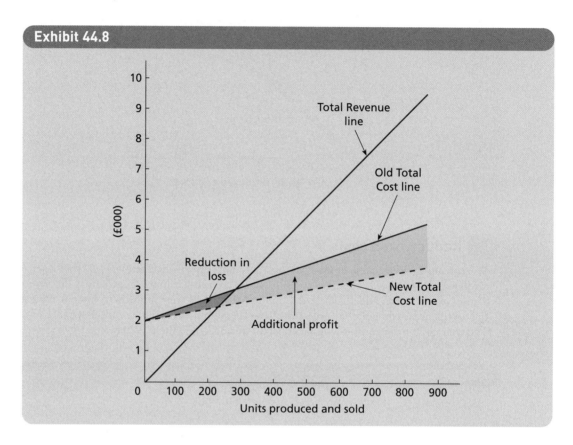

You will recall that an £800 reduction in fixed costs in Exhibit 44.7 showed a constant difference of £800 in profit compared with previously over the whole range of activity. In contrast, a reduction in variable costs (as in Exhibit 44.8) brings about different increases of profit, or reduction of loss, over the whole range of activity. The greater the activity the greater the gain with variable cost savings, whereas the gain remains constant with fixed cost savings.

(d) Increased production and sales

Reverting once more to the original position as shown in Exhibit 44.5, when sales and/or production increase, all that is required is that the lines Total Revenue and Total Cost are extended. Exhibit 44.9 shows Exhibit 44.5 with the level of activity increased by 300 units. The new profit indicated will be greater than the old profit because all extra units are being sold at a profit.

Exhibit 44.9

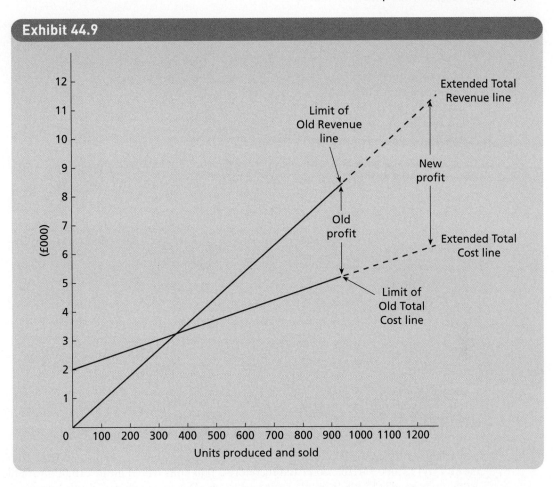

44.4 The limitations of breakeven charts

In each of the cases looked at it has been assumed that only one of the factors of variable cost, fixed cost, selling price or volume of sales has altered. This is not usually the case. An increase in price may well reduce the number sold. There may well be an increase in fixed cost which has an effect which brings down variable costs. The changes in the various factors should, therefore, be studied simultaneously rather than separately.

In addition, **where there is more than one product, the proportions in which the products are sold, i.e. the product mix, can have a very important bearing on costs.** Suppose that there are two products, one has a large amount of fixed costs but hardly any variable costs, and the other has a large amount of variable costs but little fixed costs. If the proportions in which each is sold change very much then this could mean that the costs and profit could vary tremendously, even though the total figures of sales stayed constant. An illustration of this can be seen in Exhibit 44.10:

Exhibit 44.10

In considering the breakeven analysis we may expect that the following will occur.

Fixed costs £1,000, Variable costs: Product A £5 per unit, B £20 per unit.
Selling prices: A £10 per unit, B £30 per unit.
Expected sales: A 150, B 50. Actual sales: A 30, B 90.

The expected sales are: A 150 × £10 + B 50 × £30 = £3,000.
The actual sales are: A 30 × £10 + B 90 × £30 = £3,000.

The actual sales revenue and expected sales revenue are the same, but the sales mix is different, as are the costs and profit:

			£
Expected:			
Sales			3,000
Less Variable costs:	A 150 × £5 =	750	
	B 50 × £20 =	(1,000)	
			(1,750)
Contribution			1,250
Less Fixed costs			1,000
Net profit			250
Actual:			
Sales			3,000
Less Variable costs:	A 30 × £5 =	150	
	B 90 × £20 =	1,800	
			(1,950)
Contribution			1,050
Less Fixed costs			(1,000)
Net profit			50

Variable costs are usually taken to be in direct proportion to volume, so that 1,000 units means (say) £5,000 variable costs and therefore 2,000 units would mean £10,000 variable costs, 3,000 units equal £15,000 variable costs and so on. This is often a reasonable estimation of the situation, but may well hold true only within fairly tight limits. For instance 3,100 units could mean £16,000 costs instead of the £15,500 that it would be if a linear relationship existed. This is also true of sales, because to increase sales beyond certain points some units may be sold cheaply. Thus 1,000 units might be sold for £9,000; 2,000 units sold for £18,000; but to sell 2,200 units the revenue might be only £19,100 instead of the £19,800 (2,200 × £9) that might be expected if a linear relationship existed over all ranges.

It is assumed that everything produced is sold, and that inventory remain constant. It would be difficult to do otherwise as both sales revenue and costs relate to one and the same measure of volume.

Another limitation is more of a complication than a hindrance. Organisations considering a change in the level of activity outside the current range may well be faced with changed fixed costs as a result. For example, a new warehouse may need to be leased in order to cope with the extra production. In that case, the breakeven graphs produced need to incorporate stepped fixed costs that increase to a new fixed level once the threshold in activity for the higher cost has been reached. This can result in multiple breakeven points.

44.5 Contribution graph

Exhibit 44.11 is a redrafting of Exhibit 44.5 that includes the addition of a line representing variable cost. It runs parallel to and below the total cost line. This is an alternative method of presentation.

It highlights the total contribution. The vertical gap between the Total Cost line and the Variable Cost line at any particular number of units represents the contribution at that number of units.

Exhibit 44.11

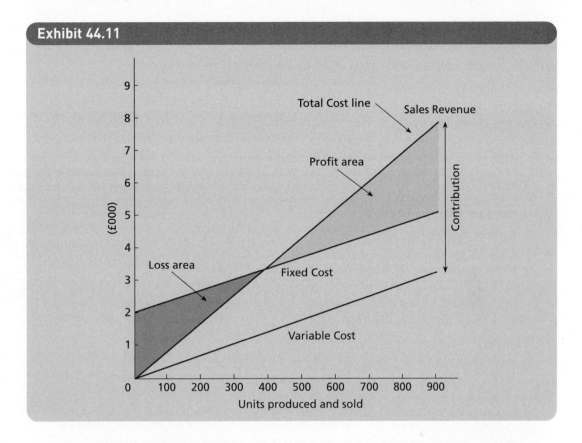

Learning outcomes

You should now have learnt:

1 How to prepare breakeven graphs and contribution graphs.

2 That breakeven analysis can be performed using either a formula or a graph.

3 How to use graphs to identify breakeven point, the margin of safety and the contribution for any level of activity.

4 How to use a formula in order to calculate the breakeven point.

5 Fixed costs are assumed to be fixed for the range of activity being considered, and variable costs per unit and sales revenue per unit are assumed to be constant within that range of activity. It is important to check whether these assumptions are correct when carrying out a breakeven analysis. If they are not, the format of the analysis should be adjusted appropriately.

6 How to use breakeven graphs to show the impact of changes in costs, volume and selling price upon profitability.

7 How to explain the relevance of contribution to decision making.

Answers to activities

44.1 3,500 units.

44.2 (*i*) (*a*) £9,000 (*b*) £19,000 (*c*) £22,000

(*ii*) (*a*) £9,000 (*b*) £18,000 (*c*) £22,500

44.3 (*a*) Loss £4,000 (*b*) Loss £1,000 (*c*) Profit £1,500 (*d*) Profit £3,500

Review questions

Advice: The very important concept of breakeven attracts quite a large number of questions. Be careful when drawing any charts, as a faulty chart will give you wrong answers for every part of your answer and you are unlikely to get marks for those wrong answers. You cannot expect examiners to assume that your faulty drawing of a graph was a simple error of draughtsmanship instead of being conceptual.

44.1 Hedges Ltd has fixed costs of £8,000. The variable costs are £4 per unit. The revenue (selling price) is £6 per unit. **You are required** (*i*) to draft a schedule as follows filling in the columns (*a*) to (*f*) for each stage of 1,000 units up to 10,000 units.

No. of units	(a) Fixed cost £	(b) Variable cost £	(c) Total cost £	(d) Revenue £	(e) Profit £	(f) Loss £
0						
1,000						
2,000						
3,000						
4,000						
5,000						
6,000						
7,000						
8,000						
9,000						
10,000						

(*ii*) **You are also required to** draw a breakeven chart from the data in this schedule. Draw it carefully to scale on a piece of graph paper. Retain your answer, you will need it for some questions which follow later.

44.2 Cover up the schedule you constructed as your answer to 44.1(*i*) and look instead at the breakeven chart constructed as the answer to 44.1(*ii*). **Answer the following:**

(*a*) What are the total costs at production levels of (*i*) 4,000 units; (*ii*) 7,000 units; (*iii*) 9,000 units; (*iv*) 5,500 units?
(*b*) What is the total revenue at (*i*) 3,000 units; (*ii*) 8,000 units; (*iii*) 5,500 units?

44.3A Look at your schedule in answer to 44.1(*i*) and **answer the following:**

(*a*) What are the total costs at production levels of (*i*) 4,000 units; (*ii*) 7,000 units; (*iii*) 9,000 units; (*iv*) 5,500 units? You will have to deduce this amount as it is not shown as a figure on the schedule.
(*b*) What is the total revenue at (*i*) 3,000 units; (*ii*) 8,000 units; (*iii*) 5,500 units?

44.4 From your breakeven chart for 44.1(*ii*), **calculate** the profit or loss that will be made at levels of (*i*) 3,000 units; (*ii*) 10,000 units; (*iii*) 4,000 units; (*iv*) 7,000 units; (*v*) 8,500 units.

44.5A From the schedule in 44.1(*i*), **calculate** the profit or loss that would be made at levels of (*i*) 3,000 units; (*ii*) 10,000 units; (*iii*) 4,000 units; (*iv*) 7,000 units; (*v*) 8,500 units (this last figure will have to be deduced as it is not a figure on the schedule).

44.6 Polemic Ltd manufacture and sell a single product. The following information is available for three financial years ending 30 September.

	Price per unit	Unit volume 000s
Sales	£	
Actual 2001	130	50
Forecast 2002	129	52
Forecast 2003	128.5	53

Costs per unit	Actual	Forecast	
Produced	2001	2002	2003
	£	£	£
Direct materials	50	55	55
Direct labour	30	31.5	33
Variable production overhead	10	11	12
Direct expenses	5	5	6
Variable sales overhead	15	16	16

Other costs for the year	£	£	£
	000	000	000
Fixed production overhead	50	55	55
Other fixed overhead	200	220	220

Additional information:
1 When the management of Polemic prepared its direct labour forecast unit cost for 2002 and 2003, direct wages were increased only by the forecast rate of inflation.
2 The trade union representatives of the production workers wished to press for a greater wage increase. They suggested that:

(*i*) Direct wages be increased at twice the rate of inflation. The effect of this would be to increase direct labour costs per unit as follows:

	2002	2003
	£	£
Direct labour	33.0	35.0

(*ii*) Unit selling prices be increased in order to cover the increased labour costs.

3 It is to be assumed that all expense and revenue relationships will be unchanged except where indicated.

Required:
(*a*) A schedule for 2001, 2002 and 2003 for Polemic Ltd showing:
  (*i*) the breakeven points;
  (*ii*) the net profit for each year.
  Base your calculations on the original labour costs.
(*b*) A graph showing a breakeven point for 2002.
(*c*) Advise Polemic Ltd's management as to their response to the trade union's claim for higher wages. Include relevant financial analysis.
(*d*) Explain the limitation of breakeven analysis.

(AQA (Associated Examining Board): GCE A-level)

→

44.7A The relationship between income/cost/volume suggests that there are four ways by which profit can be increased. These are:

1 Increase unit selling price.
2 Decrease unit variable cost.
3 Decrease fixed costs.
4 Increase volume.

Assume that the current situation for a product is as follows:

Sales volume	1,000 units
Selling price	£2 each
Variable cost	£1 per unit
Fixed costs	£500

You are required to:
(*a*) draw **four** separate breakeven charts showing the effect of the following changes on the current situation:
   (*i*)   a 10 per cent increase in volume,
   (*ii*) a 10 per cent increase in unit selling price,
   (*iii*) a 10 per cent decrease in unit variable cost,
   (*iv*) a 10 per cent reduction in fixed costs.
(*b*) Use your charts to state the additional profit resulting from **each** change.

(*AQA (Northern Examinations and Assessment Board): GCE A-level*)

44.8 At the monthly senior management meeting of Hampshire plc on 1 May 2010, various suggestions were made to improve the profit to be made by selling the firm's single product in the last quarter of the year ending 30 September 2010. The product is not subject to seasonal demand fluctuations, but there are several competitors producing similar items. In the first quarter of the year a suggestion was made that profit could be improved if the selling price were reduced by 5 per cent, and this was put into effect at the beginning of the second quarter. As the new price undercut that of the rival firms, demand increased, and the firm's breakeven point was reduced.

The following suggestions have now been raised:

(*i*)   Differentiate the product from its rivals by giving it a more distinctive shape, colour and packaging. This would increase material costs per unit by £0.30, but selling price would not be raised. Demand is then predicted to rise by 10 per cent;
(*ii*) Improve the quality of the product by strengthening it and giving it a one-year guarantee – material costs would then increase by £0.15 per unit and labour costs by £0.30 per unit. Selling price would rise by £0.40 per unit, and demand increase by 7 per cent;
(*iii*) Further reduce the selling price by 10 per cent – demand to rise by 20 per cent;
(*iv*) Pay commission plus salaries instead of fixed salaries only to all sales staff. Variable selling costs would then rise by £0.20 per unit, but fixed costs would fall by £4,100 per quarter;
(*v*) Subcontract the making of some components, and close the department responsible, making six staff redundant at an estimated cost to the firm of £12,000. 30,000 components are currently made per quarter. Each component's variable cost is £0.55. They can be bought from a recently established firm for £0.60 per unit. The department's share of the firm's fixed costs is 20 per cent and £2,500 fixed costs per quarter would cease to arise if the department were to be closed.

Data for:	First quarter	Second quarter
Number of units produced and sold	9,000	10,800
	£	£
Selling price per unit	14	13.30
Materials per unit	3.65	3.65
Labour per unit	2.10	2.10
Variable factory overhead per unit	1.40	1.40
Variable selling costs per unit	0.85	0.85
Fixed factory overhead	21,375	21,375
Fixed selling and administration costs	16,125	16,125

Required:
A. Calculate the profit made in each of the first and second quarters, showing clearly the contribution per unit in each case.
B. Draw one breakeven chart showing the total costs and total revenues for the first and second quarters. You should label clearly the two breakeven points and margins of safety.
C. Taking each suggestion independently, calculate the profit that might be made in the last quarter if each of them were to be implemented.
D. Discuss the implications for the firm of undertaking suggestions (*i*)–(*iv*), and for the firm and the local community of undertaking suggestion (*v*).
E. Explain to the senior managers how, while breakeven analysis is useful, it has limitations.

(Reproduced with the kind permission of the OCR: from *University of Oxford Delegacy of Local Examinations: GCE A-level*)

44.9A You are employed by Monarch Ltd which manufactures specialist hydraulic seals for the aircraft industry. The company has developed a new seal with the following budgeted data:

Variable cost per unit	£
Direct materials	8
Direct labour	4
Variable overheads	4
	16

The draft budget for the following year is as follows:

Production and sales	60,000 units

	£
Fixed cost: Production	260,000
Administration	90,000
Selling, marketing and distribution	100,000
Contribution	840,000

Certain departmental managers within the company believe there is room for improvement on the budgeted figures, and the following options have been suggested.

(*i*) The sales manager has suggested that if the selling price was reduced by 10 per cent, then an extra 30 per cent units could be sold. The purchasing manager has indicated that if materials requirements were increased in line, then a materials price reduction of 6.25 per cent could be negotiated. With this additional output, fixed production costs would increase by £30,000, administration by £5,000 and selling, marketing and distribution by £10,000. Other costs would remain unchanged.

(*ii*) The export manager has suggested that if the company increased overseas marketing by £15,000 then exports would increase from 15,000 units to 17,000 units. With this suggestion, distribution costs would increase by £12,000, and all other costs would remain unchanged.

(*iii*) The marketing manager has suggested that if an extra £40,000 were spent on advertising, then sales quantity would increase by 25 per cent. The purchasing manager has indicated that in such circumstances, materials costs would reduce by £0.30 per unit. With this suggestion fixed production costs would increase by £25,000, administration by £4,000 and other selling, marketing and distribution costs by £7,000. All other costs would remain unchanged.

(*iv*) The managing director believes the company should be aiming for a profit of £486,000. He asks what the selling price would be per unit if marketing were increased by £50,000, this leading to an estimated increase in sales quantity of 30 per cent. Other fixed costs would increase by £67,000, whilst material prices would decrease by 6.25 per cent per unit. All other costs would remain unchanged.

Required:
(a) Taking each suggestion independently, compile a profit statement for options (*i*) to (*iii*), showing clearly the contribution per unit in each case. For suggestion (*iv*), calculate the selling price per unit as requested by the managing director.

→

→ (b) Calculate the breakeven quantity in units if the managing director's suggestion were implemented. Draw a contribution/sales graph to illustrate your calculations.
Read from the graph the profit if 60,000 units were sold.

(c) Whilst marginal costing has a number of applications, it also has disadvantages. In a report to the managing director, outline the main applications of marginal costing and explain its disadvantages.

(Reproduced with the kind permission of the OCR: from *University of Oxford Delegacy of Local Examinations: GCE A-level*)

44.10 Magwitch Limited's finance director produced the following forecast breakeven chart for the year ending 31 May 2011:

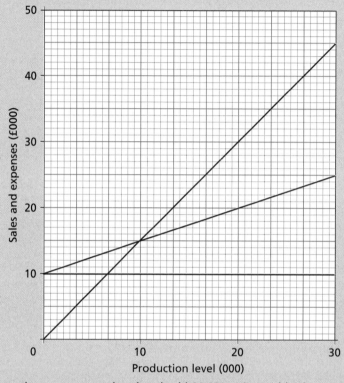

During the year the company produced and sold 20,000 units, and both revenue and expenses were 10 per cent higher than forecast.

Compeyson plc has made an agreed takeover bid for the company at a value of twelve times the net profit for the year ending 31 May 2011.

Magwitch's assets and liabilities are to be taken over at their balance sheet values, with the exception of fixed assets, which are to be revalued at £93,000.

The summarised balance sheets of Magwitch Limited and Compeyson plc at the takeover date of 31 May 2011 are as follows:

	Magwitch	Compeyson
	£000	£000
Fixed assets	32	160
Current assets	65	340
Current liabilities	(26)	(110)
	71	390
Share capital (£1 shares)	40	200
Reserves	31	190
	71	390

The terms of the takeover are that Compeyson plc will give three of its shares (value £1.80 each) for every two shares in Magwitch Limited, plus a cash payment to make up the total agreed takeover price.

Magwitch Limited will cease to trade on 31 May 2011, and its assets and liabilities will be assumed by Compeyson plc. Any goodwill arising is to be written-off immediately against reserves.

(a) Draw up a summarised profit and loss account for Magwitch Limited for the year ending 31 May 2011.
(b) Draw up a balance sheet for Compeyson plc after the takeover of Magwitch Limited has taken place.
(c) Calculate how many shares and how much cash would be received by a holder of 6,000 shares in Magwitch Limited as a result of the takeover.

(*Edexcel: GCE A-level*)

44.11A
(a) How far is it true to state that a company's breakeven point occurs where the contribution just equals the fixed costs?
(b) A company's detailed information of costs and sales has been destroyed because of a computer malfunction. The following data has, however, been gleaned from various sources:

Sales volume (units)	10,000	12,000
Costs (£):		
direct materials	30,000	36,000
direct labour	28,000	33,000
overheads	20,500	24,100

Selling price per unit at all volumes of output is £12.30

Calculate:
(*i*) the cost of an additional 2,000 units of output;
(*ii*) the variable costs of 10,000 units of output;
(*iii*) the fixed element – if any – of each component cost;
(*iv*) the breakeven point.

(*Edexcel: GCE A-level*)

You can find a range of additional self-test questions, as well as material to help you with your studies, on the website that accompanies this book at **www.pearsoned.co.uk/wood**

Interest, annuities and leasing

Learning objectives

After you have studied this chapter, you should be able to:

- explain the difference between simple and compound interest
- explain what is meant by and be able to calculate the annual percentage rate (APR)
- calculate the present value of a series of cash flows
- describe what an annuity is and be able to calculate the value of ordinary annuities
- describe the difference between operating and finance leases and be able to calculate the relevant figures to use in financial statements

Introduction

In this chapter, you'll learn about the nature of interest rates, the difference between *simple* interest and *compound* interest and how to calculate them. You'll also learn how to calculate the annual percentage rate (APR) and how to calculate the cost and value of annuities and leases. Finally, you'll learn how to apply the accounting rules relating to leases.

45.1 Different values

Would you rather be given £10 today or in 12 months' time? As time passes, money loses value due to the effects of inflation – prices generally rise over time. When a transaction involves a delay in payment for the item purchased (e.g. a new car), the (inflation-caused) loss in value of the amount paid will be recovered by the seller charging the buyer interest. The delay also represents a period during which the seller could have invested the money and earned interest. **This 'opportunity cost' of interest lost will also be charged to the buyer.**

The seller may have had to borrow money to provide the item purchased, and the interest cost incurred will be charged to the buyer. **In addition, the seller will also add interest to the amount due in order to compensate for risk** – the risk that the buyer will not pay the debt when due. Thus, the amount the buyer will be required to pay depends upon inflation, the market rate of interest, and the degree of risk in the debt as perceived by the seller.

45.2 Interest rates

If a seller adds 10 per cent interest to a debt of £100, the required payment if made 1 year later is £100 + (10 per cent × £100 = £10) = £110. The interest in this case is known as 'simple interest' – 'simple' because the rate (10 per cent) is for one year, which matches the length of the debt. Interest rates generally indicate the percentage of the amount due that will be charged as interest if the debt is unpaid for a year.

If a 10 per cent interest rate is used, but the buyer is allowed to wait two years before paying the debt, the second year's interest will be based on the amount due at the end of the first year – £110 (i.e. the original debt of £100 plus the £10 interest charged for the first year). The interest for the second year is therefore 10 per cent × £110 = £11, and the amount due at the end of the second year is the original debt (£100) + the first year's interest (£10) + the second year's interest (£11) = £121. This is known as 'compound interest' – 'compound' because the amount of interest due for years beyond the first year is calculated on the basis of how much is owed at the start of each year, i.e. the original amount plus all the interest to that date.

If a buyer offers to pay £121 in two years' time, instead of paying £100 today, and the seller charges debtors 10 per cent interest per annum, the value today to the seller of the £121 which will be received in two years' time is £100. However, if the seller uses a 20 per cent interest rate, the £121 will only be worth £84.03. On the other hand, if the seller uses a 5 per cent interest rate, the £121 will be worth £109.75. These different values can be checked by applying the same approach as with the 10 per cent interest rate.

At 20 per cent, the interest for the first year on a debt of £84.03 will be £16.80, and the amount due at the end of one year will be £100.84. The second year's interest will be 20 per cent of £100.84, i.e. £20.17, and the total due at the end of the second year will be £121.

At 5 per cent, the interest for the first year on a debt of £109.75 will be £5.49, and the amount due at the end of one year will be £115.24. The second year's interest will be 5 per cent of £115.24, i.e. £5.76, and the total due at the end of the second year will be £121.

This is not as complicated as it may appear. Easy to follow statistical tables can be used to quickly find the values involved. Alternatively, it is straightforward to prepare a spreadsheet that will provide the values required for any combination of the variables involved.

45.3 Simple interest

Simple interest on a debt of one year is, therefore, calculated using the formula:

Amount of interest (Y) = Amount due (A) × Interest rate (r)

However, simple interest also applies to periods of less than a year. In order to calculate the interest on a shorter period, the period in question is expressed as a proportion of a year, and the formula is adjusted to:

Amount of interest (Y) = Amount due (A) × Interest rate (r) × Fraction of a year (t)

Let's look at an example.

Example

Interest on a debt of £100 is to be charged at 10 per cent per annum. The debt will be repaid after 60 days. The interest due can be calculated using the formula:

$$Y = £100 \times 10\% \times (60/365)$$
$$= £10 \times (60/365)$$
$$= £1.64$$

45.4 Annual percentage rate (APR)

Sometimes, an interest rate that appears to be a 'simple interest' rate does not actually represent the 'real' rate charged. This can arise where, for example, a 10 per cent rate is charged on a debt for a year, but part of the debt must be repaid part-way through the year, and the interest charge ignores the fact that there is early payment of part of the debt. This 'real' rate is known as the 'annual percentage rate' (APR). Hire purchase agreements are examples of debts where APR must be calculated to determine the 'real' cost incurred by the debtor.

Let's look at two examples.

Example 1

Interest on a debt of £100 is to be charged at 10 per cent per annum. However, £40 must be paid after six months, and the balance plus the interest at the end of the year.

				£
The interest to be paid is	10% of £100		$= Y$	$= \underline{10}$
The amount due is	£100 for $\frac{1}{2}$ year	$=$		50
	£60 for $\frac{1}{2}$ year	$=$		$\underline{30}$
The equivalent amount due for a year is			$= q$	$= \underline{80}$
The 'real' rate of interest			$= r$	$= Y/q$
				$= 10/80$
				$= 12.5\% =$ the APR

Another typical example of APR arises when a business is owed money by its customers and it decides to sell the debt to a factor in order to obtain cash now. In these cases, the factor will pay the business an amount equal to the amount of the debt less a discount.

Example 2

A business is due £10,000 from a customer and the customer has agreed to make the payment in 90 days' time. The business approaches a debt factor who agrees to pay the amount due now, less a discount rate of 10 per cent. Applying the formula for debts of less than one year

Amount of interest (Y) = Amount due (A) × Interest rate (r) × Fraction of a year (t)

the discount charged is:

$$Y = £10,000 \times 10\% \times (90/365)$$
$$= £1,000 \times (90/365)$$
$$= £246.58$$

The debt factor will pay the business £10,000 less £246.58, i.e. £9,753.42. **However, £246.58 does not represent a charge based on the amount of the advance (£9,753.42). Rather, it is based on the higher original amount of the customer's debt of £10,000.** As a proportion of the £9,753.42 advanced by the debt factor, £246.58 represents an interest rate of 10.25 per cent. This can be seen by rewriting the formula for debts of less than one year to:

$$r = \frac{Y}{A \times t}$$

which, substituting the example values, gives:

$$r = \frac{246.58}{9,753.42 \times (90/365)} = 10.25\%$$

A similar approach is used with *bills of exchange* and *trade bill* interest rate calculations.

45.5 Compound interest and investments

As mentioned in Section 45.2, when more than a year is involved, the interest due is compounded, i.e. each year's interest charge is based on the amount outstanding, including all interest relating to previous years, at the beginning of the year.

Rather than looking at how compared interest charges to be paid are calculated, let's look at another application of compound interest – the interest earned on investments.

The graph shown in Exhibit 45.1 illustrates the difference between two investments of £1,000 at 10 per cent per annum for 20 years. In the first case, the interest is reinvested at the same 10 per cent rate and the final value of the investment is £6,727.50. In the other case, the interest is withdrawn as soon as it is paid, leaving only the original £1,000 invested, which is also the final value of the investment. However, 20 times £100, i.e. £2,000, has been received in interest over the 20 years, resulting in the overall value (ignoring inflation) being £3,000.

Exhibit 45.1

The final value of an investment that is subject to compound interest can be calculated laboriously by calculating the value at the end of the first year, calculating the interest on that amount for the next year, adding that interest to the amount at the start of the year to get the amount at the end of the year, and repeating the process for each year. However, there is a formula which enables the amount to be calculated swiftly:

Final value (V) = Amount invested (I) × $(1 + r)^n$, where n = the number of years

Example

£1,000 invested today for five years at 10 per cent would have a final value (V) of:

$$
\begin{aligned}
V &= £1,000 \times (1 + 0.10)^5 \\
&= £1,000 \times (1.1)^5 \\
&= £1,000 \times 1.61051 \\
&= £1,610.51
\end{aligned}
$$

Calculations of this type are easily performed on most calculators, or by the use of tables. Where such calculations are performed regularly, it is quite common for a spreadsheet to be used to perform the calculation, often using the structure of a compound interest table within the spreadsheet to make it clear how the numbers used were derived. A compound interest table is included in Appendix 1, but a shorter example is reproduced in Exhibit 45.2:

Exhibit 45.2 An example of a compound interest table

Compound Interest Table
Period
Length £1 compounded at the end of each period at the interest rate shown

n	1%	2%	3%	4%	5%	6%	7%	8%	9%	10%	n
1	1.010	1.020	1.030	1.040	1.050	1.060	1.070	1.080	1.090	1.100	1
2	1.202	1.040	1.061	1.082	1.103	1.124	1.145	1.166	1.188	1.210	2
3	1.030	1.061	1.093	1.125	1.158	1.191	1.225	1.260	1.295	1.331	3
4	1.041	1.082	1.126	1.170	1.216	1.262	1.311	1.360	1.412	1.464	4
5	1.051	1.104	1.159	1.217	1.276	1.338	1.403	1.469	1.539	1.611	5
6	1.062	1.126	1.194	1.265	1.340	1.419	1.501	1.587	1.677	1.772	6
7	1.072	1.149	1.230	1.316	1.407	1.504	1.606	1.714	1.828	1.949	7
8	1.083	1.172	1.267	1.369	1.477	1.594	1.718	1.851	1.993	2.144	8
9	1.094	1.195	1.305	1.423	1.551	1.689	1.838	1.999	2.172	2.358	9
10	1.105	1.219	1.344	1.480	1.629	1.791	1.967	2.159	2.367	2.594	10

n	11%	12%	13%	14%	15%	16%	17%	18%	19%	20%	n
1	1.110	1.120	1.130	1.140	1.150	1.160	1.170	1.180	1.190	1.200	1
2	1.232	1.254	1.277	1.300	1.323	1.346	1.369	1.392	1.416	1.440	2
3	1.368	1.405	1.443	1.482	1.521	1.561	1.602	1.643	1.685	1.728	3
4	1.518	1.574	1.630	1.689	1.749	1.811	1.874	1.939	2.005	2.074	4
5	1.685	1.762	1.842	1.925	2.011	2.100	2.192	2.288	2.386	2.488	5
6	1.870	1.974	2.082	2.195	2.313	2.436	2.565	2.700	2.840	2.986	6
7	2.076	2.211	2.353	2.502	2.660	2.826	3.001	3.185	3.379	3.583	7
8	2.305	2.476	2.658	2.853	3.059	3.278	3.511	3.759	4.021	4.300	8
9	2.558	2.773	3.004	3.252	3.518	3.803	4.108	4.435	4.785	5.160	9
10	2.839	3.106	3.395	3.707	4.046	4.411	4.807	5.234	5.695	6.192	10

Example

As you can see highlighted in Exhibit 45.2, if you want to know how much will be held at the end of seven years if you invest £100 at 6 per cent compound interest per annum, the table in Exhibit 45.2 shows that it would be £100 times **1.504** = £150.40.

Interest often accumulates more frequently than once a year, for example, daily, monthly, or quarterly. If so, the rate of interest used in the formula must be changed to reflect this. To do this, the number of periods is multiplied by the number of payments being made each year, and the interest rate used is divided by the same amount. The formula can then be used with these adjusted values, as shown in the following example.

Example

If £100 is invested for two years at 12 per cent compound interest paid quarterly, the interest rate used in the calculation is 3 per cent (i.e. 12 per cent divided by four). The number of periods to use is eight (i.e. two multiplied by four). Looking up the table, the amount accumulated at the end of the two years will be £126.70.

Compare that to the compounded amount if interest was paid annually, £125.40. The difference is very small. However, the investment was for a short period of time. Had it been for a longer period, the difference would have become progressively greater. When large amounts of money are being invested over a long period, an increased frequency of interest payments will have a significant effect upon the amount of interest received.

Over time, most investments change their value. Investments, whether in the stock market, houses, or anything else, are made without knowing what the rate of return (the amount earned from the investment) will be. When the investment is ended and the final amount received is known, it is often useful to know what the rate of return was over the period of the investment.

This can be done using the table. If an investment was made for five years, it is the five-year row in the table that would be consulted. In that row, you would search for the number that represents the proportion that the final amount received represented of the initial investment. The interest rate column in which that proportion lay would represent the average rate of return on the investment.

Let's look at two examples.

Example 1

If a house was bought for £100,000 on 1 January 2001 and sold for £140,300 on 31 December 2005, a five-year investment was made. The proportion that £140,300 represents of the £100,000 invested is 1.403 : 1. Looking up the table in the row where $n = 5$, a value of 1.403 can be seen in the 7 per cent interest rate column. The rate of return is equivalent to 7 per cent compound per annum. Where the proportion calculated is not shown in the table, the table can be used to identify an approximate rate which can then be adjusted in order to arrive at the accurate rate.

Example 2

If a house was bought for £100,000 on 1 January 2001 and sold for £160,000 on 31 December 2004, a four-year investment was made. The proportion that £160,000 represents of the £100,000 invested is 1.6 : 1. Looking up the table in the row where $n = 4$, a value of 1.574 can be seen in the 12 per cent column and 1.630 can be seen in the 13 per cent column. The difference between these two values is 0.056 (i.e. 1.630 − 1.574). The difference between 1.574 and the amount being searched for of 1.6 is 0.026, which represents 46 per cent of the total difference of 0.056 between the 12 per cent and 13 per cent amounts. Adding 0.46 to 12 produces a percentage return of 12.46 per cent.

Rather than using the tables to identify the rate of return, a formula can be used which rewrites the final value formula [Final value (V) = Amount invested (I) $\times (1 + r)^n$, where $n =$ the number of years] to identify r:

$$r = \sqrt[n]{(V/I)} - 1$$

Substituting the values from the last example, we can confirm the answer found:

$$r = \sqrt[4]{(160{,}000/100{,}000)} - 1$$
$$= 12.46\%$$

45.6 Annuities

Annuities are an income-generating investment whereby, in return for the payment of a single lump sum, the 'annuitant' receives regular amounts of income over a predefined term (i.e. number of years). The frequency of the payments to the annuitant will depend upon the agreement reached, but would generally be either monthly, quarterly, six-monthly or annually.

The timing of the payments to the annuitant varies from annuity to annuity. For example, some involve regular payments being made to the annuitant at the start of each period, while others make the payments at the end of each period.

In some cases, the original investment is repaid at the end of the agreed term, in others it is not. It is also possible for the agreement to include the annuitant making the investment in a series of payments, rather than in a single lump sum.

As this suggests, there is a large range of possible arrangements that can be incorporated into an annuity, and it is not possible to describe how to deal with the computations relating to each of them. However, in the next section, we will focus upon one specific form of annuity – one in which equal payments are made to the annuitant at the end of each period. From that example, the basic principles involved can be identified which can then be applied to more complex situations. As a result, there should be very few circumstances when the form of an annuity means that you find it impossible to perform the necessary calculations.

Contrary to what many people think, knowledge of how to perform annuity calculation can be a very useful business skill because many forms of business transactions, including rental agreements, hire purchase agreements and leases, involve similar calculations to an annuity.

45.7 Calculation of the value of ordinary annuities

When calculating the value of an annuity, **it can be helpful to think of it as being similar to the calculation of compound interest,** *but one period in arrears.* For example, when considering compound interest on a straightforward investment, it would be assumed that an investment of £1,000 in year two was made at the start of the year. In contrast, for an annuity, all the payments are assumed to arise at the end of a year, so interest on a payment made in year two would only start to accumulate during year three – there would be no interest in year two on that part of the annuity.

The following formula can be used to calculate the value of an annuity which provides a series of regular payments and, upon which, a set rate of interest is being earned.

$$\textbf{Value} = \textbf{Annuity per period} \times \frac{(1 + r)^n - 1}{r}$$

For example, if £1,000 is being saved at the end of each year for five years and the interest rate is 10 per cent, the amount accumulated by the end of the fifth year will be:

$$\text{Value} = \pounds 1{,}000 \times \frac{(1 + 0.10)^n - 1}{0.10}$$

$$= \pounds 1{,}000 \times 6.1051$$

$$= \pounds 6{,}105.10$$

This can be confirmed by treating each of the five payments as individual compound interest calculations:

Year	Invested £	Formula	Value £
1	1,000	$\pounds 1{,}000 \times (1 + 0.10)^4$	1,464.10
2	1,000	$\pounds 1{,}000 \times (1 + 0.10)^3$	1,331.00
3	1,000	$\pounds 1{,}000 \times (1 + 0.10)^2$	1,210.00
4	1,000	$\pounds 1{,}000 \times (1 + 0.10)^1$	1,100.00
5	1,000	$\pounds 1{,}000 \times (1 + 0.10)^0$	1,000.00
			6,105.10

Tables can also be used. The one provided in Appendix 1 also confirms that the value of an annuity of £1 for five years at 10 per cent would be £6.105, i.e. £1 times the multiplier of 6.105 given in the table in the Appendix.

Example

As an alternative to calculating the value of an annuity when the amounts paid are known, it can often be useful to know how much should be set aside regularly in order to accumulate a certain amount at the end of a given period. For example, if it was intended to purchase equipment estimated to cost £10,000 in five years' time, and a 10 per cent interest rate was being offered for regular investments over a five-year period, the annuity formula can be rewritten so as to provide the amount to set aside each year:

$$\text{Annuity per period} = \frac{\text{Value} \times (r)}{(1 + r)^n - 1}$$

For our example, this gives:

$$\frac{£10,000 \times 0.10}{(1.10)^5 - 1} = £1,637.97$$

As mentioned previously, the multiplier given in the annuity table for a five-year annuity at 10 per cent is 6.105. If £1,637.97 is multiplied by 6.105, it confirms the annuity has a final value (to the nearest £1) of £10,000. It is also possible to confirm the annuity per period does result in the correct final value of £10,000 by creating a payment plus interest table:

Annuity paid	Payment £	Interest £	Increase in fund £	Balance of fund £
end of year 1	1,637.97	–	1,637.97	1,637.97
end of year 2	1,637.97	163.80	1,801.77	3,439.74
end of year 3	1,637.97	343.97	1,981.94	5,421.68
end of year 4	1,637.97	542.17	2,180.14	7,601.82
end of year 5	1,637.97	760.18	2,398.15	9,999.97

45.8 Calculation of the present value of ordinary annuities

If faced with a choice of paying for something now, or paying for it in a series of instalments, it would obviously be useful to know which is the cheaper of the two alternatives. For example, a business may purchase a new computer costing £1,000 and have a choice of paying £1,000 now, or £200 per month for six months. At first glance, the second option appears to be more expensive because £1,200 (i.e. six times £200) would be paid instead of £1,000.

However, first impressions can be misleading. In order to be able to properly compare the two alternatives, the payments must all be discounted to arrive at their cost expressed in terms of today's money. This is known as their **present values**. Whether it really is more expensive to pay by instalments will depend on the discount rate used in the calculation.

As with the calculation of the value of an ordinary annuity, tables are available for the calculation of the present value of an ordinary annuity. A full table is provided in Appendix 1 and it shows the value now of £1 per period for n periods when an organisation uses a discount rate of r. When payments are made more frequently than once per annum, the discount rate used should be reduced accordingly – that is, if payments are half-yearly, the rate is halved; if they are made every month, the rate is divided by 12.

The formula for calculating the present value of an ordinary annuity is:

$$\text{Present value} = \text{Regular payment} \times \left[\dfrac{1 - \dfrac{1}{(1 \times r)^n}}{r} \right]$$

If a 12 per cent rate were used in the example at the start of this section, the rate of 12 per cent would be divided by 12 (because payments are made monthly) and the present value would be:

$$\text{Present value} = £200 \times \left[\dfrac{1 - \dfrac{1}{(1 + 0.01)^6}}{0.01} \right]$$

$$= £1,159.10$$

The multiplier in the table in Appendix 1 for 1 per cent over 6 periods is 5.795 which, when multiplied by the payment of £200, gives a present value of £1,159.10.

It can be shown that this is the amount required if a table of interest and withdrawals is constructed (interest is at the same rate as above – 1 per cent per month):

Period	Balance b/d £	Interest £	Payment £	Balance c/d £
1	1,159.10	11.60	(200)	970.70
2	970.70	9.70	(200)	780.40
3	780.40	7.80	(200)	558.20
4	588.50	5.88	(200)	394.08
5	394.08	3.94	(200)	198.02
6	198.02	1.98	(200)	–

45.9 Leasing

Under a lease, the lessee agrees to pay a rental to the lessor for use of something for a period of time. Lease rental payments are treated as allowable expenses for tax, whereas assets that are purchased are only eligible for a partial deduction against tax in the form of a capital allowance. The lessor claims the capital allowances on the assets leased. The lessee charges all the lease rental payments against income.

Activity 45.1

Why do you think leasing is usually financially advantageous for both the lessor and the lessee?

An organisation acquiring an asset will often consider whether leasing may be preferable to outright purchase. As the cost, expected useful economic life, anticipated scrap value, and leasing charges can all be identified, it is possible to identify the APR of the lease. That can then be used to assess whether it would be preferable to lease rather than buy the asset.

Let's look at an example.

Example

A printing machine costing £200,000 has an expected useful economic life of ten years. Scrap value of the machine is expected to be zero, as the rate of obsolescence on machinery of this type is very high. The machine could be leased for £32,547 per annum. **The APR is the interest rate that is found when the cost of the machine is equal to the present value of the annual rental payments.** That is, it is the interest rate for which the ten-year multiplier will convert £32,547 into £200,000.

£200,000 divided by £32,547 is 6.145 and, in the 10 year row of the annuity table in Appendix 1, 6.145 is the multiplier for an interest rate of 10 per cent. This is, therefore, the APR of the lease. If the multiplier being sought lies between two values in the annuity table, the APR would be identified by interpolation, you will see when you learn about accounting for leases in Section 45.11.

Normally, tax is taken into account in identifying the APR of a lease. Ignoring the time lags inherent in the tax system, as the expense is charged directly against income, if the tax rate is 40 per cent, in the above example the net of tax cost of the lease would be 60 per cent of £32,547 (i.e. £19,528) and the APR would be 60 per cent of 10 per cent, i.e. 6 per cent. This can be compared to the organisation's *cost of capital after tax* in order to assess whether to lease or purchase the machine.

So far as the option to purchase is concerned, an annualised cost approach can be used. The cost of £200,000 is assumed to occur immediately, so its real cost is £200,000. Technically, the cost is said to have occurred in 'year zero', i.e. before inflation could make any impact on monetary values.

If 100 per cent capital allowances were available on the machine, at a tax rate of 40 per cent, there would be a tax saving equivalent to 40 per cent of £200,000 in year one. '**Net present value**' (NPV) is the sum of the present values of all the cash flows. That is, it represents the net overall gain or loss on the investment in the machine after expressing all cash flows in terms of their equivalent value at year zero.

If the organisation's net of tax cost of capital is 8 per cent, the £80,000 tax saving would be discounted to £74,080 (i.e. £80,000 × 0.926), leaving a net present value of £125,920. The annualised cost is, therefore, £125,920 ÷ 6.710 (which is the annuity multiplier for 10 years at 8 per cent), i.e. £18,766. When compared to the net of tax cost of the lease of £19,528, this suggests that it might be preferable to purchase the machine.

As an alternative to the above approach, the £125,920 net present value of buying the machine (as derived in the annualised cost calculation) can be compared to the NPV of the lease payments. The net of tax NPV of leasing is the net of tax rental (£19,528) multiplied by the present value multiplier of a ten-year annuity at 8 per cent (6.710), i.e. £131,033.

45.10 Financial implications of leasing

Despite the existence of a legal obligation to continue paying rental on a lease, neither the extent of the obligation to the lessor, nor the benefits obtainable under the lease appear in the lessee's balance sheet. However, a lease often represents the equivalent of a loan. The equivalent loan is the NPV of the outstanding lease payments discounted at the pre-tax rate of interest. For example, the NPV of a ten-year lease with rental of £32,547 and a pre-tax rate of interest of 10 per cent would be £32,547 × 6.145 = £200,000.

45.11 Accounting for leases

Leases are either finance leases or operating leases. *SSAP 21: Accounting for leases and hire purchase* defines the difference between them. (You learnt about the rules of SSAP 21 in Chapter 2, Section 2.12.) The principal characteristic of a finance lease is that substantially all the risks and rewards of ownership are transferred to the lessee.

If the substance of the lease is to have the opposite effect, then it should be categorised accordingly. At the end of the day, it is the substance (i.e. what is actually happening to the risks and rewards of ownership) rather than the form of the transaction that decides whether there exists a finance or an operating lease.

Hire purchase contracts will usually be of a financing nature and treated in the same way as finance leases.

When a lease is classified as 'operating', it is deemed to still be an asset of the lessor. Both lessor and lessee take the rentals to profit or loss. The lessor should also record the asset and depreciate it over its useful life.

An asset held under a finance lease is deemed to 'belong' to the lessee, who should capitalise it and make a corresponding entry in creditors. The initial value used should be the present value of the minimum lease payments. Depreciation should then be provided over the shorter of the lease term and the asset's useful life, except in the case of a hire purchase contract, under which circumstances the asset should be depreciated over its useful life. As each payment is made, the proportion which relates to the creditor balance should be applied to reduce that balance. The rest of the payment should be treated as a lease charge in the profit and loss account for the period.

Lessors should initially record the amount due under a finance lease as a debtor using the amount of the net investment in the lease. As each payment is received, the proportion which relates to payment of the debtor balance should be applied to reduce that balance. The rest of the receipt should be treated as lease income in the profit and loss account for the period.

Operating leases are accounted for in the same way as most revenue expenditure and income. Finance leases, however, are much more complex. The rental payments comprise a mixture of capital and revenue, and they must be separated and recorded differently. An approach called the actuarial method is generally used. Under this approach, it is first necessary to calculate the real rate of interest implied in the lease. This requires that information is available concerning the rental payments, the lease period and the cash value of the asset at the start of the lease.

Example

Quarterly rental on a leased computer is £400, the lease period is 12 quarters from 1 January 2004, and the cash value of the computer at 1 January 2004 is £4,000. The interest rate implied in the lease is that which produces a present value for the 12 payments of £400 equal to £4,000. Note, the first payment is at the start of the lease, yet ordinary annuity calculations relate to payments at the end of periods. In order to bring the example into line with this assumption, the first payment is offset against the cash value, reducing it to £3,600 and the annuity is calculated over 11 periods rather than 12.

$$\text{The factor for 11 periods is } \frac{£3,600}{400} = 9$$

$$\text{From the tables} \quad 3\% \qquad\qquad = 9.253$$
$$4\% \qquad\qquad = 8.760$$

By interpolation, the gap between 3 per cent and the rate is 253/493 = 0.513, therefore, the interest rate implied in the lease is 3.513 per cent. This can be verified by substituting the rate and other information into the formula given in Section 45.8:

$$\text{Present value} = \text{Payment} \times \left[\frac{1 - \dfrac{1}{(1 + r)^n}}{r} \right]$$

$$3{,}600 = 400 \times \left[\frac{1 - \dfrac{1}{(1 + 0.03513)^{11}}}{0.03513} \right]$$

$$3{,}600 = \pounds 400 \times 9$$

Applying the rate of interest of 3.513 to the lease data produces the data in Exhibit 45.4:

Exhibit 45.4 Calculation of the periodic finance charge in the lease

Quarter		Capital sum at start of period £	Rental paid at start of period £	Capital sum during period £	Finance charge (3.513% per quarter) £	Capital sum at end of period £
2004	−1	4,000	400	3,600	126	3,726
	2	3,726	400	3,326	117	3,443
	3	3,443	400	3,043	107	3,150
	4	3,150	400	2,750	96	2,846
2005	−1	2,846	400	2,446	86	2,532
	2	2,532	400	2,132	75	2,207
	3	2,207	400	1,807	63	1,870
	4	1,870	400	1,470	51	1,521
2006	−1	1,521	400	1,121	39	1,160
	2	1,160	400	760	27	787
	3	787	400	387	13	400
	4	400	400	–	–	–
			4,800		800	

The finance charges for each year of the lease are:

		£
2004 (126 + 117 + 107 + 96)	=	446
2005 (86 + 75 + 63 + 51)	=	275
2006 (39 + 27 + 13)	=	79
		800

The overall picture in each of the three years is:

Year	Total rental £	less	Finance charge £	=	Capital repayment £
2004	1,600		446		1,154
2005	1,600		275		1,325
2006	1,600		79		1,521

In the balance sheet of the lessee, the liability under the finance lease would be:

Year	Obligations under finance lease at start of year £	less	Capital repayment £	=	Obligations under finance lease at end of year £
2004	4,000		1,154		2,846
2005	2,846		1,325		1,521
2006	1,521		1,521		–

45.12 The rule of 78

Before spreadsheets became commonplace, these actuarial method-based lease calculations were often considered too complex and, in their place, a simple rule-of-thumb approach was adopted: the rule of 78.

The '78' in its name represents the sum of the numbers 1 to 12, and is used because these calculations originally focused on twelve-month periods. Each month receives a proportion in reverse to its position. Thus, month 1 of 12 would be accorded $^{12}/_{78}$ of the total, and month 12 of 12, $^{1}/_{78}$.

Similarly to the actuarial method, under the rule of 78, earlier periods will carry the majority of the allocation. For the purpose of lease calculations, the proportion is applied to the difference between the total payments under the leasing agreement and the cash value of the asset at the start.

Using the example from Exhibit 45.4, the rule of 78 produces the following:

Quarter	Rental payment number	Rule of 78	Allocation × £800	Annual allocation £
2004 – 1	1	11	11/66 × £800 = 133	
2	2	10	121	
3	3	9	109	
4	4	8	97	460
2005 – 1	5	7	85	
2	6	6	73	
3	7	5	61	
4	8	4	49	268
2006 – 1	9	3	36	
2	10	2	24	
3	11	1	12	
4	–	–	–	72
		66	800	800

(There is no allocation to the final quarter as the payments are made at the start of each quarter.) Comparison of the two methods shows that while the rule of 78 provides a general indication of the pattern flows, it is not particularly accurate.

Year	Actuarial method £	Rule of 78 £
2004	446	460
2005	275	268
2006	79	72
	800	800

Learning outcomes

You should now have learnt:

1 As time passes, money loses value and this loss of value must be allowed for when considering long-term investments.

2 Interest rates may be simple or compound, and interest may be paid at any appropriate frequency. Compound interest will generate significantly greater values than the same rate of simple interest the longer the time period involved and the greater the frequency of interest payments.

3 How to calculate simple interest, compound interest, APR, annuities and leases.

4 The real rate of interest often differs from the apparent rate and an annual percentage rate (APR) must be calculated in order to compare alternatives.

5 Annuity calculations are useful when considering rental agreements, hire purchase and leases.

6 Operating leases are accounted for differently from finance leases.

Answer to activity

45.1 Leasing exists because both lessee and lessor can benefit from the arrangement as a result of their differing tax positions and capital-raising abilities. A small company may find it very expensive, possibly impossible, to borrow £200,000 for some new equipment, whereas a large leasing company would be able to raise the funds at a very competitive rate.

Review questions

45.1
(a) If you were lent £17,000 for 64 days at 6 per cent, how much interest would you pay?
(b) If a debt factor offered to discount a £4,000 bill of exchange at 12 per cent, and if the bill had an outstanding period of 120 days, how much would the debt factor pay for the bill?

45.2A What is the real rate of interest of discounting the bill of exchange in Question 45.1?

45.3 Interest of £600 is charged and included in a loan of £4,200, i.e. the £4,200 received included the £600 interest charged. The loan has to be repaid at £1,050 per quarter over the next 12 months. What is the real rate of interest of the loan?

45.4 If £5,000 is invested for four years at 7 per cent compound per annum, how much interest is earned over the five years?

45.5A If the interest on the investment in Question 45.4 had been compounded every six months, how much interest would have been earned over the four years?

45.6A Shares bought on 1 January 2004 for £2,500 were sold on 31 December 2008 for £4,400. What was the rate of annual compound interest on the investment?

45.7 Should you accept an offer of £50,000 for your rights over the next 12 years to the £5,000 annual rent from shop premises you own and have leased to a local company? You could invest the £50,000 at 6 per cent per annum.

→

→ **45.8A** In relation to the rental income, what rate of interest does the offer made in Question 45.7 represent?

45.9 A condition of an eight-year loan of £40,000 is that the borrower will pay equal annual amounts into a sinking fund so that it accumulates at the end of the 8 years to the amount of the loan. The sinking fund will earn interest at 5 per cent per annum. How much should be paid into the sinking fund each year?

45.10A If the interest on the sinking fund in Question 45.9 were at 7 per cent, how much would the annual payments into it be?

45.11 What is the implied interest rate if equipment can be leased for three years at £8,000 per annum and the cash price is £21,000?

45.12 The annual rental payments on a five-year lease are £11,000. If the rate of interest payable on borrowing for this purpose is 9 per cent, what is the capital value of the lease?

You can find a range of additional self-test questions, as well as material to help you with your studies, on the website that accompanies this book at **www.pearsoned.co.uk/wood**

Capital expenditure appraisal

46.1 Present value

You were introduced to the concept of present value in Chapter 45. You will recall that it is the amount that a future cash flow is worth in terms of today's money. £1,000 invested for five years at 10 per cent compound results in a final amount of £1,610.51, but what would be the value of that £1,610.51 at the date of the initial investment (i.e. today)? If it were known, it would be possible to tell whether the investment might be worthwhile.

To calculate present value, the formula to use has the same variables as that used to calculate compound interest which you learnt about in Section 45.5, but it is rewritten to reflect that it is really the reciprocal of the compound interest formula:

$$\text{Amount invested } (I) = \frac{\text{Final value } (V)}{(1 + r)^n}$$

However, it would be more appropriate to describe the amount calculated as 'present value' rather than 'amount invested' and the formula becomes:

$$\text{Present value } (PV) = \frac{\text{Final value } (V)}{(1 + r)^n}$$

Let's look at an example.

Example

A bank is offering a guaranteed return at the end of five years of £1,500 for every £1,000 invested. If you could usually expect to obtain a rate of interest of 8 per cent on your investments, what would be the present value of investing £1,000 in the bank?

$$PV = \frac{£1,500}{(1.08)^5} = £1,020.87$$

The 8 per cent interest rate used in this example is generally referred to as the **discount rate**, i.e. the rate at which the future flow of cash is discounted to arrive at its present value. As with compound interest, present value tables are generally used, and will often be created and used on spreadsheets. A present value table is included in Appendix 1. An extract is presented in Exhibit 46.1:

Exhibit 46.1 An example of a present value table

Present Value Table
Period
Length PV of £1 discounted over the period at the rate shown

n	1%	2%	3%	4%	5%	6%	7%	8%	9%	10%	n
1	0.990	0.980	0.971	0.961	0.952	0.943	0.935	0.926	0.917	0.909	1
2	0.980	0.961	0.943	0.925	0.907	0.890	0.873	0.857	0.842	0.826	2
3	0.971	0.942	0.915	0.889	0.864	0.840	0.816	0.794	0.772	0.751	3
4	0.961	0.924	0.889	0.855	0.823	0.792	0.763	0.735	0.708	0.683	4
5	0.951	0.906	0.863	0.822	0.784	0.747	0.713	0.681	0.650	0.621	5
6	0.942	0.888	0.838	0.790	0.746	0.705	0.666	0.630	0.596	0.564	6
7	0.933	0.871	0.813	0.760	0.711	0.665	0.623	0.583	0.547	0.513	7
8	0.923	0.853	0.789	0.731	0.677	0.627	0.582	0.540	0.502	0.467	8
9	0.914	0.837	0.766	0.703	0.645	0.592	0.544	0.500	0.460	0.424	9
10	0.905	0.820	0.744	0.676	0.614	0.558	0.508	0.463	0.422	0.386	10

n	11%	12%	13%	14%	15%	16%	17%	18%	19%	20%	n
1	0.901	0.893	0.885	0.877	0.870	0.862	0.855	0.847	0.840	0.833	1
2	0.812	0.797	0.783	0.769	0.756	0.743	0.731	0.718	0.706	0.694	2
3	0.731	0.712	0.693	0.675	0.658	0.641	0.624	0.609	0.593	0.579	3
4	0.659	0.636	0.613	0.592	0.572	0.552	0.534	0.516	0.499	0.482	4
5	0.593	0.567	0.543	0.519	0.497	0.476	0.456	0.437	0.419	0.402	5
6	0.535	0.507	0.480	0.456	0.432	0.410	0.390	0.370	0.352	0.335	6
7	0.482	0.452	0.425	0.400	0.376	0.354	0.333	0.314	0.296	0.279	7
8	0.434	0.404	0.376	0.351	0.327	0.305	0.285	0.266	0.249	0.233	8
9	0.391	0.361	0.333	0.308	0.284	0.263	0.243	0.226	0.209	0.194	9
10	0.352	0.322	0.295	0.270	0.247	0.227	0.208	0.191	0.176	0.162	10

Frequently, the cash flows arising from an investment arise throughout the period of the investment, not simply at the end. To calculate the overall present value of all the cash flows, each is calculated separately, and all the resulting present values are added together.

Example

An investment of £10,000 is made for five years. The net cash flows at the end of each of the five years are:

Period	Amount £
1	2,000
2	3,000
3	4,000
4	3,000
5	1,000

If the discount rate used is 10 per cent, the overall present value of the net cash flows is calculated as:

Period	Amount £	Discount factor 10%	Present value £
1	2,000	0.909	1,818
2	3,000	0.826	2,478
3	4,000	0.751	3,004
4	3,000	0.683	2,049
5	1,000	0.621	621
		Overall present value of cash flows	9,970

When compared to the initial investment of £10,000, it can be seen that this investment would lose £30 (i.e. £10,000 – £9,970). To make it easier to see this figure, these calculations usually incorporate the initial investment (which is not discounted as it is already at today's value) and produce a figure known as the net present value, or NPV. Incorporating the initial investment into this example produces the following table:

Period	Amount £	Discount factor 10%	Present value £
0	(10,000)	1.000	(10,000)
1	2,000	0.909	1,818
2	3,000	0.826	2,478
3	4,000	0.751	3,004
4	3,000	0.683	2,049
5	1,000	0.621	621
		Net present value	(30)

Many businesses have a rate of return that they require to achieve on investments. If a potential investment is not expected to achieve that rate of return, the investment will not be made. It is always possible to adopt the NPV approach in order to determine whether the return exceeds the required rate (which is shown by a positive NPV). **However, it is often useful to know what the actual rate of return is – the proposed investment may, for example, require that some additional financing be obtained that would be at a higher rate than the business's normal rate of return.**

The actual rate of return is known as the 'internal rate of return', or IRR. It is the discount rate that results in an NPV of zero. It can be calculated very easily using a spreadsheet – a table similar to the one above would be written in the spreadsheet, but the discount factor would be left blank. Then, by instigating an appropriate command, the spreadsheet would identify and insert the IRR into the table so as to arrive at an NPV of zero.

However, spreadsheets are not always available and IRR may need to be calculated manually. The method to adopt is similar to that adopted in the final example in Section 45.5 – a guess is made as to an appropriate IRR and the NPV calculation is made using that rate. If the NPV is

positive, a higher rate is selected (a lower rate is selected if the NPV is negative) and the NPV is again calculated. This continues until one positive NPV and one negative NPV are identified. The absolute difference between the two NPVs is calculated and the proportion of that difference that represents the difference between the NPV of the lower of the rates involved and zero is added to the lower rate to produce the IRR.

Example

You have been asked if you would be willing to lend £100,000 to a taxi company in order that it may expand its fleet of taxis. The money would be repaid at the rate of £30,000 per annum for four years. What is the IRR?

Step 1 is to select a rate that may be approximately correct. There is no simple way to select such a rate, and what would often be done is that the same rate would be used as the first step with most IRR calculations, and then the choice of the second rate to use would depend on how close to zero the first attempt came, and on whether the NPV it gave was positive or negative. If an 8 per cent rate is used, the following results:

Period	Amount £	Discount factor 8%	Present value £
0	(100,000)	1.000	(100,000)
1	30,000	0.926	27,780
2	30,000	0.857	25,710
3	30,000	0.794	23,820
4	30,000	0.735	22,050
		Net present value (	640)

Using the 8 per cent rate resulted in an NPV that was less than zero. The next rate chosen must, therefore, be less than 8 per cent. A 7 per cent rate produces the following:

Period	Amount £	Discount factor 7%	Present value £
0	(100,000)	1.000	(100,000)
1	30,000	0.935	28,050
2	30,000	0.873	26,190
3	30,000	0.816	24,480
4	30,000	0.763	22,890
		Net present value	1610

Therefore, the IRR lies between 7 per cent and 8 per cent. The difference between the two NPVs is 2,250 (i.e. 640 + 1,610). A zero NPV will result if the rate is set to 7 per cent plus 1,610/2,250 (as 7 per cent is 1,610 away from zero). Expressed as a decimal, 1,610/2,250 = 0.72 and the IRR is, therefore, 7.72 per cent.

46.2 Capital expenditure appraisal

Activity 46.1

If you had £5,000 to spend today and had the choice of investing it in a five-year bond with a bank, or lending it to a friend who had just opened a restaurant and who offered you 10 per cent of the profits for five years, plus the return of your £5,000 at the end of the five years, which alternative would you choose and why?

Organisations make vast numbers of short-term decisions. They make comparatively few long-term decisions. These long-term decisions involve investing resources in something and then receiving the benefits. Examples include:

● building a new production facility
● buying a new delivery truck
● sponsoring a local football team for three years
● building a bridge
● buying an airline
● making a new product
● starting a new business.

Generally, only the incremental cash payments and receipts arising from the decision to invest are relevant. The relevant costs include interest, but not items that normally appear in the calculation of profit but which do not involve cash – depreciation, for example. There are two aspects of the incremental cash flows that should be distinguished: the cash outflows resulting from the decision to invest, and the cash inflows arising as a result of investing. The difference between these two groups of incremental cash flows determines whether or not an investment is made.

The techniques used to aid the selection of the appropriate long-term decision are referred to collectively as '**capital expenditure appraisal**'. There are three generally acceptable capital expenditure appraisal techniques in common use. Two have already been introduced in Section 46.1 – *net present value* and *internal rate of return*. Collectively, these two are known as '**discounted cash flow**' (DCF) techniques, as they involve the discounting of future net cash flows of a capital project to find their present value. Both techniques assume that all cash flows occur at the end of a period.

The third technique, '**payback**', involves selecting the alternative that repays the initial investment in the shortest time, provided that it does not exceed the business's maximum acceptable payback period – its payback hurdle period. It is useful when cash resources are limited and swift repayment of the investment is vital for the maintenance of working capital. Also, because risks of problems arising increase with the length of an investment, payback reduces the risk by minimising the relevant length of investment. **In contrast to the DCF techniques, payback assumes all cash flows occur evenly over a period, other than identifying when the total investment wil be repaid.**

A fourth technique, 'accounting rate of return' (ARR), having once been very popular, is now falling into disuse as technology becomes more sophisticated, and those performing these calculations become more aware of the benefits of using the other three techniques in preference to ARR. The technique uses profits rather than cash flows and it involves dividing the average return by the average investment over the period. For example, if £10,000 is invested and the return is £30,000 over a ten-year period, there would be a return of £3,000 per year (£30,000 ÷ 10). If the £10,000 is repaid at the end of the ten years, the average investment is £10,000 (i.e. [£10,000 + £10,000] ÷ 2). Therefore, the (annual) accounting rate of return is £3,000 divided by £10,000 i.e. 30 per cent.

Although it is generally easy to calculate, ARR produces a percentage figure that is of little practical use. It cannot, for example, be compared with an organisation's cost of capital in order to assess whether a project would achieve a greater return than the cost of the capital that financed it. It also ignores the timing of cash flows – a project whose profits all arose at the start would be rejected in favour of one with a higher ARR whose profits all came at the end, even if inflation meant that those later period profits were worth significantly less in present value terms than the earlier profits of the rejected project.

Example

When considering a capital expenditure (or 'capital project') proposal, the first step is to identify all the incremental cash flows that would arise were the decision taken to proceed with the investment. As most decisions of this type involve cash flows over a number of years, once identified, the cash flows are mapped against the year in which they arise.

A new machine would cost £10,000 and installation would cost a further £1,000. It would replace an existing machine that would be sold for £2,000. The machine would generate cash income of £2,500 per annum for four years, at the end of which it would be sold for £3,000.

The cash flows are:

Period		Amount £
0	purchase + installation − sale proceeds	(9,000)
1	income	2,500
2	income	2,500
3	income	2,500
4	income (including sale proceeds)	5,500
		4,000

If the business's cost of capital is 10 per cent, that would be the discount rate used and the net present value (as previously illustrated in Section 46.6) would be:

Period	Amount £	Discount factor 10%	Present value £
0	(9,000)	1.000	(9,000.00)
1	2,500	0.909	2,272.50
2	2,500	0.826	2,065.00
3	2,500	0.751	1,877.50
4	5,500	0.683	3,756.50
		Overall net present value of cash flows	971.50

As the NPV is positive, the internal rate of return is higher than 10 per cent. A 15 per cent discount factor produces a negative NPV of £144:

Period	Amount £	Discount factor 15%	Present value £
0	(9,000)	1.000	(9,000)
1	2,500	0.870	2,175
2	2,500	0.756	1,890
3	2,500	0.658	1,645
4	5,500	0.572	3,146
		Overall net present value of cash flows	(144)

Interpolating between these two values, as in Section 46.1, the IRR is found to be 14.35 per cent. (The absolute difference is £1,115.50 (i.e. £971.50 + £144), of which approximately 87 per cent (£971.50) is represented by the proportion relating to the 10 per cent NPV. Multiplying the difference between the two discount rates (15% − 10% = 5%) by 87 per cent gives an answer to two decimal places of 4.35 per cent. This is then added to 10 per cent to produce the IRR of 14.35 per cent.) On the basis that the business's cost of capital is 10 per cent, this project will be financially beneficial. Substituting the discount rate of 14.35 per cent into the table produces a net present value of −10, the failure to reach a value of zero being due to rounding.

Period	Amount £	Discount factor 14.35%	Present value £
0	(9,000)	1.000	(9,000.00)
1	2,500	0.875	2,187.50
2	2,500	0.765	1,912.50
3	2,500	0.669	1,672.50
4	5,500	0.585	3,217.50
		Overall net present value of cash flows	(10.00)

These two DCF techniques generally arrive at the selection of the same alternative when faced with a choice between two or more projects. However, they can produce different choices, and when they do, it is the NPV choice that should be selected.

As the following schedule shows, payback on the machine occurs after 3.27 years:

Period £	Amount £	Balance £
0	(9,000)	(9,000)
1	2,500	(6,500)
2	2,500	(4,000)
3	2,500	(1,500)
4	5,500	–

Payback at 3 plus 1,500/5,500 years = 3.27 years

This will then be compared with the business's hurdle period (i.e. its maximum permitted period) for payback. If it is later than the hurdle period, the project will be rejected. When cash flow is important, for example when the cost of capital is high, or when the risks in a project increase significantly the longer it runs, payback provides a measure of how quickly the investment in the project will be repaid, any subsequent cash flows being viewed as a bonus. However, it can result in a project being selected that is considerably less profitable than another that happens to take longer to repay the investment in it. It also ignores the time value of money. ('Real' payback will always be later than revealed by calculation as later receipts are not worth so much in today's money as early ones because of inflation.)

Activity 46.2 How could you address these deficiencies to ensure payback was effectively applied?

Closer inspection of the approach reveals that payback ignores everything after the (first) breakeven point. Applied blindly, it is not concerned about whether a project breaks even overall, only that the amount invested in a project is reduced to zero at some stage. The fact that a project may break even in three years, but then requires more investment in year five, only finally breaking even in year six, can easily be overlooked when calculating payback.

46.3 Taxation

One factor often overlooked in consideration of capital projects is taxation. Items of equipment acquired will give rise to tax allowances that can be used to reduce tax payable, and any incremental profits arising from a capital project will give rise to payments of tax.

Writing-down allowances are granted in place of depreciation and, when the equipment is sold or scrapped, its tax-written-down value (i.e. cost less writing-down allowances claimed) less any amount received upon its disposal is allowed as a deduction against income for tax purposes.

Once calculated, the impact of taxation on the incremental cash flows is taken into account in the same way as any other item of incremental income or expenditure.

Example

A new machine costing £10,000 has an estimated useful life of four years, after which it will be scrapped. During those four years, it is expected to generate sales of £5,000 per annum. Production costs are anticipated to be 40 per cent of sales revenue. Working capital of £3,000 will be required for this activity, all of which will be recovered when the machine is scrapped. Depreciation is by the straight line method, i.e. £2,500 per annum starting in year 1. Corporation tax of 40 per cent is paid nine months after the end of each accounting period. A writing-down allowance of 25 per cent (reducing balance) will be available if the machine is acquired.

The expected annual profit is:

	£	£
Revenue		5,000
Production costs	2,000	
Depreciation	2,500	
		(4,500)
		500
Corporation tax		(200)
Net profit after tax		300

The expected cash flows that would be used for the capital expenditure appraisal are:

Investment (£)	Year 1	2	3	4	5
Machine	(10,000)				
Working capital	(3,000)			3,000	
Tax allowance		1,000	750	562.50	1,687.50
	(13,000)	1,000	750	3,562.50	1,687.50
Cash flows (£)					
Sales	5,000	5,000	5,000	5,000	
Production costs	(2,000)	(2,000)	(2,000)	(2,000)	
Tax (40% × £3,000)		(1,200)	(1,200)	(1,200)	(1,200)
	3,000	1,800	1,800	1,800	(1,200)
Net cash flows (£)	(10,000)	2,800	2,550	5,362.50	487.50

(The overall tax allowances are £4,000, which is 40 per cent of the cost of the equipment, for which it has been assumed that there will be no scrap proceeds. Also, the cost of the machine and additional working capital would be treated as having arisen in year 0 for the purposes of the capital expenditure appraisal techniques. They are shown in year 1 in the above table so as to clarify the timing of the tax and tax allowance cash flows.)

46.4 Annualised figures

It can be difficult comparing projects that have different lengths. To overcome this complication, it is possible to use annualised amounts. Notionally, this approach assumes that the comparison would then be made over a period that represented the lowest common multiple of the projects – a twelve-year cycle would be used for two projects, one of three years' duration, the other four. However, as will be seen, once the annualised amounts are calculated, the decision can be taken without reference to any particular length of time.

The first step is to calculate the present value of the projects and then identify the amount of the annuity for the period of each project that has the same present value as that project's NPV. For example, if a discount rate of 10 per cent is used and the NPV of the three-year project is

£500, the annuity multiplier (from the table in Appendix 1) is 2.487 and the three-year annuity with a present value of £500 is therefore £201 (i.e. £500 ÷ 2.487). If the four-year project has an NPV of £800, the four-year annuity is £252 (i.e. £800 ÷ 3.170). On the basis of these annualised amounts, the four-year project would be selected.

46.5 Relevant and irrelevant costs

When decision-making, some costs and revenues are relevant to a decision that is to be taken, whilst other costs and revenues are **irrelevant costs**. The **relevant costs** and relevant revenues are those costs and revenues of the future that will be affected by the decision, whereas irrelevant costs and revenues will not be so affected.

Take as an example a decision as to whether or not we should telephone a lot of our customers in a sales campaign. The cost of the telephone rental is irrelevant in the decision whether or not to conduct the campaign, as we will have to pay exactly the same rental whether or not we engage in the campaign. On the other hand, the cost of making the extra calls will be a relevant cost as they would not have been incurred if the campaign had not gone ahead.

With revenues, take the case of buying a new car for a salesperson. If the revenues he would help create by sales would remain unchanged no matter which car he were to have, then the revenues would be completely irrelevant in taking the decision as to the type of car to be bought.

However, to take the case of a salesperson who sells some of his products to farmers. With a four-wheel drive car he could get to farms which would otherwise be inaccessible to a two-wheel drive car. In this case the revenues would be relevant to the decision as to the type of car to be bought, as they would be affected by the decision.

46.6 Sunk costs

Sunk cost is a term which can be confusing, since it really means an irrelevant cost which has already occurred. It is a past cost, not a future cost.

Let's take the case of a machine which was bought several years ago, and now has a written-down value of £10,000. The scrap value is nil. We can either use the machine on a project we are considering or else we can scrap it. Let us suppose that the revenue from the project will be £25,000 and the future relevant costs will be £18,000. If we added the written-down value of the machine to the £18,000 costs then we would make a loss of £3,000 (£25,000 − £28,000). Looking at it that way, we would not tackle the project.

However, the cost of the machine was a past cost. If we do not use the machine on this project the only other alternative is to scrap it. Such a past cost is said to be a *sunk cost* and is irrelevant to the decision to be taken. We therefore take on the project (assuming there is no better alternative project) and are better off by £7,000 (£25,000 − £18,000).

46.7 A comparison of the methods

We will now look at a case where each of the methods already described will be used to try to select the best investment. You will see that the different methods can give different answers as to which project should be chosen.

Exhibit 46.2

ABC Ltd is wondering whether or not to invest in one of three possible projects. The initial investment will be £10,000, and the cost of capital is 10 per cent. There is no scrap value for the fixed assets used in these projects. Details of the net cash inflows are as follows:

	M £	N £	P £
Year 1	3,000	5,000	4,000
Year 2	6,000	5,000	5,000
Year 3	4,000	2,000	3,000
Year 4	–	1,600	1,000
Year 5	–	–	1,400
	13,000	13,600	14,400

1 Accounting rate of return method

$$\frac{\text{Average yearly profit}}{\text{Average investment}} \times \frac{100}{1} \qquad \frac{1,000}{5,000} = 20\% \qquad \frac{900}{5,000} = 18\% \qquad \frac{880}{5,000} = 17.6\%$$

2 Payback method

	M	N	P
	2.25 years	2 years	2 years

3 Net present value method (cost of capital 10%)

Discount factors per tables	M	N	P
		Present values (£)	
1.000	× (10,000) = (10,000)	× (10,000) = (10,000)	× (10,000) = (10,000)
0.909	× 3,000 = 2,727	× 5,000 = 4,545	× 4,000 = 3,636
0.826	× 6,000 = 4,956	× 5,000 = 4,130	× 5,000 = 4,130
0.751	× 4,000 = 3,004	× 2,000 = 1,502	× 3,000 = 2,253
0.683		× 1,600 = 1,092	× 1,000 = 683
0.621			× 1,400 = 869
Net present values	687	1,269	1,571

4 Internal rate of return

Stage 1: Use a rate of return which will give negative net present values. In this instance it is taken to be 18%.

Discount factors per tables at 18%	M	N	P
		Present values (£)	
1.000	× (10,000) = (10,000)	× (10,000) = (10,000)	× (10,000) = (10,000)
0.847	× 3,000 = 2,541	× 5,000 = 4,235	× 4,000 = 3,388
0.718	× 6,000 = 4,308	× 5,000 = 3,590	× 5,000 = 3,590
0.609	× 4,000 = 2,436	× 2,000 = 1,218	× 3,000 = 1,827
0.516		× 1,600 = 826	× 1,000 = 516
0.437			× 1,400 = 611
Net present values	(715)	(131)	(68)

Stage 2: Calculate the internal rate of return (IRR), using figures for positive present values already calculated in **3** above.

$$M \quad 10\% + \left(8\% \times \frac{687}{687 + 715}\right) = 13.92\%$$

$$N \quad 10\% + \left(8\% \times \frac{1,269}{1,269 + 131}\right) = 17.25\%$$

$$P \quad 10\% + \left(8\% \times \frac{1,571}{1,571 + 68}\right) = 17.67\%$$

If used on its own, without reference to the other methods:

1 Accounting rate of return would choose project M, as it gives highest rate of 20 per cent.
2 Payback would choose project N, as it pays back in the shortest time of two years.
3 Net present value would choose project P as it gives the highest net present value of £1,571.
4 Internal rate of return would choose project P, as it shows highest return of 17.67 per cent, which is itself higher than the cost of capital.

46.8 Uncertainty

Many of the values used in the calculations and formulae described in this chapter are, at best, objectively based estimates of future cash flows and interest rates. It is, for example, virtually inconceivable that the figures forecast in a capital expenditure appraisal will be confirmed to have been 100 per cent accurate when the project is completed.

Proposers of a course of action tend to be over-optimistic and, in order to avoid the risk of non-achievement of forecasted results, a number of measures have been adopted. The two most common are the adoption of a higher cost of capital rate than is actually required in practice, and reducing estimates of income by a fixed percentage and using the same percentage to increase all costs. However, such arbitrary adjustments can no more guarantee accuracy than the original estimates, and they will often cause the decision taken to be different from that which the original, possibly more meaningful, data would have produced.

A more rational adjustment that can be adopted is to change the amounts forecast according to their subjective probabilities. The probabilities would be provided by the proposers of a project.

Example

Estimated sales ×	Probability of occurrence =	Expected sales
£	£	
2,000	0.2	400
4,000	0.5	2,000
6,000	0.2	1,200
8,000	0.1	800
	1.0	4,400

In this case, the expected value of £4,400 will be used, rather than the most likely value of £4,000. While this approach appears more rational than the other possible methods of dealing with uncertainty, it is dependent upon the probabilities used being soundly based.

Activity 46.3

If two projects both require the same investment and one has an NPV of £100 and the other an NPV of £240, which should be selected? Would this always be the case?

46.9 Sensitivity analysis

One of the greatest benefits of spreadsheets is the facility to perform unlimited numbers of sensitivity analysis computations on a given set of data. Cash flows can be adjusted marginally to see if the change turns a positive NPV negative; interest rates can be altered to see if the same decision would be made; the timing of cash flows can be altered to see what the impact of doing so is upon NPV. Sensitivity analysis enables information generated using the formulae and methods described in this chapter to be manipulated to maximise the understanding of the flexibility and limits of that information.

The importance of discounting has been recognised by the Institute of Chartered Accountants in England and Wales, which issued Technical Release 773: *The Use of Discounting in Financial Statements*. It is an excellent source of discussion on this topic, and on its application in practice.

Learning outcomes

You should now have learnt:

1 As time passes, money loses value and this loss of value must be allowed for when considering long-term investments.

2 Net present value (NPV) and internal rate of return (IRR) usually lead to the same selection being made between mutually exclusive projects. When they differ, it is the NPV selection that should be followed.

3 Accounting rate of return (ARR) is still used, but the rate it produces cannot be compared to the cost of capital and the technique is not recommended.

4 How to calculate NPV, IRR, Payback, and ARR.

5 The relative merits of the four methods.

6 What is meant by relevant and irrelevant costs.

7 What is meant by sunk cost.

8 How to select the 'best' project for an organisation to pursue at a given time from a range of possible alternative projects.

9 How to explain why, from a financial perspective, the selected project is the 'best' one for the organisation to pursue.

10 Where alternative projects are of unequal length, annualised amounts can be calculated to enable comparison.

Answers to activities

46.1 It would depend on many factors, not least the rate of interest you would receive from the bank and the anticipated profits from the restaurant. You would need to consider the probability of the estimates concerning the profitability of the restaurant. You would also need to take into account your relationship with your friend and your own willingness to run the risk that you may not be able to recover your investment without damaging your relationship with your friend should you need the money back before the five years had passed. There are many non-financial factors that often need to be taken into account when considering long-term investments.

46.2 These deficiencies in the payback approach can be addressed by discounting all cash flows to their present values, and by ensuring that the calculation includes a check for there being multiple payback points. While the first is generally sensible, the second is essential if payback is to be effectively applied.

46.3 The project with the higher NPV should normally be chosen. Where the NPV is very small relative to the investment, it may not be so important that the one with the higher NPV is chosen. For example, if the investment required for these NPVs is £7,500 the NPVs are relatively very small indeed. Other factors would be more important, such as the likelihood that the figures would prove to be accurate; the potential impact of each alternative on the general image and reputation of the organisation; whether the projects would involve any opportunity costs that are not accounted for in the NPV calculation (such as employees being unavailable for other work), etc.

Review questions

46.1 The following project costs have been estimated relating to the upgrading of some equipment; all the costs are being incurred solely because of the project:

2004			£
January	1	One year's rent on premises paid	12,000
	31	Equipment purchased	20,000
March	31	Installation of equipment completed and paid	4,000
December	31	Costs incurred in commissioning equipment	8,000
2005			
January	1	One year's rent on premises paid	12,000
March	31	Additional commissioning costs paid	6,000
May	31	Training costs paid	3,000
June	30	Additional working capital provided	16,000
December	31	Cash proceeds from sale of old equipment	5,000

Ignoring tax, prepare a statement showing the outlays of cash on the project in 2004 and 2005. The new facility will be in full use from 1 July 2005.

46.2 Assume the company in Question 46.1 pays tax at 30 per cent, on 30 September each year, nine months after the end of its financial period. The company receives 20 per cent writing-down allowances on the cost of equipment and will receive the allowances for 2004 expenditure to be off-set against the tax payable on the profits for 2004. 100 per cent capital allowances were received on the old equipment sold in 2005 and the receipts from the sale of the old equipment must, there-fore, be treated as taxable income of 2005. Show the impact on the cash flows of these tax items.

46.3 Assuming an interest rate of 6 per cent, what is the net present value of the net of tax cash flows in Question 46.2 for 2004, 2005, 2006 and 2007?

46.4A The annual forecasted profit from a project is:

	£	£
Revenue		220,000
Labour, materials, and overheads	60,000	
Depreciation	15,000	
		(75,000)
Net profit before tax		145,000
Tax at 30%		(43,500)
Net profit after tax		101,500

Equipment with a four-year useful life and no residual value will be purchased on 1 September for £60,000. £30,000 additional working capital, which will be recovered in full at the end of the four years, will be required from 1 September. A 25 per cent writing-down allowance will be available throughout the period of the project. Tax at 30 per cent will be payable on 1 June each year, nine months after the end of the company's financial period on 31 August. Prepare a cash flow budget for the project.

46.5A If the interest rate is 7 per cent, what is the net present value of the net cash flows arising from the project in Question 46.4A?

46.6A If retained, a machine would be depreciated £3,000 for each of the next five years, at which point it would be fully written-down and scrapped. The machine could be sold at any point in the next year for £18,000, the gain being subject to tax at 30 per cent, payable the following year. If it were sold, a new machine costing £90,000 would be bought. The new machine would receive 20 per cent writing-down allowances to be offset annually against profits. It is estimated that the

→

→ new machine would save material costs of £30,000 per year compared to the current machine. Profits are subject to tax at 30 per cent, payable nine months after the end of the company's financial period. The new machinery would have a five-year life, with a residual value of zero, and would be depreciated straight line over that period. Prepare a cash flow forecast for the replacement option, and indicate how the profits reported in the financial statements would be altered were the existing machine to be replaced.

46.7 What is the payback period on the following project cash flows? (Brackets indicate expenditure.)

Year	Net cash flows
	£
0	(15,000)
1	10,000
2	6,000
3	3,000
4	1,000

46.8 Using a discount rate of 8 per cent, what is the net present value of the project in Question 46.7?

46.9 What is the internal rate of return on the project in Question 46.7?

46.10 What is the annualised amount of the net benefits from the project in Question 46.7?

46.11A What is the payback on a project requiring £40,000 initial investment that has a net cash inflow of £26,000 in year 1, £16,000 in year 2, and £10,000 in year 3?

46.12A Using a discount rate of 6 per cent, what is the net present value of the project in Question 46.11A?

46.13A What is the internal rate of return on the project in Question 46.11A?

46.14A What is the annualised amount of the net benefits from the project in Question 46.11A?

46.15A The annual profit forecast for a project is:

	£	£
Revenue		160,000
Labour, materials, and overheads	46,000	
Depreciation	24,000	
		70,000
Net profit before tax		90,000

The project requires that a new machine be purchased for £128,000. It will be depreciated using the straight line method over five years to a residual value of £8,000. The project will cease when the machine is sold for £8,000 at the end of the fifth year. Ignoring taxation, what is the accounting rate of return? (No additional working capital is required for this project.)

46.16A Assuming that all sales are for cash, what is the internal rate of return on the project in Question 46.15A?

46.17 Which of the following two mutually exclusive alternatives should be selected if a 5 per cent interest rate is used for the calculation of net present value?

	Net cash flow Year 0 £	Net cash flow Year 3 £
Machine X project	(24,000)	42,000
Machine Y project	(76,000)	138,000

46.18 Using internal rate of return, which of the two projects in Question 46.17 would be preferred?

46.19A Which of the following two mutually exclusive alternatives should be selected if a 7 per cent interest rate is used for the calculation of net present value?

	Net cash flow Year 0 £	Net cash flow Year 1 £	Net cash flow Year 3 £
Project X	(68,000)	30,000	48,000
Project Y	(58,000)	42,000	21,000

46.20A Using internal rate of return, which of the two projects in Question 46.19A would be preferred?

46.21 Equipment with an estimated useful economic life of four years has an NPV of £4,200 using an 8 per cent discount rate. What is the annualised equivalent of the £4,200 NPV?

46.22A Two mutually exclusive alternatives are available. Project X will require initial investment of £50,000 and run for three years at a cost of £8,000 per annum. Project Y will require initial investment of £110,000 and last for five years at a cost of £12,000 for the first two years and £2,000 in years three, four and five. Calculate the annualised cost of both projects over a five-year period, assuming that reinvestment in Project X would cost £4,000 at the end of year two and an interest rate of 6 per cent. Which alternative should be selected?

46.23 A machine with a four-year useful life could be purchased for £50,000. It would have zero residual value at the end of the four years. Alternatively, the machine could be rented at £15,180 per annum for four years. Assuming a tax rate of 30 per cent and that tax relief is obtained in the same period as the payments, what is the implicit interest rate in the lease?

46.24 Roadwheelers Ltd were considering buying an additional lorry but the company had not yet decided which particular lorry to purchase. The lorries had broadly similar technical specifications and each was expected to have a working life of five years.
  The following information was available on the lorries being considered:

1

	Lorries		
	BN Roadhog	FX Sprinter	VR Rocket
Purchase price	£40,000	£45,000	£50,000
Estimated scrap value after 5 years	£8,000	£9,000	£14,000
Fixed costs other than depreciation	£	£	£
Year 1	2,000	1,800	1,500
Year 2	2,000	1,800	1,500
Year 3	2,200	1,800	1,400
Year 4	2,400	2,000	1,400
Year 5	2,400	2,200	1,400
Variable costs per road mile	6p	8p	7p

→

➔

2 The company charges 25p per mile for all journeys irrespective of the length of journey and the expected annual mileages over the five-year period are:

	Miles
Year 1	50,000
Year 2	60,000
Year 3	80,000
Year 4	80,000
Year 5	80,000

3 The company's cost of capital is 10 per cent per annum.
4 It should be assumed that all operating costs are paid and revenues received at the end of year.
5 Present value of £1 at interest rate of 10 per cent per annum:

Year 1	£0.909
Year 2	£0.826
Year 3	£0.751
Year 4	£0.683
Year 5	£0.621

Required:
(a) (i) Appropriate computations using the net present value method for each of the lorries under consideration.
   (ii) A report to the directors of Roadwheelers Ltd advising them as to which specific lorry should be purchased.
(b) A brief outline of the problems encountered in evaluating capital projects.

(AQA (Associated Examining Board): GCE A-level)

46.25A Hirwaun Pig Iron Co. operate a single blast furnace producing pig iron. The present blast furnace is obsolete and the company is considering its replacement. The alternatives the company is considering are:

(i) Blast furnace type Exco. Cost £2 million.
   This furnace is of a standard size capable of a monthly output of 10,000 tonnes. The company expects to sell 80 per cent of its output annually at £150 per tonne on a fixed price contract. The remaining output will be sold on the open market at the following expected prices:

	2005	2006	2007	2008
Price per tonne	£150	£140	£140	£160

(ii) Blast furnace type Ohio. Cost £3.5 million.
   This large furnace is capable of a monthly output of 20,000 tonnes. A single buyer has agreed to buy all the monthly output at a fixed price which is applicable from 1 January each year. The prices fixed for the next four years are as follows:

	Payments per tonne of output			
	2005	2006	2007	2008
Price per tonne	£130	£130	£140	£170

Additional information:
1 Blast furnaces operate continuously and the operating labour is regarded as a fixed cost. During the next four years the operating labour costs will be as follows:

Exco £1.2 million per annum
Ohio £2.5 million per annum

2 Other forecast operating payments (excluding labour) per tonne:

	2005	2006	2007	2008
Exco	£130	£130	£135	£135
Ohio	£120	£120	£125	£125

3 It can be assumed that both blast furnaces will have a life of 10 years.
4 The company's cost of capital is 12 per cent per annum.
5 It should be assumed that all costs are paid and revenues received at the end of each year.
6 The following is an extract from the present value table for £1:

	11%	12%	13%	14%
Year 1	£0.901	£0.893	£0.885	£0.877
Year 2	£0.812	£0.797	£0.783	£0.770
Year 3	£0.731	£0.712	£0.693	£0.675
Year 4	£0.659	£0.636	£0.613	£0.592

Required:
(a) The forecast budgets for each of the years 2005–2008 and for each of the blast furnaces being considered. Show the expected yearly net cash flows.
(b) Appropriate computations using the net present value method for each of the blast furnaces, Exco and Ohio, for the first four years.
(c) A report providing a recommendation to the management of Hirwaun Pig Iron Co. as to which blast furnace should be purchased. Your report should include a critical evaluation of the method used to assess the capital project.

(AQA (Associated Examining Board): GCE A-level)

46.26 Moray Ferries Ltd own a single ship which provides a short sea ferry service for passengers, private vehicles and commercial traffic. The present ship is nearing the end of its useful life and the company is considering the purchase of a new ship.
　The forecast operating budgets using the present ship are as follows:

	2005 £m	2006 £m	2007 £m	2008 £m	2009 £m
Estimated revenue receipts					
Private traffic	2	3	4.5	6	7
Commercial traffic	3	4	4.5	5	6
	5	7	9.0	11	13
Estimated operating payments	4	5	6.5	7.5	9
	1	2	2.5	3.5	4

The ships being considered as a replacement are as described below.

1 Ship A. Cost £10m
　This ship is of similar capacity to the one being replaced, but being a more modern ship it is expected that extra business would be attracted from competitors. It is anticipated therefore that estimated revenue receipts would be 10 per cent higher in each year of the present forecast. There would be no change in operating payments.

2 Ship B. Cost £14m
　This modern ship has a carrying capacity 30 per cent greater than the present ship. It is expected that private traffic receipts would increase by £½m a year in each year of the forecast. Commercial traffic receipts are expected to increase by 15 per cent in each of the first two years and by 30 per cent in each of the remaining years.
　Operating payments would increase by 20 per cent in each year of the forecast.

Additional information:
3 The company's cost of capital is 15 per cent per annum.
4 It is company policy to assume that ships have a life of 20 years.
5 It should be assumed that all costs are paid and revenues received at the end of each year.

→

6 The following is an extract from the present value table for £1:

	12%	14%	15%	16%
Year 1	£0.893	£0.877	£0.870	£0.862
Year 2	£0.797	£0.769	£0.756	£0.743
Year 3	£0.712	£0.675	£0.658	£0.641
Year 4	£0.636	£0.592	£0.572	£0.552
Year 5	£0.567	£0.519	£0.497	£0.476

7 All calculations should be made correct to three places of decimals.

Required:
(*a*) Revised operating budgets for 2005–2009 for each of the alternatives being considered.
(*b*) Appropriate computations using the net present value method for each of the ships, A and B.
(*c*) A report providing a recommendation to the management of Moray Ferries Ltd as to which course of action should be followed. Your report should include any reservations that you may have.

(AQA (Associated Examining Board): GCE A-level)

46.27A The Rovers Football Club are languishing in the middle of the Premier Division of the Football League. The Club have suffered a loss of £200,000 in their last financial year and whilst receipts from spectators have declined over the last five years, recently receipts have stabilised at approximately £1,000,000 per season. The Club is considering the purchase of the services of one of two new football players, Jimmy Jam or Johnny Star.

Jimmy Jam is 21 years old and considered to be a future international footballer. He is prepared to sign a five-year contract with Rovers for a salary of £50,000 per annum. His present club would require a transfer fee of £200,000 for the transfer of his existing contract. With J. Jam in the team the Rovers Club would expect receipts to increase by 20 per cent.

Johnny Star is 32 years old and a leading international footballer who is prepared to sign for Rovers on a two-year contract before retiring completely from football. He would expect a salary of £200,000 per annum and his present club would require a transfer fee of £100,000 for the transfer of his existing contract. Rovers believe that as a result of signing Star receipts would increase by 40 per cent.

The rate of interest applicable to the transaction is 12 per cent and the following is an extract from the present value table for £1:

	12%
Year 1	0.893
Year 2	0.797
Year 3	0.712
Year 4	0.636
Year 5	0.567

It should be assumed that all costs are paid and revenues received at the end of each year.

Required:
A report, incorporating an evaluation of the financial result of engaging each player by the net present value method, providing the Rovers Football Club with information to assist it in deciding which alternative to adopt. Indicate any other factors that may be taken into consideration.

(AQA (Associated Examining Board): GCE A-level)

You can find a range of additional self-test questions, as well as material to help you with your studies, on the website that accompanies this book at **www.pearsoned.co.uk/wood**

The balanced scorecard

47.1 Background

Much has changed in the way that organisations operate today compared with even five years ago. The change over the past thirty years has been immense. In 1980, only the largest organisations had computers, the spreadsheet had only just been invented, the Internet was something only academics and some government employees had heard of, email was used by only a few, the *World Wide Web* was ten years away from being invented, electronic commerce was something from science fiction, and most business records were still recorded and maintained by hand.

The business environment of today is far more competitive, far more open, and far more volatile than it has ever been. In order to survive, businesses need to be far more efficient in the use of their resources, have a far better understanding of the needs of their customers, have far better organised internal systems and procedures, and have employees who have a far greater level of interpersonal skills than in the past. Above all, they need to have a well-defined organisational strategy and to have both defined the objectives that ensure the strategy is pursued and identified the measures required in order to ensure that the objectives not only are being achieved but will continue to be achieved in future.

This means that **organisations need to look beyond the historical perspective of their traditional financial reporting systems** which were mainly backwards-looking, focusing upon reporting achievements rather than upon the attainment and pursuit of objectives. They need to incorporate data capture and analysis of non-financial measures, such as customer profiles, customer satisfaction, employee performance, employee satisfaction, product quality, service quality, organisational transformation and development. They need to pay attention to the long term and think less about the short term.

One performance evaluation technique that supports this shift in emphasis and focus has emerged over the last twenty years, Kaplan and Norton's **balanced scorecard.** It bridges the strengths of the traditional financial measures of past performance with the benefits of measuring factors that impact upon or 'drive' future performance. It does so at all levels of the business, not just at the overall level typified by the traditional measures of financial performance.

47.2 The framework of the balanced scorecard

The balanced scorecard assesses performance across a balanced set of four perspectives: customers, internal processes, organisational learning and growth, and financial. It does not replace the traditional focus upon financial measurement as a critical summary of managerial and business performance. Rather, it complements it by the addition of the other three perspectives.

Thus, the traditional financial measures are still there for those that require them and for the purposes to which they are most suited but new measures are provided that enrich the information available at all levels of the organisation and so facilitate the co-ordinated achievement of organisational objectives, particularly in the long term.

The four perspectives of the balanced scorecard

Exhibit 47.1 shows the relationship between the four perspectives, and organisational vision and strategy:

Exhibit 47.1

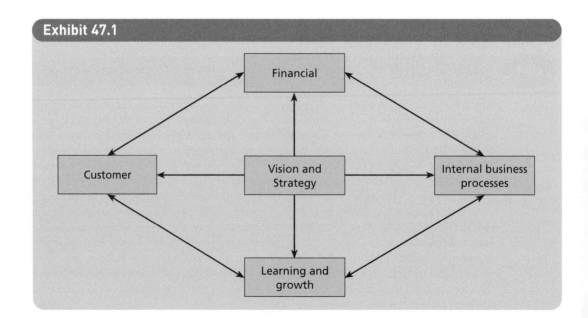

The financial perspective

Here you identify the financial objectives that the organisation wishes to pursue and develop measures that indicate how successful the organisation has been in achieving those objectives. In essence, this is the aspect of the balanced scorecard that accounting has long been associated with and includes the use of such measures as return on capital employed, earnings per share, and the other financial ratios you learnt about in Chapter 27. It answers the question, how does the organisation appear to its owners?

Examples of possible measures are:

● return on capital employed
● return on net assets
● reduction of administrative expenses
● reduction in bad debts
● reduction in debtor days
● reduction in gearing.

The customer perspective

You must identify the customer and market segments in which the organisation operates. Measurements should then be made of factors such as customer satisfaction, retention, acquisition, customer profitability and market share. It answers the question, how does the organisation appear to its customers?

Examples of possible measures are:

● customer satisfaction
● customer retention
● increasing customer base
● reduction in delivery times
● reduction in rate of goods returned by customers.

The internal business processes perspective

You need to identify and measure the internal processes that are critical to the organisation being able to improve the drivers that will attract and retain customers in targeted markets and satisfy owner expectations concerning financial returns. It answers the question, at what must the organisation excel?

Examples of possible measures are:

● reduction in quality control rejection rate
● reduced production lead times
● increased level of production capacity utilisation.

The learning and growth perspective

This identifies the human relations, technological and general systems infrastructure that the organisation must develop if it is to achieve long-term growth and organisational improvement. Appropriate measures would include those relating to the level of relevant employee skills, how up to date the organisation's IT systems and programs are, and the ability of the organisation's systems architecture to provide the information in an efficient, timely and cost-effective way. One of the key aspects in this perspective is appropriate and timely development of people and systems and development of measures to monitor and confirm that this is being done. It answers the question, how will the organisation continue to change and improve?

Examples of possible measures are:

● increased level of spending per head on employee training
● reduced employee absenteeism rate

- reduced staff turnover rate
- increased range of products
- increased proportion of new product sales as a proportion of total sales
- greater reporting flexibility in the information system
- increase in the range of information available on demand from the information system.

47.3 Measures

Two forms of measures are used in the balanced scorecard approach:

(a) *outcome measures*, which assess past performance;

(b) *performance measures (or drivers)*, which are indicators that drive future performance.

Performance measures need to be aligned to organisation strategy and, therefore, to outcomes. There is no point in having a measure that has no bearing on strategy or its pursuit. Typically, three to five measures for each of the four perspectives should be adequate. Once the organisation strategy has been identified and converted into objectives, those factors that will achieve the desired objectives (i.e. the performance measures) are identified, along with those that can confirm the objectives are being achieved (i.e. the outcome measures).

As a result of articulating the outcomes the organisation desires and pinpointing the drivers of those outcomes, the energies, abilities and specific knowledge of people throughout the organisation can be aligned to achieve the goals of the organisation.

Once they have been established, there is no reason why the measures inherent in the balanced scorecard should remain fixed. Organisational strategy may change at any time. When it does, the objectives will obviously be changed to keep them in line with the revised strategy. Clearly, the measures of both output and performance will also change as appropriate.

47.4 The relationship between the four perspectives

There needs to be a series of cause and effect relationships between the four perspectives and the factors within them. Specifically, there must be a clear and logical relationship between each performance driver and one or more of the outcome measures. If there is not, the overall strategy of the organisation cannot be achieved.

Activity 47.1 Why is this the case?

47.5 Benefits of adopting the balanced scorecard

There are a number of benefits to those organisations that adopt the balanced scorecard:

1 It provides the organisation with a strategic management system that:

(a) clarifies and encourages consensus about organisational vision and strategy

(b) communicates strategy, objectives, drives and measures of performance

(c) facilitates the linking of strategic objectives to budgets

(d) facilitates strategic reviews, especially periodic but also *ad hoc*

(e) facilitates the identification and promotion of new strategic initiatives

(f) facilitates fine-tuning and amendment of strategy in the light of performance.

In effect, the balanced scorecard provides management with a tool to focus strategy and move the organisation in a co-ordinated and transparent manner towards the achievement of its objectives.

2 **It helps people understand how they can contribute to the strategic success of the organisation.** By making it clear what items are important indicators of success, people become aware of what actually leads to the organisation achieving its objectives. They then know which aspects of their work are vital and know that to focus upon them will be beneficial to the organisation. Previously, they would have had to choose to focus upon one or more of a range of alternative activities, many of which may have made no worthwhile contribution to the achievement of the organisational goals.

3 **It guides the transformation of the organisation's vision and strategy into a set of performance measures.** The chain of development of the balanced scorecard is quite straightforward. First, the organisation's mission must be established, then its strategy to pursue its mission, then the objectives that will underpin its strategy, then output measures must be defined so that performance can be assessed and the performance measures (or drivers) established so that it can be seen whether the organisation is moving in the right direction. By creating and providing such a framework to management, the balanced scorecard approach supports the organisation's move towards a greater and more consistent performance that is in line with the organisation's objectives and strategy.

47.6 Problems that may arise in introducing the balanced scorecard

There are a number of problems that may arise when introducing the balanced scorecard. Each of them can result in its being less than successful and care needs to be taken to ensure they do not arise, or, if they do arise, that they are eliminated as quickly as possible. The problems include:

(a) **A lack of a clearly defined organisational vision or strategy.** It is very difficult to establish objectives if there is no overall organisational vision or strategy. Many organisations have no statement of their mission and many that do have developed no clear organisational strategy. This slows down implementation of the balanced scorecard, as it first requires that a mission, vision and strategy be developed and agreed. Not surprisingly, unless this is done, the balanced scorecard can do little to improve the overall ability of the organisation to achieve its strategic objectives.

(b) **Developing and implementing a balanced scorecard before appropriate objectives have been identified.** It can only be wasteful and misleading to develop a balanced scorecard in this case, as there will be aspects of it that are wasteful of resources and other aspects that simply fail to address the appropriate measures. Once the mission, vision and strategy have been developed, it will become obvious that the objectives that existed previously and formed the basis for the development of a balanced scorecard were inappropriate. At that point the incorrect balanced scorecard must be amended and replaced with one that is consistent with the 'real' objectives. As most people are naturally resistant to change, this can create human relations problems that seriously undermine the effort to install an appropriate balanced scorecard. It is far better to wait for appropriate objectives to be identified before starting to develop the balanced scorecard.

(c) **Failing to achieve consensus and acceptance at all levels of the organisation.** In this aspect, there are similarities with the need to ensure all individuals accept, understand and appropriately apply a system of budgetary control. As the extent of the measures and drivers of the four perspectives of the balanced scorecard are far greater than for a budgetary control system, the need for consensus is considerably greater. Dysfunctional responses to the balanced scorecard seriously undermine its potential to motivate development of the organisation in the directions established by the clear definition of the organisational strategy which the balanced scorecard provides.

(d) **When first attempted, definition of the objectives inherent in the financial, customer and internal business process perspectives often reveals gaps between the existing capabilities of people, organisational systems and procedures and the objectives that are sought.** Management must close these gaps by retraining employees, improving the organisational systems (often through more effective use of IT), and realigning organisational procedures and routines so that they are more compatible with the systems to which they relate.

(e) **The organisational objectives across all four perspectives must be compatible and moving in the same direction in the long term.** If the balanced scorecard is to be successfully adopted, it needs to be done with a view to the long term. For example, an objective to enhance customer satisfaction may require that employees are retrained and that systems and quality control procedures are altered so as to improve product quality.

These changes will impact the financial performance measures negatively in the short term. If the organisation has a financial strategy objective to improve return on capital employed, this will only be achieved once the changes made have resulted in increased customer satisfaction which, in turn, results in increased customer loyalty, higher demand for the organisation's products, increased profitability, and an improved return on capital employed.

(f) **The organisation's ability to offer current and accurate information to support the balanced scorecard may be undermined because it is currently capable of providing only a few of the outcomes and measures identified by the balanced scorecard analysis.** If the underlying systems and technology are incapable of providing the outcomes and measures required by the balanced scorecard, they must be reorganised and replaced if the balanced scorecard is to be implemented successfully.

(g) **The performance measures selected are not aligned with the organisation's strategy.** One cause may be a desire to retain traditional measures because they have always been used rather than to abandon them. Developing a balanced scorecard requires that management reappraise the organisation and switch the emphasis from monitoring output and performance that fails to support the organisation's strategy in a meaningful way.

Change is crucial to the successful implementation of the balanced scorecard. The difference between a traditional financial performance-related monitoring focus and the far broader and more focused balanced scorecard requires a major shift in perceptions and practices. Reluctance to change can seriously undermine the success of the balanced scorecard approach.

47.7 Strategic planning and budgeting

If you investigate when most organisations carry out these two activities, you will find that strategic planning and budgeting are typically done at different times of the year and led by different parts of the organisation.

Kaplan and Norton recommended that the budgeting process be integrated with the strategic planning process. To do so, the budgeting process should follow the strategic planning process. They also believe that the budget should represent Year 1 of a three- or a five-year plan and that companies should be budgeting not only for financial measures but for the measures in the other three perspectives as well.

They argued that by comparing the gap between where the organisation wants to be in 3–5 years and where it is today, the managers can assign new resources and strategic initiatives to close the gaps. This motivates additional spending in Year 1. Discretionary spending, both operating and capital, is aimed at closing the forecast future gaps, rather than being devoted to the pursuit of short-term gains.

At the same time, if management specify how the initial spending and investment will start to improve measures in the customer, internal business processes and learning and growth perspectives, they will provide a ready-made yardstick by which to measure performance in pursuit of these changes.

The benefit of this approach is that costs rise in the short term but in a way that does not result in the perspectives being out of balance with each other. In the long term, all the perspectives benefit.

As a result, by integrating strategic planning and budgeting, managers can reach a consensus about the trade-offs between short-term financial performance and long-term benefit. There are potentially enormous benefits to be gained by organisations that adopt such an approach over those that stick with traditional financial-based performance measures.

47.8 Adoption of the balanced scorecard

It is not surprising that the balanced scorecard is becoming increasingly adopted as a means of offering a more focused approach to performance monitoring and measurement. It provides a far more focused approach than traditional financial-based performance measures and organisations that adopt it experience a greatly enhanced synergy between their mission, strategy and objectives and the means used to measure output and performance.

It is likely that adoption of the balanced scorecard will become ever more popular as organisations of all sizes and types become aware of its potential. However, it should not be overlooked that the traditional financial measures still have a significant role to play and that the balanced scorecard adds a new and complementary dimension to performance measurement rather than offering an outright alternative.

Learning outcomes

You should now have learnt:

1 The aims of the balanced scorecard.

2 The four perspectives of the balanced scorecard.

3 The two types of measures inherent in the balanced scorecard.

4 Some advantages of adopting the balanced scorecard.

5 Some of the problems that can arise when the balanced scorecard is adopted.

6 The difference between the balanced scorecard and a traditional financial accounting-based performance appraisal system.

Answer to activity

47.1 It is very difficult to establish objectives if there is no overall organisational vision or strategy. Without a mission, vision and strategy the organisational objectives can be little more than guesses concerning whether or not they help the organisation pursue its strategy in a meaningful way. Establishing measures to achieve false objectives serves no meaningful purpose.

Review questions

47.1 What is the balanced scorecard?

47.2 Compare the balanced scorecard to traditional financial accounting-based performance measurement.

47.3 Compare and contrast the two forms of measure applied by the balanced scorecard.

47.4 Compare and contrast the four perspectives of the balanced scorecard.

You can find a range of additional self-test questions, as well as material to help you with your studies, on the website that accompanies this book at **www.pearsoned.co.uk/wood**

THE EMERGING BUSINESS ENVIRONMENT OF ACCOUNTING

Introduction

This part reviews increasingly popular recently developed approaches to managing the flow of information and data and enhancing the management of resources. It also looks at the emerging Internet-based business environment and the impact of e-commerce upon accounting.

choice and may choose to avoid dealing with organisations that look for clearer indications of demand such as allowing them to access their inventory database and automatically provide new goods when the inventory reaches its reorder level.

Not surprisingly, supply chain management is a relatively recent development and the main beneficiaries have been the larger organisations who have embraced it. While small and medium sized organisations can and do also adopt supply chain management, they have far greater difficulty in achieving the commitment of the outside entities to their objectives.

Another integrating approach, but one that is internal to the organisation, is **enterprise resource planning (ERP) system**. ERP integrates the internal functions of the organisation and achieves savings through the efficiencies that result.

An ERP system is a suite of software modules. Each relates to a function of the organisation, such as order processing, production, creditor control, debtor control, payroll, marketing and human resources. The software modules are positioned on top of a centralised database, resulting in data being entered only once into the system but being accessible to all modules within it. Because the software modules all come from the same supplier, they are fully and seamlessly integrated from the start. There is no need to bolt together a range of software from different suppliers in order to achieve data integration.

There are two groups of applications within an ERP system:

(a) **Core applications.** The applications that need to work or the organisation will be unable to function. They include production, sales, distribution and planning. These are always fully integrated within the ERP system.
(b) **Business analysis applications.** Examples include modelling, decision support, information retrieval, reporting, accounting, simulation and 'what if' analysis. Some ERP software includes these. Some provide links into the ERP system to third party software that performs tasks.

48.6 Difficulties of justifying ERP

Integrating all the functions of an organisation in this way is a non-trivial exercise. It is estimated that the implementation cost of an ERP system may be greater than £25 million and the average annual running cost of large ERP systems is more than £11 million. As with supply chain management, the benefits of such systems are hard to quantify in traditional accounting terms or through the use of traditional accounting data and techniques.

Instead, as with supply chain management, less quantifiable advantages must be considered and weighed up against the identifiable costs.

48.7 Advantages of ERP systems

The advantages of ERP systems compared with traditional information system architectures include:

● increased data consistency;
● reduced data redundancy;
● greatly enriched data, including access to qualitative data by functions that do not typically have access to it;
● greatly increased depth and breadth of data analysis;
● reduced response times to information requests;
● reduced need for manual intervention in data access and analysis;
● reduced risk of errors in data or in its analysis;
● greatly enhanced exception reporting facility (due to the increase in the range of variables that can be flagged for monitoring);
● reduced time spent analysing exception reports (as the level of detail provided by the system is greatly enhanced);

● greatly reduced lead times in report generation;
● greatly increased efficiency in materials ordering, requisition and deployment;
● much closer ties between ordering, stock control and production.

48.8 Organisational size

Since they first appeared, ERP systems have been developed in the largest organisations. Software vendors have produced their products with this in mind. However, computing power has increased and its price has dropped to such an extent that medium-sized and even small organisations can now take advantage of the software and develop ERP systems. While ERP systems are costly, the benefits are generally seen as outweighing the costs, provided the installation of ERP systems is effective and appropriate.

It is likely that within a few years, ERP software will be far cheaper and as commonplace in organisations of all sizes as general accounting packages are at present and that, in some cases, it will provide all the functionality of those accounting packages along with everything else they currently provide as standard.

48.9 ERP systems and supply chain management

Those organisations that add supply chain management to their ERP systems achieve the greatest benefit. An efficient and effective ERP system enhances the ability to integrate all the internal functions of the supply chain while also integrating other support functions, such as human resources and accounting. **Supply chain management enhances the capability of the ERP system to record and monitor all aspects of the organisation's business and bring suppliers and customers within the co-ordinated control of the organisation.**

Many organisations are moving in this direction and their accountants are being seen as playing a vital role in the success of the emerging information systems. For their part, ERP software providers have recognised the pivotal role of the accountant and have for some years funded American universities to integrate their software into accounting courses. Whether this occurs elsewhere remains to be seen. However, there is no doubt that ERP and supply chain management are two subjects that accountants need to be aware of and prepared to be involved with.

Learning outcomes

You should now have learnt:

1 What is meant by the term 'supply chain'.
2 What is meant by the term 'supply chain management'.
3 About the advantages of supply chain management.
4 What is meant by the term 'enterprise resource planning'.
5 What the differences are between an enterprise planning system and a traditional information system.
6 Why organisations that integrate their ERP systems with supply chain management stand to benefit compared with those that do not.
7 Why supply chain management and ERP systems are both important concepts for accounting and accountants.

Answers to activities

48.1 Stockholding levels would need to be established for each item of raw materials: minimum level, safety stock level, reorder level (*see* Section 38.8).

48.2 Customer service is directly affected by the speed at which delivery is made and by the amount charged for the service. It is indirectly affected by the decisions made concerning shipping raw materials in from suppliers and, once again, it is the time factor that matters. A just-in-time system that allows suppliers a week to deliver raw material orders is going to result in a level of customer service that is somewhat less than one that requires delivery within 24 hours.

Review questions

48.1 What is the supply chain?

48.2 What is meant by the term, 'supply chain management'?

48.3 What are the advantages of effective supply chain management?

48.4 Why does supply chain management bring new challenges for accounting and accountants?

48.5 What is enterprise resource planning?

48.6 What are the advantages of an ERP system?

48.7 Why will those organisations that integrate their ERP systems with supply chain management benefit more than those that introduce only one or the other or these two concepts?

You can find a range of additional self-test questions, as well as material to help you with your studies, on the website that accompanies this book at **www.pearsoned.co.uk/wood**

Chapter
49

E-commerce and accounting

Learning objectives

After you have studied this chapter, you should be able to:

- explain what is meant by 'e-commerce'
- explain what is meant by 'business-to-business' transactions
- explain what is meant by 'business-to-consumer' transactions
- describe a typical business-to-consumer transaction
- describe some of the benefits of e-commerce to sellers
- describe some of the benefits of e-commerce to buyers
- describe the impact of e-commerce upon the role of the financial accountant
- describe the impact of e-commerce upon the role of the management accountant
- describe the impact of e-commerce upon the role of the auditor, both internal and external
- explain why many retail businesses cannot afford to stay out of e-commerce

Introduction

In this chapter, you'll learn about e-commerce and its impact upon sellers, buyers and accountants.

49.1 Background

For many years, all business was undertaken face-to-face. Gradually, orders started to be placed by other means – letter, telegram, telex, fax, telephone, etc. However, when transactions were undertaken between businesses, paper was normally exchanged indicating an order was being placed and, subsequently, indicating how much the seller required to be paid for the goods ordered.

This is the business environment in which accounting developed. Accountants learnt to use the documents relating to the transaction in order to make entries in the accounting books. They ensured there was an audit trail running from the original paperwork right through to each entry in the ledger. Checking these entries was time consuming but always possible and, where original records did not exist, auditors would get very concerned as to the validity of transactions. Sometimes they accepted the word of the proprietor that transactions were valid. On other occasions, they did not and an investigation was launched in pursuit of evidence that things were recorded inaccurately.

Activity 49.1 What sorts of things were done in this investigation phase?

Other forms of business started to emerge. Ones where communication was electronic but, initially, all payment was by traditional means. Then payments too became increasingly electronic. Now, not only can communication and payment all be done electronically, but the seller may never physically possess the goods or services being sold and, in fact, the seller may not even be aware that a transaction has occurred (as the sale process is entirely automated). Also, products that were traditionally physical – books and CDs, for example – can now be sold as electronic files downloaded off the Internet directly into the customer's PC.

This is **electronic commerce** and is the environment in which an increasing proportion of business is now conducted. It was expected that the total value of e-commerce transactions would rise by 400 per cent between 2001 and 2004 to around US$5,000 billion.

In a report issued in 2001, *The Global Online Retailing Study*, the accounting firm Ernst & Young stated that online retailing is no longer an option but a *business requirement*. Retail businesses must move into e-commerce or watch their markets disappear into the hands of their competitors. That was seven years ago. If it was important then, it is even more so now. One obvious change that has occurred since 2001 is the massive switch to purchasing music by downloading it from the Internet. In 2001, this was rare: music was bought on CDs from shops. Now, shops are closing as buyers have switched to other sellers who are operating virtual shops and conducting their businesses as e-commerce organisations.

49.2 Electronic commerce

Electronic commerce can be defined as the use of electronic telecommunication technology to conduct business transactions over the Internet. It allows goods to be exchanged anytime, 24 hours a day, 7 days a week, anywhere the buyer has access to the Internet. It expands the market of every seller – in many cases, the market becomes global.

There are two principal e-commerce models:

1 **Business-to-business (B2B).** Businesses purchase from other businesses and/or sell their goods and services to other businesses; and,
2 **Business-to-consumer (B2C).** Businesses sell to consumers. For B2C to work:
   (*a*) the customer must have access to the Internet;
   (*b*) the customer must have a means of making payment electronically (normally, a credit or a debit card);
   (*c*) there must be a viable means of delivering the item(s) purchased to the consumer.

E-commerce involves the transmission of confidential, sensitive and valued information. To operate in this environment effectively, not only customers, but also business partners, must be convinced that a B2B or B2C business's systems are secure, reliable, available and properly controlled. While this is very much a necessity for effective supply chain management (Chapter 48), it is much more critical in an e-commerce environment and is the aspect of e-commerce that, more than any other, is impacting upon the role of the accountant and, in particular, the role of the auditor.

49.3 Business-to-business

B2B transactions are very similar to how transactions occur in a traditional business environment. Request for payment is often by traditional invoicing and payment follows at some date in the future.

The seller

B2B e-commerce offers the seller many advantages over a traditional business environment, including:

● cost savings by removing the need for a human salesperson to be involved in the transaction;
● faster transaction times;
● lower clerical costs as there is now a reduced level of paper records to be prepared and maintained;
● richer analysis of sales due to greatly enhanced knowledge about the pattern of sale.

However, the major differences that e-commerce can bring to this form of e-commerce lie in the ability to integrate the B2B e-commerce system into the seller's accounting system. There is a growing range of integrated software available, including many of the ERP software packages referred to in Chapter 48.

Doing so has many advantages for the seller, including:

● better credit control at the time of sale;
● better control over debtor balances;
● potential to cut costs by automating the sale process, leaving it to be triggered by the level of inventory shown in the purchaser's stock database.

The buyer

The buyer benefits from:

● faster transaction times;
● greater confidence that orders will be filled in a timely manner;
● (in many cases) a greatly increased market (geographically) in which to make a purchase;
● cost savings arising from increased competition among sellers;
● (often) visual confirmation that what is being ordered is what is required (as there is no longer a possibility that an ill-informed salesperson is dealing with the order/enquiry).

The accountant

There is less of a paper trail than under a traditional system. However, this has little effect on the day-to-day work of accountants working within the seller or buyer organisation. **Thus, accountants who work for the seller or buyer are relatively unaffected by the shift from a traditional business environment.** Transaction data is entered automatically into the accounting records rather than manually by a clerk. Thereafter, the internal accountant handles the data in the normal way and can create and provide all the 'normal' accounting information that would be provided were this a traditional business environment.

Management accountants

There is the possibility of the management accountant providing more detailed and richer information to the decision maker, as B2B transactions are information rich compared with traditional ones. For example, far more qualitative and non-financial quantitative data is available or is available from a more reliable source.

Financial accountants

Financial accountants will not experience very much change in the nature of data from that experienced under a traditional computerised accounting environment. However, when the audit is being conducted, there will be a need to be able to explain to the auditor where the data within the accounting system comes from and the controls that are in place to ensure that it is both accurate and reliable.

Auditors

In contrast to the two main groups of accountants, auditors (both internal and external) are greatly affected by the introduction of B2B e-commerce. As mentioned earlier, there is less of a paper trail than under a traditional system. In fact, there may be nothing on paper until a goods delivery note is prepared in order to ship the goods. Thus, they have an increased need to focus on the technology involved in each transaction. As a result, they need to focus on assurance. In particular, online assurance, i.e. whether the B2B system is working correctly and whether all the transaction details being recorded are accurate, reliable and complete.

This represents a major change in the nature of the audit, even where previously an organisation's accounting system was computerised. Often in that case, auditors audited around the computer – that is, they checked that what came out was what they would have expected. In a B2B organisation, they need to audit through the computer – that is, they need to be assured that the computer is doing the correct things and that there are appropriate controls in place to ensure that errors are not made. This is particularly needed in the seller organisation because there is typically no human intervention in the transaction. In this case, the assurance should, preferably, be in real time. That is, the check on the controls on transactions should be done as transactions are being processed.

49.4 Business-to-consumer

This is the side of e-commerce that is most different from the traditional business environment. The seller is represented by a computer program which responds as appropriate to enquiries made by a consumer who can not only place an order but who will also provide a shipping address and make payment, all at the same time.

The consumer accesses the Internet and navigates to the seller's website. At the website, the consumer checks the seller's catalogue for the item(s) required, often through a series of searches of the seller's stock database. This in itself may be very different from a traditional high street purchase, for the seller may actually have little or no physical stock. Instead, the seller has built a stock database of the items that can be shipped to a customer in a reasonable period of time. (You can see examples of this at sites such as **www.amazon.co.uk**.)

When the decision is made to purchase something, the customer is directed to the seller's *online transaction server*, where all the customer's information, including personal details, the item(s) required, and credit or debit card details are entered. This information, particularly the credit card information, is usually encrypted as it is received. The information is then passed to the bank that issued the credit or debit card and to the seller's bank (i.e. the bank that operates the receipt of funds in this form for the seller). If both banks accept the transaction, the seller is informed it has been accepted and provided with an order number for reference and an indication of when the item(s) will be shipped.

This B2C e-commerce system is presented in Exhibit 49.1:

Exhibit 49.1

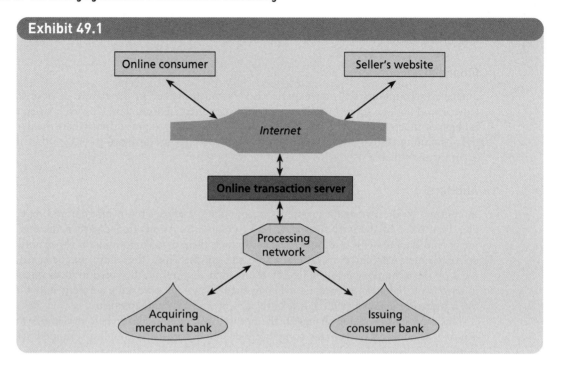

Activity 49.2

Compared with businesses operating in a traditional trading environment, what advantages concerning receipt of payment can you see for a business operating in a B2C environment?

49.5 Accountants and B2C e-commerce

B2C e-commerce has an impact upon the routine work of financial and management accountants similar to B2B. However, there are major issues with which accountants must be involved when the business first moves into a B2C environment:

1 The size of the transaction database. Is it going to be capable of handling a significant increase in transactions? In fact, what is that level of transactions likely to be?
2 The interface between the B2C systems and the accounting system.
3 The internal controls – the accountants need to emphasise the need for effective internal controls – checks built into the system to ensure entries are correct and correctly authorised – at the design stage, when it is easiest to incorporate them into the B2C system.

These are particularly difficult issues to deal with when the business is new and has no existing customer base, especially the question of size.

Auditors have similar issues to deal with as under B2B but, often, far more transactions to deal with. As individuals rather than other businesses are normally involved on the consumer side, there is a need to ensure that effective controls are in place in the system concerning credit card fraud and data security, for the liability if the system is breached may be far greater than if a B2B system is breached.

There is a further dimension for accountants to be concerned with concerning B2C transactions – globalisation.

49.6 Globalisation

Over 60 per cent of all B2C consumers resident outside the USA use B2C to purchase goods they wish to buy from sellers in other countries; over 50 per cent do so because the goods they want are not available in their own country; and 30 per cent do so because they have found goods cheaper to buy overseas.

For accountants, this adds problems concerning international tax and, for auditors especially, opens the possibility of international fraud.

49.7 E-commerce and accounting

E-commerce is changing and will continue to change the manner in which accountants carry out their role and, more importantly, it will change the nature of that role.

We already have a wide range of accounting software that eliminates the need to use traditional double entry to record transactions. Accountants have remained outside the system changes by continuing to do what they've always done and, instead, they have developed computer packages to check that the accounting software was working properly.

The accountants did not need to be retrained and, for many years, no attention was paid in the training of accountants to this shift in the environment of accounting. This was possible because business was still conducted in traditional ways. It was only the manner by which transactions were recorded that changed.

E-commerce changed this. An increasing proportion of transactions are now conducted electronically, both between businesses and between businesses and consumers. In many cases, there are no paper records and no written entries relating to these transactions. As a result, **accountants can no longer check a transaction against the original invoice or order document. Neither can they check that someone with appropriate authority has approved an order by signing an authorisation.**

Take away the paper, take away the written signature, and take away the double entry and what have you left for an accountant to do? Even more to the point, what can an auditor do to check the validity and accuracy of the accounting records?

A knowledge of double entry is still important. No financial accountant will be able to function effectively all the time without it. Accountants need to understand the entries in the accounting records and need to be able to tell if they are appropriate and correct. They also need to know how to produce financial statements and how to make appropriate adjustments to the accounting figures when doing so. Thus, there is still a need for the traditional techniques, skills and understanding that have been covered in both volumes of *Business Accounting*.

However, they now need to add further techniques, skills and understanding to their role. They need to shift towards real-time assurance – verifying that things are as they should be *in real time*. To do so, accountants need to become technologically competent. They need to know and understand the technological infrastructure of e-commerce in the same way as they have always needed to know the infrastructure of traditional business and the manner in which it is conducted and performed. They need to know how to recognise weaknesses and loopholes, and how to trap errors in an electronic business environment. They need to know how to distinguish between valid entries and those that are erroneous or falsified when the only evidence they have is electronic.

There are great changes coming in the role of the accountant. Some of the professional accounting bodies already have examinations which consider these issues, but those examinations are being sat by people who have already been working as accountants for a few years. Pre-work education always lags behind real life and it will be many years before it is normal to include these skills in accounting courses at schools, colleges and universities. Instead, they will be learnt later, on the job, by attending training courses, or while studying for the examinations of the professional accountancy bodies.

As a student of accounting, you will be wise to become aware of this changing environment and to understand how it differs from the world as presented in the classroom and in your textbooks. Don't let it take you by surprise. Look at the Internet, learn how business is conducted upon it and consider how different it is from doing business face-to-face.

Learning outcomes

You should now have learnt:

1 What is meant by 'e-commerce'.

2 What is meant by 'business-to-business' transactions.

3 What is meant by 'business-to-consumer' transactions.

4 What occurs in a typical business-to-consumer transaction.

5 About some of the benefits of e-commerce to sellers and buyers.

6 About the impact of e-commerce upon the role of the financial accountant, management accountant, internal auditor and external auditor.

7 Why many retail businesses cannot afford to stay out of e-commerce.

Answers to activities

49.1 Contacting the customer or supplier and asking for confirmation; checking inventory to confirm that it had existed; checking the existence of fixed assets; etc.

49.2 No sales take place without prior payment which is guaranteed by the issuing consumer bank. There will, therefore, be no bad debts for the seller. Also, there is far greater control over cash flows as payment will always be received on time.

Review questions

49.1 What is e-commerce?

49.2 What happens in a typical business-to-consumer transaction?

49.3 What impact is e-commerce having upon the role of the accountant?

49.4 Why can retail businesses not afford to ignore e-commerce?

You can find a range of additional self-test questions, as well as material to help you with your studies, on the website that accompanies this book at **www.pearsoned.co.uk/wood**

Interest tables

Table 1 Compound sum of £1

Year	1%	2%	3%	4%	5%	6%	7%	8%	9%	10%
1	1.010	1.020	1.030	1.040	1.050	1.060	1.070	1.080	1.090	1.100
2	1.020	1.040	1.061	1.082	1.103	1.124	1.145	1.166	1.188	1.210
3	1.030	1.061	1.093	1.125	1.158	1.191	1.225	1.260	1.295	1.331
4	1.041	1.082	1.126	1.170	1.216	1.262	1.311	1.360	1.412	1.464
5	1.051	1.104	1.159	1.217	1.276	1.338	1.403	1.469	1.539	1.611
6	1.062	1.126	1.194	1.265	1.340	1.419	1.501	1.587	1.677	1.772
7	1.072	1.149	1.230	1.316	1.407	1.504	1.606	1.714	1.828	1.949
8	1.083	1.172	1.267	1.369	1.477	1.594	1.718	1.851	1.993	2.144
9	1.094	1.195	1.305	1.423	1.551	1.689	1.838	1.999	2.172	2.358
10	1.105	1.219	1.344	1.480	1.629	1.791	1.967	2.159	2.367	2.594
11	1.116	1.243	1.384	1.539	1.710	1.898	2.105	2.332	2.580	2.853
12	1.127	1.268	1.426	1.601	1.796	2.012	2.252	2.518	2.813	3.138
13	1.138	1.294	1.469	1.665	1.886	2.133	2.410	2.720	3.066	3.452
14	1.149	1.319	1.513	1.732	1.980	2.261	2.579	2.937	3.342	3.797
15	1.161	1.346	1.558	1.801	2.079	2.397	2.759	3.172	3.642	4.177

Year	12%	14%	15%	16%	18%	20%	24%	28%	32%
1	1.120	1.140	1.150	1.160	1.180	1.200	1.240	1.280	1.320
2	1.254	1.300	1.323	1.346	1.392	1.440	1.538	1.638	1.742
3	1.405	1.482	1.521	1.561	1.643	1.728	1.907	2.097	2.300
4	1.574	1.689	1.749	1.811	1.939	2.074	2.364	2.684	3.036
5	1.762	1.925	2.011	2.100	2.288	2.488	2.932	3.436	4.007
6	1.974	2.195	2.313	2.436	2.700	2.986	3.635	4.398	5.290
7	2.211	2.502	2.660	2.826	3.185	3.583	4.508	5.629	6.983
8	2.476	2.853	3.059	3.278	3.759	4.300	5.590	7.206	9.217
9	2.773	3.252	3.518	3.803	4.435	5.160	6.931	9.223	12.166
10	3.106	3.707	4.046	4.411	5.234	6.192	8.594	11.806	16.060
11	3.479	4.226	4.652	5.117	6.176	7.430	10.657	15.112	21.199
12	3.896	4.818	5.350	5.936	7.288	8.916	13.215	19.343	27.983
13	4.363	5.492	6.153	6.886	8.599	10.699	16.386	24.759	36.937
14	4.887	6.261	7.076	7.988	10.147	12.839	20.319	31.691	48.757
15	5.474	7.138	8.137	9.266	11.974	15.407	25.196	40.565	64.359

Year	36%	40%	50%	60%	70%	80%	90%
1	1.360	1.400	1.500	1.600	1.700	1.800	1.900
2	1.850	1.960	2.250	2.560	2.890	3.240	3.610
3	2.515	2.744	3.375	4.096	4.913	5.832	6.859
4	3.421	3.842	5.062	6.544	8.352	10.498	13.032
5	4.653	5.378	7.594	10.486	14.199	18.896	24.761
6	6.328	7.530	11.391	16.777	24.138	34.012	47.046
7	8.605	10.541	17.086	26.844	41.034	61.222	89.387
8	11.703	14.758	25.629	42.950	69.758	110.200	169.836
9	15.917	20.661	38.443	68.720	118.588	198.359	322.688
10	21.647	28.925	57.665	109.951	201.599	357.047	613.107
11	29.439	40.496	86.498	175.922	342.719	642.684	1164.902
12	40.037	56.694	129.746	281.475	582.622	1156.831	2213.314
13	54.451	79.372	194.619	450.360	990.457	2082.295	4205.297
14	74.053	111.120	291.929	720.576	1683.777	3748.131	7990.065
15	100.712	155.568	437.894	1152.921	2862.421	6746.636	15181.122

Table 2 Present value of £1

Year	1%	2%	3%	4%	5%	6%	7%	8%	9%	10%	12%	14%	15%
1	0.990	0.980	0.971	0.961	0.952	0.943	0.935	0.926	0.917	0.909	0.893	0.877	0.870
2	0.980	0.961	0.943	0.925	0.907	0.890	0.873	0.857	0.842	0.826	0.797	0.769	0.756
3	0.971	0.942	0.915	0.889	0.864	0.840	0.816	0.794	0.772	0.751	0.712	0.675	0.658
4	0.961	0.924	0.889	0.855	0.823	0.792	0.763	0.735	0.708	0.683	0.636	0.592	0.572
5	0.951	0.906	0.863	0.822	0.784	0.747	0.713	0.681	0.650	0.621	0.567	0.519	0.497
6	0.942	0.888	0.838	0.790	0.746	0.705	0.666	0.630	0.596	0.564	0.507	0.456	0.432
7	0.933	0.871	0.813	0.760	0.711	0.665	0.623	0.583	0.547	0.513	0.452	0.400	0.376
8	0.923	0.853	0.789	0.731	0.677	0.627	0.582	0.540	0.502	0.467	0.404	0.351	0.327
9	0.914	0.837	0.766	0.703	0.645	0.592	0.544	0.500	0.460	0.424	0.361	0.308	0.284
10	0.905	0.820	0.744	0.676	0.614	0.558	0.508	0.463	0.422	0.386	0.322	0.270	0.247
11	0.896	0.804	0.722	0.650	0.585	0.527	0.475	0.429	0.388	0.350	0.287	0.237	0.215
12	0.887	0.788	0.701	0.625	0.557	0.497	0.444	0.397	0.356	0.319	0.257	0.208	0.187
13	0.879	0.773	0.681	0.601	0.530	0.469	0.415	0.368	0.326	0.290	0.229	0.182	0.163
14	0.870	0.758	0.661	0.577	0.505	0.442	0.388	0.340	0.299	0.263	0.205	0.160	0.141
15	0.861	0.743	0.642	0.555	0.481	0.417	0.362	0.315	0.275	0.239	0.183	0.140	0.123
16	0.853	0.728	0.623	0.534	0.458	0.394	0.339	0.292	0.252	0.218	0.163	0.123	0.107
17	0.844	0.714	0.605	0.513	0.436	0.371	0.317	0.270	0.231	0.198	0.146	0.108	0.093
18	0.836	0.700	0.587	0.494	0.416	0.350	0.296	0.250	0.212	0.180	0.130	0.095	0.081
19	0.828	0.686	0.570	0.475	0.396	0.331	0.276	0.232	0.194	0.164	0.116	0.083	0.070
20	0.820	0.673	0.554	0.456	0.377	0.319	0.258	0.215	0.178	0.149	0.104	0.073	0.061
25	0.780	0.610	0.478	0.375	0.295	0.233	0.184	0.146	0.116	0.092	0.059	0.038	0.030
30	0.742	0.552	0.412	0.308	0.231	0.174	0.131	0.099	0.075	0.057	0.033	0.020	0.015

Year	16%	18%	20%	24%	28%	32%	36%	40%	50%	60%	70%	80%	90%
1	0.862	0.847	0.833	0.806	0.781	0.758	0.735	0.714	0.667	0.625	0.588	0.556	0.526
2	0.743	0.718	0.694	0.650	0.610	0.574	0.541	0.510	0.444	0.391	0.346	0.309	0.277
3	0.641	0.609	0.579	0.524	0.477	0.435	0.398	0.364	0.296	0.244	0.204	0.171	0.146
4	0.552	0.516	0.482	0.423	0.373	0.329	0.292	0.260	0.198	0.153	0.120	0.095	0.077
5	0.476	0.437	0.402	0.341	0.291	0.250	0.215	0.186	0.132	0.095	0.070	0.053	0.040
6	0.410	0.370	0.335	0.275	0.227	0.189	0.158	0.133	0.088	0.060	0.041	0.029	0.021
7	0.354	0.314	0.279	0.222	0.178	0.143	0.116	0.095	0.059	0.037	0.024	0.016	0.011
8	0.305	0.266	0.233	0.179	0.139	0.108	0.085	0.068	0.039	0.023	0.014	0.009	0.006
9	0.263	0.226	0.194	0.144	0.108	0.082	0.063	0.048	0.026	0.015	0.008	0.005	0.003
10	0.227	0.191	0.162	0.116	0.085	0.062	0.046	0.035	0.017	0.009	0.005	0.003	0.002
11	0.195	0.162	0.135	0.094	0.066	0.047	0.034	0.025	0.012	0.006	0.003	0.002	0.001
12	0.168	0.137	0.112	0.076	0.052	0.036	0.025	0.018	0.008	0.004	0.002	0.001	0.001
13	0.145	0.116	0.093	0.061	0.040	0.027	0.018	0.013	0.005	0.002	0.001	0.001	0.000
14	0.125	0.099	0.078	0.049	0.032	0.021	0.014	0.009	0.003	0.001	0.001	0.000	0.000
15	0.108	0.084	0.065	0.040	0.025	0.016	0.010	0.006	0.002	0.001	0.000	0.000	0.000
16	0.093	0.071	0.054	0.032	0.019	0.012	0.007	0.005	0.002	0.001	0.000	0.000	
17	0.080	0.060	0.045	0.026	0.015	0.009	0.005	0.003	0.001	0.000	0.000		
18	0.069	0.051	0.038	0.021	0.012	0.007	0.004	0.002	0.001	0.000	0.000		
19	0.060	0.043	0.031	0.017	0.009	0.005	0.003	0.002	0.000	0.000			
20	0.051	0.037	0.026	0.014	0.007	0.004	0.002	0.001	0.000	0.000			
25	0.024	0.016	0.010	0.005	0.002	0.001	0.000	0.000					
30	0.012	0.007	0.004	0.002	0.001	0.000	0.000						

Table 3 Sum of an annuity of £1 for *n* years

Year	1%	2%	3%	4%	5%	6%	7%	8%
1	1.000	1.000	1.000	1.000	1.000	1.000	1.000	1.000
2	2.010	2.020	2.030	2.040	2.050	2.060	2.070	2.080
3	3.030	3.060	3.091	3.122	3.152	3.184	3.215	3.246
4	4.060	4.122	4.184	4.246	4.310	4.375	4.440	4.506
5	5.101	5.204	5.309	5.416	5.526	5.637	5.751	5.867
6	6.152	6.308	6.468	6.633	6.802	6.975	7.153	7.336
7	7.214	7.434	7.662	7.898	8.142	8.394	8.654	8.923
8	8.286	8.583	8.892	9.214	9.549	9.897	10.260	10.637
9	9.369	9.755	10.159	10.583	11.027	11.491	11.978	12.488
10	10.462	10.950	11.464	12.006	12.578	13.181	13.816	41.487
11	11.567	12.169	12.808	13.486	14.207	14.972	15.784	16.645
12	12.683	13.412	14.192	15.026	15.917	16.870	17.888	18.977
13	13.809	14.680	15.618	16.627	17.713	18.882	20.141	21.495
14	14.947	15.974	17.086	18.292	19.599	21.051	22.550	24.215
15	16.097	17.293	18.599	20.024	21.579	23.276	25.129	27.152
16	17.258	18.639	20.157	21.825	23.657	25.673	27.888	30.324
17	18.430	20.012	21.762	23.698	25.840	28.213	30.840	33.750
18	19.615	21.412	23.414	25.645	28.132	30.906	33.999	37.450
19	20.811	22.841	25.117	27.671	30.539	33.760	37.379	41.446
20	22.019	24.297	26.870	29.778	33.066	36.786	40.995	45.762
25	28.243	32.030	36.459	41.646	47.727	54.865	63.249	73.106
30	34.785	40.568	47.575	56.085	66.439	79.058	94.461	113.283

Year	9%	10%	12%	14%	16%	18%	20%	24%
1	1.000	1.000	1.000	1.000	1.000	1.000	1.000	1.000
2	2.090	2.100	2.120	2.140	2.160	2.180	2.200	2.240
3	3.278	3.310	3.374	3.440	3.506	3.572	3.640	3.778
4	4.573	4.641	4.779	4.921	5.066	5.215	5.368	5.684
5	5.985	6.105	6.353	6.610	6.877	7.154	7.442	8.048
6	7.523	7.716	8.115	8.536	8.977	9.442	9.930	10.980
7	9.200	9.487	10.089	10.730	11.414	12.142	12.916	14.615
8	11.028	11.436	12.300	13.233	14.240	15.327	16.499	19.123
9	13.021	13.579	14.776	16.085	17.518	19.086	20.799	24.712
10	15.193	15.937	17.549	19.337	21.321	23.521	25.959	31.643
11	17.560	18.531	20.655	23.044	25.738	28.755	32.150	40.238
12	20.141	21.384	24.133	27.271	30.350	34.931	39.580	50.895
13	22.953	24.523	28.029	32.089	36.766	42.219	48.497	64.110
14	26.019	27.975	32.393	37.581	43.672	50.818	59.196	80.496
15	29.361	31.722	37.280	43.842	51.659	60.965	72.035	100.815

Year	28%	32%	36%	40%	50%	60%	70%	80%
1	1.000	1.000	1.000	1.000	1.000	1.000	1.000	1.000
2	2.280	2.320	2.360	2.400	2.500	2.600	2.700	2.800
3	3.918	4.062	4.210	4.360	4.750	5.160	5.590	6.040
4	6.016	6.326	6.725	7.104	8.125	9.256	10.503	11.872
5	8.700	9.398	10.146	10.846	13.188	15.810	18.855	22.370
6	12.136	13.406	14.799	16.324	20.781	26.295	33.054	41.265
7	16.534	18.696	21.126	23.853	32.172	43.073	57.191	75.278
8	22.163	25.678	29.732	34.395	49.258	69.916	98.225	136.500
9	29.369	34.895	41.435	49.153	74.887	112.866	167.983	246.699
10	38.592	47.062	57.352	69.814	113.330	181.585	286.570	445.058
11	50.399	63.122	78.998	98.739	170.995	291.536	488.170	802.105
12	65.510	84.320	108.437	139.235	257.493	467.458	830.888	1444.788
13	84.853	112.303	148.475	195.929	387.239	748.933	1413.510	2601.619
14	109.612	149.240	202.926	275.300	581.859	1199.293	2403.968	4683.914
15	141.303	197.997	276.979	386.420	873.788	1919.869	4087.745	8432.045

Table 4 Present value of annuity of £1 per period

Year	1%	2%	3%	4%	5%	6%	7%	8%	9%	10%
1	0.990	0.980	0.971	0.962	0.952	0.943	0.935	0.926	0.917	0.909
2	1.970	1.942	1.913	1.886	1.859	1.833	1.808	1.783	1.759	1.736
3	2.941	2.884	2.829	2.775	2.723	2.673	2.624	2.577	2.531	2.487
4	3.902	3.808	3.717	3.630	3.546	3.465	3.387	3.312	3.240	3.170
5	4.853	4.713	4.580	4.452	4.329	4.212	4.100	3.993	3.890	3.791
6	5.795	5.601	5.417	5.424	5.076	4.917	4.766	4.623	4.486	4.355
7	6.728	6.472	6.230	6.002	5.786	5.582	5.389	5.206	5.033	4.868
8	7.652	7.325	7.020	6.733	6.463	6.210	5.971	5.747	5.535	5.335
9	8.566	8.162	7.786	7.435	7.108	6.802	6.515	6.247	5.985	5.759
10	9.471	8.983	8.530	8.111	7.722	7.360	7.024	6.710	6.418	6.145
11	10.368	9.787	9.253	8.760	8.306	7.887	7.499	7.139	6.805	6.495
12	11.255	10.575	9.954	9.385	8.863	8.384	7.943	7.536	7.161	6.814
13	12.134	11.348	10.635	9.986	9.394	8.853	8.358	7.904	7.487	7.103
14	13.004	12.106	11.296	10.563	8.899	9.295	8.745	8.244	7.786	7.367
15	13.865	12.849	11.938	11.118	10.380	9.712	9.108	8.559	8.060	7.606
16	14.718	13.578	12.561	11.652	10.838	10.106	9.447	8.851	8.312	7.824
17	15.562	14.292	13.166	12.166	11.274	10.477	9.763	9.122	8.544	8.022
18	16.398	14.992	13.754	12.659	11.690	10.828	10.059	9.372	8.756	8.201
19	17.226	15.678	14.324	13.134	12.085	11.158	10.336	9.604	8.950	8.365
20	18.046	16.351	14.877	13.590	12.462	11.470	10.594	9.818	9.128	8.514
25	22.023	19.523	17.413	15.622	14.094	12.783	11.654	10.675	9.823	9.077
30	25.808	22.397	19.600	17.292	15.373	13.765	12.409	11.258	10.274	9.427

Year	12%	14%	16%	18%	20%	24%	28%	32%	36%
1	0.893	0.877	0.862	0.847	0.833	0.806	0.781	0.758	0.735
2	1.690	1.647	1.605	1.566	1.528	1.457	1.392	1.332	1.276
3	2.402	2.322	2.246	2.174	2.106	1.981	1.868	1.766	1.674
4	3.037	2.914	2.798	2.690	2.589	2.404	2.241	2.096	1.966
5	3.605	3.433	3.274	3.127	2.991	2.745	2.532	2.345	2.181
6	4.111	3.889	3.685	3.498	3.326	3.020	2.759	2.534	2.339
7	4.564	4.288	4.089	3.812	3.605	3.242	2.937	2.678	2.455
8	4.968	4.639	4.344	4.078	3.837	3.421	3.076	2.786	2.540
9	5.328	4.946	4.607	4.303	4.031	3.566	3.184	2.868	2.603
10	5.650	5.216	4.833	4.494	4.193	3.682	3.269	2.930	2.650
11	5.988	5.453	5.029	4.656	4.327	3.776	3.335	2.978	2.683
12	6.194	5.660	5.197	4.793	4.439	3.851	3.387	3.013	2.708
13	6.424	5.842	5.342	4.910	4.533	3.912	3.427	3.040	2.727
14	6.628	6.002	5.468	5.008	4.611	3.962	3.459	3.061	2.740
15	6.811	6.142	5.575	5.092	4.675	4.001	3.483	3.076	2.750
16	6.974	6.265	5.669	5.162	4.730	4.033	3.503	3.088	2.758
17	7.120	5.373	5.749	4.222	4.775	4.059	3.518	3.097	2.763
18	7.250	6.467	5.818	5.273	4.812	4.080	3.529	3.104	2.767
19	7.366	6.550	5.877	5.316	4.844	4.097	3.539	3.109	2.770
20	7.469	6.623	5.929	5.353	4.870	4.110	3.546	3.113	2.772
25	7.843	6.873	6.907	5.467	4.948	4.147	3.564	3.122	2.776
30	8.055	7.003	6.177	5.517	4.979	4.160	3.569	3.124	2.778

Answers to review questions

Note: All the answers are the work of the authors. None has been supplied by an examining body. The examining bodies accept no responsibility whatsoever for the accuracy or method of working in the answers given.

Note: In order to save space, £ signs have been omitted from columns of figures, except where the figures refer to £000, or where the denomination needs to be specified. For the same reason, names of the organisations and dates are sometimes omitted, but only where they add little to an understanding of the answer.

1.1

(a) (dates omitted)

Branch Current Account

Balance b/d	72,600	Cash		110,000
Goods sent	74,200	Goods returned		2,600
Expenses paid	17,800			
Net profit	63,000	Balance c/d		115,000
	227,600			227,600

(b) Proof:

Branch assets		xxx
Less Branch liabilities		xxx
= Balance of branch current account		xxx

Indicates: Amount of money invested in branch

1.2

Branch Stock (dates omitted)

	Memo				*Memo*	
Balance b/d	40,012	28,580		Branch debtors	149,590	149,590
Goods from head						
office	170,100	121,500		Cash sales		21,000
Gross profit		48,740		Returns to HO		5,400
				Goods stolen		3,000
				Profit and loss:		
				Normal wastage		812
				Profit and loss:		
				Abnormal wastage		462
				Balance c/d	26,488	18,920
	210,112	198,820			210,112	198,820

			Branch Debtors		
Balances b/d		28,000	Bad debts		1,540
Branch stock: Sales		149,590	Discounts allowed		3,156
			Bank		131,600
			Balance c/d		41,294
		177,590			177,590

1.3

(a)(i)

		Branch Stock (Selling Prices)	
Goods from head office		Cash sales	89,940
(82,400 + 10% 8,240 =		Sales: Branch debtors	1,870
90,640 + 25%)	113,300	Goods to other branches	3,300
		Branch stock adjustment:	
		Reductions	2,250
		Balance c/d	15,940
	113,300		113,300

(ii)

		Branch Stock Adjustment * (profit margin)	
Goods to other branches	660	Branch stock	22,660
Branch stock: Reductions	2,250	(113,300 − 90,640)	
Profit and loss	16,562		
Balance c/d	3,188		
	22,660		22,660

*As cost to branch (original cost + 10%) is subject to further mark-up of 25%, therefore margin is 20%, and this is profit margin used in this account.

(b) Book stock per branch stock account   15,940
    Physical stock   14,850
                              1,090

Four possible reasons for deficiency:
(i)   thefts by customers;
(ii) thefts by staff;
(iii) wastages due to breakages, miscounting, etc.;
(iv) cash misappropriated.

(c) Figure to be taken for RST balance sheet:

Actual stock at selling price		14,850
Less 20% margin		2,970
Cost to branch		11,880
Less head office loading		
(+10%=1/11th of adjusted figure) 1/11th		1,080
Actual cost to company		10,800

Therefore *(iii)* 10,800 is correct answer.

1.5
Packer and Stringer
Trading & Profit & Loss Account for the year ended 31 December 2004

	Head Office		Branch	
Sales		39,000		26,000
Less Cost of goods sold				
Opening stock	13,000		4,400	
Add Purchases	37,000			
	50,000			
Goods to branch	17,200		17,200	
	32,800		21,600	
Less Closing stock	17,560		6,570	
	15,240		15,030	
	21,440		10,970	
Doubtful debt provision not required			20	
			10,990	
Salaries	4,500		3,200	
Administrative expenses	1,440		960	
Carriage	2,200		960	
General expenses	3,200		1,800	
Provision for doubtful debts	50			
Depreciation	150		110	
Manager's commission			360	
	11,540		7,390	
Net profit	9,900		3,600	
		13,500		
Packer: Commission	900			
Interest on capital: Packer	840			
Stringer	240			
	1,080			
	1,980			
Balance of profits: Packer ³/₄	8,640			
Stringer ¹/₄	2,880			
	11,520			
	13,500			

Balance Sheet as at 31 December 2004

Fixed assets		
Furniture	2,600	
Less Depreciation	1,110	
		1,490
Current assets		
Stock		21,810
Debtors	10,000	
Less Provision for doubtful debts	830	
		9,170
Cash and bank		3,000
		33,980
Less Current liabilities		
Creditors	6,200	
Bank overdraft	1,350	
Manager's commission	120	
		7,670
Working capital		26,310
		27,800

1.7
Nion
Trading and Profit and Loss Account for the year ending 31 October 2011

	Head office		Branch	
	£000	£000	£000	£000
Sales		850		437
Transfers to branch		380		
		1,230		
Less Cost of goods sold:				
Opening stock	8		20	
Add Purchases	914		375	
	922		395	
Add Goods from head office				
Less Closing stock	12		15	
		910		380
Gross profit		320		57
Less Expenses:				
Administrative	200		16.5	
Distribution	80.5		5	
Depreciation	35		10	
Changes in provision for doubtful debts	(6)		0.5	
		309.5		32
Net profit		10.5		25

Balance Sheet as at 31 October 2011

	£000	£000	£000	£000
Fixed assets at cost				450
Less Depreciation to date				215
				235
Current assets				
Stocks (12 + 12 + 4*)		120		28
Debtors	114			
Less Provision	6			
	114			
Cash and bank (15.5 + 13 + 50)	78.5			
	220.5			
Less Current liabilities				
Creditors		50		170.5
				405.5
Capital				
Balance at 1.11.2010				410
Add Net profit				35.5
				445.5
Less Drawings				40
				405.5

*5 × ⁴/₅

1.9

(a)

Conversion of Branch Trial Balance to Pounds Sterling

	Fl.	Fl.	Rate	£	£
Freehold buildings	63,000		7	9,000	
Debtors and creditors	36,000	1,560	8	4,460	195
Sales		432,000	9		48,000
Head office		504,260	Actual		60,100
Branch cost of sales	360,000		Below*	40,400	
Depreciation: Machinery		56,700	7		8,100
Administration costs	18,000		9	2,000	
Stock 30.6.2008	11,520		8	1,440	
Machinery at cost	126,000		7	18,000	
Remittances	272,000		Actual	29,990	
Balances at bank	79,200		8	9,900	
Selling and distribution	28,800		9	3,200	
Profit on exchange			–		1,995
	994,520	994,520		118,390	118,390

*Cost of sales: Branch Fl. 360,000
Fl. $\dfrac{12,600 \div 7 = £1,800}{347,400 \div 9 = £38,600}$
£40,400

EG Company Ltd

Trading and Profit and Loss Accounts for the year ending 30 June 2008

	Head office		Branch	
Sales		104,000		48,000
Less Cost of sales	58,400		38,600	
Depreciation	600		1,800	
	59,000		40,400	
Goods to branch	35,000	24,000		
		80,000		
Gross profit		24,000		7,600
Administration costs	15,200		2,000	
Selling and distribution	23,300		3,200	
Provison for unrealised profit on branch stock	300			
Manager's commission			114	
		38,800	5,314	
Net profit		41,200	2,286	
			43,486	
Add Balance from last year			2,000	
Balance carried forward to next year			45,486	

(b)

Balance Sheet as at 30 June 2008

	£	£
Fixed assets		
Freehold buildings at cost		23,000
Machinery at cost	24,000	
Less Depreciation	9,600	14,400
		37,400
Current assets		
Stock	30,040	
Debtors	13,360	
Bank	14,500	
Cash in transit	1,990	
	59,890	
Less Current liabilities		
Creditors*	9,809	
Working capital		50,081
		87,481
Financed by:		
Share capital: Authorised and issued		40,000
Reserves		
Difference on exchange	1,995	
Profit and loss	45,486	47,481
		87,481

*Creditors HO 9,500 + Branch 195 + Manager 114 = 9,809.

(c)

(HO Books) Branch Account

	Fl			Fl
Balance b/d	25,136	Cash from debtors	189,260	
Components	35,000	Remittances	315,000	
Net profit	2,286	Cash in transit	**24,000	
Difference on exchange	1,995	Balance c/d	528,260	
	64,417		64,417	

**This represents the profit per branch profit and loss account if it had been drawn up using florins.

1.10

(a)

Trial Balance as at 31 December 2010

	Crowns	Crowns	Rate	£	£
Bank	66,000		4	16,500	
Creditors		92,400	4		23,100
Debtors	158,400		4	39,600	
Fixed assets	145,200		5	29,040	
Head office		316,800	Actual		65,280
Profit and Loss		79,200			18,000
Stocks	118,800		4.4	29,700	
Difference on exchange			4		8,460
	488,400	488,400		114,840	114,840

1.10 (cont'd)

(b) (Books of head office) Highland Branch

Balance b/d		65,280	Balance c/d		91,740
Difference on exchange		8,460			
Net profit		18,000			
		91,740			91,740
					68,640

(c) Balance Sheet as at 31 December 2010

Fixed assets		
Current assets		
Stocks	56,100	
Debtors	58,080	
Bank	27,060	
	141,240	
Less Current liabilities		
Creditors	44,220	
Working capital		97,020
		165,660
Financed by:		
Issued share capital		86,400
Reserves		
Profit and loss	70,800	
Difference on exchange	8,460	
		79,260
		165,660

2.1

Machinery

2006			
Jan 1	Vendor	17,100	

Vendor's Account

2006						
Jan 1	Bank	2,672		Jan 1	Machinery	17,100
Dec 31	Bank	5,700		Dec 31	HP interest	1,299
Dec 31	Balance c/d	10,027				
		18,399				18,399
2007				2007		
Dec 31	Bank	5,700		Jan 1	Balance b/d	10,027
Dec 31	Balance c/d	5,229			HP interest	902
		10,929				10,929
2008				2008		
Dec 31	Bank	5,700		Jan 1	Balance b/d	5,229
					HP interest	471
		5,700				5,700

Accumulated Provision for Depreciation: Machinery

2006				2006		
Dec 31	Balance c/d	4,275		Dec 31	Profit and loss	4,275
2007				2007		
Dec 31	Balance c/d	8,550		Jan 1	Balance b/d	4,275
				Dec 31	Profit and loss	4,275
		8,550				8,550
2008				2008		
Dec 31	Balance c/d	12,825		Jan 1	Balance b/d	8,550
				Dec 31	Profit and loss	4,275
		12,825				12,825

Balance Sheet as at 31 December 2006

Machinery at cost		17,100
Less Depreciation		4,275
(included in Liabilities) Owing on HP	15,825	10,027

*17,100 − 2,672 = 14,428 × 0.09 = 1,298.52 = 1,299

2.3

(a)

Bulwell's books

Motor Lorries

2001	Granby Garages	54,000	

Hire Purchase Interest

2001	Granby Garages	11,250		2001	Profit and loss	11,250
2002	Granby Garages	8,063		2002	Profit and loss	8,063
2003	Granby Garages	4,078		2003	Profit and loss	4,078

Bank

2001	Granby (Jan 1)	9,000	
	Granby (Dec 31)	24,000	
2002	Granby	24,000	
2003	Granby	20,391	

Granby Garages

2001	Bank	9,000		2001	Motor lorries	54,000
	Bank	24,000			HP interest	11,250
	Balance c/d	32,250				
		65,250				65,250
2002	Bank	24,000		2002	Balance b/d	32,250
	Balance c/d	16,313			HP interest	8,063
		40,313				40,313
2003	Bank	20,391		2003	Balance b/d	16,313
					Interest	4,078
		20,391				20,391

Depreciation

2001	Balance c/d	12,500	2001	Profit and loss	12,500
2002	Balance c/d	25,000	2002	Balance b/d	12,500
				Profit and loss	12,500
		25,000			25,000
2003	Balance c/d	37,500	2003	Balance b/d	25,000
				Profit and loss	12,500
		37,500			37,500
2004	Balance c/d	50,000	2004	Balance b/d	37,500
				Profit and loss	12,500
		50,000			50,000

Balance Sheet as at 31 December

	2001	2002	2003	2004
Motor lorries cost	54,000	54,000	54,000	54,000
Less Depreciation to date	12,500	25,000	37,500	50,000
	41,500	29,000	16,500	4,000

Liabilities:
HP debt outstanding	32,250	16,313	–	

Charge against profit:
HP interest	11,250	8,063	4,078	
Depreciation	12,500	12,500	12,500	12,500

NB: Calculation of interest
2001 25% × £45,000 = £11,250
2002 25% × £32,250 = £8,063
2003 25% × £16,313 = £4,078

(b)

Granby's books

Bulwell Aggregates

2001	HP sales	54,000	2001	Bank – deposit	9,000
	HP interest	11,250		– instalment	24,000
				Balance c/d	32,250
		65,250			65,250
2002	Balance b/d	32,250	2002	Bank – instalment	24,000
	HP interest	8,063		Balance c/d	16,313
		40,313			40,313
2003	Balance b/d	16,313	2003	Bank – instalment	20,391
	HP interest	4,078			
		20,391			20,391

Bank

2001	Bulwell	9,000
2001	Bulwell	24,000
2002	Bulwell	24,000
2003	Bulwell	20,391

HP Interest

2001	HP trading	11,250	2001	Bulwell	11,250
2002	HP trading	8,063	2002	Bulwell	8,063
2003	HP trading	4,078	2003	Bulwell	4,078

Hire Purchase Trading

2001	Cost of lorries	43,200	2001	HP sales	54,000
	HP profit deferred c/d	6,450		HP interest	11,250
	Gross profit	15,600			
		65,250			65,250
2002	HP profit deferred c/d	3,263	2002	HP profit deferred b/d	6,450
	Gross profit	11,250		HP interest	8,063
		14,513			14,513
2003	Gross profit	7,341	2003	HP profit deferred b/d	3,263
				HP interest	4,078
		7,341			7,341

Working: Unrealised profit

Profit margin $= \dfrac{10,800}{54,000} \times \dfrac{100}{1} = 20\%$

20% × £32,250 = £6,450
20% × £16,313 = £3,263

2.5

(a)(i)

Truck Fleet Ltd

2004			2004		
Mar 31	Cash	20,000	Apr 1	Lorry	61,620
Mar 31	Balance c/d	41,620			
		61,620			61,620
2005					
Mar 31	Cash	23,981	Apr 1	Balance b/d	41,620
Mar 31	Balance c/d	21,801	Mar 31	HP interest 10% of 41,620	4,160
		45,782			45,782
2006					
Mar 31	Cash	23,981	Apr 1	Balance b/d	21,801
			Mar 31	HP interest 10% of 21,802	2,180
		23,981			23,981

2.5 (cont'd)

(ii)

Lorry

2004		
Mar 31	Truck Fleet Ltd	61,620

(iii)

Provision for Depreciation: Lorry

2004			
Mar 31		Profit and loss	24,648
2005			
Mar 31		Profit and loss	14,789
2006			
Mar 31		Profit and loss	8,873

Hire Purchase Interest

2005						
Mar 31	Vehicles and finance	4,162	Mar 31	Profit and loss	4,162	
2006						
Mar 31	Vehicles and finance	2,180	Mar 31	Profit and loss	2,180	

(b)

Balance Sheet as at 31 March 2005

Lorry at cost		61,620
Less Depreciation to date		39,437
		22,183
(Included in Liabilities) Owing on hire purchase		21,801

2.6

J Wild
Hire Purchase Trading and Profit and Loss Account for the year ending 31 March 2003

Sales at hire purchase price (1,900 × 150)		285,000
Purchases	180,000	
Less Stock (100 × 90)	9,000	
	171,000	
Provision for unrealised profit and interest*	50,160	221,160
Gross profit		63,840
Less Rent business rates and insurance	5,000	
Wages	27,000	
General expenses	5,100	37,100
Net profit		26,740

*Cash yet to be collected 285,000 − 125,400 = 159,600

Therefore profit + interest to recognise $\frac{159,600}{285,000} \times 60 = 33.6 \times 1,900 = 63,840$

∴ profit plus interest to ignore = 60 − 33.6 = 26.4 × 1,900 = 50,160

Balance Sheet as at 31 March 2003

Fixed assets			9,500
Current assets			
Stock		9,000	
HP debtors	159,600		
Less Provision: unrealised profit and interest	50,160	109,440	
Bank		7,426	
		125,866	
Less Current liabilities			
Creditors		12,600	
Working capital			113,266
			122,766

Financed by:		
Capital		
Balance at 1.10.2005		136,026
Add Net profit		26,740
		162,766
Less Drawings		40,000
		122,766

2.7

Hire Purchase Trading

2008	Cost of refrigerators	170,000	2008	HP sales (W1)	170,000
	HP profit deferred (W2)	59,500		HP interest (W1)	85,000
	Gross profit	25,500			
		255,000			255,000

W1: to separate cost from interest, it is assumed that the difference between cost price and selling price is interest. The HP sales amount is, therefore, the same as the cost of the units sold, i.e. £170,000. HP interests, therefore, £85,000.

W2: Receipts £76,500 which is 30% of the amount invoiced of £255,000. Profit (i.e. interest) is recognised at that percentage (30%) of profit received = 30% × £85,000 = £25,500 so the HP profit deferred = £85,000 − £25,500 = £59,500.

RJ
Hire Purchase Trading and Profit and Loss Account for the year ending 31 December 2008

Sales at hire purchase price (850 × 300)		255,000
Purchases	180,000	
Less Stock (50 × 200)	10,000	
Cost of goods sold	170,000	
Provision of unrealised profit	59,500	229,500
Gross profit		25,500
Less Wages and salaries	12,800	
General expenses	5,500	
Bank interest	400	18,700
Net profit		6,800

Authors' Note: it is assumed the question is asking for a separate T-account showing the HP Trading Account, plus a trading and profit and loss account. If you wish, you could simply provide the HP details in the Trading and Profit and Loss Account and include a note saying you assumed you did not need to also provide the T-account. This ambiguity in this question is quite common in questions on this topic. Be careful to ensure you make it clear that you could have prepared the T-account when you do not prepare one. Generally, examiners are looking only for the HP Trading and Profit and Loss Account unless they request a T-account. However, in this case, it is likely the T-account was also required.

Balance Sheet as at 31 December 2008

Fixed assets			10,000
Current assets			
Stock in warehouse		10,000	
Hire purchase debtors	178,500		
Less Provision for unrealised profit	59,500	119,000	
		129,000	
Less Current liabilities			
Creditors	16,600		
Bank overdraft	19,600	36,200	92,800
			102,800
Financed by:			
Capital			100,000
Cash introduced			6,800
Add Net profit			106,800
			4,000
Less Drawings			102,800

2.11
(a)(i)

Machine Hire Purchase

1.1.08	Bank	2,000	1.1.08	Machine	10,000
30.6.08	Bank	3,056	1.1.08	HP interest	7,280
31.12.08	Bank	3,056			
31.12.08	Balance c/d	9,168			
		17,280			17,280
30.6.09	Bank	3,056	1.1.09	Balance b/d	9,168
31.12.09	Bank	3,056			
31.12.09	Balance c/d	3,056			
		9,168			9,168
30.6.10	Bank	3,056	1.1.10	Balance b/d	3,056

(ii)

Machine Hire Purchase (see workings)

1.1.08	Machine HP	7,280	31.12.08	Profit and loss	4,368
			31.12.08	Balance c/d	2,912
		7,280			7,280
1.1.09	Balance b/d	2,912	31.12.09	Profit and loss	2,427
			31.12.09	Balance c/d	485
		2,912			2,912
1.1.10	Balance b/d	485	31.12.10	Profit and loss	485

(b) (Extracts) Balance Sheets as at 31 December

	2008	2009	2010
Fixed assets			
Machinery at cost	10,000	10,000	10,000
Less Depreciation to date	1,800	3,600	5,400
	8,200	6,400	4,600
Creditors			
Falling due within 1 year			
Hire purchase	3,685	2,571	
Falling due after 1 year			
Hire purchase	2,571		

Workings: Interest (sum of digits is 15)
To 31.12.2008 (5/15 × 7,280) 2,427 + (4/15 × 7,280) = 4,368
To 31.12.2009 (3/15 × 7,280) 1,456 + (2/15 × 7,280) 971 = 2,427
To 31.12.2010 1/15 × 7,280 = 485
Depreciation (10,000 − 1,000) ÷ 5 = 1,800 p.a.

3.1

Contract 349

Year to 31.03.07				
Plant	42,000	Work certified	195,000	
Materials	64,000	Plant c/d	33,000	
Wages	73,000	Stock and work in progress c/d	31,965	
Direct expenses	7,000			
Gross profit to profit and loss	73,965			
	259,965		259,965	

Year to 31.03.08				
Plant b/d	33,000	Work certified	385,000	
Stock and w-in-p b/d	31,965	Sale of plant	14,000	
Materials	82,000			
Wages	109,000			
Direct expenses	11,000			
Penalty	10,000			
Gross profit to profit and loss	122,035			
	399,000		399,000	

3.1 (*cont'd*)

Workings:

(i) Computation profit of year to 31.03.07

Contract price		580,000
Less Actual expenditure		
(64,000 + 73,000 + 7,000)	144,000	
Estimated cost of plant (42,000 − 24,000)	18,000	
Estimated expenses year to 31.03.08	198,000	360,000
Estimated total contract profit: estimate made at end of year to 31.03.07		220,000

Using formula given by question:

$$\frac{\text{Work certified}}{\text{Total contract price}} \times \text{Total estimated profit} = \text{Profit for year to 31.03.07}$$

$$= \frac{156{,}000 + 39{,}000}{580{,}000} \times 220{,}000 = \underline{73{,}965}$$

(ii) Depreciation of plant to 31.03.07 = 42,000 − 24,000 = 18,000 − 24,000 = 18,000 ÷ 18 = 1,000 per month

(iii) Work certified in year to 31.03.08 = 580,000 − 195,000 = 385,000.

3.2

Stannard and Sykes Ltd

Pier Contract Account

Contract for Seafront Development Corporation valued at £300,000

Materials: direct	58,966		Materials on site c/d		11,660
from store	10,180	69,146	Work in progress c/d		151,167
Wages		41,260			
Hire of plant		21,030			
Direct expenditure		3,065			
Overheads		8,330			
Wages accrued c/d		2,826			
		145,657			145,657
Profit and loss account (proportion of profit to date)		17,170			
		162,827			162,827
Materials on site b/d		11,660	Wages accrued b/d		2,826
Work in progress b/d		151,167			

A suggested method for prudently estimating the amount of profit to be taken to November 30 is:

$$\frac{2}{3} \times \frac{\text{Cash received}}{\text{Value of work certified}} \times \text{Estimated profit (Value of work certified less cost of work certified)}$$

Total expenditure to date		145,657
Less Materials on site at 30 November 2008	11,660	
Work in progress	12,613	24,273
Cost of work certified (*a*)		121,384
Value of work certified (*b*)		150,000
Total profit to date (*b*) − (*a*)		28,616

5.1

Bank

Application	120,000	Balance c/d	400,700
Allotment (less excess applications 40,000)	60,000		
First call (398,000 × 0.30)	119,400		
Second call (398,000 × 0.25)	99,500		
N Butt (2,000 × 0.90)	1,800		
	400,700		400,700

N Butt

Ordinary share capital	2,000	Bank	1,800
		Forfeited shares	200
	2,000		2,000

Application and Allotment

Ordinary share capital	180,000	Bank	120,000
		Bank	60,000
	180,000		180,000

Ordinary Share Capital

Forfeited shares	2,000	Application and allotment	180,000
Balance c/d	400,000	First call	120,000
		Second call	100,000
		N Butt	2,000
	402,000		402,000

First Call

Ordinary share capital	120,000	Bank	119,400
		Forfeited shares	600
	120,000		120,000

Second Call

Ordinary share capital	100,000	Bank	99,500
		Forfeited shares	500
	100,000		100,000

Forfeited Shares

First call	600	Ordinary share capital	2,000
Second call	500		
N Butt	700		
Transfer to share premium	2,000		
	2,000		2,000

Balance Sheet (extract)

Bank		2,000
Ordinary share capital		400,000
Share premium		700
		400,700

5.2

Bank

Application and allotment	128,000	Application and allotment: Refund of application monies	8,000
		Balance c/d	1,002,300
	1,010,300		**1,010,300**

Application (1.28 million × 0.10) 128,000
Allotment (1 million × 0.25 less excess application monies 20,000) 230,000
First call (994,000 × 0.35) 347,900
Second call (992,000 × 0.30) 297,600
C Lamb (8,000 × 0.85) 6,800
1,010,300

Application and Allotment

Bank: Refunds	8,000	Bank	128,000
Ordinary share capital	350,000	Bank	230,000
	358,000		**358,000**

First Call Account

Ordinary share capital	350,000	Bank	347,900
		Forfeited shares	2,100
	350,000		**350,000**

Second Call Account

Ordinary share capital	300,000	Bank	297,600
		Forfeited shares	2,400
	300,000		**300,000**

Ordinary Share Capital

Forfeited shares	8,000	Application and allotment	350,000
Balance c/d	1,000,000	First call	350,000
		Second call	300,000
		C Lamb	8,000
	1,008,000		**1,008,000**

Forfeited Shares

First call	2,100	Ordinary share capital	8,000
Second call	2,400		
C Lamb	1,200		
Transfer to share premium	1,300		
	8,000		**8,000**

C Lamb

Ordinary share capital	8,000	Bank	6,800
		Forfeited shares	1,200
	8,000		**8,000**

5.3

(a)

Cosy Fires Ltd

Application and allotment

Cash: Return of unsuccessful applications 5,000 × 0.60	3,000	Cash application for 65,000 × 0.60 =	39,000
Share capital: Due on application and allotment: 40,000 × 0.70	28,000	Cash: Balance due on allotment (see workings)*	1,975
Share premium: 40,000 × 0.25	10,000	Balance c/d: Due from allottee in respect of 500 shares: 500 × 0.35 = 175 Less o/paid on application 250 × 0.60 = 150	25
	41,000		**41,000**
Balance b/d	25	Forfeited shares	25

Share Capital

Forfeited shares: Amount called on shares forfeited: 500 × 0.70	350	Balance b/d	75,000
Balance c/d	115,000	Application and allotment	28,000
		Call	11,850
		Forfeited shares	500
	115,350		**115,350**

Share Premium

Balance c/d	10,375	Application and allotment	10,000
		Forfeited shares	375
	10,375		**10,375**

Forfeited Shares

Application and allotment	25	Share capital	350
Share capital	500	Cash: 500 × 1.10 per share	550
Share premium	375		
	900		**900**

Call

Share capital 39,500 × 0.30	11,850	Cash	11,850

5.3 (cont'd)

(b)

Share capital

Balance Sheet as at 31 May 2007

Authorised: 160,000 ordinary shares of 1 each   160,000

Issued and fully paid: 115,000 ordinary shares of 1 each   115,000
Capital reserve:
Share premium   10,375

Workings:

Due on application 0.60 × 40,000	24,000	
Due on allotment 0.35 × 40,000	14,000	
	38,000	
Received on application: 0.60 × 65,000	39,000	
Less Refunded 5,000 × 0.60	3,000	
	36,000	
Balance due on allotment	2,000	
Less		
Amount due on application and allotment 500 × 0.95	475	
Received on application 750 × 0.60	450	
	25	
	1,975	

5.5

M Ltd

Ledger Accounts (dates omitted)

Cash

Application and allotment (750,000 × 85p)	637,500	Application and allotment (Refund 125,000 × 85p)	106,250
Application and allotment (500,000 × 25p – overpaid 125,000 × 85p)	18,750		
First and final call (495,000 × 50p)	247,500		
Forfeited shares (5,000 × 90p)	4,500		

Application and Allotment

Cash	250,000	Share capital	637,500
Cash	300,000	Share premium	18,750
Cash	106,250		
	656,250		656,250

Share Premium

		Application and allotment	302,000
Balance c/d	302,000		
	302,000		302,000

Share Capital

Forfeited shares	5,000	Balance b/d	500,000
Balance c/d	1,000,000	Application and allotment	250,000
		First and final call	250,000
		Forfeited shares	5,000
	1,005,000		1,005,000

First and Final Call

Share capital	250,000	Cash	247,500
		Forfeited shares	2,500
	250,000		250,000

Forfeited Shares

First and final call	2,500	Share capital	5,000
Share capital	5,000	Cash	4,500
Share premium	2,000		
	9,500		9,500

Given Format 1 of the Companies Act 1985, there are two places where uncalled capital can be shown. These are either place A or C II (5).

If C II (5) is chosen it becomes:

Current assets

II Debtors

(5) Called-up share capital not paid   2,500
Issued share capital
1,000,000 ordinary shares of £1 each   1,000,000
Reserves
Share premium   302,000

The authorised share capital should be shown also as a note only.
The increase in share premium would also be shown as a note in the statement showing changes in reserves.

6.1

(a)

	Dr	Cr
(A1) Bank	5,000	
(A2) Ordinary share applicants		5,000
Cash received from applicants.		
(B1) Ordinary share applicants	5,000	
(B2) Ordinary share capital		5,000
Ordinary shares allotted.		
(C1) Preference share capital	5,000	
(C2) Preference share redemption		5,000
Shares to be redeemed.		
(D1) Preference share redemption	5,000	
(D2) Bank		5,000
Payment made to redeem shares.		

(a)

	Balances before Dr	Balances before Cr	Effect Dr	Effect Cr	Balances after Dr	Balances after Cr
Net assets (except bank)	20,000				20,000	
Bank		13,000	(A1) 5,000	(D2) 5,000		13,000
		33,000				33,000
Preference share capital		5,000	(C1) 5,000			–
Preference share redemption		–	(D1) 5,000	(C2) 5,000		–
Ordinary share capital		15,000		(B2) 5,000		20,000
Ordinary share applicants		–	(B1) 5,000	(A2) 5,000		–
Share premium		2,000				2,000
		22,000				22,000
Profit and loss		11,000				11,000
		33,000				33,000

(b)

(A1) Preference share capital
(A2) Preference share redemption
Shares to be redeemed.

(B1) Preference share redemption
(B2) Bank
Cash paid on redemption.

(C1) Profit and loss appropriation
(C2) Capital redemption reserve
Transfer per Companies Act.

	Balances before Dr	Balances before Cr	Effect Dr	Effect Cr	Balances after Dr	Balances after Cr
Net assets (except bank)	20,000				20,000	
Bank		13,000		(B2) 5,000		8,000
		33,000				28,000
Preference share capital		5,000	(A1) 5,000			–
Preference share redemption		–	(B1) 5,000	(A2) 5,000		–
Ordinary share capital		15,000				15,000
Capital redemption reserve		–		(C2) 5,000		5,000
Share premium		2,000				2,000
		22,000				22,000
Profit and loss		11,000	(C1) 5,000			6,000
		33,000				28,000

(c)

(A1) Bank
(A2) Ordinary share applicants
Cash received from applicants.

(B1) Ordinary share applicants
(B2) Ordinary share capital
Ordinary shares allotted.

(C1) Profit and loss appropriation
(C2) Capital redemption reserve
Part of redemption not covered by new issue, to comply with Companies Act.

(D1) Preference share capital
(D2) Preference share redemption
Shares to be redeemed.

(E1) Preference share redemption
(E2) Bank
Payment made for redemption.

	Balances before Dr	Balances before Cr	Effect Dr	Effect Cr	Balances after Dr	Balances after Cr
Net assets (except bank)	20,000				20,000	
Bank		13,000	(A1) 1,500	(E2) 5,000		9,500
		33,000				29,500
Preference share capital		5,000	(D1) 5,000			–
Preference share redemption		–	(E1) 5,000	(D2) 5,000		–
Ordinary share capital		15,000		(B2) 1,500		16,500
Ordinary share applicants		–	(B1) 1,500	(A2) 1,500		–
Capital redemption reserve		–		(C2) 3,500		3,500
Share premium		2,000				2,000
		22,000				22,000
Profit and loss		11,000	(C1) 3,500			7,500
		33,000				29,500

(d)

(A1) Preference share capital
(A2) Preference share redemption
Shares to be redeemed.

(B1) Profit and loss appropriation
(B2) Preference share redemption
Premium on redemption of shares not previously issued at premium.

(C1) Profit and loss appropriation
(C2) Capital redemption reserve
Transfer because shares redeemed out of distributable profits.

(D1) Preference share redemption
(D2) Bank
Payment on redemption.

	Dr	Cr
(A1) Preference share capital	5,000	
(A2) Preference share redemption		5,000
(B1) Profit and loss appropriation	1,250	
(B2) Preference share redemption		1,250
(C1) Profit and loss appropriation	5,000	
(C2) Capital redemption reserve		5,000
(D1) Preference share redemption	6,250	
(D2) Bank		6,250

6.1 (cont'd)

	Balances before	Effect Dr	Effect Cr	Balances after
Net assets (except bank)	20,000			20,000
Bank	13,000		(D2) 6,250	6,750
	33,000			26,750
Preference share capital	5,000			–
Preference share redemption	–	(A1) 5,000, (D1) 6,250	(A2) 5,000, (B2) 1,250	–
Ordinary share capital	15,000			15,000
Capital redemption reserve	–		(C2) 5,000	5,000
Share premium	2,000			2,000
	22,000			22,000
Profit and loss	11,000	(C1) 5,000, (B1) 1,250		4,750
	33,000			26,750

(e)

	Effect Dr	Effect Cr
(A1) Bank	7,000	
(A2) Ordinary share applicants		7,000

Cash received from applicants.

	Effect Dr	Effect Cr
(B1) Ordinary share applicants	7,000	
(B2) Ordinary share capital		7,000

Ordinary shares allotted.

	Effect Dr	Effect Cr
(C1) Preference share capital	5,000	
(C2) Preference share redemption		5,000

Shares being redeemed.

	Effect Dr	Effect Cr
(D1) Share premium account	1,500	
(D2) Preference share redemption		1,500

Amount of share premium account used for redemption.

	Effect Dr	Effect Cr
(E1) Profit and loss appropriation	500	
(E2) Preference share redemption		500

Excess of premium payable over amount of share premium account usable for the purpose.

	Effect Dr	Effect Cr
(F1) Preference share redemption	7,000	
(F2) Bank		7,000

Amount payable on redemption.

Balances for (e):

	Balances before	Effect Dr	Effect Cr	Balances after
Net assets (except bank)	20,000			20,000
Bank	13,000	(A1) 7,000	(F2) 7,000	13,000
	33,000			33,000
Preference share capital	5,000			–
Preference share redemption	–	(C1) 5,000, (F1) 7,000	(C2) 5,000, (D2) 1,500, (E2) 500	–
Ordinary share capital	15,000		(B2) 7,000	22,000
Ordinary share applicants	–	(B1) 7,000	(A2) 7,000	–
Share premium account	2,000	(D1) 1,500		500
	22,000			22,500
Profit and loss	11,000	(E1) 500		10,500
	33,000			33,000

6.3

(a)

	Effect Dr	Effect Cr
(A1) Ordinary share capital	10,000	
(A2) Ordinary share purchase		10,000

Shares to be purchased.

	Effect Dr	Effect Cr
(B1) Ordinary share purchase	10,000	
(B2) Bank		10,000

Payment for shares purchased.

	Effect Dr	Effect Cr
(C1) Profit and loss	8,000	
(C2) Capital redemption reserve		8,000

Transfer of deficiency of permissible capital payment to comply with Companies Act.

	Balances before	Effect Dr	Effect Cr	Balances after
Net assets (except bank)	40,000			40,000
Bank	48,000		(B2) 10,000	38,000
	88,000			78,000
Preference share capital	20,000			20,000
Ordinary share capital	50,000	(A1) 10,000, (B1) 10,000	(A2) 10,000	40,000
Ordinary share purchase	–			–
Non-distributable reserves	10,000			10,000
Capital redemption reserve	–		(C2) 8,000	8,000
	80,000			78,000
Profit and loss	8,000	(C1) 8,000		–
	88,000			78,000

(b)

			Dr	Cr
(A1)	Ordinary share capital		10,000	
(A2)	Ordinary share purchase			10,000
	Shares to be purchased.			
(B1a)	Profit and loss		8,000	
(B2b)	Non-distributable reserves		2,000	
(B2)	Ordinary share capital			10,000
	Transfers of profit and loss and non-distributable reserves per Companies Act.			
(C1)	Ordinary share purchase		20,000	
(C2)	Bank			20,000
	Payment to shareholders.			

	Balances before	Effect Dr	Effect Cr	Balances after
Net assets (except bank)	40,000			40,000
Bank	48,000		(C2) 20,000	28,000
	88,000			68,000
Preference share capital	20,000			20,000
Ordinary share capital	50,000	(A1) 10,000	(A2) 10,000	40,000
		(C1) 20,000	(B2) 10,000	
Ordinary share purchase	–			–
Non-distributable reserves	10,000	(B1b) 2,000		8,000
	80,000			
Profit and loss	8,000	(B1a) 8,000		–
	88,000			68,000

6.5

Workings: Opening balance 10% debentures (a/c below)

Originally issued	375,000
Less Redeemed previously	150,000
	225,000

10% Debentures

30/9	Debenture redemption	225,000	1/7 Balance b/d	225,000

Workings: Sinking fund investments (a/c below)

Appropriations to date	334,485
Interest invested (39,480 – 2,475)	37,005
	371,490
Less Sold – at cost	144,915
	226,575

Sinking Fund Investments

1/7 Balance b/d	226,575	2/8 Bank No. 2 Sale	73,215
2/8 Sinking fund: Profit (73,215 – 69,322)	3,893	25/9 Bank No. 2 Sale	160,238
25/9 Sinking fund: Profit (Cost 226,575 – 69,322 = 157,253. Sold for 160,238)	2,985		
	233,453		233,453

Workings: Sinking fund (a/c below)

Previous contributions	334,485
Interest on investments	39,480
Profit: Previous sales of investments (147,243 – 144,915)	2,328
Profit: Previous purchase debentures (150,000 – 147,243)	2,757
	379,050
Less Transfer to general reserve sum equal to debentures redeemed	150,000
	229,050

Sinking Fund A/c

30/9 Debentures redemption (Premium 1%)	2,250	1/7 Balance b/d	229,050
30/9 General reserve	236,889	7/7 No 2 Bank: Interest	1,756
		2/8 SF Investments: Profit	3,893
		13/9 No 2 Bank: Interest	1,455
		25/9 SF Investments: Profit	2,985
	239,139		239,139

No. 2 Bank A/c

1/7 Balance b/d	2,475	30/9 W Bank plc (deposit)	15,150
7/7 Sinking fund: Interest	1,756	30/9 Debentures redemption	212,100
2/8 SF investments: Sale	73,215	30/9 No. 1 Bank transfer of balance	11,889
13/9 Sinking fund: Interest	1,455		
25/9 SF investments: Sale	160,238		
	239,139		239,139

Debenture Redemption A/c

30/9 No. 2 Bank (225,000 Debentures – 15,000 B Ltd = 210,000 at 1% premium)	212,100	30/9 10% Debentures	225,000
30/9 Balance c/d (15,000 outstanding at premium 1%)	15,150	30/9 Sinking fund (premium)	2,250
	227,250		227,250

W Bank plc

30/9 No. 2 Bank	15,150		15,150

6.7

(Dates omitted – all figures shown in £000)

Application and Allotment

Ordinary shares	80	Bank	60
Share premium	20	Bank	40
	100		100

Call Account

Ordinary shares	20	Bank	18
		Investments	2
	20		20

Investments (own shares)

Call	2	Bank	11
Share premium	9		
	11		11

6.9

(*Note:* Some abbreviations are used)

(a) 10% Debentures

31.12.08	Debenture redemption	12,000	1.4.08 Balance b/d	100,000
31.3.09	Balance c/d	88,000		
		100,000		100,000

(b) Debenture Redemption Fund

31.12.08	Reserve (equal to debentures redeemed)	12,000	1.4.08 Balance b/d	20,000
			31.12.08 DRFI (profit on redemption)	1,400
			31.12.08 DR (profit on purchase)	900
31.12.09	Balance c/d	13,900	31.12.09 Bank	1,600
31.3.09			31.3.09 Profit and loss (annual appropriation)	2,000
		25,900		25,900

(c) Debenture Redemption Fund Investment

1.4.08	Balance b/d	20,000	31.12.08 Bank (sale)	11,400
31.12.08	DR Fund	1,400	31.3.09 Balance c/d	13,900
31.3.09	Bank (2,000 + 300 + 1,600) (profit on sale)	3,900		
		25,300		25,300

(d) Debenture Redemption

31.12.08	Bank (purchase)	11,400	31.12.08 10% Debentures	12,000
31.12.08	DR Fund (profit on redemption)	900	31.12.08 Debenture interest accrued	300
		12,300		12,300

(e) Debenture Interest

30.9.08	Bank (100,000 × 10% ÷ 2)	5,000	31.3.09 Profit and loss	9,700
31.12.08	Debenture redemption (interest included in price 12,000 × 10% × ¼)	300		
31.3.09	Bank (88,000 × 10% ÷ 2)	4,400		
		9,700		9,700

7.1

Deal Ltd

Profit and Loss Account for the year ending 31 May 2005

	Total	Basis of allocation	Pre-incorporation	Post incorporation
Gross profit	104,000	Turnover	36,706	67,294
Less				
Salaries of vendors	6,800	Actual	6,800	
Wages	32,400	Time	8,100	24,300
Rent	3,600	Time	900	2,700
Distribution	6,800	Turnover	2,400	4,400
Commission	2,600	Turnover	918	1,682
Bad debts	1,420	Actual	480	940
Interest	6,200	Time	1,550	4,650
Directors' remuneration	15,000	Actual		15,000
Directors' expenses	2,200	Actual		2,200
Depreciation				
Vans*	7,600	Actual	1,600	6,000
Machinery	2,300	Actual	500	1,800
Bank interest	440	Actual		440
	87,360		23,248	64,112
Net profit	16,640		13,458	3,182
	104,000		36,706	67,294

*Depreciation on vans:
Vans to 31 March 2005 20% × 3 months × 28,000 + 20% × 1 month × 12,000 = 1,600
After 20% × 9 months × 28,000 + 20% × 9 months × 12,000 = 6,000
(b) Transfer to capital reserve.
(c) Charge to a goodwill account.

7.2

Adjusted Profits

	2002	2003	2004
Profit per accounts	115,850	141,850	120,140
Add Motor expenses saved	2,350	2,475	2,575
Depreciation overcharged	6,000	3,600	1,680
Wrapping expenses saved	2,505	2,865	3,060
Bank interest	440	1,120	1,360
Preliminary expenses		4,400	8,675
	11,295	14,460	
	127,145	156,310	128,815
Less Extra management			
salaries	35,000	35,000	35,000
Investment income	2,100	2,900	4,200
Rents received	7,800	3,300	–
Opening stock	–	4,700	–
Profit on property			
	44,900	23,200	39,200
Profits as adjusted	82,245	87,210	89,615
Average profit	82,245		
	87,210		
	89,615		
	259,070 ÷ 3 = 86,357		

If 86,357 is a return of 20% on investment, then

$$\frac{86,357}{20} \times 100 = 431,785 \text{ purchase price.}$$

7.3

(a)

CK
Realisation

Freehold premises	8,000	CK Ltd: Value at which	
Plant	4,000	assets taken over	27,200
Stock	2,000	Discount on creditors	150
Debtors	5,000		
Profit on realisation	8,350		
	27,350		27,350

Capital

CK Ltd: Shares	24,150	Balance b/d	16,000
Cash	200	Profit on realisation	8,350
	24,350		24,350

CK Ltd (not asked for in question)

Realisation	27,200	Creditors	3,050
		Shares	24,150
	27,200		27,200

(b) (Narratives omitted)

Journal of CJK Ltd

Cash	5,000	
Share premium		3,000
Ordinary shares		2,000
Cash	7,840	
Discount on issue	160	
7 per cent debentures		8,000
Goodwill	7,000	
Freehold premises	10,000	
Plant	3,500	
Stock	2,000	
Debtors	5,000	
Provision for discounts receivable		150
Creditors		3,200
Provision for doubtful debts		300
Ordinary shares		24,150
Goodwill	500	
Freehold premises	5,500	
Plant	2,000	
Stock	1,600	
Debtors	3,400	
Creditors		1,500
Bank overdraft		3,500
Cash		5,000
Ordinary share capital		3,000
Formation expenses	1,200	
Cash		1,200

RP Ltd
Realisation

Freehold premises	4,500	CK Ltd: Value at which assets	
Plant	2,000	taken over	13,000
Stock	1,600		
Debtors	3,400		
Profit on realisation	1,500		
	13,000		13,000

Sundry Shareholders

CK Ltd	4,500	Share capital	4,000
Cash	5,000	Profit on realisation	1,500
Shares	3,000	Revenue surplus	2,500
	8,000		8,000

CK Ltd (not asked for in question)

Realisation	13,000	Bank overdraft	3,500
		Creditors	1,500
		Sundry shareholders: Cash	5,000
		Shares	3,000
	13,000		13,000

7.3 (cont'd)
(c)

CJK Ltd
Balance Sheet as at 1 January 2010*

Fixed assets: at cost		
Freehold premises		15,500
Plant		5,500
Goodwill		7,500
		28,500
Current assets		
Stock		3,600
Debtors	8,400	
Less Provision for doubtful debts	300	8,100
Cash at bank		3,140
		14,840
Less Current liabilities		
Creditors	4,700	
Less Provision	150	4,550
Working capital		10,290
		38,790

*This could be 31 December 2009.

8.1
(a)

Debenture Interest

2006			2006		
Dec 31	Bank	14,000	Dec 31	Profit and loss	17,500
Dec 31	Income tax	3,500			
		17,500			17,500

Income Tax

2006			2006		
Dec 31	Balance c/d	3,500	Dec 31	Debenture interest	3,500

Ordinary Dividends

2006			2006		
Jul 1	Bank	32,000	Dec 31	Profit and loss	80,000
Dec 31	Accrued c/d	48,000			
		80,000			80,000

Deferred Taxation

2006			2006		
Dec 31	Balance c/d	16,000	Dec 31	Profit and loss*	16,000

*40% of (£110,000 – £70,000) = £16,000

Corporation Tax

2006			2006		
Dec 31	Balance c/d	145,000	Dec 31	Profit and loss	145,000

(b) *Profit and Loss Account (extracts) for the year ending 31 December 2006*

Net trading profit		390,000
Less Debenture interest		17,500
Profit on ordinary activities before taxation		372,500
Less Corporation tax	145,000	
Deferred tax	16,000	161,000
Profit on ordinary activities after taxation		211,500
Less Ordinary dividends: Interim	32,000	
Final proposed	48,000	80,000
		131,500

Balance Sheet (extracts) as at 31 December 2006

Creditors: *Amounts falling due within one year*

Proposed ordinary dividend	48,000
Corporation tax	145,000
Income tax	3,500
Deferred tax	16,000

8.3
Workings:
(W1) Tax deducted from fixed interest income is $\frac{1}{4} \times$ £60,000 = £15,000
(W2) Changes in deferred taxation account.
Timing difference:

Capital allowances allowable for tax (D)		260,000
Depreciation actually charged (D)		180,000
		80,000

Transferred to deferred tax account £80,000 × 40% = £32,000

Deferred Tax

2008			2008			
Dec 31	Balance c/d	202,000	Jan 1	Balance b/d	(J)	170,000
			Dec 31	Profit and loss	(W2)	32,000
		202,000				202,000

Income Tax

2008				2008			
Nov 9	Interest received	(C1)	15,000	Dec 5	Debenture interest	(B)	40,000
Dec 19	Bank		25,000				
			40,000				40,000

Interest Received

2008			2008			
Dec 31	Profit and loss	75,000	Nov 9	Bank	(C1)	60,000
			Nov 9	Income tax	(C1)	15,000
		75,000				75,000

Skim Ltd
Profit and Loss (extracts) for the year ending 31 December 2008

Net trading profit	(A)		1,200,000
Add Fixed rate interest (C1) (gross)		75,000	
Investment income (C2) (gross)		2,000	77,000
			1,277,000
Less Debenture interest (B) (gross)			200,000
Profit on ordinary activities before taxation			1,077,000
Less Tax on profit on ordinary activities*			364,000
Profit on ordinary activities after taxation			713,000

*Notes attached to the financial statements giving make-up of this figure.

Balance Sheet (extracts) as at 31 December 2008

Creditors: amounts falling due within one year		
Proposed ordinary dividend	(K)	300,000
Corporation tax	(L)	340,000
Deferred tax		202,000

A final point concerns the difference in treatment of tax on investment income as compared with tax on other income, such as interest. It is only the tax on investment income which is treated as part of the final tax costs, while the tax on interest is simply deducted from charges paid by the company. You would have to study taxation in detail to understand why this happens.

8.5

Moontan Ltd
Profit and Loss Account for the year ending 31 December 2002

Operating profit		200,000
Income from shares in related companies	3,200*	
Other interest receivable and similar income	500**	3,700
		203,700
Interest payable and similar charges		7,000***
Profit on ordinary activities before taxation		196,700
Tax on profit on ordinary activities		106,000
Profit on ordinary activities after taxation		90,700

*£40,000 × 8% = £3,200
**£100,000 × 5% = £500
***£100,000 × 7% = £7,000

Debenture Interest

2008				2008			
Dec 5	Bank	(B)	160,000	Dec 31	Profit and loss	(B)	200,000
Dec 5	Income tax	(B)	40,000				
			200,000				200,000

Investment Income

2008				2008			
Dec 31	Profit and loss		2,000	Oct 1	Bank	(C2)	2,000
			2,000				2,000

Corporation Tax

2008				2008			
Sept 30	Bank*		272,000	Jan 1	Balance b/d	(K)	280,000
Sept 30	Profit and loss†		8,000	31 Dec	Profit and loss	(L)	340,000
Dec 31	Balance c/d	(K) (L)	340,000				
			620,000				620,000

*£280,000 owing – £8,000 reduction (K) = £272,000.
†Adjustment for amendment in tax bill.

Tax on Profit on Ordinary Activities

2008				2008			
Dec 31	Corporation tax		340,000	Oct 6	Corporation tax	(K)	8,000
Dec 31	Deferred tax	(W2)	32,000	Dec 31	Profit and loss		364,000
			372,000				372,000

Preference Dividends

2008				2008			
Jun 30	Bank	(F)	32,000	Dec 31	Profit and loss		32,000

Ordinary Dividends

2008				2008			
Mar 10	Bank	(I)	240,000	Dec 31	Profit and loss		420,000
Aug 8	Bank	(G)	180,000				
			420,000				420,000

8.6
(All in £million)

(i)

Ordinary Dividends

31.8.08	Bank (07 final)	28	31.3.09 Profit and loss	40
31.12.08	Bank (08 interim)	12		
		36		40

(ii)

Deferred Taxation

31.3.09	Balance c/d	8	1.4.08 Balance b/d	3
			31.3.09 Profit and loss	5
		8		8

8.1
(a)

Either Ltd

		£000
Profit per draft financial statements		157
(i) Stock: reduce to net realisable value	+	–
(ii) Directors' remuneration		35
(iii) Bad debt		43
(iv) Corporation tax saved on (i) + (ii) + (iii) × 50%	54	30
(v) Depreciation adjustment (W1)		30
(vi) Revaluation reserve (realised on sale)	125	
(vii) General reserve	80	
(viii) Loss brought forward (W2)		144
	259	282
	net (23)	(23)
		134

Maximum possible dividend £9,000

Preference dividend 6% £125,000

Ordinary dividend

Research and development expenditure: assumed to have been carried forward in accordance with SSAP 13 and can be justified. Failing this it would have to be a realised loss.

(b) For a plc no changes required, except that the payment should not reduce net assets below called-up share capital and undistributable reserves = 400 + 150 + 100 = 650. A further bad debt might change this position.

(W1) *Reducing balance*

Cost 1.12.2001	100,000
Depreciation 2002	25,000
	75,000
Cost 1.6.2003	25,000
	100,000
Depreciation 2003	25,000
	75,000
Cost 29.2.2004	28,000
31.5.2004	45,000
	148,000
Depreciation 2004	37,000
	111,000
Cost 1.12.2004	50,000
	161,000
Depreciation 2005	40,250
	120,750
	127,250

Total 25,000 + 25,000 + 37,000 + 40,250 =

Straight line

		2002	2003	2004	2005
Cost 1.12.2002	100,000	25,000	25,000	25,000	25,000
1.6.2003	25,000		3,125	6,250	6,250
29.2.2004	28,000			5,250	7,000
31.5.2004	45,000			5,625	11,250
1.12.2004	50,000				12,500
		25,000	28,125	42,125	62,000

Total 157,250

Extra depreciation 157,250 – 127,250 = 30,000

(W2) As profits after tax were £157,000 but were shown in the balance sheet as £13,000, this means that a deficit of £144,000 had been brought forward from last year.

10.1

(a)

Merton Manufacturing Co Ltd
Balance Sheet as at ...

Fixed tangible assets			
Freehold land and buildings at cost	(W1)	95,000	
Plant and equipment at written-down value		104,350	
			199,350
Current assets			
Stocks		25,000	
Debtors		50,000	
Bank	(W2)	14,150	
		89,150	
Creditors: amounts falling due within one year		63,500	
Net current assets			25,650
Total assets *less* current liabilities			225,000
Long-term loans: 8 per cent debentures	(W3)		150,000
			75,000
Capital and reserves			
Called-up share capital	(W4)		75,000
150,000 50p ordinary shares			

Workings:

(W1)

Capital Reduction

Ordinary shares £1 (old)			90,000
6% preference shares (old)			150,000
11½% Debentures (old)			100,000
Share premium written off			25,000
Ordinary shares 50p (new) (1 for 6 = 15,000 × 50p)		7,500	
Ordinary shares 50p (new) (1 for 3 – preference – 50,000 × 50p)		25,000	
8% debentures (1 for 3 preference)		50,000	
8% debentures (exchange for 11½%)		100,000	
Ordinary shares 50p (1 for every £4 old debenture)		12,500	
Goodwill written off		50,000	
Profit and loss written off		38,850	
Plant and equipment*		81,150	
		365,000	365,000

*Per *(vii)* of question – amount needed to balance.

(W2) Shares issued 60,000 shares × 50p = 30,000
Cash 30,000 – overdraft 15,850 = balance 14,150

(W3) See capital reduction – debit side (W1) new debentures 50,000 + 100,000 = 150,000

(W4) See (W1) 7,500 + 25,000 + 12,500 + new shares issued for cash 30,000 = 75,000

(b) (Main points)

	Old shareholdings	New shareholdings
Expected profit	22,500	22,500
Less Interest 11½%	11,500	
8%		12,000
		10,500
Taxable profits	11,000	
Less Corporation tax 33⅓%	3,667	3,500
Profits before dividends	7,333	7,000
Preference dividends – if profits sufficient	9,000	–

Before reconstruction
(Old) Preference shareholders
Before reconstruction it would have taken over 5 years at this rate before preference dividends payable, as the deficit of 38,850 on the profit and loss account would have to be cleared off first.
(Old) Ordinary shares
Even forgetting the profit and loss account deficit, the preference dividends were bigger than available profits. This would leave nothing for the ordinary shareholder.

After reconstruction
The EPS is £7,000 ÷ 150,000 = 4.67p
If all profits are distributed the following benefits will be gained:
By old preference shareholders
50,000 shares × 4.67p
£50,000 8% debentures

	2,335
	4,000
	6,335

Plus any benefits from tax credits.
By old ordinary shareholders
15,000 shares × 4.67p — 700
Plus any benefits from tax credits.

(c) Preference shareholders – points to be considered:
(i) What were prospects for income?

Based on projected earnings would have been no income for over 5 years, then earnings of 7,333 per annum if all profits distributed.

(ii) What are new prospects for income?

Total income of 6,333 per annum immediately.

(iii) Is it worth exchanging (i) for (ii)?

Obviously depends on whether forecasts are accurate or not. If the above are accurate would seem worthwhile.

(iv) What have preference shareholders given up?

Some of exchange consists of ordinary shares which are more risky than preference shares, both in terms of dividends and of payments on liquidation. Dividend will be lower than the 6% they were due previously, but it was not being paid.

(v) What have they gained?

Debenture interest payable whether profits made or not.
Likelihood of dividends much sooner than the minimum of 5 years anticipated above.

10.2

(a) *(Narratives omitted)*

	Dr	Cr
Preference share capital	37,500	
Ordinary share capital	175,000	
Capital reduction		212,500

Preference shares reduced 25p each (0.25 × 150,000) and Ordinary shares reduced by 0.875 (200,000 × 0.875).

	Dr	Cr
Capital reduction	3,375	
Ordinary share capital		3,375

Ordinary shares issued re. preference dividend arrears, 27,000 × 0.125.

	Dr	Cr
Share premium	40,000	
Capital reduction		40,000

Share premium balance utilised.

	Dr	Cr
Provision for depreciation	62,500	
Capital reduction	72,500	
Plant and machinery		135,000

Plant and machinery written down to 75,000.

	Dr	Cr
Capital reduction	176,625	
Profit and loss		114,375
Preliminary expenses		7,250
Goodwill		55,000

Profit and loss account and intangible assets written off.

	Dr	Cr
Cash	62,500	
Ordinary share applicants		62,500

Applications for shares 500,000 × 0.125.

	Dr	Cr
Ordinary share applicants	62,500	
Ordinary share capital		62,500

500,000 ordinary shares issued.

(b) *Balance Sheet as at 31 December 2005*

Fixed assets		
Leasehold property at cost	80,000	
Less Provision for depreciation	30,000	50,000
Plant and machinery at valuation		75,000
		125,000
Current assets		
Stock	79,175	
Debtors	31,200	
Bank	11,500	
	121,875	
Less *Current liabilities*		
Creditors	43,500	
Working capital		78,375
		203,375
Financed by:		
Share capital:		
Preference shares		
150,000 shares £0.75		112,500
Ordinary shares		
727,000 ordinary shares £0.125		90,875
		203,375

10.3

The Journal (narratives omitted)

	Dr	Cr
(a) Preference share capital	40,000	
Capital reduction		40,000
(b) Ordinary share capital	360,000	
Capital reduction		360,000
(c) Capital reserve	90,000	
Capital reduction		90,000
(d) Preference share capital	60,000	
Ordinary share capital	540,000	
New ordinary share capital		600,000
(e) (i) Debenture holders	400,000	
Debentures		400,000
(ii) Bank	400,000	
Debenture holders		400,000
(f) Capital reduction	490,000	
Goodwill etc.		108,000
Plant and machinery		80,000
Furniture		20,000
Profit and loss		282,000

Answers to review questions

Quality Yarns Ltd
Balance Sheet as at 31 March 2002

Fixed assets		
Intangible: Goodwill and trademarks		52,000
Tangible: Plant and machinery		350,000
Furniture and fittings		8,000
		410,000
Current assets		
Stock	230,000	
Debtors	84,000	
Bank	329,000	
Cash	2,000	
	645,000	
Creditors: amounts falling due within 1 year		
Creditors	55,000	
Net current assets		590,000
Total assets *less* current liabilities		1,000,000
Creditors: amounts falling due after more than 1 year		
Debentures		400,000
		600,000
Authorised capital: 1.75 million £1 ordinary shares	1,750,000	
Issued and fully paid share capital: 600,000 £1 ordinary shares		600,000

11.1
(a) Following is a brief answer:
(i) Such closure costs should be treated as an exceptional item, because:
● it is (probably) a material item;
● these are costs not likely to recur regularly or frequently.
(ii) This should be adjusted in tax charge for 2007. Because it is not material (probably) it does not need to be disclosed separately.
(iii) The excess should be credited to a reserve account, and a note attached to the balance sheet. Depreciation to be based on revalued amount and on new estimate of remaining life of the asset, to be disclosed in a note to the accounts.
(iv) Treat as bad debt and write off to profit and loss. Because it is a material item it should be disclosed as an exceptional item in the profit and loss account.
(v) This is a prior period adjustment. The retained profit brought forward should be amended to allow for the change in accounting policy in the current year. The reasons: (1) it is material, (2) relates to a previous year, (3) as a result of change in accounting policy. The adjustment should be disclosed in a note to the financial statements.
(b) See Section 11.23.

11.2
(i) The replacement cost is irrelevant. The stock should be shown at the cost of £26,500. This assumes historic cost accounts.
(ii) *Paramite:* Stock to be valued at direct costs £72,600 plus fixed factory overhead £15,300 = £87,900. Under no circumstances should selling expenses be included.
Paraton: As net realisable value is lower than the costs involved, this figure of £9,520 should be used (SSAP 9).
(iii) In this case there is a change of accounting policy. Accordingly a prior period adjustment will be made. On a straight line basis, net book value would have been:

Cost 160,000 less 12½% × 2 years =	120,000
Value shown	90,000
	30,000

Therefore prior period adjustment of to be added to retained profit at 1 November 2004.

For 2005 and each of the following 5 years depreciation will be charged at the rate of £20,000 per annum (FRS 3).
(iv) The cost subject to depreciation is £250,000 less land £50,000 = £200,000. With a life of 40 years this is £5,000 per annum.
This also will result in a prior period adjustment, in this case 10 × £5,000 = £50,000. This will be debited to retained profits at 1 November 2004. For 2005 and each of the following 29 years the yearly charge of depreciation will be £5,000 (FRS 3).
(v) Write off £17,500 to profit and loss (SSAP 13).
(vi) As this development expenditure is almost definitely going to be recovered over the next 4 years it can be written off over that period (SSAP 13).
(vii) As this is unlikely to happen often it is an exceptional item. Charge to profit and loss on ordinary activities under the appropriate statutory heading (FRS 3).
(viii) As this is over 20 per cent, it is material and appears to be long-term. This means that Lilleshall Ltd is an associated company and accounts should be prepared accordingly. The post-acquisition profits to be brought in are 30% × £40,000 = £12,000.

11.5
The fact that this is a partnership does not mean that accounting standards are not applicable; they are just as applicable to a partnership as they are to a limited company.
(a) (i) These should be included as sales £60,000 in the accounts for the year to 31 May 2007. This is because the matching concept requires that revenue, and the costs used up in achieving it, should be matched up. Profits: increase of £60,000.
(ii) Stock values are normally based on the lower of cost or net realisable value. In this case it depends how certain it is that the stock can be sold for £40,000. If a firm order can definitely be anticipated, then the figure of £40,000 can be used as this then represents the lower figure of net realisable value. Profit: an increase of £15,000. However, should the sale not be expected, then the concept of prudence dictates that the scrap value of £1,000 be used. Profit: a reduction of £24,000.

11.5 (cont'd)

(b) It is important to establish the probability of the payment of the debt of £80,000. If it is as certain as it possibly can be that payment will be made, even though it may be delayed then no provision is needed. Profit change: nil.

However, the effect on future profits can be substantial. A note to the accounts detailing the possibilities of such changes should be given.

(c) The concepts which are applicable here are (i) going concern, (ii) consistency, (iii) accruals, (iv) prudence.

Following on the revelations in (b) and the effect on sales so far of the advertising campaign, is the partnership still able to see itself as a going concern? This would obviously affect the treatment of valuations of all assets.

Given that it can be treated as a going concern, the next point to be considered is that of consistency. The treatment of the expense item should be treated consistently.

The accruals concept is concerned with matching up revenues and costs, and will affect the decision as to how much of the costs should be carried forward. Some revenue in future periods needs to be expected with a high degree of certainty before any of this expenditure should be carried forward. It does not seem highly likely that large revenues can be expected in future in this case. In any case 75 per cent is a very large proportion of such expenditure to be carried forward. There is no easy test of the validity of the partners' estimates. Granted that under SSAP 13 for development expenditure some of it, under very stringent conditions, can be carried forward. If the partners' estimates can be accepted under this, then profits would be increased by 75% × (50,000 + 60,000) = £82,500.

(d) The expected profit/loss is as follows:

	Project A	Project B	Project C
Direct costs to date	30,000	25,000	6,000
Overheads to date	4,000	2,000	500
Future expected direct costs	10,000	25,000	40,000
Future expected overheads	2,000	2,000	3,000
Total of expected costs	46,000	54,000	49,500
Sale price of project	55,000	50,000	57,500
Expected total profit/loss	9,000	(4,000)	8,000
% Complete	75%	50%	15%

When a project is sufficiently near completion then a proportion of the profits can be taken as being realised.

Project A is 75 per cent complete and this indicates profit being taken. Whether or not 75 per cent can be taken, i.e. £6,750, will depend on the facts of the case. If completion at the above figures can be taken for granted then it might be reasonable to do so. Prudence dictates that a lesser figure be taken.

With project B there is an expected loss. Following the prudence concept losses should always be accounted for in full as soon as they become known.

In project C it is too early in the project, 15 per cent completed, to be certain about the outcome. No profit should therefore be brought into account.

Profit, dependent on comments about project A, will therefore be increased by £6,750 − £4,000 = £2,750.

(e) This is a case where the examiner has dipped into topics from other subjects. What is needed here is a tree diagram to show the probabilities.

£15,000 0.2
£10,000 0.1 = £25,000 0.02
£20,000 0.5 = £35,000 0.10
£30,000 0.4 = £45,000 0.08

£30,000 0.5
£10,000 0.1 = £40,000 0.05
£20,000 0.5 = £50,000 0.25
£30,000 0.4 = £60,000 0.20

£40,000 0.3
£10,000 0.1 = £50,000 0.03
£20,000 0.5 = £60,000 0.15
£30,000 0.4 = £70,000 0.12

1.00

0.75

There is a probability of 0.75 of achieving £50,000 sales. As this is greater than the specified figure of 0.70 then the stocks should not be written down. Effect on profits: nil.

(f) The opening stock should be shown as the revised figure. If error had not been found this year's profit would have been £7,000 greater.

The adjustment should be shown as a prior period adjustment on the face of the profit and loss account, not in a note.

11.6

(a)
The Chief Accountant
Uncertain Ltd   Address
Dear Sir/Mr . . . ,   Date

Report on Draft Profit and Loss Account for the year ending 30 September 2006

Further to your letter/our meeting of . . . I would like to offer my suggestions for the appropriate accounting treatment of items (i) to (v).

Uncertain Ltd

(b) Draft profit and loss account for the year ending 30 September 2006

Sales		5,450,490
Manufacturing cost of sales (W1)		2,834,500
		2,615,990
Administration expenses	785,420	
Selling expenses (W2)	754,800	
Prior period adjustment	258,800	
		1,799,020
Operating profit		816,970
Continuing operations – redundancy payments	100,000	
Discontinued operations – factory closure costs	575,000	
		675,000
Profit before tax		141,970
Corporation tax (50%) (W3)		70,985
Profit for the year		70,985

Note: Dividend proposed: £125,000.

(W1) £3,284,500 – £100,000 (i) – £350,000 (iv) = £2,834,500
(W2) £629,800 + £125,000 (v) = £754,800
(W3) 50% of profits before tax

(i) Redundancy payments: £100,000
The reorganisation satisfies the requirements of FRS 3, that it had a material effect on the nature and focus of the reporting entity's operations. As a result, the costs should be shown separately on the face of the profit and loss account after operating profit and before interest, and included under the heading of continuing operations. Relevant information regarding its effect on the taxation charge should be shown in a note to the profit and loss account. If there are other exceptional items in the financial period, and the tax effect differs between them, further information should be given, where practicable, to assist users in assessing the impact of the different items on the net profit or loss attributable to shareholders.

(ii) Closure costs of a factory
FRS 3 requires that material profits or losses on the termination of an operation should be treated as exceptional and shown separately on the face of the profit and loss account after operating profit and before interest, and included under the appropriate heading of continuing or discontinued operations. In calculating the profit or loss in respect of the termination, consideration should only be given to revenue and costs directly related to it. Clearly, the costs have been identified and are known and there is a loss on the termination. It should not have been deducted from reserves; it must go through the profit and loss account.

(iii) Change of basis of depreciation: £258,000
There should only be a change in the basis of depreciation if it brings about a fairer presentation of the accounting results and financial position of the company – see FRS 15. This standard also requires that the depreciation should be shown as normal expenses, rather than as a prior period adjustment.
Because the item is a material one, and makes comparison difficult, a note as to the details should be appended to the accounts.

(iv) Additional expenses covered by fire: £350,000
These expenses are covered by FRS 21 as post-balance sheet non-adjusting events. The fire happened after the balance sheet date, and therefore did not affect conditions as at that date. The figures in this year's financial statements should not, therefore, be altered.
If the event was such as to call into question the continuation of the business, then there should be a note to the financial statements on the going-concern basis. In this particular instance this does not seem to be the case, but good practice, although not necessary, would be to give details of the event in notes to the financial statements.

(v) Bad debt: £125,000
The accounts have not yet been approved by the directors, and it does affect the valuation of assets at the year end. FRS 21 would treat it as a post-balance sheet adjusting event. It should therefore be written-off as a bad debt.
Where it is considered to be a material and unusual event, there should also be a note attached to the financial statements.

Should you like to have further discussions concerning any of the points raised, will you please contact me. I hope that you will find my comments to be of use.

Yours faithfully,
CACA

11.7

(a) (i) Post-balance sheet events (also known as 'post-reporting period' events) consists of those events, whether favourable or unfavourable, which take place between the date of the balance sheet and the date on which the financial accounts and notes are approved by the directors.

(ii) Adjusting events are post-balance sheet events which give extra evidence of what was happening at the balance sheet date. The events included may be included because they are either of a statutory nature or taken into account by convention.

(iii) Non-adjusting events are balance sheet events concerned with matters which did not exist at the balance sheet date.

(iv) A contingent asset/liability is concerned with something which seems to be apparent at the balance sheet date but can only be verified by future events which are uncertain.

(b) Adjusting events: (i) debtor's inability to pay; (ii) subsequent discovery of frauds rendering accounts incorrect; (iii) when net realisable value is used for stock valuation and later shown to be wrong when stock sold; (iv) subsequent discovery of errors rendering accounts incorrect.
Non-adjusting events: (i) change in foreign exchange rates; (ii) strikes; (iii) nationalisation; (iv) share issues.

(c) (i) A material contingent liability should be accrued where some future event will give evidence of the loss, subject to the fact that it should be able to be determined with reasonable accuracy when the accounts are agreed by the directors.

(ii) Material contingent assets should be disclosed in the financial statements if it is very probable that they will be realised.

12.1

(i) (For internal use)

Filo plc
Trading and Profit and Loss Account for the year ending 31 March 2005 (£000)

	£000	£000	£000
Sales		4,960.0	
Less Returns inwards		214.0	4,746.0
Less Cost of sales:			
Stock 1 April 2004		160.0	
Add Purchases	2,920.0		
Less Returns outwards	70.0	2,850.0	
Carriage inwards		26.0	
		3,036.0	
Less Stock 31 March 2005		208.0	2,828.0
Gross profit			1,918.0
Distribution costs:			
Salaries and wages	67.5		
Rent and business rates	15.0		
General distribution expenses	54.0		
Motor expenses	6.0		
Depreciation: Motors	35.0		
Equipment	4.8	182.3	
Administrative expenses:			
Salaries and wages	202.5		
Rent and business rates	10.0		
General administrative expenses	42.0		
Motor expenses	9.0		
Auditors' remuneration	16.0		
Discounts allowed	68.0		
Bad debts	9.0		
Depreciation: Motors	22.5		
Equipment	6.0	385.0	
			567.3
			1,350.7
Other operating income: Royalties receivable			5.0
			1,355.7
Income from shares in undertakings in which the company has a participating interest		6.0	
Interest on bank deposit		8.0	14.0
			1,369.7
Interest payable: Debenture interest		18.0	
Profit on ordinary activities before taxation			1,351.7
Tax on ordinary activities			489.0
Profit on ordinary activities after taxation			862.7
Retained profits from last year		210.0	
			1,072.7
Transfer to general reserve		30.0	
Dividend paid		240.0	270.0
Retained profits carried forward to next year			802.7

(ii) (Published accounts)

Filo plc
Profit and Loss Account for the year ending 31 March 2005 (£000)

	£000	£000
Turnover		4,746.0
Cost of sales		2,828.0
Gross profit		1,918.0
Distribution costs	182.3	
Administrative expenses	385.0	567.3
		1,350.7
Other operating income		5.0
		1,355.7
Income from shares in undertakings in which the company has a participating interest	6.0	
Other interest receivable	8.0	14.0
		1,369.7
Interest payable		18.0
Profit on ordinary activities before taxation		1,351.7
Tax on profit on ordinary activities		489.0
Profit for the year on ordinary activities after taxation		862.7

Notes to financial statements on debenture interest and movements in shareholders funds.

12.2

(i) (For internal use)

State plc
Trading and Profit and Loss Account for the year ending 31 December 2008
(£000)

	£000	£000	£000
Sales		1,860.0	
Less Returns inwards		9.0	1,851.0
Less Cost of sales:			
Stock 1 January 2008		140.0	
Add Purchases	1,140.0		
Less Returns outwards	5.0	1,145.0	
Carriage inwards		8.0	
		1,293.0	
Less Stock 31 December 2008		160.0	
Cost of goods sold		1,133.0	
Wages		88.0	
Depreciation of plant and machinery		9.0	1,230.0
Gross profit			621.0
Distribution costs			
Salaries and wages	62.0		
Rent and business rates	11.2		
Motor expenses	18.0		
General distribution expenses	12.0		
Haulage costs	4.0		
Depreciation: Motors	15.0		
Plant and machinery	7.5	129.7	

12.3

(a) **Rufford plc**

Profit and Loss Account for the year ending 31 March 2006

	Notes	£000	£000
Turnover	(1)		642
Cost of sales (60 + 401 − 71)			390
Gross profit			252
Distribution costs (33 + 19)		52	
Administrative expenses (97 + 8)		105	157
Operating profit – continuing operations	(2)		95
Loss on disposal of discontinued operations	(3)		12
			83
Income from other fixed asset investments	(4)	14	39
Other interest receivable		25	122
Interest payable	(5)		6
Profit on ordinary activities before taxation			116
Tax on profit on ordinary activities	(6)		44
Profit for the year on ordinary activities after taxation			72

Notes to the accounts:
1 Turnover is net of VAT.
2 Operating profit is shown after charging the following:

	£000	£000
Depreciation: distribution costs	19	27
administrative expenses	8	20
Auditor's remuneration		45
Directors' emoluments		12
Hire of plant		

3 Factory closure expenses.
4 Income from fixed asset investment is in respect of a listed company.
5 Interest payable is on a bank overdraft, repayable within 5 years.
6 Tax on profit on ordinary activities:

	£000
Corporation tax at 50% on profits	38
Transfer to deferred taxation	9
Overprovision in 2005	(3)
	44

7 Dividends:

	£000
Interim 5p per share	21
Final: proposed 10p per share	42
	63

8 Earnings per share:
EPS of 17.1p per share based on earnings of £72,000 and on average 420,000 shares on issue throughout the year (*see FRS 3 amendment*).

Administrative expenses

Salaries and wages	74.0	
Rent and business rates	16.8	
Motor expenses	6.0	
General administrative expenses	6.0	
Bad debts	2.0	
Discounts allowed	11.0	
Auditors' remuneration	14.0	
Directors' remuneration	36.0	
Depreciation: Motors	6.5	
Plant and machinery	4.5	176.8
Less Discounts received	14.0	162.8
		292.5
		328.5
Income from shares in undertakings in which the company has a participating interest	5.0	
Interest from government securities	3.0	8.0
		336.5
Amount written off investment in related companies	26.0	
Debenture interest	2.0	28.0
Profit on ordinary activities before taxation		308.5
Tax on profit on ordinary activities		104.0
Profit on ordinary activities after taxation		204.5
Retained profits from last year		94.0
		298.5
Transfer to debenture redemption reserve	25.0	
Dividend paid	60.0	85.0
Retained profits for the year		213.5

(ii) (Published accounts) **State plc**

Profit and Loss Account for the year ending 31 December 2008 (£000)

Turnover		1,851.0
Cost of sales		1,230.0
Gross profit		621.0
Distribution costs	129.7	
Administrative expenses	162.8	292.5
		328.5
Income from shares in undertakings in which the company has a participating interest	5.0	
Other interest receivable	3.0	8.0
		336.5
Amounts written off investments	26.0	
Interest payable	2.0	28.0
Profit on ordinary activities before taxation		308.5
Tax on profit on ordinary activities		104.0
Profit on ordinary activities after taxation		204.5
Transfer to reserves	25.0	
Dividend paid	60.0	85.0
Retained profits for the year		119.5

12.3 (cont'd)
(b)

Balance Sheet extracts as at 31 March 2006

	£000	£000
Creditors: amounts falling due within one year		
Other creditors including taxation and social security (W1)		77
Provisions for liabilities and charges		
Taxation, including deferred taxation (W2)		33
Workings:	£000	
(W1) Corporation tax for year to 31 March 2006	35	
Proposed dividend	42	
	77	
(W2) Deferred tax as given	24	
Transferred from profit and loss	9	
	33	

Capital and reserves		
Called-up share capital		550
Share premium account		55
Other reserves:		
Capital redemption reserve	16	41
General reserve	25	
Profit and loss account		45
		691

Notes:
(i) Called-up share capital consists of:

4 million £1 ordinary shares	400
150,000 preference shares of 50p each	150
	550

(ii) Land and buildings:

Cost		320
Depreciation to 31 March 2003	20	
Depreciation for year to 31 March 2004	10	30
		290

(iii) Plant and machinery:

Cost		80
Depreciation to 31 March 2003	36	
Depreciation for year to 31 March 2004	14	50
		30

13.1   Polk Ltd

Balance Sheet as at 31 March 2004 (£000)

Called-up share capital not paid			10
Fixed assets			
Intangible assets			
Development costs	52		
Goodwill	184	236	
Tangible assets			
Land and buildings	290		
Plant and machinery	30	320	
Investments			
Shares in undertakings in which the company has a participating interest		120	676
Current assets			
Stock			
Raw materials and consumables	5		
Finished goods and goods for resale	40	45	
Debtors			
Trade debtors	35		
Amounts owed by undertakings in which the company has a participating interest	12		
Prepayments	8	55	
		100	
Creditors: amounts falling due within one year			
Debentures	15		
Bank overdrafts	19		
Trade creditors	21		
Bills of exchange payable	12	67	
Net current assets			33
Total assets less current liabilities			719
Creditors: amounts falling due after one year			
Debentures	25		
Bills of exchange payable	3		28
			691

13.2   Tickers plc

Balance Sheet as at 30 April 2007 (£000)

Fixed assets			
Intangible assets			
Concessions, patents, licences, trade marks and similar rights and assets	6		
Goodwill	42	48	
Tangible assets			
Land and buildings	200		
Plant and machinery	43	243	291
Current assets			
Stock			
Raw materials and consumables	24		
Work in progress	9		
Finished goods and goods for resale	21	54	
Debtors			
Trade debtors	84		
Other debtors	3		
Prepayments and accrued income	2	89	
		143	

Creditors: amounts falling due within one year

Debenture loans	50	
Bank loans and overdrafts	3	
Trade creditors	26	
Bills of exchange payable	5	
Other creditors including taxation and social security	39	
		123
Net current assets		
Total assets less current liabilities		311

Creditors: amounts falling due after more than one year

Debenture loans	40		
Trade creditors	2	42	
Provisions for liabilities and charges			
Pensions and similar obligations	8		
Taxation, including deferred taxation	6	14	
			56
			255

Capital and reserves

Called-up share capital		100
Share premium account		60
Revaluation reserve		23

Other reserves

General reserve	30	
Foreign exchange reserve	7	37
Profit and loss account		35
		255

Notes appended to the accounts on the details of tangible assets and depreciation, also exact details of items lumped under group descriptions.

13.3

Baganza plc

Profit and Loss Account for the year ending 30 September 2007 (£000)

Turnover		19,500
Cost of sales (W1)		14,700
Gross profit		4,800
Distribution costs	600	
Administrative expenses (W2)	1,390	1,990
		2,810
Other operating income (W3)		249
Profit on ordinary activities before taxation		3,059
Tax on profit on ordinary activities (W4)		870
Profit on ordinary activities after taxation		2,189
Extraordinary item		1,500
Profit for the financial year		3,689

Earnings per share (W6)	182.4p

Note: Dividends paid £36 + proposed £720 = £756.

Workings (in £000):

(W1) Opening stock 2,300 + Purchases 16,000 – Closing stock 3,600 = 14,700
(W2) Per trial balance 400 + Research 75 + Depreciation: Property (5% × 2,700) 135 + Plant (15% × 5,200) 780 = 1,390
(W3) Dividends received 249
(W4) Corporation tax 850 + Deferred tax 40 – Overpayment last year 20 = 870
(W5) Dividends: Interim 36 + Final 720 = 756
(W6) EPS = Profit 3,689,000 ÷ Shares 1,200,000 = 307.4p

Baganza plc

Balance Sheet as at 30 September 2007

	£000	£000	£000
Fixed assets			
Tangible assets			
Land and buildings	2,305		
Plant and machinery	820	3,125	
Investments		2,000	
			5,125
Current assets			
Stocks		3,600	
Debtors		2,700	
Cash at bank		60	
		6,360	
Creditors: amounts falling due within one year			
Trade creditors	2,900		
Corporation tax (850 + 360)	1,210		
		4,110	
Net current assets			2,250
Total assets less current liabilities			7,375
Taxation, including deferred taxation (460 + 40)			500
			6,875
Capital and reserves			
Called-up share capital			1,200
Profit and loss account (2,022 – 36 + 3,689)			5,675
			6,875

14.1

X Limited
Balance Sheet at 31 March 2007

	Notes	£000	£000	£000
Fixed assets				
Intangible assets				
Development costs	(1)	35		
Tangible assets	(2)			
Freehold properties		1,040		
Plant and machinery		850		
Vehicles		285		
		2,175		
Investments	(3)			
Investments in listed shares		200		2,410
Current assets				
Stock	(4)	500		
Debtors and prepayments (see workings)		654		
Cash at bank		439	1,593	
Creditors: amounts falling due within 1 year				
Trade creditors and accrual		878		
Taxation		270	1,148	
Net current assets				445
				2,855
Total assets less current liabilities				
Creditors: amounts falling due after more than 1 year				
12% debentures 2006			500	
Provisions for liabilities and charges				
Deferred taxation	(5)	128	128	
				2,227
Capital and reserves		£000		
Called-up share capital	(6)	1,000		
Share premium		150		
Revaluation reserve		612		
Profit and loss account (see workings)	(7)	465		
		2,227		

Workings:

	£000	
Profit and loss (356 + 280)	636	
Less Bad debt (225,000 × 76%)	171	465
Debtors	825	
Less Bad debt (225,000 × 76%)	171	654

Notes to the balance sheet

1 Research and development

Research costs are written off immediately. Development costs are carried forward when there is a reasonable certainty of profitable outcome of the project and amortised over the useful life of the project.

2 Tangible assets

	Freehold property £000	Plant and machinery £000	Vehicles £000
Cost on 1 April 2006*	800	1,500	220
Disposal at cost	(320)		
Addition			200
Revaluation adjustment	612		
On 31 March 2007	1,092	1,500	420
Depreciation at 1 April 2006*	80	500	55
Depreciation on disposals	(40)		
Provision in year	12	150	80
	52	650	135
Net book values	1,040	850	285

Exam note only: Found by working backwards, leaving these figures as difference.

Note: Freehold property was valued by Messrs V & Co, Chartered Surveyors, at a market value of £1,040,000 as compared with net book value of £428,000. The valuation figure has been included in balance sheet, and £612,000 has been credited to a revaluation reserve. Depreciation for 2007 has been based on the revalued figure.

3 Investments

These had a market value of £180,000 on 31 March 2007, but as this is not considered by the directors to be a permanent fall in value, the cost figure has been retained.

4 Stock

	£000
Finished goods	250
Raw materials	200
Work in progress	50
	500

The current replacement cost of goods is £342,000.

5 Deferred taxation

Provision as at 1 April 2006	78	
Add Provision during year	50	
	128	
Less ACT recoverable	70	58

6 Share capital

1,000,000 ordinary shares of £1 each is the authorised capital, which has been fully issued and called up.

7 Reserves

	Profit and loss account	Share premium	Revaluation reserve
Balance at 1 April 2006	?	150	—
Change during the year	215	150	612
	215	150	612

14.2

Billinge plc
Profit and Loss Account for the year ending 30 June 2006

	Notes	£000	£000
Turnover – continuing operations			1,500
Cost of sales (W1)			825
Gross profit			675
Distribution costs	(2)	55	
Administrative expenses (W2)		320	375
			300
Loss on disposal of discontinued operations	(3)		30
			270
Tax on profit on ordinary activities	(4)		130
Profit from ordinary activities after taxation			140
Earnings per share	(5)		28.0p

Billinge plc
Balance Sheet as at 30 June 2006

	Notes	£000	£000
Fixed assets			
Tangible assets			
Fixtures and fittings	(7)		187
Current assets			
Stocks: Finished goods and goods for resale		100	
Debtors		500	
Cash at bank		157	
		757	
Creditors: amounts falling due within one year			
Trade creditors		64	
Other creditors, taxation and social security (W4)		100	
Proposed dividend		100	264
Net current assets			493
Total assets less current liabilities			680
Provisions for liabilities and charges			
Taxation including deferred taxation	(8)		100
			580
Capital and reserves			
Called-up share capital	(9)		500
Profit and loss account (40 + 40)			80
			580

Workings:

(W1) Opening stock		70
Purchases		855
		925
Less Closing stock		100
		825

(W2) Depreciation		340
Less disposals		20
		320
Additions		60
		380

(W2 continued)			£000
20% × 380			76
Loss on disposals	20		
Less Depreciation	(15)		
Less Cash	(3)		2
			78
Administrative expenses			242
			320

(W3) C/T for year		100
Deferred taxation		40
		140
Less Previous overprovision		10
		130

(W4) Other creditors, taxation and social security:		
Corporation tax		100

Notes to the accounts:

1 Accounting policies
(a) The financial statements have been drawn up using the historical cost convention.
(b) Turnover consists of sales to external customers less VAT.
(c) Stocks are valued at the lower of cost or net realisable value.
(d) Depreciation of fixed assets is based on cost, using the straight line method over 5 years, salvage values being ignored.
(e) Deferred taxation is at the anticipated rate, taking into account the differing periods and the probability that a liability will occur.

2 Administrative expenses include depreciation £78,000.

3 Exceptional charges have arisen of £30,000 on the closure of a factory.

4 Taxation

	£000
Corporation tax at 35% on profit for the period	100
Deferred taxation	40
	140
Less Adjustment re last year's corporation tax	10
	130

5 EPS calculated by dividing profit after taxation by number of ordinary shares on issue during the period.

6 Proposed ordinary dividend of 20p per share = £100,000.

7 Tangible fixed assets:

	£000	£000	£000
Fixtures etc. at 1.7.2005	340		
Additions	60	400	
Less Disposals		20	380
Depreciation at 1.7.2005	132		
For the period	76	208	
Less Disposals		15	193
			187

8

Deferred taxation at 1.7.2005	60
Profit and loss charge	40
	100

9 Authorised, issued and fully paid ordinary £1 shares | 500

14.6

Scampion plc
Profit and Loss Account for the year ending 31 May 2002

	£000	£000
Turnover (3,489 – VAT 259)		3,232
Cost of sales (1,929 + 330 + 51)		2,310
Gross profit		922
Administrative expenses (595 + 25 + 45)		665
Operating profit		257
Income from shares in related companies	5	
Other interest receivable (Note 2)	10	15
		272
Interest payable (Note 3)	18	
Written-off investments (Note 7)	4	22
Profit on ordinary activities before taxation		250
Tax on profit on ordinary activities (Note 4)		100
Profit on ordinary activities after taxation		150
Earnings per share (Note 5)		22.73p

Scampion plc
Balance Sheet as at 31 May 2002

	£000	£000
Fixed assets		
Tangible assets (Note 6)		1,372
Investments (Note 7)		60
		1,432
Current assets		
Stock	230	
Debtors (67 – 45)	22	
Investments (market value £115,000)	103	
Cash at bank and in hand	84	
	439	
Creditors: amounts falling due within one year (Note 8)	487	
Net current liabilities		(48)
Total assets *less* current liabilities		1,384
Creditors: amounts falling due after more than one year (Note 9)		50
		1,334
Capital and reserves		
Called-up share capital		660
Share premium account		225
Profit and loss account (Note 10)		449
		1,334

Notes:
1 Accounting policies
The historical cost convention has been used.
Provisions for depreciation are to write off the cost or valuation over the expected useful lives of the assets, by equal instalments, as follows:

Freehold buildings	40 years
Fixtures, fittings or equipment	10 years
Motor vehicles	5 years

Depreciation provisions have not been made on freehold land. The basis of the valuation of stock is at the lower of cost or net realisable value.

2 Other interest receivable
This is income from government securities £10,000.

3 Interest payable

Interest on loans repayable within 1 year	12,000
Interest on loans repayable in more than 5 years' time	6,000
	£18,000

4 Taxation
(It has been assumed that 'tax charge based on the accounts for the year' means that the profit shown of £250 is same as the taxable profits.)
Corporation tax at the rate of 40 per cent on profits has been provided for.

5 Earnings per share = $\dfrac{150}{660}$ = 22.73p

6 Tangible assets (£000):

	Valuation or cost at 31.5.06	Additions at cost	Less disposals	Depreciation to: 31.5.06	31.5.07	Net
Freehold land and buildings	1,562	50		29	5	1,178
Fixtures, fittings and equipment	141	40	400	38	18	125
Motor vehicles	117	20		40	28	69
	1,820	110	400	107	51	1,372

7 Investments

Valuation by directors of shares in related companies	64,000
Less Written off during the year	4,000
	60,000

8 Creditors

Trade creditors (487,000 – Tax 120,000)	367,000
Corporation tax	100,000
Bank loan	20,000
	487,000

9 Creditors – amounts falling due after more than one year £50,000 12% debentures repayable in 4 years' time.

10 Reserves

	Revaluation	Profit and loss
Balance 31.5.2006	150	149
Transfer to profit and loss	(150)	150
Retained profits for year to 31.5.07	–	84
	–	383

15.1
See text of Chapter 15, Section 15.2.

15.3

Lee Ltd
FRS1 Cash Flow Statement (using the direct method)
for the year ended 31 December 2004

Operating activities		
Cash received from customers	6,550	
Cash paid to suppliers	(2,875)	
Cash paid to employees	(2,025)	
Other cash payments	(600)	
Net cash inflow from operating activities		1,050
Dividends from joint ventures and associates		–
Returns on investment and servicing of finance		
Interest paid		(100)
Taxation		–
Capital expenditure and financial investment		
Payments to acquire tangible assets		(700)
Acquisitions and disposals		–
Equity dividend paid		(50)
Management of liquid resources		–
Financing		
Repurchase of debentures		(100)
Increase in cash in the period		100

Notes to the cash flow statement:
1 Reconciliation of operating profit to net cash inflow from operating activities:

Operating profit	400
Depreciation charges	500
Decrease in stocks	100
Decrease in debtors	50
Net cash inflow from operating activities	1,050

Working:
Operating profit = profit for the year (300) + interest (100) = 400

15.5
See text of Chapter 15, Section 15.2.

15.6

Nimmo Limited
FRS1 Cash Flow Statement (using the indirect method) for the year ended
31 December 2009 (£000)

Net cash inflow from operating activities		2,150
Dividends from joint ventures and associates		–
Returns on investments and servicing of finance		
Taxation		(3,200)
Capital expenditure and financial investment		
Purchase of fixed assets	(11,800)	
Sale of fixed assets	1,000	
Net cash outflow for capital expenditure		(10,800)
Acquisitions and disposals		–
Equity dividend paid		(5,100)
Management of liquid resources		–
Financing		
Issue of debenture stock		150
Decrease in cash in the period		(16,800)

Note to the cash flow statement:
1 Reconciliation of operating profit to net cash inflow from operating activities:

Operating profit	20,400
Depreciation charges	5,050
Loss on sale of fixed assets	700
Increase in stocks	(10,000)
Increase in trade debtors	(18,100)
Increase in prepayments	(100)
Increase in trade creditors	4,000
Increase in accruals	200
Net cash inflow from operating activities	2,150

Working:
Loss on sale of fixed assets = 1,000 – (5,500 – 3,800) = (700)

15.7

Track Limited

FRS1 Cash Flow Statement (using the indirect method) for the year ending
30 June 2001 (£000)

Net cash outflow from operating activities		(75)
Dividends from joint ventures and associates		–
Returns on investments and servicing of finance		–
Taxation		(230)
Capital expenditure and financial investment		
Purchase of fixed assets	(175)	
Sale of investments	150	
Sale of fixed assets	20	
Net cash outflow for capital expenditure		(5)
Acquisitions and disposals		–
Equity dividend paid		(150)
Management of liquid resources		–
Financing		
Issue of share capital		300
Net cash outflow for period		(160)

Note to the cash flow statement:

1 Reconciliation of operating profit to net cash inflow
from operating activities:

Operating profit	180
Depreciation charges	110
Profit on sale of fixed assets	(5)
Increase in stocks	(300)
Increase in trade debtors	(200)
Increase in trade creditors	140
Net cash inflow from operating activities	(75)

Workings:

Profit before tax: 670 – 530 = retained loss of 140 + tax (190) + dividends (130) = 180

Profit on sale of fixed assets = 20 – (25 – 10) = (5)

15.10

Baker Limited

(a) Forecast net cash position for the three quarters ending 30 Sept 2007

	Quarter to		
	31 March 2007 £000	30 June 2007 £000	30 Sept 2007 £000
Receipts			
Trade debtors (W1)	235	290	345
Tangible fixed assets	12	–	–
Investments	10	–	–
Debentures	–	–	50
	257	290	395
Payments			
Trade creditors (W2)	150	230	285
Administration, selling and distribution expenses	37	40	42
Tangible fixed assets	–	240	–
Investments	–	–	5
Taxation	8	–	–
Dividend	15	–	–
	210	510	332
Forecast net cash flow	47	(220)	63
Add Opening cash	80	127	(93)
Forecast closing cash	127	(93)	(30)

Workings:

W1 Trade debtors: forecast cash receivable:

	31 March 2007 £000	30 June 2007 £000	30 Sept 2007 £000
Sales	250	300	350
Less Closing trade debtors	65	75	80
	185	225	270
Add Opening trade debtors	50	65	75
Forecast cash receipts from trade debtors	235	290	345

W2 Trade creditors: forecast cash payable

	31 March 2007 £000	30 June 2007 £000	30 Sept 2007 £000
Opening stock	40	30	40
Purchases (by deduction)	190	250	295
	230	280	335
Less Closing stock	30	40	55
Cost of sales	200	240	280
Purchases (as above)	190	250	295
Less Closing trade creditors	120	140	150
	70	110	145
Add Opening trade creditors	80	120	140
Forecast cash payments to trade creditors	150	230	285

(b)   **Baker Limited**

Forecast FRS1 cash flow statement (using the direct method)
for the nine months ended 30 September 2007 (£000)

Operating activities		
Cash received from customers (W1)	870	
Cash paid to creditors (W2)	(665)	
Other cash payments (admin, selling and distrib.)	(119)	
Net cash outflow from operating activities		86
Dividends from joint ventures and associates		–
Returns on investments and servicing of finance		(8)
Taxation		
Capital expenditure and financial investment		
Purchase of fixed assets	(240)	
Sale of fixed assets	12	
Net cash outflow for capital expenditure		(228)
Acquisitions and disposals		–
Equity dividend paid		(15)
Management of liquid resources		
Addition to 90 day deposit	(5)	
Realisation of 90 day deposit	10	
Net cash inflow from management of liquid resources		5
Financing		
Issue of debentures		50
Net cash outflow for period		(110)

Note to the cash flow statement:
1 Reconciliation of operating profit to net cash inflow
from operating activities:

Operating profit	34
Depreciation charges	27
Increase in stocks	(15)
Increase in trade debtors	(30)
Increase in trade creditors	70
Net cash outflow from operating activities	86

16.1
See text Section 16.6.

16.2
See text Section 16.8.

16.3
See text Section 16.4.

16.4
See text Section 16.8.

17.1   *Consolidated Balance Sheet*

Goodwill	1,000
Stock	3,100
Bank	1,900
	6,000
Share capital	6,000

17.2   *Consolidated Balance Sheet*

Fixed assets	65,000
Goodwill: negative goodwill	(5,000)
Stock	17,000
Debtors	9,000
Bank	4,000
	90,000
Share capital	90,000

17.3   *Consolidated Balance Sheet*

Fixed assets	161,000
Stock	68,000
Debtors	37,000
Bank	9,000
	275,000
Share capital	275,000

17.6   *Consolidated Balance Sheet*

Goodwill	13,000
Fixed assets	94,000
Stock	21,000
Debtors	25,000
Bank	5,000
	158,000
Share capital	150,000
Minority interest	8,000
	158,000

17.7   *Consolidated Balance Sheet*

Goodwill: negative goodwill		(2,000)
Fixed assets (39,000 + 9,600)		48,600
Stock		19,900
Debtors		11,900
Bank		2,400
		80,800
Share capital		80,000
Minority interest (5% of 16,000)		800
		80,800

17.10   *Consolidated Balance Sheet*

Goodwill		1,000
Negative goodwill	(2,000)	(1,000)
Fixed assets		103,000
Current assets		43,000
		145,000
Share capital		110,000
Profit and loss		30,000
Minority interest		5,000
		145,000

17.11   *Consolidated Balance Sheet*

Goodwill		10,000
Negative goodwill	(17,500)	(7,500)
Fixed assets		340,000
Current assets		110,000
		442,500
Share capital		300,000
Profit and loss		40,000
General reserve		60,000
Minority interest		42,500*
		442,500

*$(1/6 \times 120) + (3/8 \times 20) = 42,500$

18.1   *Consolidated Balance Sheet as at 31 December 2003*

Goodwill (150,000 − (120,000 + 12,000))		18,000
Fixed assets		202,000
Current assets		76,000
		296,000
Share capital		100,000
Profit and loss (176,000 + 20,000)		196,000
		296,000

18.2   *Consolidated Balance Sheet as at 31 March 2005*

Goodwill: negative goodwill		
(130,000 − (150,000 + 30,000 + 15,000) × 0.7))		(6,500)
Fixed assets		282,000
Current assets		83,000
		358,500
Share capital		100,000
Profit and loss [166,000 − (70% of 6,000 = 4,200)]		161,800
General reserve		40,000
Minority interest (45,000 + 4,500 + 7,200)		56,700
		358,500

18.4   *Consolidated Balance Sheet as at 31 December 2008*

Goodwill (60,000 − (0.8 × (50,000 + 8,000 + 4,000)))		10,400
Negative goodwill (110,000 − (0.75 × (120,000 + 30,000 + 10,000)))		(10,000)
		400
Fixed assets		271,000
Current assets		124,000
		395,400
Share capital		200,000
Profit and loss		117,750
General reserve		20,000
Minority interest		57,650
		395,400

Minority interest [0.25 × (120,000 + 55,000 + 10,000)]
+ [0.2 × (50,000 + 3,000 + 4,000)] = 46,250 + 11,400 = 57,650
Profit and loss 103,000 + (0.75 × 25,000) − (0.8 × 5,000) = 117,750.

19.1   *Consolidated Balance Sheet as at 31 March 2006*

Goodwill (55,000 − (25,000 + 20,000))		10,000
Fixed assets		335,000
Current assets		
Stock (44,000 + 23,000 − 900)	66,100	
Debtors (38,000 + 16,000 − 5,000)	49,000	
Bank	10,000	
	125,100	
Less Current liabilities		
Creditors (11,000 + 6,000 − 5,000)	12,000	
Net current assets		113,100
		458,100
Financed by:		
Share capital		175,000
Profit and loss (209,000 − 900 + 45,000)		253,100
General reserve		30,000
		458,100

19.2 Consolidated Balance Sheet as at 31 December 2007

Goodwill: negative goodwill		(44,000)
Fixed assets		426,000
Current assets		
Stock $(44{,}000 + 54{,}000 - (^3/_4 \times 3{,}600))$	95,300	
Debtors $(58{,}000 - 3{,}200 + 74{,}000)$	130,800	
Bank	20,000	
	246,100	
Less Current liabilities		
Creditors $(12{,}000 + 6{,}000 - (3{,}200))$	(14,800)	
Net current assets		231,300
		613,300

Financed by:

Share capital	350,000
Profit and loss $(114{,}000 - (^3/_4 \times 3{,}600) + (^{110}/_{180} \times 54{,}000))$	144,300
Minority interest $(^{70}/_{180} \times (180{,}000 + 126{,}000))$	119,000
	613,300

19.3 Consolidated Balance Sheet as at 31 March 2003

Goodwill		4,000
Negative goodwill		(15,000)
Fixed assets		214,000
Current assets		
Stock $(80{,}000 - (^3/_4 \times 400 + 300))$	79,400	
Debtors $(55{,}000 - (3{,}000 + 2{,}000))$	50,000	
Bank	26,000	
	155,400	
Less Current liabilities		
Creditors $(36{,}000 - (3{,}000 + 2{,}000))$	(31,000)	
Net current assets		124,400
		327,400

Financed by:

Share capital	200,000
Profit and loss account	
$(81{,}000 - 300 - 300 - 12{,}000 + (90\% \times 22{,}000))$	88,200
General reserve	28,000
Minority interest $(10\% \times (70{,}000 + 42{,}000))$	11,200
	327,400

Goodwill: $85{,}000 - 90\% \times (70{,}000 + 20{,}000) = 4{,}000$.
Negative goodwill: $75{,}000 - (60{,}000 + 25{,}000 + 5{,}000) = (15{,}000)$

19.6 Pagg Group of Companies
Consolidated Balance Sheet as at 31 March 2010

			£000
Fixed assets			
Intangible assets: Goodwill (Note 1)			1,898
Tangible assets			3,500
			5,398
Current assets			
Stocks $(1{,}300 + 350 + 100 - 10)$		1,740	
Debtors $(3{,}000 + 300 + 200 - 200 - 35)$		3,265	
Cash at bank and in hand		270	
		5,275	
Creditors falling due within 1 year			
$(270 + 400 + 4{,}000 - 200 - 35)$		4,435	
Net current assets			840
Total assets *less* current liabilities			6,238
Minority interests (Note 2)			500
			5,738

Capital and reserves	
Called-up share capital	5,500
Profit and loss	238
	5,738

Notes:

1 Cost of control

		Ragg		Tagg
Consideration		3,000		1,000
Less Shares	(80%) 800		(60%) 300	
Profit and loss	(80% × 600) 480		(60% × 100) 60	
		1,280		360
Goodwill		1,720		640
Total amount written off				
to 31.3.2010	(5 years) 430		(1 year) 32	
Amount not yet written off		1,290		608
				1,898

2 Minority interests

		Ragg		Tagg
Share capital called up		1,000		500
Profit and loss		200		150
		1,200		650
	(20%)	240	(40%)	260
				500

3 Profit and loss:

Pagg		1,000
Ragg 80% of $(200 - 600)$		(320)
Tagg 60% of $(150 - 100)$		30
Goodwill (Note 1) 430 + 32		(462)
Intercompany profit on stock $(^1/_6$ of 60$)$		(10)
		238

767

20.1
2/3 Share capital and reserves 31.3.2005

Shares bought 31.3.2003	20,000	34,000
Shares bought 31.3.2005	30,000	48,000
	50,000	
		90,000
		82,000
Negative goodwill		8,000

20.3

Shares bought		120,000
Profit and loss balance 31.12.2007	62,000	
Add Proportion 2008 profits before acquisition		
7/12 × 69,000	40,250	
	102,250	

Proportion of pre-acquisition profit:

$$\frac{120,000}{200,000} \times 102,250 = 61,350$$

Paid-for shares 300,000	61,350
	181,350

Therefore goodwill is 300,000 − 181,350 = 118,650.

21.1   Consolidated Balance Sheet as at 31 March 2005

Goodwill		3,000
Fixed assets		106,000
Current assets		39,000
		148,000
Share capital		100,000
Profit and loss account (39,000 + 9,000)		48,000
		148,000

Workings: Goodwill: Cost 68,000 − 50,000 − 7,000 − Dividend 8,000 = 3,000.

21.3   Consolidated Balance Sheet as at 31 October 2003

Goodwill (Note 1)		23,100
Fixed assets		102,000
Current assets (Note 2)		60,300
		185,400
Share capital		100,000
Profit and loss: (Note 3) (54,300 + 70% of (20,000 − 9,000))		62,000
Minority interest (30% of (60,000 + 18,000))		23,400
		185,400

Workings:
(1) Goodwill: Cost 70,000 − 70% of (60,000 + 7,000) = 23,100.
(2) The current assets in Pa and Ma Ltd were increased by 70% of £9,000 = £6,300.
(3) The profit and loss reserve of Pa and Ma Ltd was increased by the dividend received of £6,300.
(4) It is presumed that the dividend was paid out of post-acquisition reserves.

21.5   Consolidated Balance Sheet of P Ltd & S Ltd as at 31 December 2006

Fixed assets		
Intangible assets		
Goodwill (see Workings)		55,000
Tangible assets (Note 1)		680,000
Current assets		
Stocks	160,000	
Debtors	138,000	
Bank	40,000	
	338,000	
Creditors: amounts falling due within 1 year		
Trade creditors	218,000	
Net current assets		120,000
Total assets less current liabilities		655,000
Capital and reserves		
Called-up share capital: ordinary shares £1 fully paid		500,000
Reserves		185,000
Minority interest		170,000
		655,000

Note 1 Tangible fixed assets

	Cost	Depreciation to date	Net
Buildings	420,000	110,000	310,000
Plant and machinery	320,000	70,000	250,000
Motor vehicles	210,000	90,000	120,000
	950,000	270,000	680,000

Workings:
(a) Goodwill

Cost of investment		250,000
Less Ordinary shares (75%)	187,500	
Reserves (75% of 50,000)		62,500
Less Dividend from pre-acquisition profits		7,500
		55,000

(b) Minority interest

Preference shares		100,000
Reserves 25% × 80,000		20,000
Ordinary shares 25%		50,000
		170,000

The proposed preference dividend could be shown as part of the minority interest.

(c) Reserves

	£
P Ltd	170,000
S Ltd 75% of extra reserves since acquisition 80,000 − 50,000 = 30,000	22,500
	192,500
Less Dividends received by P Ltd which were from pre-acquisition profits	7,500
	185,000

Note: The loan interest of £2,000 on each balance sheet is set-off and does not appear in the consolidated balance sheet. The same applies to the loan of £50,000.

21.6 Reconciling adjustments

(a) Amended profits for 2006

	X	Y
Per balances	40	28
Profit in goods in transit	(0.4)	
Profit in inventory	2.0	(2.0)
	41.6	26

Currents accounts in books of:

	X	Y
Per balances	19	(14)
Remittance not received by X	(3)	
Goods in transit		(2)
	16	16

(b) Amendments to balances

(a) Dr Bank Y	2	
Cr Current a/c with X		2
(b) Dr Profit 2006 X	0.4	
Inventory X	2.6	
Cr Current a/c with Y		3
(c) Dr Profit 2006 X	2	
Cr Inventory Y		2

(c) Amended figures in balances

	X	Y
Profits for 2006 (40 − 0.4 − 2)	37.6	
Current account (14 + 2)		16
Inventory (80 + 2.6)	82.6	
Inventory (70 − 2)		68
Bank (12 + 2)	14	
Current account (19 − 3)		16

Consolidated Balance Sheet for X plc & subsidiary Y plc as at 31 December 2006

	Cost £000	Depreciation to date £000	Net £000
Goodwill			108
Tangible fixed assets			
Freehold property	280	18	262
Plant and machinery	245	52	193
	525	70	455
			563
Current assets			
Stock (*see* Workings)		150.6	
Debtors		250	
Bank		24	
		424.6	
Less Current liabilities			
Trade creditors (130 + 80)	210		
Taxation	44		
		254	
			170.6
			733.6
Called-up share capital			
400,000 ordinary shares £1			400
Reserves (*see* Workings)			280
			680
Minority interest (*see* Workings)			53.6
			733.6

Workings:

Cost of control (remember to calculate it as on 1.1.06) £000

	£000
Cost of investment	300
Less Nominal value shares bought 80%	
Shares	120
Reserves 80% × 90	72
	192
	108

Minority interest

20% of reserves at 1.1.06 × 90	18
20% of 2006 retained profit × 18	5.6
20% of shares × 150	30
	53.6

Stock

X	82.6
Y	68
	150.6

Bank

X 10 + Y 14	24

Note: The proposed dividend is irrelevant to the preparation of the consolidated balance sheet.

22.1 Consolidated Balance Sheet as at 31 December 2003

Goodwill (650,000 – 400,000 – 60,000)		190,000
Fixed assets	810,000	
Less Depreciation	300,000	510,000
Current assets		330,000
		1,030,000
Share capital		800,000
Profit and loss account		
(190,000 – 10,000) + (48,000 + 2,000)		230,000
		1,030,000

22.3 Consolidated Balance Sheet as at 31 March 2005

Goodwill (160,000 – 80,000 – 24,000 – 30,000)		26,000
Fixed assets	230,000	
Less Depreciation	34,000	196,000
Current assets		80,000
		302,000
Share capital		200,000
Profit and loss (85,000 + 20,000 – 3,000)		102,000
		302,000

23.1 Consolidated Balance Sheet as at 31 December 2007

Goodwill		57,940
Fixed assets		617,000
Current assets		156,000
		830,940
Share capital		500,000
Profit and loss account		260,780
General reserve		50,000
Minority interest		20,160
		830,940

Minority interest

Shares in Sub1		5,000	
Shares in Sub2 37% of 10,000		3,700	8,700
Profit and loss Sub1 10% of 115,000		11,500	
Sub2 37% of 8,000		2,960	14,460
			23,160
Less Cost of shares in Sub2 for minority interest			
of Sub1 10% of 30,000			3,000
			20,160

Goodwill: Cost of shares to group in:

Sub1	115,000	
Sub2 90% of 30,000	27,000	142,000
Less Shares: In Sub1	45,000	
In Sub2 63% of 10,000	6,300	
Profit and loss Sub1 90% of 35,000	31,500	
Sub2 63% of 2,000	1,260	84,060
		57,940

23.3 Sales Ltd & subsidiaries
Balance sheet as at 31 October 2005

	Cost	Depreciation	Net
Fixed assets			
Buildings	184,000	–	184,000
	260,000	92,400	167,600
Plant (W1)	362,900	203,700	159,200
	806,900	296,100	510,800
Current assets			
Stock (W2)		247,400	
Debtors (W3)		319,200	
Bank		65,600	
		632,200	
Less Current liabilities			
Creditors (W4)		437,400	
Bank overdraft (W5)		58,100	
Corporation tax		129,100	
		(624,600)	7,600
			518,400
Ordinary share capital			200,000
Revenue reserves (W6)			189,390
			389,390
Minority interest (W8)			129,010
			518,400

Workings:

Note: S Ltd owns 75% of M Ltd & 75% × 80% = 60% of C Ltd

(W1) Plant 102,900 + 170,000 + 92,000 =		364,900
Less (Note (e)) inter-company profit		2,000
		362,900
Depreciation 69,900 + 86,000 + 48,200 =		204,100
Less 2 years on intercompany profit		
element 10% × 2,000 × 2 =		400
		203,700
(W2) Stock 108,500 + 75,500 + 68,400		252,400
– Unrealised profit (Note (d)) 20% × 25,000		5,000
		247,400
(W3) Debtors 196,700 + 124,800 + 83,500		405,000
– Inter-indebtedness (Note (f))	56,900	
(Note (f))	28,900	85,800
		319,200

(W4) Creditors (240,000 + 200,700 + 71,200)   511,900
– Inter-indebtedness (Note (f))   28,900   74,500
                                       45,600   437,400

(W5) Overdraft   69,400
– cheque in transit (Note (g))   11,300
                                                58,100

(W6) Reserves S Ltd   154,000
                   M Ltd   85,000
                   C Ltd   74,000   313,000
Add Reduction in depreciation of components
2,000 × 10% × 2 years = 400 × 60%
ownership of components   240
                                                313,240

Less Profit on machinery   2,000
Unrealised profit on stock   5,000
Pre-acquisition reserves of C Ltd on 1.4.03
60% × 60,000   36,000
Minority interest in C Ltd
40% × 74,000   29,600
Pre-acquisition reserves of M Ltd on 1.4.03
75% × 40,000   30,000
Minority interest in M Ltd
25% × 85,000   21,250   123,850
                                             189,390

(W7) Cost of control
C Ltd at date of purchase: Capital:
Ordinary shares   100,000
Reserves   60,000   160,000
M Ltd owns 80% =   128,000
M Ltd paid   128,000
                                         –
Bringing about negative goodwill
Of this 25% is owned by minority
interest of M Ltd   –

M Ltd at date of purchase: Capital 120,000
                          Reserve   40,000   160,000
S Ltd owns 75% =   120,000
S Ltd paid   120,000
Cost of control: goodwill   120,000
Overall goodwill   120,000   Nil

(W9) Minority interest
Ordinary shares: 25% M Ltd   30,000
                 40% C Ltd   40,000
                                                 40,000
Preference shares   160
Increase in profit because of
depreciation change 40% × 400
25% revenue reserves M Ltd × 85,000   21,250
40% revenue reserves C Ltd × 74,000   29,600
                                                161,010
Less 25% payment made by M Ltd
for investment in C Ltd × 128,000   32,000
                                                129,010

24.1   Brodick plc & subsidiaries
Consolidated Profit and Loss Account for the year ending 30 April 2007

	£000	£000
Turnover (1,100 + 500 + 130)		1,730
Cost of sales (630 + 300 + 70)		1,000
Gross profit		730
Administrative expenses (105 + 150 + 20)		275
Profit on ordinary activities before taxation		455
Tax on profit on ordinary activities (65 + 10 + 20)		95
Profit on ordinary activities after taxation		360
Minority interests (20% × 40 + 40% × 20)		16
Profit for the financial year		344

Note 1
Retained profits carried to next year comprise:
Brodick plc (*see* W1)   300
Subsidiaries (*see* W1)   44
                                                    344

Workings:
(W1) Retained profits b/d
Brodick (300 – (26 + 6))   300
Lamlash (40 – (20% × 40 = 8))   32
Corrie (20 – (40% × 20 = 8))   12
                                                     44
                                                    344

Note: The dividends from the subsidiary are ignored as they represent a transfer of reserves. They will be shown in the Statement of Movements in Shareholders' Funds.

24.2   Norbreck plc & its subsidiary Bispham Ltd
Consolidated Profit and Loss Account for the year ending 30 September 2007

	£000	£000
Turnover		2,150
Cost of sales		995
Gross profit		1,155
Administrative expenses		475
Profit on ordinary activities before taxation		680
Tax on profit on ordinary activities		50
Profit on ordinary activities after taxation		630
Minority interest (20% × 180)		36
Profit for the financial year		594
Earnings per share (594/900)	66p	

Norbreck plc & its subsidiary Bispham Ltd
Consolidated Balance Sheet as at 30 September 2007

	£000	£000	£000
Fixed assets			
Goodwill			72
Tangible fixed assets			1,720
			1,792
Current assets			
Stocks	550		
Debtors (280 + 150)	430		
Cash and Bank	50		
		1,030	
Creditors: amounts falling due within one year			
Trade creditors	240		
Other creditors, taxation and social security	230		
Proposed dividends (270 + 20% × 100)		560	
Net current assets			470
Total assets less current liabilities			2,352
Provisions for liabilities and charges			
Taxation, including deferred taxation			480
			1,872
Capital and reserves			
Called-up share capital			900
Profit and loss account*			852
			1,752
Minority interest (20% × £600)			120
			1,872

*700 + [80% of (200 − 10) = 152]

Workings:

	£000	£000
Goodwill		
Investment		400
Nominal value of shares (80% of 400)	320	
Profit and loss (80% of 10)	8	
		328
Goodwill on acquisition		72
Retained profits b/d		
Norbreck (700 + 360 − 570)		490
Bispham (200 + 150 − 180)	170	
− Pre-acquisition	(10)	
	160	
− Dividend paid	(150)	
	10	
− Minority interest (20%)	(2)	
		8
Retained profits of Group b/d		498
For the year (per consolidated P/L 594 − 360)		234
		732
Plus dividend received by Norbreck from Bispham		120
		852

25.1

(*a*)   Large Ltd & its subsidiary Small Ltd
Consolidated Profit and Loss Account for the year ending 30 September 2006

	£000	£000
Turnover (10,830 + 2,000 − 108)		12,722
Cost of sales and production (3,570 + 1,100 − ($\frac{2}{3}$ of 108))		4,598
		8,124
Administrative and marketing expenses	2,772	
Unpurchased goodwill written off (per Companies Acts)	50	
Research costs written off (*see* SSAP 13)	50	
		2,872
Profit on ordinary activities before taxation		5,252
Tax on profit on ordinary activities		2,504
Profit on ordinary activities after taxation		2,748
Minority interests (520 − 36) × 114		121
		2,627

(b)

Large Ltd & its subsidiary Small Ltd
Consolidated Balance Sheet as at 30 September 2006

	£000	£000	£000
Fixed assets			
Intangible assets			
Development costs	180		
Goodwill	48		
Negative goodwill (W1)	(129)	99	
Tangible assets			
At cost less depreciation		4,648	4,747
Current assets			
Stock (594 + 231 − 27)	798		
Debtors	2,620		
Bank	123	3,541	
Creditors: amounts falling due within one year			
Trade creditors		453	
Net current assets			3,088
			7,835
Capital and reserves			
Called-up share capital			6,000
Profit and loss account [(1,344 − 100) + ((472 − 36 − 72 = 364) × 475)]			1,517
Minority interest (W2)			318
			7,835

Workings:

(W1) Investment in Small cost		525
Less Share capital	600	
75% Retained earnings of 72	54	
	654	
Negative goodwill on acquisition		129

(W2) Share capital	200
25% Retained earnings of 472	118
	318

(c) In this case merger accounting is not permitted. It can only be used when 90 per cent of the consideration is given as equity share capital, and here Large obtained 75 per cent for cash.

If merger treatment had been used the profits made before the merger could be distributed as dividends.

Note: The adjustments necessary were
(a) remove intragroup sale from group revenue
(b) remove unrealised profit in inventory from net profit on Small's profit and loss account reducing it from 520 to 484 and calculating minority interest for consolidated income statement based on that account
(c) remove unrealised profit of 36 from Small's retained earnings of 472 reducing them to 676 and using the account to calculate minority interest for balance sheet
(d) remove pure research (20) and applied research (30) and unpurchased goodwill (50) from Large's balance sheet and reduce Large's retained earnings by 100 to complete the double entry
(e) remove group share of unrealised profit of 36 from inventory in Large for consolidation, i.e. reduce it by 0.75 × 36 = 27

26.1
If Q plc is unable to exercise significant influence over N Ltd, the group comprises the parent undertaking (Q) and two subsidiaries (L and M). N Ltd should be excluded from consolidation (the grounds would be 'severe long-term restrictions') and treated as a fixed asset investment at cost. However, if Q plc is able to exercise significant influence over N Ltd, it should treat it as an associated undertaking using the equity method.

26.2
(a) There are two acquisition points. Any dividends received from the pre-acquisition (of the first investment) profits should be applied to reduce the initial investment of £80,000. Similar treatment should be applied to the £110,000 investment. The investment should be shown in the P's company balance sheet at cost of £190,000 less any such dividends received (or it could be shown at valuation). Dividends received and receivable should be shown in the profit and loss account after adjustment for any pre-acquisition element.

(b) At the time the investment became 21 per cent, the net assets of the clothing company were £840,000. The company's share of this is £176,400. The premium paid on acquisition, subject to adjustment for pre-acquisition reserves distributed, is £13,600 (£80,000 + £110,000 − £176,400) and, after any such adjustment required, it should either be written off to the reserves, or capitalised and amortised. Disclosure in the company's own financial statements is as for trade investments. The group profit and loss should show the company's share of the publishing company's pre-tax profits/losses and its attributable share of the associated undertaking's tax charge on those profits/losses. The group balance sheet carrying value in respect of this investment will comprise the cost of the investment plus the company's share of post-acquisition retained profits, less any amounts written off either of these.

27.1
Solvency, profitability, efficiency, capital structure and shareholder.

27.3
Solvency	– *see* text, Section 27.3
Profitability	– *see* text, Section 27.2
Efficiency	– *see* text, Section 27.4
Capital structure	– *see* text, Section 27.6
Shareholder	– *see* text, Section 27.5

27.5
(a) stock turnover

27.7
(i) (b) and (d).
(ii) (b) and (d).
(iii) (d).
(iv) If current liabilities greater than current assets, (b) and (d); if current assets greater than current liabilities, (a) and (c).
(v) (b) and (d) but only after a customer takes up the offer.

in controlling its debtors whereas B was less efficient in controlling its creditors' payments. Overall, these two results probably cancel each other out so far as explaining A's higher rate of return.

It appears that the key factor may be the less efficient use of its assets by B. A has less than one-fifth of the resources tied up in fixed assets than B, yet has 67 per cent of B's sales and 67 per cent of B's net profit.

27.11

(a) The ratios reveal that L Ltd's relative profitability has fallen between the two years. The gross and net profit margins have both fallen, but this may be due to the new sales manager's price-cutting policy, rather than because of any change in costs.

The fall in return on capital employed is not what was hoped for from the new sales price policy. A drop from 31 per cent to 18 per cent is significant and suggests that the change in sales price policy and the investment in new machinery, although with the related increased borrowings, have led to short-term depressed returns. If the increased market resulting from the new sales policy can be retained, it would be worthwhile considering an increase in sales price to a point where a higher rate of return would be achieved.

The company appears solvent – there is no shortage of liquid assets. However, it has taken on considerably more long-term debt in order to fund the market expansion. This will have to be serviced and the level of profit should be monitored to ensure that margins do not fall further, raising the current level of risk to unacceptable levels. As 38.2 per cent (£192,000) of net profits before interest (£502,000) is already being used to meet debt interest payments, compared with only 3.8 per cent in 2002, it would not take very large changes in costs or selling price to cause this to become a major problem. The current level of gearing will also inhibit the company's ability to raise additional loan funding in future.

Profitability	2002	2003
Gross profit : sales	$\frac{540}{900} \times \frac{100}{1} = 60\%$	$\frac{1,120}{2,800} \times \frac{100}{1} = 40\%$
Net profit : sales	$\frac{302}{900} \times \frac{100}{1} = 34\%$	$\frac{310}{2,800} \times \frac{100}{1} = 11\%$
ROCE	$\frac{302 + 12}{929 + 100} = 31\%$	$\frac{310 + 192}{1,267 + 1,600} = 18\%$
Solvency		
Current ratio	$\frac{125}{36} = 3.47 : 1$	$\frac{821}{186} = 4.41 : 1$
Acid test ratio	$\frac{125 - 30}{36} = 2.63 : 1$	$\frac{821 - 238}{186} = 3.13 : 1$
Capital structure		
Capital gearing	$\frac{100}{100 + 929} = 10\%$	$\frac{1,600}{1,600 + 1,267} = 56\%$

27.9

(a) (i) Gross profit as % of sales: $\frac{400}{1,800} \times \frac{100}{1} = 22.2\%$ $\quad$ $\frac{410}{2,700} \times \frac{100}{1} = 15.2\%$

(ii) Net profit as % of sales: $\frac{60}{1,800} \times \frac{100}{1} = 3.3\%$ $\quad$ $\frac{90}{2,700} \times \frac{100}{1} = 3.3\%$

(iii) Expenses as % of sales: $\frac{340}{1,800} \times \frac{100}{1} = 18.9\%$ $\quad$ $\frac{320}{2,700} \times \frac{100}{1} = 11.9\%$

(iv) Stockturn: $\frac{1,400}{(300 + 200) \div 2} = 5.6$ times $\quad$ $\frac{2,290}{(280 + 240) \div 2} = 8.8$ times

(v) Rate of return: $\frac{60}{(240 + 230) \div 2} \times \frac{100}{1} = 25.5\%$ $\quad$ $\frac{90}{(430 + 440) \div 2} \times \frac{100}{1} = 20.7\%$

(vi) Current ratio: $\frac{409}{245} = 1.67$ $\quad$ $\frac{382}{252} = 1.52$

(vii) Acid test ratio: $\frac{209}{245} = 0.85$ $\quad$ $\frac{142}{252} = 0.56$

(viii) Debtor : sales ratio: $\frac{205}{1,800} \times 12 = 1.37$ months $\quad$ $\frac{140}{2,700} \times 12 = 0.62$ months

(ix) Creditor : purchases ratio: $\frac{245}{1,300} \times 12 = 2.26$ months $\quad$ $\frac{252}{2,250} \times 12 = 1.34$ months

(b) Business B has made more net profit (£90,000 compared with £60,000) but, in terms of capital employed, B has only managed to achieve a return of 20.7 per cent whereas A has managed a return of 25.5 per cent. A is clearly more efficient in the use of its resources. Reasons as follows – possibly – as not until you know more about the business could you give a definite answer.

(i) B managed to sell far more merchandise but at lower prices, i.e. took only 15.2 per cent net margin as compared with A's 22.2 per cent margin.

(ii) Maybe less efficient use of mechanised means in the business by B. Note that assuming A and B both use similar depreciation rates, B has more equipment and it is considerably newer than A's.

(iii) B did not have as much stock lying idle. B turned over stock 8.8 times in the year as compared with 5.6. This could indicate inefficient purchasing by A and/or a likelihood of stock outs and, so, loss of sales.

(iv) While A waited (on average) 1.37 months to be paid by customers. B managed to collect in 0.62 months on average. Money represented by debts is money lying idle. However, A took longer (2.26 months) to pay its creditors than B (1.34 months). It appears that A was therefore less efficient

(b) Current debtor collection period (i.e. debtor days) $= \dfrac{583}{2{,}800} \times 365 = 76$ days.

If the collection period were 45 days, the new debtors amount would be:

$$\frac{45}{76} \times 583{,}000 = 345{,}200$$

The amount released if a 45-day debtors collection period could be imposed would be £237,800.

28.1

(a)

Trading and Profit and Loss Accounts for the year ending
31 December 2009

	X		Y	
Sales		480,000		762,500*
Less Cost of goods sold		400,000 (+10,000)		610,000
Gross profit		80,000		152,500
Less Admin. expenses	(−10,000) 40,000		57,500	
Selling expenses	15,000	55,000	35,000	92,500
Net profit		25,000		60,000

*Assumed 25 per cent mark-up despite wrong stock valuation.

(b) Profitability:

	X	Y
Gross profit %	20%	25%

Net profit %:

$$X:\ \frac{25}{480} \times \frac{100}{1} = 5.2\% \qquad Y:\ \frac{60}{762.5} \times \frac{100}{1} = 7.87\%$$

Stockturn:

$$\frac{400{,}000}{40{,}000} = 10\ \text{times} \qquad \frac{610{,}000}{45{,}000^{*}} = 13.6\ \text{times}$$

*Adjusted to take into account inaccurate valuation.

Return on capital employed (ROCE) (previous owners)

$$X:\ \frac{25{,}000}{200{,}000} \times \frac{100}{1} = 12.5\% \qquad Y:\ \frac{60{,}000}{350{,}000} \times \frac{100}{1} = 17.14\%$$

Based on purchase price of business the ROCE for Adrian Frampton would be:

	X	Y

$$\frac{25{,}000}{190{,}000} \times \frac{100}{1} = 13.15\% \qquad \frac{60{,}000}{400{,}000} \times \frac{100}{1} = 15\%$$

All ratios are favourable for Y. If gross profit ratios remained the same in future together with other expenses then Y business is best value.

However:

(i) Can gross profit ratios of X be improved as compared with those of Y?
(ii) Can stockturn be improved?

If so, then X could be cheapest business to buy as it gives a better ROCE.

(c) (i) Need to know current assets and current liabilities in detail.
(ii) Are these similar businesses?
  Type of business
  Areas in which situated
  Competition
  Prefer several years' accounts to gauge trends
  Quality of staff and whether they would continue.

28.2

(a) 2004

	A £000		B £000		C £000	
Return on capital of 20% = Profit*		120.0		120.0		120.0
Interest *less* tax	–		24.0		66.0	
			13.2	10.8	36.3	29.7
Profit for ordinary shares		120.0		109.2		90.3
Ordinary share capital		600		400		50
Profit return (%)		20		27.3		180.6

2005

	A £000		B £000		C £000	
Return on capital of 10% = Profit		60.0		60.0		60.0
Interest *less* tax	–		24.0		66.0	
			13.2	10.8	36.3	29.7
Profit for ordinary shares		60.0		49.2		30.3
Ordinary share capital		600		400		50
Profit return (%)		10		12.3		60.6

*Profit is assumed to be after tax but before interest.

(b) High gearing accentuates the rate of return to the ordinary shareholder. In the zero-geared position of Company A the return to the shareholder simply reflects the change in profits earned on trading. In the high-geared position of Company C the return to the shareholder decreases from 180.6 per cent to 60.6 per cent, i.e. to a reduction of 66.5 per cent as profits reduce by only 50 per cent. Company B reflects an intermediate position with a relatively moderate level of gearing.

High gearing increases risk to shareholders for two reasons. First, if the profits earned are not sufficiently high to meet interest charges then the company may find itself failing since the lenders may seek a winding-up order. Second, the risk is increased simply because of exaggerated fluctuations in the returns which are accentuated in the high-geared situation.

However, it can be seen that if profits earned are higher than the interest rate, this will produce a significantly higher return to the shareholder in a high-geared company. The fact that interest is allowed as a deduction for tax purposes indicates that gearing may give an overall advantage. The market's assessment of the risk position will counter this, and will be based on the nature of the business and management.

28.4

(a) Refer to the text.

(b)

	Company A £000	%	Company B £000	%
Ordinary shares	300		800	
Revenue: Share premium	300		400	
Retained profit	400		200	
	1,000	62.5	1,400	87.5
8% preference shares	200		–	
10% loan – debentures	400		200	
12% loan – debentures			–	
	600	37.5	200	12.5
Total share capital and loan	1,600	100.0	1,600	100.0

Company A Debt : Equity = $\dfrac{37.5}{62.5}$ = 60%

B Debt : Equity = $\dfrac{12.5}{87.5}$ = 14.3%

(c) Company A is more highly geared than B since it is committed to paying a higher proportion of fixed dividend and interest payments for its profits. A higher level of gearing increases risk. (Note the answer in 28.2 (b) is appropriate.)

(d)

	A	B
Trading profit before interest	200,000	200,000
Less Interest charges	48,000	20,000
Net profit after interest charge	152,000	180,000
Preference dividend	16,000	–
Ordinary dividend	45,000	120,000
	61,000	120,000
Retained profit	91,000	60,000

28.6

(a)

	2008	2009
Equity shares	100,000	150,000
Reserves	150,000	220,000
Total equity capital	250,000	370,000
Loans	40,000	40,000
Total capital employed	290,000	410,000
Profits (net after tax)	60,000	70,000
Return on total equity	24%	18.9%

(b) To Mr C. Black

The reduction in profits from 24 per cent to 18.9 per cent of total equity needs to be analysed into its causal factors. During the year the net profits have increased but not as fast as the equity capital which has gone up by £120,000 over the year. If the increase reflected an investment late in 2008/9 it would reduce returns because a full year's profit could not be earned.

It is therefore essential to examine the nature of the investment and the future. Before shares are bought it is essential to examine future prospects. If these are good the historic analysis may not be important. However, if the new funds were used – clearly prospects may not be good and shares should not be bought.

(c) Reserves are profits retained within the business. The profits may be from revenue, i.e. from profits which could be distributed as dividends to shareholders or capital – for example where fixed amounts are revalued upwards to reflect current market value.

The creation of reserves reflects an increase in capital in the organisation which would normally be to reflect an increasing scale of operation. In this sense reserves reflect an alternative to issuing new shares. In the case of capital reserves from revaluation – these are simply 'paper adjustments' to value which do not in themselves indicate more resources in the organisation.

Revenue reserves may in fact be distributed as dividends whereas capital reserves would not normally be available for this purpose and are more akin to share capital.

28.8

(a) *Profit and Loss Accounts for the year ending 31 March 2008*

	Chan plc £000	Ling plc £000	Wong plc £000
Operating profit	300	300	300
Interest payable	–	–	(10)
Profit on ordinary activities before tax	300	300	290
Taxation (30%)	(90)	(90)	(87)
Profit on ordinary activities after tax	210	210	203

(b) Changes in profit and loss

	Chan plc	Ling plc	Wong plc
Opening balance	?	?	?
Profit for the year	210	210	203
Dividends paid: Preference	–	(20)	(30)
Ordinary	(100)	(60)	(40)
Increase over the year	110	130	133

(c) (i) *Earnings per share*

	Chan plc	Ling plc	Wong plc
Net profit after tax and preference dividend	210	210–20	203–30
Number of ordinary shares in issue	500	300	200
	42p	63.3p	86.5p

(ii) *Price/earnings ratio*

	Chan plc	Ling plc	Wong plc
Market price of ordinary shares	840	950	1038
Earnings per share	42	63.3	86.5
	20	15	12

(iii) *Gearing ratio*

$$\frac{\text{Loan capital + preference shares}}{\text{Shareholders' funds}} \times 100$$

Chan plc = Nil

Ling plc = $\dfrac{200}{300+100+130} \times 100 = 37.7\%$

Wong plc = $\dfrac{300+100}{200+100+133} \times 100 = 92.4\%$

(d) A gearing ratio expresses the relationship that exists between total borrowings (that is, preference share capital and long-term loans), and the total amount of ordinary shareholders' funds. It should be noted that other definitions of gearing are possible and are sometimes used.

Any company with a gearing ratio of, say, 70 per cent would be considered to be high geared, while a company with a gearing ratio of, say, 20 per cent would be low geared.

Gearing is an important matter to consider when investing in ordinary shares in a particular company. A *high*-geared company means that a high proportion of the company's earnings are committed to paying either interest on any debenture stock and/or dividends on any preference share capital *before* an ordinary dividend can be declared. If a company is low geared, then a high proportion of the company's earnings can be paid out as ordinary dividends.

Chan plc has not issued any long-term loans or any preference share capital. Gearing does not, therefore, apply to this company, and all of the earnings may be paid out to the ordinary shareholders.

Ling plc is a relatively low-geared company. It has no debenture stock, and only a small proportion of its earnings are committed to paying its preference shareholders. The balance may then all be declared as an ordinary dividend.

Wong plc is an extremely high-geared company. A high proportion of borrowings (in this case consisting of both debenture stock and preference share capital) means that a high proportion of its earnings has to be set aside for both its debenture holders and its preference shareholders before any ordinary dividend can be declared. As a result, if the profits of the company are low, no ordinary dividend may be payable.

If profits are rising, a high-geared company may not be a particularly risky company in which to purchase some ordinary shares, but the reverse may apply if profits are falling.

For the year to 31 March 2008, Chan, Ling and Wong's operating profit is identical. Wong is committed to paying interest on its debenture stock (which is allowable against tax), and both Ling and Wong have to pay a preference dividend (which is *not* allowable against tax).

In deciding whether to invest in any of the three companies, there are a great many other factors to be considered, including future prospects of all three companies. However, when profits are fluctuating an ordinary shareholder is more likely to receive a higher return by investing in Chan than by investing in either Ling or Wong. Similarly, an ordinary shareholder can expect a higher return by investing in Wong.

Based on the limited amount of information given in the question, therefore, an investor considering purchasing ordinary shares in only one of these three companies would be recommended to buy shares in Chan plc.

It should be noted that if profits were *increasing*, an investor would be recommended to buy shares first in Wong, then in Ling and finally in Chan. The earnings per share in both Ling and Wong are far higher than in Chan, so there is a much greater chance of an increase in the ordinary dividend, but this is not necessarily the case if profits are falling or fluctuating.

28.10

(a) (i)

Forecast Dividends

	2006 £000	2007 £000	2008 £000
Forecast profits	1,800	500	2,200
Less Corporation tax (30%)	540	150	660
	1,260	350	1,540
Dividends to be paid in the following year	1,260	350	1,540

Balance sheet extracts

	2006 £000	2007 £000	2008 £000
Shareholders' equity			
Issued ordinary shares of £1 each fully paid	6,000	6,000	6,000
Share premium account	1,000	1,000	1,000
Retained profits (1,650 + 1,260 − 630; 2,910 − 1,260 + 350; 2,000 + 3,500 + 1,540)	2,280	2,000	3,190
	9,280	9,000	10,190

Note

	2006	2007	2008
Dividends paid	630	1,260	350

(ii)

Forecast Dividends

	2006 £000	2007 £000	2008 £000
Forecast profits	1,800	500	2,200
Less interest (12% × £2m)	240	240	240
	1,560	260	1,960
Less Corporation tax (30%)	468	78	588
	1,092	182	1,372

Balance Sheet extracts

	2006 £000	2007 £000	2008 £000
Shareholders' equity			
Issued ordinary shares of £1, each fully paid	5,000	5,000	5,000
Retained profits (1,650 + 1,092; 1,742 − 1,092 + 182; 1,832 − 182 + 1,372)	1,792	1,832	3,022
	6,792	6,832	8,022
Deferred liabilities			
12% debentures	2,000	2,000	2,000

Note

	2006	2007	2008
Dividends paid	630	1,092	182

(b) (i)

If planned expansion is financed by share issue, the forecast return on shareholders' equity for the next three years will be:

2006 1,260/9,910 × 100 = 12.7%
2007   350/9,000 × 100 =   3.9%
2008 1,540/10,190 × 100 = 15.1%

(ii)

If planned expansion is financed by debenture issue, the forecast return on shareholders' equity for the next three years will be:

2006 1,092/6,792 × 100 = 16.1%
2007 182/6,832 × 100 =   2.7%
2008 1,372/8,022 × 100 = 17.1%

Note: All the above figures are, of course, net of tax and should be grossed by a factor of 100/70 if comparison with gross interest rates is to be made (on the assumption of 30 per cent tax rate).

28.10 (cont'd)

(c) The return on shareholders' equity for the year ended 30 September 2005 was 630/6,650 = 9.5 per cent (althought the shareholders only received 600 of the 630 profit so their actual return was slightly less). To have the return fluctuate between 2.7 per cent and 17.1 per cent, as it will do if the planned expansion is financed by the debenture issue, will surely unnerve all but the most sturdy shareholders. Such a violent swing from year to year will confuse, confound and alarm anyone looking at the shares as an investment.

To finance the planned expansion by a share issue does not improve matters greatly, as it will be seen that the return fluctuates between 3.9 per cent and 15.1 per cent. But since we are told that the industry is 'subject to marked variations in consumer demand' it does seem more appropriate to use share capital (by definition risk-bearing) rather than a debenture. The poor profits forecast for 2007 suggest that it would not take much of a variation from the expected results to show no profit at all, and were this to occur, is there not a possibility that the debenture holders could not be paid their due interest? Failure to pay debenture interest on time would bring in a receiver (assuming the debentures were secured); his function would then be to collect not only the unpaid interest but the capital as well, as failure to pay interest would be a breach of the conditions under which the debenture was issued.

If shareholders are to miss a year's dividends as a result of the dividend for 2005 having been paid during the year and the 2006 dividend not being paid until 2007. Under both options, the directors can expect a stormy annual general meeting, but that is far less dangerous than the entry of a receiver.

In practice, of course, it is unusual for a company to pay out all profits as dividends, and since shareholders will pay more attention usually to the level of dividends paid than to profits earned, it would make better financial sense if the 2006 dividend were maintained at or slightly above the 2005 level, enabling an addition to be made to retained profits. This in turn would enable a fund to be built up to supplement current profits for dividends and/or to redeem the debentures.

The all-shares or all-debentures choice is also an unrealistic one. Although there is much to be said for a broad share base to support what is obviously a risky business, it could make better sense to raise part of the required £2,000,000 with the use of the (probably enlarged) depreciation charge arising after the expansion had taken place could enable a debenture redemption programme to be established over the course of the next few years.

28.12

(a) (i) Shareholders

	2006	2007
Earnings per share (EPS)	$\frac{9,520}{39,680} = 24\text{p}$	$\frac{11,660}{39,680} = 29.4\text{p}$

Dividend cover (= EPS ÷ dividend per share)

2006	2007
$\frac{24\text{p}}{(2,240 \div 39,680)}$	$\frac{29.4\text{p}}{(2,400 \div 39,680)}$
$= \frac{24\text{p}}{5.6\text{p}} = 4.3$ times	$= \frac{29.4\text{p}}{6\text{p}} = 4.9$ times

(ii) *Trade creditors*

	2006	2007
Current ratio	$\frac{92,447}{36,862} = 2.5$	$\frac{99,615}{42,475} = 2.3$
Acid test	$\frac{40,210 + 12,092}{36,862} = 1.4 : 1$	$\frac{43,370 + 5,790}{42,475} = 1.2 : 1$

(iii) *Internal management*
Debtor ratio/Sales*

	2006	2007
*Assumed credit sales	$\frac{40,210}{486,300} \times 52 = 4.3$ weeks	$\frac{43,370}{583,900} \times 52 = 3.9$

Return on capital employed

	2006	2007
(before tax)	$\frac{15,254}{40,740} = 37.4\%$	$\frac{18,686}{50,000} = 37.4\%$

(b) *Shareholders*

EPS. An increase of 5.4p per share has occurred. This was due to an increase in profit without any increase in share capital.

Dividend cover. Increased by 0.6 times because increase in profit not fully reflected in dividends.

Trade creditors

Current ratio. This has fallen but only marginally and it still appears to be quite sound.

Acid test. This has also fallen, but still seems to be quite reasonable.

Internal management

Debtor ratio. There appears to have been an increase in the efficiency of our credit control.

Return on capital employed. This has stayed the same for each of the two years. The increase in capital employed has seen a proportional increase in profits.

28.14

To the Board of G plc
From   AN Other, Accountant
Subject: *Potential acquisition of either of companies A Ltd and B Ltd as subsidiaries in the machine tool manufacturing sector. Financial performances assessed.*

As instructed by you I have investigated the financial performances of these two companies to assist in the evaluation of them as potential acquisitions.

It should be borne in mind that financial ratio analysis is only partial information. There are many other factors which will need to be borne in mind before a decision can be taken.

The calculations of the various ratios are given as an appendix.

Profitability

While the main interest to the board is what G plc could obtain in profitability from A Ltd and B Ltd, all I can comment on at present is the current profitability enjoyed by these two companies.

Here the most important ratio is that of ROCE (return on capital employed). A's ROCE is 27.2 per cent as compared with B's 15.6 per cent.

Conclusions

Depending on the price which would have to be paid for acquisition, I would suggest that A Ltd is the company most suitable for takeover.

A N Other
Accountant

Appendix

(i) *Return on capital employed*

	A Ltd	B Ltd
$\dfrac{\text{Profits before interest and tax}}{\text{Capital employed}}$	$\dfrac{211}{775} \times 100 = 27.2\%$	$\dfrac{88}{565} \times 100 = 15.6\%$

(ii) *Assets utilisation ratios*

	A Ltd	B Ltd
Total assets turnover: $\dfrac{\text{Turnover}}{\text{Total assets}}$	$\dfrac{985}{1,140} = 0.9$	$\dfrac{560}{990} = 0.6$
Fixed assets turnover: $\dfrac{\text{Turnover}}{\text{Fixed assets}}$	$\dfrac{985}{765} = 1.3$	$\dfrac{560}{410} = 1.4$
Working capital turnover: $\dfrac{\text{Turnover}}{\text{Working capital}}$	$\dfrac{985}{10} = 98.5$	$\dfrac{560}{150} = 3.6$

(iii) *Profitability ratios*

	A Ltd	B Ltd
Gross profit % Turnover: $\dfrac{\text{Gross profit}}{\text{Turnover}}$	$\dfrac{335}{985} \times 100 = 34\%$	$\dfrac{163}{560} \times 100 = 29\%$
Profit before taxation and interest as % turnover	$\dfrac{211}{985} \times 100 = 21\%$	$\dfrac{88}{560} \times 100 = 16\%$

(iv) *Liquidity ratios*

	A Ltd	B Ltd
Current ratio: $\dfrac{\text{Current assets}}{\text{Current liabilities}}$	$\dfrac{375}{365} = 1.0$	$\dfrac{580}{425} = 1.4$
Acid test or Quick ratio: $\dfrac{\text{Current assets} - \text{Stock}}{\text{Current liabilities}}$	$\dfrac{220}{365} = 0.6$	$\dfrac{440}{425} = 1.0$
Debtor ratio: $\dfrac{\text{Trade debtors} \times 52}{\text{Credit sales}}$	$\dfrac{170}{985} \times 52 = 9$ weeks	$\dfrac{395}{560} \times 52 = 36.7$ weeks

(v) *Capital structure*

	A Ltd	B Ltd
Gearing ratio: $\dfrac{\text{Long-term borrowing}}{\text{Shareholders' funds}}$	$\dfrac{220}{555} \times 100 = 39.6\%$	$\dfrac{70}{495} \times 100 = 14\%$
Proprietary ratio: $\dfrac{\text{Shareholders' funds}}{\text{Tangible assets}}$	$\dfrac{555}{1,140} = 0.5$	$\dfrac{495}{990} = 0.5$

The great difference in ROCE can be explained by reference to the secondary ratios of profit and asset utilisation. Both ratios are in A's favour. The profit ratios are A 34 per cent: B 20 per cent. The asset utilisation ratios are A 0.9 per cent: B 0.6, showing that A is utilising its assets 50 per cent better than B. It is the effect of these two ratios that give the ROCE for each company.

The very low working capital employed by A Ltd very much affects the asset utilisation ratio. How far such a low working capital is representative of that throughout the whole year is impossible to say.

Liquidity

It would not be sensible to draw a final conclusion as to the liquidity positions of the two companies based on the balance sheet figures. As a balance sheet is based at one point in time it can sometimes be misleading, as a reading of figures over a period would be more appropriate.

A Ltd does appear to have a short-term liquidity problem, as the current assets only just cover current liabilities. The 'quick' or 'acid test ratio' on the face of it appears to be very inadequate at 0.6.

By contrast, B Ltd with a current ratio of 1.4 and a 'quick ratio' of 1.0 would appear to be reasonably liquid.

However, much more light is shed on the position of the companies when the debtor collection period is examined. A collects its debts with a credit period of 9 weeks. In the case of B Ltd this rises to an astonishing 36.7 weeks. Why is this so? It could be due simply to very poor credit control by B Ltd. Such a long credit period casts considerable doubt on the real worth of the debtors. There is a high probability that many of the debts may prove difficult to collect. It might be that B Ltd, in order to maintain sales, has lowered its requirements as to the creditworthiness of its customers. If the credit period were reduced to a normal one for the industry it might be found that many of the customers might go elsewhere.

The problem with debtors in the case of B Ltd is also carried on to stock. In the case of A Ltd the stock turnover is 4.3 falling to 2.8 in B Ltd. There could be a danger that B Ltd has stock increasing simply because it is finding it difficult to sell its products.

Capital gearing

A Ltd is far more highly geared than B Ltd: 93.6 per cent as compared with 14.1 per cent. A comparison with this particular industry by means of interfirm comparison should be undertaken.

Limitations of ratio analysis

You should bear in mind the following limitations of the analysis undertaken:

(i) One year's accounts are insufficient for proper analysis to be undertaken. The analysis of trends, taken from, say, five years' accounts would give a better insight.

(ii) Differences in accounting policies between A Ltd and B Ltd will affect comparisons.

(iii) The use of historical costs brings about many distortions.

(iv) The use of industry interfirm comparisons would make the ratios more capable of being interpreted.

(v) The plans of the companies for the future expressed in their budgets would be of more interest than past figures.

779

30.1

(a) T (b) F (c) T (d) F (e) T

30.4

£40,000

30.6

At 31 December 2005, accumulated depreciation is:

$$30\% \times 30{,}000 \times \frac{160}{90} = 16{,}000$$

At 31 December 2004, accumulated depreciation is:

$$20\% \times 30{,}000 \times \frac{120}{90} = 8{,}000$$

Depreciation charge for the year ended 31 December 2005 is:

$$10\% \times 30{,}000 \times \frac{160}{90} = 5{,}333$$

Hence, depreciation provision at 31 December 2005 is:

$$8{,}000 + 5{,}333 = 13{,}333$$

Backlog depreciation is $16{,}000 - 13{,}333 = 2{,}667$

30.8

Opening stock at average prices = $50{,}000 \times \dfrac{100}{80}$	=	62,500
Purchases	=	450,000
Closing stock at average prices = $70{,}000 \times \dfrac{100}{120}$	=	58,333
Current cost of sales	=	454,167
Historic cost of sales	=	430,000
Cost of sales adjustment	=	24,167

30.10

Opening working capital	=	7,000
Closing working capital	=	10,000
Change in the year	=	3,000

At average values:

Opening working capital	= $7{,}000 \times \dfrac{240}{200}$ =	8,400
Closing working capital	= $10{,}000 \times \dfrac{240}{280}$ =	8,571
Change in the year	=	171

The monetary working capital adjustment is £3,000 − £171 = £2,829

30.12

	2003 £000	2002 £000
Loan stock	200	200
Cash	145	50
Net borrowings	55	150

$$\text{Average net borrowings} = \frac{55{,}000 + 150{,}000}{2} = 102{,}500$$

	2003 £000	2002 £000
Ordinary shares	250	250
Reserves	370	340
Current cost reserve	35	30
Shareholder interest	655	620

$$\text{Average shareholder interest} = \frac{655{,}000 + 620{,}000}{2} = 637{,}500$$

$$\text{Gearing adjustment percentage is: } \frac{102{,}500}{102{,}500 + 637{,}500} = 13.85\%$$

30.14

Many accountants believe that during a period of inflation financial reports prepared under the historical cost convention are subject to a number of severe limitations. The question lists five such limitations, and a brief explanation of each one is as follows.

1 Stocks are undervalued.

Stock values are normally based on historical costs. This means that the historical closing stock will usually have cost less than its current economic value. Hence the cost of sales will tend to be higher than it would be if the closing stock was revalued at its current cost. As a result, the gross profit will be higher, and the entity may then pay out a higher level of net profit.

If the entity pays out a high level of profit and at the same time it has to pay more for its stocks (because prices are rising), it may be left with insufficient funds for it to be able to replace its stocks with the same *quantity* of goods that it had sold during the previous period. Hence it will not be able to operate at the same level of activity as it had previously experienced.

2 Depreciation is understated.

Depreciation is usually based on the historical cost of fixed assets. Such assets will normally increase in price during a period of inflation. The annual depreciation charge, therefore, may not reflect the amount needed to be able to replace the assets at their increased cost. Consequently, the accounting profit tends to be overstated, and this may mean that too much profit is withdrawn from the business. The cash resources may then prove insufficient to replace the assets at the end of their useful life. Like the stock valuation problem, therefore, the business may not be able to operate at the same level of activity that it has previously experienced.

3 *Gains and losses on net monetary assets are undisclosed.*

Net monetary assets include both long- and short-term loans made to and by the entity, for example, debentures, and trade debtors and trade creditors. During a period of inflation, an entity gains on both long- and short-term borrowings. The gain arises because although the amount originally borrowed will eventually be repaid at its face value, its purchasing power will have been reduced; for example, £5,000 borrowed in 2001 will not purchase the same quantity of goods in 2005 as it did in 2001. In 2005 the borrower may have to pay (say) £8,000 to purchase the same quantity of goods as he might have done in 2001. Hence the entity will have, in effect, gained £3,000 by borrowing during an inflationary period, because it is effectively having to pay back less in purchasing power (or in real terms, as it is known) than it borrowed.

By contrast, if the entity has *loaned* money during a similar period (perhaps by allowing its customers to buy goods on credit), it loses money because the purchasing power of the respective debts (which are fixed in monetary terms) will purchase fewer goods when they are eventually settled than they would have done when they were first incurred.

In financial reports prepared under the historical cost system, neither the gross nor the net effect of these types of transactions is disclosed.

4 *Balance sheet values are unrealistic.*

Fixed assets are normally recorded in the balance sheet at their original cost, that is, at their historical cost. During a period of inflation, the historical cost of the assets may be far less than their *current* cost, that is, at the value the entity places on them at the time that the financial reports are prepared. Hence the financial reports give a misleading impression of the entity's net worth as at the time that they are prepared.

5 *Meaningful periodic comparisons are difficult to make.*

A meaningful comparison of financial reports prepared under the historical cost convention over several accounting periods may be misleading since such accounts will normally have been prepared using, say, pounds sterling in one period and pounds sterling in all subsequent periods.

Financial reports prepared in such a way are not, however, strictly comparable. For example, £100 in 2001 is not the same as £100 in 2005, because £100 would not purchase the same amount of goods in 2005 as it did in 2001. In fact the comparison is just as meaningless as comparing financial reports prepared, say, in dollars with, say, reports prepared in euros. It is obvious to most users of such reports that 100 dollars are not the same as 100 euros, but it is less obvious that £100 in 2001 are not the same as £100 in 2005.

In order to be able to make a meaningful comparison between financial reports prepared in different time periods, therefore, it is desirable to translate them into the same currency, that is, to use the same price base. The argument behind this point is similar in principle to that used in translating dollars into euros or euros into dollars.

31.1
See text, Section 31.6.

31.2
See text, Section 31.6. Difficulties lie in trying to give these measures a value in money that would get universal acceptance. How can you place a money value on living conditions, for example?

31.3
See text, Section 31.7.

31.4
Basically, there are many things that could be done to improve the various parts of 'social well-being'. However, (*a*) benefits cost a lot of money in the short term, and (*b*) beneficial effects are felt only in the long term. Examples are better education and better housing.

31.5
See text, Section 31.10, social programme measurement.

31.7
The accountant's model of income measurement, with its reliance upon data that can be expressed in financial terms, can be said to be too narrow and fails to consider wider social and environmental issues. The air we breathe does not have a 'price' in financial terms. Yet, what businesses do may cause costs to be incurred by others as a result of their abuse of the air in their environment. Similarly, the true cost of a natural resource may never be accounted for – the rainforests being a very well known example: they are being removed upon payment of a financially stated price, but the price only satisfies the seller, it does little to replace the environment being destroyed. Thus the price being added into the cost of manufacturing paper from the trees in the rainforests does not include the social and environmental cost of their destruction.

Thus, in the income model, it could be argued only in a narrow sense of the term that 'capital' is being maintained. In reality, the destruction of natural resources that are not or cannot be replaced means that the 'capital' is being consumed and future consumption impaired as a result.

It is for reasons of this type that it can be argued that accountants ought to be involved in disclosing the effects of a company's business activities upon its environment, for only by doing so will a true view of a company's activities be revealed.

32.1
See text, Section 32.1.

32.2
See text, Section 32.3.

32.3
See text, Section 32.4.

32.4
See text, Section 32.6

33.1
See text, Section 33.1

33.2
See text, Section 33.5

33.3
See text, Section 33.6

33.4
See text, Section 33.9

34.1
See text, Sections 34.1 and 34.2

34.2
See text, Sections 34.1 and 34.2

34.3
See text, Section 34.2

34.4
See text, Section 34.3

34.5
See text, Section 34.4

34.6
See text, Section 34.7

35.1
(i) f, b. (ii) m. (iii) a, c, e, g, j; $\frac{4}{5}$ of n.t.v. $\frac{3}{4}$ of w, x. (iv) b, d, i; $\frac{1}{5}$ of n, p, q, part of $\frac{1}{4}$ of w. (v) l, r, s, z, part of $\frac{1}{4}$ of w. (vi) o, k, v, y.

35.3

Raw materials consumed (120,000 + 400,000 − 160,000)		360,000
Haulage costs		4,000
Direct labour 70% × 220,000		154,000
Royalties		1,600
(a) **Prime cost**		519,600
Factory overhead		
Factory indirect labour	66,000	
Other factory indirect expenses	58,000	
Travelling expenses	100	
Depreciation: Factory equipment	38,000	
Firm's canteen expenses	4,000	166,100
(b) **Production cost**		685,700
Administration expenses		
Salaries	72,000	
Travelling expenses	200	
Firm's canteen expenses	2,000	
Depreciation: Acctg. and office equipment	2,000	
Cars of admin. staff	1,600	
Other administrative expenses	42,000	119,800
Selling and distribution expenses		
Salaries	8,000	
Commission	1,400	
Travelling expenses	2,900	
Depreciation: Equipment	300	
Sales staff cars	3,800	
Other selling expenses	65,000	
Carriage costs on sales	7,800	89,200
Finance costs		
Interest on loans and overdrafts		3,800
(c) **Total cost**		898,500

36.1

(a) Answers to be drafted by students in proper memo form.

Introduction:

Marginal cost is:

Direct labour	3.00
Direct materials	3.50
Variable expenses	2.25
	8.75

As selling price of £10 exceeds marginal cost £8.75 we should accept (but see below)*

Proof	Without new order	With new order
Direct labour	600,000	630,000
Direct materials	700,000	735,000
Indirect manufacturing costs		
Variable	450,000	472,500
Fixed	50,000	50,000
Administration expenses	120,000	120,000
Selling and distribution expenses	60,000	60,000
Finance expenses	20,000	20,000
	2,000,000	2,087,500
Sales	2,400,000	
Sales (2,400,000 + 100,000)		2,500,000
Profit	400,000	412,500

*Depends on how other things affected besides simple accounting calculation, such as whether there is sufficient spare manufacturing capacity to produce the extra units.

(b) For extra order:

Marginal costs per unit (see (a))	8.75
Depreciation (£3,000 p.a. ÷ 15,000)	0.20
Running costs (£6,000 p.a. ÷ 15,000)	0.40
Marginal costs per unit	9.35

As £9.35 is greater than selling price £9.25 do NOT accept.

36.3

Year 1

	(A) Columbus Ltd (Marginal)	(B) Steel Ltd (Absorption)
Sales £87 × 2,700	234,900	234,900
Less Variable costs		
Direct labour £9 × 3,600	32,400	32,400
Direct materials £15 × 3,600	54,000	54,000
Variable expenses £6 × 3,600	21,600	21,600
Total variable cost	108,000	108,000
Less in (A) Valuation closing stock		
$\frac{900}{3,600} \times £198,000$	27,000	
	81,000	
Fixed indirect manufacturing costs	90,000	90,000
	90,000	198,000
Less in (B) Valuation closing stock		
$\frac{900}{3,600} \times £198,000$		49,500
Total costs	171,000	148,500
Gross profit	63,900	86,400

Year 2

	(A)	(B)
Sales £87 × 3,600	313,200	313,200
Less Variable costs		
Direct labour £9 × 3,900	35,100	35,100
Direct materials £15 × 3,900	58,500	58,500
Variable expenses £6 × 3,900	23,400	23,400
Total variable cost	117,000	117,000
Add in (A) Opening stock b/d	27,000	
Add in (B) Opening stock b/d		49,500
	144,000	166,500
Less in (A) Valuation closing stock		
$\frac{1,200}{3,900} \times 117,000$	36,000	
	108,000	
Fixed indirect manufacturing costs	90,000	90,000
	90,000	256,500
Less in (B) Valuation of closing stock		
$\frac{1,200}{3,900} \times (£117,000 + £90,000)$		63,692
Total costs	198,000	192,808
Gross profit	115,200	120,392

36.3 *(cont'd)*

Year 3

	(A)	(B)
Sales £87 × 3,300		287,100
Less Variable costs		
Direct labour £9 × 3,750	33,750	33,750
Direct materials £15 × 3,750	56,250	56,250
Var. expenses £6 × 3,750	22,500	22,500
Total variable cost	112,500	112,500
Add in (A) Op. stock b/d	36,000	
Add in (B) Op. stock b/d		63,692
	148,500	176,192

Less in (A) Valuation of closing stock

$\dfrac{1,650}{3,750} \times 112,500$ = 49,500
  99,000

Fixed indirect manufacturing costs	90,000	90,000
		266,192

Less in (B) Valuation of closing stock

$\dfrac{1,650}{3,750} \times (£112,500 + £90,000)$ = 89,100

	(A)	(B)
Total costs	189,000	177,092
Gross profit	98,100	110,008

36.5

(a) Subject to points raised in (c) the extra production should be taken on, as this results in greater profits amounting to £1,562,000. Proof is as follows:

Extra revenue 60,000 × £150		9,000,000
Less Extra costs		
Direct materials (W1)	3,141,600	
Direct labour 60,000 × 18.70 × 120% =	1,346,400	
Variable overhead 60,000 × 7.50	450,000	
Fixed costs	2,500,000	
		7,438,000
		1,562,000
Extra profit		4,488,000

(W1) 60,000 × 74.80		448,800
Less saving 10% on extra materials		
saving 10% on materials		
used on day shift		
10% × 120,000 × 74.80		897,600
		3,141,600

(b) Break-even point to justify night shift

Sale price per unit		150.00
Less Costs per unit		
Material	74.80	
Direct labour 18.70 + 20%	22.44	
Variable overhead	7.50	
		104.74
Contribution per unit		45.26

Total fixed costs $\dfrac{2,500,000}{45.26}$ = Break-even at 55,236 units

Note: No 10% reduction on materials because demand less than extra 60,000 units.

(c) (i) Would firm be able to maintain selling price of £187 on first 120,000 units per year?

(ii) Would it have been more profitable to subcontract extra units needed?

(iii) Could we diversify into a more profitable alternative product?

(iv) Could extra day facilities have been more profitable?

36.7

(a)

Arncliffe Ltd

Revenue Statement for the year ending . . .

	Crowns	Kings	Total
	60,000	25,000	85,000
Sales			
Direct costs:			
Raw mats	8,000	2,000	10,000
Labour	20,000	10,000	30,000
M/c running costs	12,000	3,000	15,000
	40,000	15,000	55,000
Contribution	20,000	10,000	30,000
Rate of contribution to sales	33.3%	40%	35.3%

(b) Best product mix for next year:

Crowns manufactured per hour = 20,000/8,000 = 2.5 per hour
Kings manufactured per hour = 10,000/2,000 = 5 per hour
Kings gives best contribution rate, so produce Kings up to maximum requirements.

	Crowns		Kings	
	Units	Hours	Units	Hours
Minimum required	6,000 ÷ 2.5	2,400	6,000 ÷ 5	1,200
Produce up to maximum of 36,000 Kings			30,000 ÷ 5	6,000
		2,400		7,200
Still (10,000 − 7,200 − 2,400) = 400 hours left, so now produce Crown	1,000 ÷ 2.5	400		
		2,800		7,200

Best mix is therefore: Crowns (6,000 + 1,000) = 7,000
Kings (6,000 + 30,000) = 36,000

Sales revenue therefore: 7,000 × £3 = 21,000 : 36,000 × £2.5 = 90,000

		Units	Hours
Contributions:	Crowns (33.3%)	7,000	
	Kings (40%)	36,000	43,000
		15,000	
		600	
Floor space costs			15,600
Insurance			27,400
Profit			

(c) Product mix with extra machine

As maximum requirements for Kings have already been met in (b), all new output will be of Crowns.

	Crowns	Kings
Sales (as before) in £	21,000	90,000
Extra (10,000 hours × 2.5) = 25,000 × £3 =	75,000	
	96,000	90,000
Contributions: Crowns (33.3%)	32,000	68,000
Kings (40%)	36,000	
	20,000	
Hire of extra machine	15,000	
Floor space costs	600	
Insurance	35,600	32,400

(d) Briefly:

(i) Market demand maintained.
(ii) Flexibility of return of extra machine if demand falls.
(iii) To see if wholesaler will guarantee minimum orders.
(iv) Are there outlets possible other than wholesaler?
(v) Selling price to wholesaler?

36.9

(a)

Paul Wagtail
Manufacturing, Trading and Profit and Loss Account
for the year ending 30 April 2009

	Marginal method		Absorption method	
Purchases of raw mats (125,000 − 2,100)		122,900		122,900
Carriage of raw materials		1,500		1,500
		124,400		124,400
Less Stock raw materials		8,900		8,900
Cost of raw materials consumed		115,500		115,500
Production wages		105,270		105,270
Prime cost		220,770		220,770
Factory overhead expenses:				
Factory power	12,430		12,430	
Factory supervisors' wages	29,600		29,600	
Factory repairs	19,360		19,360	
Factory insurance (40%)	1,920		1,920	
Factory heating & light (40%)	1,440		1,440	
Depreciation of plant	17,600	82,350	17,600	82,350
		303,120		303,120
Less Work-in-progress (W1)		11,038		15,156
Production cost of goods completed c/d		292,082		287,964
Sales		464,360		464,360
Production cost b/d	292,082		287,964	
Less Stock finished goods (W2)	18,447	273,635	18,187	269,777
Gross profit		190,725		194,583
Less Expenses:				
Administration expenses	46,700		46,700	
Distribution expenses	25,400		25,400	
Selling expenses	23,800		23,800	
Insurance (60%)	2,880		2,880	
Heating and lighting (60%)	2,160		2,160	
Depn: delivery vehicles	35,200	136,140	35,200	136,140
Net profit		54,585		58,443

Workings:
(W1) 625 × 80% = 500 equivalent making total 9,500 + 500 = 10,000

Valuations: Marginal $\dfrac{500}{10,000} \times 220,770 = 11,038$

Absorption $\dfrac{500}{10,000} \times 303,120 = 15,156$

(W2) Marginal $\dfrac{600}{9,500} \times 292,082 = 18,447$

Absorption $\dfrac{600}{9,500} \times 287,964 = 18,187$

(b) See text.

36.13

(a)

	K	L	M	N
Direct labour and materials	28	56	120	64
Variable overheads	8	16	26	24
Fixed overhead	4	8	14	12
Total cost per unit	40	80	160	100
Add Profit 10 per cent	8	16	32	20
Selling price	48	96	192	120

(b) Discontinue M. The others are above marginal cost whereas M is below it.

(c)

	(i) Followed our advice	(ii) Produced all items
Sales K 100 × £66	6,600	6,600
L 100 × £78	7,800	7,800
M 100 × £140	–	14,000
N 100 × £98	9,800	9,800
	24,200	38,200

Less Costs

Direct labour and materials

(i) (28 + 56 + 64) × 100 — 14,800

(ii) (28 + 56 + 120 + 64) × 100 — 26,800

Variable overhead

(i) (8 + 16 + 24) × 100 — 4,800

(ii) (8 + 16 + 26 + 24) × 100 — 7,400

Fixed overhead	3,800	3,800
	23,400	38,000
Net profit	800	200

Note: The net profit or loss could have been worked out using contributions per items e.g. (i) Contributions per unit (i.e. Selling price *less* Marginal cost).

K 66 − (28 + 8) = 30
L 78 − (56 + 16) = 6
N 98 − (64 + 24) = 10
46 × 100 of each = 4,600
Less Fixed costs 3,800
Net profit 800

In (ii) the contribution from M would be negative.

(d) Discontinue K and N. All other items are above marginal cost.

(e)

	(i) Followed our advice	(ii) Produced all items
Sales K 100 × £34	–	3,400
L 100 × £96	9,600	9,600
M 100 × £280	28,000	28,000
N 100 × £78	–	7,800
	37,600	48,800

Less Costs

Direct labour and materials

(i) (56 + 120) × 100 — 17,600

(ii) (28 + 56 + 120 + 64) × 100 — 26,800

Variable costs

(i) (16 + 26) × 100 — 4,200

(ii) (8 + 16 + 26 + 24) × 100 — 7,400

Fixed overhead	3,800	3,800
	25,600	38,000
Net profit	12,000	10,800

37.1

	Production departments				Service departments		
	A	B	C	D	K	L	M
Indirect lab.	8,000	12,000	16,000	4,000	3,000	6,000	8,200
Other exp.	5,400	6,200	7,200	3,000	9,000	4,000	4,000
	13,400	18,200	23,200	7,000	12,000	10,000	12,200
Apportionment of costs:							
Dept K	2,400	3,000	3,600	1,800	(12,000)	–	1,200
Dept L	3,500	–	4,500	2,000	–	(10,000)	–
Dept M	–	5,360	3,350	4,690	–	–	(13,400)
	19,300	26,560	34,650	15,490	–	–	(13,400)

(a) Overhead rates per direct labour hour

Department A $\dfrac{19,300}{4,000} = £4.825$

Department C $\dfrac{34,650}{8,900} = £3.89$

(b) Overhead rates per machine hour

Department B $\dfrac{26,560}{5,200} = £5.11$

Department D $\dfrac{15,490}{4,800} = £3.23$

37.2

Job Cost Sheet Job 351 Dept. A

Direct materials		760.00
Direct labour	112 × £5	560.00
Factory overhead	112 × £4.825	540.40
		1,860.40

Job Cost Sheet Job 352 Dept. B

Direct materials		3,597.00
Direct labour	256 × £4	1,024.00
Factory overhead	252 × £5.11	1,287.72
		5,908.72

Job Cost Sheet Job 353 Dept. C

Direct materials		2,000.00
Direct labour	390 × £6	2,340.00
Factory overhead	390 × £3.89	1,517.10
		5,857.10

Job Cost Sheet Job 354 Dept. D

Direct materials		1,998.00
Direct labour	180 × £6	1,080.00
Direct overhead	128 × £3.23	413.44
		3,491.44

Job Cost Sheet Job 355 Depts. C and B

Dept C	Direct materials		1,680.00
	Direct labour	320 × £6	1,920.00
	Factory overhead	320 × £3.89	1,244.80
Dept B	Direct materials		204.00
	Direct labour	60 × £4	240.00
	Factory overhead	40 × £5.11	204.40
			5,493.20

37.5

(a) See text, Section 37.5.

(b)

(i)

	Materials	Labour	Overhead
Finished items	4,000	4,000	4,000
W-I-P (600)	540 (90%)	450 (75%)	330 (55%)
Total units	4,540	4,450	4,330

(ii) Cost per complete unit

Material	£8,172 ÷ 4,540 =	1.80
Labour	£7,120 ÷ 4,450 =	1.60
Overhead	£5,196 ÷ 4,330 =	1.20
		£4.60

(iii) Value of work-in-progress

Material	540 × 1.80 =	972
Labour	450 × 1.60 =	720
Overhead	330 × 1.20 =	396
		£2,088

37.2

(a) Allotment: where overheads traced directly to units.

Apportionment: where overheads not directly traceable and have to be apportioned between units.

Absorption rates: the total amount of overheads calculated as being charged to each unit.

(b) Because the figures belong to the future and therefore cannot be known precisely.

(c) (i) and (ii). Note that parts (i) and (ii) illustrate two different methods in use. The method in (iii) is not in the text.

Continuous apportionment (repeated distribution) method:

Line		Production departments			Service departments	
		A	B	C	X	Y
1	Allocation per analysis	14,000	12,000	8,000	4,000	3,000
2	Allocation of X (4,000)	(35%) 1,400	(30%) 1,200	(20%) 800	(4,000)	(15%) 600
3	Allocation of Y (3,600)	(30%) 1,080	(40%) 1,440	(25%) 900	(5%) 180	(3,600)
4	Allocation of X (180)	(35%) 63	(30%) 54	(20%) 36	(180)	(15%) 27
5	Allocation of Y (27)	(30%) 8	(40%) 12*	(25%) 7	(5%) 0	(27)
		16,551	14,706	9,743		(= total 41,000)

*Rounded off

Explanation:

Steps:

(1) Allocate X overheads to others by % shown.

(2) Allocate Y overheads to others by % shown.

Keep repeating (1) and (2) until the figures left under X and Y are insignificant.

(iii) Elimination method:

Line		Production departments			Service departments	
		A	B	C	X	Y
1	Allocation per analysis	14,000	12,000	8,000	4,000	3,000
2	Allocate service dept X (35%)	1,400	(30%) 1,200	(20%) 800	(4,000)	(15%) 600
3	Allocate service dept Y (30/95)	1,137	(40/95) 1,516	(25/95) 947		(3,600)
		16,537	14,716	9,747		(total 41,000)

Explanation:

Steps:

(1) Allocate service department overheads which does largest proportion of work for other departments, i.e. department X.

(2) Allocate next service department per (1), in this case is only Y.

(3) When doing (2) nothing is charged to service departments already allocated, i.e. in this case X.

37.7 (cont'd)

(4) Note that since (3) happens the ratios in the next allocation change. As X 5% of Y is not returned then A gets 30/95 of Y, not 30% and so on.

(iv) The answer will depend on whichever approach is adopted. No one can categorically state which method is the most accurate; there is no 'ideal' method.

37.9

(a) and (b) See text.

(c) (i)   Batch No. 23

Raw materials 300 × 1.60	480
Direct labour 4.20 × 20 hours	84
Setting up of machine	21
Overheads 3.60 × 20 hours	72
Total cost	657

Cost per unit 657 ÷ 300 = £2.19

(ii)   Batch No. 23

Raw materials 300 × 1.60	480.00	
Less Received for scrap 20 × 0.86	17.20	
		462.80
Direct labour:		
Normal 20 × 4.20	84.00	
Rectification 9 × 4.20	37.80	
		121.80
Setting up:		
Normal	21.00	
Rectification	18.00	
		39.00
Overheads: Running time 3.60 × 20	72.00	
Rectification 3.60 × 9	32.40	
		104.40
		728.00

Per usable unit £728 ÷ 280 = 2.60

(iii)

Loss because of extra costs 728 − 657 =	71.00
Loss because of faulty products 657 × 20/300 =	43.80
	114.80

38.1

	July	Aug	Sept	Oct	Nov	Dec
Opening stock	148	138	156	220	280	232
Add Production	150	202	282	324	248	160
	298	340	438	544	528	392
Less Sales	160	184	218	264	296	204
Closing stock	138	156	220	280	232	188

38.2

(a)

Opening stock	144		
Add Production	?	(B)	
Less Sales total – see question			
Closing stock		(C)	
	4,650		
	150		

Missing figure (B) must be 4,800
Missing figure (C) must then be 4,656
Equal production per month 4,656 ÷ 12 = 388 units.

(b) Given figures per (a)

	J	F	M	A	M	J	J	A	S	O	N	D
Opening stock	144	202	50	128	66	94	182	360	458	336	394	332
Add Production	388	388	388	388	388	388	388	388	388	388	388	388
	532	590	438	516	454	482	570	748	846	724	782	720
Less Sales	330	540	310	450	360	300	210	290	510	330	450	570
Closing stock	202	50	128	66	94	182	360	458	336	394	332	150

Lowest closing figure is 50 units in February. It is also below 80 in April. If stock is not to fall below 80 units an extra 80 − 50 = 30 units will have to be produced in February making production for that month of 418 units; and an extra 14 will need to be produced in April making production for that month 402 units.

39.1

(a)   Took: Cash Budget

	May	Jun	Jul	Aug	Sept	Oct
Balance b/d	200	10,800	8,800	2,800		
Overdraft b/d					13,200	19,200
Receipts from debtors	800	8,000	16,000	24,000	18,000	10,000
Capital	10,000					
	11,000	18,800	24,800	26,800	4,800	(9,200)
Payments	200	10,000	22,000	40,000	24,000	14,000
Balance c/d	10,800	8,800	2,800			
Overdraft c/d				13,200	19,200	(23,200)

(b) There are the possibilities of delaying payments to creditors, delaying purchases or somehow getting debtors to pay up more quickly. Apart from these it is possible that a credit factoring firm could help in 'buying' the amounts of debtors from Ukridge.

If none of these is possible only a really fantastic product could warrant interest at 70 per cent per annum. This would rarely be the case, although there are many people whose optimism about their products exceeds their true potential profitability.

39.2

F. Jack: Cash Budget

	Jul	Aug	Sept	Oct	Nov	Dec
Balance b/d	3,600	12,309		11,343	16,731	42,822
Overdraft b/d			(1,410)			
Receipts	57,600	52,200	72,000	54,000	70,500*	72,000
	61,200	64,509	70,590	65,343	87,231	114,822
Payments (see schedule)	48,891	65,919	59,247	48,612	44,409	37,965
Balance c/d	12,309		11,343	16,731	42,822	76,857
Overdraft c/d		(1,410)				

*Includes £7,500 legacy

Payments schedule

July

Raw materials 1,050 (Jul) × £13.5	14,175
960 (Jun) × £1.5	1,440
Direct labour 1,050 × £24	25,200
Variable 960 × £3.6 + 1,050 × £2.40	5,976
Fixed expenses	1,200
Drawings	900
	48,891

Aug

1,110 (Aug) × £13.5	14,985
1,050 (July) × £1.5	15,750
1,110 × £24	26,640
1,050 × £3.6 + 1,110 × £2.40	6,444
Fixed expenses	1,200
Drawings	900
	65,919

Sept

Raw materials 1,140 (Sept) × £13.5	15,390
1,110 (Aug) × £1.5	1,665
Direct labour 1,140 × £24	27,360
Variable 1,110 × £3.6 + 1,140 × £2.4	6,732
Fixed expenses	1,200
Drawings	900
Machinery	6,000
	59,247

Oct

1,020 (Oct) × £13.5	13,770
1,140 (Sep) × £1.5	1,710
1,020 × £24	24,480
1,140 × £3.6 + 1,020 × £2.4	6,552
Fixed expenses	1,200
Drawings	900
	48,612

Nov

Raw materials 930 (Nov) × £13.5	12,555
1,020 (Oct) × £1.5	1,530
Direct labour 930 × £24	22,320
Variable 1,020 × £3.6 + 930 × £2.4	5,904
Fixed expenses	1,200
Drawings	900
	44,409

Dec

780 (Dec) × £13.5	10,530
930 (Nov) × £1.5	1,395
780 × £24	18,720
930 × £3.6 + 780 × £2.4	5,220
Fixed expenses	1,200
Drawings	900
	37,965

39.3

(a) Cash Budget

Receipts	July	Aug	Sept
Cash sales (W1)	9,600	4,800	7,200
Credit sales (W2)	17,640	14,112	7,056
	27,240	18,912	14,256
Payments			
Purchases	3,600	5,400	8,100
Direct labour	1,600	2,400	3,600
Direct production expenses	4,800	2,400	3,600
Variable selling expenses	4,000	3,200	1,600
Fixed expenses	1,820	1,820	1,820
	15,820	15,220	18,720
Balance start of month	3,900	15,320	19,012
Balance at end of month	15,320	19,012	14,548

(W1) July   800 × 40% × £30 = 9,600
     August   400 × 40% × £30 = 4,800
     September   600 × 40% × £30 = 7,200

(W2) July   1,000 × 60% × £30 = 18,000 − 2% = 17,640
     August   800 × 60% × £30 = 14,400 − 2% = 14,112
     September   400 × 60% × £30 = 7,200 − 2% = 7,056

(b) (i) Can forecast when and if money needs to be borrowed.
(ii) Can forecast when surplus funds are available so that they can be invested elsewhere.
(iii) To use as basis when dealing with supplier as to creditworthiness or bank for borrowing powers.

39.5

Receipts	July	Aug	Sept	Oct
Sales this month 20%		9,000	9,000	9,000
Sales last month 70%		32,000	31,500	31,500
Sales 2 months ago 10%			4,000	4,500
Other receipts from debtors	40,000			
	40,000	41,000	44,500	45,000
Payments				
Wages	2,000	2,000	2,000	2,000
Bank loan and interest	242	242	242	242
Drawings	500	500	500	500
Purchases	34,000	38,250	38,250	45,750
PAYE tax	500	500	500	500
Rent	1,250			1,250
Rates				2,250
Value added tax	5,000	8,150		3,950
	43,492	49,642	41,492	56,442
Current account balances				
Start of month	5,000	1,508	(7,134)	(4,126)
End of month	1,508	(7,134)	(4,126)	(15,568)

Appendix 2

39.6

(a) In brief:

Current ratio of 210,000 : 150,000 = 1.4 : 1

Acid test ratio not known. Very dangerous situation because if bank manager asks for repayment of overdraft it is unlikely it can be repaid in the short term.

Profits get ploughed back into the company in all sorts of ways, e.g. extra fixed assets, more stock. It has no direct connection with the balance at the bank. (Use cash flow statements as an illustration.)

(b) Cash Budget

	Apr	May	June	July
Receipts				
Cash sales	40,000	40,000	40,000	40,000
Credit sales	65,000	70,000	70,000	70,000
	105,000	110,000	110,000	110,000
Payments				
Purchases	60,000	58,000	61,000	55,000
Selling and administration	5,700	6,600	6,600	6,600
Administration charges	10,000	10,000	10,000	13,500
Final dividend 2009/10		7,500		
Interim dividend 2010/11				4,000
	75,700	82,100	77,600	79,100
Balance overdraft start of month	(150,000)	(120,700)	(92,800)	(60,400)
Balance overdraft end of month	(120,700)	(92,800)	(60,400)	(29,500)

(c) Would seem to be proceeding satisfactorily to eliminate overdraft.
Could be further reduced by:
(i) Issuing new shares
(ii) Getting debtors to pay more quickly
(iii) Delaying payment of creditors
(iv) Selling off fixed assets
(v) Issuing debentures.

40.1

(a) Stock Budget 2007

		Aug	Sept	Oct	Nov
Opening stock	(A)	5,000*	7,000	8,000	7,000
Add Purchases	(B)	20,000	23,500	21,500	31,000
	(C)	25,000	30,500	29,500	38,000
Less Cost of sales	(D)	18,000	22,500	22,500	27,000
Closing stock	(E)	7,000	8,000	7,000	11,000

* After special sale of £8,000 goods at cost.

To work out missing figures:

August (A) is known. (D) is 24,000 – 25%

(D) 18,000

Therefore, as stockturnover is 3,

$$\frac{\text{(D) } 18{,}000}{[\text{(A) } 5{,}000 + \text{(E) question}] \div 2} = 3$$

Therefore bottom line is 6,000 so (E) must be 7,000.
Repeat following months.

(b) Cash Budget 2007

	Aug	Sept	Oct	Nov
Receipts:				
Capital	10,000			
Soul's debtors	20,250			
Debtors		–	24,000	30,000
Special sale	8,000			
	38,250	–	24,000	30,000
Payments:				
Creditors	10,000	20,000	23,500	21,500
General expenses	700	700	700	700
	10,700	20,700	24,200	22,200
Bank: Opening	(20,000)	7,550	(13,150)	(13,350)
Closing	7,550	(13,150)	(13,350)	(5,550)

40.3

(a) Cash Budget

	July	Aug	Sept	Oct	Nov	Dec
Opening balance	30,000					18,000
Opening overdraft		(36,460)	(27,770)	(17,680)	(2,810)	
Received (see schedule)	7,200	10,800	16,400	21,600	28,800	34,400
	37,200	(25,660)	(11,370)	3,920	25,990	52,400
Payments (see schedule)	73,660	2,110	6,310	6,730	7,990	9,460
Closing balance					18,000	42,940
Closing overdraft	(36,460)	(27,770)	(17,680)	(2,810)		

Cash Receipts Schedule

	July	Aug	Sept	Oct	Nov	Dec
Cash sales	7,200	10,800	14,400	18,000	23,400	25,200
Credit sales		–	–	3,600	5,400	7,200
Rent received			2,000			2,000
	7,200	10,800	16,400	21,600	28,800	34,400

Cash Payments Schedule

	July	Aug	Sept	Oct	Nov	Dec
Drawings	1,400	1,400	1,400	1,400	1,400	1,400
Premises	60,000					
Shop fixtures	4,000					
Motor van	8,000					
Salaries of assistants	260	260	260	260	260	260
Payments to creditors			4,200	4,620	5,880	7,350
Other expenses		450	450	450	450	450
	73,660	2,110	6,310	6,730	7,990	9,460

(b)

F Tain
*Forecast Trading and Profit and Loss Account for the six months ending
31 December 2002*

Sales		148,500
Less Cost of goods sold:		
Purchases	39,570	
Less Closing stock (390 × £8)	3,120	36,450
Gross profit		112,050
Add Rent received		4,000
		116,050
Less Expenses:		
Assistants' salaries	1,560	
Other expenses	2,700	
Depreciation: Premises	1,500	
Shop fixtures	300	
Motor van	1,000	7,060
Net profit		108,990

Forecast Balance Sheet as at 31 December 2002

	Cost	Depn	NBV
Fixed assets			
Premises	60,000	1,500	58,500
Shop fixtures	4,000	300	3,700
Motor van	8,000	1,000	7,000
	72,000	2,800	69,200

Current assets			
Stock		3,120	
Debtors		33,300	
Bank		42,940	
		79,360	
Less Current liabilities			
Creditors	17,520		
Other expenses owing	450	17,970	
Working capital			61,390
			130,590

Financed by:		
Capital		30,000
Cash introduced		
Add Net profit		108,990
		138,990
Less Drawings		8,400
		130,590

40.6

(a)

Issa Ltd
*Budgeted Trading and Profit and Loss Account for the year ended
31 December 2011*

			£000
Sales			900.0
Less Cost of goods sold			
Opening stock		80.0	
Purchases (difference)		570.0	
		650.0	
Less Closing stock		65.0	585.0
Gross profit			315.0
Less Expenses			
Administration expenses		63.6	
Selling and distribution expenses (54 + 15)		69.0	
Financial charges		20.8	
Provision for doubtful debts		2.5	
Depreciation		60.0	215.9
Net profit			99.1
Gain on sale of land and buildings			150.0
Profit for the year			249.1

Note: Bonus share issue		50.0
Preference share dividends		9.0
Ordinary dividend		7.5
Total appropriation of retained earnings		66.5

(b)

Budgeted Balance Sheet as at 31 December 2011

	£000	£000	£000
Fixed assets at cost (750 – 50)		700.0	
Less Depreciation to date		204.0	496.0
Investment in Yates Ltd at cost			100.0
Current assets			
Stock		65.0	
Trade debtors	100.0		
Less Provision	7.5	92.5	
Bank		350.1	
		507.6	
Less Current liabilities			
Trade creditors	56.0		
Expense creditors	15.0	71.0	436.6
			1,032.6

		£000
Financed by:		
Ordinary share capital (200 + 100)		300.0
Share premium (150 – 50)		100.0
9% Preference shares		100.0
Retained earnings (350.0 + 249.1 – 66.5)		532.6
		1,032.6

40.6 (cont'd)

(c)

Advantages:

(i) Business can establish desired profit in advance. It can then take necessary action to try to achieve it.

Desired ROCE can be set as target.

Also helps in forecasting dividends/planning for taxation purposes/organising necessary finance/for use with financial backers.

(ii) Manage working capital to ensure its sufficiency when needed.

Ensure cash balances to seek overdrafts/loans from bank when needed.

Ensure creditors are paid on time to gain discounts. Invest surpluses as and when they may occur.

40.7 Cash Payments Schedule

	Jul	Aug	Sept	Oct	Nov	Dec
Direct materials	300	240	1,100	1,000	800	700
Direct labour	2,700	2,700	2,700	2,700	2,700	2,700
Variable indirect manufacturing expenses	1,050	1,800	1,800	1,800	1,800	1,800
Fixed indirect manufacturing expenses	450	450	450	450	450	450
Machine	2,500					
Motor vehicle			10,000			
	7,000	5,190	16,050	5,950	5,750	5,650

Cash Receipts Schedule

	Jul	Aug	Sept	Oct	Nov	Dec
Debenture					25,000	
Receipts from debtors	9,500	6,000	8,000	10,000	10,500	9,450
	9,500	6,000	8,000	10,000	35,500	9,450

(a) Cash Budget (£)

	Jul	Aug	Sept	Oct	Nov	Dec
Opening balance	35,500	38,000	38,810	30,760	34,810	64,560
Add Receipts	9,500	6,000	8,000	10,000	35,500	9,450
	45,000	44,000	46,810	40,760	70,310	74,010
Less Payments	7,000	5,190	16,050	5,950	5,750	5,650
Closing balance	38,000	38,810	30,760	34,810	64,560	68,360

(b) Debtors Budget (£)

	Jul	Aug	Sept	Oct	Nov	Dec
Opening balance	9,500	6,000	8,000	10,000	10,500	9,450
Add Sales	6,000	8,000	10,000	10,500	9,450	7,350
	15,500	14,000	18,000	20,500	19,950	16,800
Less Receipts	9,500	6,000	8,000	10,000	10,500	9,450
Closing balance	6,000	8,000	10,000	10,500	9,450	7,350

(c) Creditors Budget (£)

	Jul	Aug	Sept	Oct	Nov	Dec
Opening balance	540	1,340	2,100	1,800	1,500	1,400
Add Purchases	1,100	1,000	800	700	700	900
	1,640	2,340	2,900	2,500	2,200	2,300
Less Payments	300	240	1,100	1,000	800	700
Closing balance	1,340	2,100	1,800	1,500	1,400	1,600

(d) Raw Materials Budget (£)

	Jul	Aug	Sept	Oct	Nov	Dec
Opening stock	1,500	1,700	1,800	1,700	1,500	1,300
Add Purchases	1,100	1,000	800	700	700	900
	2,600	2,700	2,600	2,400	2,200	2,200
Less Used in production	900	900	900	900	900	900
Closing stock	1,700	1,800	1,700	1,500	1,300	1,300

(e) Forecast Operating Statement for the six months ending 31 December 2008

Pies and Cakes Ltd

Sales		51,300
Less Cost of goods sold		
Opening stock finished goods	6,840	
Add Cost of goods completed (£12 × 2,700)	32,400	
	39,240	
Less Closing stock finished goods (£12 × 770)	9,240	
		30,000
Gross profit		21,300
Less Expenses		
Fixed indirect manufacturing expenses	2,700	
Depreciation: Buildings	15,000	
Plant and machinery	5,000	
Motor vehicles	4,000	
Office fixtures	220	
		24,200
		26,920
Net loss		(5,620)

(f) Forecast Balance Sheet as at 31 December 2008

	Cost	Acc Depn	NBV
Fixed Assets			
Tangible Assets			
Buildings	300,000	135,000	165,000
Plant and machinery	52,500	35,000	17,500
Motor vehicles	40,000	18,000	22,000
Office fixtures	2,500	1,320	1,180
	395,000	189,320	205,680

Current Assets			
Stock: Finished goods		9,240	
Raw materials		1,300	
Debtors		7,350	
Cash and bank		68,360	
		86,250	
Creditors: amounts falling due within one year			
Creditors for raw materials	1,600		
Creditor for variable indirect manufacturing overheads	1,800		
		3,400	
Total assets less current liabilities		82,850	
		288,530	
Creditors: amounts falling due after more than 1 year			
Debentures		25,000	
		263,530	
Capital and reserves			
Called-up share capital		225,000	
Profit and loss (44,150 − 5,620)		38,530	
		263,530	

40.8

A (a) Debtor budget

	July	Aug	Sept	Oct
Balances from last month	52,250	52,250	49,500	51,750
Add Credit sales	24,750	24,750	27,000	33,000
	77,000	77,000	76,500	84,750
Less Paid by debtors	24,750	27,500	24,750	24,750
Balances at end of month	52,250	49,500	51,750	60,000

Note: sales are July 900, Aug 900, Sept 900, Oct 1,100. October is taken to be June figure + 10%.

(b) Raw material budget (in kg)

	July	Aug	Sept	Oct
Stock from last month	1,800	1,800	1,800	2,200
Add purchases	1,800	1,800	2,200	2,200
	3,600	3,600	4,000	4,400
Less Used	1,800	1,800	1,800	2,200
Stock at end of month	1,800	1,800	2,200	2,200

B See text, Section 40.8

$$EOQ = \sqrt{\frac{2 \times 12,000 \times £10}{£6}} = 20 \text{ units}$$

(i) Based on estimates which obviously can vary a lot from actual.
(ii) Consumption may be uneven at times; EOQ assumes even usage.
(iii) Such things as strikes, catastrophes, etc. can render it useless.

40.9

A Workings:

1 Raw materials 294,400 ÷ 64,000 = 4.6 per unit
2 Direct labour 236,800 ÷ 64,000 = 3.7 per unit
3 Power 38,400 ÷ 64,000 = 0.60 per unit
4 Repairs are 51,200 − 25% × (12,800) = 38,400 fixed. Variable 12,800 ÷ 64,000 = 0.20
5 Indirect wages 64,000 − 15% × (9,600) = 54,400 fixed. Variable 9,600 ÷ 64,000 = 0.15.

Bedford Ltd
Flexible Budget at Varying Levels of Production

	60%	70%	75%	90%	85%	Actual	Variance +(−)
Units	48,000	56,000	60,000	72,000	68,000	68,000	
Variable costs (£)							
Raw materials	220,800	257,600	276,000	331,200	312,800	310,750	2,050
Direct labour	177,600	207,200	222,000	266,400	251,600	249,100	2,500
Power	28,800	33,600	36,000	43,200	40,800	39,800	1,000
Repairs and Maintenance	9,600	11,200	12,000	14,400	13,600	14,650	(1,050)
Indirect wages	7,200	8,400	9,000	10,800	10,200	10,850	(650)
	444,000	518,000	555,000	666,000	629,000	625,150	3,850
Fixed costs							
Repairs and Maintenance	38,400	38,400	38,400	38,400	38,400	38,400	–
Insurance	1,300	1,300	1,300	1,300	1,300	1,350	(50)
Heating/lighting	1,250	1,250	1,250	1,250	1,250	1,200	50
Indirect wages	54,400	54,400	54,400	54,400	54,400	54,400	–
	95,350	95,350	95,350	95,350	95,350	95,350	–
Total costs	539,350	613,350	650,350	761,350	724,350	720,500	3,850

Briefly: generally efficient as most variances are favourable. Comment in detail on each variance.

B See text.

41.1

(a) Standard cost per unit

	X	Y	Z
Materials	4.0	6.4	4.8
Labour: Dept A & Dept B	7.0	4.2	8.4
Production cost	11.0	10.6	13.2
Overheads:			
Production (1.8 per hour)	9.0	5.4	10.8
	20.0	16.0	24.0
Administration (50%)	10.0	8.0	12.0
Selling	5.0	4.0	6.0
Standard cost	35.0	28.0	42.0
Profit (1/7 of standard cost)	5.0	4.0	6.0
Standard selling price	40.0	32.0	48.0

(b) Sales budget in units

	X	Y	Z
Budgeted at standard price	800,000	1,280,000	2,400,000
Unit selling price	40.0	32.0	48.0
Sales budget in units	20,000	40,000	50,000

(c) Production budget in units

	X	Y	Z
Needed for sales	20,000	40,000	50,000
For stock purposes	5,000	10,000	10,000
To produce	25,000	50,000	60,000

(d) Direct materials purchases budget

Materials	1	2	3	4
Product X		100,000		700,000
Product Y (kg)	900,000	300,000	500,000	
Product Z	1,440,000	480,000	360,000	
	2,340,000	1,440,000	1,080,000	1,560,000
Cost (£)	£120,000	£290,000	£234,000	£78,000

42.1

		£
(i) Net variance:	Actual cost per unit 35 × £9	315
	Standard cost per unit 30 × £10	300
	Net variance (adverse)	15
Made up of:	Favourable price variance £1 × 35	35
	Adverse usage variance 5 × £10	50
	Net variance (adverse)	15
(ii) Net variance:	Actual cost per unit 54 × £16	864
	Standard cost per unit 60 × £15	900
	Net variance (favourable)	36
Made up of:	Favourable usage variance 6 × £15	90
	Adverse price variance 54 × £1	54
	Net variance (favourable)	36
(iii) Total variance:	Actual cost per unit 38 × £28	1,064
	Standard cost per unit 30 × £24	720
	Variance (adverse)	344
Made up of:	Adverse price variance 38 × £4	152
	Adverse usage variance 8 × £24	192
	Total variance (adverse)	344
(iv) Total variance:	Actual cost per unit 28 × £18	504
	Standard cost per unit 31 × £20	620
	Total variance (favourable)	116
Made up of:	Favourable price variance 28 × £2	56
	Favourable usage variance 3 × £20	60
		116
(v) Total variance:	Actual cost per unit 310 × £5	1,550
	Standard cost per unit 280 × £4	1,120
	Total variance (adverse)	430
Made up of:	Adverse price variance 310 × £1	310
	Adverse usage variance 30 × £4	120
		430
(vi) Total variance:	Actual cost per unit 4,950 × £66	326,700
	Standard cost per unit 5,000 × £75	375,000
	Total variance (favourable)	48,300
Made up of:	Favourable price variance £9 × 4,950	44,550
	Favourable usage variance 50 × £75	3,750
		48,300

42.3

			£
(i)	Actual cost per unit	432 × £6	2,592
	Standard cost per unit	440 × £6	2,640
	Favourable labour efficiency variance		48
(ii)	Actual cost per unit	230 × £5.8	1,334
	Standard cost per unit	230 × £5.6	1,288
	Adverse wage rate variance		46
(iii)	Actual cost per unit	480 × £5.7	2,736
	Standard cost per unit	400 × £5.7	2,280
	Adverse labour efficiency variance		456
(iv)	Actual cost per unit	206 × £7	1,442
	Standard cost per unit	280 × £7	1,960
	Favourable labour efficiency variance		518
(v)	Actual cost per unit	136 × £5.1	693.6
	Standard cost per unit	136 × £5.7	775.2
	Favourable wage rate variance		81.6
(vi)	Actual cost per unit	68 × £5.6	380.8
	Standard cost per unit	60 × £5.6	336.0
	Adverse labour efficiency variance		44.8
(vii)	Actual cost per unit	154 × £5.5	847
	Standard cost per unit	140 × £5.5	770
	Adverse labour efficiency variance		77
(viii)	Actual cost per unit	200 × £6.1	1,220
	Standard cost per unit	200 × £5.8	1,160
	Adverse wage rate variance		60

42.5

(a) See text.

(b) Standard hours produced in March

Dishwashers 150 × 10	1,500
Washing machines 100 × 12	1,200
Refrigerators 90 × 14	1,260
Total standard hours	3,960

(c) (i) Standard hours × Standard hourly rate

3,960 × £4	15,840
Actual wages	18,450
Total direct labour variance	2,610 (Adverse)

(ii)

Standard pay 4,100 × £4	16,400
Actual pay	18,450
Direct labour rate variance	2,050 (Adverse)

(iii) Direct labour efficiency variance
Standard hours – Actual hours × Standard rate
3,960 – 4,100 × £4 = 560 (Adverse)

(d) Labour rate variance:
1 Higher grade labour used than necessary.
2 Job running behind time so extra people brought in to help.

Direct labour efficiency variance:
1 Using unsuitable machinery.
2 Workers slowing up work so as to get overtime rates paid.

42.7

(a) Profit Statement for the month of July 2011

	Budgeted		Actual	
Sales		1,000,000		1,071,200
Less Manufacturing costs				
Direct materials	200,000		201,285	
Direct labour	313,625		337,500	
Variable overheads	141,400		143,000	
Fixed overheads	75,000		71,000	
		730,025		752,785
Gross profit		269,975		318,415
Less Variable sales o/h	64,400		69,500	
Admin. costs	150,000		148,650	
		214,400		218,150
		55,575		100,265

(b) (i) Materials price variance
= (Standard price – Actual price per unit) × Quantity purchased
= 10.00 – 10.65 × 18,900 = 12,285 Adverse

Material usage = (Standard quantity – Actual quantity used) × Standard price
= (20,000 – 18,900) × 10 = 11,000 Favourable

Summary:	Materials price variance	12,285	(A)
	Materials usage variance	11,000	(F)
	Materials cost variance	1,285	(A)

(ii) Labour rate variance
= (Standard rate per hour – Actual wage rate) × Actual hours worked
= (6.50 – 6.75) × 50,000 = 12,500 (A)

Labour efficiency variance
= (Standard labour hours – Actual hours) × Standard rate per hour
= (48,250 – 50,000) × 6.50 = 11,375 (A)

Summary:	Labour rate variance	12,500	(A)
	Labour efficiency variance	11,375	(A)
	Labour cost variance	23,875	(A)

(c) In each case find out why the variance has occurred. Then it must be established whether the variances were outside the control of anyone in the firm or whether they were caused by the actions, or lack of action, by people in the organisation. Any necessary corrective action can then be taken.

43.1

(a) Actual overhead — 8,400
    Overhead applied to production × £6 — 9,000
    Favourable variable overhead expenditure variance — 600

(b) Actual overhead — 61,000
    Overhead applied to production 12,000 × £5 — 60,000
    Adverse variable overhead expenditure variance — 1,000

(c) Actual fixed overhead — 9,400
    Budgeted fixed overhead — 9,750
    Favourable fixed overhead expenditure variance — 350

(d) Actual fixed overhead — 16,400
    Budgeted fixed overhead — 16,320
    Adverse fixed overhead expenditure variance — 80

(e) Actual hours × Standard rate (18,100 × £4) — 72,400
    Budgeted hours × Standard rate (19,000 × £4) — 76,000
    Favourable variable overhead efficiency variance — 3,600

(f) Actual hours × Standard rate (26,000 × £6) — 156,000
    Budgeted hours (11,320 × 2 = 22,640). Standard rate (22,640 × £6) — 135,840
    Adverse variable overhead efficiency variance — 20,160

43.3

The standard variable overhead rate is:

$$\frac{£120,000}{60,000} = £2 \text{ per direct labour hour and } £2.4 \text{ per unit}$$

The standard fixed overhead rate is:

$$\frac{£48,000}{60,000} = £0.8 \text{ per direct labour hour and } £0.96 \text{ per unit}$$

The variances are:

Variable overhead
(i) Expenditure variance
    Actual overhead — 128,000
    Overhead applied to production 59,000 × £2 — 118,000
    Adverse expenditure variance — 10,000

(ii) Efficiency variance
    Actual hours × standard rate 59,000 × £2 — 118,000
    Budgeted hours × standard rate (52,000 units which
    should be produced in 52,000 × 1.2 hours = 62,400 hours × £2) — 124,800
    Favourable efficiency variance — 6,800

Fixed overhead
(i) Efficiency variance
    Actual units produced × Std rate 52,000 × 1.2 hrs per unit × £0.8 — 49,920
    Actual Labour hours × Standard rate 59,000 × £0.8 — 47,200
    Favourable fixed overhead efficiency variance — 2,720

43.3 (cont'd)

(ii) Expenditure variance

	£
Actual fixed overhead	46,000
Budgeted fixed overhead	48,000
Favourable fixed overhead expenditure variance	2,000

(iii) Capacity variance

	£
Actual hours × Standard rate 59,000 × £0.8	47,200
Budgeted hours × Standard rate 60,000 × £0.8	48,000
Adverse fixed overhead capacity variance	800
	3,920

The variances can be explained further:

Variable overhead

	£
Actual overhead	128,000
Budgeted overhead for actual production 52,000 units × £2.4	124,800
Net adverse variance (made up of favourable efficiency variance £6,800 less adverse expenditure variance 10,000)	3,200

Fixed overhead

	£
Actual overhead	46,000
Overhead based on units of production 52,000 × £0.96	49,920
Net favourable variance (made up of favourable expenditure variance £2,000 plus favourable efficiency variance £2,000 less adverse capacity variance £800)	3,920

43.5

		£
Actual units sold 168,000 × Budget price	£2.50 =	420,000
168,000 × Actual price	£2.40 =	403,200
Adverse price variance	£0.10	16,800

		£
Actual units sold 168,000 × Budget gross profit £0.30 =		50,400
Budgets units sold 140,000 × Budget gross profit £0.30 =		42,000
Favourable volume variance		8,400

43.7

Actual units sold	Budget price £	Actual price £	Unit price variance £	Budget gross profit per unit £	Total price variance £
A	1,224	6	8.20	+2.20	2.00	+2,692.8
B	2,160	9	11.60	+2.60	2.50	+5,616.0
C	216	8	10.90	+2.90	2.20	+626.4
3,600				Total price variance	+8,935.2

Actual units sold	Actual units in budget (%)	Budget sales	Variance in units	Total variance £
A	1,224	900	1,000	−100	−200
B	2,160	1,800	2,000	−200	−500
C	216	900	1,000	−100	−220
3,600	3,600	4,000	−400	−920

Actual units in budget (%)	Actual units sold	Variance in units	Budget gross profit per unit £	Total variance £
A	900	1,224	+324	2.00	+648
B	1,800	2,160	+360	2.50	+900
C	900	216	−684	2.20	−1,504.80
3,600	3,600	–		+43.2

Summary of sales variance

	£
Price variance favourable	8,935.2
Volume variance adverse	920.0
Mix variance favourable	43.2
Net favourable variance	8,058.4

43.9

(a) See text, Section 42.1.

(b) Manufacturing Account for the year ending 31 August 2009

Singleton Ltd

(i)

	Actual £	Budget £	Variance £
Raw material consumed	90,000	80,000	(10,000)
Direct labour wages	115,600	120,000	4,400
Direct expenses	6,000	5,800	(200)
Prime cost	211,600	205,800	(5,800)
Factory overhead expenses:			
Factory rent	10,000	10,000	–
Factory maintenance	6,100	6,700	600
Heating and lighting	3,900	2,900	(1,000)
Depreciation	10,500	8,900	(1,600)
Wages, maintenance labour	24,000	18,000	(6,000)
Other factory overhead	10,000	12,700	2,700
Production cost of goods completed	276,100	265,000	(11,100)

(ii) Trading Account for the year ending 31 August 2009

	£	£
Sales		405,000
Stock of finished goods 1 Sep 08	28,900	
Production cost	276,100	
	305,000	
Less Stock of finished goods 31 Aug 09	35,000	
Cost of sales		270,000
Gross profit		135,000

(c) See text.

Note to exercises on breakeven analysis:
The general idea of the questions is to get you to draw up the schedules of costs and revenues and then to draw them carefully on graph paper. It will be a waste of time if you do not use graph paper. It illustrates that accounting data can be represented in diagram form for some users in a more effective way than just using figures. It also puts over the idea that businesses exist to make a profit, and that until sufficient volume is achieved then the business will incur losses. The impact of fixed costs can be revealed quite sharply by this sort of analysis.

44.1

(i)

No. of units	Fixed cost	Variable cost	Total cost	Revenue	Profit	Loss
0	8,000	–	8,000	–	–	8,000
1,000	8,000	4,000	12,000	6,000		6,000
2,000	8,000	8,000	16,000	12,000		4,000
3,000	8,000	12,000	20,000	18,000		2,000
4,000	8,000	16,000	24,000	24,000	nil	nil
5,000	8,000	20,000	28,000	30,000	2,000	
6,000	8,000	24,000	32,000	36,000	4,000	
7,000	8,000	28,000	36,000	42,000	6,000	
8,000	8,000	32,000	40,000	48,000	8,000	
9,000	8,000	36,000	44,000	54,000	10,000	
10,000	8,000	40,000	48,000	60,000	12,000	

(ii) Similar in style to Exhibit 44.2 in the chapter.

44.2

(a) (i) £24,000 (ii) £36,000 (iii) £44,000 (iv) £30,000
(b) (i) £18,000 (ii) £48,000 (iii) £33,000.

44.4

(i) Loss £2,000 (ii) Profit £12,000 (iii) Nil (iv) Profit £6,000 (v) Profit £9,000.

44.6

(a)

(i) Break-even point = $\dfrac{\text{Total fixed costs}}{\text{Selling price per unit} - \text{Variable cost per unit}}$

For 2001 = $\dfrac{250,000}{130 - 110}$ = 12,500 units
= sales of 12,500 units × £130 = £1,625,000 sales

For 2002 = $\dfrac{275,000}{129 - 118.5}$ = sales of 26,190 units × £129
= £3,378,510 sales

For 2003 = $\dfrac{275,000}{128.5 - 122}$ = sales of 42,308 units × £128.5 = £5,436,578 sales

(ii)

Polemic Ltd
Actual & Forecast Profit & Loss Accounts for years ending 30 September (£000)

	Actual 2001	Forecast 2002	Forecast 2003
Sales	6,500	6,708	6,810.5
Direct materials	2,500	2,860	2,915
Direct labour	1,500	1,638	1,749
Variable production	500	572	636
Direct expenses	250	260	318
Variable sales overhead	750	832	848
	5,500	6,162	6,466
Contribution	1,000	546	344.5
Fixed costs			
Production	50	55	55
Overhead	200	220	220
	250	275	275
	750	271	69.5

(b) Should best be on graph paper. General idea follows:

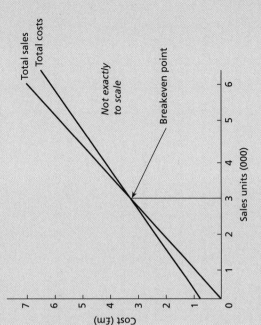

Total sales
Total costs
Breakeven point
Not exactly to scale
Cost (£m)
Sales units (000)

(c) The management of Polemic should be explaining to the union that their demand is unreasonable. As it is, profits have fallen dramatically and the break-even point in 2003 will be over three times higher than in 2001.
It is therefore almost impossible for the company to raise prices still further and maintain their level of sales. To try to do so would almost certainly mean a fall in demand and a shedding of a large part of the workforce.

(d) *See text.*

Appendix 2

44.8

A

Hampshire plc

Profit Statement for first and second quarters

	First quarter	Second quarter
Sales	126,000	143,640
Materials	32,850	39,420
Labour	18,900	22,680
Variable factory o/h	12,600	15,120
Variable selling costs	7,650	9,180
	72,000	86,400
Contribution	54,000	57,240
Fixed costs:		
Factory overhead	21,375	21,375
Selling and admin.	16,125	16,125
	37,500	37,500
Net profit	16,500	19,740

Contribution per unit $\frac{54,000}{9,000} = 6.00$ $\quad \frac{57,240}{10,800} = 5.30$

B Draw on graph paper. Breakeven points are at:

First quarter = $\frac{37,500}{14.00 - 8.00} = \frac{37,500}{6.00} = 6,250$ units

Second quarter = $\frac{37,500}{13.30 - 8.00} = \frac{37,500}{5.30} = 7,075$ units

Margins of safety above these points.

C Profit statements incorporating suggestions:

No. of units sold	(i) 11,880	(ii) 11,556	(iii) 12,960	(iv) 10,800	(v) 10,800
Sales (W1)	158,004	158,317	155,131	143,640	143,640
Materials	46,926	43,913	47,304	39,420	see (W2)
Labour	24,948	27,734	27,216	22,680	87,900
Variable factory o/h	16,632	16,178	18,144	15,120	
Variable selling o/h	10,098	9,823	11,016	11,340	
Total variable costs	98,604	97,648	103,680	88,560	87,900
Contribution	59,400	60,669	51,451	55,080	55,740
Fixed costs					
Factory	21,375	21,375	21,375	21,375	see (W3)
Selling, etc.	16,125	16,125	16,125	12,025	35,000
	37,500	37,500	37,500	33,400	35,000
Net profit	21,900	23,169	13,951	21,680	20,740
Redundancy					12,000

Workings:

(W1) Selling price per unit (i) 13.30 (ii) 13.70 (iii) 11.97 (iv) 13.30 (v) 13.30.

(W2) Per accounts of second quarter in A 86,400 + extra costs 5p per component, 30,000 × 0.5p = 1,500. Total 87,900.

(W3) Fixed costs 37,500 – saving 2,500 = 35,000. Assumed that the 20 per cent of the firm's fixed costs would still continue as they would have to be paid anyway. Question not too clear on this point.

D Briefly:

(i) Would increase profit by 21,900 – 19,740 = 2,160. Seems to be a sensible opportunity which should be considered.

(ii) Apparently increases profit by 23,169 – 19,740 = 3,429. No mention as to what the cost of maintaining the guarantee is likely to be. Until this is known it is impossible to come to a conclusion.

(iii) Fall in profit of 19,740 – 13,951 = 5,789. Should not be considered.

(iv) Increases profit by 21,680 – 19,740 = 1,940. Have to renegotiate terms of employment with sales staff. Worth considering.

(v) Firm
  (a) If we stop making components how can we be certain that suppliers will not later raise prices?
  (b) Would we have to keep larger stocks of components in case of breakdown of supply?
  (c) Possible that newly established firm has got its prices wrong and will be unable to maintain at this price for long.
  (d) Effect on morale of other employees. Local community: write generally about effects of unemployment and knock-on effects.

E *See text, Section 44.4*

44.10

(a)

Magwitch Ltd

Summarised Profit and Loss Account for the year ending 31 May 2011

Sales volume: units 20,000

	£
Sales £1.50 + 10% = 1.65 per unit	33,000
Variable costs (20 – 10) × 0.50 + 10% = 55p per unit	11,000
Contribution	22,000
Fixed costs 0.50 + 10% = 55p per unit	11,000
Profit	11,000

(b)

Compeyson plc

Balance sheet as at 31 May 2011

Fixed assets (40 + 160)		200
Current assets (65 + 340 – 24 see W2)	381	
Short-term liabilities (26 + 110)	136	
		245
		445
Share capital (200 + 60 see W2)		260
Share premium (60 × 0.80)		48
Reserves (190 – 53)		137
		445

Workings:

(W1) Purchase price $12 \times 11 =$ 132

Net assets taken over   71

+ revalued property   8

             79

Goodwill written off to reserves   53

(W2) Method of payment of purchase price   132

Shares $40 \times 3/2 = 60 \times 1.80$ 108

Cash (balance)   24

             132

(c) Shares $6,000 \times 3/2 = 9,000$ shares

Cash $6,000/40,000 \times 24,000 = £3,600$

45.1

(a) $£17,000 \times 0.06 \times \dfrac{64}{365} = £178.85$

(b) $£4,000 \times 0.12 \times \dfrac{120}{365} = £157.80$ Discount

therefore amount paid = £3,842.20

45.3

The amount borrowed is:

$4,200 \times {}^1\!/_4 =$	1,050.00
$3,150 \times {}^1\!/_4 =$	787.50
$2,100 \times {}^1\!/_4 =$	525.00
$1,050 \times {}^1\!/_4 =$	262.50
Equivalent loan for 1 year	2,625.00

$r = \dfrac{600}{2,625} = 0.2286$ or 22.86%

45.4

£5,000 will accumulate to $£5,000 \times (1 + 0.07)^4 = £6,553.98$

$£6,553.98 - £5,000 = £1,553.98$

45.7

From Table 4 in Appendix 1, the present value of an annuity of £5,000 p.a. for 12 years at 6% = $£5,000 \times 8.384 = £41,920$ or:

$$\text{Present value} = £5,000 \times \left[\dfrac{1 - \dfrac{1}{(1 + 0.06)^{12}}}{0.06}\right] = £41,919$$

As the offer of £50,000 exceeds the present value of the rent, you should accept the offer.

45.9

$$\text{Paid in per year} = \dfrac{\text{Value} \times (r)}{(1 + r)^n - 1}$$

$$= \dfrac{£40,000 \times 0.05}{(1.05)^8 - 1}$$

$$= £4,188.87 \text{ per year}$$

45.11

£8,000 × present value factor of an annuity = £21,000. Therefore, the present value factor = 21,000/8,000 = 2.625, which is 7% according to 3 year row of Table 4 in Appendix 1.

45.12

Factor present value of an annuity of £1 for five years at 9% = 3.890

$£11,000 \times 3.890 = £42,790$ capital value of the lease.

46.1

	2004	2005
Equipment purchased	20,000	
Sale of old equipment		(5,000)
Installation of equipment completed and paid	4,000	6,000
Costs incurred in commissioning equipment	8,000	6,000
Rent on premises up to completion date	12,000 (6 months)	3,000 (6 months)
Training costs		6,000
Working capital		16,000
Net cash outlay	44,000	26,000

46.2

Capital cost 2004		44,000	
2004	20% WDA	8,800	@ 30% tax £2,640 received 2005
	balance c/d	35,200	
New expenditure		15,000	excluding scrap value and additional working capital
		50,200	
2005	20% WDA	10,040	@ 30% tax £3,012 received 2006
	balance c/d	40,160	
2006	20% WDA	8,032	@ 30% tax £2,409.60 received 2007
	balance c/d	32,128	
2007	20% WDA	6,425.6	@ 30% tax £1,927.68 received 2008
	balance c/d	25,702.4	

This will continue over the life of the equipment. In 2006 the cash received from the sale of old equipment will be taxed at 30 per cent, resulting in a tax outflow of £1,500.

46.2 (cont'd)

	2004	2005	2006	2007	
Capital cash flow	(44,000)	(10,000)	3,012	2,409.50	etc.
Tax relief		2,640	(1,500)		
Tax on sale			1,512		
Net cash flow	(44,000)	(7,360)	1,512	2,409.50	etc.

46.3

	Net cash flow	Discount factor 6%	Present value
2004	(44,000)	0.943	(41,492.00)
2005	(7,360)	0.890	(6,550.40)
2006	1,512	0.840	1,270.08
2007	2,409.50	0.792	1,908.32
		NPV at start	44,864

46.7

Period	Amount	Balance
0	(15,000)	(15,000)
1	10,000	(5,000)
2	6,000	–
3	3,000	–
4	1,000	–

payback at 1 plus 5,000/6,000 years = 1.83 years

46.8

Period	Amount	Discount factor 8%	Present value
0	(15,000)	1.000	(15,000)
1	10,000	0.926	9,260
2	6,000	0.857	5,142
3	3,000	0.794	2,382
4	1,000	0.735	735

Overall net present value of cash flows = 2,519

46.9

Period	Amount	Discount factor 18%	Present value	Discount factor 20%	Present value
0	(15,000)	1.000	(15,000)	1.000	(15,000)
1	10,000	0.847	8,470	0.833	8,333
2	6,000	0.718	4,308	0.694	4,164
3	3,000	0.609	1,827	0.579	1,737
4	1,000	0.516	516	0.482	482
			121		(284)

18% discount rate gives NPV of 121
20% discount rate gives negative NPV of 284
405

The IRR is $\frac{121}{405} \times 2\% = 0.30\% + 18\% = 18.3\%$.

46.10

From Table 4 in Appendix 1, the present value of an annuity of £1 for four years at 8% is 3.312. The NPV according to 46.8 is £2,519, therefore the annualised amount = 2,519/3.312 = 760.57.

46.17

	Net present value (5%)
Machine A project	£12,288
Machine B project	£43,232

The Machine B project should be selected.

46.18

	Internal rate of return
Machine A project	20.5%
Machine B project	22.0%

The Machine B project would be preferred.

46.21

From Table 4 in Appendix 1, the present value of an annuity of £1 for four years at 8% is 3.312. Therefore the annualised amount = £4,200/3.312 = £1,268.12.

46.23

Cost of machine £50,000 × (1 − 0.3) = 35,000
Cost of leasing £15,180 × (1 − 0.3) = 10,626

Present value for four years $= \dfrac{35,000}{10,626} = 3.294$

which, interpolating between the values for 8% and 9% in Table 4 of Appendix 1 is 8.25%.

46.24

(a)(i)

BN

Roadbog	0	1	2	3	4	5
Cash inflow		12,500	15,000	20,000	20,000	20,000
Cash outflow						
fixed		2,000	2,000	2,200	2,400	2,400
variable		3,000	3,600	4,800	4,800	4,800
		7,500	9,400	13,000	12,800	12,800
Operating cash flow						
Capital	40,000					8,000
	40,000	7,500	9,400	13,000	12,800	20,800
	1.00	0.909	0.826	0.751	0.683	0.621
	40,000	6,817	7,764	9,763	8,742	12,916

NPV = 6,002 positive

FX

Sprinter

	0	1	2	3	4	5
Cash inflow		12,500	15,000	20,000	20,000	20,000
Cash outflow						
fixed		1,800	1,800	1,800	2,000	2,200
variable		4,000	4,800	6,400	6,400	6,400
Operating cash flow		6,700	8,400	11,800	11,600	11,400
						9,000
Capital	45,000					
	45,000	6,700	8,400	11,800	11,600	20,400
	1.00	0.909	0.826	0.751	0.683	0.621
	45,000	6,090	6,938	8,862	7,923	12,668

NPV = 2,519 negative

VR

Rocket

	0	1	2	3	4	5
Cash inflow		12,500	15,000	20,000	20,000	20,000
Cash outflow						
fixed		1,500	1,500	1,400	1,400	1,400
variable		3,500	4,200	5,600	5,600	5,600
Operating cash flow		7,500	9,300	13,000	13,000	13,000
						14,000
Capital	50,000					
	50,000	7,500	9,300	13,000	13,000	27,000
	1.00	0.909	0.826	0.751	0.683	0.621
	50,000	6,817	7,682	9,763	8,879	16,767

NPV = 92 negative

(ii) To the Directors of Road Wheelers Ltd
The NPV anticipated for the three vehicles is as follows:

BN Roadhog	£6,002	Positive
FX Sprinter	£2,519	Negative
VR Rocket	£ 92	Negative

On the basis of NPV assessment using a discount rate of 10 per cent the BN Roadhog appears to be the best option.

The payback position on the three vehicles is as follows:

BN Roadhog	3 years	9.3 months
FX Sprinter	4 years	3.8 months
VR Rocket	4 years	3.2 months

This indicates that the BN Roadhog recovers the cash outlay faster than the other two options which is in its favour.

Since the capital outlay on the BN Roadhog is also significantly lower than the other options this indicates a lower risk and will enhance the ROC on the balance sheet figures.

The BN Roadhog appears to be the best choice.

(b) The problems in evaluating capital projects are essentially related to the estimates involved in forecasting the revenues and costs associated with the project. In this evaluation the relative performance of the three alternatives may be more reliable than overall estimates of the environment. In some situations important factors in the decision may not be readily quantified especially in areas of new technology where many factors are unknown.

The techniques of evaluating the cash flow data are well understood but care must be taken that an appropriate 'cost of capital' is chosen and that risk is taken into account.

46.26

(a) Revised Operating Budget

Ship A

	2005	2006	2007	2008	2009
Estimated revenue receipts	5	7	9	11	13
Extra revenue 10%	0.5	0.7	0.9	1.1	1.3
	5.5	7.7	9.9	12.1	14.3
Operating payments	4.0	5.0	6.5	7.5	9.0
Net cash flow Ship A	1.5	2.7	3.4	4.6	5.3

Ship B

	2005	2006	2007	2008	2009
Estimated revenue receipts:					
Private	2.5	3.5	5.0	6.5	7.5
Commercial	3.45	4.6	5.85	6.5	7.8
	5.95	8.1	10.85	13.0	15.3
Operating payments	4.8	6.0	7.9	9.0	10.8
Net cash flow Ship B	1.15	2.1	2.95	4.0	4.5

(b) Cash flows

		Ship A	Factor 15%		Ship B	Factor 15%	
	0	(10.0)	1.0	(10.0)	(14.1)	1.0	(14.0)
	2006	1.5	0.870	1.3	1.15	0.870	1.0
	2007	2.7	0.756	2.0	2.1	0.756	1.6
	2008	3.4	0.658	2.2	2.95	0.658	1.9
	2009	4.6	0.572	2.6	4.0	0.572	2.3
	2010	5.3	0.497	2.6	4.5	0.497	2.2
	NPV			0.7			(5.0)
Assumed value of ship on market $^{15}/_{20}$ × cost		7.5	0.497	3.7	10.5	0.497	5.2
				4.4			0.2

Note: The calculation has been done with a zero assumption about cash value of ships at the end of year 5 and then with an assumed value equal to the unexplained cost value based on a 20-year life.

46.26 (cont'd)
(c) The evaluation assumes an interest rate of 15 per cent and evaluates cash flows over the first five years' life of the ships. If the assumption is that at the end of five years the ships will have no value then ship A has a positive NPV of £0.7m while B has a negative NPV of £5.0m. However, it is unlikely that the ships would be valueless at the end of year 5 and if an assumption is made to take 15/20 of the cost as the realisable value then both NPVs become positive at £4.4m and £0.2m respectively.

From this evaluation ship A looks to give a better return. It is worth noting, however, that ship B does have much higher capacity. If operating revenues were to expand more than forecast over the five years and thereafter, this ship might provide much higher returns. This operating forecast and the likely market values of the two vessels should therefore be closely examined.

47.1 *See* text.
47.2 *See* text.
47.3 *See* text.
47.4 *See* text.

48.1 *See* text.
48.2 *See* text.
48.3 *See* text.
48.4 *See* text.
48.5 *See* text.
48.6 *See* text.
48.7 *See* text.

49.1 *See* text.
49.2 *See* text.
49.3 *See* text.
49.4 *See* text.

Glossary

Abnormal losses (Chapter 37): Losses arising in the production process that should have been avoided.

Absorption costing (Chapter 36): The method of allocating all indirect manufacturing costs to products. (All fixed costs are allocated to cost units.)

Activity-based costing (Chapter 36): The process of using cost drivers as the basis for overhead absorption.

Adverse variance (Chapter 42): A difference arising that is apparently 'bad' from the perspective of the organisation. For example, when the total actual materials cost exceeds the total standard cost due to more materials having been used than anticipated. Whether it is indeed 'bad' will be revealed only when the cause of the variance is identified. It may, for example, have arisen as a result of an unexpected rise in demand for the product being produced.

Annuity (Chapter 45): An income-generating investment whereby, in return for the payment of a single lump sum, the annuitant receives regular amounts of income over a predefined period.

Articles of Association (Chapter 4): The document that arranges the internal relationships, for example, between members of the company, and the duties of directors.

Associate (Chapter 26): A company (or other entity) which is not a subsidiary of the investing group or company but in which the investing group or company has a long-term interest and over which it exercises significant influence.

Attainable standard (Chapter 41): A standard that can be achieved in normal conditions. It takes into account normal losses, and normal levels of downtime and waste.

Balanced scorecard (Chapter 47): A technique that assesses performance across a balanced set of four perspectives – customers, internal processes, organisational learning and growth, and financial.

Bonus shares (Chapter 10): Shares issued to existing shareholders free of charge. (Also known as scrip issues.)

Break-even point (Chapter 44): The level of activity at which total revenues equal total costs.

Budget (Chapter 38): A plan quantified in monetary terms in advance of a defined time period and usually showing planned income and expenditure and the capital employed to achieve a given objective.

Business-to-business (B2B) (Chapter 49): Businesses purchase from other businesses and/or sell their goods and services to other businesses.

Business-to-consumer (B2C) (Chapter 49): Businesses sell to consumers.

By-product (Chapter 37): Products of minor sales value that result from the production of a main product.

Capital redemption reserve (Chapter 6): A 'non-distributable' reserve created when shares are redeemed or purchased other than from the proceeds of a fresh issue of shares.

Capital reserve (Chapter 9): A reserve which is a balance of profit retained that can never be used for the payment of cash dividends. Examples include a capital redemption reserve and a share premium account.

Cash-based accounting (Chapter 33): A receipts-and-payments-based accounting system.

Consolidation accounting (Chapter 16): This term means bringing together into a single balance sheet and a single income statement the separate financial statements of a group of companies. Hence they are known as group financial statements.

Contribution (Chapter 36): The difference between sales income and marginal cost. (It can also be defined as sales income minus variable cost, which would virtually always produce the same answer.)

Corporate governance (Chapter 32): The exercise of power over and responsibility for corporate entities.

Corporation tax (Chapter 8): A form of direct taxation levied on the profits of companies. The rate is determined each year in the Finance Act.

Cost centre (Chapter 35): A production or service location, function, activity, or item of equipment whose costs may be attributed to cost units.

Cost of control (Chapter 17): An alternative expression to goodwill.

Cost unit (Chapter 35): A unit of product or service in relation to which costs are ascertained.

Debenture (Chapter 5): A bond or document acknowledging a loan to a company, normally under the company's seal and carrying a fixed rate of interest.

Deferred taxation (Chapter 8): Timing differences arise between the accounting treatment of events and their taxation results. Deferred taxation accounting adjusts the differences so that the accounts are not misleading.

Economic order quantity (EOQ) (Chapter 38): A mathematical method of calculating the amount of inventory that should be ordered at a time and how frequently to order it, so that the overall total of the costs of holding the inventory and the costs of ordering inventory can be minimised.

Electronic commerce (e-commerce) (Chapter 49): The use of electronic telecommunication technology to conduct business transactions over the Internet.

Enterprise resource planning (ERP) system (Chapter 48): A suite of software modules, each of which relates to a function of the organisation, such as order processing, production, accounts payable control, accounts receivable control, payroll, marketing, and human resources.

Equity accounting (Chapter 26): A method of accounting for associate entities that brings into the consolidated income statement the investor's share of the associated undertaking's results and that records the investment in the consolidated balance sheet as the investor's share of the associate entity's assets.

Favourable variance (Chapter 42): A difference arising that is apparently 'good' from the perspective of the organisation. For example, when the total actual labour cost is less than the total standard cost because fewer hours were worked than expected. Whether it is indeed 'good' will be revealed only when the cause of the variance is identified – it may be that fewer hours were worked because demand for the product fell unexpectedly.

Finance lease (Chapter 2): This is an agreement whereby the lessee enjoys substantially all the risks and rewards associated with ownership of an asset other than legal title.

Flexible budget (Chapter 40): A budget which, by recognising the difference in behaviour between fixed and variable costs in relation to fluctuations in output, turnover or other factors, is designed to change appropriately with such fluctuations.

Hire purchase agreements (Chapter 2): These are legal agreements by which an organisation can obtain the use of an asset in exchange for payment by instalment.

Holding company (Chapter 16): The outdated term for what is now known as a 'parent' entity.

Ideal standard (Chapter 41): A standard that is based upon the premise that everything operates at the maximum level of efficiency. It takes no account of normal losses, or of normal levels of downtime and waste.

Irrelevant costs (Chapter 46): Those costs of the future that will not be affected by a decision.

Job costing (Chapter 37): A costing system that is applied when goods or services are produced in discrete jobs, either one item at a time, or in batches.

Joint product (Chapter 37): Two or more products, each of which has significant sales value, created in the same production process.

Joint venture (Chapter 26): An entity in which the reporting entity holds an interest on a long-term basis and which is jointly controlled by the reporting entity and one or more other venturers under a contractual arrangement.

Limited company (Chapter 4): A form of organisation established under the Companies Acts as a separate legal entity, and required to comply with the provisions of the Acts. The members of the company, known as shareholders, are liable only to pay the full price of the shares, not for any further amount, i.e. their liability is limited.

Limiting factor (Chapter 36): Anything that limits activity. Typically, this would be the shortage of supply of something required in production, for example, machine hours, labour hours, raw materials, etc. However, it could also be something that prevents production occurring, for example a lack of storage for finished goods, or a lack of a market for the products.

Margin of safety (Chapter 44): The gap between the level of activity at the break-even point and the actual level of activity.

Marginal costing (Chapter 36): An approach to costing that takes account of the variable cost of products rather than the full production cost. It is particularly useful when considering utilisation of spare capacity.

Master budget (Chapter 40): The overall summary budget encompassing all the individual budgets.

Memorandum of Association (Chapter 4): The document that discloses the conditions governing a company's relationship with the outside world.

Minority interests (Chapter 17): Shareholders in subsidiary undertakings other than the holding undertaking who are not therefore part of the group.

Net present value (NPV) (Chapter 45): The sum of the present values of a series of cash flows.

Normal losses (Chapter 37): Losses arising in the production process that could not be avoided.

Operating lease (Chapter 2): An agreement whereby the lessor retains the risks and rewards associated with ownership and normally assumes responsibility for repairs, maintenance and insurance.

Parent (Chapter 16): Although IAS 27 should be studied for a full and proper definition, the one that will suffice for the time being is 'an undertaking which controls the affairs of another undertaking'.

Pre-incorporation profit or loss (Chapter 7): A profit or loss which arises immediately before a limited company is legally incorporated. Any such profit will be treated as capital profit not for distribution while, for sake of prudence, any such loss will be set against post-incorporation profits.

Present value (Chapter 45): The amount that a future cash flow is worth in terms of today's money.

Process costing (Chapter 37): A costing system that is applied when goods or services are produced in a continuous flow.

Provision (Chapter 9): An amount written off or retained by way of providing for depreciation, renewals or diminution in value of assets, or retained by way of providing for any known liability of which the amount cannot be determined with 'substantial accuracy'.

Public sector (Chapter 33): All organisations which are not privately owned or operated.

Relevant costs (Chapter 46): Those costs of the future that will be affected by a decision.

Resource accounting (Chapter 33): An accounting system based on normal commercial practice, including accruals and movements in cash flows.

Revenue reserves (Chapter 9): A balance of profits retained available to pay cash dividends including an amount voluntarily transferred from retained profits and crediting a named reserve account, such as a general reserve.

Rights issue (Chapter 5): An issue of shares to existing shareholders.

Share discount (Chapter 5): Where a share was issued at a price below its par, or nominal value, the shortfall was known as a discount. However, it is no longer permitted to issue shares at a discount.

Share premium (Chapter 5): Where a share is issued at a price above its par, or nominal value, the excess is known as a premium.

Shares at no par value (Chapter 5): Shares which do not have a fixed par, or nominal value.

Sinking fund (Chapter 6): An external fund set up to meet some future liability such as the redemption of debentures. Cash is paid into the fund at regular intervals to accumulate with compound interest to the required future sum.

Standard cost (Chapter 41): An estimate of what costs should be.

Standard costing (Chapter 41): A control technique that compares standard costs and standard revenues with actual costs and actual revenues in order to determine differences (variances) that may then be investigated.

Subsidiary (Chapter 16): An entity which is controlled by another entity.

Subsidiary company (Chapter 16): The outdated term for what is now known as a 'subsidiary'.

Sunk costs (Chapter 46): A cost which has already occurred and cannot, therefore, be avoided whatever decision is taken. It should be ignored when taking a decision.

Supply chain (Chapter 48): Everything within the two end-points of the continuous sequence running from demand forecasting through to receipt of payment from customers.

Supply chain management (Chapter 48): The system of control over the information and/or item flows both within and outwith the organisation that comprise the supply chain.

Variance (Chapter 41): The difference between budget and actual.

Variance analysis (Chapter 42): A means of assessing the difference between a predetermined cost/income and the actual cost/income.

Work certified (Chapter 3): The value of work-in-progress on a contract as certified by, for example, an architect or an engineer.

Index

Note: terms in bold are listed in the glossary.